Clothes
&Your Appearance

Louise A. Liddell
Memphis, Tennessee

Carolee S. Samuels, CFCS
Frankfort, Illinois

Publisher
The Goodheart-Willcox Company, Inc.
Tinley Park, Illinois
www.g-w.com

The Goodheart-Willcox Publisher Brand Disclaimer:
Brand names, company names, and illustrations for products and services included in this text are provided for educational purposes only and do not represent or imply endorsement or recommendation by the author or the publisher.

Cover photo: Dana Edmunds/Getty Images
Back cover: Fashion Institute of Technology

Part page photo credits:
Part 4—National Cotton Council of America
Part 5—Prym-Dritz Corp.

Library of Congress Cataloging-in-Publication Data

Liddell, Louise A.
    Clothes and your appearance / Louise A. Liddell, Carolee S. Samuels.
      p. cm.
    ISBN-10: 1-59070-685-4
    ISBN-13: 978-1-59070-685-5
    1. Clothing and dress. 2. Beauty, Personal. 3. Clothing trade–Vocational guidance.
  I. Samuels, Carolee S. (Carolee Stucker) II. Title.

TT507.L5 2006
646'.3–dc22   2006041068

Introduction

Clothes and Your Appearance is written for you. It will help you see how your clothes speak for you. You will learn how to choose clothes that help you look your best and send the visual message you desire. Knowing how to shop for clothes for yourself and others can help you manage your clothing dollars wisely. Facts about textiles will give you the background needed to understand fabric performance. Knowing how to keep your clothes looking their best is also an important skill you will learn.

Clothes and Your Appearance will introduce you to the exciting world of fashion. You will learn how the textiles and apparel industry has changed through the years and what is happening today. Many careers in textiles and apparel are described in this text. Skills you can develop today can lead to a successful career.

An introduction to clothing construction includes the selection and use of equipment, fabric, and patterns. Various sewing techniques are described. This edition also includes a chapter describing the serger and how to use it in constructing clothing.

Clothes and Your Appearance reflects contemporary life. Topics include current trends and the latest information. Feature articles in each chapter present additional topics you will find full of interesting historical facts, cutting-edge trends, and the newest in technology. At the end of each chapter you will find a series of questions designed to challenge your thinking about the topics covered in the chapter. Enjoy your study of *Clothes and Your Appearance* and how clothing influences your life.

About the Authors

Louise Liddell's career in family and consumer sciences includes 15 years of teaching high school in Tennessee. As Assistant Superintendent for a youth development center, she continued her work with teens. Louise's leadership roles in professional organizations include service at local, regional, state, and national levels. As president of the Tennessee Vocational Association, she received a Life Membership award in AVA for outstanding leadership. Louise is also the coauthor of the text *Building Life Skills*, as well as many magazine and newsletter articles. Louise has a bachelor's degree from the University of Georgia and a master's degree from Memphis State University.

Carolee Stucker Samuels is currently Editorial Director, Family and Consumer Sciences and Career Education, for Goodheart-Willcox Publisher, where she began as an Assistant Editor in 1986. Prior to her work as an editor, she was a family and consumer sciences teacher in Illinois and Indiana for 14 years, teaching textiles and clothing to high school students as well as adults. She is active in numerous professional organizations and has held many offices. Carolee has a bachelor's degree from Iowa State University and a master's degree from the University of Illinois.

Brief Contents

Contents

PART **4**

Fabrics and Their Care

PART 5
Sewing Techniques

Features

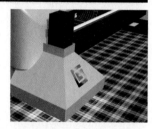

1

You and Your Clothes

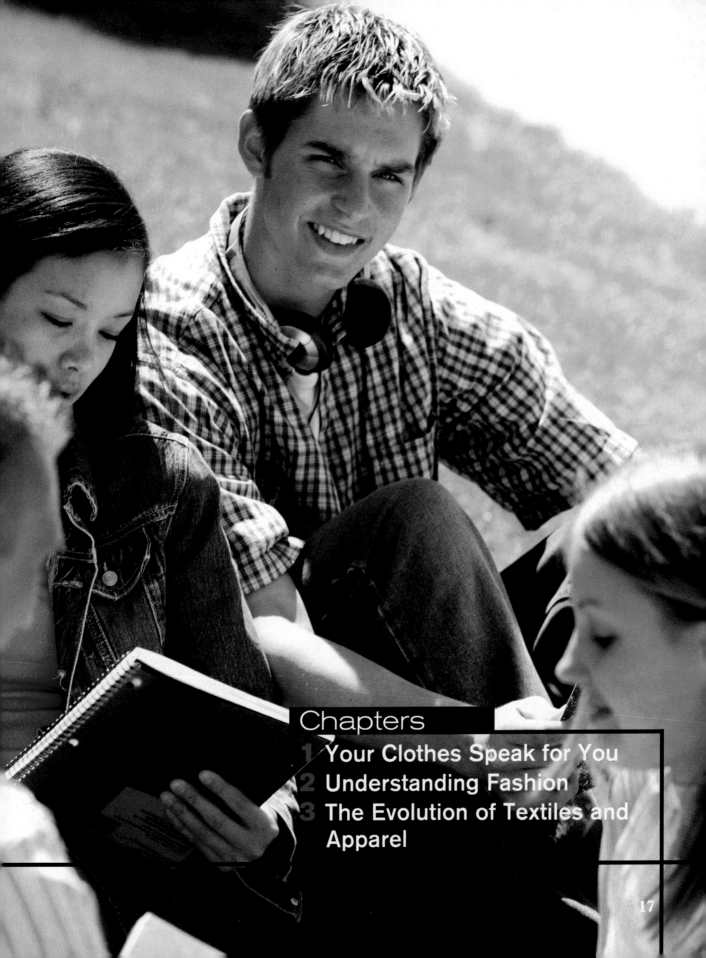

Chapters

1

Your Clothes Speak for You

Objectives

After studying this chapter, you will be able to

- describe how clothing helps satisfy human needs.
- explain how your clothes reflect your personality, your values, and your self-concept.
- describe how clothes can create positive first impressions.
- give examples of how body language conveys messages about people.
- describe how clothing can be used to play up your good points and play down your poorer ones.

Key Terms

need
modesty
conformity
peer pressure
self-esteem
self-adornment
culture
status
self-actualization
individuality
personality
traits
environment
values
self-concept
body language

Clothes are an important part of your life. You wear them every day, and they help you look your best. They can even help you feel good about yourself. They also tell other people a lot about who you are.

Your clothes can speak for you. They can express your personality, your values, and your self-concept. You can even use clothes to express your individuality. However, there are some very basic reasons why people wear clothes as well. Let's begin there.

Why People Wear Clothes

All people share certain basic human needs. A **need** is something required for a person's continued survival. These needs cause people to behave as they do. Everyone has the same basic needs. It's how people meet those needs that vary from person to person.

need
Something required for a person's continued survival.

Maslow, a noted psychiatrist, suggests that humans are motivated to satisfy five basic types of needs. He arranged these needs in order of importance from the lowest to the highest. See 1-1. The lowest needs must be satisfied before the higher needs can be met. These needs are physical; safety and security; love and acceptance; esteem; and self-actualization. The physical needs are the most basic and must be met first.

Clothing can help to satisfy physical, psychological, and social needs. Protection, comfort, and safety are physical needs. Self-adornment and identification are psychological needs. Status and prestige are social needs. Clothing can help meet all these needs.

HUMAN NEEDS

SELF-ACTUALIZATION

ESTEEM

LOVE AND ACCEPTANCE

SAFETY AND SECURITY

PHYSICAL NEEDS

1-1---
According to Maslow, the lowest level needs, which are physical needs, must be satisfied before higher level needs can be met.

Physical Needs

Protection from weather is the most important physical role played by clothing. Whether you live in a cold climate or a hot climate, clothing helps to maintain the body temperature. Eskimos wear clothing with fur linings. Warm air from their bodies is trapped in the clothing and creates a layer of warmth. People in some African countries wear long, white robes and headdresses. White reflects heat, and the long robes keep the sun from

1-2
This man's loose, flowing tunic keeps him comfortably cool in the hot climate where he lives.

1-3
This child's rain gear keeps him dry while he enjoys playing outside on a rainy day.

shining directly on the skin, 1-2. The loosely fitted garments let air circulate around their bodies. This helps to keep them cooler and more comfortable.

Where you live will often determine what types of clothing you will need for protection and comfort. If you live in Minnesota, you will need more clothing to keep you warm than if you live in Florida. Hats and gloves help keep you comfortable by helping your body retain its heat in cold weather. You may wear a cover-up at the beach to protect yourself from overexposure to the sun. Rain gear keeps you and your clothes dry, 1-3. When going on a long hike, it's a good idea to wear hiking boots to protect your feet from being blistered or injured.

Safety and Security Needs

Clothing is sometimes worn to keep you safe from harm or injury. When boating, you wear a life vest. Football and hockey players wear safety headgear. Bicycle and motorcycle riders wear helmets. Race car drivers wear special helmets and safety clothing made of flame-resistant fibers. Cyclists and runners often wear reflective-fluorescent tapes on their clothing so they are more visible to motorists, 1-4. If you have in-line skates, you probably also have knee pads, elbow pads, wrist supports, and a helmet.

Safety clothing is required in some occupations. Firefighters wear heavy boots and flame-resistant clothing. A specially designed hat is also worn. On many industrial construction sites, workers wear hard hats and safety shoes with steel reinforced toes. Road repair workers, traffic officers, and school crossing guards wear brightly colored vests so they can easily be seen. If they wear regular clothing, drivers may fail to see them, causing an accident. Agricultural workers who handle chemicals are advised to wear special gloves. Medical workers wear gloves, gowns, and masks to protect themselves and their patients from exposure to disease-causing organisms, 1-5. These coverings are then disposed of after one use.

Love and Acceptance Needs

The need for love and acceptance can influence how people choose to dress. People have a need to receive affection from others. They also want to feel like

Windmere

1-4
The reflective-flashing safety bands and belts worn by this runner and his dog keep him visible to motorists after dark.

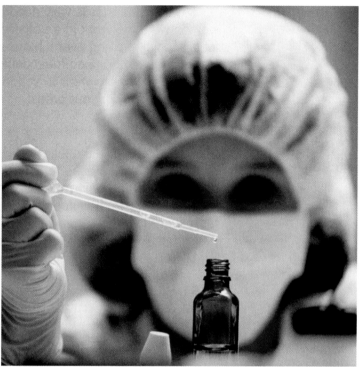

1-5
The protective clothing of this medical researcher is discarded after each use.

they belong to a group. This need guides them in their clothing choices.

Through the years, you learn from your family, friends, and teachers what is expected of you. These are *standards* that are pretty well set. They include behavior guidelines as to what is considered acceptable in this society. They also include standards of dress. These standards of dress can vary from one culture to another. They can also change over time.

Modesty

In our society, modesty is important. **Modesty** is covering the body according to what is considered proper by the society in which you live. Modesty standards may be different in other cultures. Muslim women, for instance, must cover their bodies and faces completely. Only their eyes are unveiled.

Standards of modesty can change through the years. In the 1800s, our society dictated that a considerable degree of cover-up was important for social acceptance. Women wore long dresses and layers of clothing. Today, it is acceptable for more of the legs to show. Think how swim suits have changed through the years. In earlier times, swimwear for both men and women nearly covered the entire body. In the 1960s, the bikini bathing suit became popular. Standards have changed in modern times, but a certain amount of coverage is still expected.

modesty
Covering the body according to what is considered proper by the society in which you live.

conformity
Following or obeying some set standard or authority.

peer pressure
The force that makes you want to be like friends your age (peers).

self-esteem
A feeling of personal self-worth.

self-adornment
Decorating the body in some manner.

Modesty standards vary according to the situation, 1-6. What a woman wears to work in an office will be different from what she wears for a special evening event. More skin can show in evening wear. What you wear to school also must conform to certain standards. No matter what you choose to wear to school, school authorities require a certain level of decency in your dress.

Conformity

Conformity means following or obeying some set standard or authority. People choose to conform in order to feel accepted. Peer pressure can lead to conformity. **Peer pressure** is the force that makes you want to be like friends your age (peers). For instance, you probably prefer to wear the clothing styles that other teens are wearing. You want to "fit in" with what is in style this year. Jeans are popular choices for teens. When you wear them, you feel like you're a part of the group—that you are accepted.

Attraction

Now that you are a teenager, you are more aware of the opposite sex. What you choose to wear may be influenced by your desire to attract the attention of someone you'd like to date. When you were younger, you probably didn't care as much about what you wore or how you looked. You had other things on your mind! Now, you may spend a lot of your time planning what you're going to wear to school the next day or to the game Friday night. If you're a girl, you may spend most of your money on clothes and makeup. You may be trying to attract someone's interest.

Esteem

In addition to love and acceptance, Maslow stated that people have a need for esteem. This is a need for respect, admiration, recognition, and social approval by others. It is also a need for **self-esteem**—feeling good about yourself. If you have self-esteem, you have a feeling of self-worth. You feel that you are important. Clothes can play a role in fulfilling this need.

Self-Adornment

Throughout history, people have practiced **self-adornment,** or decorated their bodies. People have followed certain practices to make themselves beautiful

1-6
Shorts are perfect for in-line skating, but they do not provide suitable coverage for most jobs.

From Humble T-Shirt to Fashion Statement

From its humble beginnings, the T-shirt has morphed into a canvas for designers. It has gone from an affordable undergarment to a vehicle for advertising. Where and when did it all begin?

Though no one knows for certain, the U.S. Navy might deserve the credit. In 1913, a crew-necked, short-sleeved, white cotton undershirt was designed to be worn under the Navy's deep, V-necked collared shirt. Because of its shape, it was called a "T". It wasn't until the late 1930s that companies including Hanes, Sears, and Fruit of the Loom started to market the shirts. In 1938, Sears proclaimed that the undershirt could also be worn as an outer garment. During World War II, the short-sleeved T-shirts gained popularity among soldiers because of their greater absorption under the arms and comfort under backpacks. Soldiers often wore them as outer garments. When the soldiers returned from the war, the shirts came home with them.

The T-shirt gained popularity in the 1950s when Marlon Brando wore one in the movie classic *A Streetcar Named Desire* and James Dean in the movie *Rebel Without a Cause.* Walt Disney was one of the first people to see the marketing value of T-shirts when he began having letters and simple designs printed on the shirts for souvenirs. With the 1960s came the popularity of tie-dying among hippies, and T-shirts were easy to buy and dye. Improvements in printing and dyeing in the '70s allowed graphic images to be printed on shirts. Rock bands and performers sold T-shirts with their images on them. The era of message T-shirts had begun. Corporations also found a new way to advertise. Imagine a walking billboard!

Enter the era of the fashion statement. When Sharon Stone paired a black T-shirt with an Armani skirt for the Oscars in 1996, the garment had truly arrived. T-shirts today come in different weights, colors, and styles. Sometimes they are plain and sometimes they are embellished. They can be layered with other T-shirts or worn under various garment styles. No matter how they are worn, they have become a staple of everyone's wardrobe. The T-shirt has truly become a classic.

culture
The beliefs and customs of a particular group of people.

according to the customs of their culture. The beliefs and social customs of a particular group of people form their **culture,** 1-7. People have painted their bodies with clay and vegetable dyes. They have inserted jewelry in their ears, noses, and lips. They have used colorful stones, metal bands, feathers, and animal teeth to decorate their bodies. Tribes in some parts of the world still carry on these practices.

Today, people still decorate their bodies, but a little differently. Cosmetics and clothes are used for adornment. Accessories such as jewelry, headbands, scarves, and neckties are also used for adornment. Beadwork, needlework, patchwork, and appliqué are some of the creative arts that are used. Some people use body piercing and tattoos as forms of self-adornment.

Status and Prestige

status
Refers to a person's position in relation to others.

People wear clothing to express status, prestige, or importance. **Status** refers to a person's position in relation to others. Some clothing symbols are used to recognize achievements. Service stripes on military uniforms show years of service in the armed forces. Ribbons, pins, and badges show achievements in scouting. Letters on school letter jackets indicate performance in athletic or academic events.

Some people choose clothes to imply they are of a higher status than others. Designer clothes are used as a status symbol for some people. The names of famous fashion designers or their logos are often printed or

1-7
These Indian women of today use jewelry and clothing to adorn their bodies following the style of their culture.

woven into garments, 1-8. Expensive jeans or athletic shoes often have the name brand where it can be seen. Some people also consider expensive jewelry and fur coats to be status symbols. They may use these symbols to indicate their achievement in life.

Identification

You can often identify people by the clothing they wear. You can easily identify police officers and mail carriers by their uniforms. Flight attendants of an airline dress alike. Hotel staff or restaurant waiters may also dress alike. In this way, they can be easily identified. Their attractive uniforms help to create a good image for their companies. Different branches of the armed forces, such as the Air Force or Navy, have specially designed uniforms for their branches, 1-9. Uniforms are also designed to show rank. A general's uniform is quite different from that of a private.

In sports, such as football, members of one team wear the same uniforms. This helps you easily identify players and teams. Imagine how confusing it would be to watch a football game if both teams dressed alike. Think about the type of clothing referees wear. You can always identify them.

Clothing and jewelry are worn by some groups to indicate a certain religious membership. Some people wear jewelry such as crosses, stars, and other religious symbols. In certain religious events, special clothing, such as prayer shawls, christening gowns, or robes, are worn.

1-8
Certain brands of blue jeans can give the wearer status.

1-9
Military uniforms are designed to identify the branch of the armed services, as well as the rank of the officer.

self-actualization
The highest level of need according to Maslow. These needs are related to success in personal achievements, expressions of personal creativity, and self-fulfillment.

individuality
What sets one person apart from others.

Sometimes special clothes are worn during certain ceremonies. At graduation, caps and gowns are worn by the graduates, 1-10. At a wedding, a bride often wears white, 1-11. At funerals, the mourners often wear black.

Self-Actualization

The highest level of need according to Maslow is self-actualization. **Self-actualization** needs are related to success in personal achievements, expressions of personal creativity, and self-fulfillment. To reach this level, the other levels of needs must be at least partially fulfilled.

At this level of need fulfillment, people may choose to express their individuality. **Individuality** is what sets one person apart from others. Where conformity is dressing like everyone else, individuality is expressing one's own uniqueness. If everyone seems to be dressing the same way, this person will choose something entirely different. He or she is rejecting peer pressure to conform, choosing instead to make a personal statement. Clothes are often used as a form of self-expression.

1-10
At a graduation ceremony, caps and gowns are traditionally worn by students to identify them as graduates.

1-11
The custom is that a bride wears the color white.

What Your Clothes Say About You

Just as no two people look exactly alike, neither do people think and feel the same. The thoughts and feelings that make you different from others are a part of your personality. Your clothes say a lot about you—your personality, your values, and your self-concept.

Your Personality

Your **personality** is everything about you that makes you unique. It includes your behavioral and emotional tendencies. Your habits and actions as well as your interests and skills are part of your personality.

Your personality is made up of many traits. **Traits** are qualities that make you different from everyone else. What traits are included in your personality? Study the chart in 1-12. Make a list of the personality traits you think belong to you. You might ask a friend to name the traits she or he would use to describe you, then compare the lists.

Influences on Personality

Why is your personality unique? It has been influenced by many factors over your lifetime. Your environment affects your personality. Your

personality
Everything about a person that makes that person unique.

traits
The personal qualities that make a person different from everyone else.

PERSONALITY **TRAITS**

Aggressive	Dishonest	Jealous	Shy
Assertive	Easygoing	Kind	Self-disciplined
Agreeable	Excitable	Lazy	Understanding
Aloof	Flighty	Loyal	Unreliable
Boring	Friendly	Mature	Tolerant
Cheerful	Faithful	Moody	Talkative
Careful	Funny	Nice	Trustworthy
Crabby	Generous	Responsible	Tense
Confident	Grumpy	Relaxed	Supportive
Capable	Gloomy	Rejecting	Thoughtful
Considerate	Greedy	Silly	Quarrelsome
Cooperative	Happy	Sincere	Warm
Critical	Honest	Self-confident	
Dependable	Introverted	Sad	

1-12
Your unique personality can be described by traits such as these.

environment
Everything around you including your family, friends, school, and community.

environment is everything around you. It includes your family, friends, school, and community. They all affect your personality in some way.

You were not born with your personality. It develops and changes as you mature. You may not have the same personality all of the time. When you are around people who you don't know, you may be reserved and talk very little. They may think you are a quiet, shy person. When you are with your friends, you may talk a lot and laugh often. You may show a different type of personality according to the occasion, 1-13.

Your personality also develops from your experiences and activities. As you grow, change, and have new experiences, your personality traits will also change. You will have new interests, new friends, and learn new skills.

Personality and Appearance

The way you dress is one way you express your personality. If you are a carefree person, you may be less concerned about what you wear than someone who always wants to look perfect. You may like to wear casual clothes most of the time. Wearing the same type of clothes as your friends may make you feel more comfortable and part of the group. On the other hand, you may like to be unique. You might enjoy wearing new or different styles of clothes that are not like your friends' clothes. This could be a way of expressing a personality that says you enjoy being original and different. What type of personality do your clothes express?

1-13
Your facial expression is a clue to your personality. Would you like to have this girl as a friend?

Your Values

Your **values** are the qualities, standards, principles, and ideals you consider important or desirable. They guide your actions and influence your decisions. They influence almost all aspects of your life in some way or another. Some of the values you have may relate to family, friends, education, wealth, and status.

Your values have been forming over your lifetime. Many of your values are influenced by your family. For instance, your family may place a high value on caring for one another, being honest, and persevering. Because of the way you were raised, you are likely to have these same values. Family values are often passed down through generations. Values are also influenced by your friends, school, and community. Cultural traditions often influence value formation.

values
The qualities, standards, principles, and ideals you consider important or desirable.

How Values Influence Dress

The decisions you make about what you wear are often influenced by your values. For example, if you value status, you might choose clothes with logos showing they were created by a popular designer. If this logo is popular with your friends, wearing clothes with this logo can give you status within your group of friends.

If you value wealth, you may buy expensive clothes to show off your wealth. On the other hand, if you value economy, you might be more inclined to buy clothes that are practical, durable, and can be laundered. You will likely look for classic styles that will not go out of fashion. You may place a higher value on education, choosing to save your money for future educational expenses. If you value entertainment, you may choose to spend more money on movies and concerts and less on clothes.

Your values will change throughout your lifetime. What you value as a teen may change during your adult years. Right now you may value clothes that are unique and trendy. In the future, as a young, working professional, you may value basic wardrobe pieces suitable for starting a career. As an older adult, you will probably place more value on comfort in clothing.

Your Self-Concept

The mental picture you have of yourself is called your **self-concept.** This is your idea of who you are and what you are like. These ideas are usually personal and private. If you like the way you see yourself, you have a *positive self-concept.* If you don't like what you see, you have a *negative self-concept.*

self-concept
The mental image a person has of himself or herself.

A Positive Self-Concept

You have a positive self-concept if you feel good about yourself and if you feel you are a worthwhile person. You enjoy life and you like people.

You feel you can accomplish many things. When you have a positive self-concept, you generally have a good outlook on life, 1-14.

What influences your self-concept? Your family, friends, environment, and experiences affect your self-concept. Your family is a strong influence in your life. Many families provide security, love, encouragement, and guidelines. This provides a sturdy base for a positive self-concept. Your friends also help you in forming your self-concept. Their support for you in what you do gives you a feeling of belonging and of being a worthwhile person. Your environment and experiences also play a major role in shaping your self-concept.

A Negative Self-Concept

Some people do not think highly of themselves. They have a negative self-concept. They think of their shortcomings and failures instead of their good qualities. When given a compliment, they shrug it off thinking they are not worthy of praise. They may be unsure of themselves and uncomfortable with others. Often, they accept the ideas of others and seldom know how they really feel. When they make a mistake, they dwell on their failure instead of learning from it.

Improving Your Self-Concept

If you have a negative self-concept, you can learn to overcome it. You *can* feel good about yourself. Think about your positive traits. Everyone has some positive traits. Try being friendly to a new student at your school or helping your neighbor with some chores. These persons may say positive things about you because of your actions. You may be complimented on your new hairstyle or on a good test score. Accept these compliments and feel good about them. Look for other good points you have. This will strengthen your self-concept. Don't sell yourself short; focus on your good qualities. Recognize your strengths. When you do something well, pat yourself on the back. If you like yourself, others will find it easier to like you, too.

Your Appearance and Self-Concept

The way you dress and your overall appearance can affect your self-concept. When wearing a new outfit, you may feel great all day. You know the color is one of your best and the style is very "in" right now. When you know you look good, you feel better about yourself.

Sometimes the opposite happens. Suppose you got up late one morning. You had to dress quickly. The

1-14.
What does this young man's expression tell you about his self-concept?

clothes you grabbed did not go together well and had some stains on them. All day long you may have felt grumpy, embarrassed, and uncomfortable because of the way you were dressed.

Studies have shown that your feelings about yourself usually show in your appearance. Clothing reflects your mental attitude. Do you try to look nice most of the time, but dress sloppily one day? You may reflect your unusual mood that day through your choice of clothing.

Some teens think that looking good is never important. They do not feel that clothes can express what is inside a person. This is the exception. Most young people who have positive self-concepts show this by dressing well.

body language
Nonverbal communication, such as facial expressions and posture.

First Impressions

Along with your self-concept, you have a public image. This is the way you look to others. Within a few seconds after meeting you, people will form their impression of you. They may guess your age, size, nationality, and whether they would like to know you better. A first impression is the way you feel about people when you first meet them. What are your first impressions of the young people in 1-15?

The way people dress is one way they give you your impression of them. Their clothing is the first thing you see. You notice their clothing before you see their faces or hear their voices.

Someone has said that clothing is a silent language—it speaks for us! Therefore, clothing is important in making a first impression. What first impression do you want others to have of you? If you want others to want to get to know you better, start with a good first impression. They will then want to learn more about you.

Body Language

What you do or say when you first meet people also helps them form a first impression of you. The way you use your body, such as your eyes, arms, and hands, communicates something about you. Your facial expressions and your posture also tell others about you. This nonverbal communication is called **body language.**

Looking people in the eye when you meet them sends a message that you are friendly. Not making eye

1-15 _____
What would be your first impression of each of the young people in this picture?

contact could say you may be shy. If you look away while they are talking, they may feel you are not listening to what they are saying. This could cause them not to be interested in getting to know you.

Gestures with your arms and hands and how you handle your body also send nonverbal messages. For instance, a clinched fist can send a message of approval or anger according to the facial expression that goes with it. Winning a contest could cause you to have a big smile and raise a clenched fist in the air over your head. The same clenched fist with a heavy frown on your face could say you are angry. Many people are not aware of how much they talk with their hands.

If your arms are folded or crossed, you may be sending a negative message. You may say you are uncomfortable or wish to be left alone. This gesture could also say you are bored. If your eyes are looking away, this shows a lack of interest or nervousness.

You can communicate a variety of emotions by your facial expressions. You may appear happy, sad, angry, interested, bored, excited, or puzzled. When a teacher asks you a question and you answer it correctly, you may have a pleased look on your face. If you cannot solve a problem, you may look puzzled.

Tapping your fingers on a table could say you are impatient. You may not be interested in what people around you are saying. Shrugging your shoulders tells people you do not know or care about what they are saying.

Your posture—the way you stand, walk, and sit—also tells others a great deal about you. People with poor posture may send a message of "I don't care." They seem to be either bored, tired, or in poor health. None of these messages may be true; poor posture can become a habit. You may not be aware of the messages you are sending if you have poor posture.

The Way You Look

Some people look great all the time. Others never look more than just "so-so." Still others could care less about their appearance and look sloppy most of the time. What makes the difference? The best looking people do not necessarily have perfect features. Their face shape, eyes, nose, ears, or mouth may not be the ideal. Neither do they always have a good body shape. What is their secret? They've identified their good and bad points. They've found ways to play up their good points and play down their bad ones.

Most young people are critical of their bodies. They seldom accept all the good points they have. Often, they think of their negative points instead of their positive ones. There are some things that cannot be changed: extra big feet, a short waist, or long arms. They need to accept these features and not dwell on them. Instead, young people should focus on their good points or assets.

Most people do not realize how many good points they have. Take a good look at yourself. Do a self-evaluation. Decide what is best about you and what you would like to make look better. Then decide what you want to cover up and what you want to show off to even better advantage.

There are many ways to accomplish this. The style of clothing you choose can help. You can also use color and design to enhance your good points and to cover up your poorer ones. You will learn how to use color and other aspects of design in later chapters. Begin by choosing clothes that express your personality and values. This is the first step in making a positive impression others are sure to remember, 1-16.

1-16
Choose clothes that reflect your values and express your personality.

CHAPTER REVIEW

Key Points

- Clothing helps satisfy human needs. These include physical needs for protection and comfort; safety and security needs; the need for love and acceptance; esteem needs; and self-actualization.

- Clothing choices are influenced by modesty, conformity, attraction, self-adornment, status, prestige, and identification.

- Your clothing choices reflect your personality, your values, and your self-concept. These are all influenced by your environment—your family, friends, school, community, culture, and religion.

- People form first impressions within a few seconds of meeting you. If this first impression is a positive one, they will want to get to know you better.

- Nonverbal communication is called body language. This is the way you use your body—your eyes, hands, arms, and facial expressions—to communicate.

- A self-evaluation of your appearance can help you identify your good points and your bad points. Then you can learn how to use clothing to enhance your best features.

To Review

1. Does everyone have the same basic needs?
2. How do clothes help meet your physical needs?
3. Which need is being met when you wear plastic goggles in chemistry lab?
4. Explain why modesty standards vary within a society.
5. Explain how peer pressure can lead to conformity.
6. Give an example of how clothing can express status or prestige.
7. Who or what influences a person's values?
8. People who only see their own weaknesses and faults are likely to have a

   _____ _____.
9. Explain how your appearance can affect your self-concept.
10. Give three examples of body language and tell what they mean.

To Do

1. Create a bulletin board showing examples of why people wear clothes. Use your creativity to write clever captions.

2. Interview employers about standards of dress in their businesses. Find out why they have these standards.

3. Research native dress or costumes worn in foreign countries. Select one item of dress typical of one particular country. Prepare a report to share with the class discussing how culture influences this dress.

4. Make a list of all the different groups to which you belong. Identify special clothing that you might wear to show that you are a member of each group.

5. Write a report describing the personality of a television character. Include both good and bad qualities. Discuss whether his or her personal appearance gives a clue to his or her personality.

6. Write a paper describing the values you have that were influenced by your family.

7. Write a paragraph "As I See Me." Do not sign your paper. Give your paper to your teacher who will then give your description to another student to read. This student will try to identify who wrote the paragraph. Was the person who read your paragraph able to identify you? Do others see you as you see yourself?

8. Make a list of the things that affect your first impression of a person. Compare lists from all class members. Make a master list naming the most mentioned things first.

9. Make a list of types of body language that can help a person to make a good impression on others. Then make a list of types of body language that can make a poor impression on others. Discuss the lists in class.

To Think About

1. Discuss the popularity of certain brand names of clothes among teenagers. Is there pressure to buy expensive clothes to achieve status in your school? Debate the pros and cons of this trend.

2. Contrast conformity versus individuality in the way a person chooses to dress. Is one better than the other?

3. Analyze factors that influence personality. Include both positive and negative ones.

4. Identify the personality traits you like most about the employees in a store where you often shop. Identify traits you dislike most in store employees. Compare and contrast the two lists of traits.

5. Do you believe a first impression is important? Defend your answer.

CHAPTER 2

Understanding Fashion

Objectives

After studying this chapter, you will be able to
- define fashion terms.
- explain fashion cycles.
- summarize the social, religious, political, economic, and technological influences on clothing design.

Key Terms

fashion
style
fashion trend
classic
fad
fashion cycle
trendsetter
societies
customs
heritage
ready-to-wear
economics
technology

One of the most exciting aspects of clothing is fashion. A **fashion** is a particular style of apparel that is popular at a given time. What is in fashion is going to influence your clothing choices.

Fashion reflects a time and a place. What is considered fashionable today is quite different from what was in fashion 100 years ago. What is in fashion in this country is often different from what is fashionable in other countries around the world.

It is important to understand fashion concepts and terms as you begin your study of fashion. The influences on fashion design will also be explained in this chapter.

fashion
The particular style of clothing that is popular at a given time.

style
Type of garment that has specific characteristics that make it unique.

fashion trend
The direction in which a particular change or fashion is moving.

Fashion Terms

Many clothing terms may be familiar to you. Sometimes people use these terms interchangeably, but they each have a specific meaning. Some of the key clothing terms are style, fashion, classic, and fad.

Style

A **style** refers to a particular design, shape, or type of garment or apparel item. Specific characteristics help identify a garment as a certain style. These styles have common names that are used by people in the fashion industry.

There are different styles of pants, dresses, skirts, necklines, collars, and sleeves. An A-line skirt is different than a pleated or gathered skirt. Each is a distinct style. Sweater styles include the pullover and the cardigan (open front), 2-1. A parka is a style of coat. The pockets, hood, and length make it different from other coat styles. Jeans are a style of pants.

Fashion

A fashion is a style that is currently popular with consumers. Most people prefer to wear the clothing styles that are in fashion at the present time. What is fashionable this year may not be in fashion a few years from now. Often a fashion reappears that was popular a long time ago. This is why you may have heard the saying, "Fashion repeats itself."

A **fashion trend** is the direction in which a particular change or fashion is moving. It is a

2-1
The pullover is a popular sweater style.

2-2_____
The bare midriff and low rise jeans are fashion trends popular with teens.

comparison of what is in fashion this year as compared to previous years. A fashion trend gains popularity and soon becomes accepted by more and more people. Typically a fashion trend lasts for three to seven years. There are fashion trends for different markets. For example, a fashion trend for the teenage market might be different from a trend in women's career wear, 2-2.

As a fashion changes, the details of the basic styles change, too. In men's suits, the width of lapels, the shape of pockets, and the location and number of buttons all change with fashion. However, the basic style of the suit remains the same, 2-3.

Fashions in neckties change often. Sometimes wide ones are in fashion. In other years, narrow ties are popular.

Fashion changes quickly today because of instant communication. However, more and more people wear styles they like even if those styles are not in fashion. Personal satisfaction is more important to some people than what is considered fashionable.

This attitude did not always exist. For instance, when high heels first became fashionable, almost all women wore them whether they were comfortable or not. They simply accepted the current fashion. Today, though high heels are popular, other heel heights are also in fashion. Women can select the style or height they like. People today are freer to choose the styles they prefer.

Classic

A **classic** is a style that stays in fashion for a long time. A tailored shirt and a simple pullover sweater are classics. A navy blue blazer is a classic. Metal, white, or blue buttons on the blazer may be seen in different years. Lapels may be wide or narrow. However, the classic blazer stays in fashion. Blue, white, black, or faded jeans may be the fashion from time to time. The legs of the jeans may be wide, tapered, or narrow. However, jeans are a classic, 2-4.

Many other clothes have become classics. Among these are caps, polo shirts, trench coats, business suits, and tuxedos. A tuxedo may have wide or narrow lapels, and it may be made of a variety of colors and fabrics. In any variation, the classic style can still be recognized.

Fabrics, designs, and colors also become classics. Linen, crepe, velvet, seersucker, suede, and corduroy rarely go completely out of fashion. Plaids, dots, checks, and striped designs are classic patterns. Navy blue and gray are classic colors that are seen year after year.

2-3_____
The details of the double-breasted jacket, such as the width of the lapels, change with fashion.

Fad

A **fad** is something new in clothing that quickly becomes popular, but only for a short time. It may appeal to many people for a short period of time, but it fades quickly. Many times fads are extremely unusual styles or accessories. Often they are popular with teens, 2-5.

At one time, blue jeans and sneakers were fads. However, they were so well liked by teens and adults that their popularity lasted. They are now considered classics.

Smart consumers are careful not to spend too much of their clothing money for fad items. These items are fun to wear, and you might feel good wearing "the latest" fashion. However, fad items should be purchased only when you have extra money.

A fad can be a color. Perhaps one season everyone seems to be wearing hot pink. The next season hot pink is seldom seen. Black jeans may be popular one season and not the next.

classic
A style that stays in fashion for a long time.

fad
Something new that is popular for only a short period of time.

McCall's 3490

2-4
Denim jeans are classics that have been in fashion for a long time.

2-5
Which of the styles shown here, popular with teens, may be fads that will quickly be out of style?

fashion cycle
The periodic return of specific styles and general shapes.

trendsetter
A person who takes the lead or sets an example.

Fads can also be accessories. Gold chains may be worn by everyone for a few seasons. Then they are less popular, and colored beads or leather bracelets may take their place, 2-6.

The next time you go shopping, look for styles, fashions, classics, and fads. Save most of your money for styles that will last. Watch for the latest fashion details within a basic style. Spend less on fads that will be out of fashion next year. Invest more in classics for a long-lasting wardrobe.

Fashion Cycles

A **fashion cycle** is the periodic return of specific styles and general shapes. This means that fashions go through periods of being popular, and then they go through periods of being unacceptable, or "old-fashioned." Fashions are popular, then they disappear, and later return again to popularity.

A fashion cycle often begins when a designer creates a new style. The style is introduced to the fashion industry in the form of high-priced garments. People who are *fashion leaders* buy these garments at the start of the cycle. These are people who like to be seen in the latest fashions and can afford to buy designer clothes. Movie and television stars often buy these garments because they want to be noticed. They also have the money to buy new fashions and discard them when newer styles are introduced. See 2-7.

New fashions are often worn by trendsetters. A **trendsetter** is a person who takes the lead or sets an example. They aren't afraid to try new styles. They can be teens as well as adults, but they are usually leaders in their respective social groups. Their clothing styles are soon copied and worn by many others.

In the next stage of the fashion cycle, the fashion becomes affordably priced and gains popularity with the general public. Soon the fashion is seen everywhere. All of the major retailers are promoting the style and carrying various versions at different prices. More people are feeling comfortable with the style and are adding it to their wardrobes. It is during this stage that the majority of people are wearing the style. At the same time, the fashion leaders and trendsetters are looking at the next fashion style.

Before long, the style's popularity declines. It is worn by everyone, and has become boring. Often this is because a newer fashion has come along. Soon, the style disappears altogether.

2-6   Colorful flip-flops may be a fad that will quickly be replaced by another fad.

After many years pass, the style may reappear at the beginning of a new cycle. The style might not be exactly the same; new and different details will be added.

Clothing details go through fashion cycles. The width of lapels, neckties, and pant legs change from wide to narrow to wide again over time. Skirt lengths are sometimes near the ankles one year and just above the knees another year. At still other times, all lengths can be seen.

In the past, fashion cycles moved slowly. For example, three basic dress silhouettes or shapes went through the fashion cycle about every 100 years. These silhouettes were the bell, back fullness, and tubular. See 2-8. These silhouettes were repeated, but with new and different features each time. Each period of dress had features that set it apart from other time periods. Men's fashion cycles could be seen through the changes in the widths of lapels, neckties, and pant legs.

Today, fashions cycle at a faster rate because society is changing faster. It is not unusual for fashion cycles to occur every 20 to 30 years. As technology develops, clothing production improves. These changes mean that more styles are available at a quicker rate. The

Fashion Cycle Silhouettes

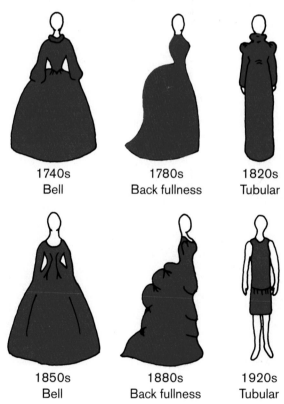

| 1740s | 1780s | 1820s |
| Bell | Back fullness | Tubular |

| 1850s | 1880s | 1920s |
| Bell | Back fullness | Tubular |

Photo by Irving Solero. Courtesy of the Museum at the Fashion Institute of Technology, New York

2-7
These two dresses, designed by Halston in the 1970s, were worn by the actress, Lauren Bacall.

2-8
The bell, back fullness, and tubular silhouettes have been repeated throughout the years.

increase in worldwide communication now makes it easier to see what other people around the world are wearing.

Influences on Fashion

You can tell a great deal about people by the clothes they wear. For thousands of years, people in different societies wore clothes unique to their culture, 2-9. **Societies** are groups of people with broad, common interests who live and work together. The beliefs and social customs of a particular group of people form their culture. Traditions are handed down from one generation to the next as **customs.** These customs form a part of a person's cultural **heritage**—the background and traditions acquired from predecessors.

Many events throughout history have influenced the fabrics used, the designs created, and the uses made of clothing throughout the world. Some influences have been social and political. Others are related to a country's economy. Technological advances have also played an important part.

Social and Cultural Influences

Throughout the centuries, social changes have brought about changes in fashion. Social changes due to modernization have occurred from the earliest civilizations to modern times. What people wore reflected their lifestyles and values, as well as the technology available to them.

Early people lived in small, isolated groups. They often wore animal skins as clothing. Members of tribes who were considered to be brave warriors or outstanding hunters wore special animal skins, such as tiger or lion, to show how important they were. Other tribe members wore caribou, bear, moose, or elk skins. Elaborate headdresses, tattoos, and ornate jewelry were also used to display a special status within a group. Feathers, shells, and vegetation were used in dress as well. Clothing was made with a simple technology using few tools and limited skills. Families were close, and young people learned customary dress from their elders.

As people developed agricultural skills, they began to grow natural fibers. Technology

Photographer: Marla C. Berns

2-9
These Waja women from Nigeria, photographed in 1982, continue to use gourds to carry food. They also use decorated gourd bowls to protect their infants from the hot sun as they carry them on their backs.

led to spinning and weaving to produce fabrics. Social life still centered around the family, but wealth increased. Dress became a way to distinguish between social classes. Farm families wore rough, homemade garments. Wealthy merchants and planters and their families wore expensive clothing made of imported fabrics.

For many centuries, the nobility in Europe wore clothing that showed they were the highest class in their society. Clothing was elegant and extravagant with lots of lace, beads, and embroidery. The fine fabrics used were made of imported silks and linens, 2-10.

The Industrial Revolution began in England during the eighteenth century and rapidly spread to other countries. Agriculture declined as offices and factories took over. Elegant knee breeches, brocaded vests, and fancy waistcoats for men gave way to black coats, long trousers, and high top hats. While men's attire became somber, women were wearing layers of petticoats and tight-fitting corsets, 2-11.

There was still a wide gap between the rich and the poor classes. Farmers and factory workers had very few clothes. A woman might

973.399.a-.c Photograph courtesy of the Royal Ontario Museum, © ROM

2-10

This silk gown decorated with silver thread and lace was worn between 1740 and 1760.

Open Robe, 1789: Gift of Mrs. Henry Wheeler de Forest in memory of her husband. *Court Suit, 1780s:* Gift of E. Coster Wilmerding. Museum of the City of New York. 54.209ab; 50.256a-h

2-11

In 1789 these garments were worn to George Washington's inaugural ball. The woman's dress shows the tight bodice common in the late 1700s.

have one dress for special occasions. The rest of the time she wore dark, cotton garments, 2-12. A man had one suit for church and funerals.

In the early 1900s, technology led to widespread and rapid change. Electricity led to many laborsaving devices in the home. Women were beginning to venture into the work world as teachers, nurses, and clerks. With the invention of the typewriter, a new career opened for them. Ready-made, mass-produced clothing became available. The shirtwaist was the first ready-to-wear fashion item available to women. **Ready-to-wear** is clothing made in factories in standard sizes. The shirtwaist was a tailored white linen blouse.

ready-to-wear
Clothing made in factories in standard sizes.

An increased interest in sports for women led to the creation of new styles that were less cumbersome and let women move more freely, 2-13. The interest in physical fitness led to more clothing items designed for physical activity, such as jogging suits and running shorts.

Today, people in Western societies are freer to dress as they wish. There are general social standards regarding dress, but the rules are less rigid. The trend is toward more casual dress, even for office workers. There is a wide variety in types of clothing available due to mass production. More people have more wealth, allowing them to buy more clothes than in earlier generations.

Media influences how people dress—plays, movies, music, books, and television programs. When a clothing style is shown on television or in newspapers, people become more aware of it. They may decide that they like this style of dress and want to adopt it.

Religious Influences

In almost all societies, religion influences how people dress. For instance, religious customs require Muslim women to wear veils in public to hide their faces from strangers. Amish people believe in plain clothing to go with their simple lifestyles.

In most cultures, robes, masks, or other accessories are worn for religious ceremonies. In some cultures, these clothes are even thought to help the religious leaders perform their jobs.

Historical Influences

Many historical events have influenced fashions. These are political, economic, and technological.

Political Influences

For centuries, kings and queens set fashions that were followed by members of their courts. They wore elegant, elaborate garments made of fine linens and colorful silks. Certain colors, such as purple, were reserved for royalty

From the collection of American Textile History Museum, Lowell, Mass. Photographer: Anton Grassl
1100.19.3-AB, 1100.63-A-B, 1996.24.3-A-B

2-12
These dresses were typical of those worn by women around 1900.

only. The purple dye that came from the shellfish, mollusk, was rare, difficult to obtain, and therefore expensive.

Rulers wanted their clothing to be superior to that of their subjects. During the Middle Ages, people were divided into different classes. Some countries passed *sumptuary laws.* These were laws that regulated what each class of people could wear. Sometimes laws were also made to force people to buy products made in their own country.

Wealthy, powerful nations also influenced clothing styles. In the 1600s, France became a European power. Soon it became the fashion leader of the world. Other countries copied the French designers' creations. Even today, France is still considered a fashion leader.

A great change occurred in clothing styles after the French Revolution, which took place in the late 1700s. As France changed from a monarchy to a democracy, people wanted to have a say in what kinds of fashions were designed. The elegant fashions of the French nobility, 2-14, were replaced by simpler fashions.

Napoléon Bonaparte became Emperor of France in the early 1800s. His wife,

Marjorie Russell Clothing and Textile Center, Nevada State Museum, Carson City. Photographer: Scott Klette

2-13

Can you imagine swimming in this swimsuit in 1910? It was not long before less bulky swimsuits became popular.

North Wind Picture Archives

2-14

The elaborate dress of the French nobility is illustrated by this gentleman and lady of Louis XIV's court.

Empress Josephine, made the Empire style world famous. Her dresses had low necklines and high waistlines, often with drawstrings. Many women worldwide quickly adopted this style, 2-15.

During World War I, women contributed to the war effort by working in offices, shops, and factories. Clothing needed to be less cumbersome and restrictive than in the past. Bustles, high necklines, and full sleeves disappeared. The result was a "boyish" look that included short-cropped hair and loose clothing. See 2-16. Bloomers were worn by women factory workers.

During World War II, civilian use of fabric was restricted since it was needed for military use. New fashions were limited to specific amounts of fabric. Women's clothing styles became shorter, sleeveless, and collarless. Zippers and trims were not allowed. After the war, the "New Look" became fashionable thanks to Christian Dior, a French designer. Dresses had longer, fuller skirts, 2-17. During the 1950s, the ideal woman had a full, shapely figure. Fashions were designed for the mature woman.

North Wind Picture Archives

2-15--
This gown illustrates the Empire style that was popular in the 1800s.

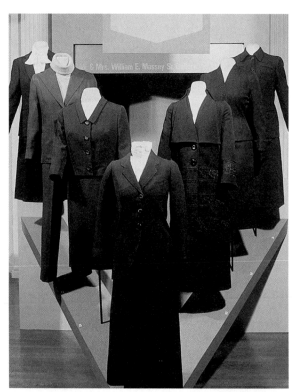

Valentine Museum

2-16--
This display of women's suits shows how styles changed from 1912 (center) to one worn in 1986 (left, back).

The start of the 1960s saw another radical change in fashion. Because more than half of the population was under the age of 25, this group demanded its own look. That look was designed for skinny, boyish figures. The miniskirt was introduced by Mary Quant in 1960. Bright colors and patterns with colorful stockings became popular. See 2-18.

During the Vietnam War in the late 1960s and early 1970s, many young people started the "hippie" movement to protest the war. Their clothing was very casual, emphasizing comfort and practicality. There was less interest in status dressing. Faded, tattered jeans were worn by both men and women along with tie-dyed clothing. "Unisex" dressing (similarity of dress worn by the sexes), which began in the 1950s, became more common.

In the early 1970s, President Richard Nixon went to China to resume relations with the Chinese government. Soon afterward, the mandarin collar and Asian designs became fashionable in clothing and jewelry.

economics
How a society chooses to produce, distribute, and consume its goods and services.

Economic Influences

Economics is how a society chooses to produce, distribute, and consume its goods and services. Goods, such as apparel, come to you

Fine Arts Museums of San Francisco, Gift of Mrs. Eloise Heidland, 1982.18.4a-b; Hat gift of Mr. E. J. Larson, 1984.24.5.

2-17—————————————————————————————
Christian Dior designed this afternoon ensemble in 1948. It illustrates the long, full skirts for which he was known.

Emilio Pucci, *Braniff Airlines Hostess Uniforms*, 1965-66, Texas Fashion Collection, University of North Texas. Photo by Michael Bodycomb.

2-18—————————————————————————————
Italian designer Emilio Pucci was known for his vibrant colors and patterns. In 1965, he designed this special collection for Braniff Airlines hostesses.

Christian Dior: A Name Synonymous with Fashion

One of the most famous fashion designers of all time was Christian Dior. He was 31 years old when he began sketching fashion designs in Paris in 1938. Though his career was temporarily halted during World War II, in 1947 he opened his own fashion house for "truly elegant women." His first collection was launched this same year. Fashions during and after the war had been subject to fabric restrictions leading to short skirts and conservative designs. Christian Dior made a sensation with his truly feminine silhouette—wide rustling skirts with a daring mid-calf length setting off a tiny waist and rounded shoulders. The line became known as "The New Look" and symbolized the end of the war. The fashion look was an instant hit, and Dior's name became known worldwide.

Though The New Look dominated the fashion scene for several years, Dior continued to create variations on his basic theme throughout his twenty-two collections. All of his designs featured tasteful elegance, but were also in keeping with the demands of modern life, making his clothes easy to wear. Every garment Dior designed was fully lined to make sure the structure was well supported. Each design started with a study of the fabric, followed by a hundred or so sketches before it reached its final form.

Dior dressed the most elegant women of the time—the Duchess of Windsor, Marlene Dietrich, Britain's Princess Margaret and Princess Grace of Monaco, to name but a few. Dior felt his designs were for all women, for any day and any hour. He designed each garment for a particular time and place, whether a travel suit, an afternoon dress, a ball gown, or a tea. See one of his designs in 2-17.

Christian Dior died in 1957 at the age of 52. In only a very short time, he had become one of the most famous men in the world. The House of Dior continued after his death through another famous designer, Yves Saint Laurent.

Christian Dior's childhood home at Granville in France is now the Christian Dior Museum, the only museum dedicated to a couturier.

largely through the economic activities of producers. They make and sell goods and services to satisfy consumer needs and wants. The exchange of goods and services takes place within the framework of an economic system. There are two basic types of economic systems today.

Thousands of years ago, however, these systems didn't exist. People made clothing from the natural resources that were available. Later, they learned to grow fibers that could be spun and woven into fabrics. Some people were more skilled at spinning and weaving than others. They found that their skills could be bartered. Bartering is trading your skills or goods for another person's skills or goods. Bartering provided the society with better goods and services.

The two types of economies common today are the market economy and the command economy. The type of economic system of a country influences fashion choices. In the U.S. and most European countries, the market economy system exists. A *market economy* is a system in which private individuals and businesses respond freely to the needs of the marketplace. This is also called the *free enterprise system.* Manufacturers try to respond to the needs of their customers. Consumers are important in this system. What they choose to buy affects the profits of the manufacturers. Competition exists between manufacturers, creating lots of choices for consumers. Due to competition, new clothing designs come out every season. Manufacturers advertise their new designs to get you to choose their clothes. A wide variety of types of retailers provide many options for consumers.

In a *command economy,* the state or some other central authority controls economic activities. This type of economy is usually found with socialist or communist forms of government. The central authority decides who will produce manufactured goods and how much they will produce. The government also sets the prices of goods and services. The needs and wants of consumers are not always considered. This often leads to limited choices for consumers. Because there is no competition, prices are fairly firm. Fashions change very slowly in this type of economy.

Within the market economies, a significant change has occurred in the last half century that has influenced fashion. More and more women are working outside the home. Families have two paychecks, which has resulted in increased buying power. More clothing is available because families have more money to buy new fashions. Women also buy more clothes as required for their jobs. As people buy more clothes, there is more money in circulation, and the economy is better.

A more recent economic trend has been the increased spending money of teens. Teens have more spending money today than ever before. Manufacturers recognize this trend, and aim their advertising to this very important market segment. Most teens who work spend a large portion of their money on clothes.

Technological Influences

technology
The manner of accomplishing a task using current technical methods or knowledge.

Technology is the manner of accomplishing a task using current technical methods or knowledge. Technological influences on fashion have been significant. Methods of technology used in the production of clothing have changed dramatically from early times.

During the Stone Age, people made stone tools to kill animals for food and their furs. Later, they invented needles made from bone. This technological advance enabled them to sew skins together and make better clothing. The simple invention of the eyed sewing needle is perhaps the single most important technological event to influence clothing production.

Spinning and weaving were later developed. All spinning and weaving was done by hand until the invention of foot- and water-powered machinery in the 1700s. This development was followed by the invention of the sewing machine in the 1800s.

Today, machinery and procedures are constantly being improved and developed. The development of manufactured fibers from chemicals is a major technological advance of the twentieth century. Rayon, acetate, nylon, and polyester fibers were developed that were less expensive, looked better, and were easier to care for. New fabrics have been developed that provide greater comfort when worn. Stretch fabrics are now commonplace, and many items of clothing are being made using fabrics that have built-in stretch. Today's fabric finishes have improved the appearance of fabrics and their ease-of-care qualities.

Another recent technological advance is the use of computers in textile design and manufacturing. Because of computers, all aspects of fashion design and production can be done faster and with greater accuracy. Manufacturing plants are entering a robotics age where specially designed machines handle many manufacturing processes formerly done by people. Retailers use computers to keep accurate and up-to-the-minute track of inventory and sales.

Fashion Trends Today

Social, religious, political, economic, and historical events continue to influence today's fashions. Economic conditions and world events always play a role in determining what people wear, but these events cannot always be predicted.

Fashion designers look to various sources for inspiration. Designers often study history to get ideas. They might look at historic costume collections for ideas to translate into designs for today. They create new designs using details from the past. Designers also get ideas by studying different cultures. They incorporate these ideas into their designs. They might visit art exhibits for inspiration. They study nature for ideas to translate into fashion.

Designers are also observers of the world around them. What is happening in the world that they can translate into fashion designs? For example, current movies and popular television shows can inspire fashion ideas. After the movie *Flashdance* was released, wearing sweatshirts with the sleeves and neck cut off became popular. Designers pay attention to what the top musical performers are wearing. Young people like to copy what these celebrities are wearing, so designers copy these designs for the ready-to-wear market. Sports figures are also observed. They often are hired by manufacturers to wear and promote their fashion designs.

Designers also observe lifestyles and living patterns. They want to design garments that meet the everyday needs of people. Exercise and fitness is a current trend. Designers focus on creating garments that are comfortable to wear while people work out. Fabrics that move with the body and absorb moisture are used in these designs. Some famous designers of the 20th century are listed in 2-19.

Sometimes, instead of new fashion ideas being created by fashion designers, they come from the street. For instance, jeans and military surplus clothing started out as "street" fashions. Later, designers and trendsetters caught onto these fashions and made them "new" fashions.

20TH CENTURY **DESIGNERS** AND THEIR CONTRIBUTIONS TO **FASHION**

Giorgio Armani: menswear, especially unstructured suits, and some womenswear

Geoffrey Beene: American designer of elegant, superbly cut, couture apparel; licenses many other products

Bill Blass: American designer of elegant eveningwear as well as classic sportswear; licenses many products

Coco Chanel: the "Boyish Look" following World War I and her collarless suits

Liz Claiborne: women's sportswear and officewear

Oscar de la Renta: designs elegant men's and women's clothes in New York and Paris

Hubert de Givenchy: women's eveningwear, suits, and dresses

Christian Dior: the "New Look" following World War II

Gucci: handbags, shoes, and other leather goods with the "GG" logo

Jean-Paul Gaultier: daring, form-fitting, controversial designs for younger men and women; often unisex

Halston: women's clothing and accessories

Tommy Hilfiger: American designer who began with menswear; now designs casual womenswear, accessories, and home fashions

Donna Karan: simple women's clothing with sculptured shapes

Calvin Klein: jeans and sportswear

Ralph Lauren: the "Polo" logo and the American and English country look

Mary Quant: designed for young people in the 1960s; miniskirts and tights

Yves Saint Laurent: sophisticated, restrained designs for men and women

Emanuel Ungaro: designs soft, form-fitting apparel in many colors and patterns

Vera Wang: American designer known for exquisite bridal gowns and evening dresses

2-19
This is only a partial list of fashion designers whose names may be well-known to you.

CHAPTER
REVIEW

Key Points

- A fashion is a particular style of apparel that is popular at a given time. A classic style stays in fashion a long time, but a fad is popular for only a short time.

- Fashions go through cycles of being popular, and then they disappear for awhile, and later return to popularity.

- Many events throughout history have influenced the fabrics used, the designs created, and the uses made of clothing. Some influences have been social, religious, and political. Others are related to a country's economy. Technological advances have also played a part.

- Today's fashion designers look to various sources for inspiration. They study historic costumes, different cultures, and nature. They are also observers of the world around them—lifestyles, living patterns, and entertainers.

To Review

1. Which of these is *not* a style?
   A. A pleated skirt.
   B. A black coat.
   C. A bow tie.
   D. A double-breasted suit.

2. Explain the difference between a classic and a fad.

3. (True or False) If you want to build a long-lasting and exciting wardrobe, choose lots of fads.

4. List the four stages of the fashion cycle.

5. Why do fashions cycle at a faster rate today than they did in the past?

6. Give an example of a recent fashion trend that reflects a social influence.

7. Give an example of a historical event and how it influenced fashion.

8. In which type of economic system does the consumer play an important role?

9. List two developments in technology that have led to more and improved fabrics and apparel.

10. Where might a fashion idea come from before it is picked up by designers?

To Do

1. Collect pictures from magazines and newspapers of styles, fashions, classics, and fads. Arrange the four groups of pictures on a bulletin board.

2. Make a list of current fads. Vote to see how many students think each item will become a fashion.

3. Interview three older people. Ask each to list different fashions that he or she recalls cycled one or more times.

4. Look at current fads and fashions in fashion magazines. Then look in a history of costume book to see which fashion details from the past are being used today.

5. Survey adults to learn what type of clothing they wore when they were your age. Compare your findings in class discussions.

6. Collect pictures or make drawings of fashions worn at various times in history. Tell how each was influenced by political, economic, or technological events in history.

7. Interview an older adult who remembers World War II. Ask how the war effort influenced fashions and fabrics during that time.

8. Ask a local fashion buyer to speak on trends in fashions.

9. Research a popular fashion designer and prepare a report for the class. Try to find out what inspires and influences his or her designs.

10. Prepare a report on current fashion trends. Use fashion magazines, newspapers, television, and the Internet as sources of information.

To Think About

1. What are some of the current fashion trends for women? men? teens? Which do you think will remain "in fashion" the longest?

2. Does your school have a group of students that you consider to be trendsetters?

3. Which historical event do you think had the greatest impact on apparel design? Explain your answer.

4. Clothing in earlier times often reflected a person's wealth and status. Do you think clothes reflect wealth and status today?

5. Well-worn jeans and T-shirts have been popular with teens for some time now. Why are these styles so popular with young people? Do you predict this will change anytime soon?

CHAPTER 3

The Evolution of Textiles and Apparel

Objectives

After studying this chapter, you will be able to

- describe how textiles and apparel have evolved from prehistoric times to the present.
- explain early developments in the home sewing industry.
- explain the differences between natural and manufactured fibers.
- describe the three segments of today's textile and apparel industry.
- describe ways computer systems are used in the textile and garment-making industries today.
- summarize the provisions of the Fair Labor Standards Act and the Occupational Safety and Health Act.
- explain the impact of the apparel industry on world economies.

Key Terms

textiles
fiber
natural fibers
piecework
mass production
manufactured fibers
synthetics
merchandising plan
fashion centers
apparel marts
CAD
CAM
computer imaging
pattern grading
robotic machine
retailers
fashion merchandising
fashion promotion
Fair Labor Standards Act
Occupational Safety and Health Act
sweatshop
exports
imports
balance of trade
trade surplus
trade deficit

This chapter tells the story of the development of the textile and apparel industry. **Textiles** are products made of cloth. The basic unit of all textiles is the **fiber.** Since time began, people have used textiles to cover their bodies.

In the United States, clothing and accessories make up the largest share of textile production. The next largest share is used in industrial products. Textiles are used to make conveyor belts, filters, and space suits. Nose cones, football field turf, and even artificial hearts are made from textiles, too. The third largest share is used in floor coverings—carpets and rugs. The rest are used in other home furnishings. These include draperies, curtains, and upholstery fabrics, as well as bath and kitchen towels, blankets, sheets, and pillowcases. See 3-1 for a partial list of the many uses for textile fibers.

One of the biggest business success stories of the last 200 years is the amazing growth of the textile and apparel industry. It is one of the largest industries in the United States. In recent years, however, foreign textile companies are competing for more of this market. Many U.S. mills have had to slow down their production or close altogether. More apparel manufacturing is also being done in foreign countries, affecting U.S. apparel producers.

textiles
Products made of cloth.

fiber
Basic unit of all textiles.

USES FOR TEXTILES

Home Furnishings	Medical Uses	Industry
Sheets	Adhesive tape	Conveyor belts
Pillowcases	Bandages	Filters
Blankets	Antibacterial wound dressings	Safety nets
Bedspreads		Electronic circuit boards
Towels	Surgical gowns and masks	Protective garments for firefighters, police, and military
Rugs	Disposable sheets	
Carpets	Artificial hearts and arteries	Protective gloves for chefs
Lampshades	**Transportation**	Building insulation
Tablecloths	Tire cords	Hoses
Napkins	Seat belts	Mailbags
Curtains	Seat covers	
Draperies	Air bags	
Upholstery	Brake linings	
Flags	Boat sails	

3-1 All of these items have something in common. They are all made of textiles.

natural fibers
Fibers made from natural sources (plant or animal) and changed slightly during processing. Cotton, wool, silk, and linen are the most common natural fibers.

The History of Textiles and Apparel

From the Stone Age to the Space Age, the types and uses of textiles have changed greatly. To appreciate textile and apparel production today, you need to know a bit about the history of textiles and apparel.

Early Wearing Apparel

Fiber fragments have been found in archaeological excavations dating back thousands of years. Pictures found on the walls of caves show that people in the Stone Age used animal skins as clothing. These sources give evidence about some of the earliest uses of textiles and clothing.

Historians know that prehistoric people living in cold climates used animal skins to cover their bodies. As people learned to make and use tools, they applied these skills to the making of clothing. Animal skins were softened by rubbing them with stones or beating them with sticks. Needles were carved from bones. Thread was made from tendons of animal muscles. People were able to use these tools to sew sections of skin together to form more closely-fitted garments, 3-2.

Early people living in hot climates wore clothing as protection from the hot sun. These people made garments from trees and plants. They gathered bark from certain trees and soaked it in water. The bark was then pounded into a thin sheet and treated with oils. This produced a soft, strong fabric that could be used to make clothes. Soft grasses were also used to make garments and other items. Grasses were gathered and laced or woven together to form loose-fitting garments, hats, fishing nets, and baskets.

In ancient times, groups of people wandered from one place to another hunting food. Later, people began to live together and villages were settled. By living in one place, people had more time to develop skills. They learned how to grow plants and raise animals for food.

The raising of plants and animals led to the development of fabric making using natural fibers. **Natural fibers** are fibers taken from nature, such as cotton, flax, wool, and silk. People discovered the seed pods of cotton plants and the inner section of flax plants contained fibers. They discovered the hair of sheep and the cocoons of silkworms were fibers, too. They learned how to use these fibers to make cotton, linen, wool, and silk fabrics.

3-2
Early people used animal skins as garments.

For hundreds of years, cotton, flax, wool, and silk were the only fibers in use. All fibers were spun into yarns by hand. The weaving of yarns to make fabrics was done by hand, too.

The Industrial Revolution

In colonial days, tailors and dressmakers made clothing mainly for wealthy people. Clothing took many hours to make and was expensive. Most families took care of their own needs for cloth and garments. They spun yarns and wove fabrics using spinning wheels and looms in their own homes. The handwoven fabric was cut into pieces and sewn into garments by hand.

In England in the late 1700s, the production of textiles began to change. This time period signaled the start of the *Industrial Revolution*. This was a movement marked by major changes in the economy due to the invention of many machines. This movement was also sparked by the introduction of steam power and the development of the factory system.

In 1769, Richard Arkwright invented a spinning frame. It combined several hand-operated spinning devices into one large machine that was driven by water power. Sixteen years later, in 1785, Edmund Cartwright invented a steam-powered loom. Then the spinning and weaving steps were brought together under one roof in a textile mill. Inside the mill, raw materials were made into finished cloth. The first successful textile mill in the United States was built in 1789 by Samuel Slater.

In the years that followed, many other machines were invented that affected the textile industry. The use of these machines allowed fewer people to produce more fabric than ever before. Study chart 3-3 to see some significant inventions of this period.

INVENTIONS IN THE TEXTILE INDUSTRY

1733 John Kay–Flying shuttle
A tool used to weave the crosswise threads back and forth on a loom. Before this invention, the shuttle was moved by hand. On wide fabrics, two weavers operated the shuttle. With Kay's shuttle, the weaver pulled a stick and the shuttle automatically moved across the loom, hence the name the "flying" shuttle.

1769 Richard Arkwright–Water frame
This spinning machine was powered by water instead of by manpower. It was faster than hand spinning.

1770 James Hargreaves–Spinning jenny
Until this time, yarns were spun on a single rod called a spindle. The spinning jenny had eight spindles so a spinner could spin eight yarns at the same time.

1779 Samuel Crompton–Spinning mule
Features of the spinning jenny and water frame were combined into a huge machine. It could produce as much yarn as 200 spinners.

1785 Edmund Cartwright–Power loom
This loom was powered by steam instead of by operators using their hands.

1785 Thomas Bell–Cylinder printing
This invention allowed repetitious designs to be printed rapidly on cotton fabrics. Before this time, designs were block printed by hand.

1793 Eli Whitney–Cotton gin
A machine that separated the cotton fibers from the seeds. Before this time, this was done by hand using various crude tools.

1804 Joseph Marie Jacquard–Jacquard loom
This loom allowed the operator to weave different patterns in fabric automatically.

3-3
Machines invented during the Industrial Revolution had a great impact on the development of the textile industry.

Although the production of fabrics had evolved greatly, most garments were still being made one at a time. Until the mid 1800s, many companies paid women to sew for them in their homes. They were paid a certain amount for each garment or each step they finished. This was called **piecework.**

During the Civil War, **mass production** started to take over. Garment factories were built where many garments could be made at the same time. Instead of one person sewing an entire garment, several people shared the job. Each person sewed only one part of the garment. A worker might sew only leg seams or collars. Then the item was passed to someone else to complete another step. This continued until the garment was completed.

One of the inventions that greatly increased production was the band knife machine. Until the advent of this machine, garment pieces had been cut out by hand using shears or a short knife. This machine could cut around pattern pieces through many layers of fabric. Hundreds of pattern pieces were cut out at the same time.

Mass production made it possible to finish garments faster. Each worker became more skilled and could work faster at his or her particular step. Mass production made more clothes available to more people at lower prices than ever before. Production increased and factories were operating around the clock to produce ready-made clothing.

New methods of textile and garment production are continually found. Today, more and better fabrics can be made faster and at less cost than at any time in the past. When you wear a new garment, think of it as the latest advance in an old art. See 3-4.

Developments in the Home Sewing Industry

Two major developments greatly affected the home sewing industry. These were the invention of the sewing machine and the availability of paper patterns.

The Sewing Machine

Years ago, all garments were stitched by hand with a needle and thread. As early as the mid 1700s, attempts were made to develop a machine to sew fabrics. In 1830, a Frenchman, Barth´elemy Thimonnier, patented a single-thread sewing machine. A number of these machines were made and used to make army uniforms. However, the machines were destroyed by a mob of tailors. The tailors were afraid they would become unemployed because of the machines.

piecework
Work done one piece or one step at a time for which payment is made at a set rate per unit.

mass production
A manufacturing process that allows large numbers of items to be made at the same time.

The McCall Pattern Co.

3-4
Extensive research and progress in technology have produced beautiful, easy-care fabrics.

The first really usable sewing machine did not come about until 1846. In this year, Elias Howe designed a two-thread sewing machine. This machine had an eye-pointed needle and an underthread shuttle. This design allowed stitches to be "locked" into the fabric.

The first sewing machine that could sew continuously was developed by Isaac Singer in 1851. Howe's machine was powered by a hand crank, but Singer's model used a foot treadle to make it run. This allowed the sewer to use both hands to guide the fabric. Electric motors were added to sewing machines in 1889.

Paper Patterns

During the time that all sewing was done at home, people exchanged patterns with each other. They were cut from muslin or newsprint and were fitted to the body. Sewers made the pattern pieces larger or smaller as needed to fit family members.

Commercial paper patterns became available to home sewers during the middle of the nineteenth century. One tailor, Ebenezer Butterick, had many requests for patterns he was using. Butterick was the first to make patterns that were graded for different sizes. He decided to duplicate and sell them. He first created heavy cardboard templates, but soon realized he couldn't fold and ship the heavy patterns. Ebenezer tried lighter papers and discovered that tissue paper was ideal to work with and to package. In 1863, he started a company to send patterns to customers by mail order. The company is still in business today selling Butterick patterns.

In 1869, James McCall added another improvement to the graded pattern business. He used drawings as guides to cut patterns from tissue paper. In 1919, printed patterns were first sold by McCalls. See 3-5.

The Development of Manufactured Fibers

Manufactured fibers are fibers not found in nature. They are a fairly new development. Experimental production of manufactured fibers began around 1850. Rayon, originally sold as "artificial silk," was the first manufactured fiber to be developed. It was first commercially produced in the United States in 1910.

manufactured fibers
Fibers not found in nature. Rayon, acetate, and triacetate are made from cellulose. Other manufactured fibers are made primarily from carbon, oxygen, hydrogen, and nitrogen.

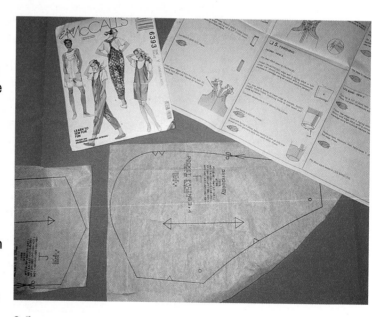

3-5
This is today's version of the paper patterns introduced in the 1860s.

Rayon is produced from cellulose, the fibrous substance in all plants. At first, linters were used as the source of cellulose. (Linters are the small fibers left on cotton seeds after ginning.) Later, wood from softwood trees was used. Two other manufactured fibers are also made from cellulose: acetate and triacetate.

synthetics
Manufactured
fibers.

The other manufactured fibers are sometimes called **synthetics.** They are made completely from chemicals. Four elements form the basis for these fibers. They are carbon (from petroleum or natural gas), hydrogen (from water), nitrogen (from air), and oxygen (from air).

The first fiber to be made completely from chemicals was nylon. It was made in 1938 by the Du Pont Company. Other synthetic fibers include polyester, olefin, acrylic, modacrylic, rubber, and spandex.

During the last 30 years, almost 250 different fibers have been manufactured. Synthetics now account for 94 percent of worldwide fiber production. Only 14 percent of the synthetic fibers are made in North America, down by 9 percent over the last 20 years. Asian countries produce 65 percent of the world's supply. Manufactured fibers are used to make a wide range of textile products. See 3-6.

Today, more manufactured fibers are used to make clothes than natural fibers. Often, the two types of fibers are used together to take advantage of the good characteristics of each type.

TEXTILE **TECHNOLOGY**

- In the Arctic, the Army uses three-dimensional nylon fabrics for insulated shelters. These shelters keep the inside temperature at 50 degrees when it's as low as 65 degrees below zero outside.

- Olefin and acrylic sandbags are used as crash barriers on highways and on levees to prevent flooding.

- Aramid, a manufactured fiber that is lighter and tougher than steel, is used to make vests and helmets worn by police officers and soldiers. A seven-layer vest weighs only 2 ½ pounds. It can deflect a knife slash and stop a bullet fired from a gun ten feet away.

- Olefin and polyester fabrics control erosion on steep slopes, line roadside ditches, and reenforce streambeds and shorelines.

- An olefin fiber that is ten times stronger than steel is used to reenforce hoses and power belts.

3-6
These are just a few of the many examples of the amazing uses of textiles today.

The Textile and Apparel Industry Today

The textile and apparel industry today consists of three segments. The first segment is the textile industry where the fabrics used for apparel and other uses are produced. The second segment is apparel production. This includes all the steps in turning fabrics into apparel, including the design process and garment manufacturing. The third segment is the retail segment. It includes all the business activities involved with selling fashion items to consumers.

Textile Production

The textile industry includes all the people and processes involved in making fibers and fabrics. The ranchers who raise sheep for wool and the farmers who grow cotton are part of this industry. The chemists who develop manufactured fibers are part of the textile industry, too.

The textile industry is one of the oldest and largest in the nation. The long road from fibers to fabrics requires many processes and thousands of workers.

You may think of textiles as only clothing. This is the largest use of textiles, with home furnishings following close behind. But there are also many other uses of textiles. See 3-7. The space program, transportation, personal safety, sports, and medicine could not have advanced to the present level without the textile industry.

The first stage in the production of textiles is producing the fibers. The natural fibers of cotton and linen come from cotton and flax plants. Wool comes from the fleece of sheep, and silk comes from cocoons spun by silkworms. Manufactured fibers are produced by various chemical companies.

The second stage of textile production takes place in textile mills where the fibers are spun into yarns. Most of these mills are located in the states of North Carolina, South Carolina, and Georgia.

Fabric production is next. Textile mills also weave or knit yarns into fabrics. Looms and knitting machines produce unfinished cloth.

The final stage is fabric finishing. Fabrics are dyed and printed, as well as given special treatments that give the desired performance characteristics. Fabrics may be water repellent, fireproof, or wrinkle resistant.

The fabrics are now ready for sale to apparel manufacturers or other companies requiring fabrics in their products. Some fabrics go to supply

3-7
Towels and washcloths are some of the home products that make up the third largest use of textiles.

Nanotechnology in the Apparel Industry

Apparel that battles bugs, soothes with aloe vera, and fends off odors! Can it be? Yes, thanks to fiber innovations brought to us through the science of nanotechnology. **Nanotechnology** involves the transformation of materials at the molecular level, atom by atom. In other words, finishes are not added to the fabric. These characteristics result from alterations to the molecular structure of the chemicals that are used to form the fibers.

Most fiber enhancements are developed to address common consumer complaints about fabrics. Though some of these enhancements have been around for years, they were not durable. After a few washings, the treatment was no longer effective. They also compromised the style, drape, comfort, and feel of the fabric. Today, consumers can have it all.

The complaints and their innovative solutions include the following:

Static electricity: When applied to polyester, this treatment reduces static cling and repels statically attractive substances, such as dog hair, lint, and dust. Your clothes won't cling to you, and no more static shocks.

Stains: New innovations have led to fabrics that repel stains as well as release stains, so you're protected on defense and offense. Spill resistance keeps stains from soaking in, while stain release allows them to easily come clean. If coffee spills on your pants, it just beads up and rolls right off.

Insect bites: When heading for the woods, clothes treated with a substance from chrysanthemums will repel insects. No more bites from mosquitoes, ticks, ants, flies, and chiggers! Look for "Buzz Off" clothing by Orvis.

Moisture: You will look and feel cool all day long with new natural and synthetic fabrics that provide moisture wicking. Fabrics pull perspiration away from the skin, keeping the body cooler, dryer, and more comfortable. The fabrics "breathe." When it's hot, they let air in. When it's chilly, the fibers close up.

Odors: No one wants smelly socks, so you can get ones that have a new odor-fighting component. Gore-Tex even makes scent-suppressing clothing for hunters. Towels treated with Microban fend off mold, mildew, and odor-causing bacteria. Antimicrobials inhibit the growth of the micro-organisims that cause odors and stains.

Irritation: Moisturizing socks and aloe-enriched intimates soothe the skin thanks to technology that involves microcapsules. Microcapsules included in the fabric rupture on movement, contacting the skin.

Who knows what lies ahead as science continues to tackle common consumer complaints.

the needs of the home sewing market. Coordination of this stage in the textile segment takes place in sales offices and showrooms usually located in New York City.

Environmental Efforts of Textile Producers

Many fiber manufacturers are doing their part to protect the environment. *Lyocell* is a new manufactured fiber made from wood pulp from trees grown in replanted forests. The chemical agents used to produce the fiber are recycled. The fiber itself, which is biodegradable, is strong and absorbent.

Recycled plastic bottles are being made into a polyester fiber. The bottles are sorted, cleaned, chopped, melted, and extruded into fibers. The fibers are made into fabrics used in upholstery, sportswear, denim, thermal underwear, and other items. See 3-8.

The American Textile Manufacturers Institute (ATMI) began a program in 1992 to encourage U.S. textile companies to strengthen their commitment to the environment. *Encouraging Environmental Excellence* (E3) challenges textile companies to go beyond simply complying with environmental laws. Participating companies must develop a policy and set goals to reduce

Source: National Association for Plastic Container Recovery

3-8
By recycling empty plastic soda bottles, you can play a role in protecting the environment.

American Textile Manufacturers Institute

3-9
The E3 logo signifies this company is taking extra steps to protect the environment.

merchandising plan
The producer's plans for creating a line of designs for a given season.

fashion centers
Cities such as New York, Los Angeles, Dallas, Chicago, Atlanta, and Miami where retail store buyers come during fashion weeks to view the new collections and make their selections.

apparel marts
Large buildings in Atlanta, Dallas, and Chicago where many garment manufacturers have showrooms and sales offices.

waste and conserve water and energy. They must also work with their customers and suppliers to encourage pollution prevention and waste minimization. The E3 logo can be displayed on their products, advertising the companies' commitment to the environment. See 3-9. The Environmental Protection Agency (EPA) has recognized the companies in this program for their outstanding job of reducing waste and improving the environment.

Apparel Production

Apparel production includes all the people and processes involved in designing and making garments. It begins with the fabrics that eventually become items of apparel. The designing of garments, pattern making, cutting, sewing, assembling, and distribution of finished items to stores are all included in the process.

Apparel production is the second largest manufacturing industry in the United States. The largest concentration of garment factories is in the Middle Atlantic region. The state of New York alone has hundreds of factories that produce garments. The leading manufacturers have design and marketing offices there as well. On the West coast, Los Angeles is the headquarters for the garment industry. In addition, small garment factories are located throughout the United States.

Apparel production begins with a **merchandising plan**—the producer's plans for creating a line of designs for a given season. There are four production seasons: Spring, Summer, Fall I, and Fall II (Winter). The firm's staff tries to predict what their customers will buy. Apparel designers interpret these trends and create sample designs. These samples are shown to retail buyers who then make their selections.

During *market weeks,* the retail store buyers come to the **fashion centers** to view the new collections and make their selections. The U.S. fashion centers are New York, Los Angeles, Dallas, Chicago, Atlanta, and Miami. In several large cities, such as Atlanta, Dallas, and Chicago, there are **apparel marts.** These are buildings where many garment manufacturers have permanent showrooms and sales offices. The manufacturers show their collections and take orders from the buyers for their retail stores.

The designs that are selected are then readied for production. Master patterns are made for the standard sizes. Fabrics, fasteners, thread, and trims are ordered. The cutting and sewing begins about six months before the clothes will appear in retail stores.

Layers of fabrics are cut using computerized knife cutters, water-jet cutters, or lasers, 3-10. *Lasers* use intense beams of light that vaporize the fabric, making fast and precise cuts.

Most of the sewing is done in assembly-line fashion. A piecework system is used in which one person does one specific task, often using a specialized machine. Bundles of collars may be taken to one station and sleeves to another. Later in the assembly line, the parts are sewn together by other workers.

Following a final inspection, the garment is steam pressed. Labels or hangtags are attached. The garments are now ready to be shipped to the stores that ordered them.

Technological Advances in Apparel Production

One of the most important technological advances of the twentieth century is the development of computers. Computers have touched nearly every area of life, and textiles and apparel are no exception. In fact, computers are playing a bigger part in the design and manufacture of apparel than in most other industries.

A system called CAD/CAM has revolutionized the garment industry, saving time and reducing costs in all areas. **CAD (computer-aided design)** is used to create textile and garment designs. **CAM (computer-aided manufacturing)** is used to control the steps in producing finished textiles and garments.

Textile designers develop designs, patterns, weaves, and suggest color combinations for fabrics. Fashion designers design clothing and accessories to be made from those fabrics. Both of these designers can use CAD systems to help create the looks they want. As they enter design commands into a computer, their design appears on a monitor. Details are changed until the designer is satisfied.

Textile designers can change the design of a fabric with the proper computer commands. Plaids can be made smaller or larger. Colors can be changed to find the right tint or shade the designer wants.

Computer imaging is a program many fashion designers use. This program has a three-dimensional effect. It allows an image on the display screen to

CAD (computer-aided design)
A computer system used to create textile and garment designs on a display screen.

CAM (computer-aided manufacturing)
A computer system used to control specific steps in the production of textiles and garments.

computer imaging
A computer program that allows an image on a display screen to be turned to any angle in a three-dimensional effect.

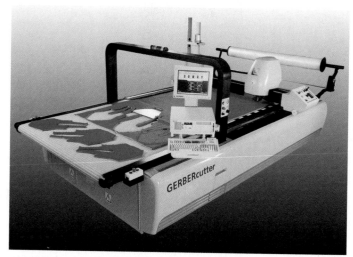

Gerber Technology

3-10 _____

Today's high-speed computerized cutting machines can cut single layers or multiple layers of fabric quickly and precisely.

be turned to any angle. The fashion designer can sketch a garment design on the display screen. Then it can be turned so all sides of the design can be seen, 3-11.

Pattern makers use CAD systems, too. Pattern pieces can be drawn on the computer screen. The designer may decide to change the shape of the sleeve or move darts to a different location. The pattern maker can input these changes. The computer will automatically change all pattern pieces to go with the changes. Different sizes can be made with only the touch of a few buttons on the computer keyboard. This step is called **pattern grading.**

CAM systems are used in all areas of textile production. Textile makers use computerized machines for knitting, weaving, dyeing, and finishing fabrics.

CAM systems can control all areas of garment making, too. Many garment manufacturers use computers to determine the best layouts for pattern pieces on fabric. Data is entered into the computer as to width of fabric and the amount on each bolt. Pattern pieces are shown on the display screen and moved into position. Plaids and stripes can be matched by computer. Grain lines and nap are automatically checked. Pattern pieces are placed to make the best use of all of the fabric in order to avoid waste.

When the computer operator is satisfied with the layout, a printout is made. This printout is called a *marker,* 3-12. It is used as a cutting guide. The pattern size and name of each piece is listed as the marker is being printed.

Garments may not be made at the same place as the patterns are made. Some companies have computers that have a telecommunications feature. This allows the marker to be sent electronically to the garment manufacturer.

A computer can control the knife cutters, water-jet cutters, and laser beams used to cut layers of fabric. The speed of the cutting device is adjusted according to fabric thickness and the number of pieces being cut. The sizes and shapes of garment pieces are programmed into the computer. The cutters are then preset to cut around the pieces.

Robotic machines are operated by computers. They are being used to completely and automatically assemble and package garments. An operator stationed at a computer terminal controls the

pattern grading
The process of adjusting pattern pieces to make garments in a range of sizes. This process is now computerized.

robotic machine
A machine that operates automatically and is controlled by a computer.

Gerber Technology

3-11_____
Three-dimensional pattern design software enables designers to view 2-dimensional patterns on a 3-dimensional human form to check fit and drape. The image can be viewed from all angles by rotating the form.

system. Garment pieces are moved from one workstation to the next when the operator presses a button. One machine will sew, another will trim, and another will press. At the end of the line, garments are labeled and packaged.

CAM systems keep track of inventories, operating costs, and production information. Different terminals throughout a manufacturing plant feed information into the main system. At any time, plant managers have access to information about anything and everything that is going on in the plant.

As computer systems become more advanced, their uses in the textile and apparel industry will become even more amazing. In the future, who knows how quickly a computer-designed fashion will make it to a retail outlet.

Gerber Technology

3-12

CAD systems can automatically generate markers to maximize fabric use.

The Retail Segment

The third segment in the textile and apparel industry is the retail segment. After the garments are produced, they are ready for sale to consumers. **Retailers** buy the garments from the manufacturers and sell them to customers. Retailers include department stores, discount chains, specialty stores (carrying specific kinds of apparel), and mail-order companies, 3-13.

Fashion merchandising includes all phases of planning, buying, and selling apparel. It is the central function of retailers. An important part of selling is fashion promotion. **Fashion promotion** includes advertising, setting up window and store displays, media publicity, and special events, such as fashion shows. All of these efforts are planned to increase clothing sales and to move the merchandise ordered by the retailer.

Factors Influencing the Apparel Industry

Several factors are influencing today's apparel industry. Some of these are the result of factory conditions and policies that existed in the early years of apparel manufacturing. These conditions and practices helped lead to the enactment of laws to protect workers. Another factor is the impact of the apparel industry on world economies.

retailers
Businesses that buy from manufacturers and sell goods to customers.

fashion merchandising
A field that includes all the phases of planning, buying, and selling clothes and accessories.

fashion promotion
A field that includes all the efforts made to inform people through advertising of what is new in fashion and convincing them to buy it.

3-13
Retailers make up the third and final segment of the textile and apparel industry.

Laws to Protect Apparel Workers

Earlier in this chapter you read about the first textile mills built in the late 1700s. At that time, labor was scarce. About 90 percent of Americans were farmers. To meet labor needs, whole families were brought to the mills to work. Children as young as four or five years old worked at the looms. The *Lowell system* hired young, unmarried women to work in the mills. They were well paid by the standards for the period.

European immigration increased the labor supply in the mid 1800s. Nearly three-fourths of U.S. factory workers were employed in the mills and factories of New England and the middle states. Most produced cotton, wool, and silk textiles. Conditions in the factories deteriorated as demands for more production increased. The mills were unsanitary, unhealthful buildings. The average workday was 12-15 hours. Some states passed laws to regulate child labor, but they were minimal. The abundant labor supply continued to keep wages low. Early attempts to form labor unions were considered illegal acts by the courts.

By the early 1900s, child labor continued to be a serious problem. According to the 1900 census, one out of three workers in Southern cotton mills was a child under 16. Children worked all night at the looms. Few safety devices existed on the dangerous looms, causing long hair to get caught. Industrial accidents were frequent occurrences. Public awareness of the ages of these children and the hours they worked led to the first state labor laws in the early 1900s. At least 38 states set a minimum age of 12 years and a workday of ten hours for children in factories. This was an improvement, but a long way from today's standards.

It wasn't until 1938 that a federal law was passed—the **Fair Labor Standards Act.** It established a minimum wage and a maximum work-week of 40 hours. The minimum wage is raised from time to time to keep workers' wages in line with the cost of living. The act also forbade employment of children under 16 in many jobs. These provisions were designed to protect the educational opportunities of the young. It also prevented them from working in jobs that might be hazardous to their health. See 3-14 for key features of the Child Labor Standards of the Fair Labor Standards Act. All employees who work for employers involved in interstate commerce are covered by this law. States may have stricter laws that cover all workers.

Many companies improved working conditions in the 1920s. They installed safety devices and improved sanitation. It wasn't until 1970, however, that the federal **Occupational Safety and Health Act** was passed. This act calls for safe and healthful working conditions. The Occupational Safety and Health Administration (OSHA) was formed to set and enforce job safety and health standards. OSHA requires each employer to provide a safe place to work. Employers also are responsible for following OSHA standards and making sure employees follow safety procedures. If employers do not comply, OSHA can force a court appearance and fines. Some of the responsibilities of both employers and employees are listed in 3-15.

Fair Labor Standards Act
A 1938 federal law that established a minimum wage and a maximum work week of 40 hours. It also included child labor regulations.

Occupational Safety and Health Act
This 1970 act calls for safe and healthful working conditions in the workplace. The Occupational Safety and Health Administration (OSHA) was formed to set and enforce job safety and health standards.

FAIR LABOR STANDARDS ACT: CHILD LABOR PROVISIONS

- 18-year-olds can work at any job for any number of hours.

- 16- and 17-year-olds can work at any nonhazardous job for any number of hours. (Hazardous jobs include operating motor vehicles or power-driven machinery, working with explosives or nuclear materials, and many jobs in construction, demolition, meat processing, and other fields.)

- 14- and 15-year-olds may work outside school hours in various nonmanufacturing, nonmining, and nonhazardous jobs, but for no longer than three hours per school day or 18 hours per school week. Their work may not begin before 7 a.m. or extend past 7 p.m.

- Young people of any age may deliver newspapers or work for parents in a nonfarm business. They may also perform in radio, television, movie, or theatrical productions.

3-14
These provisions are important in safeguarding the health of young workers and preventing work from interfering with their education.

sweatshop
A manufacturing plant that may use child labor, pay less than minimum wages, not pay overtime, or have unclean or unsafe facilities.

Although most apparel manufacturers follow safe and fair employment practices, some sweatshops exist in this country (and other countries). A **sweatshop** is a manufacturing plant that may use child labor, pay less than minimum wages, not pay overtime, or have unclean or unsafe facilities. Unethical employers operate in this manner to keep their labor and manufacturing costs low. They may employ illegal immigrants who are afraid to object to their working conditions for fear of being returned to their native countries. Oftentimes these workers are hindered by their inability to speak and understand English.

Today, U.S. sweatshops operate as small subcontractor businesses in the cities with major apparel centers. These cities are Los Angeles, New York, Dallas, Miami, and Atlanta. Be aware that garments made in these sweatshops may still bear the "Made in the U.S.A." label. Though efforts are made to shut down these operations, they still continue to exist.

Impact of the Apparel Industry on World Economies

exports
Products sent out of a country to other countries.

Almost all of the early textile products—coarse and cheap fabrics—were exported to China. **Exports** are products sent out of a country to other countries. Most of the cotton crop was also sold overseas. Finer

RESPONSIBILITIES FOR A SAFE WORK **ENVIRONMENT**

Employer Responsibilities:
- Provide a workplace free from recognized hazards that could cause death or serious physical harm.
- Comply with all standards, rules, and regulations under OSHA.
- Make sure employees have and use safe tools and equipment.
- Post signs to warn of potential hazards.
- Establish and update safe operating procedures.
- Provide health and safety-related training.
- Keep records of work-related injuries and illnesses.

Employee Responsibilities:
- Read the OSHA poster.
- Comply with all standards.
- Follow all employer safety and health rules.
- Use or wear prescribed protective equipment.
- Report hazardous conditions to supervisor.
- Report job-related injuries or illnesses to employer.

3-15
Both employers and employees must do their part in keeping the workplace safe.

clothes were imported. **Imports** are products that come into a country from foreign sources. In the 1700s, exports exceeded imports in value so the U.S. had a "favorable" balance of trade—more exports than imports. A country's **balance of trade** is the relationship between the value of its imports compared to its exports. This **trade surplus** (exports exceeding imports) allowed money to flow into this country in payment. By 1865, however, most of the textiles and cotton crop remained in this country to satisfy the growing need of American consumers.

Today, the U.S. exports millions of dollars in textiles and apparel products each year. However, we import three times this amount. The result is a **trade deficit,** or negative trade balance. This fact significantly impacts world economies.

There are several reasons for this imbalance in trade. One reason is the low wages paid in some developing countries compared to the high wages paid in the U.S. Low-wage countries can mass-produce garments more cheaply. They can then sell these garments in the U.S. at a lower price than garments made here. For many countries, apparel manufacturing is a major revenue source. Often, apparel factories are the largest employers. Many people in developing countries rely on this industry to provide their basic needs. U.S. companies also must comply with government safety regulations and provide benefits to employees not provided in some foreign countries. Even with transportation and tariff costs, retailers still often choose to do business offshore. For a foreign-produced garment that sells for $100, $50 might go to the retailer in the form of a markup, $35 to the manufacturer, $10 to the contractor, and $5 to the garment worker. Two-thirds of the apparel worn by Americans is made in foreign factories.

Apparel production is labor intensive, so the U.S. is at a disadvantage when competing with low-wage countries. Clothing factories can be set up inexpensively in some countries and little technology is needed. The result has been a decrease in apparel production in this country as more garments are imported, leading to some unemployment in the industry. Nearly 300 U.S. textile plants have closed in the last five years while employment has fallen 40 percent. The closings have prompted the U.S. textile industry to urge the government to enact trade restrictions, particularly with China. *Quotas,* which set limits on imports, have been enacted through 2008. Proponents of free trade oppose such agreements.

On the other hand, some U.S. companies are taking advantage of the cheap labor supply outside of the United States. They have chosen to open their own production facilities in foreign countries to manufacture their garments. Nike products, for example, are manufactured by more than 400 factories in 43 different countries. A garment could be designed in New York, made of fabric woven in Australia, cut in Hong Kong, sewn in China, and marketed in Germany.

Because so many garments are now imported, laws passed in the 1980s require textile and apparel products to be labeled showing where they were made.

imports
Products that come into a country from foreign sources.

balance of trade
The relationship between the value of a country's imports compared to its exports.

trade surplus
Exports of a country exceed its imports, allowing money to flow into the country in payment.

trade deficit
Imports of a country exceed its exports, causing a negative trade balance. Money flows out of the country in payment for imports.

CHAPTER REVIEW

Key Points

- Early people used animal skins for clothing. The raising of plants and animals led to the development of fabrics using natural fibers.

- The Industrial Revolution led to the production of textiles using spinning frames and steam-powered looms. Mass production greatly increased garment production, as did the invention of the sewing machine. The first manufactured fiber was produced in 1910.

- The textile and apparel industry consists of three segments: textile production, apparel production, and the retail segment. The textile industry includes all the people and processes involved in making fibers and fabrics. Apparel production includes all the people and processes involved in designing and making garments. Retailers then buy the garments from the manufacturers and sell them to customers.

- Apparel production begins with a merchandising plan for creating a line of designs for a given season. During market weeks, the designs are on display at fashion centers and apparel marts. Buyers select the designs they want to sell in their retail stores.

- Computers are now involved in almost every aspect of the design and manufacture of apparel.

- Early child labor abuses, long work weeks, and low pay in the textile mills were an important factor in the passing of the Fair Labor Standards Act in 1938. The Occupational Safety and Health Act has led to safer and healthier working conditions.

- The U.S. exports more textiles and apparel than it imports, creating a trade deficit. One reason is the low wages in developing countries. The result has been a decrease in apparel production in this country as more garments are imported.

To Review

1. List five uses of textile products other than clothing.
2. How were animal skins prepared and sewn in prehistoric times?
3. Name four natural fibers.
4. Name four inventors and their inventions that affected the textile and apparel industry.
5. What was the first manufactured fiber to be developed?
6. What is included in fabric finishing?
7. What happens during market weeks?
8. Identify and describe the computer systems that have revolutionized the garment industry.
9. What is fashion merchandising and how does it relate to fashion promotion?
10. List the three main provisions of the Fair Labor Standards Act.
11. What is required by the Occupational Safety and Health Act?
12. Explain how wages have affected the balance of trade for textiles and apparel.

To Do

1. Find or draw pictures of many new and different uses of textile products. Arrange them on a bulletin board.

2. Write a two-page research report on archaeological evidence of textile and garment use by prehistoric people.

3. Pretend you are an inventor from the Industrial Revolution. Give an oral "sales presentation" to the class. Use visual aids to explain how your invention works. Try to convince your audience why they should give your invention a try. Conduct Internet or library research to prepare for your presentation.

4. Work in a small group to research the development and uses of one of the manufactured fibers. Give a panel presentation to the class.

5. Pretend you are a textile designer. Use a computer and a drawing program to create a fabric design on the screen. If you do not have access to this type of software, draw your design on paper.

6. Find out more information on the Encouraging Environmental Excellence Program of the American Textile Manufacturers Institute and prepare a report for the class. You can visit their Web site at atmi.org/programs.

7. Invite an OSHA representative to speak to the class on employers' and workers' rights and responsibilities under OSHA. You can also visit the following U.S. Department of Labor Web site for information on safe working conditions: dol.gov.

8. Take ten items of clothing from your closet. Read the labels to see where the garments were manufactured. Tally your results. Total the results for all members of the class. Create a chart listing the garment sources. What conclusions can you draw from this survey?

To Think About

1. What was the impact of mass production during the Industrial Revolution?

2. What have been the effects of the increased use of computers in the textile and apparel industry? Do you think there are any downsides to this change in the industry?

3. What can you, as a wearer of apparel, do to save natural resources and protect the environment?

4. What are the costs and benefits of providing a safe work environment for employees? for employers?

5. What are the ethical issues involved in the decision by some manufacturers to move their apparel production facilities to developing countries?

2

Managing Your Apparel Dollar

Chapters

CHAPTER 4

Planning a Wardrobe

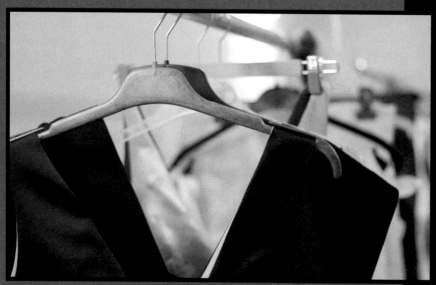

Objectives

After studying this chapter, you will be able to

- explain the goals of wardrobe planning.
- make an inventory of your clothes.
- evaluate your clothes inventory to determine your clothing needs.
- demonstrate how to mix and match clothing to create new outfits.
- explain how accessories can extend your wardrobe.
- prioritize clothing needs and wants.
- identify factors that affect your clothing preferences.
- select appropriate clothing for different occasions and activities.

Key Terms

wardrobe
wardrobe plan
inventory
evaluate
mix-and-match
  wardrobe
accessories
order of priority

It's probably happened to you. A friend calls and invites you to go somewhere special. You hang up the phone, and it suddenly hits you. You shout, "I have nothing to wear!" You look in your closet and shake your head. Nothing seems right for the occasion. That's when you think to yourself, "Why didn't I plan for something like this so I'd have the right clothes to wear?"

A simple solution to this dilemma could have been a wardrobe plan. In this chapter, you will learn how to look at the clothes you have and decide what you need to add to meet your needs. With careful planning, you will be more likely to have the right clothes for any occasion. With planning, you can also get more of the clothes you want with the amount of money you have to spend. Planning also helps you make the most of the clothes you already have. It guides you in choosing new clothes to fit your lifestyle. This chapter will show you how to develop your wardrobe planning skills.

Your Wardrobe Plan

A **wardrobe** is all the clothes and accessories a person has to wear. A good wardrobe does not just happen. Careful planning is needed. A plan is defined as a method used to achieve a goal. With a **wardrobe plan,** you will know what clothes you have now and what you will need to add in the future.

In planning a wardrobe, the major goal is to have the appropriate clothes for any activity that might come your way. You want your wardrobe to include suitable clothes for all your activities—at home, at school, and for special occasions.

Another goal of planning is to make better use of the clothes you already have. Before you buy a new garment, you should know how it will fit into your wardrobe. With planning, you will be able to see which of your garments go well with other garments. Your outfits will seem to double in number.

A third goal in planning your wardrobe is to create a buying plan. When you go shopping, you'll know what you're looking for. This will save you time and money. You won't waste time looking for items you don't really need. You won't waste money buying clothes you forgot you already had or won't wear. You will know what you need to add to your wardrobe so you can make wise purchases.

A Look at Your Clothes

A good wardrobe plan will help you make better use of your present wardrobe. Most people are not aware of how many clothes they really have. Your first step in making a wardrobe plan is taking an inventory of the clothes you already have, 4-1. An **inventory** is a count or listing of certain items—in this case, clothing and accessories. Have you ever made an inventory of all your clothing? Making a clothing inventory can be fun and can

wardrobe
All the clothes and accessories a person has to wear.

wardrobe plan
A plan that includes the clothes you have now and what you will need to add in the future.

inventory
An itemized list of goods, possessions, or resources. A wardrobe inventory is an itemized list of clothes and accessories.

Nancy Henke-Konopasek

4-1
Take a look at your wardrobe before you shop to see what you already have.

give you a feeling of self-confidence and organization. You may even find a surprise in the back of your closet!

It is a good idea to take your clothing inventory at the beginning of a season or school year. The chart in 4-2 can serve as a guide for your inventory. You may want to add more rows or columns. Include all of your clothes and accessories. Group your clothes by type. For instance, put all of your pants together, your shirts together, and your shorts together.

List of My Clothes	Description	How I Like It	Condition	What I Need to Add or Do
Suits (guys)	none	don't like		
Sport Coats (guys)	1–plain brown	OK	like new	
Dresses (girls)				
Skirts (girls)				
Slacks	1–tan 1–plaid	like alot don't like	good too small	1–pair plain-colored
Jeans	4 pairs	great	3–good 1–worn out	1–new pair
Shirts/Blouses	3–plain 5–pattern	like patterned ones best	2–too small	2–new shirts
Sweaters				
Jackets				
Coats	all weather	fits my needs	good	
Shoes/Boots	1–pair for school 1–pair boots	OK my favorite	beat up pretty good	new shoes
Underwear				
Socks				
Jewelry				
Belts				
Other				

4-2
This partially complete chart may help you get started on a clothing inventory of your own.

In addition to listing everything, ask yourself these questions. Which clothes do you enjoy wearing? Which ones help you look your best? Which ones fit your personality? Your answers to these questions will depend on how the clothes are made, how they fit you, how you feel in them, the color, the type of fabric, and the design. Your answers will help you have a better idea as to your clothing likes and dislikes.

Evaluating Your Wardrobe

As you complete your wardrobe inventory, evaluate each item. To **evaluate** means to determine the worth of something. After you list each item, tell how you like it. Do you enjoy wearing the item, or do you seldom, if ever, wear it? Does it go with other items in your wardrobe, or do you need something to wear with it?

evaluate
To determine the worth of something.

Evaluate the condition of each item. Is it like new, or is it almost worn out? Does it need to be cleaned? Does it need to be repaired? If there are garments that need repair, put them in a special section. Indicate what needs to be done. Is a seam coming loose or a button falling off? As you find time, you can work on them. If items need to be dry cleaned, put these aside, too.

Evaluate the fit of each item. Have you outgrown some of your clothes? Some of your clothing will be outgrown and can be passed on to someone else.

When your inventory is complete, you can do an overall evaluation of your wardrobe. In the last column of your inventory, explain what action you will take. For instance, you can now see what clothes you have and what, if any, new ones you need to add. You may find that you have more clothes in good condition than you thought you had. You may discover that you can mix and match more garments to create additional outfits. You can also decide what to do with garments that need to be repaired or discarded. Indicate who might welcome your discarded items.

Now look at the garments under each listing in your wardrobe inventory. Do you find you have too many of one type of clothing and not enough of another? For instance, are all of your shirts suited to jeans and only one to dress slacks? Do you find you have enough dress-up clothes for the number of times you need them?

What else can you learn from your chart? Perhaps from the comments under the heading "How I Like It," you can tell what type of clothing you like best. These garments are probably best suited to your figure type or build, skin coloring, and personality. Deciding what you like best when there is so much to choose from is an accomplishment. Now when you shop for new clothes, you will know the types of clothing you enjoy wearing. This will help you make wise purchases.

Trends Making News

Teen-age Trendsetters

In today's booming economy, clothing manufacturers are targeting teens and preteens because of their huge numbers. In 2003, there were 33 million 12- to 19-year-olds in the U.S. population. This number has been growing every year since 1992, and is expected to top off in 2010. At that point, there will be almost 35 million teens in the U.S., more than ever before.

Not only are there many teens, but their buying power is tremendous. According to Teenage Research Unlimited, a teen-oriented marketing firm, teens spent $159 billion in 2005. About 40 percent of this money was spent on clothing.

These two factors have made teens a prime target market. Research shows that 68 percent of teens go to shopping malls each week, spending about three and one-half hours there. They spend about $103 per week. Every manufacturer and retailer wants a piece of this action. In addition, they want to establish a relationship with these young buyers to build brand loyalty that will stay with them into their adult years.

Because of the dollars at stake, stores want to be sure they have what teens are buying when they are buying them. This means retailers have to plan ahead for the items to be designed, manufactured, and shipped to them. To be sure they don't miss this opportunity, manufacturers watch teen-age trendsetters. They invite them to fill out questionnaires on the Web or in magazines. Some companies even hire groups of teens to meet with executives where they try products and talk about fashions.

Companies look for the 20 percent of teens who are innovative enough to start new fashion trends. Marketers call one group "Edge" kids—those that start new trends. A second group is called "Influencers." Members of this second group look at the new trends and decide whether they will adopt them. If they do give their approval, the remaining 80 percent of teens will latch on to the style. In the meantime, the Edge kids are on to a new look.

Mixing and Matching

Mixing and matching is an easy way to make more outfits from the clothes you own. A **mix-and-match wardrobe** is a wardrobe in which the garments have been coordinated (put together) to add variety and to create more outfits. Even if you combine only a few garments in mix-and-match outfits, you can give the impression of having more clothes, 4-3.

Look through your wardrobe. Do you find that a certain color is repeated in many of your clothes? If so, you could use that color as a foundation as you build your mix-and-match wardrobe.

Perhaps many of your clothes are blue. You could choose to develop a red, white, and blue color scheme. You could begin with a few basic garments including blue jeans, navy pants, a white top (shirt or blouse), a red print top, and a red V-neck sweater. You could wear blue jeans with either the white or the red print top. You could add the sweater to either outfit. That makes four different outfits. Change the blue jeans to navy pants, and you have four more!

mix-and-match wardrobe
A wardrobe in which garments can be combined with many other garments to create several different outfits.

Try New Combinations

Study your wardrobe carefully. Select a pair of slacks and see how many shirts, sweaters, and vests look good with them. Imagine combinations you have not thought of before. Hold the combinations together to see the effect. How would a belt or tie look with an outfit? With this try-and-see method, you may find new, unexpected combinations.

Sport coats and slacks for guys can be interchanged to make other outfits. A plaid sport coat could be worn with several different pairs of slacks. If the slacks are the same color as one of the colors in the plaid, the effect is even better. The same coat could be worn with jeans for some activities. Add a vest or sweater and you'll have another outfit. Suppose a young man's wardrobe includes a pair of jeans, corduroy slacks, and khaki pants. He also has a plaid shirt, T-shirt, western shirt, solid color shirt, and jacket. How many different combinations could you make for him?

For girls, skirts, pants, blouses, vests, sweaters, and jackets can be mixed and matched. A skirt could be teamed with a lacy blouse for a dressy occasion. The same skirt could then be teamed with a sweater to create

The McCall Pattern Co.

4-3 By combining the jacket with either a skirt or slacks, you can create outfits for different occasions.

a super outfit for school. If a girl has a plaid skirt, a solid color suit, a plaid shirt, a dressy blouse, slacks, and jeans, how many different combinations could you make for her?

When you have the chance to add something to your wardrobe, get clothes that mix and match with those you already have. A few additions can create many new outfits, 4-4.

accessories
Items such as shoes, scarves, legwear, handbags, billfolds, hats, neckties, jewelry, and belts; the items needed to complete an outfit.

Accessories Can Stretch Your Wardrobe

You can get more from your clothes with the use of **accessories.** These include belts, jewelry, scarves, hats, neckties, handbags, and shoes. They do not usually cost as much as other clothing items, and the choices are endless.

Accessories add variety to your wardrobe. For instance, you can make the same outfit look either dressy or casual, depending on the accessories you wear with it. They can also help you coordinate your wardrobe. If you have black pants, you may plan to wear a white shirt or blouse with them. You can look even better by adding a tie or scarf that has black in it. To repeat a color from your outfit in accessories gives your outfit a coordinated look.

Another advantage of using accessories is that they can help you keep up with the latest fashion. Since they are less expensive than most garments, you can afford to buy them more often. Watch the newspapers, magazines, and stores for the new fashions. Then look for an accessory that will help give an old outfit that new look, 4-5.

Look through your wardrobe and decide what it will take to "tie it all together." What could you select that could be worn with many outfits and improve the looks of each one? You would not want to spend money on items that will seldom be used or worn. This is when planning can really be worthwhile.

©Spiegel 2000

4-4
These basic pieces can be mixed and matched in many ways to create several outfits.

Prioritize Your Needs and Wants

Now that you have a better picture of your present wardrobe, you can see what you need to add to it. Make a list of the clothes that you need to replace because you have either outgrown them or worn them out. Also list the clothes that will help you fill in some missing pieces in your wardrobe. As you make your list, consider both your needs and your wants.

Simplicity Pattern Co.

4-5
Trendy accessories have given this outfit a new look.

You may find it difficult to distinguish between needs and wants. Few people would be happy if they had only things they need. Your actual clothing needs are few, but your wants are unlimited.

A *need* is something you have to have for your existence. The most basic clothing need is to cover your body for protection from the environment. For instance, you need a warm coat if you live in a cold climate. There are varying degrees of need, however. You may need to buy a required gym uniform for school. A certain outfit may be required where you work. You also need to wear certain styles of clothes for reasons of modesty. These are all examples of clothing needs.

A *want* is a desire for something that will give you more satisfaction than you have now. Wants are endless. You may want clothes for attractiveness, enjoyment, variety, or self-confidence. Many wants result from wishing to have something because somebody else has it, 4-6.

Your peer group and close friends also influence your clothing wants. You like to dress as they do, and certain clothes help to accomplish this. These clothes may seem like a need to you, but your parents may consider them wants.

Manufacturers use advertisements to make consumers want their products and fashions. Merchants set up attractive displays in stores to convince customers that they want certain merchandise. In 4-7, the display

4-6
Is this garment likely to fulfill a want for this young woman?

shows several styles of tops and pants. When you first see it, you might think that you would like to have one of the garments. If you think back to your clothing needs, you might be able to resist the tempting display.

As you review your list of wardrobe needs and wants, list them in **order of priority.** That means you will list them from the most important to the least important. Some items may be needed right away, while others can wait. Most people have a limited amount of money to spend on clothes. Therefore, they will need to buy the most important items first. This would be an item of top priority. After the needed items are purchased, some of the wanted items can be added if there is still money available. These would be items lower on the priority list.

order of priority
Items are listed from the most important to the least important.

Your Clothing Preferences

Few people like to wear exactly the same clothes as someone else. Instead, they like to show their individuality. You choose clothes based on your needs, but you also consider your personality, activities, and the climate where you live. Do you like your clothes to be noticed, or do you prefer to wear what everyone else is wearing? Do you need special clothes for dressy occasions, for certain sports, or for your hobbies? Do you need warm clothes for cold winters or extra swimsuits for all those days on the beach? The answers to these questions will help you choose the clothes that are right for you.

4-7
Attractive displays may cause you to confuse your clothing needs and wants.

Your Personality

The clothes in your wardrobe should express your personality. When shopping for clothes, has a friend ever held up an item and said, "This looks like you"? If so, your friend was saying that the clothing matched your personality.

Your clothes should help you say, "I am trying to be me. This is how I feel about myself." You want to wear clothes that are in style, but you also want to choose the styles that express your personality. For example, some girls may express passive and timid personality traits by choosing soft, sheer fabrics and small, delicate designs. More forceful personalities may be expressed with a minimum of design details, strong colors, and rough textures.

Many young men like to wear casual outfits like the ones shown in 4-8. They feel neat, but comfortable. As they create these outfits, they are expressing their personalities.

Girls can wear casual outfits based on jeans or slacks, 4-9. They also have the option of showing their femininity by wearing skirts or dresses. They can express the businesslike side of their personalities by wearing suits.

Your Activities

Your clothing choices are influenced by your activities—where you go and what you do. Your most frequent activity is attending school. Therefore, most of your clothes will be chosen for school wear. These same outfits can be worn for most leisure activities, such as attending

Wal-Mart Stores, Inc.

4-8
Most young men feel more comfortable in casual outfits such as these.

4-9
These girls are dressed for fun, choosing clothes that express their personalities.

4-10
This couple is dressed for a special dance at school.

Wal-Mart Stores, Inc.

4-11
A day flying kites on the beach calls for shorts, T-shirts, and sandals.

ball games, going shopping or to the movies, or just hanging out with friends.

If you work part-time, you may need special clothes for your job. A uniform may be required, or sturdy work pants. If you participate in sports, you may need clothing for these activities. Sports clothes will need to be comfortable, protective, and durable.

The clothes you choose may be completely different than those of the person sitting beside you. Your friend may need hiking boots, but you might not need them if you never go hiking. Some people do not need dressy or fancy clothes. Casual clothes and jeans are acceptable for the parties and events they attend. Other people who go to many church activities and special events need several dressy outfits.

Compare the people in 4-10 and 4-11. They have planned different activities, so they have chosen different clothing. They are all suitably dressed for what they will be doing.

Your Climate

Different climates create different clothing needs. In some areas, temperatures are fairly warm all year. In these places, people do not have to give much thought to seasonal clothing. They can wear most of their clothes during any season.

In other sections of the country, people must have some clothing that is comfortable in warm weather and other clothes for cold weather. They will probably spend more money for clothes than people in mild climates. A winter coat could be a major expense. Boots, hats, scarves, and gloves are other expenses for people living in cold climates.

In many areas, medium-weight clothing is appropriate for the climate. You can add extra sweaters and lightweight jackets to medium-weight garments when days are cold. Several layers will give more warmth than one heavy garment. This is because air is trapped between the layers and becomes warm from the heat of your body. In some sections of the country, a lightweight coat is all that is needed. One with a heavy zipout lining is a good choice for those who live in a colder climate. It can be worn during fall, winter, and spring.

When looking for a coat, style and fit are your first considerations, followed closely by quality and cost. Select a color that can be worn with many outfits. It should not show soil easily since dry cleaning bills can add up quickly. Few people buy a coat every year, so keep in mind that you will be wearing your coat for a long time.

The layered look is great for adjusting to different temperatures. It is a popular, attractive, and practical fashion for both guys and girls. Shirts, sweaters, and jackets can be combined in several different ways, depending on the weather. In 4-12, the man's outfit began as a basic T-shirt and jeans combination. Then he added a long-sleeved, collarless knit pullover and a wool shirt. He can adjust this layered outfit to be comfortable as the temperature changes.

Selecting Appropriate Clothes

Dressing appropriately means wearing clothes that are suitable for the occasion. This includes clothes for school, relaxing with friends, working around home, and special occasions. The accepted customs of your community will also affect what is appropriate clothing for you.

During your teenage years, you are trying to establish your own identity. You want to make your own decisions and do things your own way. There is a strong feeling to want to do as your friends do. Peer group pressure is strongest at this time.

At this age, the selection and wearing of clothes often causes conflicts between parents and their teenagers. They may not understand why you want to wear the clothes that you select.

You want to convince the adults in your life that you are growing up. You act mature when you accept responsibility for what you do. Dressing suitably for your activities is one part of being responsible. This means that you realize there are certain types of clothes that should be worn for the different things

Pendleton Woolen Mills

4-12

The layered look is well suited to changing temperatures as the day goes on.

you do, 4-13. In most areas, jeans, T-shirts, and sweatshirts can be worn to school, the movies, or to attend a sports activity. However, these outfits might not be appropriate for a religious service.

School Clothes

Most of your clothing is bought for school wear. This same clothing can be appropriate for other activities such as shopping, movies, spectator sports, babysitting, and visiting friends. As school clothes become worn, they can be worn as you do chores such as mowing the lawn or washing the car.

It is impossible to say what should be worn to which places for all teenagers. Although dress codes are seldom written, you generally know what you can and cannot wear to school. For instance, when a student's clothing distracts other people, it is unsuitable. If a girl wore a skimpy top, it would be hard not to stare at her. You would wonder how she is feeling about herself. She may be creating the wrong impression. Different parts of the country accept more casual, informal wear than others.

For school and informal activities, both guys and girls have many options. The group of teens in 4-14 look ready for a day at the beach or party. The girl in 4-15 has just finished classes for the day. The typical way of dressing at her school is comfortable jeans, shirts, sweaters, and jackets.

Simplicity Pattern Co.

4-13
Dressing appropriately for the occasion and the community in which you live shows you are responsible.

4-14
This group of teens is dressed for a party at the beach.

Special Occasions

Many school clothes can be changed into special occasion clothing with the addition of accessories. A sport coat, jewelry, a scarf, or a necktie can be added for a dress-up look.

Some dress-up occasions call for clothes different than those worn to school. Although many parties are casual, some are planned to be "dress up." This may mean that sport coats, suits, neckties, or dresses are to be worn.

When they need to look more businesslike, young men may choose to wear a suit or sport coat. With a well-planned wardrobe, young men can mix and match their garments. They can combine different slacks, shirts, sweaters, and sport coats. They can create in-between outfits like the one shown in 4-16.

Parties at the end of school or during holidays could give you a chance to dress up. Some teens think it is a special feeling to get dressed up in their best clothes. Many people seem to have a better self-concept and are happier when they are dressed up. When they are dressed appropriately, they are able to relax and have a good time, knowing they are wearing the right clothes.

Other occasions where special clothing, other than school clothing, is worn could be to weddings, religious services, and some elegant restaurants. If you are not sure of the type clothing to wear to an event, ask some-one who knows. The person who is responsible for the event is the best one to ask. Otherwise, ask several of your friends what they plan to wear. You might feel uncomfortable wearing a dress-up outfit if you arrive at a party and everyone else is in jeans.

Community Customs and Clothing

Communities vary in what is appropriate and accept-able clothing for different places and activities. In some states, the law requires customers to wear shoes and shirts to be admitted to restaurants and stores. Some elegant dining places require coats and ties. If you wish to eat there, you must accept their standard of dress.

Wearing what is expected by the majority of people is important. This may not be what is most comfortable for you. However, you will feel more at ease when you are appropriately dressed.

4-15_____
Shirts, jeans, and book bags are popular with teens for school wear.

4-16_____
Sometimes a dress shirt and tie are all that is needed for an office job.

CHAPTER REVIEW

Key Points

- With a wardrobe plan, you will know what clothes you have now and what you will need to add in the future.

- A wardrobe plan requires an inventory of your present clothes. As you look at each item in your wardrobe, evaluate it. Consider its condition and whether or not you can still wear it. You may have outgrown some items. Some items will need to be repaired or cleaned. See where the gaps are in your clothing inventory.

- Two ways to get more out of your wardrobe are to mix and match items to make more outfits and to wear different accessories.

- Clothing needs and wants should be listed in order of priority. This will help you plan your clothing purchases, making better use of your time and money.

- You choose clothes based on your needs, but you also should consider your personality, your activities, and the climate where you live.

- Dressing appropriately means wearing clothes that are suitable for the occasion.

- Communities vary in what is appropriate and acceptable clothing for different places and activities.

To Review

1. List three goals of wardrobe planning.
2. What is the first step in planning your wardrobe?
3. When is a good time to take an inventory of your wardrobe, and what should you include in your inventory?
4. Name three things you might consider when evaluating each item in your wardrobe.
5. Explain the difference between a need and a want.
6. The most basic clothing need is _____.
7. List three factors that influence your clothing preferences.
8. The layered look is practical because _____.
   A. it is popular
   B. it is attractive
   C. it can be adjusted according to the weather
   D. it is inexpensive
9. Who should you talk to if you don't know what to wear to an event?
10. When you are dressed appropriately, you are more likely to feel _____.

To Do

1. Make a list of the clothes that should be included in a student's wardrobe. List the number of garments and put them in an order of priority.

2. Take an inventory of your clothes. Then make a wardrobe plan. Write a summary of the results of your clothing inventory and wardrobe plan.

3. Make one list of clothing needs and one of clothing wants. Divide into groups to discuss the difference between needs and wants.

4. Cut out six photos of garments from advertisements, magazines, or catalogs. Mount them on paper and number each item. List all the possible outfits you could make by mixing and matching the different items.

5. Set an imaginary clothing allowance for a year. Make a wardrobe plan based on this amount of money. Use clothing catalogs to see how much your clothing items will cost. Compare your plan with those of your classmates.

6. Select an occupation and plan a suitable wardrobe for a person in that occupation. Explain your choices.

7. Collect pictures that illustrate your personality in your clothing preferences. Give a reason for each selection.

8. The layered look is practical and fashionable. Collect examples of the layered look that are suitable for your climate and arrange a bulletin board display.

9. Collect pictures of people and react to their clothing choices. List various activities. Indicate which people are dressed appropriately for each activity.

To Think About

1. Think about a clothing purchase you made that you now regret. How might a wardrobe plan have helped you make a better clothing purchase?

2. How can a wardrobe plan save you both time and money?

3. Make a list of clothes you would like to buy. Which are needs and which are wants?

4. Describe your personality. What clothing styles, fabrics, and colors seem to express your personality?

5. As a class, plan a dress code for your school. Justify your decisions.

CHAPTER 5

Clothing Decisions and Choices

Objectives

After studying this chapter, you will be able to

- list factors that affect your clothing decisions.
- use the decision-making process to make clothing decisions.
- describe factors affecting family clothing decisions.
- explain the stages in the family life cycle and how they impact clothing decisions.
- analyze factors to consider when deciding to sew or buy garments.

Key Terms

decision-making process
goals
resources
human resources
nonhuman resources
alternatives
family life cycle
priorities
compromise
budget

Making clothing decisions and choices is like putting a puzzle together. You have to add the pieces one by one. A good wardrobe plan will help you see which parts fit together. You do not want any extra pieces that will not fit into the finished product. You must decide which pieces to add.

A few of the right additions to your wardrobe can make a big change, 5-1. Learning to use the decision-making process can help you with your decisions. Making wise decisions about the clothes you and other family members need can help you make the right choices.

Decision Making

Decision making is the process of making a choice. You make many decisions about clothing every day. Some are minor decisions, while others are major decisions. What to wear to school each day is a minor or simple decision for most teens. Whether to wear a sweater or a jacket may not be a major decision either. However, what clothes to buy and how much to spend may be more important decisions. Whether to sew some garments and what to give away to someone else may also be in the important decision category. Some of these decisions may be made quickly, while others might require some thought.

When you were younger, your clothing decisions were made for you. Now that you are older, you will probably assume more and more responsibility for your clothing decisions.

Factors Affecting Your Clothing Decisions

What do your appearance, your activities, your clothing budget, fashion trends, and peer pressure have in common? They are all factors that can affect your clothing decisions.

- *What looks good on you.* When making clothing decisions, you'll want to choose those garments that look good on you. Evaluate the clothes in your wardrobe. Are they right for your body shape? What colors look best with your skin tone? Test new colors near your face to see the effect. You may decide you need a change.

Pendleton Woolen Mills

5-1 You can wear any of these separates with other clothes to make a new outfit. This is the basis of good wardrobe planning.

- *Your activities.* Your activities play a major role in your clothing decisions. Based on your wardrobe plan, you may have decided that you needed clothes for school. Maybe you needed clothes for work, sports, and some special occasions, 5-2.

- *The amount of money you have to spend.* Your clothing budget will affect the decisions you make about clothes. Few people have an unlimited amount of money to spend on clothes. If you plan your clothing budget wisely, you can buy the clothes you really need and save for the more costly items that you do not need right away. A spending plan helps you acquire the clothes that you need and want.

- *Fashion trends.* Fashion trends can also influence your clothing decisions. Most people want to wear clothes that are the current fashion. Before deciding to follow the latest fashion trend, think about it. Is it just a fad? Will this new fashion look good on you? Can you afford it?

- *Peer pressure.* Your friends are often your peers. You may enjoy being with your friends and like to have their opinions about the clothes that you buy. However, sometimes peer pressure may be a pitfall to decision making when buying clothes. Your friends may try to persuade you to buy a garment that might not be a good choice for you. This could be a garment that will not go with anything else in your wardrobe. It could be a fad item that costs more than you should spend. When you shop for clothes, keep your best colors and styles and what you already have in mind. It's fine to listen to your friends' opinions, but the final decision is yours. See 5-3.

5-2
Sometimes your activities help you decide what to wear.

The Decision-Making Process

Making decisions is usually easier if you have a plan for making them. If you follow the decision-making process, your decisions will be easier. The **decision-making process** is a series of steps you go through to help you make choices. These steps can be followed for either minor or major decisions. Here are the steps to follow:

1. State the problem to be solved.
2. Set goals for what you want to accomplish.
3. Identify your resources.
4. List the alternatives or options that are available.
5. Make your decision.
6. Carry out your decision.
7. Evaluate the results of the decision you made.

State the Problem to Be Solved

Be specific about what you must decide. Otherwise, you may have trouble deciding how to solve the problem. The problem could range from what you will wear to school tomorrow to how you will coordinate your wardrobe. State the problem. For instance, "I need to decide what to wear with my new shirt" or "I need a jacket, another pair of jeans, and a pair of school shoes to round out my wardrobe." These are better statements than saying "I need new clothes for school." Stating the problem in detail will help you know what to consider when making your decision, and you will make a better decision.

Set Goals

Goals are what you want to accomplish. Establish specific goals for what you want to attain. Then determine the goal you hope to reach from the decision you will make. For instance, your goal may be to add a jacket, a pair of jeans, and a pair of school shoes to your wardrobe before school starts.

Identify Your Resources

Resources are the objects or abilities that you can use to reach your goals. You may have both human resources and nonhuman resources. **Human resources** are all the resources you have within yourself such as skills, knowledge, and experience. **Nonhuman resources** are the material things you have or can use to achieve your goals. These include money, tools, time, and community resources.

decision-making process
A series of steps that you go through to help you make choices and solve problems.

goals
Something a person wants to accomplish.

resources
The objects or abilities that can be used to reach goals.

human resources
All the resources you have within yourself such as skills, knowledge, and experience.

nonhuman resources
Material things you have or can use to help you achieve goals, such as money, tools, and time.

5-3
It's fun to shop with friends, but make your clothing decisions based on what you really need and how much money you can spend.

Trends Making News

Casual Confusion

It was supposed to be easy—dressing casually for work. Now, many young people are confused by what to wear. Casual dress for work began with the high-tech companies, but by the early 1990s, it started creeping into the rest of the work world. At first, companies allowed employees to forgo suits and ties on Fridays only. Now, nearly 51 percent of large companies are casual five days a week.

The problem is that everyone interprets "casual" differently. Some people believe its taking off your suit jacket and tie. Others show up for work in ragged T-shirts, bare midriffs, or gym clothes. The situation has gotten so bad at some companies that consultants are being hired to teach employees what is appropriate for work and what is not.

Most companies now have casual dress codes that help employees know what is appropriate and what is not. Most companies discourage the following:

- Worn-out sneakers
- Flip-flops
- Shorts
- Pool or beach clothes

Don'ts for women include
- Very short dresses and skirts
- Pants that reveal the navel
- See-through clothing
- Low-cut upper clothing
- Halters, camisoles, and tank tops

Don'ts for men are
- Gym wear
- T-shirts or sleeveless shirts
- Ripped or unkempt clothing

Dressing down at work is more comfortable and can be less expensive. It also gives you the chance to express your individual style, but you still need to use good judgment. Respect the people you are around and the culture of the company where you work.

Make a list of all your resources. Do you know how to sew? This is a human resource. Do you have money available from a part-time job or an allowance? Do family members or friends offer you secondhand clothes? Do you have time to sew or carefully shop for the items you want? These are all types of nonhuman resources, 5-4.

List the Alternatives

There are usually several ways to solve a problem or reach a goal. These are **alternatives.** Explore all of your options and weigh their advantages and disadvantages. A good way to test alternatives is to ask yourself some questions. Would you want to make a jacket? Do you want to shop for jeans and shoes now or wait until they go on sale? How would you feel about wearing secondhand jeans or a secondhand jacket? Do you have the skills to mix and match new garments with those in your present wardrobe to create new outfits? This could extend your wardrobe.

alternatives
Various ways to solve a problem or reach a goal.

Make Your Decision

After carefully thinking about the advantages and disadvantages of each alternative, decide which is best. Perhaps you will decide to sew the jacket and buy the shoes on sale. Your cousin, who has grown several inches this year, may have offered you a pair of good secondhand jeans. Your decisions have been made.

Carry out Your Decision

To carr out your decision means to turn your words into action. The quicker you carry out your decision, the quicker your goal will be met. Since you know you will be making a jacket, you can shop for a fabric that will coordinate with other items in your wardrobe. You can also begin looking for shoes that are on sale. Perhaps, with the money you saved by getting the jeans secondhand and sewing the jacket, you could buy accessories to further extend your wardrobe.

Evaluate the Results

Think about the decisions you have made. Were they successful decisions? Did the decisions solve the problem? Did you meet your goal? Are you satisfied with the results? What would you have done differently? By carefully evaluating your decisions, your future decision-making skills will be improved. When you evaluated your decisions about the jacket, jeans, and shoes, were you happy? Although it took a lot of thought, you now have three great additions to your wardrobe.

5-4
The time you have to shop and carefully compare merchandise is a type of nonhuman resource.

Factors Affecting Family Clothing Decisions

In making family clothing decisions, the same decision-making process can be used. However, instead of applying the process to just your needs, it is applied to the needs of the family.

Several factors affect family clothing decisions. These include the stage in the family life cycle; family values, goals, and priorities; family resources; and the budget for clothes. How all of these factors are managed will determine how successful a family's clothing decisions will be.

Stage in the Family Life Cycle

family life cycle
Stages in the life of a family beginning with marriage.

Families change through the years. From being newly married couples to being grandparents, families grow in size. Households often grow from two people to many people. After a few years it is back to two again, and then one. These changes occur in stages that make up the **family life cycle.** Clothing needs change as families go through these stages. See 5-5.

Beginning Stage	Childbearing Stage	Parenting Stage	Launching/Mid-years Stage	Aging Stage
		Substages		
■ Married couple without children	■ Couple with child(ren) up to 30 months old. ■ Couple with child(ren) up to 2 1/2 to 6 years old.	■ Couple with child(ren) 6 to 13 years old. ■ Couple with child(ren) 13 to 20 years old.	■ Couple with child(ren) leaving home. ■ Couple with child(ren) away from home until couple retires.	■ Couple from time of retirement until death of both spouses.

5-5
Family life follows a series of stages, and clothing needs change throughout these stages.

The first stage of the family life cycle is the *beginning stage.* It begins when a couple first marries. They establish a home together. Both the husband and wife may be employed, so they have money to spend on themselves. They also have time to pursue leisure activities. The couple will buy clothes suited to their work needs. They may also need special clothes for their leisure activities.

The second stage of the family life cycle begins when the couple has a child. This is called the *childbearing stage.* Many adjustments are made during this stage as the couple assumes their new roles as parents. More demands are made on their time, money, energy, and freedom. This stage continues until all children are born. The first baby will have many clothing needs. The next child can wear some of the clothes of the firstborn. Because babies and young children grow fast, they need clothes more often than adults do.

The family enters the third stage of the family life cycle when the first child begins school. This is called the *parenting stage.* More changes occur in the family. School activities, sports events, and social activities lead to a busy family life. More demands are made on time, money, and energy. When children go to school, their clothing needs often increase. In addition to play clothes, school clothes are needed. When children enter their teen years, they spend more time with their friends and less time with their family. Teens are involved in more social activities and may work part-time. They will sometimes need more clothes for their many activities.

Family members involved in organizations or sports may need special clothes. For instance, if members of a family are involved in skiing, they might need hats, gloves, jackets, pants, and boots. If children belong to organizations such as Scouts or Little League, special uniforms may also be needed. See 5-6. Family members' hobbies and activities should be considered when determining family clothing needs.

Sometimes, special clothing needs arise for special occasions or holidays. For instance, a wedding often calls for special clothes. Special clothes may also be needed if a family will be going on a vacation, 5-7.

5-6

Little League uniforms might be required by children involved in baseball.

5-7

Sometimes people buy special clothes to wear on a family vacation.

The fourth stage of the family life cycle begins when the first child leaves home. This is called the *launching stage.* Children may leave for school, work, or marriage. Young people planning to attend college often need clothes for their college wardrobes. Young adults entering the job market will need clothes appropriate for their jobs. As the children leave, parents have more time and space for themselves. They may have more money to spend on their own interests. Since their income is usually highest at this stage, they may do more traveling. This is the *mid-years stage.*

When the couple retires, they enter the *aging stage.* Depending on their health, they may continue to be active in a variety of ways. They may pursue hobbies, do volunteer work, or participate in sports. A person who is retired may need more casual clothes. As their health declines, their needs for special services will increase. Their clothing needs are often related to their health.

As you can see, throughout the various stages of the life cycle, family clothing needs change. New clothing needs arise at each stage of the life cycle.

Family Values, Goals, and Priorities

priorities
Ranking of the importance of items or options.

A family's values and goals will affect clothing decisions. Family attitudes about clothes, their tastes, and their activities will all influence a family's priorities. Families set **priorities** based on what is most important to them.

Setting family clothing priorities and achieving goals are most effective if each member of the family has a part in the process. Parents usually lead the planning process. When children reach a level of understanding, they should be encouraged to participate, too. The family should decide what is most important to the family as a unit and to each member. Family members should be urged to think and talk about their values as well as their clothing needs and wants.

Setting family clothing priorities and goals has advantages. Each family member learns to balance his or her own needs and wants against those of others. Everyone learns to compromise. In a **compromise,** everyone agrees to give up a little until an agreement is reached.

compromise
An agreement that requires each person to give up a little.

Family members should begin by listing clothing items the family needs and wants most. Estimate the cost of each item and when it will be needed. This will help in establishing priorities and goals.

It's a good idea to try to find a balance between family goals. For instance, it may be nice if each member of the family had new summer clothes, but winter coats may be needed later in the year. Perhaps one member of the family wants an expensive outfit for a special occasion while another member of the family wants clothes for school or work. A family decision-making session should take place. Family values, goals, and priorities should be discussed. A decision that is best for the family should be reached.

Managing Family Resources

After family clothing goals and priorities have been discussed, a family should consider their resources. Resources are the objects or abilities that families can use to reach goals. Skills, time, and money are all resources that can help meet family clothing needs.

Just as families differ, the resources available to each family differ. A family may lack a resource such as money, but perhaps family members can use other resources such as time or skills to compensate. For instance, sewing clothes or careful shopping could save the family money. (You will learn more about sewing and shopping skills in later chapters.) Family members can learn to do their own clothing repairs and alterations instead of paying someone else to do them. Recycling or redesigning garments could save money and enlarge wardrobes. (Recycling and redesigning ideas are given in Chapter 17.) Clothes can also be shared among family members or handed down from one family member to another.

Budgeting for Clothes

Used wisely, money is an important resource. A **budget** is a spending plan that can help families manage money. A budget gives a family a clear picture of how much money is available to meet needs. Many items are included in a family budget. Keep in mind that clothing is only one of these

budget
A spending plan that can help people manage money.

items. Other items include food, housing, health care, transportation, personal items, and recreation, 5-8.

Some families set up clothing budgets on a monthly, seasonal, or yearly basis. However the budget is set up, family members need to consider

- the total amount of money the family has to spend

- the total amount of nonclothing expenses

- the amount the family wants to budget for clothes after meeting essential needs such as housing and food

Once a family decides how much money is available for clothing, a record of clothing expenses should be kept. Clothing expenses include the cost of all garments plus their regular upkeep—laundry, dry cleaning, and repairs. This list can be reviewed to see if spending patterns need to be changed. The family may want to reduce spending on clothes or reduce spending in other areas such as recreation.

Families can save money on clothes by buying well-made garments that won't have to be replaced often. You may have to pay slightly more for a garment that is well-made, but the extra expense will pay off in the long run. Inexpensive clothes are often poorly made. Seams may not be sturdy, hems may come loose, and fasteners fall off. If the garment cannot be repaired easily, it may need to be discarded after only a few wearings. The

5-8

In addition to clothes, the family budget must also include items such as food, housing, and transportation.

dollars saved in the purchase price will be lost if the garment is only worn a few times.

It's a good idea to buy clothes that can be laundered so dry cleaning bills can be avoided. Having to dry clean a garment each time it is soiled adds to the total cost of that garment. It is far less expensive to launder a garment at home. This factor should be considered when clothes are purchased. Read the labels to determine care requirements. If many items need to be dry cleaned each year, this will impact your clothing budget.

The list of expenses reflects family spending patterns. This will help in planning future expenses. Big budget items like winter coats or a new career wardrobe may require extra planning. A family can start preparing for these needs several months in advance. A certain amount of money can be set aside weekly so that it is available when the items are needed.

Every few months, the family budget should be evaluated. A budget is not a rigid plan that cannot be changed. When there is a need to change the budget, family members should discuss it and make adjustments. A budget can be a useful tool if it is used to help a family meet needs based on family values, goals, and priorities.

To Sew or To Buy

Now that you have learned about the decision-making process, you can apply it to sew or buy decisions regarding clothing. How do you decide whether to make a garment or buy one? It's a good idea to consider several factors. These include your sewing skills, how much money is available, the type of design you want, whether or not you enjoy sewing, obtaining a good fit, and the amount of time available. Answering the questions in figure 5-9 may help you to make your decision. After answering these questions, apply the decision-making process to your decision.

You may find that each option has both advantages and disadvantages. You may choose to sew some items and buy others ready-made. For example, you may want to sew those clothes that are easier

TO SEW? TO BUY?
FACTORS TO CONSIDER

	How would you rate your sewing skills?
	How much money would it cost to make the garment? How much money would it cost to buy the garment at a store?
	How do the current fashions in the stores look on you? Would you rather wear a personal, original design?
	Do you see sewing as a fun activity or as a chore?
	Do you wear a standard size that requires little, if any, alterations? Are you "in between" sizes, or do you find that ready-made garments just don't fit you like they should?
	When do you need the garment? What would require the most time—shopping for the garment or sewing the garment? Do you have enough time to shop for a pattern, fabric, and notions and to make the garment?

5-9
Before making a decision about sewing or buying a garment, ask yourself these questions.

to make, such as pants, skirts, and T-shirts. You may want to buy items that may be more difficult to sew, such as shirts, blouses, and jackets.

You may choose to sew some of your clothes because sewing is one of the best ways to build up a wardrobe. Sewing is a skill, as is playing the guitar, throwing a football, or riding a horse. Certain skills are easier for some people than for others. However, with patience and practice, you can learn any skill, including sewing.

If you sew, you could have about twice as many clothes for the same amount of money, 5-10. In most cases, you can sew clothes of better materials for less money than if you buy the same types of ready-made clothes. You would also know how well they are constructed.

Sometimes, sewing is the only way to get the garment you want—the right color, style, and fit. You could make clothes that reflect your interests and personality. Your clothes would look great, and you could have fun making them, 5-11.

Fit is one of the most important factors in a clothing decision. When you buy ready-to-wear clothes, you can try them on before you buy them. If you sew, you can take careful measurements to help ensure a good fit. You can also make adjustments to the fit as you go along.

Both shopping for ready-made garments and sewing garments take time. When deciding whether to sew or buy, you need to know how soon you will need the garment. If you need a garment tomorrow, you will probably have to buy it. If you have some spare time, sewing may be a wise choice. If the design is simple, it may not take long to sew. You can also do hand sewing of hems and buttons while you are watching a TV program or listening to music.

You may want to think about recycling before buying something new. You may be able to restyle some of last year's outfits to have this year's new fashion. Some other advantages of sewing are listed in figure 5-12.

Simplicity Pattern Co.

5-10

Compare the cost of ready-made clothing with what you can sew yourself. Often clothes you make will fit better and be of better quality for less cost.

Simplicity Pattern Co.

5-11
Sometimes sewing is the only way to have the garment you want. You can have fun making and wearing your own clothes.

ADVANTAGES
OF SEWING

- Have a feeling of pride and accomplishment.
- Make accessories for your own room and home.
- Make gifts and garments for your family and friends.
- Have an interesting hobby and outlet for your creativity.
- Earn money by sewing or altering clothes for friends.
- Select ready-made clothing more intelligently.
- Alter your ready-mades so they will fit better.
- Consider a future career in the clothing field and perhaps a part-time job very soon.

5-12
These are just some of the advantages of being able to sew. Can you think of others?

CHAPTER REVIEW

Key Points

- Decision making is the process of making a choice. You make many decisions about clothing every day. Some are minor decisions, while others are major decisions. Many factors need to be considered when making clothing decisions.

- Making decisions is usually easier if you have a plan for making them. If you follow the decision-making process, your decisions will be easier. The decision-making process is a series of steps you go through to help you make choices.

- Goals are what you want to accomplish. Establish specific goals for what you want to attain. Then determine the goal you hope to reach from the decision you will make. Look at the resources you have to help you reach your goal.

- There are usually several ways to solve a problem or reach a goal. These are called alternatives.

- Families change through the years. These changes occur in stages that make up the family life cycle. Clothing needs change as families go through these stages.

- Families need to consider their values, goals, priorities, and resources when making clothing decisions. All of these factors will influence the amount of money to set aside for meeting family clothing needs.

- The decision-making process can be used to help you decide whether to sew a garment or buy it ready-made.

To Review

1. Give two examples of minor decisions and two examples of major decisions related to clothing. Label each decision as minor or major.
2. Name five factors that can affect your clothing decisions.
3. List the seven steps of the decision-making process.
4. What is the difference between a human resource and a nonhuman resource?
5. Name two stages of the family life cycle and explain what the family clothing needs might be during each of these stages.
6. Give three examples of family resources.
7. Name three items family members need to consider when setting up a budget.
8. Name six factors to consider when deciding whether to sew or buy a garment.

To Do

1. Choose a partner and role-play situations about the factors that affect decisions about clothes. Let the class decide which influence you are using.

2. Present a wardrobe problem to the class. Use the decision-making process to solve it.

3. Divide into groups. Plan a clothing purchase using the decision-making process.

4. If you are given a monthly clothing allowance, make a budget for the next six months. List your goals, the money you have to spend, and what you would like to buy during this time frame. How will this budget help you reach your goals?

5. Interview your parents to find out how much your family budgets for clothes each year. What advice do they have for managing clothing costs?

6. Pretend that you are going to college. Plan a wardrobe budget with a given amount of money.

7. If some class members already know how to sew, ask them about the advantages of sewing.

To Think About

1. Rank the five factors that affect clothing decisions in order of importance for you. Which has the greatest influence on your clothing decisions? Why? Which factor influences your decisions the least? Why?

2. Think of an important decision you recently made. Do you think using the decision-making process would have helped you make a better decision? Why or why not?

3. What human and nonhuman resources do you have? How might you use these resources?

4. Which stage of the family life cycle is your family in? Explain your answer.

5. Divide into two groups. Debate which is better—sewing clothes or buying clothes.

CHAPTER

Consumer Rights and Responsibilities

Teenagers are important consumers in today's market. A **consumer** is a person who uses goods and services. You are a consumer of goods every time you buy an article of clothing for yourself. You are a consumer of services when you have a garment dry-cleaned. During your teen years, you will accept more and more responsibilities. You will choose and buy more of your own clothes, 6-1. Getting your money's worth in the clothes you buy is a goal of smart consumers.

Labels and Hangtags

Do you read the labels and hangtags attached to the textile items you buy? Time, effort, and money were used to develop them. Laws were passed to enforce them. They tell you what to expect from the product and how to care for it properly. Understanding labels and hangtags will help you make wiser clothing decisions.

Fabrics and garments are labeled for four basic reasons:

- to identify the product
- to help businesses sell products
- to help consumers make wise purchases
- to explain proper care methods for the product

Labels are small pieces of ribbon or fabric, firmly attached to the inside of garments, that provide important information. Labels remain attached to a garment as it is used. The newest replacement for sewn-in labels are garments that are tagless. The required information about the garment is inside the clothing. It is stamped onto the fabric through heat-transfer technology. By law, labels must state the fiber content, care instructions, and country of origin. They may also list the fabric construction, special finishes, performance standards, size, brand name, and guarantees.

Hangtags are the larger tags of heavy paper or cardboard that are attached to purchased clothes. They are not required by law to be provided by manufacturers. They are removed before the garments are worn. Some information on labels is often repeated on hangtags. The trademark,

consumer
A person who uses goods and services; a buyer of goods and services.

labels
Small pieces of ribbon or fabric, firmly attached to the inside of garments, that provide important information required by law.

hangtags
Tags made of heavy paper or cardboard that are attached to purchased clothes.

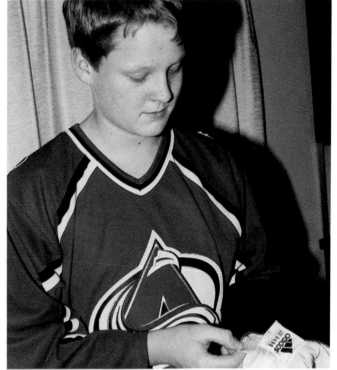

Nancy Henke-Konopasek

6-1 --

Many teens are responsible for selecting their own clothes. Labels and hangtags help them make wise purchases.

6-2 Note the many kinds of information provided on labels and hangtags.

size, style number, price, and special features may also be listed on hang-tags. See samples of labels and hangtags in 6-2.

Using Labels and Hangtags

Labels are attached so they will not be seen while you wear the garment. They are usually found at the back of the neckline of shirts, blouses, dresses, and sweaters. Look for them at the back center of the waistband on skirts and slacks. Men's suits and sport jackets often have labels on the inside pocket at chest level. Some jackets and coats have the label on the front facing below the waistline. You may have to search, but the labels can be found.

Tagless garments are shown in 6-3. Most tagless garments are T-shirts, knit tops, and underwear. About ten percent of all clothing is now tagless.

Labels and hangtags are meant to help you. Make use of them. Smart shoppers save hangtags. They write the date and place of purchase and a short description of the garment on them. They may be kept in the laundry area for easy reference.

Federal Legislation to Help Consumers

Consumers have not always had the help of hangtags and labels. They were not really needed until manufactured fabrics appeared on the market. Then the confusion began. People did not know how to care for the new fabrics. They could not tell what fiber was used in a fabric just by looking at it. Consumers and fabric and clothing manufacturers were confused.

The government stepped in to settle the confusion. Three of the regulations that deal with clothing are the

- Textile Fiber Products Identification Act, amended in 1969
- Care Labeling Rule, 1972, revised in 1984
- Flammable Fabrics Act, 1953, amended in 1967

The Textile Fiber Products Identification Act

The **Textile Fiber Products Identification Act (TFPIA)** requires labels to tell what fibers are in the textiles. The Federal Trade Commission (FTC) was given the task of enforcing the regulations. The manufactured fibers were divided into 22 **generic groups.**

Textile Fiber Products Identification Act
Requires labels to tell what fibers are in the textiles.

generic groups
Groups of manufactured fibers that are chemically alike.

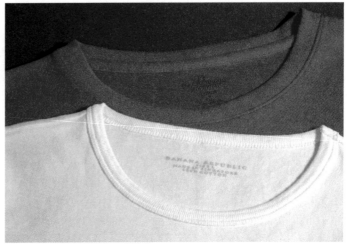

Jack Klasey

6-3 --

Tagless garments include required label information, but are more comfortable to wear.

Fibers that are chemically alike make up a generic group. In 1996, lyocell became the first new generic fiber group in 30 years to be approved by the FTC. The 22 generic groups of fibers are listed in 6-4.

Each generic group can include many different fibers. Although the fibers are chemically alike, there are slight differences. Manufacturers want their fiber to have special characteristics. Each fiber has a **trademark** to set it apart from others. For instance, olefin is a generic name. The olefin fibers used to make indoor-outdoor carpet are different than the olefin fibers used in upholstery fabrics. Manufacturers give a trademark to each kind of fiber. Herculon and Marvess are two of the olefin trademarks. Study 6-5 for other examples.

The TFPIA requires that all clothing and household textile products be labeled to show

- the generic name of every fiber in the item unless a fiber weighs less than 5 percent of the total fiber weight
- the percentage of each fiber, by weight
- the name or other identification of the manufacturer
- the country of origin, if the textile product is imported

trademark
Identifying name, symbol, or design that sets a manufacturer's product apart from similar products or competitors.

The Care Labeling Rule

The **Care Labeling Rule** requires that all clothing labels (except hosiery) give clear, uniform, and detailed instructions for care and maintenance. This rule was issued by the Federal Trade Commission. Care labels must appear on all items of clothing except those made of suede or leather. The care label must be attached firmly to the garment, be easy to find, and readable for the useful life of the garment.

Care Labeling Rule
A rule issued by the Federal Trade Commission that requires all clothing (except hosiery) give clear, uniform, and detailed instructions for care and maintenance.

GENERIC FIBER GROUPS

Acetate	Lastrile*	Nytril*	Spandex
Acrylic	Lyocell	Olefin	Triacetate*
Anidex*	Metallic	Polyester	Vinal *
Aramid	Modacrylic	Rayon	Vinyon
Azlon*	Novoloid	Rubber	
Glass	Nylon	Saran	

* Not currently produced in the U.S.

6-4

The Federal Trade Commission has assigned 22 generic names to the various types of manufactured fibers according to the chemicals used to make them.

Manufacturers can use a distinct care label for their products. Labels can be any color, style, or shape as long as they follow the standards set by law. They can be fused, glued, or sewn to the garment. They must be made so they do not ravel.

Care instructions are printed on a label or woven into it. They may be printed directly on the fabric if they will remain readable for the life of the garment. Many manufacturers print the care instructions on the back of their own brand labels. This is legal if the label states "Care Instructions on Reverse Side."

The 1984 revised rule requires labels to include the following information:

- method of washing (by hand or machine)
- water temperature (cold, warm, or hot)
- method of drying (machine, hang, or lay flat)
- drying temperature (low, medium, or high)
- type of bleach when all types cannot be used safely
- use of iron and ironing temperature when necessary (cool, warm, or do not iron)

All dry-cleaning instructions must specify the best type of solvent for cleaning when some solvents might damage the article being cleaned.

The care label should warn you of what method(s) cannot be used. If a care label gives washing instructions but does not warn against dry-cleaning, you should be able to dry-clean the garment.

This rule applies to fabrics as well as to ready-made garments. The ends of fabric bolts are coded to give you care instructions.

Exemptions may be granted for

- articles whose utility or appearance may be impaired by a permanent label
- articles which are completely washable under normal circumstances
- articles which are intended to sell at retail for $3.00 or less

In 1997, the Care Labeling Rule was once again revised. Manufacturers may use certain care symbols in place of words on labels. (These symbols are shown in Chapter 16.) This allows American-made products to be marketed with the same care labels throughout North America.

Generic Name	Trademark
Acetate	Estron Celanese Chromspun MicroSafe
Acrylic	Acrilan Creslan Orlon Duraspun
Lyocell	Tencel Lenzing
Metallic	Lurex
Modacrylic	SEF Plus
Nylon	Anso Antron Cantrece Crepeset Zeftron
Olefin	Herculon Spectra
Polyester	Dacron Fortrel CoolMax Microloft Trevira
Rayon	Galaxy Viscose Fibro Zantrel
Spandex	Lycra Cleerspun

6-5
Within each generic group there are several tradenames. Each one represents a fiber with slight variations.

The Flammable Fabrics Act

The **Flammable Fabrics Act** was passed to regulate the manufacture and sale of all highly flammable wearing apparel fabrics. It was
directed at prohibiting the sale of very hazardous, or "torch-type" fabrics.
The act is enforced by the Consumer Product Safety Commission.

The Flammable Fabrics Act has been expanded many times. Specific
standards have been added for carpets, rugs, mattresses, children's
sleepwear, and some upholstery fabrics.

Treating fabrics to reduce flammability does not prevent them from
burning. Almost every fabric will burn when exposed to a flame. Treating
fabrics reduces the danger of burning. Consumers still need to take precautions and reduce fire hazards.

Consumers must be warned if the flame-resistant properties of a garment will be destroyed by laundering methods. For instance, children's
sleepwear must be washed using a detergent instead of soap. This is
because soap can destroy the flame-resistant properties of the fabric.

In the future, there may be more flammability standards. New standards for blankets and for upholstered furniture have been discussed.
Many manufacturers are working on new fibers and finishes to make
more fabrics flame-resistant.

Your Rights as a Consumer

As a consumer, you have the right to expect certain things from the
goods and services you use. During the 1960s, President John F.
Kennedy defined the rights of the consumer as the right to safety, the
right to be informed, the right to choose, and the right to be heard.

- The *right to safety* means that you have the right to be protected
  from goods and services that can be harmful to your health or life.

- The *right to be informed* is the right to be given true facts and information about products so you can make wise choices. Advertising,
  articles in newspapers, and product labels are some sources of information. Understanding certain terms related to consumer behavior
  will help you be a more informed consumer. See 6-6.

- You have the *right to make choices* according to your needs and
  wants. These choices should be from a wide variety of goods and
  services from more than one producer.

- The *right to be heard* means you can speak out if you feel products
  you buy are unsatisfactory. There are agencies that will listen to you
  and help you get action to settle your complaint.

During the 1970s, President Richard Nixon added another right—the
right to redress. This means that consumers who have had problems
with goods and services have the right to have the problems corrected.
Suppose you have paid for products or services that turned out to be

GLOSSARY OF **CONSUMER TERMS**

advertisement. A paid public announcement offering goods, services, and ideas for sale.

as is. Merchandise is to be sold in its present condition regardless of defects, flaws, or imperfections.

catalog. A listing and description of products and services for sale by retail stores or mail-order houses.

comparison shopping. Looking at different brands and models of the same or similar products in several stores to compare prices, quality, features, and store services before buying.

consumer. One who uses goods and services; buyer of goods and services.

consumer protection. A type of aid related to consumer interests provided by law, by government agencies, or by private individuals or organizations.

credit card. An identifying card entitling the holder to charge goods and services and in some cases to borrow money.

customer. One who buys or does business with a particular store or firm.

custom-made. Something made to the individual order of a customer or to fit particular specifications set by the customer.

dealer. One who buys products from a manufacturer or wholesaler for resale to the final user.

discount. The amount deducted from an amount due; reduction from usual price of an item or service.

false advertising. Any advertising which is misleading in a material respect, including false representation of the contents or benefits of a product as well as the failure to reveal any consequences which are likely to follow from its use.

guarantee. A statement given to the buyer by the seller at the time of sale. It lists certain standards of quality or performance for the product and promises remedial action (repair, replacement, refund, etc.) if the product fails to meet these standards during a specified period of time.

high pressure. Usually refers to selling techniques that are intense, strong, persuasive, and difficult for customers to withstand.

impulse buying. Generally, unplanned consumer purchases or "spur-of-the-moment" buying of merchandise on display or on sale.

lifestyle. A way of living which is characteristic of an entire society or segment of a society.

loss leader. Items sold below cost to attract customers to a store with the hope that they will buy other items at regular prices. (Illegal in some states.)

made-to-order. Goods made up after a customer places an order.

mail order. Order for merchandise which is normally sent and received by mail.

markdown. A reduction below the original price of an item.

needs. Those goods and services considered essential for living.

open stock. A term indicating that a particular product or pattern will continue to be available for a long period of time and that it may be purchased individually as well as in sets. The term usually refers to china, glassware, silver, etc.

packaged goods. Products which are bought and sold in prepared packages.

(continued)

6-6

Understanding these terms will help you to be a more informed consumer.

GLOSSARY OF **CONSUMER TERMS**
(CONTINUED)

product testing. A process by which consumer products are checked and tested before being sold to the public, usually during the development stage of new products.

promotion. The activities designed to increase the sale of certain products or services or to improve business of a specific store or business organization.

purchase. To obtain goods, property, or service in exchange for money or credit.

refund. A repayment of money.

retail. The business of selling for use (to consumer) as opposed to selling for resale, such as sales by wholesalers, producers, or manufacturers.

retailer. An individual or organization in the business of selling goods and services at retail or to consumers.

retail store. A business establishment engaged in selling to consumers or households but not including catalog or mail-order sellers.

sell. To transfer goods or perform services for a price.

service charge. A fee added to the price of goods or services for some added service connected with the sale such as delivery, credit, or installation.

shopping mall. A number of retail stores and service businesses grouped in a single location for shopping and parking convenience.

trade association. An organization of business firms in the same or related fields. They work together to promote their common interests.

trademark. An identifying name, symbol, or design which sets a product apart from similar products of competitors.

warranty. A statement by manufacturers or sellers of a product or service concerning their responsibility for quality, characteristics, and performance of the product or service. The term is used interchangeably with guarantee.

wear and tear. The deterioration of property or equipment which results from ordinary use and aging.

wholesale. The selling of goods in large lots or bulk to a retailer for resale to consumers.

will call. A way of buying goods in which the buyer leaves a deposit or partial payment for the goods and the merchandise is set aside. When full payment is made, the seller gives the goods to the buyer. Also called *layaway plan.*

6-6
Continued

unsatisfactory. If the store or business will not satisfy you, certain agencies will advise you on whom to contact and what action to take.

Another consumer right was added by President Gerald Ford—the *right to consumer education.* Several agencies were created to help consumers buy wisely. You should know how to evaluate and compare products before making a purchase. Consumer education programs give advice through articles, reports, and seminars. They can give you buying tips and suggestions about buying wisely. They also warn against fraud and give advice about action that can be taken concerning consumer complaints.

Consumer Protection Agencies and Organizations

You have learned about several acts that have been passed to safeguard consumer rights. Several government agencies and organizations have been created to enforce these laws. Some also set standards. A **standard** is a set of criteria established by authorities who judge products to verify certain levels of quality. The following are some of the government agencies:

standard
A set of criteria established by authorities who judge products to verify certain levels of quality.

- The *Federal Trade Commission (FTC)* promotes free and fair competition by preventing deceptive practices, false advertising, and unfair trade practices. It enforces consumer protection legislation.

- The *Food and Drug Administration (FDA)* protects the public against impure and unsafe foods, drugs, and cosmetics.

- The *National Institute of Standards and Technology,* previously called the National Bureau of Standards, works with industry to develop and apply technology, measurements, and standards. Products have to pass safety standards before they can be sold.

- The *Consumer Product Safety Commission* protects the public against risk of injury from consumer products, sets safety standards, and promotes research into product-related injuries or deaths.

In addition to these government agencies, several private nonprofit groups have been formed that help consumers. Trade organizations representing various industries also benefit consumers through their work. These include the following:

- *Better Business Bureaus* are private organizations supported by business and professional groups. They (1) provide reports on businesses to help consumers with purchases; (2) help resolve consumers' disputes with businesses; and (3) promote ethical business standards and self-regulation of business practices.

- The *International Organization for Standardization* has developed textile standards to certify the quality of goods and services internationally.

- The *American Society for Testing and Materials* develops voluntary standards for products and materials, including textiles.

These groups work to improve standards in many fields, including textiles and clothing. They conduct research to find which new products consumers want. They test fabrics and garments for quality and durability. This helps both the producer and the consumer by developing better products.

Consumer Responsibilities

Consumers have responsibilities as well as rights. The people who make and sell goods and services expect certain things from you as a consumer. See 6-7 for a list that outlines your consumer rights and responsibilities.

- You have the *responsibility to use products safely and to guard against carelessness.* Keeping safety in mind, especially around fire hazards is the consumer's responsibility. For instance, a fuzzy sweater could become enveloped in flames in seconds if touched by a lighted match.

- You have the *responsibility to seek out information and to use it when buying.* When manufacturers or businesses provide information about a product or service, you have the responsibility to seek it out. You also have the responsibility to use this information when buying the product or paying for the service. When you are choosing a product or service, you should consider your needs and wants in order to get the best product or service from the wide variety available.

- You have the *responsibility to buy wisely from the wide variety available.* Smart consumers are smart shoppers. Before they buy, they read labels and hangtags. These provide product information for the customer. This information helps the shopper make a wise purchase. They look for the features they want. See 6-8. They check to see if

CONSUMER RIGHTS AND **RESPONSIBILITIES**

- The right to safety...and the responsibility to guard against carelessness, especially around fire hazards.
- The right to information...and the responsibility to seek it out and to use it when buying.
- The right to selection...and the responsibility to buy wisely from the wide variety available.
- The right to be heard...and the responsibility to let legitimate dissatisfactions be known.
- The right to redress...and the responsibility to have problems corrected.
- The right to education...and the responsibility to seek it out and use it.

6-7 ⎯⎯⎯⎯⎯⎯⎯⎯⎯⎯⎯⎯⎯⎯⎯⎯⎯⎯⎯⎯⎯⎯⎯
Consumers should be aware of their rights and responsibilities.

6-8 ⎯⎯⎯⎯⎯⎯⎯⎯⎯⎯⎯⎯⎯⎯⎯⎯⎯⎯⎯⎯⎯⎯⎯
Examine clothes before you buy. Careful shopping will assure you of getting the quality you want.

Shoplifting— A Cost to Everyone

In the most recent nationwide survey of retailers, a record annual loss of nearly $9 billion due to customer theft was reported. This amount would be even higher if it weren't for antitheft systems such as electronic article surveillance (EAS) devices and closed circuit television systems.

Who is stealing and what are they taking? Nearly 60 percent of all shoplifters are 18 or over. This means that almost one-third are between the ages of 13 and 17. This younger group is most likely to steal items they can't afford or are prohibited from buying. Compact discs, cosmetics, trendy clothes, cigarettes, and consumer electronics are most often stolen.

Why do people steal? Simply stated, they steal to get something for nothing. This is like getting a gift, which gives them a "lift." For teens, the reasons often relate to pressures they feel from family, peers, or school. Most teens say they don't know why they do it. Some say to have nice things, or because they are being pressured by friends. Others just want to see if they can get away with it. Some are angry, depressed, confused, bored, or just mad at the world and want to strike back.

Though people usually know it's wrong, when life is stressful they become more vulnerable to temptation. Shoplifting is one of many inappropriate ways of coping with stress. Some people overeat, drink too much, use drugs, or withdraw.

Because shoplifting can be addictive, swift and unforgiving action on the part of retailers and the court system is necessary. Retailers also are moving to more technologically sophisticated loss prevention systems. For apparel, thin label-like electronic circuits designed as labels applied directly to apparel by the manufacturers is the most likely answer.

buttons are sewn on well, buttonholes are made neatly, zippers zip easily, and stripes match at the seams. They ask questions before they buy. They buy only the garments that meet their standards. Study the list of shopping tips in 6-9.

- You have the *responsibility to let legitimate dissatisfactions be known*. If a product does not perform as advertised and expected, it is the responsibility of the consumer to let it be known. Otherwise, the manufacturer may not be aware of the problem.

As a consumer, you also have the responsibility to follow care instructions recommended on the hangtags and care labels. This will help the product to perform as the manufacturer has designed it to perform. Manufacturers are required to sew care labels into garments. Suppose a care label in a shirt says dry clean only. If you wash the shirt and it shrinks, you cannot make a claim to anyone about the shrinkage.

Handling a Complaint

The strong interest in consumer protection, coupled with advanced technology, has created new standards for textile products. Your

10 EASY TIPS TO FOLLOW
BEFORE YOU BUY

- Is the fiber content right for your needs? (Look at labels.)
- Is the garment washable? Does it have to be dry cleaned? (Look at labels and tags for instructions.)
- Is the garment colorfast? (Look at labels and tags. Ask questions before you buy!)
- Is the garment wrinkle-resistant? (Look at tags for claims. Then, just to make sure, crumple a corner in your hand. Does it bounce back? It should.)
- Will fabric pill? (Look at a small area after you have rubbed it together in a circular motion. Hold it at an angle. Any fuzzing or pilling?)
- Will fabric snag? (Look for long stitches or loose loops in fabric.)
- Is the garment well-constructed? (Look at buttons, buttonholes, stitching, dangling threads, width of seams, hem.)
- Will the garment fit? Will it sag or bag? (Look at fabric after you have wrapped it tight around your fist. It should flatten right out without buckling.)
- Is there a guarantee or warranty? (Look at tags, and read the fine print carefully!)
- Are you buying from a reliable retailer? (Look up a store's return policy before purchasing. Why be sorry later?)

Monsanto Textiles Co.

6-9--

Smart consumers find the answers to these questions before they buy clothes.

responsibilities as a consumer are to be informed and to care for your purchased goods properly. If a product does not perform as it should, you should inform the right people. When buyers and sellers work together, products can be improved.

You may buy something that you cannot wear because it is of poor quality. The sweater shown in 6-10 was bought in haste. Later the purchaser discovered a button was missing. Since an extra button was not supplied, all of the buttons would have to be replaced. The blouse shown in 6-11 was found on a sale table. There was soil on the collar that may or may not wash out.

In cases like this, a complaint is in order. You may not like to complain, but you do not want to feel that you have made a "bad buy." Go to the store where you bought the item. Bring the item and the sales receipt. Return the garment to the proper person. This could be the manager, department head, or clerk in customer service. These people are the decision makers. They want to know about customer complaints. Then they can correct the problem before it happens again. Most stores will gladly replace your purchase or refund your money. The item is often returned to the manufacturer for credit on the store's account.

6-10
A button is missing from this sweater. What would you do about it?

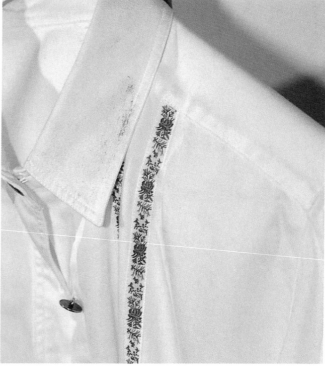

6-11
This blouse was on a sale table. Notice the soil on the collar. As a smart shopper, inspect garments before you buy.

What should you do if you are not satisfied with how your problem is handled? Write a letter to the store. Read and study the sample complaint letter in 6-12. Notice the information that should be included in such a letter.

If you are not contacted within the time specified in your letter, write to the manufacturer. You can obtain names and addresses from your library information center or reference books at the library. You can also use the Internet to do a search for the company. Many manufacturers have their own Web sites that will provide you a way to contact the company.

If the above suggestions do not work, contact a consumer protection agency for help. You may contact a local newspaper, radio, or TV station if there is a consumer reporter. The Better Business Bureau can also advise you.

Consumers, retailers, and manufacturers must work together for the benefit of each other. Manufacturers want their products to perform well so retailers will want to continue to sell them. Retailers want to offer quality products and services so they will have satisfied, happy customers. Consumers want to feel they have made good buying decisions.

Sample Complaint Letter

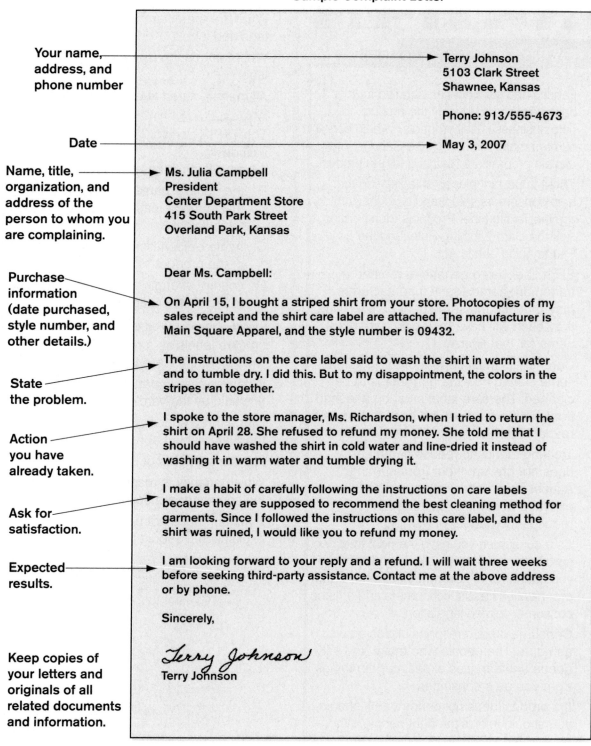

Your name, address, and phone number → Terry Johnson
5103 Clark Street
Shawnee, Kansas

Phone: 913/555-4673

Date → May 3, 2007

Name, title, organization, and address of the person to whom you are complaining. →
Ms. Julia Campbell
President
Center Department Store
415 South Park Street
Overland Park, Kansas

Dear Ms. Campbell:

Purchase information (date purchased, style number, and other details.) → On April 15, I bought a striped shirt from your store. Photocopies of my sales receipt and the shirt care label are attached. The manufacturer is Main Square Apparel, and the style number is 09432.

State the problem. → The instructions on the care label said to wash the shirt in warm water and to tumble dry. I did this. But to my disappointment, the colors in the stripes ran together.

Action you have already taken. → I spoke to the store manager, Ms. Richardson, when I tried to return the shirt on April 28. She refused to refund my money. She told me that I should have washed the shirt in cold water and line-dried it instead of washing it in warm water and tumble drying it.

Ask for satisfaction. → I make a habit of carefully following the instructions on care labels because they are supposed to recommend the best cleaning method for garments. Since I followed the instructions on this care label, and the shirt was ruined, I would like you to refund my money.

Expected results. → I am looking forward to your reply and a refund. I will wait three weeks before seeking third-party assistance. Contact me at the above address or by phone.

Sincerely,

Terry Johnson
Terry Johnson

Keep copies of your letters and originals of all related documents and information.

6-12
Sometimes it may be necessary to write a complaint letter.

CHAPTER REVIEW

Key Points

- Fabrics and garments are labeled for four basic reasons: to identify the product, to help businesses sell products, to help consumers make wise purchases, and to explain proper care methods for the product.

- Three important pieces of legislation that help consumers select and care for clothing are the Textile Fiber Products Identification Act, the Care Labeling Rule, and the Flammable Fabrics Act.

- Each fiber has a generic name and a trademark name. Many manufacturers may produce the same generic fiber, but they each will have their own trademark name for that fiber.

- Care labels must appear on all clothing items stating how the garment is to be cleaned. The care label must be attached firmly to the garment, be easy to find, and readable for the useful life of the garment.

- Treating fabrics to reduce flammability does not prevent them from burning. Almost every fabric will burn when exposed to a flame. Treating fabrics reduces the danger of burning.

- As a consumer, you have the right to expect certain things from the goods and services you use. Several government agencies and organizations assist consumers and enforce consumer-related legislation.

- Consumers have responsibilities as well as rights. The people who make and sell goods and services expect certain things from you as a consumer.

- If a product does not perform as it should, you should inform the right people. When buyers and sellers work together, products can be improved.

To Review

1. What are the differences between hang-tags and labels?
2. What information is required to be on a label?
3. All manufactured fibers are divided into 22 _____.
4. The TFPIA does NOT require that labels include _____.
   - A. care instructions
   - B. the generic name of every fiber that makes up at least five percent of the total weight
   - C. name or identification of manufacturer of the product
   - D. country of origin, if product is imported to the United States
5. List the six items of information required on care labels as a result of the 1984 revision of the Care Labeling Rule.
6. Where is care information found for fabrics sold by the yard?
7. Name three specific products covered by the Flammable Fabrics Act.
8. List the six rights of consumers.
9. Which agency is responsible for enforcing consumer protection legislation?
10. If an item does not perform as expected, explain what should be done first.

To Do

1. Collect hangtags and labels for a bulletin board display. Note the information that is required and the information that is not required.

2. Divide into groups. Write a care label that could be applicable to a certain fabric or garment. Compare with other groups.

3. Visit a fabric store. Ask the salesperson to let you examine ends of fabric bolts. Record the information and share it with other class members.

4. Find the costs of dry-cleaning different garments. Compare to laundering costs.

5. Invite a local firefighter to speak to the class about fire hazards related to clothing.

6. As a class, research and develop a brochure listing local sources for consumer assistance. Look in the Yellow Pages of the phone directory. Also use the Internet to see what services your community offers.

7. Invite a staff member of the Better Business Bureau to talk to your class about the functions of the organization.

8. Ask a clothing department or store manager to visit your class. Ask about policies related to returned merchandise and the do's and don'ts of returning merchandise. Also ask how consumers use label information.

9. Role-play correct and incorrect ways to return defective merchandise to a store.

To Think About

1. Think about an experience you have had with a fabric or garment that failed to wear or perform as you expected. What could you have done differently as a consumer?

2. Why is it important to save hangtags from the clothes you buy?

3. What would it be like to buy clothes and other textile items without any labels or hangtags on them? What kinds of problems could you have?

4. Consumers have responsibilities as well as rights. Review each of the consumer responsibilities again. Do you feel you carry out these responsibilities as a consumer? Do you carry out some responsibilities better than others?

5. Write a sample letter to a store manager about a disappointing purchase. Compare letters for clarity and detail with classmates.

CHAPTER 7

Your Choices as a Consumer

Key Terms

department stores
specialty shops
chain stores
discount stores
off-price
  discount stores
factory outlet stores
overruns
irregulars
seconds
thrift shops
resale shops
mail-order
  shopping
online shopping
comparison shopping
impulse buying
bargain
finance charge
debit card
credit
regular charge account
revolving charge account
layaway buying

Objectives

After studying this chapter, you will be able to

- identify and compare the features of different types of stores.
- identify and compare the features of non-store shopping.
- describe how to comparison shop and avoid impulse buying.
- explain the role of advertising in your buying decisions.
- define the types of sales stores will have.
- describe various ways you can pay for your purchases.

You have many choices today when you need to buy clothes. Most clothing purchases are made in retail stores. There are a wide variety of types of stores that sell clothes and accessories. Each type has advantages and disadvantages.

You can also shop for clothes from your home. If you have one of several forms of technology in your home, you can make purchases without ever leaving home. You can also shop almost 24-hours a day. All you need is a phone, television, fax machine, or computer with a modem.

Consumers also have more options today when they are ready to pay for their purchases. With so many choices, it pays to be an informed consumer.

department stores
Stores that sell a variety of items and clothing in a wide range of styles, qualities, and prices.

Types of Stores

Why do you like one store better than another? Is it because it carries a wider selection of clothes? Are the salespeople there more helpful? See 7-1. Do they treat you as an important person rather than someone who is too young to know anything? Maybe you shop in a certain store because your friends shop there. Perhaps it is located in a shopping mall close to your home.

There are many types of stores that carry clothing. Compare the features as well as prices to find which type suits you best.

Department Stores

Department stores offer one-stop shopping. They sell a variety of clothing, shoes, and accessories in a wide range of styles, qualities, and prices. A department store offers clothing for infants, children, teens, and juniors as well as styles for older persons. In addition, they may sell a wide variety of products for the home such as furniture, carpet, lamps, and linens. Luggage, jewelry, and cosmetics are also sold.

Department stores generally sell designer names and manufacturer brands that are recognized by consumers as being quality products. They may also carry their own *private label* (house brand) merchandise that is made specifically for

7-1
Courteous and helpful salespeople can attract customers to a store.

that store. This allows the store to specify the qualities they want in these products. Many large department stores also have "budget-priced" clothing departments.

Department stores feature service for their customers. They have salespeople who provide you with personal assistance. They will help you find your size, get the proper fit, and arrange for alterations. You pay for your purchases in the same area where the items are located. It is also easy to return your purchases if you are unhappy with what you bought.

Many services may be offered such as credit accounts, alterations, gift wrapping and mailing, and home delivery. There is usually a charge for these services. Customers decide if it is worth the cost to them to use these services.

Specialty Shops

Specialty shops sell specific kinds of merchandise. For instance, they may sell only junior-size dresses or boys' and men's pants or infants' wear. Shopping centers and malls are

7-2

Malls offer climate-controlled shopping. A variety of specialty shops are often located in malls.

specialty shops
Shops that sell specific kinds of merchandise.

good places to find specialty shops, 7-2. If you need a certain item that is not available, the store may be able to get it for you. The service is good, and the salespeople know their merchandise. For people with limited time to shop, specialty shops are ideal. Prices are sometimes higher than in other stores.

A *boutique* is a type of specialty store that features a limited type of unique apparel or accessories. These stores are small, pricey, and give personal service.

Chain Stores

Chain stores are groups of 12 or more stores owned and managed by a central office. The stores carry the same line of products at similar prices. Some chains are department stores, such as Sears Roebuck and JCPenney. Other chains are more like specialty shops, selling a single product category, such as men's or women's clothes. The Limited and Gap are examples of chain clothing stores.

All of the stores in the chain will have a similar look to them. Private label merchandise may be made exclusively for the stores. Because of their buying power, manufacturers offer lower prices to chain stores. This leads to lower retail prices.

chain stores
Groups of 12 or more stores owned and managed by a central office and carrying the same line or products.

Discount Stores

Discount stores have lower prices than department stores. They can get better prices because they buy in larger quantities. Discount stores carry a wide range of clothing and household items. The quality of clothing can range from high to low. Items may have something slightly wrong with them, but are still wearable. This could be a pulled thread or a place where the color is not the same. Discount stores also sell clothes from manufacturers who produced more than their dealers ordered. These clothes could be first quality, but because they are "extras," they are sold at lower prices.

These stores are the department stores' greatest competition. In recent years, discount stores have done more to improve their image. Some stores have greeters to welcome you when you enter. They may have film developing, snack bars, and banking facilities within them. They have convenient hours and are open in the evenings, on weekends, and most holidays.

Generally, discount stores offer less personal service than department stores. There is little personal assistance. You are on your own to find your style preferences and sizes. Large overhead signs direct you to the proper department. Once you have selected your items, you take them to the front of the store where the checkout counters are located. The buildings are large and simply decorated. Dressing rooms may be sparse. Special services, such as gift wrapping and home deliveries, are not offered.

discount stores
Stores where items are sold at lower prices than department stores.

Off-Price Discount Stores

Another type of discount store is becoming more common. **Off-price discount stores** feature brand-name or designer merchandise at below-normal prices. You may have a TJMaxx, Marshalls, Syms, or Designer Depot store near you. Off-price stores sell moderate to higher-priced merchandise that sometimes have the labels cut to protect the manufacturers' products sold in other stores at full price.

Buyers for off-price discount stores do not place orders for their merchandise. Instead, they buy what's available during the season when most

off-price discount stores
A type of discount store that features brand-name or designer merchandise at below-normal prices.

factory outlet stores
Stores operated by manufacturers that sell only their own merchandise.

overrun
Item that was produced by a manufacturer but not ordered by retailers.

irregulars
Items with slight defects.

seconds
Items that are soiled or have flaws.

thrift shops
Shops that carry leftovers from other stores and some out-of-style garments.

other buyers are placing orders for the next season. They buy whatever they can and sell it immediately. As a consumer, you can enjoy reduced prices for brand-name goods at these stores. However, you cannot predict what you will find when you shop.

Factory Outlet Stores

Factory outlet stores are stores operated by manufacturers that sell only their own merchandise. See 7-3. The prices are often less than those at department stores because the clothing comes directly from the factory. There is no wholesaler or "middle person" involved. They are often located near their factories. They generally do not locate near the stores that sell their full-price merchandise.

Factory outlet malls feature only stores of this type. They are usually located in outlying areas.

Some factory outlets offer first-quality items from the current season, shipped weeks after the same items went to the department stores. They also sell last season's lines and manufacturers' overruns. **Overruns** are items that were produced by the manufacturer but not ordered by retailers. Half of all outlets are now carrying clothes produced specifically for those stores, accounting for about 10 percent of their inventory. Know the prices of items you're looking for before you go. Not everything at an outlet is a bargain. Return policies are not as liberal at outlet stores compared to full-price stores.

You'll also find irregulars and seconds in outlet stores. The labels or price tags on the garments will indicate if the items are **irregulars** or seconds. An irregular means that there is a slight defect in the garment. Look carefully for the defect and decide if it will affect the wearing quality of the garment. **Seconds** are items that are soiled or have flaws. A poorly sewn seam or a hidden flaw in a garment could be a good buy. You could repair the seam. The flaw could be in a spot that would not show as the garment is worn. Soiled garments can be cleaned.

Thrift and Resale Shops

Thrift shops carry leftovers from other stores and some out-of-style garments. Some clothing may have been owned by others. Thrift shops are often run by not-for-profit organizations to raise money for charitable causes. Search for flaws and signs of quality to be sure you are spending your money wisely.

Resale shops are just what their name implies. The clothing has been owned and worn before. It is

7-3
Some name-brand manufacturers run factory outlet stores. You can find some very good buys at these stores.

being sold again. Clothing that has been outgrown or is no longer worn is brought to these stores. Some resale shops sell donated items. Others sell on *consignment.* That means a portion of the sale price goes back to the original owner of the garment. The remainder of the sale price goes to the shop. Shops will carry items on consignment for about 30 days. If the item does not sell after that time, the price is reduced. If it still doesn't sell, it can be returned to the owner or donated to charity. Many resale shops have a no-return policy, so try the items on. Inspect clothes for spots, missing buttons, and broken zippers.

Your choice of stores depends on you. Which has the garments you like best? In which stores do you feel comfortable and enjoy shopping? You may decide to shop in different stores for different items.

resale shops
Stores that sell clothing that has been owned or worn before.

Non-Store Shopping

If you don't want to leave home or you want to shop in the middle of the night, you may want to try non-store shopping. You have several choices: mail-order shopping, online shopping, television shopping, or personal selling.

Mail-Order Shopping

Mail-order shopping is one way to shop at home. Items are ordered from a catalog by phone, fax, or mail, 7-4. This type of shopping has become a way of life for many consumers. There are several reasons for the increased growth of catalogs. These include the widespread use of credit cards and the number of people in the workforce who now have less time for shopping at retail stores. With mail-order shopping, you can take your time choosing the items you want when you have the time to shop.

Catalogs often offer a better assortment of clothing items than local stores. Many catalogs include designer fashions. Prices vary, but they usually compete with department stores.

There are advantages and disadvantages to mail-order shopping. The following are some of the advantages:

mail-order shopping
A type of shopping that allows a person to shop at home by mail.

- Shopping by mail is convenient. There are no parking problems or time limits for store openings and closings.

- Catalog services are usually quite good. Returns can usually be made with no questions asked. (Check the company policy in the catalog to see if you can return items for a refund or credit.)

- Each item of clothing is shown and described. The fabrics, sizes, colors, prices, and details are listed. This catalog information is often more complete than what a store salesperson could give you.

7-4
Mail-order catalogs offer the convenience of shopping at home.

- Orders are easily placed by phone, practically any time, day or night, through toll-free numbers and credit cards. Orders can also be mailed or faxed.

Some disadvantages are the following:

- There is often a delivery charge added to the price of your purchase. Taxes may or may not be charged depending on the state in which you live.
- Perfect fit may be a problem, as you are not able to try the garment on before you buy it.
- There may be a slight difference in color when the garment arrives. Photos are taken of each item, but the exact color is difficult to reproduce on paper.
- If you have to return an item, you will have to repackage it and return it for an exchange, a refund, or credit. Often, you must pay the shipping cost of returning the item.
- You will have to wait for your order to be delivered, which is inconvenient if you need something right away.

Some stores have catalog departments in their retail stores. You can find what you want in a catalog, and place your order there. You may return to pick up the order later or pay to have it mailed to you.

Never send cash along with your order. It could be lost or stolen, and it would be difficult to prove you sent it. Pay by credit card, check, or money order. Stores may have different policies concerning payments. See 7-5 for some additional hints for catalog shopping.

Online Shopping

The area of greatest growth in non-store shopping is the use of the Internet for online purchases. Nearly 75 percent of households have Internet access, and half will make purchases online. Most shopping is done for books and computer equipment, but apparel is quickly becoming a popular category. The total amount spent will reach $117 billion in 2008.

Though this is only five percent of all retail sales, the Internet impacts sales even though purchases may not be made online. Many consumers comparison shop online to find the best prices for the products they want to buy. Once they have narrowed down their choices, they often make the purchase at a local retail store. Some Web sites even consolidate listings from reliable merchants. They will show a range of prices for the same product, be it an iPod or a trendy leather purse.

For online shopping, you need a computer with a modem. You also need to subscribe to an Internet service provider. More and more retailers have Web sites where their merchandise is shown and sold. At these Web sites, you can view three-dimensional pictures of clothing styles and read descriptions of the items. Information on colors, sizes, styles, and prices

HELPFUL HINTS FOR CATALOG **SHOPPING**

- When ordering, ask about special services, like free color swatches, hemming, or advice on coordinating outfits.

- Sizes differ from one catalog to another, so take your measurements and follow the sizing directions on the order form. Ask the operator if the style runs full or snug, long or short. Also watch for sizing clues such as *fitted, relaxed fit,* or *oversize.*

- Mailing charges can add up. A low-priced item may not be a good buy after postage and handling are added. If ordering several items, do so at one time to keep charges as low as possible.

- Ask the operator when your order will be shipped (usually within a day or two) and the approximate arrival date. In case of problems, write down the date ordered, item details, and order number.

- Ask about the return policy. Most catalogs accept returns, but you won't get your original mailing charge refunded. Many catalogs now offer free returns and enclose a labeled package for your use.

7-5
Catalog shopping can be a convenient way to shop, but follow these helpful hints.

are given. To purchase an item, you key in your selections. You pay by entering your credit card number, although some sites will bill you by mail. Currently, there is a no-tax policy on Internet purchases. Merchandise is delivered to you within a few days.

Many of the advantages and disadvantages of online shopping are similar to those of catalog shopping. It is convenient and can be done at any hour of the day or night. It can be hassle free, depending on the design of the Web site. Some Web sites are easier to "navigate" than others, 7-6. They have clear connection paths that allow you to move quickly to the product you want with just three clicks of the mouse. Some sites will send you electronic notices of items on sale or special offers at your request. Sites may provide "wish lists" where people can "window shop" and create an online record of items they like, making gift shopping easier.

Nordstrom.com

7-6
Shopping online can be more satisfying if the Web site is easy to navigate.

A disadvantage in buying clothing online is that you cannot feel the fabric or try on the clothes. Some retailers have attempted to overcome this problem by allowing visitors to try clothes on a personal model created on screen to mimic the shopper's own body traits. Some sites allow you to view fabric swatches up close. Others allow you to see both the front and back of a product. At some sites, if you select one item, other items will be shown that coordinate with your initial selection.

.com Shopping— Buyer Beware

In 1996, electronic commerce (e-commerce) began with a relatively small number of "shoppers" making purchases over the Internet. E-commerce has exploded since then. Well-designed Web sites have made shopping online a popular alternative.

Yet there are problems with shopping online that you, the consumer, need to be aware of. There are honest merchants and there are dishonest merchants. There are safety and security concerns, even as there are when you shop at your local mall. This is especially so if you do a search for a very specific item and end up at a Web site for a company that is unknown to you. Remember, anyone can set up shop on the Internet. Very few safeguards are currently in place to protect consumers. Therefore, you need to be extra cautious. Be sure of the following before you agree to any purchase and enter your credit card number. Does the site

- provide complete information about the company, such as the kind of business it is, what it sells, where it is located, and how you can contact them?
- provide enough details about the product so you know exactly what you are buying?
- provide complete information on the cost of the item including shipping, handling, and any taxes?
- provide any warranties or guarantees?
- allow you to print a record of the transaction?
- provide confirmation by e-mail within one business day that your order has been received?
- notify you of stock status and approximate delivery time?
- explain the return policy and how you can receive a credit?
- provide credit card transactions through a secured server?
- have a customer service person you can call or e-mail with any complaints or problem?

If you can answer yes to all of these questions, then you can be fairly sure your online shopping experience will be a positive one.

An early concern of consumers was the safety of providing a credit card number online. Experts now claim that it is safe to make credit card purchases from established online retailers. The company's software encrypts all personal information into bits of code that only the customer and the business can view. Look for a symbol such as an unbroken padlock or key or the words Secure Sockets Layer (SSL) at Web sites. These indicate that the company is using a system to secure your payment information. If you buy from a certain site often, your credit card information can be saved. This information will automatically be entered for you each time you make a purchase, saving checkout time.

Television Shopping

Several television channels show products that are available for purchase. A wide variety of products are sold in this manner, including clothing and accessories. Many home shopping programs feature jewelry. The products are displayed, modeled, and described in detail. Viewers call toll-free numbers to place their orders. Most require payment by credit card, and the orders are shipped to your home.

Television shopping is convenient, but some people may order items they don't really need or cannot afford. Celebrity hosts entice people to buy. Personal testimonials by satisfied customers are also used to promote the sale of products.

Personal Selling

Clothing items, jewelry, accessories, and cosmetics are also sold in the home through *personal selling.* Parties or showings are scheduled in private homes, either for groups or individuals. Items are modeled or displayed, and orders are taken by a sales representative. The items are then delivered in person or through the mail. The merchandise is generally of a high quality, but may also be high in price. Customers sometimes feel pressure to buy if the party is held by a friend. If you attend a party, be sure you won't feel pressured to buy something you don't really need.

Shopping Strategies

When you are ready to begin shopping, there are a number of strategies that will help you get the most for your money. Few people have unlimited funds for clothing purchases. Using some of these strategies will help your clothing dollar go farther.

Do Comparison Shopping

comparison shopping
Looking at different brands of the same or similar products in several stores to compare prices, quality, features, and store services before buying.

A smart shopper compares qualities and prices in different stores before buying. This is called **comparison shopping.** The young woman in 7-7 is comparing tops. She wants one with the right details at the right price.

Begin your comparison shopping by studying newspaper advertisements for items you need and keep prices in mind. Mail-order catalogs are a good reference in comparison shopping. Then when you visit stores, you will be ready to compare garments. Read the labels to be sure you are comparing items with similar qualities.

Compare nationally advertised brands with lesser-known brands. Lesser-known brands often cost less. If the quality is equal, the lesser-known brand is a better buy. When you are not sure about the quality of a product, you may be smart to buy the nationally advertised one. A well-known brand name usually assures you of good quality.

Comparison shopping takes time. You must have patience and a real desire to get the best value for your money. The results make it worthwhile. You will have a feeling of satisfaction when you know you have made the right purchase. Going with a friend can make comparison shopping more helpful. See 7-8.

7-7
After comparison shopping, this young woman has found the top she wants. It is the right style, size, color, and price.

7-8
Comparison shopping is more fun when you are with a friend.

Avoid Impulse Buying

People often buy clothes without a plan. **Impulse buying** is buying something as soon as you see it. You do not stop to think about your needs. You may not consider if you have something in your wardrobe that you can wear with it. You buy it because it is pretty, because someone else has one, or because you happen to have enough money with you.

Do not let advertising displays, as in 7-9, or special sale signs influence you. Impulse buying will cause you to spend too much money on clothing. Besides, you may not be happy with your purchase when you return home. It is smarter to make a list of planned purchases before you begin to shop. Then if you find a sale price on a garment that you had planned to buy anyway, you will have found a true bargain.

impulse buying
Unplanned consumer purchases or "spur of the moment" buying of merchandise on display.

Use Advertisements Wisely

Advertising has the power to "create" wants by making products seem desirable. Clever slogans, songs, and phrases are composed to catch your attention. Photos and drawings are shown to heighten your interest.

Many clothing ads are aimed at young people. Teens can be fashion leaders. They begin new clothing trends, and adults often follow. An example is the widespread use of denim today. Teens started this trend by wearing denim jeans. Then they bought denim purses, backpacks, jackets, skirts, and hats. Before long, denim was worn by everyone. See 7-10.

Pendleton Woolen Mills

7-10
Many denim clothing ads are aimed at young people. Still, denim clothes are worn by people of all ages.

7-9
Attractive store windows are designed to draw you into a store to make a purchase.

The advertising industry gives major financial support to newspapers, magazines, radio, television, and the Internet. These methods of communication help the advertiser reach you, the consumer. Competition between companies is stiff. They want you to spend your money for their products. They also want you to be satisfied so you will buy their products again.

Advertisements can be a big help to you. They often contain vital information that can help you with your buying decision. For instance, if you were buying a pair of pants, you would want to know the fiber content, care required, brand name, sizes available, and price. You would need to know what stores carried the item. Informational ads also tell you the advantages of a product and show you how to use products correctly. New products are often introduced in this manner.

Advertisers also look for ways to entice you to buy their products. They try to appeal to your "hidden needs" for individuality, adventure, and fantasy. They may use words that lead you to believe that wearing these garments will make you a trendsetter. Words such as "just in," "latest designs," and "new" encourage you to buy. Advertisers also may ask well-known actors or sports figures to model their garments. These types of ads are called *endorsements.*

Infomercials and advertorials blur the lines between advertising and information. *Infomercials* are television presentations that advertise a product under the guise of a product demonstration by a host or "expert." *Advertorials* attempt to "hide" advertising in the form of an article or short story in a magazine or newspaper. (Look for the word "Advertisement" in small letters at the top of the page.) No matter how convincing the expert or how appealing the article, it is important to remember that infomercials and advertorials are still just forms of advertising.

Ads also announce sales. Some of the sales they announce are a help and can save you money. Unfortunately, not all sales are bargains.

Know Your Sales

When stores plan sales, they try to convince you that you need their merchandise. Their ads tell you the sale is an opportunity to find great bargains. However, a sale is a **bargain** only when you can save money on items you need. By being able to evaluate sales, you will be a better shopper and will save money.

bargain
A sale in which money is saved on items needed.

Most stores have many sales during a year. Many are scheduled during slow seasons to lure shoppers into stores. Sometimes all stores will have sales at the same time, such as before and after holidays. Other sale days are chosen by individual stores. Sales are labeled *Store-Wide Sale, Bargain Days, Anniversary Sale, Manager's Sale,* and other catchy titles. Some stores have a sale each week! Free gifts and chances for prizes are sometimes offered to entice customers into stores during sales. All of this leads you to wonder if you can really save money at these sales. The answer is yes if you know your sales and are familiar with prices.

Plan your purchases before you go to a sale. It is hard to think clearly about what you need when you are surrounded by people. The confusion may cause you to change your mind about trying to save money.

Salespersons may find it difficult to keep merchandise straight on tables. People are careless about "digging" to find what they want. If you are willing to search through the piles, you can find bargains.

Look at the hangtags to see if the price has really been lowered. See 7-11. A 50 percent markdown is a real bargain if the garment is still in good condition. But 10 percent off is not a great savings. It would be a bargain only if it is exactly what you want.

Clearance, inventory, and end-of-season sales can be real money-savers. Look for these types of sales:

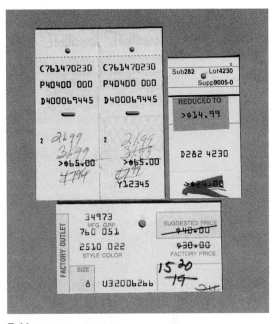

7-11
Check sale markdowns to see if you are really getting a good deal. Remember, a sale is a bargain only if it is something you really need and want.

- *Clearance sales* are planned when a store wants to sell items to make room for new merchandise.

- *Inventory sales* are held before stock is counted or after it is counted. In either case, an inventory sale is held to reduce a store's inventory.

- *End-of-season sales* are held to make room for new merchandise for a new season.

- *Pre-season sales* feature items that are ahead of the season, such as coats sold at the end of summer. Because you are buying the item early, stores offer them at sale prices. After the sale, prices return to the full retail price.

- A *special-purchase sale* offers products that have been bought especially for the sale. By buying large amounts, the store can offer items to you for less than regular price. This type of sale usually offers fewer bargains than other sales.

- *Going-out-of-business sales* indicate that the owner is closing the store for some reason. All of the merchandise must be sold. Prices may be good, but items cannot be returned.

Irregulars or seconds are sometimes good buys. Take your time and inspect any item before you buy it. If imperfections exist that you will not accept, it is best to find them before you leave the store. Many sale items cannot be returned. Ask before you buy.

Sales can help both stores and consumers. Stores need to sell the products. They have to make room for the newer ones. Consumers like to get the products they need at reduced prices. Study the sale ads of stores near you to find those that offer real sale bargains.

Paying for What You Buy

After careful shopping, you are ready to pay for your purchases, 7-12. The cashier may ask you if you want to pay with cash, check, or credit. You may want to put your purchases on layaway. The decision is yours, but you need to know the pros and cons of each option.

Paying with Cash

finance charge
An extra charge you pay for the use of credit.

Paying for clothing with cash is the quickest and easiest way to buy. You can buy what you like no matter where you shop because all stores will take cash as payment. Paying with cash has several advantages. There are no finance charges when you pay with cash. (A **finance charge** is the price you pay for credit.) Also, you will not go into debt because you will only spend the amount of cash you have.

Paying with a Check

As with cash, you can avoid finance charges by paying by check. Using a check is a way of paying for something without using cash. You can put your money into a bank account and write checks on the account to pay for your purchases. As you write a check, you are actually letting the bank pay your bill from your account. Your check gives the store the right to collect the money you owe. Guidelines for writing a check are given in 7-13.

Sometimes banks have a service charge for checking accounts, or they may charge a certain amount for each check written. Check with banks to find the checking account that best suits your needs.

If you plan to pay for your purchases by check, find out the store's policy regarding checks. Some stores will not accept checks. Others may require that you show several pieces of identification such as a credit card and a driver's license before they will accept a check.

As you write a check, write clearly in ink. Study the details of the check in 7-14 to understand how to write a check correctly. Be sure to keep an accurate record of all checks you write to help you remember whom you paid, how much you paid, and when you paid.

7-12_____
Cash, check, or charge? You may have several options of how you will pay for clothing.

HOW TO WRITE A **CHECK**

- Write clearly with ink.
- Date the check with month, date, and year.
- After words "Pay to the order of," write the name of the store to whom you are paying the money. Ask the clerk for the correct title to use. If you are unsure of spelling, ask for help.
- Write the amount of the payment in numerals, close to the dollar sign. Make your first number as close as possible to the sign.
- Write the amount of the payment in words at the beginning of the next line. After the dollars amount, write the word, "and." The amount of cents may be written as 25/100, or 00/00, or no/100. Draw a line through the space that is left in the line.
- Sign the check exactly as you signed the signature card when you opened the account.
- Record the amount of the check and the name of the store to whom the check was written. Also record the date and what you purchased.

7-13
Study these guidelines to learn how to write a check.

Payee's name

Date

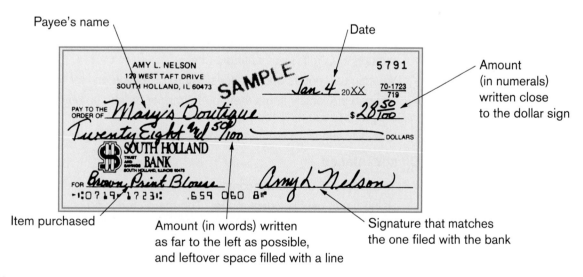

Amount (in numerals) written close to the dollar sign

Item purchased

Amount (in words) written as far to the left as possible, and leftover space filled with a line

Signature that matches the one filed with the bank

7-14
Checks should be written neatly and correctly to avoid errors.

debit card
A card issued by banks that allows the user to deduct money electronically from the user's bank account in payment for goods or services.

Debit Cards

Banks may also provide you with a debit card (or check card), which looks much like a credit card. When a **debit card** is used, the money is deducted electronically from your bank account without you writing a check. If you use a debit card, you need to record the transaction in your checkbook so you can keep track of your balance. When you receive your bank statement, also check these transactions for accuracy.

Using Credit

credit
A promise to pay in the future for what is purchased today.

Buying on **credit** is a promise to pay in the future for what you buy today. When you buy on credit, a card is usually presented instead of cash or a check. People often purchase clothing on credit because it can have several advantages. Buying on credit can have disadvantages, too. For a list of advantages and disadvantages of using credit, see 7-15.

Types of Credit

regular charge account
A charge account that allows a person to charge purchases in exchange for a promise to pay in full within 10 to 30 days after the billing date.

The two major types of retail credit are the regular charge account and the revolving charge account. With the **regular charge account,** you may charge purchases in exchange for your promise to pay in full within 10 to 30 days after the billing date. You will receive a bill or statement. If you pay on time, there is no finance charge.

BUYING ON **CREDIT**

Advantages

- It is convenient. You do not have to carry large amounts of cash nor go through the process of writing a check.
- You can use goods and services before or as you pay for them.
- You can buy costly items that you might not be able to buy with the amount of cash available.
- It usually simplifies exchanges, returns, and telephone orders.

Disadvantages

- You reduce your future income.
- Using credit usually costs money. The more credit you use and the more time you take to repay, the more you must pay in finance charges.
- You may be tempted to overspend because of impulse buying.
- Failure to pay promptly could result in a poor credit rating.

7-15

Using credit has both advantages and disadvantages.

The **revolving charge account** allows you to make purchases up to a limit set by the creditor and the customer when the account was opened. If you pay in full, there is no finance charge. If you do not pay in full, there is a finance charge on the unpaid balance. You are required to make at least the minimum payment each month. This amount is specified on the bill.

Credit Cards

Credit cards are most often used to make credit purchases. Many stores issue their own credit cards. Other cards are issued by financial institutions such as banks and by credit card companies. Sometimes a membership fee is charged for these cards. They often specify a *credit limit.* This is the maximum amount of money a customer can owe the credit card company at one time.

When you apply for credit, you will be asked to complete an application form. You will be asked questions that indicate your ability to pay for the use of credit. Questions about your income, your bank accounts, where you live, how long you have lived there, and other credit cards you have may be asked. You must be 18 years old in order to have a card in your own name.

Read the credit contract before signing. Sign only when you are sure you understand all the terms and obligations and can meet those terms and obligations. You will want to know what the annual percentage rate is that will be applied to any unpaid balance. Also note the minimum amount you must pay each month and how much time you have to make your payments. Penalties can be added if payments arrive after the due date. These can add up quickly.

Layaway Buying

Layaway buying is placing a small deposit on an item so that the store will reserve it for you. Sometimes the deposit is at least 10 percent of the cost of the item. Payments are made each week or month until the full amount is paid. When you make the last payment, you receive your item. Usually there is no interest charge on the unpaid balance of layaway purchases. However, there may be a service charge.

Layaway buying can be an advantage if you need a major item. Suppose you will need a coat for next season. While shopping you find a coat that is a good buy, but you don't have enough money to buy it now. You could put the coat on layaway. The disadvantage of layaway is having to wait weeks or months before you can get your item. Also, if you fail to complete the payments, you will lose the item, and in some cases, the money you have already paid. Be sure to check the store's layaway policy before making a layaway purchase.

revolving charge account
A charge account that allows a person to make purchases up to a limit set by the creditor and the customer when the account was opened.

layaway buying
Placing a small deposit on an item so that the store will reserve it for a buyer.

CHAPTER REVIEW

Key Points

- Most clothing purchases are made in retail stores. There are a wide variety of types of stores that sell clothes and accessories. Each type has advantages and disadvantages.

- If you want to shop from your home, you can use a non-store shopping option. You have several choices: mail-order shopping, online shopping, television shopping, or personal selling.

- When you are ready to begin shopping, there are a number of strategies that will help you get the most for your money. You should do some comparison shopping, comparing qualities and prices in different stores, before you buy. Avoiding impulse buying can also help you stay within your budget.

- Advertisements can help you learn more about a product, but they can also create wants by making products seem more desirable.

- There are many kinds of sales, but a sale is a bargain only when you can save money on items you need.

- You have many options for paying for your purchases. You can pay with cash, a check, a debit card, or a credit card. Using credit allows you to have an item immediately with the promise that you will pay at a later date.

To Review

1. What is the main feature department stores offer their customers?
2. What is the difference between a regular discount store and an off-price discount store?
3. Why are prices usually lower at factory outlet stores?
4. Name three advantages and three disadvantages of mail-order shopping.
5. How have online merchandisers made it safe for customers to give their credit card numbers when making purchases?
6. When comparison shopping, what two things should you compare?
7. Why is it a good idea to avoid impulse buying?
8. Advertising _____.
   A. is not important to consumers
   B. is a financial support for communication media
   C. is usually aimed at middle-aged people
   D. is a dirty business that tries to deceive consumers
9. How do sales help both stores and consumers?
10. What methods of paying for purchases do not have finance charges?
11. What is the main difference between regular charge accounts and revolving charge accounts?
12. List one advantage and one disadvantage of layaway buying.

To Do

1. Debate the advantages of one type of store versus another.

2. Select different types of stores for comparison shopping. Decide on a particular item that can be found in each type of store. Work in pairs or teams. Set up guidelines and questions, comparing prices, quality, and services. When the project is completed, compare your results. What are the advantages and disadvantages of each store? Where would you purchase the item?

3. Ask a store manager to visit your class. Prepare questions to ask about policy related to returned merchandise, sales, shoplifting, etc.

4. Bring clothing advertisements from different sources to class. List the kinds of information given and terms designed to create wants. Make an attractive bulletin board display.

5. Compile a list of advertising slogans that you think influence people to buy.

6. Ask someone from a newspaper office or radio station to discuss the code of ethics used in advertising copy.

7. Write a TV commercial to sell a garment or accessory of your choice. Present the commercial to the class.

8. Select an item of clothing that you could buy online. Visit three Web sites that offer the item. Compare the offers at each site, and decide from which vendor you would buy the item. Compare such items as cost, availability, qualities, shipping charges, shipping date, return policy, and method of delivery. Write a report explaining your selection.

9. Figure the differences in cost and convenience for a coat that you can buy for $150 cash; buy on credit at 18 percent annual interest; buy on layaway, paying $25.00 per month.

To Think About

1. Where do you and your friends like to shop the most? What makes this your favorite place?

2. Watch a home shopping television show. What methods are used to entice you to buy? What are the advantages of shopping in this way? What are the disadvantages?

3. Is every sale item a bargain for you? Explain your answer.

4. What makes an effective retail Web site? Visit several Web sites and make a list of the strengths and weaknesses of each one. What ideas would you use if you were designing your own retail Web site?

5. Obtain a credit card application. Why do you think each question is asked?

CHAPTER 8

Get Your Money's Worth

Objectives

After studying this chapter, you will be able to
- select clothes that fit properly.
- evaluate standards of quality construction in garments.
- judge the appearance and fit of a garment.
- make decisions concerning alterations.
- judge the fit, quality, and care of accessories.

Key Terms

quality
alterations
fine jewelry
costume jewelry

Have you ever been faced with the problem of choosing between two clothing items you like? The decision is easier when you know which points to compare.

One of the points to consider is fit. Which item fits you the best? Even clothes that are the same size may fit you differently. You need to be able to evaluate points of fit in a garment to make the best selection.

To get your money's worth in clothing, you also need to understand the term quality. The **quality** of an item depends on the degree to which it meets certain standards of excellence. The words high, medium, and low can be used to describe quality. A garment of low quality will not perform as well as one of high quality. A low-quality garment may not look as good, fit as well, or wear as long as a high-quality garment.

Quality and fit are only two of the factors you should consider when buying clothes. These are some other questions you may ask yourself. Does it look right on me? Is it appropriate for my activities? Will I wear it often enough to get my money's worth? Does it fit into my wardrobe plan? How will I care for it? Do I have accessories that will go with it?

quality
The performance characteristics of an item.

Getting the Right Fit

You know what size you wear, right? Then why is it that some garments you try on in your size seem to fit and others do not? The answer is the way different apparel manufacturers interpret standard sizes. Standard measurements for the garment industry were established more than 30 years ago. However, the average woman weighs 164 pounds today, up from 140 pounds in 1960. People have also become more tubular in shape. Though height has increased, so have the hips and waist.

Each manufacturer may design for different body proportions, based on their target market. Some target teens, while others design for career women. Therefore, some may design more ease into their garments. Others may design for close-fitting looks. There is also the practice of *vanity sizing* where manufacturers cut clothes larger and label them smaller. A woman who is a true size eight might fit comfortably into a size four. This makes her feel good about her figure.

Begin your search for the right fit by finding the size category for your body structure. Height, weight, build, and key body measurements are used to determine size categories. Within these categories, a range of sizes is offered. The chart in 8-1 gives descriptions and size ranges of various categories.

When you try on a garment, it should feel comfortable on you. It should not be too tight, too loose, too long, or too short. If you are trying on pants, be sure to sit down to make sure there is enough ease in the seat. Try on the garment with the shoes you plan to wear. This can affect skirt lengths and pant cuffs. Look in a three-way, full-length mirror. Once you are satisfied with the fit, you can look closer at the quality of the construction.

SIZE RANGE **CATEGORIES**

Female Size Categories

Figure Types	Sizes	Proportions
Subteen girls	7-16	For girls whose figures are average; undeveloped in bust and hips. Height approximately 4'2" to 5'.
Slim girls	7S-16S	For girls whose figures are slim; undeveloped in bust and hips.
Girls plus	8 1/2-18 1/2	For girls whose figures are heavier; undeveloped in bust and hips.
Teen girls	7-14	For girls whose figures are beginning to mature and be longer waisted. Height approximately 4'9" to 5'5".
Junior	3-17	For girls and women who are short-waisted, have fully developed bust and hips, and small waist. Height approximately 5'3" to 5'6 1/2".
Junior petite	3P-17P	Junior figure with height 5'2" and under.
Junior tall	3T-17T	Junior figure with height 5'7" to 5'11".
Misses	6-20	For girls and women, fully developed, with average figures and proportions. Height approximately 5'4" to 5'8".
Misses petite	6P-20P	For short and slim girls and women. Height under 5'4".
Tall misses	6T-20T	Height over 5'8".
Women's	18-60	Large proportions. Height 5'5" to 5'9".
Half sizes	12 1/2-24 1/2	Heavier, short-waisted girls and women. Height under 5'5".

(Sometimes Misses sizes are: Petite, sizes 2-6; Small, sizes 8-10; Medium, sizes 12-14; Large, sizes 16-18; Extra large, sizes 20-22; XX Large, size 24.)

Male Size Categories

Boys regular	8-20	For boys of average frame and proportions.
Slim boys	8S-20S	For small frames and thin body.
Husky boys	8H-20H	For boys who have a fuller body in proportion to height.
Student	26-30	Average frame to proportions; physique is beginning to mature; narrower seat in proportion to waist.
Men's (related to chest measurement)	30-48	For boys and men who are fully developed. Height 5'7" to 5'11".

(Sometimes Men's sizes are: Extra small, sizes 30-32; Small, sizes 34-36; Medium, sizes 38-40; Large, sizes 42-44; Extra large, sizes 46-48. Short men, for men of heights 5'3" to 5'7"; Tall men, for men of heights 5'11" to 6'3".)

8-1

Getting the right fit begins by finding the right size category for your body structure.

Judging Garment Quality

The quality of a garment must be considered when making a buying decision. The quality can generally be described as high, medium, or low. Quality often determines how the garment looks, how well it fits, and how long it will wear.

Levels of Quality

High-quality garments will have the best construction features, use the best materials, and reflect good design. Attention to details in the construction of the garment can be seen. Plaids and stripes are matched at the seams. The fabrics and trims are some of the best available. The principles of good design are used in the styling of the garment. The higher prices of these garments reflect these quality features.

Medium-quality garments have good, reliable construction features. Garments are well made and durable. Quality fabrics are used. They generally reflect good design. These garments will be in the medium price range.

The *lowest-quality* garments will not be as well made. The quality of the construction is poor, and fabrics may not hold up well when worn and cleaned. Principles of good design may not be followed. These are generally the lowest-priced garments.

You may want different levels of quality for different garments. You would be smart to buy a high-quality coat or jacket if you plan to wear it for several seasons. If you want a shirt that is the latest fad, one of lower quality with a lower price could be your best buy. You must decide which quality will meet your needs.

Price is sometimes an indication of quality, but not always. An alert shopper can often find good quality products at low prices. Shop in several stores before you make a purchase.

General Standards of Quality

There are a number of construction details that you should look at when judging the quality of a garment. A checklist for judging quality construction is given in 8-2.

You'll first want to look closely at the fabric. Evaluate the quality of the fabric for evenness of color and pattern. Check to see that the fabric has no defects. Also consider the appropriateness of the fabric for the garment.

The cut of the garment should be evaluated. Is the fabric cut with the grain? Is their ample fabric used in the garment? Do plaids, stripes, and checks match?

Seams, seam allowances, and stitching are important to check. Seams should be neat and smooth with ample seam allowances. Stitching should be straight and neat. Thread color should match the fabric and be suitable in weight.

JUDGING **QUALITY**

Construction Features	Quality Indicators
Cut and Fabric	■ Fabric is free from flaws or irregularities. ■ Garment pieces cut with the grain. ■ Fabric appropriate for garment type and style. ■ Stripes, plaids, checks, and other designs matched at seams.
Seams	■ Generous allowances for seams. ■ Flat, even in width, wide enough to withstand strain and permit alterations. ■ Double row stitching to reinforce stress points, such as armpits, crotch, waist, neckline. ■ Smooth outside seams and darts. ■ Raw edges finished.
Stitching	■ Short, continuous, and straight. ■ Securely fastened at the ends. ■ Thread of the right weight, color, and fiber for the fabric.
Reinforcements	■ Extra stitching, bar tacks, metal rivets, or tape at points of strain. ■ Reinforced underarm seams, openings, slits, pockets, knees, and elbows in work clothes, sportswear, and children's play clothes.
Hems	■ Flat, even in width, invisible on the right side. ■ Carefully finished and evenly stitched on inside. ■ Even in length.
Buttonholes	■ Cut with grain of fabric. ■ Smooth and properly placed. ■ Right size and type for the garment. ■ Firmly stitched and trimmed with no loose threads or frayed edges. ■ Evenly spaced with reinforced corners.
Buttons, Hooks and Eyes, Snaps	■ Firmly attached and properly spaced. ■ Right size and type for garment. ■ Extra buttons often included for high-quality clothes.
Trim and Decoration	■ Suited to the garment, well placed, and firmly attached. ■ Same care requirements as garment.
Zippers and Closures	■ Smooth, flat, securely stitched. ■ Right size, type, strength, and color for garment. ■ Smooth sliding zippers and easy to operate closures.
Linings	■ Smooth, properly inserted. ■ Right weight and texture for garment with same care requirements.
Interfacing	■ Properly placed, hidden, and securely attached. ■ Made of materials right for the garment and its care requirements.
Pockets	■ Flat, smooth, and properly matched to garment. ■ Reinforced corners and firmly woven linings.
Collars and Lapels	■ Collar points neatly finished and do not curl. ■ Collar top slightly turned over undercollar around seam edges. ■ Lapels lying flat to the chest with graceful roll and smooth edge.

8-2

Become familiar with these items for judging the quality of garment construction.

Hems are also important to check. They should be an even width and an appropriate depth for the design of the garment. If you think you might want to lengthen the garment at some time, check to see if this would be possible. Hemming stitches should not show on the outside of the garment.

There are other features to check as well. Look again at the checklist shown in 8-2.

Specific Points to Check

The following standards may help you evaluate specific styles of garments the next time you shop. *Standards* are measures used for comparing products in quality, fit, performance, and price.

Standards for Buying Shirts and Blouses

When choosing a shirt or blouse, as in 8-3, look for

- ample room across the chest or bust, back, and shoulders
- shoulder seams that come to the end of the shoulder bone
- tops that are long enough to stay tucked in jeans, skirts, or slacks
- armholes that are large enough for arms to move freely
- collars with even, sharp points
- smooth topstitching
- buttons sewn on securely and placed directly under buttonholes
- well-made buttonholes
- neat, even cuffs that fit comfortably around wrists
- pockets that are securely sewn on flat without wrinkles

Standards for Buying Sport Jackets and Suits

Before you buy a sport jacket or suit, as in 8-4, be sure

- it fits across the back shoulders smoothly, with no wrinkles or bunching
- the armholes are large enough for an undershirt, shirt, and sweater to be worn underneath
- the outside stitching is smooth

8-3
Check for quality construction when buying shirts and blouses.

8-4
A sport jacket worn with jeans gives a more casual look.

Slacks will give you more wearing comfort if you try them on to check for fit when you buy them.

- the jacket fits smoothly across the chest area when buttoned
- the pocket corners are reinforced
- you see about one-half inch of shirt cuffs below jacket sleeves
- the collar fits closely around the neck without gaps
- any pattern in the fabric matches at center, side seams, and pockets
- the buttons are sewn on securely with a shank beneath so they button easily and smoothly
- linings and interfacings are used as needed to give strength, support, and better shape to the garment

Standards for Buying Jeans and Slacks

When shopping for jeans or slacks, as in 8-5, check to see that

- you can walk and sit comfortably in them
- the seat area fits smoothly without bagging or binding
- the crotch length is just right—not too long or too short
- the waistband has a double thickness of fabric
- there is reinforced stitching at bottom of zipper and corner of pockets
- the zipper has a locking pull tab so it will not unzip by itself
- seams are straight and not puckered
- the slacks hang straight without wrinkling
- you can follow the instructions given on the care label

Standards for Buying Dresses and Skirts

Before choosing a skirt or dress, as in 8-6, see if

- it is cut with enough fabric so it does not look skimpy
- the garment feels good on your body
- it hangs straight from the waistband without cupping under the hips
- the waistline fits snugly at your natural waistline
- the waistline does not roll up (It rolls if it is too tight in the hip area.)
- the bustline darts (if present) point toward the highest point of the bust
- zippers work smoothly and have a lock tab
- the seams are wide enough to alter, if needed

Alterations

Suppose you want to buy a garment, but it doesn't quite fit. Perhaps it can be altered. **Alterations** are changes made in the size, length, or style of a garment. They can make a garment larger, smaller, shorter, or longer. Buttons and trims can be added, moved, or changed.

When you are deciding whether or not to buy a garment that needs alterations, there are some factors to consider. Some alterations are easy to do, while others are more complicated and are seldom effective or successful. If you can make the alterations yourself, it may be worthwhile. If you have to pay someone to make the alterations, you need to consider this cost in the overall cost of the garment.

It is important to check seam widths. If a garment is to be made larger, the seams must be wide enough to accomplish this. When a garment is to be made longer, check to see if there is enough hem width to let it down.

Alterations easy to do include lengthening or shortening a garment, leveling an uneven hem, shortening sleeves, or taking in some seams.

Major alterations in ready-to-wear clothing may not be effective or worthwhile. For instance, if a jacket is too full or too tight across the shoulders, major alterations would be required, 8-7. The sleeves might have to

alterations
Changes made in the size, length, or style of a garment so it will fit properly.

Pendleton Woolen Mills

8-6
When your clothes fit properly, they help you look your best.

Pendleton Woolen Mills

8-7
Jackets are more difficult to alter than dresses or skirts.

be removed and adjusted. The lining and shoulder pads would need to be adjusted. Unless you are an experienced sewer, this alteration is usually not recommended. If you hire someone to make these alterations, it will be expensive.

If a garment is too large in the waistline, you will probably have to remove the waistband. The seams and the waistband would need to be adjusted. The zipper area may also need to be altered.

Unless ready-to-wear garments requiring major alterations are exceptionally good buys, it is best to avoid them. Too much altering can change the looks of a garment, and it may never look just right.

Buying Accessories

Accessories are fun to choose and wear. Accessories include shoes, legwear, handbags, billfolds, neckties, jewelry, and belts. They are the items you need to complete an outfit. Accessories add variety to your wardrobe. The right ones can change a plain, dull outfit into the latest look, 8-8. You can take the same outfit and make it casual or dressy, depending on the accessories you wear with it.

Before you shop, look over your wardrobe and make some decisions about what kinds of accessories you could use. Consider the main colors in your wardrobe. To repeat a color in your outfit and in your accessories helps give you a coordinated look.

Keep in mind your size and body build when selecting your accessories. For instance, small persons look better wearing small accessories. Large accessories seem to overpower them.

Most accessories cost less than clothes. If you buy several of them, the prices can add up to a lot of money. Knowing more about accessories will help you get the most for your money.

Shoes

Shoes are the most important accessory in your wardrobe. They should be chosen with care. You may need new ones because your present pair is worn out or too small. A special occasion or a new outfit may be your reason for buying new shoes. In any case, look before you buy. There are hundreds of styles from which to choose, 8-9.

8-8
Choosing the right accessories can give an outfit a complete look.

Shoes can be expensive. The ones you wear most often should be comfortable and of good quality. You can spend less money on the shoes that you seldom wear.

Good fit is the most important feature of shoes. Good-fitting shoes provide comfort and correct support to your feet. If fitted correctly, they will not be too short, too loose, or too tight.

Poorly fitted shoes can cause foot disorders. These include bunions, corns, calluses, and ingrown toenails. They cause discomfort and can contribute to poor posture. Do not rush when buying shoes. Since feet tend to swell during the course of the day, try to buy shoes toward the end of the day when your feet are largest.

At better shoe departments, you can have your feet measured. You should stand to have your feet measured. Since one foot is often larger than the other, shoes should be fitted to the larger size. Innersoles or pads can be placed in the shoe of your smaller foot for better fit and comfort. When trying on shoes, wear the same type of socks or hose that you plan to wear with the shoes you buy.

Shoes vary in width as well as length. They are often sized by both a letter and a number such as 7A or 9D. The number refers to the length of the foot. The larger the number, the larger the shoe will be. Half sizes of each number such as 7 1/2 are available. The letter refers to the width of the shoe. The width AAA (triple A) would be very narrow, while EEE (triple E) would be quite wide. There are special stores that offer shoes in unusual sizes and widths.

8-9
There are many styles of shoes to choose from. Select the right style for your needs.

Don't buy according to size. Buy according to fit. One manufacturer's 8B may be another's 7C. A size made by one manufacturer may not fit as well as the same size made by another manufacturer.

Walking in shoes helps you to judge the comfort and fit. Try on both shoes and walk in them, 8-10. The widest part of the shoe should fit the widest part of your foot.

When you stand, shoes should be one-half to three-fourths inch longer than your foot. Check the fit in the instep, in the heel, and over the arch. Examine the material and construction. Will this style, color, and quality fit your needs?

Choose shoes that flatter your feet. If your feet are large and wide, plain, dark colors are best for you. Choose styles that are plain or that have narrow straps. Light-colored shoes will make your feet seem larger than they are.

8-10
Try on shoes to be sure they will be comfortable to wear.

Highlights in History

A Sneaking Success

You probably have a pair of sneakers in your closet. You may even have several pairs, each designed for a different sport. You might use one pair when you're playing basketball and a different pair for walking. But where and when did they first appear?

The first shoes that combined canvas with rubber soles were made in the United States in the late 1800s. American tire companies Goodyear and U.S. Rubber developed the manufacturing process called *vulcanization*. This process uses heat to meld rubber to cloth in a sturdy, permanent bond. The first rubber-soled shoes were called *plimsolls* because the high, rubber sole looked like the Plimsoll line. This was the load-line marking around the side of cargo ships.

From 1892 to 1913, U.S. Rubber was manufacturing 30 different brands. The company decided to make just one brand. When choosing a name, the first choice was Peds, from the Latin word meaning foot. Since that name was already trade-marked, they selected the name Keds. Keds® were the first mass-marketed canvas-top "sneakers." An advertising agent nicknamed them sneakers because the rubber-soled shoes allowed you to sneak up on people! All other shoes at that time made noise when you walked.

The first athlete to endorse a sneaker was Charles "Chuck" Taylor in 1923. Sales of Converse All Star sneakers increased dramatically when the Chuck Taylor ankle patch was added to the shoe. By the beginning of this century, Nike was paying Tiger Woods and Michael Jordan tens of millions of dollars to wear their shoes.

Sneakers have come a long way from their humble beginnings. Today's shoes are designed to assist the athlete in specific demands of the sport. Sports medicine has influenced the design of shoes to improve performance while preventing injury. Motion-control devices, new shock-absorbing materials, and many other features are now incorporated into sneakers. One brand continuously adjusts the shoe's cushioning while you run.

Never buy shoes that you have to "break in." Shoes should not be even a little uncomfortable when you buy them. Do not accept a salesperson's statement that the shoes will feel better after you have worn them a few hours.

Types of Shoes

Many people feel that they need at least several types of shoes. These may include casual, dress, and athletic shoes.

Casual shoes should be selected carefully. These are the shoes you will probably wear most often. Casual shoes are often worn to school. They should be comfortable and give your feet support.

Dress shoes often last longer than casual shoes since they are not worn as often. A basic or classic style is a smart buy since it will remain fashionable longer. Young and adult men wear many of the same shoe styles for dress. High heel shoes are popular as dress shoes for women. The higher the heel is, the more weight that is thrust on the ball of the foot. This could cause foot problems. High heel shoes can also cause unsteadiness, which can increase the likelihood of a twisted ankle or a strained back. If high heels are selected, care should be taken to wear them only for short periods of time.

Athletic shoes are a popular choice for many members of the family. These shoes are carefully designed for different sports such as basketball, tennis, aerobic exercise, walking, and running. See 8-11. Athletic shoes are now worn to school and other everyday activities.

Some shoes are fads. Often, they are extreme styles and provide poor foot support. For instance, platform shoes are sometimes popular. Some styles of platform shoes are so extreme they cause many people to sprain their ankles. Other shoes start out as fads and become classics. Two examples are clogs and sandals.

Caring for Your Shoes

Your shoes will last longer and look better when they receive proper care. Leather shoes should be polished when needed, 8-12. If they get wet, take them off as soon as possible. Dry them away from heat. They may shrink or stiffen if they dry near heat.

Shoes of manufactured materials can be cleaned with a damp cloth. Fabric shoes can be washed with a mild

8-11
When buying athletic shoes, consider the type of sport or activity for which they will be worn.

8-12
Leather shoes will keep their shine and always look good when kept polished.

detergent and soft brush. Some can be cleaned in automatic washing machines and dryers. Check directions for care of your new shoes when you buy them. You can save money by taking good care of your shoes.

Legwear

Fashions in legwear change as quickly as in clothing. Your choices are many. Consider your activities, the clothes you own, what looks best on you, and the money you have to spend.

Young men's socks vary in length. The three common lengths are ankle, mid-leg, and knee. Sometimes they are called short, medium, and long lengths. Socks are sized according to the distance from heel to toe. Sizes usually range from 8 to 13. Stretch socks are popular since they will fit feet of any size. Correct size is important. Socks that are too short can be uncomfortable and can cause physical damage. Ingrown toenails are often caused by short socks.

The choice of color and design is yours. Bold designs and bright colors appeal to many. Bulky yarns can be used to create novelty effects. Dark, solid colors are a good choice for most occasions.

Most socks are made of manufactured fibers. They hold color well and are easy to launder. Socks made of wool, wool blends, and cotton are available. They are more absorbent than synthetics. Wool socks must be washed in lukewarm or cool water, using a mild detergent. Drying flat or with a cool temperature setting in the dryer will keep them in good shape. They cost more than socks made of manufactured fibers.

In choosing legwear, girls have more decisions to make. They can choose between socks, hose, and tights. If they select socks, they can choose anklets, or knee-highs of either bulky or smooth knit. Then they make the same size, color, and design decisions as men. Novelty patterns can be fun for both guys and girls. See 8-13.

Pantyhose and knee-length hose are worn with skirts, dresses, and slacks. The sizes for hose are different from those for socks. They are often sized according to height and weight. Charts are often on the hosiery package to help you make the right decision. Your hose and socks will also last longer if they fit correctly.

Tights are popular for winter wear with skirts and shorts. Tights come in different colors, designs, and weights. Tights are made of cotton, nylon, polyester, or wool. Lycra and spandex fibers add stretch.

Butterick Company, Inc.

8-13
The bright stripes in these tights make them fun for girls to wear.

Hose and tights should be washed with care. If you wash them by hand, remove your rings and check for rough fingernails. Use mild detergent and warm water. Rub toes between fingers to remove perspiration and odor. Rinse well. Wrap in a towel to remove excess moisture. Hang them on a smooth rod to dry.

Mesh bags are available to hold hose and tights if they are put in an automatic washer. Wash them with other delicate garments. Hang to dry.

Handbags

Most young women have at least one handbag or purse in their wardrobes. Your activities, body size, and personal taste are the main factors in choosing a handbag.

Handbags are available in all sizes and shapes, 8-14. They are made of various materials including leather, vinyl, fabric, and cord. Shoulder bags have a long strap that hangs over your shoulder. It leaves your hands free to carry or do other activities. A smaller purse is the "wallet on a string." It has a strap that is worn over the shoulder and across your chest. Sections inside provide for credit cards, keys, a pen, and money. Another purse is the waist or belt pack. It fastens around your waist with an adjustable strap and buckle. It is a hands-free way to carry your money and credit cards. Leather backpacks are another popular option.

Before you buy a purse, examine it closely. Look for rough seams or edges. Check the fastener. It should open easily and close securely. Look for handy compartments that help keep your belongings in order. Check how securely the handles are attached to the purse. Handles attached to rings are often more durable.

Brightly colored purses might be fun to carry. If your budget is limited, a purse in a neutral or basic color would be a better choice. It would look right with more of your outfits.

Billfolds

Billfolds are made of leather, vinyl, or fabric. Leather billfolds are often the most expensive, but they last longer than those made of fabric or vinyl. Billfolds can range in price from low to expensive.

Billfolds for women often have a compartment for coins as well as bills. The area for coins may be small or the entire length of the billfold. A section

8-14
A classic leather handbag can be used for several years.

for photos and cards is often included. Snaps, clasps, or zippers are used for fasteners.

Men usually carry their billfolds in their pants pockets. Some billfolds are suedelike on the outside to help prevent pickpocketing. The rough finish makes it difficult for someone to slip it out of the pocket. Men's billfolds contain a compartment for bills and a section for cards and photos.

When buying a billfold, check for quality. Be sure bindings are sewn securely and that no rough edges are present. Check zippers and clasps. Do they open and close easily? Does the size of the billfold fit your needs and spaces for carrying it?

Neckties

The only function of the necktie is for appearance. It can express the wearer's individuality and personality. A conservative man may prefer to wear ties of dark colors either in solids or small patterns. An outgoing man will select bolder patterns and brighter colors.

Fashions in neckwear change just as other fashions do. Look at the many patterns of neckties in 8-15. Neckties change in width, color, design, and fabric. Both long and bow neckties have been popular. You can buy neckties that are pre-tied, or you can tie your own. Study 8-16 until you can tie a perfect tie.

8-15

An endless variety of neckties is available. Choose one to match your personality as well as your jacket.

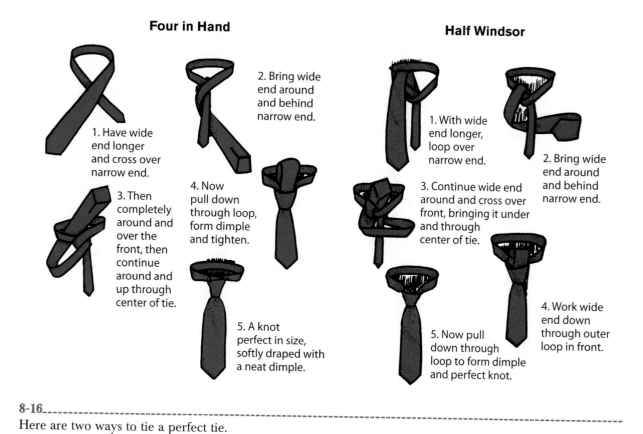

Four in Hand

1. Have wide end longer and cross over narrow end.

2. Bring wide end around and behind narrow end.

3. Then completely around and over the front, then continue around and up through center of tie.

4. Now pull down through loop, form dimple and tighten.

5. A knot perfect in size, softly draped with a neat dimple.

Half Windsor

1. With wide end longer, loop over narrow end.

2. Bring wide end around and behind narrow end.

3. Continue wide end around and cross over front, bringing it under and through center of tie.

4. Work wide end down through outer loop in front.

5. Now pull down through loop to form dimple and perfect knot.

8-16
Here are two ways to tie a perfect tie.

Many neckties are washable. Others must be dry-cleaned. Check the care label to see how to clean yours.

Scarves

Scarves can be used to keep your neck warm, to protect your coat collar from soil, and to add interest to your outfit. They are available in wool, wool-blends, cotton, silk, and other fibers. The fabrics range from thick, warm, and bulky to thin and flimsy.

A new way to wear scarves appears as fashions change. Shapes, colors, and sizes vary with the season. Squares, triangles, and rectangles are sometimes small, sometimes big.

Adding a bright scarf to an outfit can give it a new, lively look. Scarves can be used in many ways as shown in 8-17.

Scarves add individuality to your clothing. They help you create more outfits from your same garments. Because of the wide selection and low price of scarves, you can use these fashion accessories as your imagination and creativity dictate.

8-17
Scarves can stretch your wardrobe by changing the look of your outfits.

Jewelry

Costume or fashion jewelry is distinguished from fine jewelry only by the material used to make it. **Fine jewelry** is usually made from gold, silver, or platinum. It may contain precious or semiprecious stones. Diamonds, rubies, sapphires, and emeralds are types of *precious stones*. Jade, garnet, opal, and amethyst are types of *semiprecious stones*.

Costume jewelry is designed to wear with current fashions. It is usually made from inexpensive materials. Few teens can afford fine jewelry, but may be able to afford costume jewelry, 8-18.

The wide variety of designs, colors, and shapes makes looking at jewelry fun, but they make your final choice difficult. Planning will help. Decide what you need and what will go with several of your outfits. Know how much money you can afford to spend. Then look for the jewelry that will show your individuality.

Jewelry is both functional and ornamental. Watchbands, cuff links, and tie tacks are types of functional jewelry. Ornamental items are rings, bracelets, necklaces, and earrings.

Belts

Belts can have a function or they can be decorative, 8-19. They are available in many materials. Leather, vinyl, metal, and fabric are some of your choices. There are wide, narrow, stretchy, thick, thin, heavy, and lightweight styles. Designs are varied. Belts are worn by both guys and girls.

Belt sizes correspond to waist measurements, but men should buy belts two inches larger than their waist size. Try on a belt before buying it. Keep your overall body size in mind. A belt that is wide and heavy might look better on a large person.

Leather is labeled either top grain or split. *Top grain leather* has the natural animal grain. It is smooth and expensive. *Split leather* is from portions of hides or skins that are split into two or more thicknesses. It is rough, so many people prefer it to have a suede finish.

Belts should be cleaned as needed. If they become heavily soiled, cleaning is more difficult. Cleaning methods for belts, like those for shoes, vary with the materials used to make them.

fine jewelry
Jewelry usually made from gold, silver, or platinum.

costume jewelry
Jewelry designed for wear with current fashions and usually made from inexpensive materials.

8-18
Costume jewelry is popular with teens because of its affordability.

8-19
Belts can be both functional and decorative.

CHAPTER REVIEW

Key Points

- Two key factors to consider when buying apparel are fit and quality. To find the right size, begin with the size category for your body structure. Then find the size closest to your measurements. Try on every garment you purchase as sizes can vary with each manufacturer.

- The quality of a garment can be described as high, medium, or low. You may want different levels of quality for different garments. Price is sometimes an indication of quality, but not always.

- Evaluate the following construction details when judging the quality of a garment: fabric, cut, seams, seam allowances, stitching, hems, fasteners, linings, pockets, and special features.

- When deciding whether or not to buy a garment that needs alterations, consider how complicated they will be. You may be able to make simple alterations yourself. If you have to pay someone to make the alterations, it will add to the overall cost of the garment.

- Accessories add variety to your wardrobe. You can take the same outfit and make it casual or dressy. Choose accessories carefully to evaluate their quality. Know how to care for them.

To Review

1. The _____ of an item depends on how well it meets certain standards of excellence.
2. Why does the same size not always fit you the same way?
3. Give two suggestions to follow when trying on garments.
4. How does a high-quality garment differ from a low-quality garment?
5. What should you look at when evaluating the fabric in a garment?
6. List five points to check before buying jeans or slacks.
7. Name three alterations that would be easy to do.
8. List four items that are considered accessories.
9. _____ is the most important consideration when buying shoes.
10. How are shoes sized?
11. What is the purpose of wearing neckties?
12. (True or False) Costume jewelry is more expensive than fine jewelry.
13. Which of the following is an example of functional jewelry?
    A. earrings
    B. rings
    C. cuff links
    D. necklace

To Do

1. Measure your hips, waist, and chest or bust following the instructions given in Chapter 18. Using a size chart from a catalog, determine your size category or figure type. Then determine your size. Have you been buying the right size?

2. Bring a garment to class, and evaluate its construction using the checklist in figure 8-2. Rate the garment's quality as high, medium, or low.

3. Shop for a similar garment, such as a shirt or blouse, at several different stores. Note the price of each garment, and compare the quality features. Decide if price is an indication of quality. Write a report stating which garment you would buy and why.

4. Have a student bring a suit to class and model it. Judge the fit according to the buying guide. Have other students model blouses, shirts, jeans, skirts, and dresses. Use the standards for buying to evaluate these garments.

5. If some of the items in activity 4 do not fit, decide if they could be altered. What alterations would be necessary? Could they be done by a beginning sewer, or would they need to be done by a professional alterationist?

6. Visit a shoe department or store. Ask the clerk to discuss materials used, proper foot measurements, and shoe fit. Examine the quality of shoes on display. Compare prices.

7. Bring a necktie to class and practice the different knots.

8. Practice several different ways to wear a scarf.

9. Invite a representative from a local department store to speak to your class about buying clothes and accessories. Prepare a list of questions to ask the person about how to choose quality items.

To Think About

1. Do you think manufacturers should be required to follow strict standards in sizing their garments?

2. Why is price not always an indication of quality?

3. Is a low-quality garment ever a good buy? Explain your answer.

4. Can you get better quality in a garment if you sew it yourself?

5. Is it wise to pay more for high-quality accessories than for high-quality clothing? Explain your answer.

CHAPTER 9

Selecting Clothes for Family Members

Objectives

After studying this chapter, you will be able to

- identify the factors that affect clothing decisions for family members of all ages.
- choose appropriate clothing for children, adults, and older people.
- identify garment features and fabrics appropriate for people with disabilities.

Key Terms

flame resistant
self-help features
hook-and-loop tape
disability

Life is a series of stages. As each stage in life changes, so do clothing needs. People have different clothing needs as they pass through the various stages of life. For instance, when you were a baby, your wardrobe was quite different than it is now. A grandparent's wardrobe would also be a lot different from yours.

All members of a family want clothes that are comfortable, safe, and attractive. They also want clothes that are suitable for their activities and that require little care. See 9-1.

Suppose that you want to select a clothing item for a baby, parent, grandparent, or a person with a disability. What would you buy or make? You would need to take some important factors into consideration. With a few guidelines, your selection can be both useful and pleasing.

Selecting Clothes for Children

Years ago, children were dressed like small adults. We now know children have clothing needs all their own. Some adults may be willing to sacrifice comfort and freedom of movement for fashion, but children are not.

Clothing needs for children vary with their stages of growth and development. Children's clothing should provide freedom of movement, safety, and room for growth. Equally important are comfort and ease of care.

9-1
Family members of all ages need clothes to fit their lifestyles.

flame resistant
A term used in relation to fabrics that are self-extinguishing or easy to extinguish.

Whether you are selecting clothes for an infant, toddler, preschooler, or school-age child, you will want to consider proper fit. The best way to check for proper fit is to have the child try on the garment at the time of purchase or as you are sewing it. When this isn't possible, garments should be selected by the child's measurements and weight, not by the child's age. Look for clothing that provides for normal growth. Choose garments with adequate sleeve and garment length so they won't be too short within a few weeks or months. Clothing that fits properly is not so tight that it restricts movement or so loose that it causes falls.

When selecting children's clothes, consider the comfort of the garments. Children like smooth, soft clothing best. They will not wear clothes that are rough, scratchy, or itchy. Sleeves, neckbands, and waistbands should be snug, but not binding. Knit fabrics are good choices for young children because they give and stretch.

Safety is a critical factor to consider when buying children's clothing. A popular children's clothing feature that proved to be dangerous was the drawstring, often located at the neck or waist. These strings could get caught in cribs or playground equipment leading to strangulation. In 1995, the Consumer Product Safety Commission required the industry to eliminate these drawstrings from all children's clothing. A recall was placed on any clothing made prior to 1995 that still had these drawstrings. If an older item of clothing is obtained that has a drawstring, parents are advised to cut or remove the string.

While shopping for children's sleepwear, you'll notice tags or labels on these garments stating that they meet flame-resistant standards. These are standards set by the federal government. This does not mean that these garments are fireproof. **Flame resistant** means if they were accidentally ignited, they would burn very slowly, and when removed from the flame, would be either self-extinguishing or easy to extinguish.

Care requirements are important whether you are selecting clothing for children or adults. Washability is important—both for convenience and for economy. Easy-care, soft, durable fabrics that require little or no ironing are good fabric choices for children's clothes, 9-2.

Certain guidelines should be kept in mind when selecting children's shoes. Proper fit of shoes, socks, or booties is essential to good foot growth. Buy the size of shoe that fits. Proper fit

9-2
Children are active. They need clothes that are easy-care, soft, and durable.

should allow at least 1/2 inch from the end of the toe to the end of the shoe. Since children's shoe sizes change rapidly, new shoes need to be purchased often to avoid discomfort.

Infants

When selecting clothes for an infant, it is often tempting to get carried away when you see all the cute outfits that are available. Before buying a garment for an infant, consider the needs of a growing baby. Many factors influence the selection of baby clothes. Comfort, ease of care, fabric type, construction, size, and season of the year or climate are all important.

As you shop for baby clothes, your major concern should be the baby's comfort. Keep in mind that a baby's skin is sensitive and delicate. Clothes that won't chafe and that are easy to change are a good choice.

Another major concern is ease of care. Since babies are often changed several times a day, baby clothes should be easy to wash and dry.

Fabrics used for baby clothes should be soft, absorbent, and light-weight. Knitted fabrics offer more comfort and ease of movement than woven ones, 9-3. Knit garments are popular because of the built-in stretch that "grows" with the baby.

Most infants double their weight in the first three or four months. Because of this rapid growth, try to select clothes that have been designed with growth features that adjust to a baby's increasing size and weight. For instance, some two-piece sleepers have a double set of snaps at the waist. Clothes that grow with a baby are a good investment.

Dressing and undressing is easier if a baby's clothing has neck openings, zippers, snaps, or buttons. Pullover garments should have stretchable necklines. Pants should have snap crotches for easy diaper changing. For safety reasons, avoid loose buttons or snaps that can be pulled off the garment and swallowed. All trims should be firmly attached.

When selecting undershirts for babies, wraparound or snap-on styles are good choices. Look for undershirts that feature seamless underarms.

Stretch terry coveralls and baby jogging suits are suitable for play. Be sure that they allow lots of room for movement and growth. Most coveralls have a snap closure that extends down the leg for easy dressing.

For greater warmth, blanket sleepers are available. These are useful in cooler weather when a baby is likely to kick off the covers and needs extra warmth, 9-4. For older babies, sleepers should have rubber-soled feet to prevent slipping and falling.

9-3
Knit garments are comfortable for infants and allow some room for growth.

The McCall Pattern Company

9-4
Blanket sleepers keep a baby warm during the night.

Babies' most essential clothing items are diapers. When selecting diapers, you may choose cloth diapers or disposable diapers. Cloth diapers are made of absorbent cotton. They may be prefolded, fitted, or flat. Cloth diapers must be washed, but they can be used many times. Disposable diapers are made of paper and plastic with an absorbent inner fiber. Some disposable diapers draw moisture away from the skin.

Disposable diapers are convenient. They are used once and thrown away.

Vinyl (plastic) pants are usually worn over cloth diapers. Vinyl pants should be flexible and soft to allow for comfort and a good fit.

When selecting baby clothes, the garment label and package information are good guides. Age, weight, height, or general sizes are often given. For infants, clothing sizes may be listed by age in months or by descriptive terms, such as small, medium, or large. Weight is usually a more accurate guide than age or general size. When trying to decide whether to select a newborn size or a larger size, it is best to look ahead to the slightly larger sizes for growing babies.

The climate and season of the year are important considerations when selecting baby clothes. For instance, winter garments bought for a baby born in the summer may be outgrown by the time the baby needs them.

Toddlers and Preschoolers

Unlike infants, who don't care what they wear as long as they are comfortable, toddlers and preschoolers are more interested in their clothes. Their clothing needs are based on growth, active movement, and their improving abilities to dress themselves. Comfort is still important, however. Toddlers' and preschoolers' clothes should be comfortable, safe, durable, functional, and attractive.

When selecting clothes for toddlers and preschoolers, growth features are important. At this stage, children tend to grow faster in height than in width. Therefore, the length of the waist, arms, and legs will change more quickly than the width of the shoulders, chest, and hips. Clothes that provide built-in growth features include

- adjustable or stretchable shoulder straps
- raglan or sleeveless styles
- elastic inserts
- stretch or knit fabrics

Highlights in History

Pink and Blue for Children's Clothing

Pink for girls and blue for boys. How clearly we stick to this guideline as we carefully select clothes for babies and decorate their nurseries. Where did this idea come from, and how long has it been around?

Believe it or not, little boys wore pink as recently as the 1940s. Pink and blue were first associated with gender in 1916 in an article in *Infants' and Children's Wear Review.* It stated "the generally accepted rule is pink for the boy and blue for the girl." The colors were still used interchangeably for boys and girls until after World War II. By 1950, a combination of public opinion and manufacturers' clout ordained pink for girls and blue for boys.

Even with this mandate, it was still permissible for girls to wear blue, but not for boys to wear pink. This points out the continuing notion that if a garment's trim or color is equated with feminine clothing, it is unacceptable for boys.

By the 1970s, parents pushing a nonsexist child-rearing movement pressed manufacturers for gender-free children's clothes. The result was the elimination of anything feminine such as the color pink or ruffles. In contrast, colors and trims previously acceptable for boys only were considered gender-free.

Boys' attire has become increasingly less feminine during the 20th century whereas female clothing has become more masculine. The male-only trouser, for example, is accepted for women and girls in nearly every social situation today. It wasn't until 1970, however, that pants were finally accepted by school and office dress codes.

- undefined waistlines in one-piece garments
- large hems that can be let down as the child grows
- two-piece outfits

Comfort and safety are of special concern when selecting clothes for toddlers and preschoolers. Clothes should be made of soft, absorbent, flame-resistant fabrics. The garments should fit properly and have a non-binding, simple design. For safety reasons, clothing, especially outer clothing, should be brightly colored so children can be clearly seen by motorists.

Toddlers and preschoolers like bright colors and designs. These give children an opportunity to learn to recognize colors, shapes, and symbols.

Toddlers

Since toddlers have not developed a waistline and some still wear diapers, simple styles that allow for fullness and maximum freedom of movement should be selected. One-piece garments that fall from the shoulders are practical. Snap crotches on pants help make changing diapers easier, 9-5.

Design features should be functional as well as decorative. For instance, shoulder straps should cross in the back to prevent them from sliding off the shoulders.

self-help features
Easy-to-work openings and closures in clothes that make it easier for children to dress themselves.

During the toddler stage, children begin to learn to dress themselves. Clothing with **self-help features** will encourage independence as children learn to dress and undress themselves. Easy-to-work openings and closures for quick changes are necessary during toilet learning. Elastic waistbands are especially good for these children. Pull-on garments with large neck and armhole openings are easiest for toddlers to handle. When toddlers learn to snap, button, or zip clothing, they are proud of the new skills they have mastered.

Toddlers clothing sizes are 1T, 2T, 3T, and 4T. These sizes are based on age, but it is best to go by height, chest, and waist measurements, as well as weight. Toddlers do not always wear the size based on their age. See 9-6 for clothing sizes for toddlers.

Preschoolers

Because preschoolers are still growing quickly and moving actively, freedom of movement in clothes and proper fit are still necessary. When selecting clothes for preschoolers, look for styles that allow them to move freely. Jumpsuits are practical garments for preschoolers because they

9-5
Clothes with undefined waistlines and snap crotches are ideal for on-the-move toddlers.

CLOTHING SIZES FOR TODDLERS

Toddler Size	Height (in inches)	Chest (in inches)	Waist (in inches)	Approximate Weight
1T	29 1/2 to 32	20 to 20 1/2	19 1/2	25 lb.
2T	32 1/2 to 35	21 to 21 1/2	20	29 lb.
3T	35 1/2 to 38	22 to 22 1/2	20 1/2	33 lb.
4T	38 1/2 to 41	23 to 23 1/2	21	38 lb.

9-6
The measurements listed above are used to determine clothing sizes for toddlers.

allow for mobility, 9-7. Preschoolers can also wear shirts and pants with elastic waistbands or belts because their waistlines are now more defined.

Dressing skills improve during the preschool years. Preschoolers are able to manipulate fasteners such as buttons, snaps, nylon tape closings, and zippers. They may still have trouble with small fasteners or with fasteners on the back of a garment. Look for design features that help children identify the front from the back of a garment. For instance, a V-neckline at the front of a shirt or an appliqué design on the front of a shirt or pants can help children identify the front from the back.

Clothing can help preschoolers develop a sense of self-identity from comments they receive about their clothes. Allowing preschoolers to help select their clothes ensures that they will wear the clothing. A color-coordinated wardrobe is a good idea. This way, almost any garments that a child chooses to wear together will look good. Preschoolers like garments with pockets. Pockets should be easy to reach and big enough to hold favorite small toys or other items.

Preschoolers wear sizes from 2 to 6X. Though these are related to age, it is again best to go by height rather than age. See 9-8.

School-Age Children

School-age children are most comfortable when they wear clothes similar to those of their friends. Older

9-7
One-piece overalls are a good choice for preschoolers who are learning to dress themselves.

CLOTHING SIZES FOR PRESCHOOLERS

Children's Size	Height (in inches)	Chest (in inches)	Slim Waist (in inches)	Regular Waist (in inches)
2	32 1/2 to 35	21	18	20
3	35 1/2 to 38	22	18 1/2	20 1/2
4	38 1/2 to 41	23	19 1/4	21 1/4
5	41 1/2 to 44	24	20	22
6	44 1/2 to 47	25	20 1/2	22 1/2
6X	47 1/2 to 49	25 1/2	21	23

9-8
Garments in sizes 2 to 6X are for preschoolers who are taller and more slender than toddlers.

9-9
When selecting clothes for children, keep safety in mind. These brightly colored outfits are both comfortable and easily seen.

brothers and sisters or TV and movie heroes also influence what school children like to wear. Dressing like others helps school-age children to feel that they belong. Conforming to certain styles of dress is an important aspect of belonging to a group. Clothes that do not conform may cause ridicule from peers.

It's a good idea to allow school-age children to help to select their own clothes. By helping to choose what clothes to buy and what to wear each day, children develop decision-making skills.

When selecting clothes for school-age children, consider their opinions about colors and styles. Children are alert to what other children are wearing. They will likely enjoy clothing that looks like that worn by their friends. Select items that will fit into a child's wardrobe. Children should be aware of which outfits are for school, play, or special occasions.

Clothes for school-age children should be appropriate for their activities. School-age children like to play. Their clothes should hold up under rough wear. Select clothes that are durable and require little care.

As children become more skillful in dressing themselves, select clothes with smaller buttons and zippers. These help children to develop coordination.

Safety is another factor to consider when choosing clothes for school-age children. Clothes should be in bright colors motorists can easily see, 9-9. Caps or hats that do not obstruct vision are good choices. Reflective-fluorescent tapes are helpful safety features that can be added to a garment. They can be used for a decorative effect. Stitch them to children's outdoor wear, rainwear, and Halloween costumes.

Selecting Clothes for Adults

There are a number of factors to consider when adults select their clothes. These include their occupations, interests, and activities.

Often, the major clothing needs of adults are determined by their occupations, 9-10. The clothes that adults wear to work depend on the kind of work they do. Bankers, salespeople, receptionists, or managers often come in contact with the public. The way they dress has an influence on how the people they meet feel about them and their companies. Their companies want them to make a good impression because this could affect the success of the company.

Many professional and business people wear suits, 9-11. Men often wear ties. Some office workers may wear dress slacks or dresses, shirts or blouses, sweaters, or blazers. Most office workers wear similar clothing. In some offices, you will see more casual clothing than in other offices.

People who do physical work need durable clothes. Farmers, painters, factory workers, auto mechanics, and construction workers are examples of adults who need durable clothes. Their clothing must be sturdy enough to withstand hard wear and frequent laundering. Well-made garments in wash-and-wear fabrics are suitable.

Some adults are employed in jobs that require safety clothing such as hard hats, earplugs, eye goggles, and safety shoes. Welders, miners, brick masons, and certain factory workers need these types of clothes.

Special clothing or uniforms may be needed in some jobs such as those in the medical field, airlines, restaurants, or post office. The clothing may be furnished by the employer or purchased by the employees.

Adults may have leisure interests and activities that require special clothes. Adults who spend a lot of time outdoors fishing or golfing would have different clothing needs than those who prefer reading or attending plays

9-10
An adult's occupation often determines clothing needs. What type of occupation do you think this woman has?

9-11
A suit is common attire for men and women in business.

Simplicity Pattern Co.,

9-12

A special evening event might require a dressier outfit such as this one.

9-13

A down jacket, knit hat, boots, and gloves are good to wear while clearing snow—even by the youngest helpers!

and concerts. See 9-12. For adults with special interests, gardening gloves, a beach towel, a tennis racket cover, a chef's apron, a sun hat, or a pair of athletic socks could be appropriate. If the person does home chores such as shoveling snow and mowing the lawn, types of clothes that are appropriate for the climate would be worn, 9-13.

For men, shirts come in neck and sleeve measurements. Slacks have a waist measurement and an inseam to end of leg measurement. Sweaters are sized small, medium, large, and extra-large.

Women's dress, skirt, and slacks sizes often range from 4 to 20. Some specialty shops and some department stores offer larger sizes, petite sizes, and half-sizes. Blouses are sized according to the bust measurement. Women's sweaters come in small, medium, large, and extra-large.

Some parents stay at home to care for their children. In this case, fewer and more casual clothes may be needed than if a parent worked outside of the home. As a homemaker, a parent may need clothes for caring for children, shopping, caring for the home, gardening, and preparing food. Clothes should be casual and easy to clean. Many stay-at-home parents are active in volunteer work. They may need clothes similar to those of office workers or more casual outfits, depending on what type of volunteer work they do.

Selecting Clothes for Older Adults

When older adults select clothes, they consider their lifestyles. How do they spend most of their time? If they are at home most of the time, they may need only casual clothes. If they are always on the go, attending community events and religious services or traveling, they may need more extensive wardrobes, 9-14.

Basic garments usually suit retired or elderly people better than the latest styles or fads. Older people are generally more conservative in their dress. They want basic clothing that will stay in style longer and can easily be changed for a new look with accessories. Jewelry, scarves, or belts could give an outfit a new look.

Clothing for the elderly may have many of the characteristics of clothing for young children. These include safety features, large openings, fabrics that feel soft to the skin, and fasteners that open and close easily.

Arthritis, which causes pain and stiffness in the joints, affects many elderly people. They may not be able to raise their arms over their heads for back closures or to manipulate zipper pulls or buttons. Clothing that makes dressing and undressing easier for them, such as slip-on shoes and pre-tied neckties are appropriate. Pull-on slacks and pants with elastic waistlines are a good choice. Wraparound garments that tie in front are easy to wear. Hook-and-loop tape fasteners can be used in many areas instead of buttons. **Hook-and-loop tape** has tiny hooks on one strip and loops on the other that hold together when pressed with the fingers. Hook-and-loop tape fasteners on belts are easier to fasten than buckles.

As people become older, they may be less active. Their blood circulation may slow down. This may cause them to be more sensitive to cool temperatures. They may need items such as sweaters, robes, or warm slippers.

9-14
Active older adults need clothes suited to their interests and activities.

hook-and-loop tape
A type of fastener that has tiny hooks on one strip and loops on the other that hold together when pressed with the fingers.

disability
A condition that interferes with a person's ability to perform tasks like walking or lifting. It may be the result of an injury, an illness, or a birth defect.

Selecting Clothes for People with Disabilities

If you have ever had a sprained arm or a broken leg, you may have a small idea about what a disability is like. A **disability** is a condition that interferes with a person's ability to perform tasks like walking or lifting.

Some people are born with disabilities. Other disabilities are the result of illness or injury. Disabilities may last a lifetime or a limited period of time.

Clothes selected for people with disabilities should promote comfort and independent living, 9-15. Clothing should be as attractive and fashionable as possible. At the same time, it must be functional. Clothing styles for people who are able to dress themselves should be easy to put on. Clothing should contribute to the dignity of people who may have to depend on others for personal care.

Finding ready-to-wear garments or patterns that meet the special needs of people with disabilities is often difficult. Alterations or adaptations may be necessary to make clothing easier to put on and more comfortable to wear.

People with disabilities have unique clothing needs. Select, alter, or construct clothing that someone with a functional limitation can manage conveniently. People with physical disabilities may have limited hand movement or they may be unable to move their arms freely. Some may have trouble fastening garments with back openings. They may need larger arm openings because they are unable to reach to put their arms into sleeves. This is why styles with raglan sleeves are a better choice than those with set-in sleeves.

It may also be difficult or impossible for people with disabilities to button garments. People with limited hand movements or limited vision may have trouble aligning and buttoning buttons. Using hook-and-loop tape (Velcro) can make fasteners and closures more convenient. It is available in long strips that can replace zippers. It is also available in small pieces that can be used in place of snaps or buttons.

People with low vision may have trouble distinguishing the back of a garment from the front. Look for design features, such as a V-neckline or a design on the front of a garment, that would make identification easier. It might be difficult for people with low vision to identify colors. Stitching small pieces of different widths of rickrack or other trims to the inside of garments help mark them. All garments that can be worn together can be marked with the same size or type of trim.

When selecting clothes or patterns for people with disabilities who can dress themselves, look for front openings or wraparound styles. Fasteners and closures using hook-and-loop tape, zippers with ring pulls, and longer length zippers

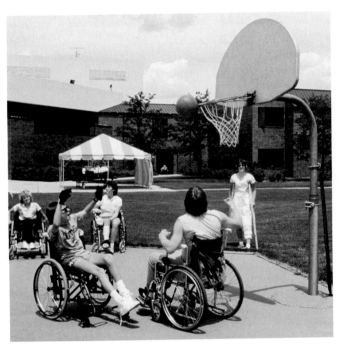

9-15
Clothing that is comfortable and easy to put on can help people with disabilities lead independent lives.

provide more convenient openings. Elastic waistlines or garments with no waistline are more comfortable for people who must be in one position for long periods of time.

Often clothing must fit over braces or a cast on a leg, 9-16. Slacks should have elastic waists. Adding zippers to the inseams of slacks will also aid in dressing.

Durable fabrics should be chosen, especially if a brace is worn. The friction caused by braces can be hard on most fabrics. You can adapt the garment by fusing or stitching an extra layer of fabric to the inside of the garment to reinforce areas that receive a lot of wear. Leather patches or large appliqués can be added to the outside of garments to reinforce areas of friction.

Easy-care fabrics should be selected. Heavy fabrics may be too bulky for people who use a wheelchair, crutches, or a walker. Fabrics that cling are not suitable because they do not allow adequate freedom of movement. Moderate-weight knit fabrics are a good choice because they provide comfort and ease of movement. See 9-17 for a list of features to look for in selecting or adapting clothing for the physically disabled.

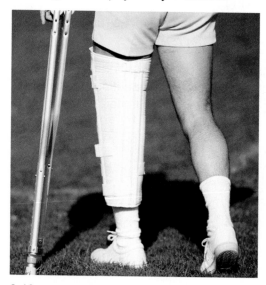

APPAREL FEATURES FOR PEOPLE WITH DISABILITIES

When buying apparel for people with physical disabilities, look for the following features. Sometimes garments can be modified to add some of these features. Also consider these points when constructing garments for people with disabilities.

Garment Features
- Large arm openings
- Raglan or dolman sleeves
- V-necklines
- Large necklines with drawstrings
- Front or side openings
- Wraparound styles
- Elastic waists, drawstrings, or no waistline at all
- Few fastenings, especially above mid-chest level
- Hook-and-loop fasteners or large hooks
- Longer length zippers
- Zippers with ring pulls, or add to existing pull
- Large pockets and long shirttails
- Reinforced areas that receive wear

Fabrics
- Durable
- Soft and absorbent, but not scratchy
- Moderate weight that provides warmth
- Knits that give but do not cling
- Prints that don't show stains
- Easy to launder; little or no ironing needed

9-16_____
A cast creates special challenges for finding clothes that fit over the cast.

9-17_____
Look for these features when buying clothes for people with disabilities.

CHAPTER REVIEW

Key Points

- Clothing needs for children vary with their stages of growth and development.

- Many factors influence the selection of baby clothes. Comfort, ease of care, fabric type, construction, size, and season of the year or climate are all important.

- Toddlers and preschoolers are more interested in their clothes. Their clothing needs are based on growth, active movement, and their improving abilities to dress themselves.

- School-age children are most comfortable when they wear clothes similar to those of their friends. Dressing like others helps school-age children to feel they belong.

- There are a number of factors to consider when adults select their clothes. These include their occupations, interests, and activities.

- Clothing for the elderly may have many of the characteristics of clothing for young children. These include safety features, large openings, fabrics that feel soft to the skin, and fasteners that open and close easily.

- People with disabilities have unique clothing needs. Select, alter, or construct clothing that someone with a functional limitation can manage conveniently.

To Review

1. List five factors to consider when selecting clothes for children.
2. For proper fit, clothes for a child should be selected according to the child's _____ and _____.
3. List three features you would look for when buying clothes for an infant.
4. List three types of built-in growth features in clothes for toddlers and preschoolers.
5. Clothing with self-help features will encourage _____ as children learn to dress and undress themselves.
6. Why should school-age children be allowed to help select their own clothes?
7. Often, adults' major clothing needs are determined by their _____.
8. What is the main factor that determines the clothing needs of older people?
9. Clothes selected for people with disabilities should _____.
    A. promote dependent living
    B. promote comfort and independent living
    C. be attractive as well as functional
    D. Both B and C above.
10. Name three construction features you would look for when selecting a garment for a person who has limited vision.

To Do

1. Bring several children's garments to class. Discuss the features that are good and those that could be improved.

2. Invite a parent to bring a baby or a toddler to class. Ask the parent to demonstrate dressing the child showing the features that should be included in clothing designed for easy dressing.

3. Interview someone who has a small child. Ask what factors were considered in selecting clothes for the child.

4. Interview three school-age children about their choices in clothing. Ask about their favorite colors, styles, and fabrics. Write a report.

5. Invite a person who has assumed the dual role of homemaker and wage earner to discuss his or her wardrobe needs.

6. Invite a member of an association for retired people to speak to the class about choosing clothing for older people.

7. Interview someone who has had a broken leg, foot, or arm. Write a short report about how the disability affected the person's clothing selections.

8. Invite a person with a disability to speak to the class about the adaptations or alterations that must be made to his or her clothing for comfort, convenience, and/or proper fit.

9. Bring in a selection of clothing items. Explain how each could be modified or altered to make it suitable for a person with a physical disability.

10. Using the Internet, find companies that sell clothing for people with physical disabilities. Ask for copies of their catalogs. Compare the variety and quality of items offered for sale, then give the catalogs to persons, families, or agencies that might use them.

To Think About

1. What are the advantages and disadvantages of using cloth diapers versus disposable diapers? Which are more expensive? Which has the greatest impact on the environment? Which would you choose and why?

2. How can parents help their children learn to dress themselves?

3. At what age do you think children start to become aware of how their clothes look to others? Do you remember when you reached this age?

4. How are the clothing needs of the very old and the very young similar? How are they different?

5. If a friend of yours broke an arm, what suggestions could you give to modify his or her clothes?

3

Looking Your Best

Chapters

CHAPTER 10

Colors for You

Objectives

After studying this chapter, you will be able to
- define basic color terms.
- describe the relationship of the colors in the color wheel.
- identify the basic color schemes.
- choose colors that enhance your skin tone, hair, eye color, and body shape.
- select colors that reflect your personality, moods, and feelings.

Key Terms

hue
value
tint
shade
intensity
neutrals
color wheel
primary colors
secondary colors
intermediate colors
complementary colors
warm colors
cool colors
color scheme
monochromatic color scheme
analogous color scheme
complementary color scheme
split-complementary color scheme
triad color scheme
accented neutral color scheme

Color affects you in many ways. Look at 10-1 and 10-2. Try to imagine how each would look if everything were colorless. Color is everywhere. It is hard to visualize life without it.

Few people are aware of the power of color. For instance, studies have shown that the color red can increase your appetite. Have you ever seen red carpets or furniture in a restaurant? The color was not chosen accidentally. It was planned to encourage you to order more food! Red is also used in many store displays to attract shoppers to certain areas.

When shopping for clothes, color may be the first thing that attracts you to a particular garment. The range of colors is almost limitless. Some are light; others are dark. Some are bright; others are dull. Understanding these properties of color can help you choose colors that will enhance your features. You will be able to make better clothing decisions when you can choose the colors that are best for you.

Understanding Color Terms

Color has three properties or qualities. The first is hue. **Hue** is the name of a color, such as red, green, or blue. The other two qualities are value and intensity. **Value** is the lightness or darkness of a color. Each color has a wide value scale from light to dark. Different values are formed when white or black is added to a color. A **tint** is made by adding white to a color. For instance, pink is a tint of red. A **shade** is made by adding black to a color. Maroon is a shade of red, navy is a shade of blue, and brown is a shade of orange.

hue
The name of a color.

value
The lightness or darkness of a color.

tint
Light value of a color made by adding white to the color.

shade
Dark value of a color made by adding black to the color.

10-1
Many of the colors in nature can be found in our clothes.

10-2
The colors of food add to their appeal.

intensity
The brightness or
dullness of a color.

The dress and handbag in 10-3 are based on the same color of violet. The difference is in the values of the color. A tint is used in the dress and wrap. A shade is used in the handbag.

Intensity is the brightness or dullness of a color. Flag blue is bright, and denim blue is dull, but both are blue. A bright color is more intense than a dull color. Adding more of the dominant color makes a color more intense. Adding some of a color's complement will make the color less intense. (See next section.) For instance, adding a little bit of green to the color red will make the red look "grayed."

The color blocks in 10-4 and 10-5 will help you compare tints and shades. The color blocks in 10-6 and 10-7 will help you compare bright and dull intensities.

10-4_____
The value (lightness or darkness) of any color can be changed. When white is added to a color, the result is a tint.

Simplicity Pattern Co., Inc.

10-3_____
Different values of
the hue violet are
used to create this
attractive ensemble.

10-5_____
A shade is made by adding black to a color.

10-6

Colors look more intense when more of the dominant color is added.

10-7

A color looks less intense (grayed) when some of its complement is added to it.

Black, white, and gray are called **neutrals.** White is the absence of color. It reflects light. Black absorbs all color and light. When white and black are used together, the contrast produces a dramatic effect, 10-8. When white and black are blended, they form gray, another neutral. In clothing, beige is also considered a neutral.

You can wear black, white, gray, and beige with all colors. Neutrals are often used as basic colors in planning a wardrobe. You can mix and match them with various colors to produce a pleasing look. When a small amount of color in an outfit is used with a neutral, the color becomes more vivid.

White and light-colored clothing feel cooler because white reflects light. This is why people often wear white clothes in tropical climates or in the

neutrals
Black, white, and gray are neutrals. White, the absence of color, reflects light. Black absorbs all colors. Gray is a blend of black and white.

color wheel
A chart that shows the relationship among colors or hues.

primary colors
The three colors from which all other colors can be made; red, yellow, and blue.

secondary colors
Colors made by combining equal amounts of two primary colors; orange, green, and violet.

summer. Since black absorbs light, it makes black and dark-colored clothes feel warmer. This is why dark clothes are popular in cold climates.

The Color Wheel

The **color wheel** shows the relationship among colors or hues, 10-9. Red, yellow, and blue are the basic or **primary colors.** Each is a pure color. No other colors can be combined to make any of these. They are placed equal distances from each other on the color wheel, forming a triangle.

All other colors can be made from the three primary colors. Orange, green, and violet are called **secondary colors.** They are made by mixing equal amounts of two primary colors. Red and yellow make orange; yellow and blue make green; and red and blue make violet (purple). They are located evenly between each primary hue on the color wheel.

The McCall Pattern Co.

10-8_____
A dramatic effect is achieved when black and white are used together.

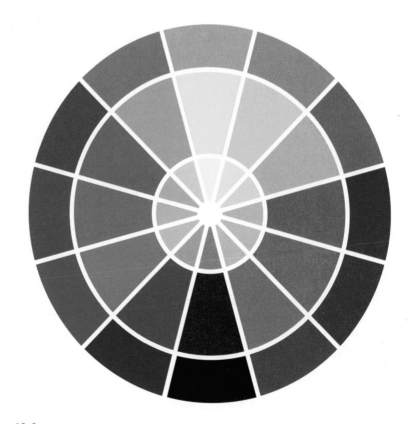

10-9_____
Colors in a color wheel are arranged in a circle to show how they relate to one another. Each color seems to "belong" between its neighbors. The inner ring shows tints of the colors. The outer ring shows shades of the colors.

You can make new colors by combining equal amounts of a primary and a secondary color. These are called **intermediate colors.** These are red-violet, blue-violet, blue-green, yellow-green, yellow-orange, and red-orange. Locate them between a primary and secondary hue on the color wheel. See 10-10 to locate the primary, secondary, and intermediate colors on the color wheel.

Complementary colors are colors located opposite one another on the color wheel. They have the greatest contrast and look brightest when used together. Red and green are complementary colors, as are yellow and violet. Look at the color wheel to identify other complementary colors. To lower the intensity of a color, you add some of its complementary color. When mixed together, as in paints or dyes, any pair of complementary colors in equal amounts will produce gray.

Warm and Cool Colors

Look at the color wheel again. You will notice that one side looks cool and one side looks warm. Red, orange, and yellow are considered **warm colors.** They are bright and cheerful, and suggest activity. Many people like to wear warm colors.

Blues, greens, and purples are the **cool colors.** Restful, relaxing, refreshing, cool, soothing, and serious are terms often used to describe these colors. Long-term hospital patients may stay in rooms painted soft green or blue-green. These colors help them feel relaxed and comfortable.

Warm, light, and bright colors appear to *advance,* or come toward you. When an object moves closer to you, it becomes larger in appearance. Look around you. A warm color is likely to catch your eye first. This is why

intermediate colors
Colors made by combining equal amounts of a primary color and a secondary color; red-violet, blue-violet, blue-green, yellow-green, yellow-orange, red-orange.

complementary colors
Colors located opposite one another on the color wheel.

warm colors
Red, yellow, and orange.

cool colors
Blue, green, and purple.

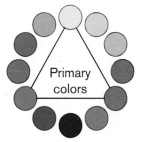

The primary colors are yellow, blue, and red.

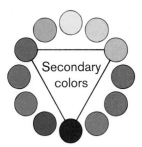

The secondary colors are orange, green, and violet.

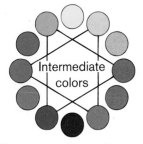

The intermediate colors are yellow-green, blue-green, blue-violet, red-violet, red-orange, and yellow-orange.

10-10
Primary, secondary, and intermediate colors can be determined by their location on the color wheel.

warm colors are used for traffic signs and danger signals, 10-11. Hunters wear red or orange caps so they can be seen easily. Red and orange flags are used on construction projects. Traffic police wear yellow raincoats.

Advertising designers use this knowledge of color in their work. Notice how many food products have yellow or red in their labels when you are in a food store. The advancing colors quickly attract your attention.

Cool, dark, and dull colors appear to *recede* (move away). As an object moves away from you, it appears smaller. That is why a person can look thinner in a blue outfit than in a red one. Slacks made in dark, cool colors will help de-emphasize large hips. Look at 10-12. Can you see how warm colors appear to advance and cool colors recede?

Color Schemes

color scheme
An appealing combination of colors.

Appealing combinations of colors form **color schemes.** You can use the color wheel to see how various color schemes are formed. Designers often base their fabric and clothing designs on these time-tested color schemes. Refer to Figure 10-13 as you read about the different color schemes.

10-11
Black on yellow is the most distinct color combination. These colors are used on warning signs for traffic.

Haan Crafts

10-12
Notice how the warm colors in this photograph catch your eye before the cool colors or neutrals.

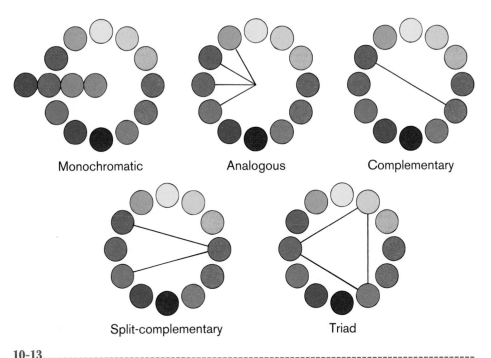

Monochromatic   Analogous   Complementary

Split-complementary   Triad

10-13
These examples illustrate the various types of color schemes.

Monochromatic

A one-color scheme is called the **monochromatic color scheme.** It is formed when several tints, shades, and intensities of one color are used together. For instance, you might use pink, red, and maroon together to form a monochromatic scheme. Someone wearing a pale blue shirt, navy jeans, and pure blue socks would have created a monochromatic outfit.

Analogous

Adjacent colors are the colors that are next to each other on the color wheel. They are closely related and always blend well. When adjacent colors are used together, they form an **analogous color scheme.** You can find analogous color schemes in nature. An example of a natural analogous color scheme is the yellows, oranges, and reds of autumn leaves.

Complementary

Colors that are opposite each other on the color wheel form a **complementary color scheme.** An example is shown in 10-14. When put side by side, complementary colors make each other look brighter. For instance, the complement of blue is orange. When the two colors are used together, both seem brighter. Red and green are stronger when used

monochromatic color scheme.
A color scheme using several values and intensities of one color.

analogous color scheme.
A color scheme using adjacent colors on the color wheel.

complementary color scheme.
A color scheme using colors opposite each other on the color wheel.

split-complementary color scheme
A color scheme using one color with the two colors on the sides of its opposite complement.

triad color scheme
A color scheme using three colors that form an equal-sided triangle on the color wheel.

accented neutral color scheme
A color scheme using a neutral color combined with a bright accent color.

together, as are yellow and violet. If you want to be noticed, this is a combination to choose. Using tints and shades in complementary colors will make a subtle, but pleasing combination.

Split-Complementary

A **split-complementary color scheme** combines one color with the two colors on the sides of its opposite complement. An example would be red combined with yellow-green and blue-green. This combination is a little less bold than a complementary scheme, but still provides vivid contrast.

Triad

The **triad color scheme** uses three colors that form an equal-sided triangle on the color wheel. Using the three primary colors (red, yellow, and blue) or the three secondary colors (green, orange, and violet) together would make a triad color scheme, 10-15. When using this vivid color harmony, it is best to use a large amount of one color and lesser amounts of the other two. You can also use less intense colors for an attractive combination.

Accented Neutral

When a neutral color is combined with a bright color accent, an **accented neutral color scheme** is used. Black, white, gray, or beige can be used with any bright color for a pleasing look. This is also a very versatile combination when mixing and matching various pieces in a wardrobe.

Pendleton Woolen Mills

10-14
The contrast of complementary colors, such as blue and orange, makes the colors look brighter.

10-15
These school uniforms illustrate the triad color scheme of red, yellow, and blue.

By changing the accent color, you can give an outfit an entirely new look. A black sweater and slacks can be changed instantly with a bright colored belt or scarf.

Choosing Your Best Colors

There are hundreds of colors in your life; each is a little different. Knowing about color is called color sense. You were not born with it, but you can easily acquire it. See 10-16 for some guidelines to help you.

Your choice of color will depend on your personal coloring, body shape, personality, and present wardrobe. The season of the year or a special occasion may also be a factor. Select colors that look good on you, give you self-confidence, and make you feel your best.

Colors for Your Skin Tone

How can you decide which colors are best for you? Your personal coloring, which includes your skin tone, is one factor to consider. If you choose the right colors for your clothes, you can enhance your skin tone.

COLOR SELECTION GUIDELINES

- Decide which color does the most for you.
- Select a neutral or a basic color for your clothing. Beige, navy blue, or black are often used.
- With beige—try brown, orange, rust, black, dark green, blue-green, white, and coral.
- With navy blue—use bright green, red, white, pink, yellow, coral, and light blue.
- With black—any color can be used. Because of the sharp contrast, some tints and shades will be better than others.
- Use your basic color selection for items that cost the most money and can be worn several years—coats and suits.
- Use light and bright colors to play up your good features. Use dull, dark colors to play down your bad features.
- Use bright colors in small amounts to add interest and for accent. Do not use too many at a time; a spotty effect will result.
- Plan your clothes so that you will be able to "mix-and-match." This way you will have several different outfits and save money.

10-16

Follow these guidelines to help you choose your best colors.

Skin contains brown, yellow, and red pigments that determine skin tone. Your skin tone will reflect more of one pigment than of another. Darker skinned people have more brown pigment than lighter skinned people. There are many variations of skin tone ranging from very fair to very dark.

Skin color also has blue or yellow *undertones.* You may be able to see these undertones in the coloring of the inside of your wrist. People with blue undertones will look best in cool colors. People with yellow undertones will look best in warm colors. Some cosmetic manufacturers market products designed for warm and cool skin tones.

Colors for Your Hair and Eyes

Another important consideration in selecting your best colors is the color of your hair and eyes. Your hair can take on a new glow with the right colors. Color can also affect the color and brightness of your eyes. See 10-17.

You can emphasize your hair and eye color in two ways. You can choose clothes in tints or shades of your hair or eyes. For instance, beige or tan would emphasize brown hair color.

The second way to emphasize hair and eye color is to choose clothes in complementary colors. For instance, a red shirt will help emphasize green eyes.

Most eyes contain a touch of several colors. Some eyes seem to change color when different colors are worn. For instance, hazel eyes will seem greener when green is worn. Blue eyes may seem bluer when a blue garment is worn. Color does not influence brown eyes as much as other eye colors.

Your Seasonal Coloring

Your personal coloring is sometimes described as one of the four seasons of the year. If you have winter or summer coloring, you have blue undertones in your skin color. If you have spring or autumn coloring, you have yellow undertones. See 10-18.

There are more people with *winter coloring* than with any other seasonal coloring. People with winter coloring

10-17
Hair and eye color can be enhanced by the colors you wear.

THE SEASONAL APPROACH TO YOUR PERSONAL COLORING

Your Season	Winter	Summer	Autumn	Spring
Skin Coloring	Blue Undertones Milk white (colorless) White (with slight undertone) Beige (with slight sallowness) Rosy beige Olive Black Freckles: Dark brown, gray	Blue Undertones Light beige (with a little tinge of pink) Light beige (no color, slightly pale) Rosy pink Dark brown Freckles: medium to dark brown	Yellow Undertones Pure ivory Peach Golden beige Coppery beige Coppery brown Golden black Freckles: golden blond or light brown	Yellow Undertones Ivory Peach Peachy pink Peachy beige Light beige Golden beige Peachy brown Brown Freckles: light golden brown
Hair Coloring	Black (with blue cast) Brown (medium to dark, maybe red highlights) Blond (white) Salt and pepper Silver-gray white (snow)	Platinum Blond Ash blond Smoky blond Smoky brown (or reddish cast) Dark brown (taupe cast) Blue-gray	Red Reddish brown Golden brown Golden blond Charcoal black Bronze or metallic gray	Yellow blond Golden blond Strawberry blond Redhead Auburn Golden brown Golden gray
Eyes	Black Dark brown Brown (with a reddish cast) Hazel (with varying shades of gray, green, blue) Green (with blue or green combination) Medium blue Dark blue	Blue (clear, sky blue, aqua, may have white flecks) Gray-blue (may be chameleon) Soft pale gray Green (may have white flecks) Hazel (with flecks)	Dark brown Golden brown Hazel (brownish-green) Deep to pale green (gold, brown, or citron flecks) Jade green Peacock blue	Clear/bright blue Aqua blue (with turquoise) Bluish-green Clear green Light brown Golden to topaz brown

10-18

Find your personal colors in this chart to determine your seasonal coloring.

usually have dark hair and eyes. They can wear true black or pure white. Bright, vivid, contrasting colors with blue undertones are their best colors, 10-19. Faded or muted colors are not good choices. Silver or pewter tones in jewelry look best.

People with *summer coloring* have hints of pink in their skin. They might easily sunburn. Their eyes are normally very blue; some might have shades of green or hazel. Their hair is usually ash to light blond with light to golden blond highlights. Soft, cool colors look best on people with summer coloring. Silver or pewter toned jewelry flatters their skin tones.

People with *spring coloring* have the most delicate coloring of any season. Their hair color is often light to strawberry blond, pale brown, or reddish brown. Their eyes are usually blue but can be shades of blue-green. People with spring coloring look best in clear, bright colors in medium to light shades. They should not wear muted or faded colors. Gold jewelry tones are best.

People with *autumn coloring* can have ivory or peach colored skin, and they may have freckles. Their hair may be light or dark brown with auburn or red highlights. People with autumn coloring often have brown eyes, but hazel, green, or blue-green eyes are also common. These people can wear muted as well as vivid colors. They look best in the colors of fall foliage. Gold jewelry looks great with the autumn colors.

Your personal coloring determines the colors that look best on you. If you have winter or summer coloring, you look best in cool colors. If you have spring or autumn coloring, warm colors are best for you to wear. Many colors will look great with your personal coloring.

What is your seasonal coloring? Put fabric drapes of colors best for the different seasons around your shoulders. Cover any clothes you are wearing. Study the effects in a large mirror to determine which colors look best on you. Do some colors enhance the blue or yellow undertones of your skin? Do the colors that look best on you seem to fall into a warm or cool category? The best colors for you will enhance your personal coloring. See 10-20.

Cotton Incorporated

10-19
Clear, vivid navy blue looks attractive with the blue skin undertones and dark hair of this woman classified as a winter season type.

Colors for Your Body Shape

Color is one of the best ways to make the most of your body shape. Body shape is called *figure* for girls and *physique* for guys. Colors can be used to your advantage if you follow some simple guidelines.

Light, warm, and bright colors make an object appear larger. If you want to look heavier, choose these types of colors. Most people can wear white and off-white, but it will make an area appear larger. If you want to emphasize your broad shoulders, select a garment with white or a light color in that area.

The dark, cool, dull colors tend to make objects appear smaller. If you want to look slimmer, use this to your advantage. Blue jeans will be more slimming than light-colored khakis. A dark green shirt will make you look smaller than a bright red one.

By using a single color in an entire outfit, you can look taller and slimmer. The eye is carried from top to bottom without a break, giving the illusion of greater height. The traditional business suit gives this effect. If two contrasting colors are used in an outfit, the eye will stop where one color ends and the other begins. This tends to shorten the figure. When a person wears a shirt or jacket with a contrasting color in the slacks or skirt, the figure appears shorter. You can use these guidelines in making your figure appear taller or shorter. See 10-21.

You can also choose colors to emphasize your best features. A small amount of a light or bright color can call attention to your eyes, hair, or complexion. Maybe a small waist is your best feature. Draw attention to that part of your body, and use subdued colors elsewhere. The eye is automatically drawn from the less attractive areas to your best features.

Butterick Company, Inc.

10-20 Choosing the right colors for your clothes accentuates your personal coloring.

Simplicity Pattern Co.

10-21

Notice how the matching top and skirt on the left gives the illusion of more height compared to the contrasting top and pants outfit on the right.

Perhaps you have found a color that you like and that is right for your body shape. However, you find little of this color in your clothes. You cannot toss everything out and start over! Plan carefully to add this color to your wardrobe. Stick to a one-color addition to avoid confusion. Try to see what other clothes you now own that could be worn with new clothes of this color. See 10-22.

Colors and Your Personality

Your personality often influences colors you wear, 10-23. People who wear more warm colors than cool colors are usually described as outgoing. They are often lively, active, and energetic. They love bright colors. They feel light-hearted and cheerful when wearing bright colors.

Other people may feel shy and uncomfortable in such bright colors. Orange or red could overshadow their personalities. Cool or conservative colors might make them feel more at ease. They feel better in the calming look of blues and greens.

EFFECTS OF COLOR ON YOUR **BODY SHAPE**

- Wear neutrals to draw attention away from your body. Add color in accessories.
- Black and navy blue are slenderizing.
- If you are tall and thin, wear two- or three-piece outfits in contrasting colors.
- To appear taller, wear an outfit of only one color, especially a cool color.
- Bold, bright colors and white make an area appear larger; they seem to add weight.
- A small person should wear separates that are one color or are an analogous color scheme. A scattered look will result if too many different colors are worn.
- If you are short-waisted, select colored tops that continue below your waistline.
- Multicolored or light shoes will draw attention to the feet and make them appear larger.
- Wide, light-colored belts will make a waistline appear larger.
- A one-color outfit is the most flattering on a heavier person.
- Turtlenecks make long necks appear shorter.

10-22
These are some of the effects of color on your body shape.

10-23
The colors you choose to wear may reflect something about your personality.

Look at the clothes you own. You may be able to tell whether you prefer warm or cool colors. Do you see more of one type of color than another?

Some colors make you feel good because you are sure you look nice in them. Suppose you receive a compliment on what you are wearing. The color of the outfit probably flatters your personal coloring. The color of a garment should enhance the appearance of the person who wears it. Your personal likes and dislikes and your tastes influence the colors you select to wear. Wearing the colors that do the most for your looks can have a positive effect on your personality.

Blue Rules as the Most Popular Color

The color blue came in as the country's most popular color in a study done by Pantone, Inc., a color communication company. Nearly 35 percent of the 2000 people polled chose the color that evokes a soothing, calming tranquility. Perhaps this color choice reflects the stressful state of today's world.

Second to blue was green, chosen by 16 percent of those polled. It is considered fresh, clean, and revitalizing. It also signifies ecology and the preservation of nature—a current social concern.

The third most popular color was—surprisingly—purple, which just edged out red by 1 percent. The 18- to 29-year-olds consider purple to be sexy. Red is still viewed as the most exciting color, while black is considered mysterious and sophisticated.

When it comes to apparel, 37 percent of the people surveyed chose blue as their favorite color for casual clothing. Grays and blacks were preferred for business suits, but were the second favorite color for casual clothing (13 percent). Blues were the second favorite color for business attire.

Bright orange was the least favorite color overall, but found its highest acceptance among teens. Young people like this in-your-face, look-at-me color. A sulfuric yellow-green was the second most disliked color among adults, but it, too, was a favorite with teens.

So what's your favorite color? Whatever it is today may change as you get older as color preferences do tend to reflect a person's age.

Color and Its Meanings

Some colors are associated with certain feelings or moods. Studies show that people associate certain traits and emotions to specific colors. Red, for example, is a vibrant color. It is associated with anger, power, danger, passion, war, and love. It makes you feel good and full of energy. Why are fire trucks, stoplights, and many emblems red?

Orange is a warm, lively color. It expresses courage, friendliness, hospitality, and energy.

Yellow is cheerful and bright, 10-24. Over the years it has been associated with prosperity, cowardice, deceit, wisdom, and warmth.

Green is the color of spring. It is restful and refreshing. Green has been associated with luck, envy, life, and hope.

Blue is cool, calm, and dignified. It expresses serenity and formality, and it gives a feeling of spaciousness. It is often associated with depression, as a "blue Monday."

Purple is the color of royalty, mystery, humility, and dignity. It expresses opulence, wisdom, and suffering.

Neutrals are also associated with various feelings. Black is a mysterious, sophisticated, and strong color. It may symbolize wisdom, evil, and death. In our culture, people often wear black for funerals.

White is serene and cool. It is the symbol of innocence, purity, faith, and peace. This is why white is worn for weddings, baptisms, and confirmations.

10-24
Yellow is a bright, cheerful color.

CHAPTER REVIEW

Key Points

- Understanding the properties of color can help you choose colors that will enhance your best features. You will be able to make better clothing decisions when you can choose the colors that are best for you.

- Color has three properties or qualities: hue, value, and intensity.

- The color wheel shows the relationship among colors or hues. Colors on the wheel are classified as primary, secondary, or intermediate colors. Half of the colors are considered warm colors and the other half are cool colors. Colors opposite each other on the color wheel are complementary colors.

- Designers have found that the most appealing combinations of colors fall into six basic color schemes: monochromatic, analogous, complementary, split-complementary, triad, and accented neutral.

- Your best colors are those that enhance your personal coloring and body shape. Consider your skin tone, hair, and eye color when choosing colors for your wardrobe. Using a color selection system based on the four seasons of the year can help you choose the right colors for you.

- Light, warm, bright colors make a person look heavier. Dark, cool, dull colors make a person appear slimmer.

- Some colors are associated with certain feelings or moods. Studies show that people associate certain traits and emotions to specific colors.

To Review

1. The brightness or dullness of a color describes its _____.

2. Name the secondary hues.

3. In a complementary color scheme, the color _____ is used with yellow.

4. An analogous color scheme uses colors that are _____ on the color wheel.

5. Give an example of a triad color scheme.

6. Everyone has either _____ or _____ undertones in their skin coloring.

7. Name two ways to use color to emphasize your hair and eyes.

8. People with summer coloring might have _____ skin.
   A. rosy pink
   B. golden brown
   C. peachy beige

9. What three types of colors should you choose if you want to appear smaller?

10. Give an example of how color can indicate your mood.

To Do

1. Arrange a color wheel on the bulletin board. Group samples of fabric or paper under such words as value, intensity, cool, and warm. Caption: "Put a Little Color in Your Life."

2. Using tempera paints, make a color wheel of primary, secondary, and intermediate colors.

3. Using fabric, construction paper, or paint, make a grouping of a complementary color scheme, an analogous color scheme, and a monochromatic color scheme. Discuss and compare your color schemes with others.

4. Working in groups, take turns holding different colors next to your face. Use fabric swatches, colored paper, or items of clothing. Which colors do your classmates say look best on you?

5. Bring samples of fabric prints and plaids to class. Identify the color scheme that was used in each fabric.

6. Select a color scheme of your choice. Describe an outfit using it. Sketch the outfit. Would this be a good outfit for you to wear? Explain.

7. Select three garments. Describe the colors, and tell if they are good colors for you and why.

8. Select colors for a wardrobe that you can mix-and-match. Explain your selections to class members.

9. Check the clothes you own. Decide which colors you have in quantity. Are these your best colors? What changes or additions would you like to make?

10. From extra readings or an Internet search, report to class on colors that
    A. are used as symbols
    B. reflect tranquility and peace
    C. arouse passion
    D. are used as warnings

To Think About

1. Find out what colors are "in" this season. You might use the Internet to find this information. If these colors do not enhance your features, what can you do to be fashionable and still look your best?

2. What is your best feature? What can you do with color to play up your best feature?

3. What are some of the physical effects of color? What are some of the emotional effects of color?

4. What color would you wear to an important job interview? Explain your choice.

5. Think up some descriptive color names that would affect people's emotions and make them want to buy a garment in that color.

CHAPTER 11

Making Design Work for You

204

Objectives

After studying this chapter, you will be able to

- describe the elements of design and their use in clothing design.
- describe the principles of design and their use in clothing design.
- explain how the principles of design relate to the design elements.
- use the elements and principles of design in selecting clothes and accessories appropriate for your figure type and size.

Key Terms

design
elements of design
line
structural lines
decorative lines
optical illusion
shape
form
texture
principles of design
balance
proportion
rhythm
emphasis
harmony

A **design** is an arrangement of elements or details in a product or work of art. Paintings, buildings, and even cities are designs. The clothes you are wearing are designs. *Designing* is the art or practice of creating designs.

You may be attracted to a certain outfit because it is well designed. The overall effect is pleasing; all of the elements seem to belong together. The colors are right, the fabric is right, and the design is right. A fashion designer using the elements and principles of design you will study in this chapter is carefully planning the outfit in 11-1.

How can knowing about good design help you? First, it will help you to recognize a well-designed garment or ensemble. Second, it will help you select the designs that look best on you. By clever use of design, you will be able to show off your best features and camouflage your not-so-good ones. If you know you look good, you will feel good about yourself.

design
An arrangement of elements or details in a product or work of art.

Elements of Design

The **elements of design** are color, line, form, and texture. They are sometimes referred to as the building blocks of design. Each of these elements plays an important role in clothing design. You can apply your knowledge of the elements of design as you select, buy, or construct clothes. You already explored the element of color in Chapter 10. Now you will learn about line, form, and texture.

elements of design
Color, line, form, and texture.

Fashion Institute of Technology

11-1

A fashion designer uses the elements and principles of design to achieve an attractive result.

Line

Lines give direction to a design and break larger areas into smaller ones. Lines also create movement in a design, carrying your eye from one area to another. They can be vertical, horizontal, diagonal, or curved, 11-2.

- *Vertical lines* lead your eye up and down. They give the feeling of height, dignity, and strength.

- *Horizontal lines* carry the eye across from side to side. Horizontal lines suggest a feeling of calm relaxation.

- *Diagonal lines* are angled or slanted. They suggest activity and excitement, 11-3. They are not common, so they attract attention.

- *Curved lines* are lines that gently bend. They create the appearance of softness and fullness.

The lines found in garments can be either structural or decorative. **Structural lines** are formed as the pieces of a garment are sewn together. Seams, darts, pleats, tucks, or the edges of the garment may form these lines. They are easily seen if a plain fabric is used. Sometimes structural lines are the main design element in a garment.

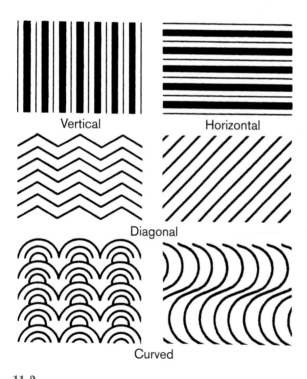

Vertical

Horizontal

Diagonal

Curved

11-2

These are just a few of the types of lines found in clothing.

The McCall Pattern Company

11-3

The combination of horizontal and diagonal lines in this dress creates an interesting effect.

Decorative lines are those that are applied to the garment to add interest. Braid, fringe, ruffles, edgings, top-stitching, lace, tabs, flaps, appliqués, and buttons all form decorative lines. The designer adds these features to a garment to create the design. Sometimes decorative lines are used to accent structural lines. For instance, top-stitching may be used along a neckline, seam, or cuff.

decorative lines
Lines added to a garment to add interest.

Using Lines to Create Illusions

The most important line to you is the outline or *silhouette* of your body. Knowing your silhouette will help you to decide how you want to use line in your clothing to play up or play down your good and bad points.

The lines formed in garments can be used to create optical illusions. An **optical illusion** is a misleading image or visual impression presented to the eyes. Look at the illustration in 11-4. Though each rectangle is the same, the one on the right looks longer and narrower than the one on the left.

optical illusion
A misleading image or visual impression presented to the eyes.

The clever use of line can give an illusion that you have a different body shape than you really have. You can select clothes to make you look shorter, taller, larger, or smaller by using lines correctly.

Wearing clothes with vertical lines will make you look taller and thinner. Study the illustrations in 11-5. Notice how the eye moves upward, giving the illusion of slim height. A vertically striped dress can make a girl seem taller because of the unbroken line that is created. Likewise, a vertically striped shirt or jacket can make a guy seem taller.

The vertical lines may be from stripes in the fabric. They can also be any fabric design that is up and down—circles, dots, or prints. The structural and decorative lines of the garment may be vertical, 11-6. Seams, buttons, pockets, cuffs, and trimmings may be in an up-and-down line.

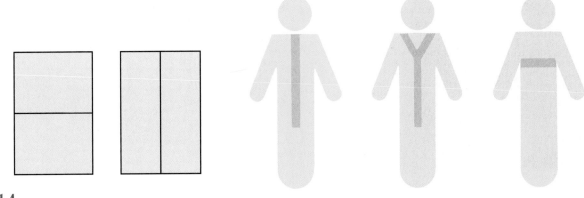

11-4
An optical illusion causes your eye to sense that the left rectangle is shorter than the right one.

11-5
For a taller and thinner look, select vertical lines that keep the eye moving upward.

Not all vertical lines will make the figure appear slimmer. If the lines are spaced far apart, the figure will appear larger. This is because the eye goes back and forth between the lines, giving the illusion of more width. Look at the illustration in 11-7. Notice how the wide panel gives a wider look to the body. The narrow panel makes the body look more slender.

Horizontal lines tend to make the figure appear shorter and wider. Look at the illustrations in 11-8. Your eye tends to move from side to side, making the body appear wider and shorter. If a garment has horizontal stripes that carry the eye from side to side, the body will appear wider and therefore larger or heavier.

If you feel you are too tall and too thin, select garments that have horizontal stripes. You will seem less tall and thin. A wide contrasting belt will make you seem shorter. The belt will seem to cut you in two. Wide, bold stripes across narrow shoulders will make a person appear to have broader shoulders. A girl with wide hips should not choose horizontally striped skirts. Her hips will seem even wider. Overweight people will seem even larger in bold plaids than in clothes with narrow, vertical stripes.

If there are diagonal lines in a garment and they are nearly vertical, they will make you look taller. If they are mostly horizontal, they will make you look wider or larger. However, the effect is not as strong as with vertical or horizontal lines.

The McCall Pattern Co.

11-6
The unbroken vertical movement in this pantsuit carries the eye upward, creating the illusion of slim height.

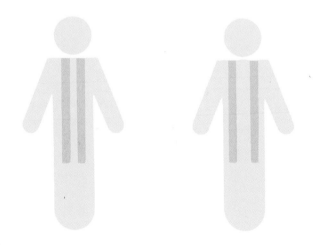

11-7
Not all vertical lines have the same effect. If they are spaced far apart, the figure will appear wider and heavier.

11-8
For a shorter, more rounded look, select lines that keep the eye moving from side to side.

Rolled collars on sweaters and round collars on garments are popular uses of curved lines. Curved lines can also be seen in pockets, trims, necklines, scarves, and caps or hats.

Different effects can be achieved by using curved lines. A person's square face will look less square with a rounded neckline. A long, thin neck will seem to become shorter if a person wears a turtleneck or rolled neck sweater. If you have a pointed chin, a V-neckline will only make it seem more pointed. A high or round neckline would be better.

Form and Shape

The outline of an object is its **shape,** which is made up of lines. If you stand in front of a lighted area near a wall, you can see your shape on the wall as a shadow. This shape is called your silhouette. When you are seen from a distance, people see only your outline or shape.

When a two-dimensional shape takes on a third dimension, it becomes a **form** or mass. Form is the three-dimensional shape of an object. If an object has height, weight, and depth, it has form. Form makes up the enclosed area of a design. Along with your body shape, the clothes you are wearing help to create form.

A form or silhouette that will be in fashion from year to year is determined by many factors. One year the form may be a "natural" look. Clothes may follow the shape of the body. Another year, padded shoulders, which give a squared form, may be popular.

Several forms or shapes are common in clothes. These include the full form, tubular form, and bell form. Some clothes, such as a full skirt or

shape
The outline of an object made up of lines.

form
The three-dimensional shape of an object.

texture
How a fabric feels
and how it looks on
the surface.

Simplicity Pattern Co.

11-9_____
The bell-shaped form is attractive on all figures.

The McCall Pattern Co.

11-10_____
A variety of textures are used to create this attractive ensemble.

pants with wide legs, produce a *full form.* These clothes would make a person look larger and heavier. Clothes having a *tubular* form are more vertical. A straight dress without a defined waistline, straight-leg pants, or a suit appears tubular. They would tend to make a person look taller and thinner. Clothes that produce a *bell-shaped form* look good on most people, 11-9. Flared skirts and pants are examples of bell forms.

Texture

How a fabric feels and looks on the surface is called **texture.** The yarn, weave, and finish determine a fabric's texture. Some words used to describe texture are smooth, dull, rough, shiny, nubby, soft, fuzzy, delicate, crisp, pebbly, scratchy, swishy, and shaggy.

How can texture help you to play up and play down your size and features? Follow these guidelines:

- Fuzzy, loopy, or shaggy surfaces are usually thicker and bulkier. They will add visual size to the area where you wear them.

- Stiff, crisp textures make you look bigger because the fabric stands away from the body. They do, however, conceal some figure problems.

- Soft, clingy fabrics reveal your body's silhouette, calling attention to heavy areas.

- Smooth, flat textures will make you appear smaller than you are.

- Shiny textures tend to add weight or size because they reflect light and emphasize body curves.

- Dull surfaces absorb light so they will make you appear smaller.

Combinations of textures are interesting, 11-10. A bulky sweater to emphasize the shoulders can be worn with smooth-textured slacks to de-emphasize hips or seat. Decide which textures look best on you.

Fabrics may have a design woven into them or printed on them creating a pattern. The fabric may be a stripe, plaid, floral, or geometric print. The designs may be large or small, light or dark, bold or subdued. If the pattern or design is large and bold, the texture will be secondary. The applied design will be more important than the texture.

Large, bold patterns call attention to the area where they are used. This will increase your apparent size, especially if bright or contrasting colors are used. Quiet, small, overall prints tend to make you look smaller.

Virtual Reality Puts You in the Fashion Picture

One of the drawbacks of shopping for clothes online is you can't try them on to see how they will look on you. That may be less of a problem now that there are Virtual Dressing Rooms™. This latest technology, available now at some Web sites, allows you to virtually "try on" clothing and accessories. You can even apply makeup and experiment with new hairstyles and colors on a model that reflects your own measurements, features, and skin tone. You can sample and mix and match an entire digital inventory of clothes, accessories, hairstyles, makeup, and eyeglasses.

You use your own face and body measurements, creating a photorealistic lifelike image. Body shapes (hourglass, pear, apple, lanky) and types (petite, misses, women's, men's) are selected. A built-in fashion advisory offers advice on fashion selections. Recommendations for appropriate styles and colors based on your body type and skin tone are provided. Accessories to go with an outfit might also be suggested. Finally, the correct garment size based on the manufacturer's lines is provided.

Shopping for cloths online can be more fun and satisfying when you can put yourself on the computer screen.

Other new features to look for at fashion Web sites include the following:

- shopping services that keep a file of your sizes, tastes, and past purchases.
- two shoppers at two different computers can browse together and add items to a single "shopping cart."
- e-mail announcements of special sales and promotions.
- the mailing of free fabric swatches if you want to check out the color or feel of a fabric.
- "zoom" technology that allows shoppers to see product details.
- a "live chat" option that allows you to talk directly to a customer service representative. Receive outfit suggestions or help in finding certain items. You can talk by phone (if you have a second line) or by live text.

What other innovations await the online shopper?

principles of design
Guides that tell how the elements of design should be combined. Balance, proportion, rhythm, and emphasis are the principles of design.

balance
The arrangement of objects in an even, pleasing way with equal visual weight on both sides.

Principles of Design

The **principles of design** are guides that tell how the elements of design should be combined. Balance, proportion, rhythm, and emphasis are the principles of design. When these are used correctly, harmony, the goal of design, is achieved.

The principles of design are used in both creating and judging a design. They serve as guides in using the design elements of color, form, line, and texture. These principles are kept in mind and used by designers as they work.

By learning how to use each design principle, you will be able to analyze the design of the clothing you select. You will be able to see why you should avoid a particular combination of colors, lines, or textures and why others would be more pleasing.

Pendleton Woolen Mills

11-11

A classic Western-style shirt is an example of formal balance with both sides of the garment identical.

Balance

When you look at something that has **balance,** you will see that objects are arranged in an even, pleasing way. There is equal visual weight on both sides. There is equal balance on either side of an imaginary center line. Balance can be created in garments and outfits by using the elements of design. Color, line, form, or texture can be used separately or together to achieve balance.

One way to balance a garment is to have it exactly alike on both sides. This equal balance is called *formal balance,* or symmetrical balance. See 11-11. Formal balance is easy to achieve. It can be seen in many garments and outfits. Many of your shirts, blouses, pants, jackets, coats, and sweaters have formal balance; one side is identical to the other side. Skirts with the same number of pleats on each side of the center have formal balance. A shirt with an identical breast pocket on each side also has formal balance.

Balance can also be achieved when the design elements are different on both sides. This unequal kind of balance is called *informal balance* or asymmetrical balance. Informal balance is not as easy to create as formal balance, but it is usually more interesting. The sides are not alike, but neither side overpowers the other. With informal balance, there is less monotony, and the visual weight is still equal. Each side is different, but to the eye, the design appears to be balanced. A jacket with an off-center closing on one side balanced with a pocket on the other side is an example of informal balance. See 11-12.

proportion
The relationship between one part to another and of all the parts to the whole.

Proportion

Proportion is the relationship between one part to another and of all the parts to the whole. This includes sizes, spaces, shapes, and visual weight. When an outfit has pleasing proportion, it looks right for the person wearing it.

Clothing and accessories should be in proportion to your size and body shape. If you have a small body shape or are short, you should avoid styles that seem to overpower you. Garments with huge pockets, big collars, large buttons, and wide lapels are not proportioned to your size. If your legs are short, a short jacket will make your legs look longer. A longer jacket would make your upper body seem longer and your legs shorter. A large plaid sports shirt would look just right for a tall, thin person. If a small, short person wears it, it would seem out of proportion to his or her size.

When selecting accessories, keep proportion in mind. Accessories include handbags, shoes, boots, ties, belts, and jewelry. A large handbag will look completely out of proportion to your size if you are a small-framed girl. A large belt looks better if you are tall. If you are short, a narrower belt would be more in proportion to your figure.

Unequal proportions are considered to be more interesting than equal ones. See 11-13. When a jacket or shirt is exactly the same

The McCall Pattern Co.

11-12
This dress is an example of informal balance. The side closure balances the ruffle.

rhythm
The feeling of movement created by line, shape, or color.

length as the skirt or pants length worn with it, the effect is uninteresting. Stripes on fabrics that are equal in width are not as interesting as those that vary in width. An uneven number (three or five) of buttons on a jacket or coat are more pleasing than an even number (two or four).

To decide what is good proportion, you will need to look at many garments and outfits. Looking at pictures in newspapers and magazines will give you practice. You can study your own clothes and the clothing you see others wear. With practice, you will be able to achieve the best proportion for you.

Rhythm

Rhythm in design is the feeling of movement created by line, shape, or color. It causes your eye to move smoothly from one part of the design to another. Each part of the design seems to belong to or go with another part.

Rhythm in design is somewhat like rhythm in music. In music, a sound is repeated, a regular beat is heard, and rhythm is produced. However, in design, we see rhythm rather than hear it. Rhythm in design is achieved by repetition, gradation, and radiation of colors, lines, and shapes as well as textures. See 11-14.

You achieve rhythm through *repetition* when lines, colors, forms, or textures are repeated in a design. One color in a plaid may be selected as a trim or used in buttons. Because of the repetition of color, your eye is lead from one area to another. This creates rhythm and causes you to look at each part of the outfit.

When lines are repeated, rhythm is achieved. See 11-15. Curved pockets on a coat go with the curves of the coat hem or the rounded lapels. Contrasting trim on a jogging suit may be repeated on both the shirtsleeves and the legs of the pants.

Rhythm can also be achieved by varying the rhythm through *gradation*. For instance, stripes may be close together at the top of a sweater and gradually become wider apart at the bottom. This can be from light to dark colors, small to large sizes, larger to smaller sizes, or from horizontal to vertical lines.

Another way to achieve rhythm in design is by radiation. *Radiation* occurs when lines extend outward from a central point. In clothing, gathers at the neck-

Butterick Co., Inc.

11-13
The short contrasting jacket shows good use of proportion in this outfit—a good choice for someone short. The size of the print is also in proportion to the girl's small figure.

line of a sweater or dress create lines toward the waistline. Your eye is drawn toward the face because it is close to the center of interest or where the lines form.

When rhythm is achieved, your eye moves from one part to another part with a steady movement. This is why it is important for plaids and stripes to be matched at seams. Unmatched stripes and plaids can destroy the rhythm of an outfit. The uneven breaks in the fabric design would cause your eye to stop at that point.

Emphasis

Interesting designs have one part that stands out more than any other part. This is called the center of interest or **emphasis.** Your eye is drawn to this area and it is the first thing you see.

Emphasis should play up your best features and draw attention away from your poorer features. Emphasis can be achieved with color,

emphasis
The center of interest.

Simplicity Pattern Co.

11-15
The repetition of lines in this dress creates rhythm, which causes the eye to move the length of the dress.

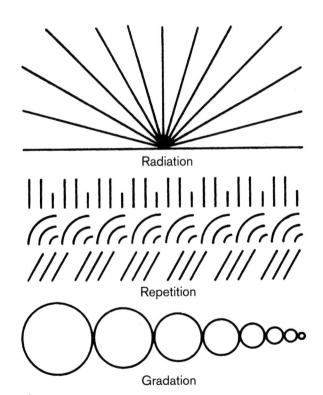

Radiation

Repetition

Gradation

11-14
Rhythm can be achieved in a variety of ways.

harmony
A sense of unity achieved when the elements of design are used according to the principles of design, creating a pleasing visual image.

design details, texture, or accessories. Lace, ruffles, and unusual shapes in buttons and trims attract attention to the areas in which they are placed.

Emphasis can be added to a plain blouse and skirt or a shirt and pants with an accessory. A tie, pin, or neck jewelry can improve the looks of the outfit by providing a point of emphasis. See 11-16.

A contrasting belt would emphasize a waistline. Is that what you want to highlight? A thick middle with a protruding tummy may need to be camouflaged. A bright print tie or scarf at the neckline will pull attention away from your body shape and to the neckline.

If you want to appear shorter, an area of emphasis at the waistline or hemline may do this. If you want to look taller, place the area of interest high on the body. This draws the eye upward instead of downward.

Achieving Harmony

Harmony is achieved when the elements of design are used according to the principles of design, creating a pleasing visual image. All parts of a design look as if they belong together as in 11-17. The line, color, form, and texture harmonize with each other. The design is harmonious when it is well balanced, has a sense of rhythm, and is in good proportion. Everything looks suited to the whole—there is a sense of unity. The design also enhances the coloring, body shape, and personality of the wearer.

All parts of an outfit should be considered when you are striving for harmony. Jeans and leather jackets go together. A leather jacket over a fancy party dress would be less harmonious. A plaid, cotton flannel sports shirt would look better with the collar open than with a necktie.

Simplicity Pattern Co.

11-16
The contrasting belt on this dress provides a point of emphasis.

Accessories can help an outfit achieve harmony. Too many accessories can also spoil the effect. Repeating colors from a garment by adding a belt or jewelry can be pleasing. Guys and girls could wear boots, jeans, a western belt and shirt for a harmonious, casual look.

Just as harmony is the goal of good design, wearing garments and outfits that make you look your best should be your goal. You can use your knowledge of the design elements and design principles to improve your good points. You will also be able to draw attention away from your less-than-perfect features. The bottom line is to select clothing that creates the best total look for you.

Simplicity Pattern Co.

11-17_____
Harmony is achieved when all aspects of an ensemble create a pleasing visual image and all parts of the design seem to belong together.

CHAPTER REVIEW

Key Points

- A design is an arrangement of elements or details in a product or work of art. The clothes you are wearing are designs.
- The elements of design are color, line, form, and texture. They are sometimes referred to as the building blocks of design.
- Lines in garments can be vertical, horizontal, diagonal, or curved. They may be structural or decorative. These lines can create optical illusions that may mislead the eyes.
- The form or shape of a garment can make a person look larger or smaller. The texture of a fabric can also be used to play up and play down a person's size and features.
- The principles of design are balance, proportion, rhythm, and emphasis.
- When the principles of design are used correctly, harmony, the goal of design, is achieved.

To Review

1. Explain the difference between structural lines and decorative lines in garments.
2. Give three examples of lines in garment features that can make a person appear taller and slimmer.
3. Name two fabric textures that would make you appear heavier.
4. Explain how the principles of design relate to the design elements.
5. Explain the difference between formal and informal balance.
6. Name three design features you would avoid if you were choosing clothes or accessories that would be in proportion to a small figure.
7. _____ proportions are considered to be more pleasing and interesting.
8. Give an example of how rhythm can be achieved in a garment. State the type of rhythm you used in your example.
9. What principle of design is created with a bright red tie worn with a white shirt?
10. Explain how harmony is achieved in a design.

To Do

1. Plan a bulletin board titled "Select the Right Designs for You." Use fabric swatches with various textures, lines, and colors. Group them according to different body shapes such as tall/thin, short/heavy, small-framed, large-framed, etc.

2. Collect as many fabric samples as possible of textures and designs. Describe each texture and design in class. Identify those that would make a person appear heavier and those that would make a person appear slimmer.

3. Collect pictures of clothing from magazines, pattern books, and catalogs that illustrate the different principles of design. Mount pictures on paper. Comment as to whether you feel the examples are excellent, fair, or poor. Support your opinions.

4. Find examples of formal and informal balance in this textbook.

5. Find pictures of outfits or garments that show the design principle of emphasis. Identify the item of emphasis on each outfit.

6. Demonstrate the principle of proportion by having two students of different heights try on several sweaters or jackets of different lengths.

7. Create a fabric design on white construction paper using paint or felt-tip pens. If you have access to a CAD program on a computer, create the design using the computer. Analyze the design. Ask class members for comments.

8. Collect ten pictures of people in various outfits. Decide which outfits have harmony and which do not. Give reasons for your answers. Also decide which outfits would make a person look taller and slimmer and which would make a person look shorter and heavier.

To Think About

1. How is design everywhere you look?
2. Is there a difference between good design and bad design?
3. Can good design be taught, or is a person born with a "sense of design?"
4. If you were a fashion designer, which element of design would you consider most important? Why?
5. Which form or silhouette seems to be in fashion this year?

CHAPTER 12

Taking Care of Your Body

Objectives

After studying this chapter, you will be able to
- practice good health and grooming habits.
- describe types of skin and skin care.
- explain causes and treatment of acne.
- summarize skin protection practices.
- practice dental hygiene.
- use MyPyramid in making food choices.
- describe eating disorders.
- describe ways to maintain proper body weight.
- explain the benefits of regular exercise and adequate rest.

Key Terms

grooming
deodorant
antiperspirants
acne
dermatologist
plaque
tartar
nutrition
nutrients
MyPyramid
anorexia nervosa
bulimia
calories

Everyone wants to look good. This doesn't mean you have to have beautiful features. You don't have to be born with good looks. There are things you can do to make the best of what you do have.

Whether you like it or not, your looks affect and reflect everything about you. This includes your mood, self-esteem, schoolwork, and friends. If you know you look good, you feel good. You can then forget about how you look and focus on living your life.

If you were asked to select some well-groomed persons in your class, it would probably be easy. They would look great—not necessarily beautiful or sensational—but great! Their skin, hair, nails, and teeth would be clean. They would be wearing neat, appropriate clothes that "do something" for them. You might select persons who look like the teens in 12-1. The key to looking great is being well groomed.

grooming
Taking care of your body through good health habits and personal cleanliness.

Body Cleanliness

Since the definition of **grooming** is "to take care of," the first step in a good grooming program is to take care of you. Good health and good looks go hand in hand. If you feel good, you will try harder to look good.

When people look at you, they see skin. They have to see it; it is on display. And you do have a lot of it! If you are of average size, your skin weighs about 8 pounds. If you could spread it out flat, it would be about 18 square feet in size. Your skin has many jobs, including the following:

- keeping your body temperature at the proper level

- protecting your body from bacteria

- excreting (discharging) body wastes

- repairing itself

Since skin is so important, it is to your advantage to take good care of it.

A Daily Bath or Shower

Taking good care of your skin means keeping it clean. A bath or shower is needed every day. All your efforts toward being well groomed are wasted if you are not clean. Bathing keeps your skin pores open. If they are clogged, blemishes will result.

12-1
Being well-groomed–having clean skin, hair, nails, teeth, and clothes–is important to these teens.

The method of bathing you use is a personal choice. You may like a shower, 12-2. It takes little time, and you can shampoo your hair at the same time. A relaxing bath may suit you.

The purpose of a bath or shower is to get clean. Every part of your body should receive attention. Skin folds and creases need special care, since perspiration and airborne dust accumulate in these areas. Use plenty of mild soap. Water alone will not wash away body oils, perspiration, and dirt. Remove all traces of soap to prevent your skin from becoming too dry.

Deodorants and Antiperspirants

A daily bath does not guarantee you will be free of body odor. The most offensive odor comes from perspiration. To perspire is normal and natural. Perspiration removes body wastes through the pores of the skin. It also helps to regulate body temperature. Perspiration or sweat by itself is odorless. However, when bacteria on the skin react with it, an unpleasant odor results. More bacteria are in a moist area than on dry skin. Therefore, the underarm area is the main source of body odors.

Many teens are bothered by a heavy flow of perspiration. When you become nervous, excited, or upset, it increases. You are aware of the circle of wetness on your clothes. This is often embarrassing.

To prevent odors from forming, use a good deodorant or an antiperspirant. When you are near others, you want to be free of body odor, 12-3.

12-2_____

A daily shower or bath using a mild soap is necessary for body cleanliness.

12-3_____

When you are close to someone, it is important that you are free of body odor.

A **deodorant** controls odor, but it allows you to perspire normally. It stops odor by killing bacteria on the skin. You may have to try several brands before you find one that is effective for you. If you perspire more than normal, the moisture will wash away or dilute the deodorant, making it ineffective.

Antiperspirants may be the answer to the problem of excessive perspiration. **Antiperspirants** reduce the flow of moisture. They contain a metallic salt that clogs the pores and prevents moisture from forming. Do not use them anywhere except under the arms. If a rash appears, stop using the antiperspirant. The brand may be too strong. Try other brands until you find the right one for you. You can buy deodorants and antiperspirants as spray-on, roll-on, stick, gel, cream, or powder. Many products are specially developed for men or women.

Deodorant soaps are available. If you are aware that you have an odor problem, you may need this type of soap. They remove odors better than regular soap. However, using them does not reduce the amount of perspiration.

Persons who have an offensive odor are seldom aware of it. Sometimes a person looks good, but has a body odor. If you cannot control perspiration by commercial products, see your doctor.

deodorant
Personal care product that controls body odor while allowing the person to perspire normally.

antiperspirants
Personal care products that control perspiration by reducing the flow of moisture.

Special Care for Facial Skin

The best way to care for your facial skin is to keep it clean. Washing it in the morning and again at night is important. Keeping your face clean cannot be overstressed. See 12-4.

Good health helps your skin look smooth and healthy. You need plenty of fresh air, exercise, and sleep. Proper foods in the right amounts are important, too.

All people have one of four basic skin types: oily, dry, combination, or normal. When you know your type, you will be able to set up your own skin care program. What is good for one person may not be right for another person.

Types of Skin

Deciding what type of skin you have may be easy. If you have a problem with pimples, you may have oily skin. If your skin is flaky and tight after washing, it is dry.

12-4
A clear complexion begins with clean skin.

If you are unsure of your skin type, here is a simple test to help you decide. Wash your face and wait 15 minutes. Cut several one-inch squares of facial tissue. Touch one each to your forehead, nose, chin, and cheeks. Check each square for oil. If there is none on the tissue squares, your skin is dry. If all of the squares become slightly transparent, your skin is oily. (Your skin is normal if the tissue squares absorb only a little bit of oil.) If the tissues on your cheeks are dry, but the ones on the forehead, nose, and chin are slightly transparent, you have combination skin. This type of skin is the most common.

Caring for your skin does not necessarily mean doing what your sister, brother, or best friend does. Plan and follow a routine suited to your own skin type.

Care of Oily Skin

Oily skin is the type most teenagers have. Glands are pumping too much oil to the skin surface. Flakiness around only the nose area is a sign of oily skin. This is really excess oil that has dried from exposure to air. If you have oily skin, your nose, forehead, and chin have an oily shine within an hour after washing. In the mornings, your entire face is oily. Blackheads may be seen on your nose and chin. Check other characteristics in 12-5.

Oil that sits on top of skin can clog skin pores. The oil must be removed often and thoroughly to prevent skin problems. Wash your face several times daily. Use soap made for oily skin. Rinse thoroughly with warm water. An astringent may be used if the skin is very oily.

Care of Dry Skin

Dry skin does not affect most people until they are past 20. However, some teenagers may show signs of dryness. Young men who have just started shaving may have dry skin areas.

If you have dry skin, flakiness will appear all over your face. Other symptoms are shown in 12-6. You do not have enough natural oil in your skin to hold moisture. You need to restore moisture to your tight, drawn skin. This is especially important after washing your face.

Keeping your skin clean is always basic to a good complexion. Wash at least twice daily. Use soap made for dry skin. You may want to use lotion or a moisturizer in the morning, at night, or anytime your skin feels dry.

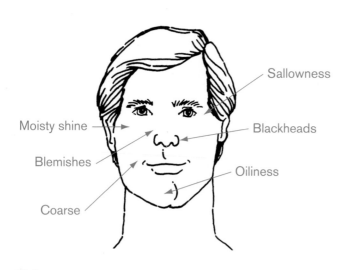

Sallowness

Moisty shine

Blackheads

Blemishes

Oiliness

Coarse

12-5.
Problems develop for teens in the oily skin group. Frequent cleansing is necessary.

Care of Combination Skin

Combination skins have oil in the "T-zone" area as shown in 12-7. The forehead, nose, and chin areas are oily. The rest of the face is dry.

Follow the guidelines for oily skin to treat your oily areas. Avoid scrubbing around the eyes and the cheeks. All dry areas will need moisture, as when caring for dry skin. Applying lotion or moisturizer at night will help.

Care of Normal Skin

A few lucky teens have no skin problems. Their complexions are clear, soft, and smooth. Their skin care routine may include a thorough cleansing in the morning and again at night. A protective moisturizer can prevent chapping during cold weather.

Acne

Few teens escape complexion problems. Nearly 85 percent of adolescents and young adults between the ages of 12 and 24 develop acne. **Acne** is a disorder of the skin's oil glands that results in plugged pores and outbreaks of lesions. No one has died from this disease, but it makes most teens miserable at one time or another. Severe cases of acne can cause deep pitting and scarring.

Acne occurs when the *sebaceous (oil)* glands, which produce an oily substance called *sebum,* work overtime. These glands are connected to

acne
A disorder of the skin's oil glands that results in plugged pores and outbreaks of lesions.

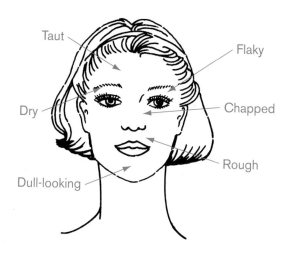

12-6
Note the characteristics of dry skin. Few teens have this problem.

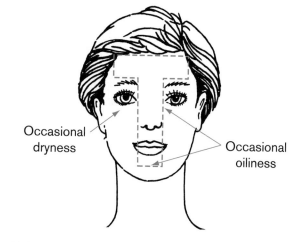

12-7
You may have a combination type of skin—part oily and part dry. The oily area is known as the "T-zone."

hair-containing canals called *follicles.* See 12-8. Normally the sebum emp-ties onto the skin surface through the follicle opening, carrying shed cells to the skin surface. If cells from the lining of the follicle shed too fast and clump together, the sebum cannot reach the skin's surface. A plug called a *come-do* forms below the surface of the skin. It is light in color and called a *white-head.* If the comedo reaches the surface of the skin and opens up, the tip looks dark and is called a *blackhead.* The mixture of oil and cells causes bacteria to grow, resulting in inflammation (swelling, redness, and pain). Inflamed, pus-filled lesions called *pimples* may form. The most severe degree of acne is the *cyst.* This is a hard bump under the skin that results from an infection in deep skin tissue. Scars may appear after cysts go away.

Causes of Acne

You can inherit a tendency to get acne just as you inherit the color of your eyes or the shape of your nose. Rising hormone levels are another cause of acne. During the teen years, there are rapid changes in body chemistry and an increase in hormone development. Certain hormones,

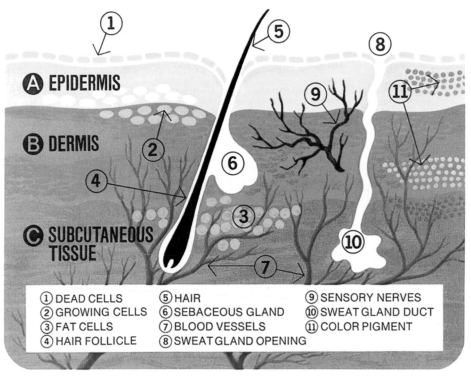

Carson Chemical Co.

12-8.
Acne occurs when sebum from the sebaceous glands cannot reach the skin's sur-face through the hair follicles.

called *androgens,* cause the oil glands to enlarge and make more sebum. After puberty, boys produce 10 times as much androgen as girls. Therefore, more boys than girls develop severe cases of acne.

Several factors can contribute to acne or make it worse. Friction and pressure can cause acne. Football players have more acne on their shoulders where shoulder pads have pressed. Tennis players who wear sweatbands on their foreheads can find more acne there. Resting your chin or the side of your face in your hand while reading can sprout a new crop. Even oily hair that touches your forehead can cause blemishes.

Many young women notice more pimples near the start of their menstrual periods. Greasy cosmetics may trigger acne in some people. Environmental irritants, such as industrial oils, grease, and chemicals, may make acne worse.

No one has proved that foods such as chocolate, nuts, or cola drinks cause facial blemishes. Doctors say that emotions have more effect on blemishes than food does. Have you had a flare-up just before exams or after a disagreement with a friend? Anger, tension, or nervousness could be the reason.

dermatologist
Doctor who specializes in diseases and disorders of the skin.

Treatments for Acne

There are various degrees of acne. The mildest and most common form is oily skin and whiteheads. Simply washing your face twice daily can often clear up this form of acne, 12-9. You may want to apply an over-the-counter (sold without a doctor's prescription) topical medication. Topical medications are applied directly to the skin. Depending on the type of medication used, they may keep bacteria from forming, loosen plugs, reduce oil production, or help shed dead cells.

When a severe case of acne develops, you should visit a dermatologist. A **dermatologist** is a doctor who specializes in diseases and disorders of the skin. Dermatologists cannot cure acne, but they can help control it. New, successful treatments are available.

Since there are many forms of acne, there are many treatments. The dermatologist will give you details on how to care for your particular condition and type of skin. You may be given antibiotics, such as tetracycline and erythromycin, or tretinoin, a type of drug that contains vitamin A. Other types of treatment may also be used.

For all forms of acne, most doctors recommend that you gently wash your skin with a mild cleanser twice a day. Wash the skin again after heavy exercise.

12-9
Cleanliness is needed for a clear complexion. Wash your face at least twice a day.

Avoid strong detergent soaps. Do not scrub your skin with rough scrubs or pads. Scrubbing may make your acne worse. Shampoo your hair every day if it is oily. If you wear cosmetics, choose those that are oil free.

Do not pick or squeeze pimples. You can make them worse, and there is a better chance of leaving a scar. Frequent rubbing and touching of skin lesions should be avoided.

Your Skin and the Sun

Most people enjoy spending time in the sun, 12-10. They enjoy working outside, exercising outside, or just sitting outside and enjoying the fresh air. The sunshine feels good. The sun also helps the body produce vitamin D. However, 10 to 15 minutes of sun two to three times a week provides you with a healthy dose.

Studies show that the sun gives off ultraviolet (UV) rays that can cause permanent damage to the skin. Exposure to these rays can lead to dry, wrinkled, and prematurely aged skin. A more serious concern is skin cancer. Cataracts, a form of eye damage that clouds vision, can result from UV radiation. Recent research has also shown that repeated exposure to UV rays may cause long-lasting damage to the body's immune system.

12-10
If you spend time in the sun, keep your skin healthy by protecting it from the sun's rays by using a sunscreen.

Trends Making News

Sunscreen Use on the Rise

The use of sunscreens is improving. Teens' use of sunscreen is also on the increase. According to a recent study, 72 percent of teenagers say they use sunscreen at least some of the time. Only about 40 percent say they use sunscreen often or all of the time. Guys are less likely than girls to use it. Reasons given for not using sunscreen include the belief they never burn, it's inconvenient, or they want a dark tan.

Unfortunately, teenagers won't see the effects of sun damage until they reach their 40s and 50s or later. By then, the damage is done.

Many teens are tempted to lie in a tanning bed to achieve a tan. This practice must be avoided. Tanning beds and lights are just as dangerous as tanning in the sun. Sunless tanning lotions, creams, and sprays are a relatively safe alternative.

If you are going to be outdoors during mid-day, check the Ultraviolet Index (UVI). UVI is a number from one to eleven that indicates the amount of UV rays reaching the earth's surface at any point in time. The daily UVI number is listed in newspapers and on TV weather forecasts. If the UVI number is five or higher, you should always protect yourself with sunscreen, hat, and sunglasses.

Special sun-protective clothes are now available, though they are sold mostly through catalogs. These items are made of fabrics that are lightweight and breathable, and yet shield you from UV rays. Look for UPF (ultraviolet protection factor) shirts, pants, and shorts if you plan to spend extensive time in the sun.

Another new device is now available that will let you know when you have had too much sun. You place a dime-sized patch on your skin or clothing when you plan to spend time in the sun. The patch changes color when you have had too much sun. It measures the total accumulated dosage of UV rays that are being absorbed by your body. As absorbed UV radiation reaches a certain level, the patch turns color to match the color of the sticker's edge. There are two types of patches: one for use with sunscreen and one for use without. They also come in six skin types, ranging from very light for people who burn easily to very dark for those who seldom burn.

PROTECTING YOUR SKIN FROM THE **SUN**

- Avoid exposure to the sun between the hours of 10:00 a.m. and 3:00 p.m. If you must be in the sun then, upgrade your sunscreen to a higher SPF.

- Use a sunscreen with a high SPF on sensitive areas such as the face, neck, shoulders, bathing suit lines, tops of feet, inside elbows, backs of knees, and ears. Lips need extra protection.

- Apply ample sunscreen to clean, dry skin at least a half hour before going out into the sun. Reapply after swiming or heavy sweating.

- A family of four should use a four-ounce bottle of sunscreen during one day at the beach.

- Snow, sand, water, and concrete reflect UV rays, increasing exposure. The sun can even damage the skin when you are in the shade.

- If you are taking medication, it may chemically alter your skin's tolerance to the sun. You may need to avoid being in the sun when taking some medications to avoid sunburn.

- Wear a wide-brim hat and tightly woven, loose-fitting clothing that keeps your skin covered.

- Wear sunglasses that block 99-100 percent of UV radiation to prevent eye damage.

12-11

To protect your skin and keep it healthy, follow these guidelines.

No one, not even someone with the darkest black skin, is immune to sunburn, premature aging of the skin, or skin cancer. Although many of the sun's worst effects do not appear until later in life, it is very important to protect children from overexposure to UV rays. Studies increasingly suggest a link between early exposure and skin cancer as an adult. Children need special care since they spend more time outdoors than adults and can burn more quickly.

Sunscreens are available to help prevent skin damage from the sun. Sunscreens are rated as to the degree of protection. The higher the Sun Protection Factor (SPF) number marked on a product, the more protection you will receive. Products marked SPF 15 are best. To be effective, apply sunscreens before you go out in the sun. Apply again after washing, swimming, or heavy sweating, or every two hours. Everyone who spends time in the sun, regardless of skin type, should use a sunscreen. Do not use sunscreens on children younger than six months of age. They should avoid too much time outdoors. Some tips for protecting your skin are given in 12-11.

Taking Care of Your Teeth

Every time you smile, your teeth become an important part of your appearance. To have healthy teeth and gums, you must follow a complete program of *dental hygiene.* This is the care of your teeth and gums.

Brushing, flossing, eating the right foods, and visiting a dentist regularly are all part of good dental hygiene. Good dental hygiene habits that you practice while you are young will stay with you for the rest of your life. They will ensure that your teeth do, too!

Teeth should be brushed after each meal. If this is not possible, swishing water in your mouth several times will help. A toothbrush with soft bristles is better than a toothbrush with hard ones. Soft bristles can do a better job of removing food particles that are caught between the teeth. Using a toothpaste containing fluoride helps to prevent tooth decay, 12-12. A mouthwash doesn't substitute for a good brushing. It only tastes good and is refreshing.

Your teeth should be flossed daily. Using dental floss helps remove food that is lodged between teeth that regular brushing may not be able to remove. Care should be taken not to cut into the gums with the thread. If you do not know how to floss or brush properly, ask your dentist.

Brushing and flossing remove plaque from the teeth. **Plaque** is a thin layer of film on teeth that contains harmful bacteria. The bacteria causes tooth decay and gum disease. This problem usually starts between the teeth. If plaque is left on the teeth, it builds up and becomes a hard, crusty substance called **tartar.** A dentist or a dental hygienist must remove tartar.

It is important to see a dentist twice a year to have your teeth cleaned and checked. Problems can be found and solved before they become serious. The cost of regular checkups is small compared to the cost of repairing neglected teeth.

plaque
A layer of film on teeth that contains harmful bacteria, which can cause tooth decay and gum disease.

tartar
A hard, crusty substance that results when plaque is left on the teeth.

12-12
Practicing good dental hygiene can help you have healthy teeth and gums.

Good Health and Good Looks

Being clean is important, but that is only one part of good grooming. The foods you eat, your body weight, and the amount of exercise and sleep that you get affect your health and looks. Good looks begin with good health.

Eating Right

The way you look and feel depends a great deal on the foods you eat. By eating the right foods, you will feel good and have more energy. When you eat the right foods, you are practicing good nutrition. Good **nutrition** means eating a variety of nourishing foods that will keep your body working properly. **Nutrients** are substances that you get from foods that help your body to grow and stay healthy. Nutrients include carbohydrates, proteins, fats, vitamins, minerals, and water. A well-balanced diet includes all of these nutrients.

nutrition
Eating a variety of nourishing foods that will keep the body working properly.

nutrients
The substances that a person gets from foods that help the body to grow and stay healthy.

MyPyramid
An individualized food guidance system that will help you eat a well-balanced diet.

MyPyramid

MyPyramid is an individualized food guidance system that will help you eat a well-balanced diet. By logging on to MyPyramid.gov, and entering your age, sex, and activity level, you will learn what you should be eating each day. The recommendations are divided into five main food groups:

- grains
- vegetables
- fruits
- milk
- meat and beans

When you enter your personal data at MyPyramid.gov, the plan selects a food intake pattern that is right for you. Your food plan includes daily amounts from each of these food groups. Many teens require 2,000 calories daily. The amounts shown in 12-13 are for a 2,000 calorie eating plan. Oils are also included because they supply essential nutrients. They are also high in calories, so should be consumed in moderation.

Choosing nutritious snacks is also a part of eating right. When planning snacks, avoid those that are high in sugar, salt, and fat. Instead, choose foods that are high in nutritional value. You can choose from a variety of nutritious snacks. Some nutritious snacks are shown in 12-14.

Eating Disorders

Abnormal eating behavior is an eating disorder. Anorexia nervosa and bulimia are both eating disorders that can cause serious health problems.

Anorexia nervosa is a disorder in which a person avoids eating. Some victims avoid food to the point of starvation. A person with anorexia nervosa has a distorted self-concept. A victim of this disorder feels fat no matter how thin he or she is.

anorexia nervosa
A disorder in which a person avoids eating.

GRAINS	VEGETABLES	FRUITS	MILK	MEAT & BEANS
For a 2,000-calorie diet, you need the amounts below from each food group. To find the amounts that are right for you, go to MyPyramid.gov.				
Eat 6 oz. every day	Eat 2½ cups every day	Eat 2 cups every day	Get 3 cups every day	Eat 5½ oz. every day

USDA

12-13

At MyPyramid.gov, you can learn the amount of food you should eat from each of the five main food groups. The amounts shown here are for a 2,000 calorie eating plan.

12-14

Fruits make a great nutritious snack.

bulimia
An eating disorder where victims eat large amounts of food and then expel the food by vomiting or purging.

Bulimia victims go on food binges. They eat large amounts of food. Then they get rid of the food by vomiting or purging (using laxatives). As with anorexia nervosa, victims of bulimia always feel the need to be thinner.

Both of these disorders can cause serious health damage. Persons need medical care and psychological counseling in order to get well.

Your Body Weight

Your daily activities, your inherited physical characteristics, such as your height and build, and your eating habits determine your body weight.

Overweight

Are you overweight? One of the big problems with some teens today is weighing too much for their body size. You should not worry if you weigh a few pounds more than you would like. However, if you have a lot of weight to lose, you should try to do something about it.

If you are overweight, you probably eat more food than you need for your lifestyle. Your daily activities are not enough to burn up or use all the calories food gives you. **Calories** are the units of energy or "body fuel" provided by the foods you eat. The number of calories that you need daily depends on your age, body size, rate of growth, and energy level.

calories
The units of energy or "body fuel" provided by the foods a person eats.

Overeating is a habit that is difficult to break. You need willpower and determination. You have to resist snacks and some foods you like. Your family and friends influence your eating habits. Unless they know that you are trying to develop new eating habits, they may make it difficult for you to break your old habits. They will still expect you to eat as you have in the past.

If you have a serious problem, you should consult your doctor. By testing, he or she can tell if anything other than overeating is your problem. If a doctor or dietitian gives you a diet, stick to it.

One or two pounds of weight loss a week is a safe amount. Diets that cause faster weight loss are unsafe. After you finish with them, your weight often returns. This is discouraging. These are called "fad" or "crash" diets. Most are not medically approved and could result in other health problems. They tend to make many people nervous, tired, cranky, miserable, and depressed.

By reducing the amount of food you eat, you will lose weight slowly. Between-meal snacks are a good place to start cutting down your caloric intake. At the same time, add exercise to your daily routine, 12-15. Develop a realistic plan for weight loss and follow it carefully. Keep in mind the MyPyramid recommendations. Your weight loss will be permanent if you will form good health habits.

Underweight

Being underweight can also be a problem. There are many reasons why teens are underweight. The most common are poor eating and health habits. Others could be nervousness and tension. The last two

12-15_____
Adding exercise to your daily schedule will help you meet your weight-loss goals.

can either make you eat too often and too much, or not often enough. If you are seriously underweight, check with your doctor. He or she may find a cause that can be corrected medically.

Think through a day's activities. Keep a list of the foods you eat. Compare these to see if you are eating enough for the energy you need. Then compare the list of foods you eat to your MyPyramid recomendations. Are you eating the right foods?

To gain weight, set up a plan and follow it daily. Eat foods that are high in calories. Instead of eating three times daily, eat five times whether you are hungry or not. Drink water or tea between meals rather than with your meal. Save the room for food. You can snack between meals, but try not to ruin your appetite.

Learn to relax. Try not to get involved with problems that cause you to be nervous or emotional. This will rob your appetite, and it will interfere with good digestion. Schedule some time each day to relax. A short break after school would be good.

Exercise

Exercise is an activity performed for physical conditioning. Running, jogging, and walking are all good forms of exercise. You learned years ago that regular exercise is important. You know that a good game of basketball, tennis, or softball is fun and good for your health. It exercises your lungs, strengthens your heart and other muscles, and burns fat. It also helps you relax and reduces stress levels. Both guys and girls need active sports for exercise.

With so much time spent in a classroom, when is there time to exercise? You should make time for exercise. Perhaps you could substitute some activities for a few television programs or hours spent at the computer. Walking, tennis, dancing, swimming, and bicycling are good forms of exercise, 12-16. You might invite a friend to go on a walk with you, or take your pet for a walk, 12-17. If you walk outside, you will get fresh air that is good for your health.

Sleep

To feel healthy, energetic, and happy, you must get enough sleep. Most teenagers need 8 to 10 hours nightly. You may need more or less than your friend needs, 12-18.

Lack of sleep can make you feel drowsy and lazy. You may not be able to stay awake during class. You will often feel irritable and tired. Your eyes may be red and puffy. Dark circles could appear under them.

12-16
Bicycling is a great form of exercise.

12-17
Hiking is great exercise and fun. You can improve your health while enjoying nature.

Since sleep can help you look and feel better, it makes sense to get as much of it as you need. With careful planning, you can get enough sleep almost every night. Feeling great and looking good will make it worthwhile.

12-18
Getting enough sleep at night is important if you want to look and feel your best during the day.

CHAPTER
REVIEW

Key Points

- The key to looking great is being well-groomed. The first step in a good grooming program is to take care of yourself. Good health and good looks go hand in hand.

- A daily bath or shower keeps your skin clean. Using a deodorant or antiperspirant prevents body odors from forming.

- All people have one of four basic skin types: oily, dry, combination, or normal. Your skin-care program should be based on your skin type.

- Acne is a disorder of the skin's oil glands that results in plugged pores and outbreaks of lesions. It cannot be cured, but treatments are available to help control it.

- The sun gives off ultraviolet (UV) rays that can cause permanent damage to the skin. Sunscreens should be used to prevent skin damage from the sun.

- To have healthy teeth and gums, you should follow a program of dental hygiene. This includes brushing, flossing, eating the right foods, and having regular dental checkups.

- The way you look and feel depends a great deal on the foods you eat. Following the MyPyramid food guidance system will help you select the right foods for keeping your body working properly. The eating disorders of anorexia nervosa and bulimia can cause serious health problems.

- Your daily activities, your inherited physical characteristics, such as your height and build, and your eating habits determine your body weight.

- Regular exercise and adequate sleep are important to overall good health.

To Review

1. Name two functions of the skin.
2. _____ contain a metallic salt that clogs the pores and prevents moisture from forming.
3. Describe the combination skin type.
4. The most severe degree of acne is a

   _____.
   A. cyst
   B. pimple
   C. whitehead
   D. blackhead
5. Name two causes of acne.
6. What do doctors recommend for the daily care of skin with all forms of acne?
7. List two ways overexposure to the sun's rays can affect a person's health.
8. Name the three factors that determine your personalized food intake pattern when you log on to MyPyramid.gov.
9. A person trying to lose weight should

   _____.
   A. eat only snacks and skip all meals
   B. follow a "crash" diet
   C. try to lose only one or two pounds a week
   D. ignore MyPyramid recommendations; you can eat anything
10. Persons trying to gain weight should

    _____.
    A. eat foods high in calories
    B. eat only three times a day
    C. drink lots of water at every meal
    D. ignore the MyPyramid reccomendations; they can eat anything
11. Name two benefits of exercise.
12. Inadequate sleep will _____.
    A. make you feel drowsy and irritable
    B. make your eyes look red and puffy
    C. make it difficult for you to stay awake during class
    D. All of the above.

To Do

1. Design a bulletin board titled "Good Looks Begin with Good Health." Write tips on cards and place alongside related illustrations.

2. Find male and female resource persons who will speak on the importance of good grooming to get and keep a job.

3. Make a daily and weekly schedule of good grooming activities.

4. Do the simple test described in this chapter to determine your skin type. Then write a paragraph describing how you should care for your particular skin type.

5. Ask a dermatologist to speak to the class about acne—its causes and treatments.

6. Draw a sketch of a cross section of skin. Label each part. Explain how acne develops.

7. Write phrases that are related to good grooming and good health practices. Begin each with a different letter of the alphabet. Examples: Avoid the sun's rays between the hours of 10:00 a.m. and 3:00 p.m. Brush your teeth twice daily. Give your list to your teacher. A master list can be made for the school paper.

8. Invite a dentist or dental hygienist to visit the class to discuss the importance of proper care for your teeth.

9. Divide into small groups. Select one of the food groups from MyPyramid and write a TV commercial to sell the food group to the public. Use creative ways, such as good snack ideas, to make the food group more appealing. Present your commercial to the class.

10. Log on to MyPyramid.gov and enter your personal data to create your own food intake pattern. Print a copy of your food intake pattern and make adjustments in your diet to follow the recommendations.

To Think About

1. Explain the following statement: Your looks affect and reflect everything about you, including your mood, self-esteem, schoolwork, and friends. Do you agree with this statement?

2. Would you cancel a big date or stay home from an important event if you had a severe breakout of acne? Why or why not?

3. Many people like the look of sun-tanned skin. Now that more is known about the health risks of exposure to UV rays, what can be done to change this unhealthy ideal?

4. Many teens do not exercise as much as they should. Why is this, and what can be done about it?

5. How do your family and friends influence your eating habits?

13

Taking Care of Your Appearance

Objectives

After studying this chapter, you will be able to

- explain the proper procedure to follow for shaving.
- describe various eye problems and types of corrective lenses.
- list the steps in a manicure and a pedicure.
- identify foot problems and their solutions.
- explain the steps to follow in caring for your particular type of hair.
- identify hair problems and solutions for them.

Key Terms

nearsighted
farsighted
contact lenses
cuticle
manicure
emery board
hangnails
pedicure
podiatrist

Your eyes, hands, and feet are the only ones you will ever have. They deserve some special care. Do you need corrective lenses? Which kind would you prefer? How do you give yourself a manicure or a pedicure? Can you recognize foot problems? Do you know how to cure them? This chapter will help you answer these questions.

You will also learn the proper way to shave and the best care for your hair. Each is an aspect of your overall appearance. You want to appear as pleasant and attractive as possible so other people enjoy being in your company. Whether you are with family members, classmates, or coworkers, they will appreciate a clean and well-groomed appearance. It's unpleasant being around someone with dirty hands, fingernails, or hair.

Shaving

Shaving improves both your appearance and cleanliness. Young men's facial hair begins to darken and become coarse as they enter their teens. This happens at different ages. When it does, they should begin to shave. Girls may want to begin shaving their legs and armpits during their teen years.

When shaving, you need to take care not to harm your skin. Skin is sensitive, especially if it is blemished or dry. Before you begin shaving, wash the area to remove natural oils and perspiration. It's a good idea to shower or bathe before you shave. Then soften the hair by applying a gel, cream, or lather. These preparations have lubricants and other ingredients that soothe and protect the skin while shaving and keep the hair moist. Wait for two minutes before shaving to allow the water to fully soften the hair.

Begin with a sharp blade. A dull blade is your skin's worst enemy. Dull blades cause cuts and irritation and prevent a close shave. As you shave, use short, careful strokes, 13-1. Shave in the direction that feels most comfortable. This may be in the same direction as your hair grows. Shaving against the growth lifts the hair and small sections of skin. The result may be ingrown hair and razor rash.

When you have finished shaving, rinse carefully to remove all traces of shaving cream and hair. Then apply an after-shave lotion or a skin balm to soothe the freshly shaved skin.

Before shaving armpits and legs, girls should moisten their skin with shaving cream or water.

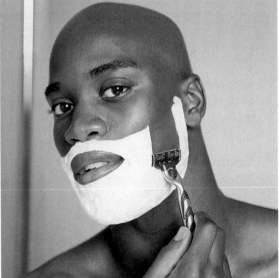

Gillette

13-1

Use plenty of shaving cream and a sharp blade to get a smooth shave.

Take short strokes, using razors with sharp blades. Apply a moisturizing cream or lotion after shaving to leave your skin soft and smooth.

Both men and women can use electric shavers. They may be better for sensitive skin. They are initially more expensive than razors. There are many models available. Some will trim sideburns neatly. Others, made for women, can be adjusted to shave both armpits and legs. You may want to apply a preshave lotion to prepare your skin before shaving. When you finish, wash with warm water. Then apply an after-shave lotion or cream.

The Eyes Have It

About one-third of all teenagers in America today wear some form of corrective lenses. (Eyeglasses and contact lenses are corrective lenses.) When you are told you need them, many questions pop into your mind. Why do I need them? How will I look with glasses—better or worse? Should I ask for contact lenses? Are soft contact lenses better for me?

Who Needs Corrective Lenses?

There is no such thing as perfect eyesight. Even people with 20/20 vision do not see perfectly. If you have 20/20 vision, you can see at 20 feet what a person with average vision sees at the same distance. If you can see at 20 feet what the average person can see at 40, 60, or 80 feet, your vision is 20/40, 20/60, or 20/80. In these cases, you may need corrective lenses.

Corrective lenses cannot cure poor eyesight, but they do help you see well. People who can help you with eye care have three different titles. See 13-2 to see who does what.

When you have trouble seeing clearly, you make your eyes try harder. This injures your eyes, and you develop eyestrain. Your eyes may be tired. They may burn, itch, ache, and look red. Your eyelids may feel puffy or grainy on the inside.

There are often other problems when you make your eyes work too hard. Repeated headaches, having a hard time keeping your mind on your work, tension, or nervousness may result. If these symptoms sound familiar, you probably need glasses.

KNOW YOUR EYE CARE **SPECIALISTS**

Opticians grind lenses according to the prescription given to them. After you select the frames, they put the lenses in them and fit the glasses to you.

Optometrists examine your eyes for vision problems. This includes a testing session. They can prescribe eyeglasses or contact lenses. If you have an eye disease, they can spot it but cannot treat it.

Ophthalmologists (sometimes called oculists) are physicians. They specialize in eye care. All defects, disorders, and diseases come under their care. They can also perform eye surgery.

13-2

Who's who in eye care.

If you are **nearsighted,** you can see things that are near you, but you cannot see things clearly from a distance. Does the writing on the chalkboard look blurred when you sit in the back of the classroom? Do you find yourself straining, squinting, and frowning in order to see? If so, you should have your eyes checked. You are probably nearsighted.

The opposite problem is being farsighted. If you are **farsighted,** you can see things that are far away from you. You have trouble seeing at close range. Reading is more difficult for you. As people grow older, they often become more farsighted.

nearsighted
Able to see things that are near more clearly than things far away.

farsighted
Able to see things that are far away more clearly than things that are near.

Eyeglasses

Many teenagers wear eyeglasses. Choosing the type and style of frame for both function and fashion is a big decision. Eyeglass frames are more durable now and are often made of such materials as titanium. Lenses are thinner, lighter, stronger, and more impact-resistant. Lens options include antireflective coating, light-changing tints, and line-free bifocals.

The frame has to fit well, or it will bother you. If the sidepieces or bows are too short or too long, opticians can adjust them. If your glasses slide down your nose, the bows may be too long. Sometimes the shape of a nose makes it impossible to wear certain styles comfortably. Be sure the frames you choose will fit your facial features.

Contact Lenses

The most common reason for buying contact lenses is to improve appearance. **Contact lenses** are vision correction devices that are worn directly on the eye. Some people get contact lenses for convenience. There are many times when glasses are a bother. Walking in a rainstorm, looking in a microscope, and playing football are only a few of them. They can also fog up or break.

contact lenses
Vision correction devices worn directly on the eyes.

Contact lenses can be rigid or soft. Some need to be removed daily while others can be worn for extended periods of time. These lenses can be worn for several days up to a week. Your doctor will be able to recommend the type of contact lenses that is right for you.

All contacts are made of thin porous plastic. They are shaped to fit over the surface of the eyeball. The surface of the eyeball has no blood supply to furnish oxygen. It depends on exposure to oxygen in the air to keep the eye healthy.

The first contact lenses were called hard contact lenses. They were made of an inflexible plastic material. Hard lenses provided excellent vision, but kept oxygen from reaching the cornea. (The *cornea* is the clear front eye tissue that covers the iris and pupil and admits light.) Hard lenses have become obsolete.

In 1979, *rigid gas permeable (RGP)* lenses were introduced. These lenses are made of a breathable plastic that is custom fit to the shape of the cornea. This type of plastic allows some oxygen to pass through to the surface of the eyeball. This lets the eyes "breathe" and stay healthy. The shape of the discs is very important. The curve on the inside fits the surface of the eyeball. The outside is shaped to correct and improve vision.

Soft contact lenses are clear flexible discs made of a gel-like plastic that contains varying amounts of water, 13-3. They are soft and flexible when they are either in your eyes or stored in a saline (salty) solution. When they become dry, they are hard and brittle. Soft lenses, introduced in 1971, mold themselves to the shape of the eyeball. Therefore, no dust particles can get between the lens and the eye. This prevents scratches to the eye.

It is sometimes difficult to adjust to RGP lenses. Some people try and give up. At first, a schedule of wearing them for short periods of time is followed. People may blink too often, tilt their head, and have tears. After two to four weeks, most people are comfortable with the lenses.

Adjusting to soft contact lenses is easier than adjusting to RGP lenses. In some places, you can get soft lenses in one visit to the optometrist. Your examination and fitting are done the same day. A checkup in a week or so is important.

Soft contact lenses need more care than hard ones and must be replaced often. Many people find caring for them too much trouble. They have to be cleaned every night. If they become dry, they will be damaged or split, and will have to be replaced. Disposable contact lenses are available. These contact lenses are worn for brief periods, from one day to two weeks. They are then discarded and replaced with new ones.

Contact lenses are safe if you follow your doctor's instructions carefully. Your hands should be clean when you insert or remove them from your eyes. If you drop a lens, moisten your fingertip and gently touch the lens surface. Never use saliva to wet your lenses. It may irritate your eyes or blur your vision. Instead, use the wetting and soaking solutions recommended by your doctor.

Bausch & Lomb

13-3
Soft contact lenses are made from a water-absorbing plastic material. They adjust to fit your eye.

Sunglasses

Ultraviolet rays of the sun can damage your eyes. To prevent damage to your eyes, be sure to wear sunglasses whenever you are out in the sun, 13-4. When skiing, sun-goggles or sunglasses are a must. The snow reflects the ultraviolet rays back up into your eyes and could cause severe damage. Sunglasses should be dark enough so that you cannot see your eyes through them when you look in a mirror.

Your Hands Tell On You

People do notice your hands—more than you may think. They play an important part in how you express yourself, so they deserve some attention.

To have well-groomed hands, you must keep them clean. Hands must be washed many times daily. It is surprising how often they get dirty. The palms of hands contain many sweat glands. As hands perspire, they collect dirt and stains. Hands can also collect bacteria. The only solution is to wash them frequently throughout the day.

There are few oil glands on the backs of hands. That is why dryness, chapping, and roughness are common problems. Hand lotions help to prevent these problems. You may use lotion whenever your hands are dry, especially after washing them. When you are outside in very cold weather, wear gloves to protect your hands.

13-4

Take care of your eyes by protecting them from the sun's rays.

Fingernails

From time to time, most nails get a few ridges, ruts, or bumps. Some you can control, others you cannot. Horizontal ridges across the nail are usually caused by rough treatment around the **cuticle** or base of the nail. White spots are caused by air pockets forming in the nail as it grows. They are harmless, and you cannot do much to stop them.

cuticle
The skin at the base of the nail.

The growing part of your nail is close to your first knuckle. As it grows, it forces the rest of the nail into sight. Nails grow only about a quarter inch a month.

Manicures

Well-kept fingernails are a part of good grooming. A weekly manicure will help keep them in top shape. A **manicure** is a treatment for the care of hands and fingernails. It is not limited to girls. A manicure is important for everyone.

manicure
A treatment for the care of hands and fingernails.

Giving yourself a manicure is easy. It takes only a few minutes and can make a big difference in your appearance. Just follow these steps.

1. Gently clean under the nails. Do not use a file that has a sharp point. You may tear the skin and leave the area open to infection.

2. Smooth edges and shape nails with an emery board. **Emery boards** are pieces of thin cardboard covered with a grainy paper. Move it in one

emery board
Pieces of thin cardboard covered with a grainy paper used to smooth edges and shape nails.

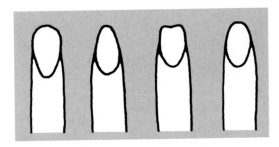

13-5
Balloon-shaped nails make fingers look
stumpy. Pointed nails have no support from
the sides and break easily. Nails without any
shape give hands a sloppy look. An oval shape
is best. It is graceful, but sturdy.

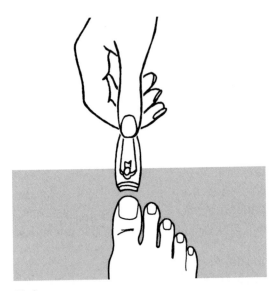

13-6
To avoid ingrown toenails, trim toenails
straight across.

hangnails
The tiny, loose
pieces of skin along
the side of nails.

pedicure
A treatment for the
care of feet and
toenails.

direction only. Sawing back and forth will damage nails. Try to achieve an oval shape as
shown in 13-5.

3. Scrub nails in warm, soapy water with a small
    nail brush. Gently push back cuticles with a cuti-
    cle stick or a terrycloth towel.

4. Clip away **hangnails** (the tiny, loose pieces of
    skin along the side of nails).

5. Rub on hand lotion. Reapply after hand washing
    to keep cuticles soft.

Appreciate Your Feet

Each of your feet contains 26 bones, 27 liga-
ments, and 19 muscles. All must be finely balanced
to carry your weight through the 65,000 miles you
will walk during your life. With all this walking, it's
important to take care of your feet.

Pedicures

Your feet should receive daily care. Scrub them
well each time you take a bath or shower. Dryness is
a problem because feet have very few oil glands.
After your bath, dry them well. You may want to rub
on an oil or lotion.

Pedicures are treatments for the care of feet,
just as manicures are for hands. When you have
time, give yourself a pedicure. Follow these steps:

1. Soak feet in warm, soapy water.

2. Scrub toenails and heels with a small, stiff brush.

3. Dry thoroughly, especially between toes.

4. Gently push back cuticles.

5. Trim toenails straight across, 13-6. Leave them
    slightly longer than the tip of the toe.

6. Smooth edges with an emery board.

7. Massage (rub with fingers) the feet. It relaxes
    the muscles, improves blood circulation, and
    keeps the feet smooth. Lotion or oil will make
    the job easier.

Shoes

Doctors say that many adult foot problems begin during childhood. Young feet grow fast and often change shoe sizes during each year. Shoes may be outgrown before they are worn out. If new shoes are not purchased, feet will be pinched, and toes will be cramped. As a result, feet may be permanently misshapen.

Continuous pressure from shoes can cause pain as well as damage. If your shoes are hurting your feet, have your feet measured the next time you buy shoes. Always stand in order to get your correct foot measurement.

There are special shoes for almost every activity. Tennis, golf, dancing, and football all require a different type of shoe. When you buy shoes, keep in mind the job you want them to do. If you need shoes for school, look for shoes that offer comfort. If you are going hiking or mountain climbing, you should have a pair of shoes that will protect and support your feet. See 13-7.

podiatrist
Physician who specializes in foot problems.

Foot Problems and Solutions

Since people spend so much time on their feet, many types of foot problems can occur. Many problems can be treated with home remedies or products available at your local pharmacy. A foot doctor should treat serious foot problems. He or she is called a **podiatrist.**

A *corn* is a painful, cone-shaped overgrowth of skin. It usually occurs on toe joints or between toes. Some corns are painful even when nothing touches them. Others may hurt only when pressure is applied. Corns between the toes are called "soft corns." Foot moisture makes them rubbery instead of hard.

Why do people have corns? When shoes put pressure on a certain spot, protective tissue builds up. When the tissue gets high enough, it puts pressure on the nerve below and causes pain. If you know which pair of shoes caused the corn, discard them. The corn will soon go away.

13-7
If you enjoy hiking, you may want to buy shoes like these. They are designed to protect and support your feet.

Trends Making News

Backpacks— A Real Pain in the Back

Backpacks came on the school scene because they were a great way to tote home stacks of books. Unfortunately, books are getting heavier and homework demands require students to carry them back and forth to school almost daily. It is not unusual for some preteens to carry packs that weigh as much as 50 percent of their body weight. This kind of weight can cause muscle strain, neck and shoulder pain, low back pain, or acquired scoliosis (curvature of the spine).

Most backpacks weren't designed for carrying the amount of weight placed in them. There's a disconnection between the weight the bags are carrying and the design of the pack.

To avoid back pain, check the weight of your backpack by placing it on a bathroom scale. It should weigh less than 10 percent of your body weight. Also check to see if the backpack has an internal frame to help distribute the weight. The shoulder straps should be tight enough so the pack touches your back. Don't wear the pack over one shoulder. This shifts all the weight to one side, which causes pain and muscle spasms. Better still, try one of the new wheeled backpacks, which look like small carry-on luggage, and avoid the pain altogether.

Some schools are finding other ways to address the problem. For example, a set of textbooks is kept in each classroom for in-class use only. Each student also has a text at home to use for homework assignments. In this way, books do not have to be carried back and forth. It saves wear and tear on the books so they last longer, and students have fewer back problems. This has also been a solution for those schools that are doing away with lockers for security reasons.

A *callus* is similar to a corn but larger. It is usually on the side or bottom of the foot. Soaking in hot, soapy water will soften the area. A brush or rough pad can be used to help remove the excess, hardened skin. You may need several treatments before it is gone.

A *bunion* results when the big toe folds under the second one. This can be hereditary, but poorly fitted shoes and tight stockings can make it worse. Here again, your feet respond by building up a pad or protective tissue. If it is painful, a doctor should see it.

Ingrown toenails bother many people. They can be very painful. The most common cause of this problem is trimming the big toenail incorrectly. Other causes could be shoes or socks that are too small. When the toenail has been trimmed in a wedge shape, soft tissue grows over it at the corners. Pressure from shoes and stockings cause the pain that results. Trimming or filing the nail straight across will prevent the ingrown problem from occurring. Toenails should extend a little beyond the flesh, just like fingernails, but the corners should be seen.

Foot odor is a problem for many people. One reason is that air cannot circulate in shoes, especially those made of manufactured materials. When feet perspire, air and moisture are trapped, causing the odor. A medicated, deodorant foot powder put in shoes after each wearing will help the odor problems. If you wipe the insides of shoes with a soapy cloth before treating them, the results are even better. Shoes and socks should be changed daily. If possible, do not wear the same shoes every day. A day off will give them time to dry and air out. Also, keep feet clean.

Athlete's foot is a fungus that grows on moist skin. If there is a break or crack in the skin, the fungus attacks quickly. It is very contagious. You can even get athlete's foot by walking barefoot in public places. To keep athlete's foot under control, your feet should be kept as dry as possible. When you dry after each shower, give special attention to the areas between your toes. Once the infection starts, it is difficult to stop. The skin peels and itches. It can spread over and under the toes and cause foot odor. Medication is needed to destroy the fungus.

Heads up for Good-Looking Hair

In an effort to look good, teenagers spend more time on their hair than any other area of grooming, 13-8. They comb it, shampoo it, and style it to keep it looking clean and attractive.

13-8
Teenagers often spend extra time making sure their hair looks good.

Clean, shiny hair that is styled right for you will help you look great, 13-9. Some styles help to cover up less-than-attractive features. Hair can hide ears that stick out or a forehead that is too wide. Hair can also frame a pretty face or show off lovely eyes. Where else can you find such a built-in asset? You can make your hair work for you.

Hair Facts

Hair is composed of proteins. Its condition and color are determined before it reaches the surface of your scalp. Your general health and the food you eat affect the growth of your hair. Eating the right foods will keep your hair in good condition. The amount of proteins, vitamins, and minerals you eat may be less than you need. If so, your hair may be dull, dry, and hard to manage.

Hair has two parts—the shaft and the root. The *shaft* is the part you see. It is dead tissue. It does not have a blood supply or nerve endings. The shaft is made up of three layers as seen in 13-10.

- The *cuticle,* or outer layer, protects the hair. Its overlapping cells look like shingles on a roof.

- The *cortex,* or middle layer, is made of long, thin cells. It contains the pigment that gives color to hair. Dark hair has more pigment in the cortex than blond hair.

- The *medulla,* or center core, is an empty space. Some hair does not have a medulla.

The *root* is the living part of the hair. It is below the scalp surface. Here the hair receives its nourishment for growth from the blood. There is an oil sac close by that lubricates the hair and protects it. The amount of oil given off is affected by age, diet, medications, blood circulation, and emotions.

Hair grows about one-half inch per month or six to seven inches each year. Trimming the hair does not make it grow faster. A hair stays on the head from two to six years. It is then pushed out and replaced by a new one. A loss of 40 to 60 hairs a day is normal. The average head has from 90,000 to 140,000 hairs. Some myths and facts about hair are given in 13-11.

13-9
You look great with clean, shiny hair in a style that is right for you.

Analyzing Your Hair Type

Before you can choose the best treatment and style for your hair, you should know some facts about the hair you have. What is the texture? Is it fine or coarse? Is it thick or thin? Is it curly or straight?

Pull one hair from your head. Look at it. Is it rough and thick or silky and thin? Fine hair is narrow and will break easily. It is usually limp and without much body. A strand of coarse hair is large and wide. It is often strong when it is in good condition. If it is wiry, it may be hard to manage.

Take a look at your whole head of hair. How much do you have? Persons with thin hair have fewer strands of hair than people with thick hair. The terms thin and thick refer to the whole head of hair, just as the terms fine and coarse refer to each strand. You may have thin, coarse hair; thin, fine hair; thick, fine hair; or thick, coarse hair.

To see if your hair is thick or thin, lift it up and look at the roots in a mirror. Can you easily see your scalp? If so, you probably have thin hair. Short to medium length hairstyles are usually better for thin hair. They make the hair seem thicker. The weight of long hair pulls the hair down, making it seem even thinner.

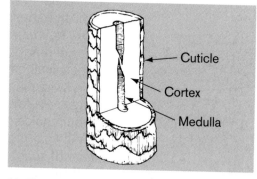

Cuticle

Cortex

Medulla

13-10
The hair shaft consists of the cuticle, which protects the hair. The cortex contains the color pigment, and the medulla is empty space.

MYTHS AND FACTS ABOUT **HAIR**

Myth:	Fact:
The more you cut your hair, the faster it will grow.	Cutting does not affect the growth cycle of hair.
If you shampoo every day, your hair will become oilier.	It is just the reverse. Oily hair often has to be washed every day.
Permanent waving will cause dandruff.	Dandruff is a scalp condition and has nothing to do with the chemicals in permanent waves.
When hair reaches a certain length, it will stop growing.	Hair growth is ongoing. You do not notice the growth of long hair as much as you do short hair.
If you have your hair cut when you are sick, it will not look as good as when you are well.	Illness can dull the hair, but a good haircut always looks good.
If you pull out one gray hair, five more will grow in its place.	Only one hair at a time grows from a single follicle.
Hair grows from the ends.	Growth starts from the roots, which are under the scalp.

13-11
Knowing about hair can help you separate myths from facts.

Hair Care

Your hair enhances your appearance only when it is clean, shiny, and lively, 13-12. A few minutes of skillful, daily care will keep it that way.

Shampooing

Many teenagers have oily hair. The amount of oil coming from the scalp is different for each person. There is no way to stop it despite all the claims of products on the market. Some hair becomes oily after only one day. Oily hair collects dirt quickly and looks lifeless and stringy. Hard brushing will make hair oilier, so shampooing daily may be the only solution.

Dry hair can feel like straw. If not conditioned, it becomes dull and lifeless. It breaks, splits easily, and has lots of static electricity when it is brushed. Hair can become dry from exposure to too much sun or chlorine in swimming pools. Using high temperatures when drying hair can also cause it to become dry.

Your choice of shampoos depends on your hair and the hardness of water in your area. Most shampoos are made with synthetic detergents instead of soap. This helps shampoos clean hair better, especially in hard water.

Synthetic detergents remove dirt well, but they can harm hair. To prevent this, conditioners are added. *Conditioners* are products that help improve the condition or quality of your hair. The goal is to get a shampoo that will clean well and still be mild. Shampoos for oily and dry hair differ in the amount and strength of synthetic detergents and conditioners. Read the labels of shampoos to find the best one for you, 13-13.

Rinsing

Rinsing is as important as shampooing. Rinse several times with warm water. Any shampoo left in the hair will leave a dulling film on the hair or cause the scalp to flake and itch.

You may want to use a creme rinse or conditioner. Your hair will be softer, more manageable, and tangles will comb out easily. These products also stop static electricity so flyaway hair will be easier to control.

Always use clean combs, brushes, and towels when caring for your hair. You do not want to add dirt after you have worked to remove it. See 13-14 for a review of hair-washing steps.

13-12
Beautiful hair is clean, healthy, and well styled. This young woman's hair enhances her beauty.

Hair Tips for African-American Teens

For African-American teens, there are special ways to care for and style hair. There are two hair characteristics to consider. The first is the wave pattern. Many African-Americans have very curly hair. Unless this type of hair has a fine texture, the extra curl gives it enough body to stand up well. The second characteristic is its texture. The hair is more porous. It absorbs moisture more readily.

Shampooing

Oil-based shampoos add shine and make hair easier to control. When using them, begin by massaging the scalp with the fingertips. Do not use a circular motion. Slide the fingers through the hair as though you were combing it. This prevents tangles and makes hair easier to comb. There is also less hair breakage.

A conditioner should be used after each shampoo. Select a light one rather than one that is thick and heavy. Conditioners give the hair strength and shine. They also make the hair easier to manage.

Hair that is naturally very curly is often dry and weak. It can be difficult to control. Use a comb with wide teeth to untangle hair. A brush

13-13
If you swim frequently in chlorinated pools, you may need to choose a shampoo with a conditioner.

TEN STEPS TO CLEANER HAIR

1. Wet hair with lukewarm water.
2. Apply shampoo and rub to a rich lather.
3. Massage scalp gently but firmly using fingertips—not fingernails. (Nails can scratch scalp or snag and tear hair shafts.)
4. Gently work shampoo through the rest of the hair for a few minutes. Lots of lather helps spread the cleaning agent through the hair.
5. Rinse thoroughly with warm water until hair is completely free of shampoo. This is the most important step for shiny hair.
6. If hair tangles easily, use a conditioner. Work through wet hair to the ends. Rinse well.
7. Gently squeeze hair to remove excess water.
8. Use a towel to blot and partially dry hair.
9. Comb with a wide tooth comb to remove tangles.
10. Wash hair as often as needed. This may be once a day or at least two or three times a week.

13-14
To have good-looking hair, it's a good idea to establish a hair-washing routine such as this one.

13-15
Hair that is conditioned and neatly styled will enhance your appearance.

13-16
A close cut natural hairstyle is good looking and easy to wash and style.

can be used to lift hair from the scalp when styling. Setting hair at night will make it easier to comb in the morning, 13-15.

Styling

There are many different hairstyles. The *fade* is a popular style for African-American men. It is trimmed very short on the sides and fuller on the top. The close cut hairstyle pictured in 13-16 is great for active people because it is easy to wash and style. The style you choose should be one that you like and that looks good on you.

Braids are popular and fun to wear. They are made by separating a square of hair at the center front of the head. The hair is braided tightly toward the face. Then braids are made down the front of each side of the face. The hair behind each braid is combed forward to hide the part where the braids begin.

If the hair is straightened, permanents are often given for soft curls and better control. The hair can be set on hot rollers, or it can be blow-dried and then styled with a curling iron.

Hair Problems

Two hair problems may give you some concern. Dandruff is quite common, but head lice occur less often. Both can be treated.

Dandruff is flaking of the scalp. The cause of dandruff is unknown. People with all types of hair can have dandruff. If you have a dandruff problem, it will be especially noticeable on the shoulder area when dark clothing is worn. Special dandruff-control shampoos are available. Follow the directions carefully. Be sure to rinse your hair well after washing.

Head lice are tiny insects that can become a problem on the scalp. Lice are difficult to see. You can detect them by their eggs, which are called *nits.* Lice attach the small, white nits to strands of hair near the scalp. They cannot cause serious illness, but they do cause severe itching.

Although head lice cannot jump or fly, they are usually transmitted on items such as combs and hats. This is why you should avoid sharing combs, brushes, hats, and other items that touch your hair. Unclean hair is not a factor in getting lice. Lice can live in even the cleanest of hair.

Head lice cannot be shampooed out of the hair. Special medications to treat lice are available at drug stores.

CHAPTER REVIEW

Key Points

- Shaving improves both appearance and cleanliness. Because the skin can be sensitive, hair should be softened with water and shaving cream first. Sharp blades should be used with short, careful strokes.

- Corrective lenses, including eyeglasses and contact lenses, are used to correct the vision of those who are nearsighted or farsighted. Contact lenses, which are made of thin porous plastic, can be either hard or soft.

- To have well-groomed hands, you must keep them clean. Wash them frequently throughout each day. A manicure will keep fingernails looking their best.

- Caring for your feet includes regular pedicures, wearing shoes that fit properly, and recognizing and treating foot problems when they occur.

- Knowing your hair type (thin, thick, coarse, fine, oily, dry) will help you select the best style and the most suitable shampoo and conditioner.

To Review

1. Shave in the _____ direction as your hair grows.
2. (True or False) Eyeglasses can cure poor eyesight.
3. Name the eye care specialist who can care for all defects, disorders, and diseases of the eye.
4. People who are _____ can clearly see things that are far away.
5. Why do hands become dry and chapped so easily?
6. What is the best shape for fingernails? for toenails?
7. A corn is _____.
    A. a painful, cone-shaped overgrowth of skin
    B. usually on the side or bottom of the foot
    C. the result of the big toe folding under the second one
    D. caused by trimming the big toenail incorrectly
8. Anyone can get athlete's foot. What can you do to prevent it?
9. Name and describe the three parts of the hair shaft.
10. The hair root is nourished by _____.
11. Why is thorough rinsing of the hair as important as shampooing?
12. List two hair problems and describe how to solve them.

To Do

1. Ask an optician, optometrist, or ophthalmologist to speak to your class. Learn about corrective lenses—the history, latest developments, and future expectations.

2. If someone in class is wearing contact lenses, have them relate their experiences with adjustments, limitations, and care.

3. Research and compare the advantages and disadvantages of the various types of hard and soft contact lenses.

4. Plan a "stop biting your fingernails contest." Check weekly to determine progress. Decide on appropriate rewards and penalties.

5. Plan for a cosmetologist to visit your class for a manicure or pedicure demonstration.

6. Have a hair stylist visit your class to discuss hair care procedures for various hair types.

7. Ask an African-American student to demonstrate braiding hair.

8. Research popular hairstyles of the past. Report to class with sketches or pictures.

9. Arrange a display of hair care products. Have several examples of each product. Compare prices and information on labels. Discuss reasons for differences. Decide which products are suited to each hair type.

10. Collect magazine and newspaper advertisements for hair care products. Compare statements made about the products. Do they seem to be factual or an effort to get people to buy the products?

To Think About

1. Some employers prefer their male employees be clean-shaven with short hair. Do you think employers have the right to make this request? Should the place of employment make a difference? Would it matter to you?

2. Some people choose to wear contact lenses instead of eyeglasses because they do not like the appearance of glasses. Which would you choose? Why?

3. Are there places of work where the cleanliness of employees' hands and fingernails are more important than others? Give some examples.

4. First impressions count a lot when interviewing for a job. Should a person's grooming and appearance count that much? Why or why not?

5. If a friend of yours was not as well groomed as he or she could be, and it was causing people to talk, how could you tactfully help your friend?

4

Fabrics and Their Care

Chapters

259

CHAPTER 14

From Fiber to Yarn

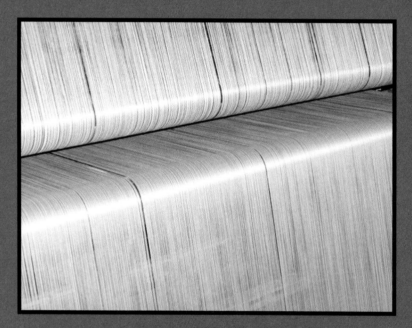

Key Terms

yarn
fabrics
cellulosic fibers
protein fibers
cotton
carding
drawing
combing
linen
ramie
jute
wool
woolen yarns
worsted yarns
Wool Products Labeling Act
virgin wool
recycled wool
silk
spinneret
filament
staple fibers
texturing

Objectives

After studying this chapter, you will be able to

- list fiber characteristics that affect appearance and performance of fabrics.
- explain the sources, production steps, and characteristics of the natural fibers.
- outline the processes involved in the production of manufactured fibers.
- list the characteristics and end uses of manufactured fibers.

Fibers are the basic units of all textiles. When fibers are put together to form a continuous strand, a **yarn** is made. Yarns are woven or knitted together to make **fabrics.**

Look at 14-1 to see the relationship among fibers, yarns, and fabrics. You can see the same thing by pulling a "thread" from any scrap of fabric. This is a yarn. Untwist the yarn to find the tiny, individual fibers.

There are two main groups of fibers. Natural fibers are made from natural sources—plants and animals. Common natural fibers are cotton and wool. The other group of fibers is manufactured from chemicals in factories. These are called manufactured fibers. Common manufactured fibers are nylon and polyester.

yarn
A continuous strand made of fibers.

fabric
Textile product usually made by knitting or weaving yarns together.

Fiber Characteristics

Each fiber has its own characteristics and properties, depending on its source or chemical composition. The fiber may also be short, long, straight, or curly. These fiber characteristics greatly affect the appearance and performance of the fabrics they become.

Knowledge of fiber characteristics will help you select the fiber most appropriate for its end use. The characteristics you would look for in a fiber to be used for sportswear will be different from one you would select for eveningwear. Fibers chosen for carpets or bed linens will require different characteristics than those chosen for bath towels.

As you read about the various fibers in this chapter, you will learn about their characteristics. These include the following:

- strength—the ability to withstand pulling and twisting

- shrinkage—the ability to maintain size

- warmth—the ability to maintain body temperature

- durability—the ability to hold up to repeated usage

- absorbency—the ability to take in moisture

- wrinkle resistance—the ability to resist creasing

- resiliency—the ability to spring back when crushed or wrinkled

Keep these characteristics in mind as you select the best fiber for your particular apparel and household needs.

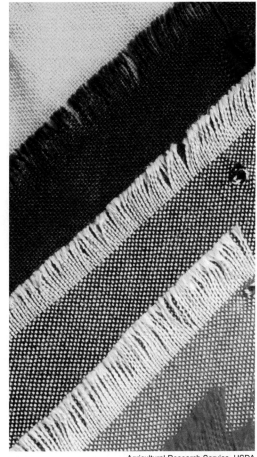

Agricultural Research Service, USDA

14-1 Fibers are combined to make yarns, and yarns are combined to make fabrics.

Natural Fibers

Cotton, linen, wool, and silk are the most common natural fibers. Natural fibers vary in quality depending on the kind of animal or plant and the growing conditions. They must be cleaned before they can be made into yarns. Supplies of natural fibers vary, according to the season. They each have unique characteristics that cannot be copied by science. Therefore, natural fibers are still an important part of today's textile story.

There are two categories of natural fibers as shown in 14-2. **Cellulosic fibers** come from vegetable (plant) sources. There are many kinds of cellulosic fibers, but few of them are used in clothing. Cotton, flax, and ramie are the main cellulosic fibers used for apparel.

cellulosic fibers
Fibers made from vegetable (plant) sources.

The other category of natural fibers is the protein fibers. **Protein fibers** come from animal sources. Wool and silk are the main protein fibers. Others are called specialty hair fibers. These include mohair and cashmere fibers from the goat family; camel, llama, alpaca, vicuña, and guanaco hairs of the camel family; and angora hair from the rabbit family. Supplies of the specialty hair fibers are smaller than wool supplies, so they are more expensive.

protein fibers
Natural fibers made from animal sources.

Cotton

cotton
A natural cellulosic fiber obtained from the cotton plant.

Cotton is the natural fiber made from the cotton plant. Throughout history, cotton has played a major role in everyday life. It was and still is the most widely used natural fiber. Cotton has many features that make it great for clothing, 14-3. It is inexpensive and can be used in many ways. Cotton is strong and launders well, though it may shrink unless given a special treatment. It is soft and absorbent, making it a good choice for towels, diapers, and underwear. It keeps the body cool in warm weather, so it is a popular choice for summer clothes. Two disadvantages of cotton are that it wrinkles easily unless given a special finish, and it mildews if stored when damp.

The cotton plant can be grown in any part of the world where the growing season lasts six or seven months. The United States leads in cotton production, followed by India and China.

Cotton comes from the seedpods of the cotton plant. After the blooms fall from the plant, the seedpod or *boll* grows. Snow-white fibers form from the seeds inside. When it is ripe, the boll bursts open. Many bolls are on one stalk or plant, 14-4.

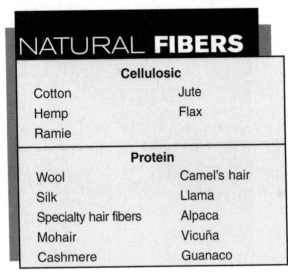

NATURAL **FIBERS**

Cellulosic	
Cotton	Jute
Hemp	Flax
Ramie	

Protein	
Wool	Camel's hair
Silk	Llama
Specialty hair fibers	Alpaca
Mohair	Vicuña
Cashmere	Guanaco

14-2
Of all the natural fibers, cotton, linen, wool, and silk are used most often in clothes.

14-3

Cotton helps to keep you cool on warm, sunny days.

14-4

When the cotton ball is ripe, it bursts open and is ready to harvest.

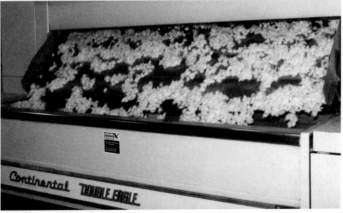

14-5

At the cotton gin, revolving circular saws separate the seeds from the cotton.

After picking, cotton is taken to a *gin.* This machine separates the fibers from the seed, 14-5. The cotton is compressed into 500-pound bales.

Once cotton reaches the mill, it goes through many cleaning and separating steps. After most of the impurities are removed, the fibers are shaped into a lap. The *lap* is a continuous layer of fibers that is wrapped around and around a cylinder. A carding machine is a spinning cylinder covered with short, wire points. **Carding** pulls the fibers from the lap, cleans them, and straightens them. Then the machine shapes them into a much thinner web of fibers. These fibers go through a funnel-shaped device that molds them into a *carded sliver* (a soft rope-like strand slightly thicker than your finger). See 14-6.

carding
A process that pulls the cotton fibers from the lap, cleans them, and straightens them.

drawing
A process that combines many carded slivers of cotton into a single drawn sliver, which is then stretched.

combing
A process that makes fibers even more parallel and removes any short fibers. This leaves longer fibers that make smoother, stronger yarns called combed sliver.

Drawing is the next step. In **drawing,** many carded slivers are combined into a single drawn sliver. The drawn sliver is "stretched" so it is about the same diameter as one of the carded slivers.

For finer cottons, combing follows drawing. **Combing** is done to make fibers even more parallel and to remove any short fibers. This leaves longer fibers, which make smoother, stronger yarns. The product of combing is *combed sliver.* See 14-7. Drawn (or combed) slivers are fed into a roving frame where the cotton is twisted slightly and pulled to become a smaller strand. This strand is called *roving.* It is about the size of your pencil.

Finally, spinning machines pull the roving finer, add more twist, and wind it on bobbins. The tightly wound yarns are ready to be formed into fabric. See 14-8. Study 14-9 as a review of the process of making cotton yarns.

Cotton has had a great deal of competition from manufactured fibers in recent years. New treatments and finishes have helped cotton regain popularity. In addition, combinations with manufactured fibers have improved garment performance. For instance, some cotton denim used to make jeans is now washed many times in an ammonia solution, making it very soft. Shrinkage of cotton denim has been controlled so the jeans you buy will not shrink as much.

Linen

linen
A cloth made from the cellulosic fiber called flax.

Flax is the fiber used to make **linen.** It was probably the first cellulosic fiber used for making fabric. The Egyptians grew fields of flax along the Nile River 4000 years ago and made it into fine cloth. Pieces of linen

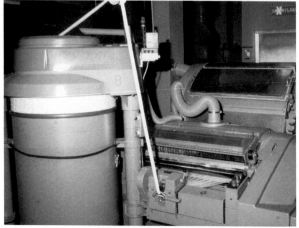
National Cotton Council of America

14-6
Carding machines separate the fibers from the lap and pull them into a thin web. The web is molded into a soft ropelike strand called a carded sliver.

National Cotton Council of America

14-7
The combing machine further straightens the fibers to make smoother, stronger yarns called combed slivers.

have been found in the tombs of the Pharaohs. Egyptian mummies, wrapped in linen, are still seen in museums. Today, Belgium, Ireland, and New Zealand produce most of the linen.

Linen is used for tablecloths, kitchen towels, handkerchiefs, draperies, upholstery, and clothing, 14-10. It is known for its durability and absorbency. Linen is often an expensive fabric. This is because it is imported and making linen from flax takes much time and effort. Some of the work is still done by hand.

The flax plants shown in 14-11 are ready to be harvested. Machines pull flax plants from the ground. They are never cut, as fibers will discolor. Threshing machines remove the seeds, and the flax stalks are allowed to dry in the sun. Then they are tied into bundles and soaked in dew or water for one or two days. This loosens the outside woody stalk from the flax fibers. The bundles are dried again.

When the flax stalks are dry, they are retied and taken to be *scutched*. In this step, rollers crush the stalks. This completes the separation of the soft flax fibers from the harsh straw.

National Cotton Council of America

14-8

In the spinning frame, the roving is pulled and twisted into yarn and wound on bobbins.

Cotton: Fiber to Yarn

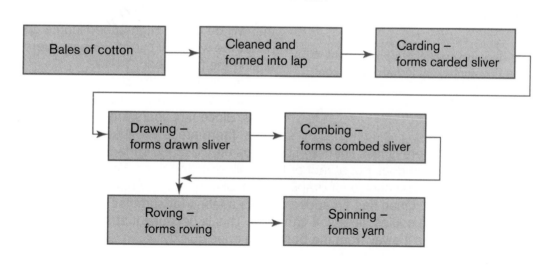

14-9

The steps in cotton production are shown above.

Irish Linen Guild

14-10
Linen is durable and extremely beautiful and has a distinctive texture.

Irish Linen Guild

14-11
Mature flax stalks are about three feet tall. Machines pull them from the ground and lay them in rows.

Irish Linen Guild

14-12
Different finishing treatments can produce the crisp elegance of a fine damask tablecloth or the cool comfort of linen clothes.

Next, the fibers are *hackled* or combed. This process separates the short fibers called "tow" from the long fibers called "line." Then they pass through a drawing machine where they are combined into a continuous wide ribbon called a sliver. The drawing process is repeated until all the fibers are parallel in small, ropelike strands. Finishes can be applied to give linen different properties, 14-12.

Finally, the linen yarns are spun. The method used depends on the kind of fabric that will be made. High-speed looms operate under the watchful eye of linen weavers, producing the final fabric, 14-13.

Flax fibers are the strongest of the natural fibers. They are also smooth, durable, and lustrous. Since flax fibers are longer than cotton ones, there are fewer fiber ends in a yarn. There is less lint from fiber ends on the fabric surface. This means that linen does not attract or hold soil as cotton does. For this reason, linen is a good choice for draperies, upholstery, and clothing.

Linen has an added plus as a fabric for summer clothes since flax is the coolest fiber you can wear. This is because it absorbs body heat, carries it away from the body, and dries quickly.

Linen wrinkles easily. A special finish can solve this problem, but the finish reduces the absorption and coolness of the fabric.

Ramie

Ramie is often called "China grass." It comes from a shrubby plant often grown in China and India. It has rodlike stems and heart-shaped leaves. The fibers are obtained from the stems of the plants, similar to the harvesting of flax for linen.

The ramie fiber is strong, lustrous, absorbs moisture, and dries quickly. In the past, it was mainly used for making ropes, canvas, and fire hoses because of its strength. Today, combined with other natural fibers and manufactured fibers, ramie is gaining popularity for use in clothing. Ramie adds strength to fabrics such as cotton, rayon, and silk, while these fibers give a soft feel to the fabric.

Jute

Jute also comes from a plant. It is a rough, coarse fiber and has a natural odor. The main use of jute is for making burlap bags, but it is also used for decorative household items and accessories. Bulletin boards and lampshades are often covered with burlap fabric.

Jute is not a strong fiber, and the fiber weakens with age. It wrinkles easily and produces lint. Jute takes dyes readily and is quite inexpensive.

Wool

Wool is made from the fleece (hair) of sheep or lambs. It is the most common animal fiber worn today, but its use goes back to early times. Crude wool fabrics have been found in ruins of the Stone Age. Even then, people knew that the fleece of sheep was softer and warmer than the skins of other animals. Sheep were the first animals to be domesticated (raised for their fleece).

Wool is the warmest fiber. It is a natural insulator, so it protects your body from changes in temperature. The fibers trap air, preventing the transfer of heat and cold. The items shown in 14-14 are all wool.

A fabric made of wool is strong and durable, but lightweight. It can absorb moisture without making you feel wet. It is also resilient, recovering its original shape and size after being stretched. The wrinkle-resistance of wool is another desirable characteristic. These factors make it a comfortable fabric for clothes.

The first step to produce wool is to shear the sheep, 14-15. If possible, the fleece is removed in one piece. The quality varies from different places on the sheep. The best comes from the shoulders and sides. The poorest

Irish Linen Guild

14-13

High-speed looms weave the linen yarns into the final fabric.

ramie
A fiber often called "China grass." It comes from a shrubby plant often grown in China and India.

jute
A rough, coarse natural fiber that has a natural odor. It is used for burlap.

wool
A natural protein fiber made from the fleece of sheep or lambs.

American Sheep Industry Association

14-14

Blankets, jackets, and sweaters are often made of wool—the natural insulator.

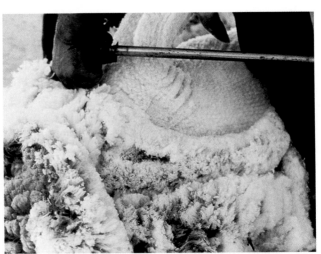

American Sheep Industry Association

14-15

Once a year, fleece is taken from the sheep by an expert shearer using an electric clipper.

woolen yarns

Wool yarns made from short fibers (less than two inches).

worsted yarns

Wool yarns made from combed sliver using longer fibers.

is from the lower legs. Quality also depends on the health of the sheep and the climate.

At the wool mill, many steps are needed to produce yarn. First, the fibers are graded and sorted according to quality. To remove the natural oil, they are *scoured* or washed in detergent or soap. The oil taken out is *lanolin.* It is refined and used in cosmetics, shampoos, and ointments.

Wool is carded to straighten fibers. After carding, the longer fibers are combed. The carded sliver is made into **woolen yarns** that use the short fibers (less than *two* inches). Yarns made from combed sliver (called *top* in the case of wool) are called **worsted yarns.** Worsted yarns are made using longer fibers. See 14-16.

See 14-17 to compare woolen and worsted yarns. The fibers in woolen yarns lie in all directions, giving a twisted, loose look. They have a somewhat fuzzy surface. These yarns are used for making flannels, tweeds, and soft fleece fabrics.

The longer fibers in worsted yarns are tightly twisted. This produces a closely woven, hard-surfaced fabric. Worsted fabrics are lighter in weight and smoother than woolen fabrics. Gabardine, challis, and sharkskin are examples of worsted fabrics.

Wool Labeling

Consumers cannot know how much and what type of wool is in a fabric simply by looking at it. To protect consumers and manufacturers, the

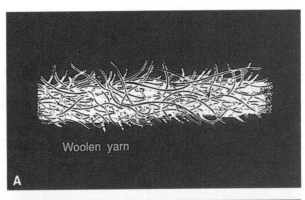

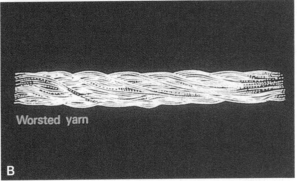

International Wool Secretariat

14-17 --
Woolen yarns are made from carded sliver (A).
Worsted yarns are made from combed sliver called
"top" (B).

American Sheep Industry Association

14-16 --
The scoured wool is being carded to straighten the
fibers (A). Then the longer fibers are combed to
make a combed sliver for worsted yarns (B).

Wool Products Labeling Act was passed in 1939. The law was passed to
overcome confusion and misinformation about the wool used in products.
Any textile product that contains some wool must list the percentage and
type of wool present. The country of origin must also be listed. The term
wool means that the fiber has never been used before for a fabric or garment. Some manufacturers call this **virgin wool.**

Recycled wool is wool fibers from previously made wool fabrics.
Recycled wool can be from two sources. It might be from a product that
was made but never used. This is called *reprocessed wool* and may
come from unused garments or cutting scraps. If made from wool that
was previously used, it is called *reused wool.*

When wool is recycled, the quality can be lowered. A low price may
be more important than appearance or durability. Recycled wool is often

Woolmark label

Woolblend mark

The Wool Bureau, Inc.

14-18
The Woolmark label is used on fabrics made of pure wool. The Woolblend mark is used on fabrics made predominately of wool.

silk
A natural protein fiber obtained by unwinding the cocoons of silkworms.

used in winter gloves, interlinings of coats, and picnic blankets. A small amount of recycled wool mixed with other fibers does not mean the product is inferior. You must decide how you will be using the product. It may meet your particular needs.

The Wool Bureau, Inc. is a trade organization of wool growers. They developed two symbols to readily identify wool products and wool blends. Products made of 100 percent wool use the *Woolmark* trademark. Products that include wool and other fibers use the *Woolblend* mark, 14-18. For fabrics to be identified with these symbols, products must meet certain performance standards.

Silk

Silk is the protein fiber obtained by unwinding the cocoons of silkworms. The silk fiber is the longest natural fiber, sometimes reaching a thousand yards or more.

Silk is one of the strongest fibers. A strand of silk is two-thirds as strong as an iron wire of equal size. While it is strong, it also has a natural shine or luster giving fabrics a luxurious look. It is very elastic and resists wrinkling. Silk is so smooth that dirt does not cling to it. Though silk is washable, the dyes used often are not. Most care labels advise dry cleaning garments made of silk.

Japan is the leading producer of raw silk today. China, Italy, France, and India also produce large amounts of silk. The United States does not produce raw silk because of the high cost of labor. However, it is the world's largest manufacturer of silk products.

Some of the steps in silk production are shown in 14-19. A silk moth lays from 200 to 500 eggs early in the summer. As soon as the tiny worms hatch, they begin eating mulberry leaves. They eat their own weight in leaves each day. After about five weeks, they have grown to about 3 inches long and 1/2 inch thick.

At this time, the silkworm stops eating and begins to spin its cocoon. First, it spins the outer covering of the cocoon. Then it begins to wind the silk strand around its body. The silkworm is soon out of sight. If left undisturbed, the worm will turn into a tiny moth and force its way out of its cocoon in two or three weeks. Since this would break and ruin the silk thread, it is killed by heat before this can happen.

The cocoon is unwound either by hand or by machine. A few threads are put together and wound on a reel. Later, the silk from these reels is twisted tightly into skeins, tied in bundles, and baled. It is then ready for the manufacturers of silk cloth.

(A) Silk moths come out of their cocoons and mate.

(B) This female has laid her clutch of eggs from which caterpillars, also called silkworms, will hatch.

(C) The silkworms grow by eating mulberry leaves.

(D) Full-grown silkworms find an empty "frame" provided by the silk farmer to spin their cocoons. These frames make harvesting of the cocoons quick and efficient. Threads from four or five cocoons are wound together on a reel. Later, they can be either wound onto cones or twisted into skeins.

SERICULUM, Sebastopol, CA

14-19
Silkworms produce silk strands as they spin their cocoons. The silk yarns are then sent to cloth manufacturers.

Highlights in History

The Discovery of Silk

According to legend, a young Chinese Empress named Si Ling-Shi discovered silk. One day, as she sat in the garden drinking tea, she noticed a fat, white worm on a leaf of a mulberry tree. It moved its head back and forth while spraying a fine white thread from two tiny holes below its mouth. As she watched, she saw the worm wrap the thread around itself forming a cocoon. She caught it and dropped it into her cup of hot tea. When it softened, she saw the fiber floating in the tea. As she lifted it, the cocoon unwound into a long thread.

There are many versions of this story. No one knows which one is correct. From records we do know that for about 3000 years after the discovery of the silkworm, only the Chinese knew how to make silk. They named the lustrous cloth "Si" for their Empress. Si is still the Chinese name for silk.

The Western world was mystified as to how silk was made. They speculated as to whether it came from a vegetable, animal, or mineral. Envoys were sent to China to discover this secret, but without success. Other countries had to buy the silken material and then unravel it to obtain the silk threads. The threads were then rewoven into lengths of silk, which were exchanged for more than their weight in gold. Very little silk could make its way to Rome and Europe. This increased its value, and the price could only be paid by the wealthiest people. Silk was in such demand and so costly that it was known throughout the world as the "cloth of kings."

In the third century A.D., Japan once again sent an envoy to China to either bribe or capture some of their silk-weavers and bring them to Japan to teach the process to the Japanese. This led to the beginning of the silk industry in Japan. Eventually, the silkworm eggs were smuggled to other countries of the world, and sericulture (silkworm cultivation) flourished.

Silk is covered by a natural gum, which must be removed by washing. This is done so dyes will give brilliant, uniform colors. The washing process makes some yarns very thin and lightweight. Salts from tin, lead, or iron can be added to make the fabrics from these yarns heavier. This fabric is called *weighted silk.* One way to tell if silk is weighted is to shake the fabric and see if it rustles. Too much weighting weakens the silk.

Short threads from broken cocoons are also used. They are spun in much the same way as cotton fibers. This *spun silk* is used in making rough-textured fabrics. Spun silk is not as strong or lustrous as reeled silk.

A summary of the advantages, disadvantages, and uses of the natural fibers is shown in 14-20. Reviewing these fiber characteristics will help you select the best fiber for your particular use.

NATURAL FIBER CHARACTERISTICS AND USES

Fiber and Source	Advantages	Disadvantages	End Uses
Cotton **Cotton plant**	inexpensive; supply unlimited comfortable—cool in warm weather absorbent—soaks up water easily; good for towels and underwear no static electricity buildup withstands high temperature; does not scorch easily when ironed; can be boiled to sterilize versatile; dyes and prints well can be combined with other fibers wide variety of uses	mildews if put in damp storage area or put away damp wrinkles easily unless a special finish is added shrinks in hot water if not treated weakened by wrinkle-resistant finishes, perspiration, and long exposure to sun	clothing—all kinds of underwear and outerwear; socks, shirts, dresses, jeans, coats home furnishings— towels, wash- cloths, sheets, bedspreads, cur- tains, slipcovers, tablecloths, rugs
Linen **Flax plant**	strongest of natural fibers comfortable; absorbs moisture from skin and dries quickly smooth, lustrous stands high temperatures, will not scorch easily when ironed durable; withstands frequent laundering lint-free; used for dishtowels, cloth for medical profession	expensive if of good quality wrinkles easily unless treated creases hard to remove shines if ironed on right side mildews, rots, and has color loss	clothing—suits, dresses, handkerchiefs home furnishings— draperies, kitchen towels, table- cloths, upholstery *(continued)*

14-20
This chart summarizes the advantages, disadvantages, and end uses of the natural fibers.

NATURAL FIBER
CHARACTERISTICS AND USES *(Cont.)*

Fiber and Source	Advantages	Disadvantages	End Uses
Ramie **China grass**	strong lustrous dries quickly durable absorbs moisture	wrinkles easily stiff and wirelike coarse	cords, twine, rope, canvas, fire hoses home furnishings— combined with other fibers for draperies, uphol- stery fabrics combined with other natural and manufactured fibers in wearing apparel
Wool **Sheep fleece**	warmest of all fibers, but lightweight highly absorbent (absorbs moisture without feeling wet) wrinkle resistant holds and regains shape creases well durable combines with other fibers successfully	expensive will shrink and mat when moisture and heat are applied special care is needed; most fabrics must be dry cleaned attracts moths and carpet beetles absorbs odors burns easily; press at low temperature	clothing—outer- wear, sweaters, suits, skirts, athletic socks home furnishings— rugs, carpets, upholstery, blankets
Silk **Cocoon of** **the silkworm**	luxurious look and feel strong but lightweight very absorbent comfortable in all climates resists wrinkling soil resistant combines well with other fibers	usually requires dry cleaning yellows with age weakened by long exposure to sunlight, detergents, and perspiration attacked by insects such as silverfish spotted by water unless specially treated requires low temperature for pressing expensive	clothing—wedding dresses, evening gowns, blouses, scarves, neckties, and lingerie home furnishings— lampshades, pillow cushions, wall hangings, draperies, upholstery

14-20
Continued

There is another new natural fiber that you might find in apparel.
Bamboo is being made into a fiber that is both durable and soft. It has a
natural sheen, is antibacterial, breathable, and biodegradable. It is often
blended with cotton in knit fabrics.

Manufactured Fibers

Manufactured fibers surround you. They are in your clothes, on your furniture, at your school, and in your car. They can be as small as a spider's web or as large as the ropes that moor an ocean vessel.

Rayon was the first commercially produced fiber. It was followed by acetate. These fibers, along with triacetate and lyocell, are made from cellulose, the fibrous substance in plant life. They are called *cellulosic fibers.*

Combining molecules of nitrogen, oxygen, hydrogen, and carbon makes most other manufactured fibers. These are called *noncellulosic fibers.* The molecules are linked in various ways to form chemical compounds called *polymers.* The noncellulosic fibers are sometimes called *synthetic fibers* since they are made from chemicals. See 14-21 for a list of the generic names of the most common manufactured fibers. (Refer to Chapter 6 for more information on the generic names and trademark names of manufactured fibers.)

Manufacturing Fibers

The raw materials and chemicals used to make manufactured fibers can vary. They all go through the same basic steps before they become fibers:

1. The solid raw material is changed to a liquid.
2. The liquid is *extruded* (forced or pushed) through a spinneret.
3. It hardens in the form of a fiber.

In step one, the raw material becomes a thick liquid (like honey). Softwood trees are the most common source for rayon and acetate. The wood is cut into small wood chips. These are dissolved by chemicals to form the thick liquid.

The other manufactured fibers begin as a solid mass of chemicals, which is chopped into small pieces. These are either melted or dissolved by chemicals to form the liquid.

The second step is to extrude the liquid through a spinneret. A **spinneret** is a small nozzle with many tiny holes, similar to a bathroom showerhead, 14-22. As the thick liquid is *extruded* (forced) through the spinneret, each tiny hole forms one fiber. Several fibers join to make a filament, 14-23.

MANUFACTURED FIBERS		
Cellulosic Fibers		
acetate		rayon
lyocell		triacetate
Noncellulosic Fibers		
acrylic	metallic	rubber
anidex	modacrylic	saran
aramid	nylon	spandex
azlon	nytril	vinal
glass	olefin	vinyon
lastrile	polyester	

14-21

These are the generic names of the most common manufactured fibers.

14-22

The metal spinneret has very tiny holes. Thick liquid solutions are pushed through the holes to form fibers.

spinneret
A small nozzle with many tiny holes through which a thick liquid is extruded, making manufactured fibers.

filament
A long continuous strand of fiber.

staple fiber
Short strand of fiber.

A **filament** is a continuous strand of fiber. Any manufactured fiber can be made in filament form. Silk is the only natural fiber that is a filament. Other natural fibers are short and are called **staple fibers.** Manufactured filaments can be cut to make staple fibers.

In the third step, the filament is hardened. The process of extrusion and the formation of filaments is called *spinning.* Some filaments pass from the spinneret directly into a chemical bath where they become solid *(wet spinning).* Others harden after the chemical that was used to change it to liquid has evaporated in warm air *(dry spinning).* Some filaments harden as soon as they come in contact with cool air *(melt spinning).*

The next step varies, depending upon the type of yarn that will be made. To make filament yarns, a few filaments are twisted together into yarns. Then the yarns are wound onto spools, as in 14-24. To make staple yarns, filaments are cut into short lengths and later spun into yarns.

Fiber Modifications

Two factors affect the properties of manufactured fibers. One is the chemicals used to make the fiber. This factor remains fairly constant. The other is the way the fiber is treated during production.

Before, during, and after the three basic production steps, there are countless ways to alter the fiber. The cross-sectional shape can be changed. It might be round, trilobal, pentagonal, or octagonal. Each shape results in fibers with different characteristics. The fiber can be thick or thin. The color, luster, wrinkle-resistance, absorption, strength, and pliability can all be varied during the fiber-making process. Fibers can be blended or combined with other manufactured or natural fibers.

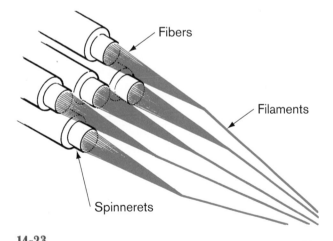

14-23
Fibers formed by the holes of the spinneret combine to form a filament.

American Textile Manufacturers Institute

14-24
After the dry spinning process, fibers are formed into yarn and wound onto spools.

Yarns can be made from a single filament or from many filaments twisted together. They can be twisted, crimped, coiled, or looped to vary the appearance and stretch. This is called **texturing.** See 14-25.

The list of fiber modifications grows longer each year. Scientists in textile labs continue to find new and better fibers to meet new needs and requirements.

texturing
Twisting, crimping, coiling, or looping fibers to vary the appearance and stretch of yarns.

Characteristics of Manufactured Fibers

Although manufactured fibers can be modified in many ways, each kind of fiber has some typical characteristics. The following are the characteristics of some of the most popular manufactured fibers.

Rayon

Rayon is much like cotton. It is soft, comfortable, absorbent, inexpensive, and versatile. It is easy to dye, and it drapes well. A special treatment increases its strength and resistance to shrinking and wrinkling.

Rayon is used for almost all kinds of clothing. Lingerie, shirts, blouses, dresses, slacks, coats, and work clothes are some of the common uses, 14-26. In the home, rayon is used for bedding, rugs, curtains, draperies, upholstery, and tablecloths. It is also used in many nonwoven, industrial, and medical products.

J.C. Penney Co., Inc.

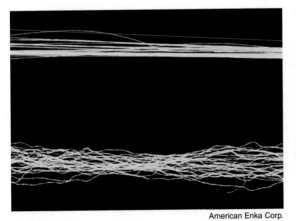

American Enka Corp.

14-25_____
The filament yarn shown at the top in this illustration has not been textured. The same yarn after being textured adds bulk and stretch to fabrics.

14-26_____
Rayon is often used in clothing. It is soft, easy to dye, and drapes well. Here it is blended with nylon.

Care instructions for rayon garments vary. Some require dry cleaning. Some should be washed by hand. Some can be washed and bleached like cotton. Check the care labels.

Lyocell

Though *lyocell* has a separate generic name, the Federal Trade Commission classifies it as a subcategory under rayon. It has similar characteristics as rayon, as well as similar uses. A common trademark name you will see for lyocell is Tencel.

Lyocell is a versatile fiber with many desirable properties. It is breathable and generally comfortable to wear. It is also very absorbent. It can take high ironing temperatures, but will scorch. Lyocell has moderate resiliency. It does not wrinkle as badly as cotton or linen. Some wrinkles will hang out if the garment is placed in a warm, moist area. Slight shrinkage is common. Lyocell has strength and durability. It dyes well, has a luxurious hand, and a soft drape.

Lyocell was initially expensive to manufacture, so its use was mainly in designer apparel. As costs have come down, it can now be found in more affordable apparel. It is used in various fabrics, including denim and gabardine. It is often used in women's garments as well as men's shirts. It is also used in some home products, such as towels and sheets.

Most lyocell garments can be either hand or machine washed and tumble dried. However, some fabrics are best dry cleaned. Some touch up ironing may be necessary at a medium to high temperature.

Acetate

Acetate looks and feels luxurious. It is crisp and drapes (handles) well. It can be dyed in a wide range of colors. With special dyes, acetate will not fade or change color. It is resistant to moths and mildew. It is inexpensive, but it is weak.

Clothing uses of acetate include neckties, scarves, shirts, blouses, dresses, evening gowns, lingerie, and garment linings. In the home, it is used for draperies, upholstery, and quilted products such as comforters and mattress pads. It is also used in cigarette filters.

Most acetate garments should be dry cleaned. (Check the care labels.) If you do launder them at home, handle them with care. Use warm water with mild suds. Do not twist the garment. Press while slightly damp on the wrong side of the fabric. Use a cool iron. Acetate will melt under high heat.

Triacetate

Triacetate is similar to acetate in appearance. It can be very lustrous. It is more resistant to sunlight, wrinkles, and shrinkage than acetate. Permanent creases and pleats can be made in triacetate fabrics using a special heat treatment.

Triacetate is often used in lightweight knits. Garments of triacetate include dresses, shirts, blouses, and clothes that require permanent pleats.

Caring for triacetate garments is easy. Most can be machine washed and dried. (Pleated garments should be washed by hand.) If any ironing is needed, a low temperature may be used.

Nylon

Nylon is very strong and durable. It is elastic, but keeps its shape. It is lightweight, lustrous, and easy to dye. Because nylon is low in absorbency, static electricity is a problem. It also is uncomfortable in hot weather, and provides little warmth in cold weather. Pilling may also be a problem.

Many garments are made of nylon, 14-27. Some are hosiery, lingerie, casual tops, dresses, raincoats, and skiwear. Carpets, draperies, and upholstery are home uses. Nylon has many other uses such as thread, seat belts, racket strings, ropes, tents, and tire cord.

Most nylon garments can be machine washed and dried at low temperatures. They dry quickly. Use warm water and a fabric softener. Remove garments from the dryer as soon as it stops. Wash light-colored nylon items alone. They pick up colors from darker items if washed together.

14-27--
Nylon skiwear is lightweight, durable, and comfortable.

J.C. Penney Co., Inc.

14-28--
Polyester is often blended with cotton to create comfortable, easy-care clothing.

Polyester

Polyester is very resistant to wrinkles, stretching, shrinking, bleach, sunlight, moths, and mildew. It is strong and easy to dye. With a special heat treatment, it will hold permanent creases. Polyester is versatile. Almost any texture and appearance can be achieved in polyester fabrics. It also has disadvantages. Pilling may be a problem. Oily stains are difficult to remove. Absorption is quite low which makes these fabrics uncomfortable in hot, humid weather. Static electricity is also a problem because of low absorbency.

Polyester can be used alone or blended with other fibers (especially cotton) in clothing, 14-28. It is used for shirts, blouses, children's wear, dresses, insulated garments, lingerie, permanent press garments, slacks, and suits. In the home, it is used for carpets, curtains, and sheets. Thread, fiberfill, fire hose, ropes, tire cord, and sails are other uses.

Most polyester items can be machine washed and dried. Use warm water and a fabric softener. Remove promptly from the dryer.

Olefin

Olefin is the lightest fiber made. It floats on water and has very low absorption. It resists wrinkles, soil, water-based stains, mildew, and insects. Olefin is a strong, durable fiber and it is inexpensive. The disadvantages are that it is difficult to dye and it melts at fairly low temperatures.

Knitted sport shirts and sweaters are made of olefin. In the future, more garments will be made of olefin. Indoor/outdoor carpeting is the largest single use of the fiber. Carpet backing, slipcovers, and upholstery are other home uses. Industry uses olefin for filters, sewing thread, envelopes, and rope.

Machine wash olefin items in lukewarm water. Use a fabric softener. If you machine dry, use a very low setting and remove items promptly. Most carpet stains can be removed by blotting with an absorbent tissue.

Acrylic

Acrylic is often used as a replacement for wool. It is soft, warm, and lightweight. It keeps its shape well. It resists sunlight, chemicals, and wrinkles. It can be treated to keep a permanent crease. Pilling and static electricity may be problems.

Many sweaters are made of acrylic. Other uses are dresses, infant wear, slacks, athletic wear, and socks, 14-29. Blankets, carpets, draperies, and upholstery are some home uses. It is also used in hand knitting yarns.

Wash delicate items by hand in warm water. Gently squeeze out water. Smooth out wrinkles, and hang to dry. (Lay sweaters flat to dry.) If the care label suggests machine washing, use warm water and a fabric softener. Machine dry at a low setting, and remove promptly.

Modacrylic

Modacrylic is flame resistant. It also resists shrinkage and chemicals. It is soft, warm, and easy to dye. Fibers can be molded and keep their

Pineapple Appeal

14-29

Fleece for athletic wear is often made of acrylic.

shape. One problem is that the fiber softens at low temperatures.

Modacrylic is the fiber used to make fake fur. It is also used for deep-pile coats and trims and for wigs. In the home, it is used in blankets, carpets, flame-resistant draperies, and wall coverings. Other uses are filters, paint rollers, and stuffed toys.

Furlike items should be dry cleaned. Check the care label. If a modacrylic item can be washed, use warm water, mild suds, and a fabric softener. Use a very low setting on the dryer, and remove promptly.

Rubber

Rubber is defined as a manufactured fiber in which the fiber-forming substance is composed of natural or synthetic rubber. Natural rubber is made from a thick liquid called *latex,* which comes from rubber trees. Rubber is used to make items such as waterproof coats, boots, and gloves. It is also used in some elastic waistbands and as a backing for rugs.

Be sure to check care labels in garments containing rubber. Body oils, perspiration, and exposure to light will weaken rubber. It is most often laundered and dried at low temperatures. Often, items made of rubber should be laundered instead of dry cleaned. The dry-cleaning chemicals may cause damage.

14-30
Swimsuits and exercise wear often contain spandex where stretch is desired.

Spandex

Spandex is elastic-like rubber, but is made entirely from chemicals. Spandex has good stretch and will go back into shape easily. Since spandex is resistant to sunlight, oil, perspiration, and abrasion, it is better than rubber for most uses. Many former uses of rubber in clothing have been replaced by spandex. Spandex is used for both woven and knitted fabrics. Some uses are in swimsuits, underwear, ski pants, and many other articles where stretch is needed, 14-30.

High temperatures in washing machines and dryers can cause spandex to lose some of its stretching power, and it may take on a gray tint. Bleach and the chlorine in swimming pools may also damage it. That is why it is important to rinse a swimsuit thoroughly as soon as possible after swimming in a chlorine pool.

See figure 14-31 for a summary of the characteristics and uses of these manufactured fibers.

MANUFACTURED FIBER
CHARACTERISTICS AND USES

Generic Name	Advantages	Disadvantages	End Uses
Rayon	very absorbent drapes well dyes and prints well soft comfortable versatile inexpensive	wrinkles easily unless treated low resiliency heat sensitive will mildew shrinks in hot water unless treated stretches weak when wet	blouses dresses shirts lingerie sportswear bedding curtains tablecloths
Lyocell	soft strong absorbent dyes well drapes well biodegradable luxurious hand	susceptible to mildew moderate resiliency slight shrinkage	dresses shirts blouses bedding towels
Acetate	silklike luster/feel drapes well resists moths, mildew, pilling inexpensive easy to dye	poor abrasion resistance weak heat sensitive special care for cleaning	dresses blouses linings lingerie shirts scarves neckties
Triacetate	resists wrinkles and fading easy care resilient can be heat set lustrous does not shrink	nonabsorbent weak static buildup low abrasion resistance	blouses dresses lightweight knits pleated garments

Nylon	very strong
	lightweight
	dries quickly
	durable
	resilient
	resists mildew, moths, chem-
	  icals, wrinkles
	retains shape
	colorfast
	easy care
		low absorbency
		surface pills
		damaged by sun
		picks up oils and dyes in
		  wash
		static buildup
		heat sensitive
			casual tops
			hosiery
			lingerie
			skiwear
			slacks
			windbreakers
			dresses
			raincoats
			carpets
			upholstery
			(continued)

14-31

The advantages, disadvantages, and end uses for many manufactured fibers are summarized in this chart.

MANUFACTURED FIBER
CHARACTERISTICS AND USES *(Cont.)*

Generic Name	Advantages	Disadvantages	End Uses

Polyester	resilient
	colorfast
	strong/durable
	easy care
	resists wrinkles, abrasion,
	  bleach, perspiration,
	  mildew, moths
	can be heat set
	does not stretch or shrink
		low absorbency
		spun yarns pill
		takes oily stains
		static buildup
			permanent press
			  fabrics
			fiberfill insulation
			shirts and dresses
			suits
			underwear
			sportswear
			children's wear
			carpets

Olefin	resists abrasion, chemicals,
	  stains, mildew, pilling,
	  wrinkles, static
	not affected by weather,
	  aging, perspiration
	strong, durable
	very lightweight
	inexpensive
		heat sensitive
		poor dyeability
		nonabsorbent
			knitted socks,
			  sportswear,
			  sweaters, shirts
			nonwoven fabrics
			  for industrial
			  apparel
			filler in quilted
			  goods
			disposable diapers
			carpets

Acrylic	resembles wool lightweight soft, fluffy warm, bulky resilient resists sunlight, moths, chemicals, mildew, wrinkles	low absorbency static buildup surface pills heat sensitive	sportswear sweaters infant wear knitted garments blankets carpets draperies
Modacrylic	bulky, warm easy to dye resists wrinkling, flames, chemicals retains shape soft, lightweight	heat sensitive static buildup weak surface pills	furlike fabrics coats knitwear sportswear fleece fabrics wigs

Spandex	very elastic
	resistant to lotions, oils, per-
	  spiration, sun, abrasion
	lightweight
	strong, durable
	soft, smooth
	easy care
		nonabsorbent
		yellows with age
		heat sensitive
		harmed by chlorine bleach
			swimwear
			skiwear
			underwear
			support hose
			exercise and
			  dance wear

14-31

Continued

CHAPTER
REVIEW

Key Points

- Fibers are the basic units of all textiles. There are two main groups of fibers. Natural fibers are made from plants and animals. Manufactured fibers are made from chemicals in special manufacturing processes.

- Each fiber has its own characteristics and properties, depending on its source or chemical composition. A knowledge of fiber characteristics will help you select the fiber most suitable for its end use.

- Cotton, linen, wool, and silk are the most common natural fibers.

- There are two categories of natural fibers. Cellulosic fibers come from plant sources and protein fibers come from animal sources.

- The Wool Products Labeling Act was passed to help consumers know how much and what type of wool is in the fabrics they buy.

- There are two categories of manufactured fibers—cellulosic fibers (rayon, acetate, lyocell, and triacetate) and non-cellulosic fibers (nylon, polyester, spandex, as well as others).

- Manufactured fibers can be modified in many ways to change their color, luster, wrinkle-resistance, absorption, strength, and pliability. They can be modified in other ways as well.

To Review

1. Explain the relationship among fibers, yarns, and fabrics.
2. What is absorbency, and why might you want this characteristic in a fabric?
3. List two advantages of cotton.
4. Which fiber is used to make linen?
5. _____ is the coolest natural fiber; _____ is the warmest.
6. The major natural protein fibers are _____ and _____ .
7. Name the oil obtained from the processing of wool and two of its uses.
8. Explain the difference between reprocessed wool and reused wool.
9. Why is silk not produced in the United States?
10. Name two key characteristics of silk.
11. What are the sources for the manufactured cellulosic fibers and the noncellulosic fibers?
12. List the three basic steps in manufacturing fibers.
13. What two factors influence the properties of manufactured fibers?
14. List one characteristic and one use for each of the 10 major manufactured fibers.

To Do

1. Make a bulletin board display that shows the steps in making yarns from either natural or manufactured fibers.

2. Collect samples of fabrics made from various fibers. Identify and compare characteristics.

3. Find pictures of end uses for the different fibers. Display them on a bulletin board.

4. Visit a fabric store and compare prices of fabrics made from different fibers.

5. Hold a piece of cotton fabric in one hand and a piece of polyester fabric in the other. Squeeze both for five seconds, then compare. Which is more wrinkle-resistant?

6. Place a tablespoon of water on each of two plates. Place a linen sample on one plate and a nylon sample on the other. Which absorbed more water?

7. Unravel some manufactured fabrics to see if the fibers have been texturized.

8. Look at various natural and manufactured fibers and yarns under a microscope. Identify and compare them.

9. Cut two identical samples of wool fabric. Record the measurement. Wash one sample in cold water and the other one in hot water. Dry the samples by squeezing in a towel. Measure each again. Was there a change? What characteristic of wool caused this difference?

10. Research the Internet to find some of the most recent innovations in fiber manufacturing and characteristics. Prepare a report for the class.

To Think About

1. Do you or any of your friends or family members have any fiber prejudices? For example, does anyone ever say "I hate polyester" or "I only choose clothes made of natural fibers"? If so, why do you think this happens?

2. Would you buy a wool product that contained recycled wool? Why or why not?

3. Make a list of end uses for fibers. Include both clothing items and household uses. Then recommend a fiber for each use. Explain why you made each choice.

4. Efforts are being made by some fiber manufacturers to save the environment. Do you think enough is being done? Would you look for fiber manufacturers who are making special efforts to conserve natural resources?

5. If you were a textile chemist, what new fiber characteristic would you try to develop? Why?

CHAPTER 15

From Yarn to Fabric

Objectives

After studying this chapter, you will be able to

- explain how fibers are combined to make various types of yarns.
- identify and describe different ways in which yarn is made into fabrics through weaving, knitting, or other processes.
- describe various ways color and design can be added to fabrics.
- explain the performance to be expected from different finishes applied to fabrics.

Before a yarn becomes part of a finished fabric, it goes through many steps. The yarn itself can vary in size, strength, and texture. It can be made into fabric in several different ways.

The appearance and performance of a textile product depends on its fiber content, type of yarn, fabric construction, added color, and finishes. These factors can be varied to make millions of different fabrics. The fiber content was discussed in Chapter 14. In this chapter, you will learn how fibers are made into yarns and yarns into fabrics.

Yarns

Fibers are spun together to make yarns, 15-1. Yarns are combined to make fabrics. The type of yarn used has a big effect on the finished product.

Spun yarns are made from short, staple fibers. They have a rough surface. Some of the tiny fiber ends stick out, making it look fuzzy. All natural fibers except silk are made into spun yarns. All manufactured fibers can be cut to staple length and used for spun yarns.

Have you ever had a sweater that pilled? That sweater was made of spun yarns. **Pills** are tiny balls of fiber that appear in places of wear such as elbows and cuffs. They can be cut off or smoothed with an emery board or fine sandpaper. When you wear the sweater again, more pills may form. Some new fibers do not pill.

Monofilament yarns are made from a single filament. The clear, plasticlike thread used to hem some ready-to-wear garments is a monofilament yarn. These yarns are also used in hosiery.

Multifilament yarns are made from a group of filaments. Silk and all manufactured fibers can be made into multifilament yarns for most kinds of clothing.

Twist in Yarns

The amount of twist added to a yarn varies. Twist is needed to hold the fibers or filaments together. Twist is also added to increase the strength of the yarn.

spun yarn
Yarn made from short, staple fibers.

pills
Small balls of fiber that form on the surface of a fabric.

monofilament yarns
Yarns made from a single filament.

multifilament yarns
Yarns made from a group of filaments.

American Sheep Industry Assoc.

15-1

Spinning machines combine fibers to make yarns, which will then be woven into fabrics.

Microfiber— A New Name in Textiles

A new term has been showing up on more and more garment and fabric labels recently. That word is *microfiber*. Whenever you see this word on a label, you will notice the fabric is extra smooth, soft, and silky, and the fabric weave is barely visible. Microfibers have been one of the most important developments in textiles in recent years. The technology to extrude extremely fine filaments that are still strong and uniform led to their development. These microfibers are even finer than silk as you can see in this diagram.

In addition to their luxurious feel, they have some outstanding performance characteristics. Microfibers are popular for raincoats and jackets because they are lighter and more comfortable than conventional fibers. The small filaments are packed so close together they form an effective wind barrier. This barrier prevents loss of body heat. In addition, the nonwetting surface of the fibers causes water to bead up. These beads are larger than the spaces between the yarns so the water is locked out.

Silk

Microfiber

Moisture vapor can still escape, keeping the wearer dry and comfortable. Fabrics made of microfibers can breathe well. Chemical treatments and coatings are not needed to provide water resistance.

Microfiber yarns are made from most major generic fibers, particularly nylon, polyester, acrylic, and rayon. Watch for this term to show up more and more in the apparel and fabrics you buy.

- Very low twist yarns are often used for multifilament yarns. The fibers used in this kind of yarn are strong, so the twist is used only to hold the filaments together.
- Low twist, spun yarns are "fluffy." They are used to make bulky, soft, and fuzzy fabrics. They are fairly weak and form pills easily.
- Average twist is the most common twist for yarns made of staple fibers.
- High twist yarns are hard and compact. These yarns are less common today. Yarns with high twist are used in fabrics called voile and crepe.

Textured Yarns

Filament yarns from all manufactured fibers (except rayon and acetate) can be textured. This makes the yarns less smooth. They are crimped, looped, or coiled to achieve some properties of the spun yarns. Texturing yarns makes them more absorbent and more comfortable with more bulk and stretch. They have less static buildup. The development of texturing has been a major factor in the widespread acceptance of manufactured fibers.

Single, Ply, and Cord Yarns

The relationship among single, ply, and cord yarns is shown in 15-2. The product of the first twisting step is a single yarn.

Twisting two or more single yarns together makes a **ply yarn.** Each part of the yarn is called a ply. Ply yarns are larger and stronger than single yarns. Home knitting or crocheting is done with ply yarns.

When ply yarns are twisted together, the result is a **cord yarn.** Ropes are often made from cord yarns.

Blends and Combinations

Many textiles today have a mixture of natural and manufactured fibers. These are called blends or combinations.

When different staple fibers are spun together into a single yarn, a **blend** results. When two different single yarns are twisted into a ply, a **combination yarn** results.

Blends and combinations are used to obtain fabrics with better performance, better appearance, or lower prices. By adding acrylic to a wool fiber or

ply yarn
Yarn made by twisting two or more single yarns together.

cord yarn
Yarn made by twisting ply yarns together.

blend
Yarn made by spinning different types of staple fibers together into a single yarn.

combination yarn
Yarn made by twisting two different types of single yarns into a ply yarn.

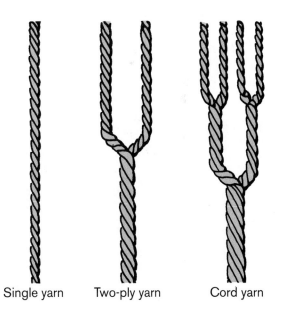

Single yarn   Two-ply yarn   Cord yarn

15-2
Fibers are first twisted into single yarns. Another twisting step combines single yarns into ply yarns. A third twisting step forms cord yarns.

weaving
Process of interlacing yarns at right angles to each other to make fabric.

woven fabric
Fabric made by interlacing yarns at right angles to each other.

yarn, the cost can be reduced. Since acrylic neither shrinks nor attracts moths, both of these problems can also be lessened.

Many shirts are a blend of 65 percent polyester and 35 percent cotton. The amount of each fiber used is important. This 65-35 blend takes advantage of the good characteristics of both fibers and lessens the effect of the bad characteristics. Cotton feels good next to the body. It is cool and absorbent, and it does not pill. However, cotton wrinkles easily and shrinks. Polyester is strong and wrinkle-resistant. It dries quickly and does not shrink. A fabric with the best characteristics of each fiber is the result when they are blended.

Fabrics

The two most common methods of making fabric are weaving and knitting. Other methods are used such as felting and bonding. From only a few construction methods come many different fabrics, 15-3.

Weaving

Weaving is the process of interlacing yarns at right angles to each other to create a **woven fabric.** It is done on machines called *looms,* as in 15-4. Weaving was done by hand for hundreds of years. Your great-grandparents may have had a loom in their home. A few handlooms are still used. Some are large, but most handlooms used today are small. Hand-woven products are usually costly, specialty items. An example is the small rugs made by Indians in the Southwest.

15-3
A variety of fabrics can be produced by weaving, knitting, felting, and bonding.

American Sheep Industry Assoc.

15-4
High-speed looms can weave thousands of yards of fabric in a very short time.

Two sets of yarns are used. The lengthwise ones are the **warp yarns.** The crosswise yarns are the **filling yarns.** The warp yarns are threaded onto the loom. They must be strong and durable to withstand the strain they bear during the weaving process.

The filling yarns pass over and under the warp yarns. When they reach an edge, they turn back and weave across the warp yarns in the other direction. The turned filling yarns along each side of the woven fabric forms the **selvage.** It is very strong and will not ravel.

The filling yarns are usually weaker than the warp yarns. Therefore, if the fabric has low-twist or "special effect" yarns, they will be in the filling.

In woven fabrics, the filling yarns stretch more than the warp. This is why the grain of fabric is important in clothing. **Grain** is the direction the yarns run. Garments need to stretch more across your body than up and down. Therefore, the *crosswise grain* is along the filling. The *lengthwise grain* is along the warp. See 15-5.

Large and complex designs are woven on Jacquard looms. See 15-6. The design of the fabric is programmed on a series of punch cards. The cards control the warp yarns, raising or lowering them to create the woven design.

Damask, brocade, and tapestry fabrics are made on the *Jacquard loom.* They are used for clothing and home furnishings such as bedspreads and upholstery. Towels with hotel names as the woven design are also made on these looms.

Smaller patterns can be woven into a fabric with a *dobby attachment.* It can be added to a regular loom. A plastic tape is punched with holes. These holes control the warp yarns to produce the design.

warp yarns
The longer yarns that run the length of fabric.

filling yarns
The shorter yarns that run crosswise in woven fabric.

selvage
Turned filling yarns along each side of a woven fabric.

grain
The direction the lengthwise and crosswise yarns run.

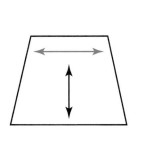
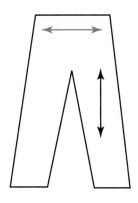

15-5_____
Because filling yarns (blue) stretch more than warp yarns (black), garments are made with the filling yarns going around the body. Warp yarns are used in the lengthwise direction.

Somet S.p.A., Bergamo, Italy

15-6_____
A Jacquard loom makes it possible to weave intricate patterns.

Three Basic Weaves

Weaving has been defined as the process of interlacing yarns at right angles to each other. You can create different effects by passing the filling yarns over and under different numbers of warp yarns. This creates three basic types of weaves. They are the plain weave, the twill weave, and the satin weave.

Plain Weave

plain weave
A weave made by passing a filling yarn over one warp yarn and then under one warp yarn.

Passing a filling yarn over one warp yarn and then under one warp yarn makes the **plain weave.** The netting of a tennis racket is an example of the plain weave. Review Figure 15-7 as you read about the various weaves.

Generally, plain weave fabrics are strong, durable, and easy to sew. They wrinkle more and absorb less moisture than fabrics of other weaves.

Using large yarns with small ones, textured yarns, or a special finish can change the effect. You can also get a different look by working with more than one yarn at a time. This is called the *basket weave.* It is made by passing two or more filling yarns over and under two or more warp yarns. In the *leno weave,* two warp yarns cross over each other before each filling yarn. Fabrics made with this weave are lacelike in character. Uses include sheer curtains and thermal blankets. Plain weave fabrics are listed in 15-7.

Twill Weave

twill weave
A weave made when the filling yarns float over one and under two or more warp yarns.

The **twill weave** is made when a yarn in one direction *floats* (passes) over two or more yarns in the other direction. Each float begins one yarn over from the last one. The floats can be either filling or warp yarns. Twill weave fabrics have a distinct diagonal line or wale. The twill weave is shown in 15-7.

Twill weaves are very durable, resist wrinkles, and hide soil. They are less stiff than plain weave fabrics that have the same number of yarns.

There are many ways to vary twill weaves. The floats can be long or short. The angle of the wale can be steep, average, or reclining as shown in 15-8. Large, high-twist, or textured yarns also create different looks. The wale goes "up and right" in wool and acrylic fabrics. It goes "up and left" in cotton and cotton blend fabrics such as denim jeans. When the wale changes direction, a zigzag look appears. This is called a *herringbone twill.* Twill weave fabrics are listed in 15-7.

Satin Weave

satin weave
Weave made by floating a yarn from one direction over four or more yarns from the other direction and then under one yarn.

The **satin weave** is made by floating a yarn from one direction over four or more yarns from the other direction and then under one yarn. Each float begins two yarns over from where the last float began. It is used to make fabrics with a smooth surface. See 15-7.

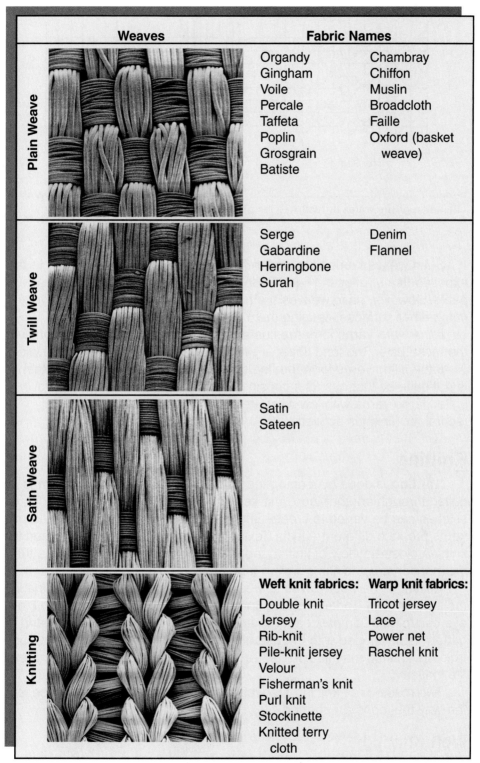

Weaves	Fabric Names	
Plain Weave	Organdy Gingham Voile Percale Taffeta Poplin Grosgrain Batiste	Chambray Chiffon Muslin Broadcloth Faille Oxford (basket weave)
Twill Weave	Serge Gabardine Herringbone Surah	Denim Flannel
Satin Weave	Satin Sateen	
Knitting	**Weft knit fabrics:** Double knit Jersey Rib-knit Pile-knit jersey Velour Fisherman's knit Purl knit Stockinette Knitted terry cloth	**Warp knit fabrics:** Tricot jersey Lace Power net Raschel knit

American Textile Manufacturers Institute

15-7

Compare these magnified views of the various weaves and knitted fabric.

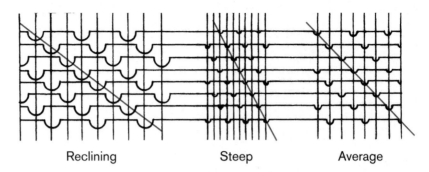

Reclining   Steep   Average

15-8

The angle of the wales in twill weaves may be reclining, steep, or average.

Satin weave fabrics are known for their luster. The luster is due to the exposed floats reflecting light. Satin weaves feel smooth and are drapable. However, satin weaves are not very durable. The floats tend to catch other surfaces, causing them to snag or break.

If the warp yarns form the floats, the fabric is called *satin.* To achieve the most luster, the long floats are made of filament fibers with low twist.

If the filling yarns form the floats, the fabric is called *sateen.* Sateen is not quite as lustrous as satin since spun yarns are used. To improve luster, large yarns with low twist are used in the filling and a special (schreiner) finish is applied.

Knitting

knitting
Looping yarns together with a knitting machine to produce fabric.

Knitting is done by looping the yarns together. One loop of yarn is pulled through another loop, just as you would knit at home. The loops or stitches can be varied to create different patterns and textures. Different yarns produce different effects. Textured filament yarns are often used in knits. A close-up view of knitted fabric is shown in 15-7. You can see that it is not constructed like a woven fabric.

Knitting is new compared to weaving. It was first done by machine in the 16th century. Today, modern knitting machines move faster than the eye can follow. Complex patterns and fine yarns are used. An idea and pattern is developed with the use of a computer. The computer then controls the knitting machine. Knits are a big and exciting part of today's textile industry.

Two methods of knitting are weft (filling) and warp. The difference is the way the loops are formed.

Weft Knitting

weft knitting
Process of knitting in which loops are made as yarn is added in the crosswise direction of the fabric.

In **weft knitting,** the loops are made as yarn is added in the crosswise direction. This can be done by hand or by machine.

Weft knitting machines can be either circular or flat. Circular machines knit the fabric in the shape of a tube, 15-9. Socks, tights, and hosiery are made on specially designed circular machines. These machines are computerized. Therefore, hundreds of shapes and sizes can be produced.

Generally, flat knitting is more complex than circular knitting. Flat knitting can be done in various ways to produce different effects. Stitches can be added or dropped, changing the fabric width. This creates the shape of the garment, so little sewing is needed to produce the final garment. Sweaters, dresses, and other knit garments are knitted on these machines, as well as separate collars, cuffs, and trims. Some weft knits are listed in 15-7.

The most common type of weft knit is the *single knit.* These knits are made on a single needle knitting machine. The most common type of single knit is jersey. Single knits stretch in both directions and can stretch out of shape. Hosiery, T-shirts, and lingerie are usually made of single-knit fabrics.

Another kind of weft knit is the *double knit.* It is used in children's, men's, and women's clothing as well as in household goods. Two sets of needles are used on a weft knitting machine. Although it is called "double" knit, it cannot be separated into two layers. The result is a sturdy fabric that will not stretch or sag. It has enough "give" to be comfortable. Other weft knit fabrics are rib-knit, pile-knit jersey, velour, purl knit, and stockinette.

warp knitting
Process of knitting in which loops are made by one or more sets of warp yarns.

American Textile Manufacturers Institute

15-9_____
A circular knitting machine produces fabric in a tubular form.

Warp Knitting

In **warp knitting,** the loops are made by one or more sets of warp yarns. Each set of warp yarns is as wide as the fabric. An entire row of loops is made at one time. Then the warp yarns are raised to make the next row. Vertical rows of loops are the product.

Warp knitting is the fastest way to make cloth. Warp knits are made on flat machines, 15-10. The knit designs and colors to be used are programmed by computer. Warp knit fabrics are listed in 15-7.

Warp knits tend to be less elastic and lighter in weight than weft knits. If a loop is broken, weft knits will "run" or "ladder." Warp knits will not run, but any knit will snag when a loop is pulled. Bringing the pulled loop to the inside

American Textile Manufacturers Institute

15-10_____
Warp knitting provides lighter and more delicate material than weft knitting. Lingerie, swimsuits, and exercise wear are often made in this manner.

of the garment where it will not show can solve this problem. Common warp knit fabrics are tricot jersey, lace, power net, and raschel knit.

Knitted Fabrics

Why are knits popular? One reason is the development of manufactured fibers. They are well suited for knitting. Another reason is that most people today want clothes that are comfortable to wear. Knits answer that need for comfort. They adjust to the shape of your body. They stretch as you sit, walk, reach, and bend.

Knitted fabrics can be warm in the winter or cool in the summer, depending on the fiber, yarn, and finish used. Caring for them is easy, too. They resist wrinkling and most can be washed if you follow the care instructions. Little or no ironing is needed, 15-11.

Knitted fabrics are very versatile. They can be made from any fiber and any yarn. Most woven fabrics can be copied by a knitted one.

Seamless Knit Garments

One of the newest trends in knitting is making seamless garments. This may be the next generation of clothing because these garments feel good, are comfortable, and slim the body. The current fashion trend is for tighter-fitting clothes for both men and women.

Regular knitting machines produce yards of fabric that have to be cut and sewn. A normal garment may require 17 different operations and each stage must be checked for quality. The seamless machines produce individual garments from yarn that is fed into the machine. Computer commands allow for different stitching patterns in various sizes. These special knitting machines can create a garment in one or two operations. Seamless garments take 30 to 40 percent less time to make than cut-and-sew versions. Currently, eight percent of lingerie is seamless, but that figure is expected to increase. Knit tops, skirts, and T-shirts are also popular seamless garments.

Other Fabric Constructions

Yarns are made of fibers, and fabrics are made of yarns, right? Well, that is a good rule. But like all rules, it has exceptions. Not all fabrics are woven or knitted. Some fabrics are made directly from fibers. A few fabrics do not even have fibers!

The McCall Pattern Co.

15-11 Knitted garments are popular because they stretch, resist wrinkling, and are easy to care for.

Felt

Felt is made from short wool fibers. Wool fibers have overlapping scales. Under a microscope you would see they look like fish scales. As heat, moisture, and pressure are applied to the fibers, the scales interlock to form a solid mass.

A story is told of how felting was discovered. Shepherds put fleece from their sheep in their sandals for warmth. The heat, moisture, and pressure from their feet caused the wool to become a solid mass of wool fibers or felt.

Felt fabrics are thick, stiff, and warm. They are not as strong as woven or knitted fabrics. Felt is easily molded into any shape. It is used for hats, handicrafts, and household items. See 15-12.

15-12--
Felt is commonly used to make hats because it can be molded into the desired shape.

Nonwoven Fabrics

Fibers other than wool can be made into a web fabric much like felt. In some cases, adhesives hold the staple fibers together. For many of the manufactured fibers, heat is used to "melt" the fibers together.

Nonwoven fabrics are often used for disposable items. They are less costly than woven or knitted fabrics. Some uses of nonwoven fabrics are diapers, hospital sheets, operating gowns, bandages, towels, and cleaning cloths. A nondisposable use is for interfacings in garments.

Most nonwoven fabrics are made in the U.S. because of the technology involved in producing the fabrics. The largest growth in the use of nonwovens is as personal and household "wipes." Many people buy wipes because of their antibacterial and disinfecting qualities. One third are sold as baby wipes, one third for personal use, and the other third are used for cleaning. Floor cleaners, glass cleaners, and mopheads are popular uses.

Films

Films are not made of fibers. They are thin sheets of vinyl and urethane. They are often used as a coating on other fabrics. Films are low cost and waterproof. They can be finished to look like leather or any woven fabric.

Fabrics with a urethane coating are easy to sew and easy to clean. They are durable and will remain soft in cold weather. They will not crack or scuff.

Films and film-coated fabrics are used for raincoats, umbrellas, purses, shoes, tablecloths, and upholstery.

Bonded Fabrics

Bonding is the process of permanently fastening (gluing or laminating) one fabric to another. A bonded fabric is often more stable.

felt
Fabric made from short wool fibers that interlock to form a solid mass when heat, moisture, and pressure are applied.

films
Fabrics made of thin sheets of vinyl and urethane.

bonding
The process of permanently fastening one fabric to another.

quilting
The process of adding a layer of padding between two layers of fabric held together with stitches.

greige goods
Unfinished fabric ready to be dyed or printed.

dyes
Coloring agents used to add color to fibers, yarns, fabrics, or garments.

colorfast
Able to resist a change in color in spite of a certain influence such as washing, dry cleaning, perspiration, sunlight, or rubbing.

Tricot knit is often used as the backing fabric. It is inexpensive and allows some stretch. Sometimes a layer of foam is attached to a layer of fabric to add warmth. Bonded fabrics have more body than single fabrics, and they wrinkle less. They are easy to sew. They will not fray or ravel, and they do not need to be lined.

Garments of bonded fabrics are warm without being heavy. They are often used for skiwear and winter coats.

Quilted Fabrics

Quilting is the process of adding a layer of padding (batting) between two layers of fabrics, 15-13. The three layers are then held together with rows of machine stitching creating a pattern. Sometimes a machine that uses heat to weld the layers together creates a quilted look without the stitching.

Adding Color

After the cloth is woven or knitted into fabric, it is still in an unfinished state. The unfinished fabric is called **greige** (pronounced "gray") **goods.** The fabric is ready to be dyed or printed.

Color is a major part of any textile item. As you shop for clothes, the first thing you notice is color. You want colors that are in fashion and that look good on you.

Dyes are coloring agents that are used to add color to fibers, yarns, fabrics, or garments. Today, dyes are used to produce five million different colors. Computers are programmed to match these colors. This system saves time and prevents mistakes.

Some dyes come from natural sources, and some are manufactured. No dye is colorfast to everything. (**Colorfast** means the color will remain in spite of a certain influence such as washing, dry cleaning, perspiration, sunlight, or rubbing.)

The fastness of a color depends on the chemical makeup of the dye, the fibers used, and the method of adding the dye. These factors must all work together. You cannot be sure a garment is colorfast just by looking at it. Read the care label. It should warn you if the product is not colorfast under certain conditions.

Dyeing

Dyeing is one way to add color to textile products. The basic dyeing methods are fiber dyeing, yarn dyeing, and piece dyeing.

J.C. Penney Co., Inc.

15-13_____
The fabric used in these vests is quilted. There is a layer of padding between two fabric layers.

Fiber Dyeing

If fibers are dyed before they are spun into yarns, the process is **fiber dyeing.** This can be done in two ways. Manufactured fibers are solution dyed. Natural fibers are stock dyed.

In **solution dyeing,** the dye is added to the thick liquid before it is forced through the spinneret. In **stock dyeing,** the dye is added to the loose fibers.

Yarn Dyeing

Some yarn is dyed before being formed into fabrics. This is called **yarn dyeing.** After spinning, the yarns are tightly wound on tubes, and then placed in the dye bath. Most fabrics that are plaid or striped, as in 15-14, are yarn dyed. Generally, yarn dyeing costs less than fiber dyeing, but more than piece dyeing.

Piece Dyeing

This is the most common method of dyeing. Color is added after the fabric has been made. **Piece dyeing** allows manufacturers to follow fashion trends closely. They can wait until the last minute to choose the dye colors. Most, but not all, piece-dyed fabrics are a solid color.

Some dyes will color one type of fiber, but not another. Different dyes can be combined in a single dye bath. When a fabric made of more than one fiber is placed in that dye bath, it can become a stripe or check. This is called *cross dyeing.*

Suppose a red dye for acetate and a blue dye for rayon were mixed in a dye bath. Suppose that an acetate/rayon fabric had been woven in a special way. If this fabric were placed in that dye bath, a red and blue stripe fabric might be made. That is the magic of cross dyeing.

A more recent trend is *garment dyeing.* The finished garment is made of undyed yarns and the entire garment is dyed after it is constructed. This allows manufacturers to make fast deliveries to retailers of particular colors that are popular.

Printing

Color can also be added to fabrics by printing. Printing is the process of adding color, pattern, or design to the surface of fabrics. You can tell whether fabrics have been colored in a dye bath or by printing. The wrong side of most printed fabrics is much lighter than the right side. Both sides of dyed fabrics are the same color.

fiber dyeing
Process of dyeing fibers before they are spun into yarns.

solution dyeing
The process of dyeing manufactured fibers by adding dye to the liquid before the fiber is forced through the spinneret.

stock dyeing
Process of adding dye to loose fibers.

yarn dyeing
A dyeing process in which yarns are first wound onto spools and then placed in a dye bath.

piece dyeing
Process of adding dye after the fabric has been made.

Somet S.p.A., Bergamo, Italy

15-14

These warp yarns have been dyed. The finished, woven fabric is striped Jacquard.

There are many ways to print cloth. Two common methods are roller printing and rotary screen printing.

In *roller printing,* the design is etched on copper rollers. A separate cylinder is used for each color. As the cloth passes through the rollers, each one transfers its color and pattern to the fabric.

Rotary screen printing is one of the newest and fastest printing methods. The design is transferred onto a cylinder-shaped screen. There is a screen for each color. Dye is forced through a pattern of holes in each screen. The cylinders roll over the fabric, leaving the design.

Finishing

All fabrics receive some kind of finish. A **fabric finish** is any treatment given to fibers, yarns, or fabrics that make the final product look, feel, or perform differently. Finishes can be applied with heat, pressure, or chemicals.

Not all finishes given to fabrics last for the life of the garment. The following terms indicate how long a finish will last:

- *permanent finish:* lasts for the life of the garment
- *durable finish:* lasts through several launderings or dry cleanings
- *temporary finish:* lasts only until the fabric is washed or dry-cleaned
- *renewable finish:* a temporary finish that can be replaced or reapplied

Finishes make textile items more beautiful and more useful. They cannot improve the quality of the fabric itself. Fabric quality depends on the quality of the fibers and yarns and on the method of construction.

Each of the many different finishes gives certain characteristics to a fabric. Read labels to see what finishes have been applied. Some of the finishes are designed to affect the performance of the fabric. Others affect the appearance or texture of the fabric.

Finishes That Affect Performance

The following finishes are designed to affect the performance of the fabric. Children's play clothes often have several of these finishes applied, 15-15.

Antistatic

This chemical treatment prevents static electricity. This is done so garments will not cling to the wearer.

Crease Resistant and Wrinkle Resistant

These finishes are much the same. They involve treating fabrics with resins, a special group of chemicals. Resins are "baked" onto cotton, rayon, and linen fabrics. They help fabrics resist wrinkles, but they also

15-15
Children's clothes benefit from finishes that make them easier to resist soil and stains.

make fabrics weaker and less absorbent. Stains are more difficult to remove from fabrics with resin finishes.

Durable Press and Permanent Press

Many manufactured fibers achieve a durable-press finish without resins. High temperatures are used to "heat set" fabrics or garments. The desired shape, creases, and pleats are permanent, but wrinkles are resisted. If care instructions are followed, ironing is unnecessary.

Flame-Resistant

The Flammable Fabrics Act lists general requirements for all clothing and specific ones for children's sleepwear, carpets, rugs, and mattresses. As a fabric burns, this chemical finish works by cutting off the oxygen supply or changing the chemical makeup of the fibers. This causes the flame to extinguish itself.

Mildew-Resistant

A metallic chemical is applied to fabrics to prevent mildew.

Mercerization

Cotton and rayon fabrics are chemically treated to improve luster, strength, and absorbency.

Moth-Repellent

Chemicals can be added to dye baths to slightly change wool fibers. Moth and carpet beetle larvae will not eat the changed fibers.

Preshrunk

Fabrics are shrunk by moisture and heat. Later, when consumers buy the fabrics or garments, they will not shrink more than three percent unless otherwise stated.

Sanforized®

This trademark means that fabrics have been processed so they will not shrink more than one percent in either direction.

Soil-Release

This finish allows fabrics to be more easily "wetted." This helps detergents release soil. It is often used with durable-press finishes.

Stain-Resistant

This finish causes fabrics to repel food, water, and other substances by reducing absorbency. Stains can be lifted or sponged off easily.

Water-Repellent and Waterproof

This finish is applied to tightly woven fabrics to help them resist water. The finish cannot resist heavy rain or long exposure to rain. It is not a permanent finish, but it can be renewed.

Water-repellent finishes are not the same as waterproof fabrics. Waterproof fabrics are films or film-coated fabrics. No water can soak into these fabrics. They are cheaper, but less comfortable than fabrics with a water-repellent finish.

Finishes That Affect Texture

These finishes are a few that are used to change the appearance or texture of the fabric.

Calendering

Heat and pressure are applied to fabrics to produce a smooth, polished surface.

Napping

Napping raises the short, loose fibers on the fabric surface. Fiber ends are pulled from low-twist, spun yarns. A soft, fuzzy surface is made.

Sizing

Starch or resin is applied to fabrics to increase weight, body, and luster. It is a less expensive way to improve the appearance of a fabric, but it often washes out.

Weighting

Addition of metallic salts to silk increases the fabric weight and crispness.

Select fabrics with finishes that will meet your various performance requirements.

CHAPTER REVIEW

Key Points

- Fibers are combined to make yarns. Yarns are combined to make fabrics. The yarns used can be spun yarns, monofilament yarns, or multifilament yarns.

- The amount of twist added to a yarn affects the strength of the yarn. Filament yarns can be textured, making the yarns less smooth. Two or more yarns can be twisted together to form ply yarns.

- The two most common methods of making fabric are weaving and knitting. Other methods include felting, bonding, and quilting.

- Weaving is the process of interlacing yarns at right angles to each other to create a woven fabric. Different effects are achieved by passing the filling yarns over and under different numbers of warp yarns.

- Knitting is the process of looping yarns together to form a knitted fabric. The loops or stitches can be varied to create different patterns and textures.

- Greige goods are either dyed or printed to add color and pattern to the fabric. There are many methods used to dye and print fabrics.

- A fabric finish is any treatment given to fibers, yarns, or fabrics that make the final product look, feel, or perform differently.

To Review

1. Which are made from staple fibers?
   A. Spun yarns.
   B. Monofilament yarns.
   C. Multifilament yarns.

2. Name two reasons for adding twist to a yarn.

3. Which list is arranged from the smallest to the largest yarn?
   A. Single, cord, ply.
   B. Single, ply, cord.
   C. Ply, cord, single.
   D. Cord, ply, single.

4. When different staple fibers are spun into a single yarn, the result is a _____.

5. In woven fabrics, the lengthwise yarns are the _____ yarns. The crosswise yarns are the _____ yarns.

6. Name the three basic weaves and one fabric made from each.

7. What is the basic difference between weaving and knitting?

8. List three uses of nonwoven fabrics.

9. Which type of fabric is NOT made of fibers?
   A. Woven fabrics.
   B. Nonwoven fabrics.
   C. Felt.
   D. Films.

10. Explain two methods of dyeing.

11. In _____ printing, the design is etched on copper rollers.

12. Describe four finishes for textile items.

To Do

1. Unravel some fabric samples. Identify the kinds of yarns used.

2. Look through a catalog of ready-to-wear clothing. Make a list of the fiber blends that are listed.

3. Using narrow strips of colored paper, construct small samples of basic weaves. Display. Discuss characteristics of each.

4. Collect samples of fabrics that have been woven or knitted by different methods. Identify the methods used.

5. Display various samples of felt, films, nonwoven fabrics, bonded fabrics, and quilted fabrics. Also display pictures of their end uses.

6. Examine several fabric samples. Tell which ones were dyed and which ones were printed.

7. Research various natural dyeing techniques used many years ago. Experiment with the processes using pieces of muslin fabric. Display the fabrics along with a description of how they were dyed.

8. Divide the class into two groups. Have a "spelling bee" game using textile terms from this chapter and their definitions.

9. Make several large tic-tac-toe designs on a sheet of paper. In each square, list different fabrics, weaves, dyeing methods, and finishes. Then visit a fabric department or store. Place an X in each square that matches the description of a fabric you find. See who finishes first.

To Think About

1. If you were creating a blended yarn, which two fibers would you choose? What characteristics would they bring to a fabric?

2. Debate the advantages and disadvantages of woven fabrics versus knitted fabrics. Which wins the debate?

3. List three types of garments. What kind of fabric construction would be best for each of these garment types? What finishes would you like the fabrics to have for each of these garments?

4. If a garment has a flame-resistant label on it, do you think people are likely to be more careless around open flames? Why or why not?

5. You are a textile scientist. What new fabric finish would you invent and why?

Keeping Clothes Looking Their Best

Maytag

Objectives

After studying this chapter, you will be able to

- explain the importance of daily clothing care.
- choose the laundry product best suited to a certain laundry task.
- select and use clothing care equipment.
- demonstrate how to remove various types of stains.
- explain how using information on care labels can help you to obtain good laundry results.
- describe how to properly and safely wash and dry clothing.
- explain the difference between pressing and ironing.
- use the services of a professional dry cleaner.
- describe methods of storing clothes.

You have probably taken a great deal of time to select, purchase, or sew the clothes you wear. Some items of clothing receive only occasional wear, but many items are worn regularly. In order to save your investment of time and money, you need to take good care of your clothes. To keep them looking their best for a long time, there are simple clothing care practices you need to do every day. Your clothes also need to be laundered properly to maintain their appearance.

Most clothing items today are easier to care for than in past years. New fibers and fabric characteristics have made weekly laundry chores easier. Laundry care products have improved through the years, and new products appear regularly. All are designed to do a better job of keeping your clothes looking their best. You need to have knowledge of these products and how to use them. Then you will always have clean clothes ready to go whenever you need them.

Daily Clothing Care

What do you do with your clothes at the end of the day? Instead of tossing them onto a chair, take a minute of your time and put your clothes and accessories where they belong. Do they need to be cleaned? Do they need a repair? Can they be worn again? You are the one who knows what your clothes need, and right then is the time to make the decisions. See 16-1.

After you finish wearing a garment, do a quick inspection. First, check for stains. If you remember spilling food on your clothes, now is a good time to do some preliminary stain removal. For most washable items, a quick rinse in cool water will go a long way to prevent permanent stains from forming. You will learn more about stain removal later in this chapter.

Next, check for any repairs that might be needed. Did you notice a button starting to come loose? Did you catch your heel in a hem, causing a few stitches to come loose? If so, set the garment aside so you will remember to make the repair before you need to wear the garment again.

If the garment can be worn again, put it on a hanger or in a drawer. Heavier

KEEPING YOUR CLOTHES READY TO WEAR

Decide if a garment is to be worn again before cleaning.

Remove any stains or spots.

Place garments together that need repairs. If they are put in a special place, they can be found when you have time to work on them.

Put dresses, jackets, shirts, and coats on hangers.

Fold pants over hanger or use pants hangers.

Fold sweaters. Place in drawer or on shelf.

If shoes are damp from wearing, let dry before putting them away.

Wipe dust or dirt from shoes before putting them in the closet.

16-1
Keep your clothes ready to wear by following these tips.

garments should be placed on padded hangers or broad hangers shaped of wood or plastic. Empty all pockets. Close zippers and buttons to keep them from becoming wrinkled or twisted in a crowded closet. Brush dust and lint off garments with a clothing brush or lint roller. Fold sweaters carefully and put them in a drawer. They could stretch out of shape on a hanger.

If the clothing item is soiled and needs to be laundered, place it in a clothes basket or hamper. Having a place designated for dirty laundry in your bedroom or bathroom will remind you when the laundry needs to be done. It may also help you resist the temptation to just toss your dirty clothes on the floor or a chair.

Some soiled items will need to be dry-cleaned. Your family may have a special place to put clothing items that need to be taken to a dry cleaner.

Clothing Care Products

To keep your clothes looking their best, it is a good idea to keep some laundry and stain removal products on hand. At the minimum, you should have a good laundry soap or detergent. There are some additional laundry aids, however, that can solve specific laundry problems. Knowing what these products are and what they can do will help you in selecting the right product for your needs. Some products are designed to remove stains on clothing.

Look at the display in 16-2. Only a few of the many laundry products on the market are shown. Do you know how to use each type of product?

16-2

There are numerous laundry products available to help clean and care for clothes.

Water Softeners

Some sections of the country have hard water, and other areas have soft water. **Water hardness** refers to the amount of minerals, usually calcium and magnesium, contained in the water. Hard water is preferred for drinking, but it is a problem when washing clothes. A soap scum or film often forms when you use soap in hard water. Do you find a ring around your bathtub when the water is drained? If so, you probably have hard water.

Many families in hard water areas use a **water softener,** which is a product or device used to soften the water. Some families have a water-softening system installed in their homes if their water is very hard. By doing this, all the water that comes into their house is softened. Others purchase packaged water softeners that remove or inactivate calcium and magnesium ions present in the water. These products may be powders or liquids. Powders are added to the wash or rinse water when doing the laundry. Liquids are added to rinse water only. The result is whiter, cleaner, and softer clothes.

Laundry Detergents

Detergents are made from petroleum and natural fats and oils. Their primary purpose is to remove dirt from laundry items. There are many types of detergents on the market. Choose the one best suited to your needs. Some are high-sudsing and others are low-sudsing, but suds are not needed to clean clothes. Some are called *general purpose* or *heavy-duty laundry detergents.* These are suitable for all washable fabrics from heavily soiled work clothes to lightly soiled lingerie. Others are called *light-duty detergents.* These are designed for lightly soiled items and delicate fabrics, as well as baby clothes. Some detergents are called *combination detergents.* These are detergents that do two jobs, such as removing dirt and bleaching or softening.

Some detergents are concentrated. They come in smaller packages because you use less product. These may be referred to as *ultra detergents.* Another category of detergents is designed for use in cold water. These detergents help consumers reduce their energy bills by using cold water instead of hot water.

The newest category of laundry detergents are designed for the new high-efficiency front-loading washers. These washers require the use of a detergent designated as *high efficiency (HE).* HE detergents are formulated to be low-sudsing and quick-dispersing. Excess suds in HE washers would "cushion" the tumbling action, which can impact proper cleaning.

16-3
Measure the recommended amount of detergent for your type of washer and your wash load.

water hardness
The amount of minerals, such as calcium and magnesium, contained in water.

water softener
A product or device used to soften water.

detergent
A chemical mixture made from petroleum and natural fats and oils used to remove dirt from clothes.

All detergents are available as liquids or powders. Follow the directions on the package to find the amount of detergent to use. For best results, measure the detergent as in 16-3, rather than just pouring it into the machine.

Enzyme Presoaks

enzyme presoak
A laundry product specially formulated to help remove stains before washing.

An **enzyme presoak** is used for soaking the laundry before washing. These products help remove many difficult stains, especially those with a protein base. Baby formula, blood, dairy products, eggs, and grass stains can be removed with the use of an enzyme product. Though these powders are usually used to soak laundry before washing, they can also be added to the wash cycle in addition to the detergent. This boosts the cleaning power of the detergent.

Bleach

bleach
A laundry product that removes stains and whitens or brightens fabrics.

Bleach is a chemical mixture that removes stains and whitens or brightens fabrics. With proper laundering, bleach is seldom necessary for the weekly wash. Bleach can shorten the life of a garment by weakening the fibers if it is used too often. There are two types of bleaches: chlorine bleach and oxygen bleach.

Chlorine bleach is identified by the word "hypochlorite" or "liquid household bleach." It is the more powerful of the laundry bleaches. It disinfects as well as cleans and whitens. Use it in wash water according to the manufacturer's directions. Caution! Never use it on wool, silk, spandex, or any garment with a label that warns against its use. Check care labels on garments. Many advise "Do Not Bleach."

Chlorine bleach can be used on white fabrics and colorfast washables. Do not pour chlorine bleach directly on clothes. Instead, put it in the water before you add the clothes. Follow directions on the container to decide how much to use.

Many teenagers use bleach to get a tie-dyed look in T-shirts or jeans. However, the bleached spots become holes if the bleach stays on the item too long.

Oxygen bleach is identified by the words "perborate" or "all-fabric." It is mild and can be used on most colored fabrics. Follow directions. You may need to soak the garment.

Blueing

blueing
A product used to counteract the natural yellowing in some fabrics.

Blueing is another product used to counteract the natural yellowing in some fabrics, particularly white and black fabrics. It is dark blue in color and is available in liquid form. Blueing is added to the washer at the start of the wash or in the final rinse. Bleaches and detergents often include blue flakes for the same purpose.

Fabric Softeners

Fabric softeners, a popular laundry aid, give softness and fluffiness to fabrics. Fabric softeners cause a thin, invisible, lubricating coating to form over each fiber. As a result, garments will be soft and have few wrinkles. Many add a pleasing fragrance. Clothes will be easier to iron and nicer to wear. Fabric softeners may reduce the effectiveness of flame retardancy on fabrics, such as children's sleepwear.

Sometimes in cold, dry weather, garments made from manufactured fibers have a tendency to cling to the body. Does your shirt, sweater, slip, or skirt make snapping noises when you take it off? This is caused by static electricity. Using a fabric softener can reduce it. Other antistatic products are available. Some can be sprayed from aerosol cans.

Fabric softeners are available in two forms. Liquid products are added to the final rinse of the washer cycle. To be effective, they should not be used with any other laundry products in the rinse cycle. They should be diluted and added directly to the rinse water. Do not pour on fabrics as staining can occur. Always use the amount suggested by the manufacturer.

Dryer-added fabric softeners are designed to be added to a load of clothes in the dryer. Some are in the form of a small nonwoven sheet of synthetic fabric or polyurethane foam. These are saturated with a softener, and the heat of the dryer transfers the softener to the clothes. A new sheet is used each time. A packet-type fabric softener is attached to a fin of the dryer drum.

Starch

Starch produces a crisp, smooth surface on fabrics. It is available in dry, liquid, or spray forms. If collars or cuffs appear wrinkled or puckered, a light application of spray starch before ironing should give them a smooth look. The dry and liquid forms are mixed with water. Starch is most effective on cotton or cotton-blend fabrics. With manufactured fibers and durable press finishes, starch is rarely needed.

Prewash Soil and Stain Removers

Products that help remove oily stains and heavy soil are called **prewash soil and stain removers.** They are available in pump spray, liquid, gel, stick, or aerosol forms. They contain solvents that penetrate the fibers and dissolve grease and oil stains. Prewash products are especially effective on oil-based stains on polyester fabrics. For instance, when a prewash spray is used on the neck edges of shirt or blouse collars, they become cleaner, 16-4. To get the best cleaning action, be sure to follow the directions on the label.

fabric softener
Laundry product used to make garments soft and fluffy and to reduce wrinkles and static electricity.

starch
A laundry product that produces a crisp, smooth surface on fabrics.

prewash soil and stain removers
Products that help remove oily stains and heavy soil from fabrics.

Little Kids, Inc.

16-4 Little children often get stains on their clothing. Treat all stains as soon as possible so they will be easier to remove.

Solvents or Cleaning Fluids

solvent
A liquid substance used to dissolve greasy stains.

Sometimes, a **solvent** is used to dissolve stains. Use solvents to remove makeup and greasy stains. There are many brand names, but most are labeled "cleaning fluid" or "spot remover." Some are flammable, and some are poisonous. Read all label warnings. Use them only in a well-ventilated place.

agitation
The action that helps to loosen and remove soil from clothes during the wash cycle.

Clothing Care Equipment

Special equipment is needed to care for your clothes. These include washing machines, clothes dryers, irons, and ironing boards. You may have this equipment at home, but they are also available for use in self-service laundries. Apartment buildings may have laundry rooms where this equipment is available for tenants' use.

Washers and Dryers

Many families have their own washing machines and dryers. Automatic models have dials or push buttons you can set according to your wash load. These settings include:

- fill level
- water temperatures for wash and rinse cycles
- soak time
- wash cycles that determine agitator speed and length of washing time

Most models offer three cycles: regular, gentle, and permanent press. These generally determine the length and amount of agitation. **Agitation** is the action that helps to loosen and remove soils from the clothes during the wash cycle. Top-loading washers are the most common. The laundry is completely submerged in water. An agitator moves the laundry back and forth to loosen soils. Deluxe models also include features for dispensing fabric softener, presoak product, bleach, and detergent. These models also offer a wider range of water levels and more temperature combinations. Less expensive models have fewer features. They are less convenient, but they can make your clothes just as clean as the deluxe models.

The newest washing machines are high-efficiency front-loading washers, 16-5. These washers use a "tumbler" system with no agitator. The tub rotates back and forth, moving

Maytag Corporation

16-5_____
New front-loading washers are more energy efficient because they use only a small amonut of water

the water and detergent through the laundry to remove soil. Only a small amount of water is used, saving energy. The Department of Energy is expected to impose water and energy regulations on clothes washers within the next few years. This led to the development of these machines. All load through the front and spin horizontally. There is no center agitator. They are capable of removing more water, thus cutting drying time.

Automatic washing machines often have matching automatic dryers. Dryers usually have regular, permanent press, and air fluff cycles. The regular cycle is for items that are not sensitive to heat. Permanent press cycles provide a cool-down time with no heat at the end to reduce wrinkles. The air fluff cycle provides tumbling in unheated air.

Some families use commercial washers and dryers. They take their clothes to self-service laundries. The machines there are coin-operated. Several can be used at one time. This can reduce the time spent doing laundry.

Irons and Ironing Boards

In addition to a washer and dryer, an iron and ironing board may be needed. Irons generally have both dry and steam settings and a wide variety of fabric settings. The dry setting is used at low temperatures for fabrics sensitive to heat. If the fabric is already damp, a dry iron setting can be used. Steam settings are used when you need to iron or press with steam. The soleplate of the iron has holes that allow steam to escape, 16-6. Some models have a button that is used to give a shot of steam or water. Most use distilled water to avoid buildup of mineral deposits, but some can use tap water.

An ironing board is an asset. Most adjust to your height for comfort. Make sure the board is sturdy and does not rock as you iron. Use a padded cover. Padding is usually foam or a felted pad. Covers are given a silicone treatment to prevent burning and increase wear. Replace both when wear starts to show as tears and burned areas can damage your clothes as you iron.

Outsmarting Stains

A **stain** is a spot or discoloration caused by various liquids or solid materials. If you find a spot or stain on a garment, do something about it quickly. Do not wait to find it

stain
A spot or discoloration caused by various liquids or solid materials.

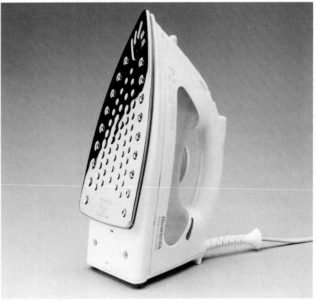

Rowenta

16-6_____

Steam irons have holes that allow steam to escape. The combination of heat and moisture effectively removes wrinkles.

again just as you are ready to go somewhere. Removing stains is easier than you may think. Most common ones can be removed if you are prompt, patient, and persistent.

Treat stains as soon as you see them. Fresh stains come out more easily than old ones. You cannot see some stains until they have been in the garment for a while. Then a yellow spot appears. Ironing over a stain will often make it impossible to remove. Take your nonwashable garments to the dry cleaners as soon as possible. Be sure and tell them what the stain is if you know.

Try to find out what the stain is. Use the stain removal procedure that is recommended for the stain and the type of fabric. Otherwise, you may damage your garment or set the stain. If it is worth saving, it is worth a little extra time and effort. Stains on durable press fabrics are sometimes difficult to remove. This is because of the chemical finish that is on them.

You may have to try to remove the stain several times before you succeed. If the first treatment does not work, try a different method. Knowing what the stain is will speed the process.

Successful Stain Removal

You are more likely to remove a stain if you use the right products. In the laundry area, you should keep detergents, prewash soil and stain removers, bleaches, solvents, clean white cloths, and white paper towels or facial tissues. A chart as in 16-7, with a listing of stains and removal procedures, should also be in this area.

A GUIDE FOR REMOVING **STAINS**

Adhesive Tape
Scrape with a dull knife. Apply cleaning fluid or prewash stain remover. Rinse, and then wash with detergent.

Ballpoint Ink
Laundering will remove some types of ballpoint ink, but it sets other types. To see if the stain will wash out, find a similar scrap of fabric. Mark it with the ink and wash it. Pretreat with a prewash stain remover. Denatured (rubbing) alcohol will remove some types of ink. Place stain face down on paper towels and apply alcohol. When stain is removed, wash as usual.

Blood
Soak fresh stains in cold water. Rinse. For dried stains, pretreat or soak in warm water with enzyme product. Rub a heavy-duty detergent into the spot, and then launder as usual. If the stain remains, rewash using bleach safe for the fabric.

(Continued)

16-7
This guide lists some methods you can use to remove common stains.

A GUIDE FOR REMOVING **STAINS** *(Cont.)*

Candle Wax
Rub the stain with ice and scrape off as much wax as possible. Then place the stain between several layers of white paper towels. Press with warm iron. If any stain remains, apply cleaning fluid or pre-wash stain remover. Launder.

Car Grease, Oil
Most of these stains can be removed by rubbing a heavy-duty detergent or prewash stain remover into the stain. Wash in hottest water safe for fabric. If the stain remains, put cleaning fluid on it and wash again.

Chewing Gum
Make the gum hard by putting ice on it. Remove as much as you can with a dull knife. Put prewash stain remover or cleaning fluid on the remaining spot. Then launder.

Chocolate
Soak stain in warm water with a product containing enzymes or treat with prewash stain remover. Rinse. If stain remains, work heavy-duty detergent into the stain. Then rinse thoroughly. If the stain looks greasy, apply cleaning fluid.

Coffee or Tea
Soak in enzyme presoak product or oxygen bleach. Use the hottest water that is safe for the fabric. Wash.

Cosmetics
Apply undiluted, heavy-duty liquid detergent to stain. Work with your fingers to form suds. Rinse well. Or, pretreat with prewash stain remover. If the garment is not washable, use a spot remover. Rub the edges of the stain lightly with a cloth. This will prevent a circle from forming.

Deodorants and Antiperspirants
Rub liquid detergent on stain. Wash in the hottest water safe for the fabric. Pretreat heavy stains with prewash stain remover. Allow to stand 5 to 10 minutes.

Grass
Pretreat or soak in product containing enzymes. Wash garment as usual. If stain remains, use bleach according to manufacturer's directions.

Ice Cream or Milk
Pretreat or soak stains using product containing enzymes. Soak for at least 30 minutes or several hours. Launder. Repeat if necessary.

Nail Polish
Use nail polish remover. Before using, test a scrap or small area to be sure it will not cause damage. Do not use remover on acetate or triacetate fabrics. Place stain face down on paper towels and apply remover to back of stain.

Fruit—Fruit Juices, Soft Drinks, Punches
If possible, sponge with cool water as soon as stain occurs. Soak with enzyme presoak, rinse. Bleach the garment, if possible. Apply white vinegar if bleach cannot be used. Launder again.

Perspiration
Presoak by wetting the area and applying heavy-duty detergent or use a prewash stain remover. Wait one hour. Then wash in hot water. Stubborn stains may respond to product containing enzymes or oxygen bleach.

Scorch
Launder using bleach that is safe for fabric in hot water.

16-7

Continued

There are water-based stains and oil-based stains. Water-based stains include fruit, vegetables, soft drinks, coffee, and tea. Oil-based stains include cosmetics, grease, candle wax, motor oil, and tar. Water-based stains are removed by a wet process, usually detergent and water. Stains are generally soaked in cool water for a period of time. To remove oil-based stains, use a dry process with a solvent or spot remover if the garment cannot be washed.

Many oil-based stains can be removed from washable garments if pretreated with a liquid laundry detergent. First, wet the stained area. Then pour undiluted detergent on it. Wait a few minutes before washing or rinsing the garment. You may need to soak it longer or use a heavy-duty detergent.

When using a solvent or dry-cleaning fluid, first place the stained area on an absorbent surface—a soft cloth, paper towels, or facial tissues. Put the stained side down so the stain can be washed out of the garment, not through it.

Dampen a soft cloth or pad of cotton with the solvent. Apply the solvent to the stain using a soft brushing or tapping motion. Work outward from the center. Brush the edges often to prevent a circle from forming around the stained area. Changing the absorbent pad under the fabric will keep the stain from going back into the fabric.

Stain Removal Cautions

Keep the following safety precautions in mind when removing stains:

- Read instructions on all products and keep them in their original labeled containers.
- Always keep cleaning materials beyond the reach of children.
- Do not mix or combine stain removal products, such as ammonia and chlorine bleach. Some mixtures can release irritating gases.
- Solvents, such as cleaning fluid and denatured alcohol, should be used only in a well-ventilated room. Keep them away from open flame and pilot lights.
- Clothes treated with solvents should be rinsed before washing.

Doing Laundry the Right Way

laundering
The washing of clothes with water and laundry products.

In many homes today, all of the adult members work outside the home. Everyone must help with the duties of homemaking. Perhaps you could help with the family laundry. **Laundering** is the washing of clothes with water and laundry products. To do your laundry the right way, there are specific steps to follow.

Read the Care Labels

First, read the care label. If you do not know the best way to wash, dry, or iron a garment, you can refer to its care label. Care labels are often found at the center neckline or in a seam. They are permanently attached to the garments. These are the manufacturers' recommended methods of safely caring for the garments. They are your best guide for what to do and what not to do. The terms found on these labels are explained in 16-8.

Prior to 1972, there were no care labels in garments. Instructions for care were on hangtags that were removed from the garments. In 1972, the Federal Trade Commission issued the Care Labeling Rule. This law required

UNDERSTANDING
CARE **LABELS**

	When label reads:	It means:
Machine Washable	Machine wash	Wash, bleach, dry, and press by any customary method including commercial laundering and dry cleaning.
	Home launder only	Same as above, but do not use commercial laundering.
	No chlorine bleach	Do not use chlorine bleach. Oxygen bleach may be used.
	No bleach	Do not use any type of bleach.
	Cold wash Cold rinse	Use cold water from tap or cold washing machine setting.
	Warm wash Warm rinse	Use warm water or warm washing machine setting.
	Hot wash	Use hot water or hot washing machine setting.
	No spin	Remove wash load before final machine spin cycle.
	Delicate cycle Gentle cycle	Use appropriate machine setting; otherwise wash by hand.
	Durable press cycle Permanent press cycle	Use appropriate machine setting; otherwise use warm wash, cold rinse, and short spin cycle.
	Wash separately	Wash alone or with like colors.
Non-Machine Washing	Hand wash	Launder only by hand in lukewarm (hand comfortable) water. May be bleached, may be dry-cleaned.
	Hand wash only	Same as above, but do not dry-clean.
	Hand wash separately	Hand wash alone or with like colors.
	No bleach	Do not use bleach.
	Damp wipe	Clean surface with damp cloth or sponge.

(Continued)

American Apparel Manufacturers Assoc.

16-8

This explanation of care terms will help you understand them.

UNDERSTANDING
CARE LABELS *(Cont.)*

	When label reads:	It means:
Home Drying	Tumble dry	Dry in tumble dryer at specified setting–high, medium, low, or no heat.
	Tumble dry Remove promptly	Same as above, but in absence of cool-down cycle, remove at once when tumbling stops.
	Drip dry	Hang wet and allow to dry with hand shaping only.
	Line dry	Hang damp and allow to dry.
	No wring No twist	Hang dry, drip dry, or dry flat only. Handle to prevent wrinkles and distortion.
	Dry flat	Lay garment on flat surface.
	Block to dry	Maintain original size and shape while drying.
Ironing or Pressing	Cool iron	Set iron at lowest setting.
	Warm iron	Set iron at medium setting.
	Hot iron	Set iron at hot setting.
	Do not iron	Do not iron or press with heat.
	Steam iron	Iron or press with steam.
	Iron damp	Dampen garment before ironing.
Miscellaneous	Dry-clean only	Garment should be dry-cleaned only.
	No dry clean	Use recommended care instructions. No dry-cleaning materials to be used.

American Apparel Manufacturers Assoc.

16-8

Continued

that all wearing apparel (except hosiery) give clear and complete directions for regular care and maintenance on permanent labels attached to garments. In 1984, the Care Labeling Rule was revised. The information listed on labels had to be more detailed and complete. A label that recommends washing must state the washing method, such as machine or by hand. The safe water temperature must also be listed, along with safe drying and ironing methods. Only a few exceptions were allowed.

Beginning in 1997, certain care symbols could be used on labels instead of words. A chart of these symbols is shown in 16-9. Laundry mistakes have been greatly reduced because of the Care Labeling Rule. (See Chapter 6 for more details.)

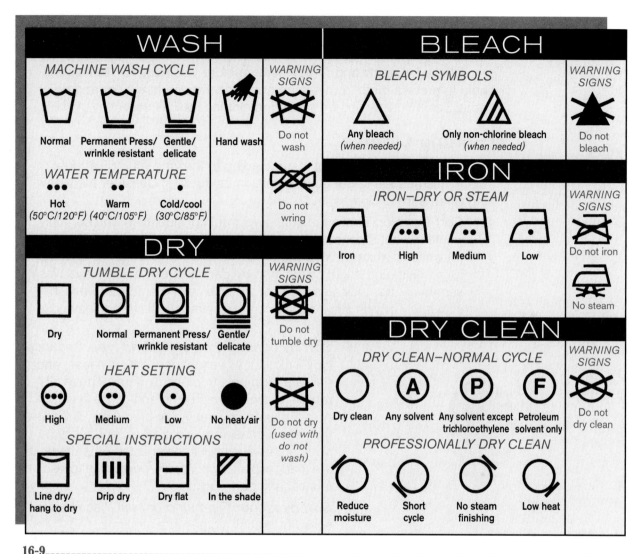

16-9

Look for these symbols on care labels in your clothes.

Preparing Clothes for Washing

Look carefully at each garment before washing it. Remove all items from the pockets—folded notes, gum, and pencils. A facial tissue left in a pocket will cover your clothes with lint.

If a large metal fastener or buckle cannot be removed from an item, it can be tucked inside the fabric and basted in place. Sometimes items can be hooked or buttoned shut or secured inside a pocket. This prevents damage to the washer basket, to other clothes, and to the item.

Loosely tie together long belts, strings, sashes, or stockings. Turn knits inside out to prevent snagging. Close zippers, hooks and eyes, and buttons. Shake dirt from cuffs of slacks.

Check for stains and remove them before washing, 16-10. This will help to prevent them from setting permanently with hot water and dryer heat. See 16-11 for tips on preparing clothes for washing.

Sorting Clothes

sorting
Grouping clothes in piles according to the way they will be laundered.

Sorting is grouping clothes according to the way you will launder them. It is needed to get good results in laundering. Consider the following when sorting clothes:

- *Sort by color.* This is the most important consideration. You certainly wouldn't want a noncolorfast item mixed in with a white load. Separate (1) white or white-background prints that are colorfast, (2) light colors, (3) medium and bright colors, and (4) dark colors. If a label says *wash separately,* this indicates the item will lose color. Be sure to wash it separately or with similar colors until you are sure it will not leave dye in the water.

- *Sort by construction and fabric type.* Separate loosely knit or woven fabrics, sheers, laces, and delicate garments from sturdy items. These all require a shorter wash time and gentle agitation. Also separate any heavy lint-producers, such as flannel pajamas, terry cloth robes, and fuzzy sweatshirts. They will transfer lint to other items in the load, especially corduroy, permanent press fabrics, and dark socks.

- *Sort by amount and kind of soil.* Place heavily soiled or greasy clothes in a separate load. If washed with lightly soiled items, they will make the lightly soiled items dingy. Whites may look gray or yellow, and colors may become dull.

If possible, include large and small garments in each pile, 16-12. This allows for better washing action.

If you have a heavily soiled, white garment, it may be wise to wash it by itself. Many light-colored, manufactured fibers (especially nylon) will absorb dirt from the wash water and look gray or dingy.

Little Kids, Inc.

16-10
The chocolate stain on this toddler's shirt will be difficult to remove. Be sure to pretreat before laundering.

Washing Clothes

After sorting the laundry into wash loads, you are ready to begin. Most of the laundry can be washed in automatic washers. Some will require hand washing.

Preparing Clothes for Washing

- Make sure all pockets are empty. Turn them inside out.
- Turn down cuffs and brush away lint and dirt.
- Remove pins, buckles, and other hard or sharp objects to avoid scratching the washer basket or snagging other items.
- Close zippers, snaps, and hooks to avoid snagging other items in the load.
- Tie strings and cords so they won't tangle.
- Mend tears, loose hems, and seams.

16-11

Taking steps like these before washing can pay off with better results.

Machine Washing

The following are the steps you should follow when washing clothes by machine.

Choose and Add Laundry Products

Choose the laundry products you will need for your wash load. A detergent will be needed to remove the dirt. Read and follow the label directions on the container for best results. Measure the recommended amount using the specially designed bottle cap or other device provided with the detergent. If a device is not provided, use a standard measuring cup. Pour the detergent into the washer tub following the manufacturer's instructions.

The amount of detergent recommended is based on an average load. This is five to seven pounds of clothes, moderately soiled, and washed in moderately hard water. If any of these conditions are changed, the amount of detergent should be adjusted.

If you are using any other laundry additives, follow the instructions on the container for their use. Some products, such as oxygen bleaches, should be added to the wash water before clothes are added. Fabric softeners are usually added to the rinse water.

Nancy Henke-Konopasek

16-12

Sorting clothes is a necessary step before washing them.

Load the Washer

When you load the washer, be careful not to put too many clothes in it. It is better to under load than to overload. Garments need room to move about easily in the water and detergent to get their cleanest. Do not wind large items around the agitator or the tub. They can become tangled.

If the garments are heavily soiled, wash only a few at a time. Bulky clothes take up room even if they are lightweight. If you decide to launder a blanket, wash it by itself.

Select the Water Level

The water level should match the size of the load. You want to be sure there is ample water for the movement of the clothes. Choose a lower water level for smaller wash loads. This saves energy and prevents wasting water.

Select the Wash Temperature

The water temperatures you select will be based on the items you are washing, 16-13. Water temperature affects cleaning, wrinkling, and color and size retention. Hot water (130°F) does the best job of removing soil and disinfecting. However, hot water can cause colors to run and garments to shrink. Hot water also increases wrinkling. Wash sturdy whites, diapers, colorfast items, and heavily soiled permanent press items in hot water.

Using warm water (90°F) will reduce shrinkage, color loss, and wrinkling. Water at this temperature does not sanitize clothes; a disinfectant would need to be added to the wash water. Use warm water for moderately soiled, permanent press, and noncolorfast items. Some silks, washable woolens, and manufactured fibers are washed in warm water.

Cold water (80°F or cooler) does not clean as well as hot or warm water. Cold water does reduce wrinkling and fading of colors. Wash only noncolorfast and lightly soiled items in cold water.

Using cold water for rinsing will reduce wrinkles. It will also help to conserve energy used in heating water. Even when hot or warm water is used for the wash cycle, use cold water for rinsing to save energy.

CORRECT WATER TEMPERATURES

Water Temperature	Items to Wash
Hot Water	Sturdy whites, diapers, colorfast items, and heavily soiled permanent-press items.
Warm Water	Moderately soiled, permanent press, and noncolorfast items. Silks, washable woolens, and manufactured fibers.
Cold Water	Noncolorfast, lightly soiled items. Dark colored items that are lightly soiled.

16-13
Laundering clothes in correct water temperatures will help clothes retain their colors and appearance.

Select the Agitation Speed or Wash Cycle

Choose an agitation speed suitable for the items you are washing. Agitation is necessary for soil removal, but too much can damage delicate items. Machines may have a "cycle selection" using *regular* or *normal, delicate,* and *permanent press,* or "wash speed selection" with *regular* and *gentle* selections.

Normal or regular agitation should be used for all but delicate items. Choose gentle speeds for delicate loads. The permanent press cycle usually has normal agitation, but also includes a cool-down rinse to minimize wrinkling. Wrinkling of permanent press items may occur at higher speeds.

Today, most washers shut off when the door is opened. Still, never put your hand inside the washer until it has stopped. See 16-14. For a review of steps in laundering, see 16-15.

Hand Washing

A care label may state that a certain garment should be hand washed. This garment could have delicate trims or have colors that run when washed. A garment such as a sweater may be loosely knitted. This type of garment may look better and last longer if washed by hand.

Many wool garments have care labels that suggest washing by hand. Machine washing may cause them to shrink or become matted. Women often wash their hose by hand.

When you wash clothes by hand, wash only one or two garments at a time. Pretreat spots and stains. Use the temperature of water suited to the fabric. Add the detergents in the amount suggested on the package label. Swish the detergent around with your hand until it has dissolved. Force the water through the garment by squeezing it several times with your hands. This dissolves the soil and lifts it out of the garment into the water. Badly soiled areas may need to be rubbed between your fingers to remove the soil.

Rinse several times to get all of the detergent or soap out of the garment. Rinse as many times as necessary until the water is clear and there are no remaining suds. Rolling the garment in a large towel can remove most of the water. Either hang the garment on a rustproof hanger to dry or lay the garment to dry on a clean towel in the flat position.

NEVER put your hand inside the washer while it is running. Motors are powerful, and parts move at high speed. *You can be hurt!*

16-14_____
Safety is a must when operating a washer.

STEPS IN
LAUNDERING

1. Read care labels.
2. Treat spots, stains, and very dirty areas.
3. Sort clothes.
4. Choose and add the right amount of laundry products.
5. Load the washer.
6. Select the water level.
7. Select the appropriate water temperatures.
8. Select the appropriate wash cycle.

16-15_____
If you follow these steps, you will have good laundry results.

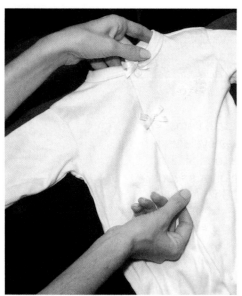

Made and Grown in USA

16-16

Promptly remove clothes from the dryer to prevent wrinkling. Carefully hand press clothes to shape.

Nancy Henke-Konopasek

16-17

As soon as clothes are removed from the dryer, hang them on hangers or fold them neatly.

Drying Clothes

Most clothes that are washed together can be dried together. An automatic dryer is the easiest and quickest way to dry clothes. Clothes can also be dried without using a dryer. Line drying, flat drying, and drip drying are other recommended methods of drying clothes.

Machine Drying

Drying clothes seems simple if you have an automatic dryer. You just throw clothes in, set the dial, and come back when you have time. Right? Wrong! There is a little more to doing a good job than that.

First, learn how to use the dryer. Study the information that came with the dryer if it is available.

Before you put the clothes in the dryer, make sure they can all be tumble dried. Read the care labels of the garments. Some cannot be dried in a dryer. Another method of drying may be recommended, such as line drying, drip drying, or drying flat. Labels also include a recommended dryer temperature, such as high, medium, low, or no heat.

Overloading the dryer causes clothing to become wrinkled and twisted. High temperatures could ruin buttons and trims and shrink some clothes. Cotton garments can withstand higher temperatures than those made of manufactured fibers. Set controls for "regular." Fabrics with wrinkle-resistant finishes require low temperatures. Heat will dissolve the chemicals used for these finishes. Set the control on "permanent press." The permanent press cycle provides a cool down period at the end to minimize wrinkling.

An average load of clothes needs about 25 to 30 minutes of drying time. Heavier items such as jeans, sweatshirts, and towels may need more than 30 minutes. Lingerie and other delicate garments require a lower temperature and about 10 to 15 minutes of drying time.

Remove the clothes as soon as the dryer stops, 16-16. This will help prevent wrinkling. Most garments will be ready to wear. If clothes lie in the bottom of the dryer until they are cool, you will probably need to iron them. Be sure to clean the lint filter after each use.

Hang any garments you can on hangers, 16-17. Smooth the seams, collars, and cuffs. Fold flat items while they are still warm to eliminate even more wrinkles. Be sure the clothes are completely dry before you put them away. Damp clothes can cause mildew and foul odors.

Line Drying

You may prefer to dry your clothes outside on a clothesline. In fact, many care labels suggest line drying or state "Hang to dry." As you hang the clothes, shake them, smooth out the wrinkles, and straighten the seams. Use clothespins on places where the imprint will not show, such as the bottoms of shirts or waistbands. You may want to use plastic hangers if you are hanging garments inside. If the garments are outside, take them from the line as soon as they are dry. Long exposure to the sun may cause some clothes to fade.

Flat Drying

Garments that are likely to shrink or stretch out of shape may keep their shapes better if they are allowed to dry in a flat position. See 16-18. Much of the rinse water can be removed by wrapping the garment in a large towel for a few minutes. Roll the garment in the towel and press it with your hands. Unroll and shape the garment on a clean, flat, absorbent surface. Never place a garment on newspaper. The ink from the print will stain the garment. Dry the garment away from direct heat.

Drip-Drying

In drip-drying, garments are not squeezed, wrung, or twisted to remove the water. After rinsing, lift the garment from the water and place it on a plastic or rustproof hanger. Hang the garment over an area that will not be damaged by water. For instance, you may choose to drip-dry garments over the bathtub, in the shower, or outside.

Pressing and Ironing

What is the difference between pressing and ironing? The terms are sometimes used for doing the same task.

Ironing is the process of removing wrinkles from damp, washable clothing. Heat and pressure are used to smooth the fabric. A gliding motion moves the iron over the fabric. Entire garments are dampened and then ironed after laundering.

Pressing is the process of removing wrinkles from clothing using steam and a lifting motion. The iron does not glide across the fabric. This could be done just before wearing a garment. It is also used for wool items. Pressing is also done when people sew clothes. They press seams open as they sew them.

ironing
The process of removing wrinkles from damp, washable clothing using a gliding motion.

pressing
The process of removing wrinkles from clothing using steam and a lifting motion.

16-18 _____
This sweater was laid to dry in its original shape on a towel. This method of drying is called flat drying.

After several washings, even minimum-care garments look better after ironing. Steam irons make the job easier, but follow the safety guidelines given in 16-19. Some steam irons have a spray button that, when pushed, supplies an extra mist of moisture. This can help remove stubborn wrinkles. If a steam iron is not available, a damp cloth placed carefully over small sections at a time will work equally well. Steam and heat are more effective than pressure in removing wrinkles.

Most irons have a dial showing temperature settings according to the fabric. Follow this guide since some synthetics melt under a hot iron. If you think the heat of the iron may damage your garment, press a seam first as a test. Cottons and linens require higher temperatures.

Iron all of your delicate or low-temperature garments first. This saves time waiting for high temperatures to cool. Ironing on the wrong side of fabrics will prevent shine on the face of the garment.

Iron small areas, such as sleeves, collars, and cuffs, before going to the large sections. There will be less wrinkling of parts already ironed. Iron with the grain of the fabric (usually from top to bottom). The garment will be less likely to stretch. Use a gliding motion. Let heat instead of pressure iron for you. You will not tire as quickly. See 16-20.

Follow these safety precautions when using a steam iron:

- **Fill the iron with water before plugging it in. Do not overfill or the water may boil out.**
- **Make sure the iron cord cannot be tripped over or pull the iron off the board.**
- **Steam is extremely dangerous! Keep your hands and face away from the steam.**
- **Place the iron on its heel rest after each use.**
- **Turn off the iron and allow it to cool before unplugging it. Unplug the iron after each use.**
- **Empty any remaining water before storing the iron.**

16-19

Prevent burns and other injuries by following these safety precautions when using a steam iron.

16-20

Use a gliding motion when ironing, and let heat instead of pressure do the work for you.

When using an iron, insert the plug into the outlet firmly before turning the iron on. When finished, turn the iron off, then unplug it by grasping the plug. Do not yank the cord because this will eventually damage it, leading to a possible electrical shock.

Dry Cleaning

The care labels on some clothes state that they must be dry-cleaned instead of laundered. This usually includes wool and silk garments. Suits, coats, and some dresses are often dry cleaned. Professional dry cleaners also know how to clean special materials such as leather, suede, fur, and imitations of these.

Dry cleaning is a process of cleaning clothes using organic chemical solvents instead of water. This type of cleaning can be done by professional dry cleaners.

dry cleaning
A process of cleaning clothes using organic chemical solvents instead of water.

Professional Dry Cleaning

Professional dry cleaners use large machines that look like washing machines. The clothes are placed in the machine and are tumbled. The chemical solvent flows through the clothes and removes the dirt and soil. After a period of time, the solvent drains from the machine, and the clothes tumble dry.

Professional dry cleaners remove stains and spots before garments are cleaned. Special chemicals and methods are used for different stains. This is why it is very important to point out any stains to the dry cleaner and, if possible, identify the stain, 16-21. Be sure to point out any stains that are light in color. If overlooked, these stains could turn brown with the heat used in drying during dry cleaning.

More services are offered by professional dry cleaners than just cleaning. Often, plastic trims and buttons must be removed before cleaning because the chemical solvent may melt or misshape them. If the cleaners remove them, they will also replace them after the garment is cleaned. If a water-repellent coat no longer repels water, the cleaners can add a new finish to replace the old one at an additional cost.

16-21
Professional dry cleaners remove stains and spots from garments. Identify stains when you drop garments off.

What's New in Cleaning Clothes?

While textile manufacturers are finding new ways to improve stain and wrinkle resistance, manufacturers of cleaning products and appliances are coming up with new innovations as well. The following are some of the newest products available to help you clean your clothes.

Dry cleaning is expensive, but now you can do some dry cleaning at home in your own dryer. Special kits can be purchased that contain the supplies you need, including a stain remover. You can place up to four garments in the reusable bag provided. A specially moistened cloth is placed in the bag, which is activated by the heat of the dryer. Within 30 minutes, clothes are smooth and most odors and stains removed.

On-the-spot stain removers are another convenient product gaining in popularity. Options include rollers, felt tip stain absorbers, squeeze bottles with brush tops, sprays, and towelettes. Products you can carry with you or keep in your desk to treat emergency spills can sometimes mean the difference in preventing a permanent stain from ruining a garment.

New appliances are also available. You have already read about the new high-efficiency washers, but there are also new appliances for drying clothes. Maytag's Neptune Drying Center combines a traditional dryer on the bottom with a drying cabinet above. Using warm air infused with steam, the cabinet offers a gentler way to dry, with less shrinkage. You can lay sweaters flat to dry on removable shelves, or hang shirts on special hangers that conform to clothes so they won't get stretched out. As clothes dry, the rod gently shakes back and forth to prevent wrinkles from forming.

Whirlpool's Personal Valet® is an at-home dry-cleaning appliance that looks like a small cabinet. It can be located in a bedroom, walk-in closet, or laundry room. Hang up to three garments of any fabric type inside the system. Then add a special solution and press start. A penetrating mist of the special clothes care formula circulates through the fabrics, smoothing wrinkles and cleaning away odors. In 30 minutes, garments are ready to wear.

Dry cleaners press most garments after they are cleaned. Pressing is done with special equipment. Garments are placed on forms and steam is blown through the garment from inside the form. Wrinkles are pressed or blown out in this manner. Garments that have pleats and creases, like skirts and pants, are pressed with large pressing machines that use pressure and steam.

Clothing Storage

Once a garment has been cleaned, it is ready to be stored. Garments can be placed on hangers and hung in closets or folded and stored in drawers or on shelves, 16-22.

If you wish to hang a garment for storage, select an appropriate hanger based on the garment's style and weight. Wire hangers may be used, but check for rust, peeling paint, or rough edges that can snag delicate items. Plastic tubular hangers are preferred for lightweight, firmly woven shirts and blouses. Padded hangers would be better for sheer fabric blouses and dresses. Jackets, suits, and tailored garments call for wide, shaped wood or plastic hangers that provide more support. Slacks can be suspended from the cuff or hem using specially designed hangers. Otherwise, place slacks over the horizontal bar of a plastic tubular hanger instead of a wire hanger to prevent creases from forming at the thigh.

Sweaters and stretchable garments should be folded and stored in drawers or on shelves rather than on hangers, 16-23. Hanging these garments would cause them to stretch and lose their shape. Fold garments at

Originally published in *Lowe's Creative Ideas* magazine. Copyright 2006 SPC Custom Publishing.

16-22

This well-organized closet provides many options for clothing storage including hangers, shelves, drawers, and hooks.

construction lines. If garments must be stacked, place heavier items at the bottom. Some smaller items can be rolled rather than folded, reducing wrinkles and saving storage space. This works well for underwear and socks.

With our modern climate-controlled buildings and transportation facilities, people wear less seasonal clothing than they did years ago. Today, year-round clothing is popular and more practical. However, there are still times when you need special clothes if you have cold winters. These coats, sweaters, and clothing need to be stored when winter is past.

Select a storage area that is dry and away from direct sunlight. Attics are usually better than basements. Dampness in a basement can cause mildew and musty, unpleasant odors, which are difficult to remove.

Cloth garment bags and cardboard boxes are good containers for storing out-of-season clothes. If you label the boxes, you can find what you need quickly. Tissue paper placed between folds will help prevent wrinkling.

The most important thing to remember about storing any clothing is to store only clean clothes. It is impossible to see all the soiled spots on a garment. There could be a soft drink spill that does not show. It can turn yellow or brown during storage and be impossible to remove later. If insects find the spot, they will eat it as well as some of the fabric. It would be smart to have your winter clothing dry-cleaned before you store it.

16-23
Knits can stretch out of shape on hangers. They will keep their shape if stored in drawers or on shelves.

Storing winter garments takes more effort than storing summer clothes. Wool is the warmest fiber, so it is used in many winter garments. Wool is expensive, and it requires special care if it is to look nice for several seasons.

Moths are pests that attack woolen garments. They appear mysteriously in closets and storage areas. They lay eggs on clothing. When the eggs hatch, the larvae eat the wool. Dry cleaning will destroy any moth eggs or larvae. This is another reason for cleaning clothes before storing them. Tightly seal bags and boxes with tape to keep moths from damaging the clean garments.

Repellents for moths are available. There are cake, flake-crystal, and marble forms. All are effective if used according to manufacturers' directions. Garments must be placed in sealed containers for the products to be effective. Many have an odor, so clothes will have to be aired before you can wear them.

Silverfish is another pest that will eat soil spots as well as fabrics. Cleanliness is the best treatment for keeping them away. An all-purpose insect spray may be needed for closets and storage areas.

Caring for Accessories

Gloves, scarves, handbags, hats, and caps become soiled, too. If you clean these items before they are heavily soiled, they will look nice for a long time. They will also be easier to clean.

Gloves can be made of leather, manufactured fibers, cotton, wool, or a combination of these. Warm water with a mild detergent can be used to clean them. Put the gloves on your hands. Wash as if you are washing your hands, rubbing the heavily soiled spots. Rinse well. Roll in a towel to remove as much moisture as possible. Unroll and lay flat on a towel to dry. If they seem hard or stiff when they dry, rub between fingers to soften them.

Leather handbags require a special leather cleanser. Follow the directions on the package. Plastic items can be wiped clean with mild soap. Fabric tote bags or backpacks can be scrubbed lightly with a soft brush and mild suds. Rinse well. Then blot with a towel and hang to dry.

Most hats and caps can be washed by squeezing suds of mild detergent and warm water through them. Do not twist or wring. Gently squeeze out suds. Rinse well. To dry, smooth and reshape them with your hands. Stuff them with tissue or crumpled brown paper while drying.

CHAPTER REVIEW

Key Points

- Keep some laundry and stain removal products on hand, such as laundry detergent. There are some additional laundry aids that can solve specific laundry problems. These include enzyme presoaks, bleaches, fabric softeners, and prewash soil and stain removers. Learn how and when to use these products to keep your clothes looking their best.

- Having access to a washer, dryer, iron, and ironing board will give you the needed equipment to care for your clothes.

- Most common stains can be removed if you are prompt, patient, and persistent. The key is to remove stains as soon as you see them.

- Reading care labels will provide you with the information you need to properly care for your clothes. Washing, drying, ironing, and dry cleaning recommendations are given.

- When washing clothes, you will need to make decisions about sorting, laundry products, the water level, the wash and rinse temperatures, and the wash cycle. Clothes can be dried using machine drying, line drying, flat drying, or drip-drying. Some will require ironing.

- Some clothes will need to be dry cleaned. You can use a professional dry cleaner or do it yourself using a coin-operated dry cleaning machine.

- If clothes are to be stored for a period of time, they require some special care.

To Review

1. If you have hard water, how will a water softener improve the look and feel of your clothes?
2. Explain the differences between chlorine bleach and oxygen bleach.
3. Name the three most common wash cycles available on automatic washers and explain how they differ.
4. Why is it important to remove stains as soon as possible after they occur?
5. Remove _____ stains by the wet process and _____ stains by the dry process.
6. Give two safety precautions you should use when removing stains.
7. What change was made in the Care Labeling Rule in 1997?
8. What three factors determine how clothes should be sorted before washing?
9. Why should a heavily soiled white garment be washed separately?
10. Which water temperature does the best job of removing soil and disinfecting?
11. Give an important safety rule you should always remember when loading a washer.
12. Why should permanent press garments be dried at low temperatures with a cool-down period at the end?
13. Explain the differences between ironing and pressing.
14. When ironing a shirt, you should _____.
    A. iron the largest area first
    B. iron with the grain of the fabric
    C. use a lifting motion
15. When having your clothes dry cleaned, why is it important to point out any stains to the dry cleaner?
16. Why should you store only clean clothes?

To Do

1. Bring empty bottles and boxes of laundry products for study of information on labels. Make a chart listing the types of clothing care products and their uses.

2. Plan a visit to a laundromat. Let your teacher explain how the heavy-duty equipment is to be used. Investigate the coin-operated dry cleaning equipment.

3. Visit a local appliance center. Compare features of different washers and dryers. Study prices. Decide which would be a better buy.

4. Compare the cost of owning laundry equipment versus doing your laundry in a commercial establishment. Discuss advantages and disadvantages.

5. If laundry equipment is available in the family and consumer sciences department, give a demonstration of removing a stain, washing a durable press shirt, washing a nondurable press shirt, and comparing pressing and ironing techniques.

6. Bring a variety of garments to class. In small groups, read the care labels and describe how each garment should be cleaned.

7. Find examples of garments ruined as a result of improper clothing care methods. If possible, display these items in class with an explanation of how the damage to the clothes could have been prevented.

8. Visit a commercial laundry and dry-cleaning plant. Inspect products used. Ask questions about spot and stain removal. Have them explain what they are doing to preserve the environment and safely dispose of solvents.

To Think About

1. Visit a store that sells laundry products. Compare prices of the various laundry products and what they are designed to do. Are the new combination detergents and products a better buy? Explain your findings.

2. Pretend someone had removed all of the care labels from your clothes. How would you feel? What could you do?

3. Have you ever had a laundry disaster? Describe what happened. Then describe what you should have done.

4. Create a brochure for someone who has never done laundry before. What key points would you include to help them through the process?

5. Design the perfect closet—one that would solve all of your storage needs. What would it look like?

CHAPTER

Repair, Redesign, and Recycle

Reproduced courtesy of Coats & Clark

Objectives

After studying this chapter, you will be able to

- expand your wardrobe by repairing, redesigning, and recycling garments.
- demonstrate clothing repair techniques.
- alter garments to improve their fit.
- restyle and update garments to better fit your wardrobe needs.
- use garment redesigning methods such as adding appliqués, embroidery, trims, dyeing, or painting.
- list ways clothes can be recycled.

Key Terms

patching
redesigning
restyling
appliqué
fusible fabric
embroidery
tie-dyeing
recycling
patchwork

Look at the clothes in your closet. Do you have some garments that just hang there month after month? Whenever you select something to wear, do you skip over these clothes? Some could have loose buttons, rips, or tears that need to be repaired. Others are in good condition, but you may just not like to wear them. The legs of jeans may be too wide, too narrow, or too short. Perhaps a garment is the wrong color or style. Maybe you have outgrown it, or it is in poor condition.

There are ways to revive these clothes. Three methods are by repairing, redesigning, and recycling. Take one garment at a time, and look at it carefully. You can have fun using your creative abilities and your sewing skills. Some garments could come to life in a completely new form. Your ideas and handiwork could make an old garment better than something new.

patching
A garment repair technique in which a small piece of fabric is sewed over a hole.

Repairing Clothes

What do you do with your clothes that need to be repaired? Do you ignore them and toss them in the laundry basket? Do you hide them in the back of your closet? A better solution is to repair the garments right away. See 17-1. If that is not possible, you should put them in a special place. Then when you do have time, you can repair all of the items at once. Keeping all of your supplies together in one location can also save time.

Fix That Hole

When holes appear in garments, patches are needed. **Patching** is the technique of sewing a small piece of fabric over a hole in a garment. Patches are often used on garments to add color and interest. No one has to know that there is a hole beneath the patch. Do you have a hole in the elbow of a sweater or jacket? You can cover it with an oval-shaped, leatherlike patch to give it a new look.

You can even use a decorative appliqué to patch a small hole. Leftover scraps of fabric in your home can be cut into any shape and used as patches. Iron-on materials in a matching color or in a new design cover holes quickly and easily. They can be purchased in fabric or craft stores.

A patch can be used to fix a tear in the center of a garment. A sewing machine gives faster and stronger repairs than hand sewing, but either method can be used. Trim the damaged portion to a

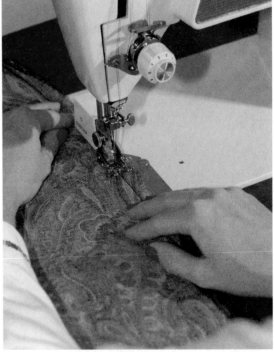

17-1
Some stitches have come loose along a seam in this skirt. Repairing the seam right away means the skirt will be ready to be worn when needed.

square or rectangle and replace it with a similar or contrasting fabric. Cut the fabric patch about one inch larger than the hole it is to repair. Turn under the edges around the patch, and topstitch for extra strength. See 17-2.

You can use a chain-stitch to repair sweaters and other knitted garments. Use matching yarn and a darning needle. Run the yarn invisibly around the area and across the hole as shown in 17-3A. Next, starting at the top, chain stitch down across yarns as shown in 17-3B. Run the yarn back invisibly, over and under, to the top and begin the second row. Repeat until the hole is filled.

A snag is simple to repair. Insert a small crochet hook or needle threader through the back of the fabric directly under the snag and grasp the loop of fabric. Pull it through to the underside. Then smooth any puckers by gently pulling the fabric.

Repair That Rip

A small rip has a way of becoming a big rip! Delaying a repair job just makes it more difficult. If rips are not repaired before the garment is laundered, they will probably be longer rips afterward. Stretching may also occur.

A few stitches by hand or with the sewing machine may be all that is needed. If the rip were in an area that receives much stress, such as the seat or crotch of pants, a double row of stitches would be better. Use a double thread for extra strength if you are sewing by hand. If you do not have the exact color of thread, use a darker shade rather than a lighter one.

Look at 17-4. The seam in the seat of these slacks is ripped. To mend the rip, turn the pants inside out. Pin the seam together and sew

17-2.
After the garment edges around the patch have been turned back, top-stitching is done to add strength.

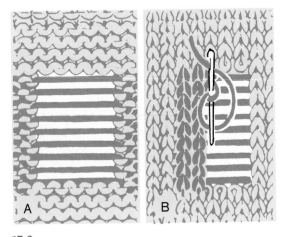

17-3.
Knitted garments can be repaired by using chain stitch darning.

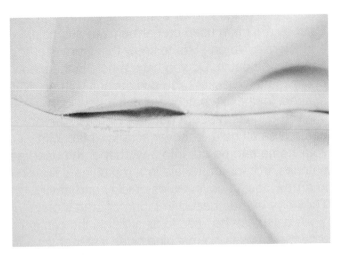

17-4.
Rips in a seam are easy to repair.

with short stitches and strong thread. A second row of stitches placed close to the first row will reinforce the seam to prevent future rips. See 17-5. Do not pull stitches too tight if you are hand sewing. Tight stitches may break again under stress.

Another quick way to fix a tear is to use the zigzag stitch on a sewing machine. Stitch down the length of the tear to hold the edges together. This is quick and easy to do, but should only be used on work or play clothes.

Quick Repairs

Loose buttons can cause problems. The time for action is when you first notice them. Resew them immediately. If you do not have time, remove the loose buttons and put them where you can find them later. It is usually difficult to replace a lost button with an identical one. See 17-6 for the steps of sewing on buttons.

The hooks and eyes as well as the snaps should be kept in good repair on your clothing. Study 17-7 to see how they should be attached.

Having a repair box could save you time and effort. Most repairs can be made in a few minutes if the equipment is handy. Scissors, needles, buttons, snaps, hooks and eyes, light and dark thread, and a thimble are the items you need.

(A) Button placement: Close opening of garment. To mark placement of button, place a pin through buttonhole. Slip buttonhole over the pin to open.

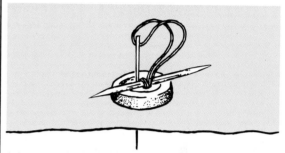

(B) Sew-through button: Place a pin or toothpick on top of the button. Bring needle and thread through the fabric and button, over the pin and back through the fabric. Repeat five or six times.

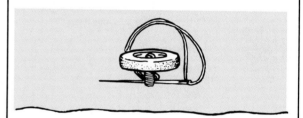

(C) Remove pin and pull button up. Bring threaded needle between garment and button. Wind thread around stitches several times to make a shank. (Shanks raise buttons from garment to allow room for the button hole to fit smoothly beneath it.) Pass thread to underside of garment and fasten securely.

(D) Shank button: Shank buttons need an additional thread shank, but it can be smaller than the shank for sew-through ones. Sew the button on loosely. Then wind the thread under the button to form the thread shank.

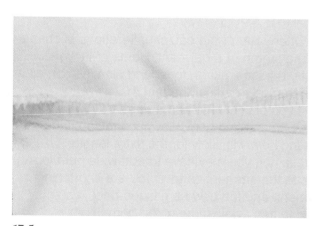

17-5
A double row of stitching reinforces the seam.

17-6
Mark the placement of the button. Then follow these steps to secure the button.

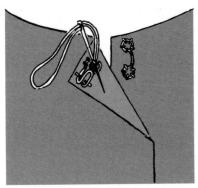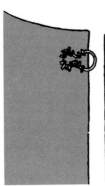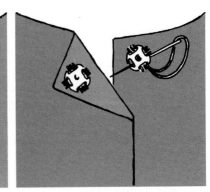

(A) Hook and eyes: Use the bar eye for edges that lap.

(B): Use the round eye for edges that meet.

(C): Snap: Use snaps for closings where there is very little strain.

17-7

Attaching hooks and eyes and snaps is easy.

Nancy Henke-Konopasek

17-8

Garments may be easily lengthened if there is enough hem allowance.

Altering for Better Fit

If a garment doesn't fit well, it may need to be altered. An alteration is a change made to a garment so that it will fit properly. A garment is altered to decrease or increase its length or width. Perhaps you like a pair of slacks or jeans, but you just don't feel right wearing them because they are too long or too short. Maybe you have a nice skirt or pants, but you avoid wearing them because the waistband is too loose or too tight. Some simple alterations may make the garments fit better, and you will enjoy wearing them more often.

Altering Length

Often, one of the easiest alterations is changing the length of a garment. Hems of jackets, pants, dresses, skirts, tops, and sleeves can all be hemmed to adjust the length.

If you plan to lengthen a garment, be sure to check the existing hem allowance to see if the existing hem will allow for the extra length, 17-8. If there is not, you may have to add wide hem facing tape to the garment edge. If you are shortening a garment, and the new hem is too deep, you may need to trim away some of the hem depth.

To alter the hem of a garment, remove the existing hem. Press out the crease. If you are lengthening the garment, be sure you are able to remove the crease in the fabric. You may have to clean the garment or use a spot remover. Next, try on the garment. Ask a friend or family member to pin the hem in place. Follow the instructions for hemming given in Chapter 21.

Altering Width

Changing the garment width can be a minor or a complex task. Sometimes, all that is needed is to move a hook or button. Other times, both sides or the front and back of a garment need to be changed.

Remove the stitching in areas that need adjustment. Pin new seams in place. Be sure to evenly distribute the decrease or increase among all seams. The more seams that a garment has, the easier it will be to alter its width. Try on the garment, and check the fit.

When letting out a garment, or making it larger, sew the new seam outside the old seam in the seam allowance. It is important to always check the width of a seam allowance to be sure it is wide enough to sew a new seam. When taking in a garment, or making it smaller, sew the new seam inside the old seam or within the garment itself. After making the new seams, remove the old stitching and press.

Redesigning Clothes

Redesigning a garment means to change it in its appearance or function. Redesigning is a good way of expanding your wardrobe at little or no cost. Redesigning includes restyling, adding decorative features, or changing the color of a garment.

Redesign shirts and blouses by changing long sleeves to short sleeves or by dyeing them. You can add decorative trim to an old garment or dye it a new color. Liven up a tired-looking jacket by adding a decorative touch such as an appliqué. Give an updated or original fashion look to T-shirts by tie-dyeing or painting. Through redesigning, you can add your personal touch to any garment.

Restyling

By **restyling** a garment, you can give it a new and different look. The easiest way to restyle jeans that are too short is to cut off the lower part of the legs. Jeans then become a pair of "cut-offs." See 17-9. You can also restyle pants that are too short. Cut them off to the

redesigning
To change a garment in its appearance or function.

restyling
Giving a garment a new and different look.

Nancy Henke-Konopasek

17-9

Making "cut-offs" of jeans that have become too short for you is easy to do.

17-10------------------------------------
A new purse and vest have given this outfit the latest fashion look.

17-11------------------------------------
Leaf appliqués have given this vest a unique look.

length you like best: walking shorts or short-shorts. Be sure to allow enough length for a hem. If pant legs are flared and the fashion is straight legs, make the legs straight. Restitch both the outer and inner seams. Be sure that the amount you take in is exactly the same for both legs.

By removing the sleeves from a sweater or jacket, you can make a vest. The armholes will have to be finished with overcasting or by sewing a folded trim over the edges. Change long sleeves into short sleeves by cutting off the old sleeves and hemming the edges. A coat can be restyled into a jacket by cutting off the lower edge and rehemming the garment. New buttons may be added for an updated look.

Some dresses may be made into jumpers by removing the collar and sleeves. Finish the cut edges. If a dress has a full skirt, you may want to slim it down with larger side seams. If the skirt is narrow, you could make side slits starting at the hem.

Updating with Accessories

Wear new accessories with old garments to give them a new look. Look through fashion magazines, pattern catalogs, and displays in stores to find the latest trends. A new belt, scarf, necktie, or jewelry can update last season's styles, 17-10.

Appliqués, Embroidery, and Trims

Appliqué is done by sewing one or more small pieces of contrasting fabric to a larger piece of fabric or a garment. Appliqués add a decorative touch to your clothes. They are made of small pieces of fabric that are cut into any shape, 17-11. If you need help with ideas, borrow some from ready-mades.

The appliqués can be made from a pattern. You can buy appliqué patterns in fabric stores, or you can draw your own designs. Your trees, houses, animals, or flowers do not have to look real. Use your imagination and have fun. It can be fun to create your own designs. Draw the design on paper first. Then cut it out and use it as a pattern when cutting the fabric.

Using a zigzag stitch on a sewing machine or the serger is a good and easy way to finish the edges of an appliqué. For a neat look, you can trim close to the stitching. When you sew the appliqué to the garment, fewer stitches will be needed to keep the edges from fraying.

When applying an appliqué or trim to a garment, first pin it in place. In this way, you can try different placements and choose the best location. Curves are easier to attach than points. If your appliqué has points, sew it on the garment with close stitches. Hand embroidery stitches can also be used to apply an appliqué.

Another way to apply an appliqué to a garment is to use **fusible fabric.** This sheer fabric is covered with a thin layer of plastic adhesive. Cut a piece of fusible fabric the same size or a bit smaller than the appliqué. Place it between the appliqué and the garment. Apply steam with an iron and the fusible fabric will fuse (join) the other two fabrics. The appliqué will stay attached to the garment even when it is washed or dry cleaned.

A garment can also be restyled by adding embroidery. **Embroidery** is decorative stitching that creates a pattern or a design on the fabric. It can be done by hand or by machine. The newest sewing machines have decorative stitches programmed into them. Some use separate cards with different design motifs that you insert into the machines. Either of these methods can give your garments a personal touch, 17-12. You can learn more about embroidery in Chapter 25.

appliqué
Sewing one or more small pieces of fabric to a larger piece of fabric or a garment to add a decorative touch.

fusible fabric
A sheer adhesive-coated fabric that joins two other fabrics together when ironed.

embroidery
Decorative hand or machine stitching that creates a pattern or a design on the fabric.

17-12
Colorful embroidery can add a unique touch to denim jeans.

Trims are very popular today and can be used to give your clothes a unique look, 17-13. Trims can be purchased by the yard or in packages. Choose from braids, rickrack, bias tape, foldover braid, or knitted bands. Some trims are designed to give a decorative edge to a garment. These include fringe, piping, and pre-gathered ruffles.

Whenever you use a decorative technique such as trim, consider applying it to more than one area of the garment to create a total effect. For instance, if you use decorative trim at the hem of a garment, repeat the use of the trim on the sleeves or the collar. Trims can also be used to cover the crease line created by lowering a hem. Measure the area to be trimmed, then add at least 1/2 yard so you will have enough extra to join the ends and go around corners and curves.

Dyeing

A fun and easy way to change the look of some of your clothes is by dyeing or recoloring them. You can make a light garment darker or a dull one brighter.

Dye can be bought in liquid or powder form. Many colors are available. Interesting effects can be made with combinations of colors. Use your creativity.

Dye only clothes that are washable. Some fibers will not take dye. Measure the garments you think may shrink. After dyeing, measure them again. You may need to press or stretch them to get them back into shape. For knitted garments, such as sweaters, you should draw the entire outline on paper so you can match the shape after dyeing.

Be sure to have enough dye on hand for the amount of fabric you plan to dye. Check the package for directions. Use hot water, rinse thoroughly, and dry.

Tie-Dyeing

Tie-dyeing is a method of dyeing where sections of fabric are folded or gathered and tied tightly with string or wrapped with rubber bands. When the fabric is dyed, the tied or wrapped portions resist (do not absorb) the

To-Sew

17-13. Adding colorful trims and braids is a great way to redesign a garment to give it a new look.

Tie-Dyeing: A Fun Way to Design Your Own Fabric

Be your own textile designer with a package or two of dye! Use the stripe, donut knot, and rosette knot to create these interesting patterns.

Stripe: Lay fabric on a flat surface. Mark the pieces where you want stripes. Gather the fabric and tie tightly. Use many strings or rubber bands for a wide stripe, or a single string or band for a narrow stripe.

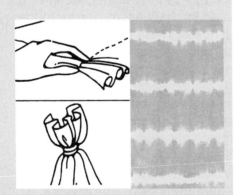

Rosette knot: Pull a section of fabric. Fasten tightly with string or rubber bands. Add more ties to get the sunburst variation shown here.

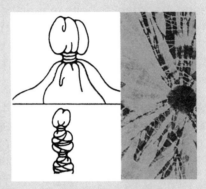

Donut knot: Begin as if you were making a rosette knot. Then push the center through to the other side. Secure tightly with string or rubber bands.

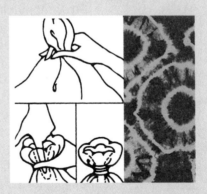

Let your imagination run wild and create unique designs on fabrics you can then sew into garments or frame as pieces of art.

For more ideas and specific instructions, visit the Web site ritdye.com.

tie-dyeing
Sections of fabric
are tied tightly with
string or rubber
bands and dyed
causing the tied
portions to resist the
dye, resulting in a
design.

recycling
To reuse in some
manner.

dye, resulting in a design. Tie-dyeing is a resist type of fabric dyeing. Tie-dyeing was one of the earliest known methods of decorating fabric. It is still popular today, 17-14.

Tie-dyeing can be done before or after a garment is made. It is a thrifty way to change some tired-looking garments and a neat way to have something that is one-of-a-kind. The excitement is often from the surprise of your finished product. All types of garments plus fabric handbags, backpacks, belts, shoelaces, and socks are possibilities. Always follow the directions of the dye manufacturer.

Fabric Painting

Another fun way to add color to your clothes is to paint them. Colors can be applied with a brush, pen, marker, or direct from a tube. Designs can be painted with acrylic oil paints. These paints are washable. They come in ready-to-use tubes. Many colors are available. Some are designed to create a raised area on the fabric.

You can have fun creating your own designs on items such as jogging outfits, T-shirts, jeans, or canvas bags. You can also purchase patterns to follow.

Recycling Clothes

How many clothes do you throw away each year? Studies show that each person annually discards 35 pounds of clothes or other textile items. This amounts to 8.5 billion pounds in this country alone. Though many items are donated to charities, most go into the trash and end up in landfills. There are companies, however, that recycle textile products. **Recycling** means to reuse. About 25 percent of discarded textile products are currently being recycled in this manner. Some communities have developed collection sites especially for textiles. Is your community one of them?

Instead of discarding your clothes, find ways to extend their usefulness. You can pass clothing along for someone else to use. You can also make something entirely new out of a garment. Recycling clothes is a way of conserving resources.

Passing Clothes Along

You may have some garments that are in good condition. If you cannot wear them or redesign them, you may want to consider passing them along to someone else.

Simplicity Pattern Co., Inc.

17-14.
The fabric used to make this top was tie-dyed to give it a unique look.

17-15

Clothes are often recycled among family members. Since children outgrow more clothes than they wear out, the clothes are often passed on to younger sisters and brothers.

In many families, passing clothes along to younger sisters or brothers has been a custom for years, 17-15. Families often pass clothes on to relatives or friends when their families can no longer use them because of size. Your size often changes at a rapid rate until you are well into your teen years. Therefore, you will probably outgrow more clothes than you will wear out completely.

Friends sometimes have a swap party. They bring garments they no longer wear to the party. Each person trades a garment or garments for someone else's garments. Clothing that is no longer the right thing for you may be a real find for someone else. For instance, you may bring a blue jacket that you no longer wear to the party. Your friend likes the jacket. You may want to trade the jacket for the gray sweater your friend has brought to trade. You could both add something to your wardrobes without spending any money.

There are many charitable groups that give or sell clothing at a small cost to those in need. Your usable, but unwanted, clothing could help these families. Some of these organizations are Goodwill, Red Cross, Salvation Army, and various religious groups. In many cases, they may help families who have lost their belongings in a flood, fire, or other disaster. Knowing

patchwork
Small pieces of fabric cut into shapes then sewn together by hand or machine to form a pattern.

that someone who needs it is using your unwanted clothing can be a good feeling. Some organizations have a pick-up service to collect donations of clothing. Such donations are usually tax deductible.

You may also want to sell your unwanted clothes. You can earn some money by selling clothes to used clothing stores. Yard and garage sales, flea markets, and bazaars can be fun and profitable. Several persons or families often plan them.

New Life for Old Clothes

When you are sure you can no longer wear a garment and neither can anyone else, what can you do with it? It may be possible to recycle the usable section of the garment. Use the fabric to make items such as potholders, makeup pouches, or shoe bags. These items could be useful as gifts for others or for your own use at little or no cost, 17-16.

Sometimes fabric from old clothes can be used to make clothes for children. For instance, an old dress may be used to make a shirt for a child.

If you have outgrown a pair of jeans, you might use them to make a tote bag or backpack. Cut off the legs just below the crotch. Turn inside out and sew the legs together. Tote bags and backpacks are popular for carrying school supplies. You can also use other outgrown clothes to make tote bags.

Patchwork

Through patchwork you can use your artistic talents. **Patchwork** is sewing pieces and shapes of fabric together. They are often of different textures and designs. Patchwork quilts are popular. However, you could make a patchwork covering for your bed without quilting it. The covering would be like a bedspread. You can also make tote bags, place mats, stuffed toys, and pillows from patchwork. Clothing, such as a vest, can be made by using patchwork designs.

Patterns and ideas are available in craft stores and magazines. Be sure to use fabric that is firmly woven. Each section should be similar to other sections in terms of care. For instance, denim and heavy cotton flannel would require the same care.

Reproduced courtesy of Coats & Clark

17-16
You can recycle fabric from garments into useful items, such as this organizer made from the legs of cut-off jeans.

Tyke Corporation

Simplicity Pattern Co.

17-17_____
What fun it is to play "dress-up" with old clothes. Some old clothes can be used for Halloween costumes, too.

17-18_____
Some fabrics can be recycled to make stuffing materials for stuffed animals.

Other Uses for Old Clothes

Children love to play "dress-up." A box of old clothes can provide many hours of fun. Old clothes make good sources of play and masquerade costumes, too, 17-17.

When garments are too worn to be recycled into other useful items, they can be used for cleaning cloths. Household rags may be needed for washing woodwork, dusting furniture, or washing the car. Be careful to cut off any buttons or other fasteners that could scratch furniture or the paint on a car. Old buttons and fasteners can also be recycled for later use.

Fabrics made of 100 percent cotton or cotton blends often make the best rags because they are soft and absorbent. Fabrics made of other fibers that are not suitable as rags can be used for stuffing pillows and toys, 17-18. Use your imagination to come up with new and different ways to recycle clothes.

CHAPTER REVIEW

Key Points

- There are three ways to revive your clothes: repairing, redesigning, and recycling.

- Repair holes and rips and reattach loose buttons, fasteners, and hems when you first notice them. Then they will be ready to wear when you next need them.

- A garment can be altered to decrease or increase its length or width so it fits better.

- Redesigning includes restyling for a new look, adding decorative features such as appliqués or trims, or changing the color of a garment.

- Recycling means to reuse. With clothing, this means finding ways and methods of extending the use of garments. This may be passing clothes along to others or finding new uses for the fabric in the clothes.

To Review

1. Explain the steps in repairing slacks or jeans that have a hole in the knee.
2. When would chain-stitching be used to repair a garment?
3. In repair work, if you do not have the exact color of thread, should you use a lighter or darker one?
4. If there is not enough hem to lengthen a garment, what can you do?
5. (True or False) When letting out a garment, or making it larger, sew the new seam inside the old seam allowance.
6. How could you restyle a long-sleeved shirt whose sleeves are too short for you?
7. List the correct order of these steps.
    A. Draw a design for an appliqué on paper.
    B. Trim close to stitching.
    C. Sew it on garment with small stitches.
    D. Cut your design out of fabric.
    E. Use a zigzag stitch to finish the edges.
8. What kind of paint can you use to "paint" fabric?
9. List three ways you could restyle or recycle worn jeans.
10. List four ways you could recycle garments you no longer wear.

To Do

1. Bring an article of clothing to class that you no longer wear. As a class, decide how to repair, redesign, or recycle each garment brought to class.

2. Bring a garment to class that you have repaired, redesigned, or recycled. Describe the technique you used.

3. Assemble a clothing repair box. Give a reason for including each item.

4. Caption a bulletin board "Cures for Sick Clothes." Display pictures of redesigned garments.

5. Create an original design for an appliqué or fabric painting project.

6. Arrange for a demonstration of a new electronic sewing machine that does machine embroidery almost automatically.

7. Make a list of recycling ideas by having each person contribute one. Have the list published in the local or school newspaper.

8. Have a clothing swap party. Take pictures for a bulletin board.

9. Bring clean clothing that you no longer wear to class. Sort it according to age groups. Deliver the clothing to a charitable organization.

To Think About

1. Do fewer people do their own clothing repairs today than in earlier times? What might be the reasons?

2. Do you have any clothes that you cannot wear because they need a simple repair? What skills would you need in order to do these repairs?

3. Why do you think teens took to the worn and frayed look in jeans? Do you think this is a fad or will it remain popular for some time?

4. Do you admire people who can find clever ways to redesign or recycle old clothes? Why or why not?

5. Do you think it is important to recycle everything you can?

PART 5

Sewing Techniques

Chapters

CHAPTER 18

Figure Types and Pattern Sizes

Objectives

After studying this chapter, you will be able to
- determine your figure type and pattern size.
- take accurate body measurements.
- select a pattern that fits you.
- explain the importance of pattern ease.

Key Terms

figure types
standard sizes
body measurements
unisex
multisized patterns
wearing ease
design ease

When you look around you, you see students of all sizes and shapes. Some are more mature in growth than others of the same age. You can find tall, short, thin, and stout people all in the same group.

You may not be able to wear the same size of clothing as the student beside you. Ready-to-wear clothes as well as clothes patterns are made in many sizes to suit the many types of people. The difficult part of choosing clothes or patterns is getting ones that fit.

Determining Your Figure Type

All pattern companies group patterns under **figure types** according to height and proportion. The female figure types are Girls', Girls' Plus, Junior, Misses', Miss Petite, Women's, and Women's Petite. For males, the figure types are Boys', Teen Boys', and Men's. See 18-1 and 18-2.

figure types
Sizing standards used by pattern companies to group figures according to height and proportion.

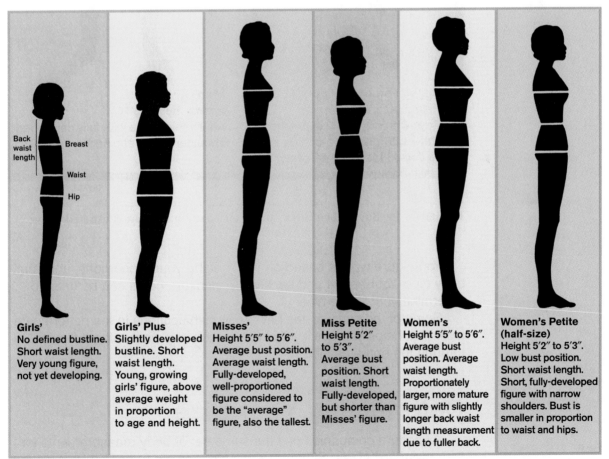

Girls'
No defined bustline. Short waist length. Very young figure, not yet developing.

Girls' Plus
Slightly developed bustline. Short waist length. Young, growing girls' figure, above average weight in proportion to age and height.

Misses'
Height 5'5" to 5'6". Average bust position. Average waist length. Fully-developed, well-proportioned figure considered to be the "average" figure, also the tallest.

Miss Petite
Height 5'2" to 5'3". Average bust position. Short waist length. Fully-developed, but shorter than Misses' figure.

Women's
Height 5'5" to 5'6". Average bust position. Average waist length. Proportionately larger, more mature figure with slightly longer back waist length measurement due to fuller back.

Women's Petite (half-size)
Height 5'2" to 5'3". Low bust position. Short waist length. Short, fully-developed figure with narrow shoulders. Bust is smaller in proportion to waist and hips.

Labels on first figure: Back waist length, Breast, Waist, Hip

The McCall Pattern Company

18-1
The figure types for girls and women are illustrated above.

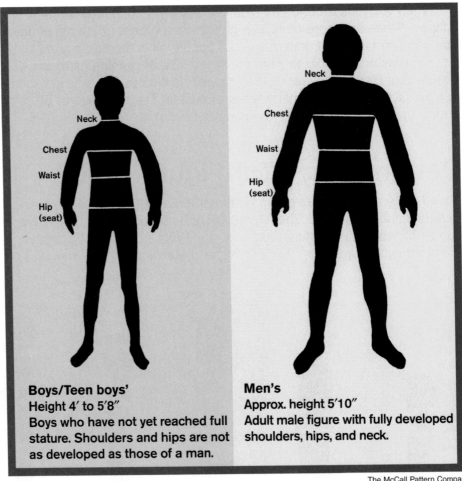

Boys/Teen boys'
Height 4' to 5'8"
Boys who have not yet reached full
stature. Shoulders and hips are not
as developed as those of a man.

Men's
Approx. height 5'10"
Adult male figure with fully developed
shoulders, hips, and neck.

The McCall Pattern Company

18-2
The stature for Boys', Teen Boys', and Men's pattern sizes are illustrated above.

Your figure type is based on your height, your proportions, and your body type. Your height and back waist measurements can be used to determine your figure type.

Some of the figure types have their own sections in the pattern catalogs. This helps you quickly find the section you want without flipping through the entire catalog.

Determining Your Size

standard sizes
The set of body measurements used by most pattern companies.

All pattern companies use the same set of body measurements for their **standard sizes**. Standard sizes also remain the same from issue to issue of the catalogs. Pattern sizes may or may not correspond to ready-to-wear sizes. The sizes of ready-to-wear garments vary from one garment manufacturer to another.

Bust or chest, waist, and hip or seat measurements determine pattern sizes. There are different sizes in each figure type. The measurements for each figure type for girls and women are shown in 18-3. The measurements for men's and boys' sizes are also listed in 18-3.

Some patterns are designed for either males or females. The styles are often more classic and would look good on either a male or female figure. These sizes are called **unisex.** They are made for figures within the Misses', Men's, Teen Boys', Boys', and Girls' size ranges. See 18-3 for these measurements.

unisex
Patterns that are designed for either males or females.

PATTERN SIZES AND BODY MEASUREMENTS

Inches

Girls'/Girls' Plus—For growing girls who have not yet begun to mature.
Girls' Plus are designed for girls over the average weight for their height and age.

	Girls'					Girls' Plus				
Sizes	7	8	10	12	14	8½	10½	12½	14½	16½
Chest	26	27	28½	30	32	30	31½	33	34½	36
Waist	23	23½	24½	25½	26½	28	29	30	31	32
Hips	27	28	30	32	34	33	34½	36	37½	39
Back waist length	11½	12	12¾	13½	14¼	12½	13¼	14	14¾	15½
approx. height	50	52	56	58½	61	52	56	58½	61	63½

Junior—For the young miss figure, about 5'2" to 5'5" in height without shoes.

Sizes	3/4	5/6	7/8	9/10	11/12	13/14	15/16	17/18	19/20	21/22	23-24
Bust	28	29	30½	32	33½	35	36½	38½	40½	42½	44½
Waist	22	23	24	25	26	27	28	29½	31	33½	35½
Hip–7² below waist	31	32	33½	35	36½	38	39½	41½	43½	45½	47½
Back waist length	13½	14	14½	15	15⅜	15¼	16⅛	16⅛	16⅝	16⅞	17⅛

Misses'/Miss Petite—For well-proportioned, developed figures.
Misses' about 5'5" to 5'6" without shoes. Miss Petite under 5'4" without shoes.

Sizes	4	6	8	10	12	14	16	18	20	22	24	26
Bust	29½	30½	31½	32½	34	36	38	40	42	44	46	48
Waist	22	23	24	25	26½	28	30	32	34	37	39	41½
Hip–9² below waist	31½	32½	33½	34½	36	38	40	42	44	46	48	50
Misses-Back waist length	15½	15½	15¾	16	16¼	16½	16¾	17	17¼	17⅜	17½	17¾
Miss Petite-Back waist length		14	14½	14¾	15	15¼	15½	15¾	16	16¼	16⅜	16½	16⅝

Women's/Women's Petite—for larger, more fully mature figures.
Women's about 5'5" to 5'6" without shoes. Women's Petite under 5'4" without shoes.

Sizes	Women's	16W	20W	22W	24W	26W	28W	30W	32W
	Women's Petite	36	38	40	42	44	46	48	50
Bust		40	42	44	46	48	50	52	54
Waist		33	35	37	39	41½	44	46½	49
Hip–9² below waist		42	44	46	48	50	52	54	56
Women's back waist length		17⅛	17¼	17⅜	17½	17⅝	17¾	17⅞	18
Women's Petite back waist length		16⅛	16¼	16⅜	16½	16⅝	16¾	16⅞	17

(continued)

18-3
Pattern sizes and body measurements for both male and female figures are given in this chart.

PATTERN SIZES AND BODY **MEASUREMENTS**

Inches								
Boys's & Teen Boys'—For growing boys and young men who have not reached full adult stature.								
Sizes	7	8	10	12	14	16	18	20
Chest	26	27	28	30	32	33½	35	36½
Waist	23	24	25	26	27	28	29	30
Hip	27	28	29½	31	32½	34	35½	37
Neck band	11¾	12	12½	13	13½	14	14½	15
Approx. height	48	50	54	58	61	64	66	68
Shirt sleeve	22⅜	23¼	25	26¾	29	30	31	32

Men's—For men of average build; about 5'10" without shoes.										
Sizes	32	34	36	38	40	42	44	46	48	50	52
Chest	32	34	36	38	40	41	44	46	48	50	52
Waist	27	28	30	32	34	36	39	42	44	46	48
Hip	34	35	37	39	41	43	45	47	49	51	53
Neck band	13½	14	14½	15	15½	16	16½	17	17½	18	18½
Shirt sleeve	31	32	32	33	33	34	34	35	35	36	36

Unisex—For figures within Misses', Men's, Teen-Boys', Boys' and Girls' size ranges.							
Sizes	XXS	XS	S	M	L	XL	XXL
Chest/Bust	28-29	30-32	34-36	38-40	42-44	46-48	50-52
Hip	29-30	31-32	35-37	39-41	43-45	47-49	51-53

18-3
Continued

Once you know your figure type, you can easily determine your pattern size. All you have to do is measure carefully.

Body Measurements

body measurements
The actual dimensions of the body.

Body measurements are the actual dimensions of your body. They should be taken over your undergarments or a well-fitting garment. Remove any bulky garments, sweaters, or belts. You may want to have a friend measure you. Stand or sit erect and still. The tape measure should be snug, but not tight. Measure each area twice to ensure accuracy.

Make a chart of your own to record your measurements. You will use the chart later to make any needed adjustments on your pattern. It will also be helpful when you select patterns in the future.

Measuring Females

Tie a string, cord, or narrow elastic around the waist. Then bend over from side to side. The string will fall at your natural waistline. Keep the string in place while your measurements are taken. Measure the body as shown in 18-4.

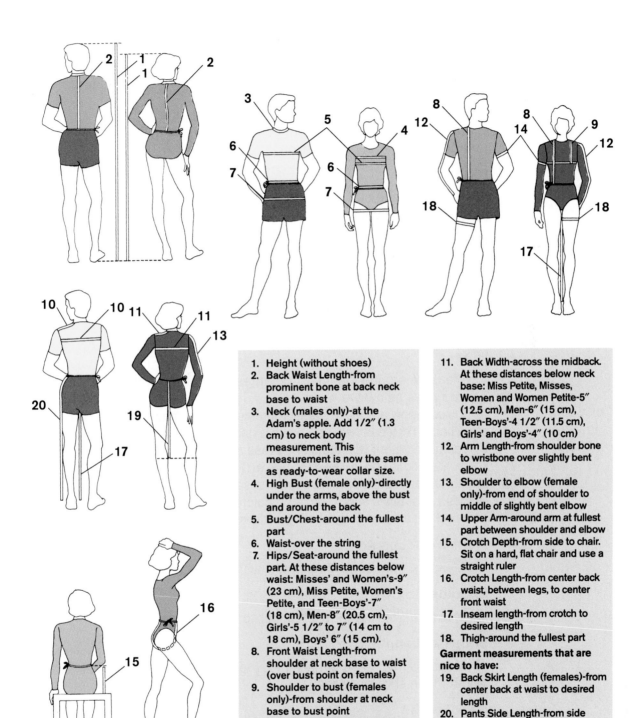

1. Height (without shoes)
2. Back Waist Length-from prominent bone at back neck base to waist
3. Neck (males only)-at the Adam's apple. Add 1/2″ (1.3 cm) to neck body measurement. This measurement is now the same as ready-to-wear collar size.
4. High Bust (female only)-directly under the arms, above the bust and around the back
5. Bust/Chest-around the fullest part
6. Waist-over the string
7. Hips/Seat-around the fullest part. At these distances below waist: Misses' and Women's-9″ (23 cm), Miss Petite, Women's Petite, and Teen-Boys'-7″ (18 cm), Men-8″ (20.5 cm), Girls'-5 1/2″ to 7″ (14 cm to 18 cm), Boys' 6″ (15 cm).
8. Front Waist Length-from shoulder at neck base to waist (over bust point on females)
9. Shoulder to bust (females only)-from shoulder at neck base to bust point
10. Shoulder Length-from neck base to shoulder bone
11. Back Width-across the midback. At these distances below neck base: Miss Petite, Misses, Women and Women Petite-5″ (12.5 cm), Men-6″ (15 cm), Teen-Boys'-4 1/2″ (11.5 cm), Girls' and Boys'-4″ (10 cm)
12. Arm Length-from shoulder bone to wristbone over slightly bent elbow
13. Shoulder to elbow (female only)-from end of shoulder to middle of slightly bent elbow
14. Upper Arm-around arm at fullest part between shoulder and elbow
15. Crotch Depth-from side to chair. Sit on a hard, flat chair and use a straight ruler
16. Crotch Length-from center back waist, between legs, to center front waist
17. Inseam length-from crotch to desired length
18. Thigh-around the fullest part

Garment measurements that are nice to have:
19. Back Skirt Length (females)-from center back at waist to desired length
20. Pants Side Length-from side waistline to desired length along outside of leg

18-4

In order to sew garments that fit, you need to take accurate measurements.

Height

Figure types are based on measurements without shoes. Stand against a wall. Mark height of head lightly on wall. Measure from mark to floor.

Back Waist Length

Measure from the prominent bone you can feel at the base of your neck to the string at the waistline.

High Bust

Bring the tape straight across the back, directly under the arms and above the fullest part of the bust.

Bust

Measure across the fullest part of the bust and straight across the back at the tips of the shoulder blades.

Waist

Measure over the string or elastic at the waist.

Hips

Measure around the fullest or largest part of the body. This is usually 7 to 9 inches below the waist.

Listed below are some measurements that you may not find on pattern size charts. They can help you make a garment that fits well and looks good. By comparing them with the same areas on pattern pieces, you will see what, if any, alterations you will need to make. (Remember that pattern pieces are slightly larger than body measurements so you can move comfortably in your clothes.) Alterations should be done before cutting your fabric. You will save time and get a better fit by altering patterns instead of garments.

Front Waist Length

Measure from base of neck to waistline.

Shoulder to Bust

Measure from center of shoulder to highest point of bust.

Shoulder Length

Measure from base of neck below ear to tip of shoulder. This is the length of the shoulder seam.

Back Width

With the tape 4 to 5 inches (depending on figure type) below base of neck, measure the distance from armhole to armhole.

Arm Length

Measure from shoulder bone to wristbone, over slightly bent elbow.

Shoulder to Elbow

Measure from end of shoulder to middle of slightly bent elbow.

Upper Arm

Measure around arm at fullest part between the shoulder and elbow.

Crotch Depth

Measure from side waist to chair. (Sit on a flat chair and use a ruler.)

Crotch Length

Measure from center back waist between the legs to center front waist.

Inseam Length

Measure the inseam of the leg to the desired length. You could also measure the inseam of a pair of your pants that fit well to get this measurement.

Thigh

Measure around the fullest part.

Back Skirt Length

Measure from the elastic around the waist at the center back to the desired length. Remember to allow for the hem when you are comparing measurements on your pattern.

Measuring Males

Tie a string, cord, or narrow elastic around the waist over a shirt. Then measure the body as in 18-4.

Height

Stand tall, without shoes, against a wall. Put a ruler on top of the head. Lightly mark position on wall. Measure the distance between the mark and the floor.

Back Waist Length

Measure from the prominent bone you can feel at the center back neck base to your waistline.

Neck

Measure around the neck at the Adam's apple. Add 1/2 inch to the neck measurement. This is the shirt neck size. It is also a ready-to-wear shirt measurement.

Chest

Measure around the fullest or largest part of the chest.

Waist

Be sure to measure at the exact waistline as this determines size.

Hips (Seat)

Measure around the fullest part of the seat—about 7 inches below the waistline for boys and 8 inches for men.

Front Waist Length

Measure from base of neck to waistline.

Shoulder Length

Measure from base of neck below ear to tip of shoulder. This is the length of the shoulder seam.

Back Width

With the tape 4 to 5 inches (depending on figure type) below base of neck, measure the distance from armhole to armhole.

Arm Length

Measure from the large bone at the back of your neck along the shoulder, over bent elbow down to the wrist bone. This is also a ready-to-wear shirt measurement.

Upper Arm

Measure around arm at fullest part between the shoulder and elbow.

Crotch Depth

Measure from side waist to chair. (Sit on a flat chair and use a ruler.)

Crotch Length

Measure from center back waist between the legs to center front waist.

Inseam Length

Measure the inseam of the leg to the desired length. You could also measure the inseam of a pair of your pants that fit well to get this measurement.

Thigh

Measure around the fullest part.

Pants Side Length

Measure from the natural waistline down the outside of the leg to the desired length.

Trends Making News

Junior Pattern Sizes Make a Comeback

In the mid 1990s, Junior sizes did a short disappearing act from pattern catalogs. Decreased demand for Junior sizes led the major pattern companies to drop them from their catalogs. About this same time, the shift was made to multisize patterns to keep costs of patterns from sky-rocketing.

By 1999, however, Junior sizes reappeared. The major pattern companies realized they needed to encourage teens to learn to sew. They reintroduced Junior sizes into their catalogs, but with some slight changes from the earlier Junior body measurement charts. Because teen girls mature much earlier today, their measurements are not as straight up and down as they used to be. Instead, their figures are curvier—similar to Misses' sizes. Girls this age have more of a waist in relation to bust and hip size. The new Junior size chart reflects these changes.

That's not all that the pattern companies changed. To entice teens to sew, Junior pattern styles are now very trendy, sporty, and playful. Teens have definite ideas on how they want to dress. It's a part of their desire to develop their own sense of identity. These new styles will definitely not appeal to moms! The designs are unique, exciting, and cutting edge—just what today's teens are looking for.

multisized patterns
Patterns having several sizes printed on the same pattern tissue.

Selecting a Pattern That Fits

Now you are ready to choose patterns that will fit you. You have determined your figure type and have taken your body measurements. Compare your measurements to the pattern measurements listed under your figure type. (Refer back to 18-3.)

Most people are not a perfect size. If you fall between two sizes, keep the following points in mind:

- If you are small boned, choose the smaller size. If you are large boned, choose the larger one.
- If you like a close fit, choose the smaller size. If you prefer a loose fit, choose the larger size.
- If the silhouette is close fitting, choose the larger size.

For females, the bust is the most important measurement when choosing a pattern for a blouse, dress, coat, or jacket. Girls should look for the size with the bust measurement closest to their own if they do not fit any group exactly. Waist and hip sections of a pattern are easier to alter than shoulder and bust darts. The pattern will lose its original look if too many alterations are made.

The hip measurement is more important than the waist measurement in selecting patterns for skirts, slacks, and shorts. Waistlines are fairly easy to adjust. Therefore, select your pattern by the hip measurement. However, if skirts are not fitted in the hip area, the waist measurement should be used.

Pattern sizes for Boys', Teen Boys', and Men's are different. For slacks or shorts, buy your pattern by the waist measurement. For shirts, use the neck measurement.

Sport coats and vests should be bought by chest size. For a snug fit, pick a smaller size; for a looser fit, a larger one. Some young men might prefer a closer fit while older men might prefer extra room.

Unisex styles are designed and sized to look good on both males and females. Unisex patterns are selected by the chest, bust, or hip measurement and sized for a looser fit than female and male patterns, 18-5. If you prefer a closer fit, you might select a smaller unisex size. Likewise, if you prefer more room or an extremely baggy look, you might choose a larger unisex size.

Many patterns are multisized. **Multisized patterns** have several sizes printed on the same pattern tissue. The cutting line is selected for the size that fits your

The McCall Pattern Co.

18-5_____
These unisex patterns are designed with a looser fit to suit both male and female figures.

body. These patterns help you if you have a different size top and bottom. You can follow the cutting lines for the size you are in each body area.

Pattern Ease

You could not wear slacks that measure exactly the same as your body. When you measure the hip section of a pattern, you may find it to be from two to three inches larger than the hip measurement listed on the pattern. This extra room is called **wearing ease.** It is planned so your clothes will be comfortable. Ease is important in both men's and women's patterns. Without ease, garments would be too tight, uncomfortable, and unattractive. Unflattering wrinkles and pulls would occur. It would be impossible to sit, walk, or bend in your clothes.

Wearing ease varies from measurement to measurement. The waist will have 1 inch of wearing ease. Hips generally have 2 1/2 inches of ease and the bust or chest between 2 1/2 and 3 1/2 inches. The larger sizes have more ease, as do coats and jackets.

Another type of ease is called **design ease.** This is an extra amount of fullness the designer used to give the garment its special look or silhouette. When the fashion look features body skimming fit, there will be less design ease in patterns, 18-6. When a looser, less traditional look is in style, there will be more design ease built into the patterns. Design ease varies from a little extra—a few tucks or pleats—to a lot. For example, trouser styles may have flat fronts, small tucks at the waistline, or deeper, fuller pleats. The resulting hip width will be different in each style.

There are several ways you can determine the amount of design ease in a pattern. First, study the artwork or photographs on the pattern envelope to see how close or full the garment appears. You can also read the written descriptions of the garment on the pattern envelope. Look for the following descriptive terms: *close-fitted, fitted, semi-fitted, loose fitting,* or *very loose fitting.* These will give you an idea of the amount of ease in the garment. Another way is to compare your actual body measurements to the finished garment measurements. These are printed on the tissue pattern and/or on the back of the pattern envelope.

Patterns designed for knitted fabrics only have less ease allowance than other patterns. Some "give" is supplied by the fabric itself. A regular amount of ease would be too much. Besides, knitted garments are usually worn closer to the body than garments made of woven fabrics. This is true of both male and female patterns.

wearing ease
Extra room allowed in patterns for wearing comfort.

design ease
An extra amount of fullness provided in patterns to give the garment its special look or silhouette.

Simplicity Pattern Co., Inc.

18-6 The designer of this pattern allowed less design ease for a body skimming fit.

CHAPTER REVIEW

Key Points

- Pattern companies group patterns under figure types according to height and proportion.

- All pattern companies use the same set of body measurements for their standard sizes.

- Body measurements are the actual dimensions of your body. They should be taken over your undergarments or a well-fitting garment.

- Most people are not a perfect size. The size you choose should be based on your bone structure, the fit you prefer, and the closeness of the silhouette. It also depends on the type of garment you are sewing.

- All patterns have a certain amount of ease added to them to make them comfortable and attractive.

To Review

1. List five terms used to identify pattern figure types.
2. How are figure types determined?
3. All brands of patterns follow the same measurements for the same size. Ready-to-wear garments do not. Why not?
4. What is the correct method of measuring height? waistline?
5. What are the advantages of altering a pattern to fit rather than altering the garment?
6. How is shirt neck size determined for men and boys?
7. Why should girls select patterns closest to their bust size?
8. By what measurement are men's slacks bought?
9. Explain the difference between wearing ease and design ease.
10. Name three ways you can judge the amount of design ease in a pattern.

To Do

1. Select a partner and measure each other. Make two measurements in the same place to assure accuracy. Record on a personal measurement chart.

2. Bring ready-made garments to class. Measure them in the same areas as your body measurements. Compare the measurements and determine the amount of ease allowed. Decide if each measurement is wearing ease or design ease.

3. Measure pattern pieces and corresponding areas of ready-made garments of the same size. How much difference do you find?

4. Make an oversized chart showing how to take measurements for males and females. Post it on a bulletin board.

5. Compare two patterns of the same size—one designed for knitted fabrics only and one designed for woven fabrics. (Make sure the styles are somewhat alike.) How much difference in ease do you find?

To Think About

1. Ready-to-wear garment manufacturers have attempted to standardize sizes, but there still is a great deal of variation. In contrast, the major pattern companies have agreed on a set of standard body measurements for their sizes. Why do you think the garment manufacturers have not shown this same willingness to make their sizes the same?

2. When you took your measurements and determined your pattern size, it may have been one or two sizes larger than the one you are accustomed to in ready-to-wear. Does this bother you? Will anyone know what size you are wearing once your garment is made?

3. How often do you think teens should take their measurements? Why?

4. What is currently in fashion concerning design ease in garments? Are garments today more close-fitting or loose-fitting? Which do you prefer?

CHAPTER 19

Looking at Patterns

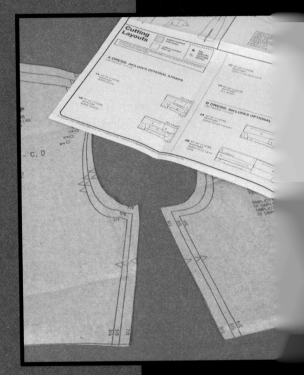

The pattern catalog and your pattern give you ideas about styles, fashions, possible fabrics, and accessories. A **pattern** includes tissue paper pieces to follow when cutting out your fabric. It also includes step-by-step instructions for constructing the garment. With the help of your pattern, you can buy your supplies and cut, mark, and sew your garment successfully.

pattern
Tissue paper pieces to follow when cutting out fabric for making a garment.

Pattern Catalogs

Your first look at pattern catalogs may surprise you. They are huge. Each of the major pattern companies has its own catalogs. They are all similar in format and size, but the patterns are different. If you look through all of them, you will surely find the pattern you want.

Many popular patterns remain in the catalogs for months or even years. Others that do not sell well are dropped. Four major catalog issues come out each year, but new patterns are introduced monthly.

Stores receive the catalogs many weeks ahead of the date shown on the cover. This gives people who make their own clothes time to complete them for the coming season. For instance, the catalog for winter holiday fashions appears on the counters in September. By the middle of January, the spring issue is available.

In 19-1, the format of a typical catalog is shown. The tabs at the right tell you what is in each of the sections. Although the book is large, you are interested in only a few sections of it.

Inside the Pattern Catalog

Few people use all the benefits of a pattern catalog. It offers much more than pattern choices. Suppose that you already know your pattern number, but you want to see it illustrated. You can find it listed in the numerical index. This is in the back of the book. All of the patterns are listed by number in numerical order. The page numbers are then given, so you can find your pattern easily.

Many photographs and detailed drawings are shown in the catalog. They give you ideas for garment variations and possible fabrics, 19-2. All outfits shown in the catalog are accessorized.

19-1
The patterns in pattern catalogs are divided into many sections. This helps you find the type of pattern you want quickly.

Nationally available merchandise is used. Home sewers see how outfits can be completed. The sources of accessories (hats, purses, shoes, jewelry, scarves, belts, and trims) may be listed under "Accessory Credits" in the back of the catalog.

The garment sketches in pattern catalogs show you the shape or form of the garment. This helps you better determine if a particular style is good for you. The sketches also show textures, colors, or designs that would look good in the garment, 19-3.

A measurements page is also in the back of the catalogs. All of the charts for different pattern sizes are shown. Illustrations show how to take body measurements correctly. If you are not sure which pattern size to buy, this is the place to look.

Understanding Your Pattern

A pattern is to someone making a garment what a blueprint is to someone building a house. It shows the *what, when,* and *how.* As in a blueprint, a basic plan is given. This helps you build or put together a successful finished product—a garment. Take good care of your pattern. You may want to use it again.

Most stores will not let you return or exchange patterns. Study the pattern in the pattern catalog until

Simplicity Pattern Co., Inc.

19-2

Photographs like this often appear in pattern books. They give you ideas of possible fabrics you might use.

Simplicity Pattern Co., Inc.

19-3

This sketch was made by a graphic artist at the pattern company. It will be used in the pattern catalog or for the pattern envelope.

you are certain it is the one you want. If the store does not have the size you need, select another pattern, or look for it in another store. You want your garment to fit.

Your pattern has three main parts—the envelope, the cutting and sewing instruction sheet, and the tissue pattern pieces. Each part has helpful information.

Pattern Envelope

The front of the envelope shows the brand or company name. It may also give the pattern number, figure type, size, and price. A sketch and sometimes a photograph of the garment you plan to make are shown, 19-4. You often see more than one view, as in 19-5. These views give you an

The McCall Pattern Company

19-4
The front of a pattern envelope can give you important information as well as show you what the finished garment should look like.

The McCall Pattern Company

19-5
Pattern envelopes sometimes show photographs of different garments that can be made from the same pattern.

idea of different fabrics, designs, and details that can be used. For instance, a shirt pattern may show long sleeves, short sleeves, and no sleeves; collar and no collar. You can choose the combination you prefer. Most of the information on the envelope front is also shown in the catalog. You will have made some decisions before you ask for your pattern.

The pattern illustration can help you decide a fabric design to buy. If a garment is shown in a stripe or plaid, it means you can use that fabric design if you wish. Suppose you want to use a stripe and the picture does not show stripes. Look on the back of the envelope. Any fabrics and designs that are not suitable will be listed, along with a list of suggested fabrics.

Part of the back of your pattern envelope deals with the amount of fabric you need to make the garments. Usually, the width of your fabric is listed so you can easily find the length you need. If your fabric width is not listed, use a conversion chart like the one in 19-6. A conversion chart is usually provided in the pattern catalogs.

Many other kinds of information are also found on the back of the envelope. See 19-7. If your pattern requires lining or interfacing, the amount needed is listed. Standard body measurements are also given. They can be used as a reference if you make pattern adjustments for your body shape.

CONVERSION CHART FOR DIFFERENT WIDTHS OF **FABRIC**

Fabric Width	35"–36"	39"–42"	44"–45"	52"–54"	58"–60"
	$1^3/_4$	$1^1/_2$	$1^3/_8$	$1^1/_8$	1
	2	$1^3/_4$	$1^5/_8$	$1^3/_8$	$1^1/_4$
	$2^1/_4$	2	$1^3/_4$	$1^1/_2$	$1^3/_8$
	$2^1/_2$	$2^1/_4$	$2^1/_8$	$1^3/_4$	$1^5/_8$
	$2^7/_8$	$2^1/_2$	$2^1/_4$	$1^7/_8$	$1^3/_4$
Yardage	$3^1/_8$	$2^3/_4$	$2^1/_2$	2	$1^7/_8$
	$3^3/_8$	$2^7/_8$	$2^3/_4$	$2^1/_4$	2
	$3^3/_4$	$3^1/_8$	$2^7/_8$	$2^3/_8$	$2^1/_2$
	$4^1/_4$	$3^3/_8$	$3^1/_8$	$2^5/_8$	$2^3/_8$
	$4^1/_2$	$3^5/_8$	$3^3/_8$	$2^3/_4$	$2^5/_8$
	$4^3/_4$	$3^7/_8$	$3^5/_8$	$2^7/_8$	$2^3/_4$
	5	$4^1/_8$	$3^7/_8$	$3^1/_8$	$2^7/_8$

19-6

If your fabric is narrower or wider than your pattern shows, this chart can help you select the amount you need to buy. For example, if your pattern envelope calls for $1^3/_4$ yard of 36-inch fabric and your chosen fabric is 60 inches wide, you will need only 1 yard.

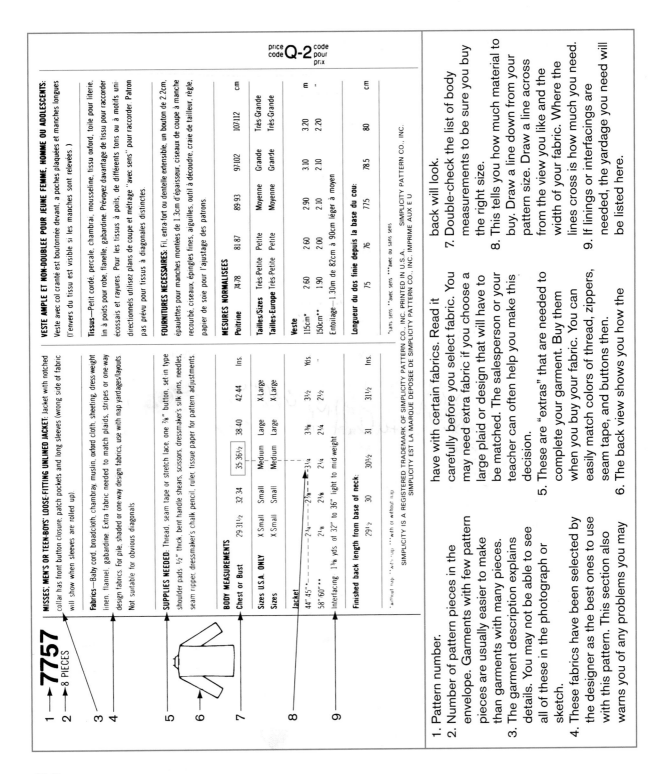

1. Pattern number.
2. Number of pattern pieces in the envelope. Garments with few pattern pieces are usually easier to make than garments with many pieces.
3. The garment description explains details. You may not be able to see all of these in the photograph or sketch.
4. These fabrics have been selected by the designer as the best ones to use with this pattern. This section also warns you of any problems you may

have with certain fabrics. Read it carefully before you select fabric. You may need extra fabric if you choose a large plaid or design that will have to be matched. The salesperson or your teacher can often help you make this decision.
5. These are "extras" that are needed to complete your garment. Buy them when you buy your fabric. You can easily match colors of thread, zippers, seam tape, and buttons then.
6. The back view shows you how the

back will look.
7. Double-check the list of body measurements to be sure you buy the right size.
8. This tells you how much material to buy. Draw a line down from your pattern size. Draw a line across from the view you like and the width of your fabric. Where the lines cross is how much you need.
9. If linings or interfacings are needed, the yardage you need will be listed here.

19-7
The back of your pattern envelope contains important information.

notions
Items other than fabric that become part of a garment. Thread, fasteners, and interfacing are examples.

The information on the back of the pattern envelope also includes the notions you need to complete your garment. **Notions** are the items other than fabric that become part of a garment. These include such items as thread, fasteners, and interfacing. They are listed under "Notions" or "Supplies Needed." The size and amount needed of each notion are also listed. Read this information carefully to make sure you buy the needed notions.

Cutting and Sewing Guide Sheet

cutting and sewing guide sheet
A printed sheet that gives detailed instructions on how to make a garment.

In your pattern envelope, you will find one or more printed sheets. These **cutting and sewing guide sheets** give detailed instructions on how to make your garment. You will want to keep them handy as you work. See 19-8. Cutting layouts, explanations of marking symbols, and a few general directions are given on the first page.

Also on the first page you will find line drawings of all the pattern pieces. Each piece will have a letter or number on it. This makes it easier to identify the pieces needed for the view you are making.

The next section usually includes some general directions. A pattern markings section explains the symbols used on pattern pieces such as cutting lines, grain lines, notches, and dots. Another section shows how to

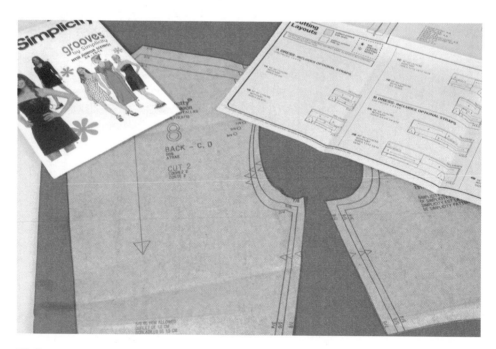

19-8
Your guide sheet gives step-by-step directions for making your garment. Sketches are shown to help you understand procedures.

lengthen or shorten pattern pieces for a proper fit. Other suggestions for preparing your fabric and pattern may be given, as well as any special cutting notes. A fabric key may be included. It explains what the various shadings on the guide sheet mean. They show the different layers of fabric and the printed and reversed sides of pattern pieces.

Cutting layouts show you how to correctly place the pattern pieces on your fabric. Layouts are given for different views and sizes. They are also given for various widths of fabrics and fabrics with a nap. Find the layout for your garment and draw a circle around it. Often there are special notes in the cutting layout section to make cutting and marking easier. Be sure to read these carefully before you begin.

The sewing directions section takes you step-by-step through the process of making your garment. Each part should be completed before going on to the next. It will make the construction of your garment easier if you read through all the steps before you begin sewing. You will have a better idea of what must be done and how it will be done.

Pattern Pieces

Inside your pattern envelope you will also find the pattern pieces needed to make your garment. Pattern pieces are made of tissue paper. Handle them carefully so they do not tear. Select the pieces you need for your garment by referring to the guide sheet. Refold the others, and put them in the envelope.

Look at a pattern piece. You will see terms and markings that you may not know. Many of them are explained on your cutting and sewing guide sheet. Understanding these symbols will help you avoid costly mistakes. They help you cut, mark, and sew correctly.

The pattern number, size, view number, name of piece, and identification letter are listed on each pattern piece. In addition, many symbols are used. See 19-9. The bold outline around each piece is the **cutting line.** Most patterns have several sizes printed on one pattern piece. If so, you will see several cutting lines representing each pattern size. You will use the cutting line for your size. If you are not using a multisized pattern, just inside the cutting line may be a broken line that represents the **stitching line.** If you are using a multisized pattern, it will not show a stitching line.

1. Cutting line.	5. Adjustment lines.
2. Center front.	6. Fold line for dart.
3. Buttonhole placement.	7. Dart stitching line.
4. Grain line	8. Dot.
	9. Notch.

19-9 _____

These pattern symbols are found on most pattern pieces. Multisized patterns may show as many as five cutting lines.

cutting line
The bold outline around the edge of each pattern piece.

stitching line
The broken line just inside the cutting line on single-sized pattern pieces.

Did You Know?

Patterns— New Kinds, New Places

Someone new to sewing may be surprised at the many kinds of patterns available for home sewing. Look through any of the large pattern catalogs at your local fabric store and see what all you can sew. Here is a sampling:

- bridal gowns and tuxedos
- maternity clothes
- children's clothes from baby layettes to christening gowns
- scrubs and other apparel for medical workers
- lingerie and sleepwear
- costumes for children and adults, from Halloween costumes to historical clothes
- women's clothes from earlier decades, such as the 40s and 50s
- home decor items including pillows, slipcovers, bedspreads, window treatments, placemats, chair cushions, nursery items, and more
- purses, backpacks, hats, and gloves
- stuffed toys and beanbags
- craft items from doll clothes to quilts
- pet accessories

If you can't get to a store to look at pattern catalogs, you can view most pattern selections online. All of the major pattern companies have Web sites where you can browse their pattern selections and then order patterns online.

There are also many Web sites that offer free patterns and sewing project directions. You can find patterns for simple items that you can print or download from the Web. Many sewing machine and serger manufacturers provide projects at their Web sites, including Baby Lock, Elna, Janome New Home, Pfaff, and Viking Husqvarna. Craft and quilt projects are also available online. It doesn't take much of a search online to find all types of interesting and easy sewing projects and patterns. Have fun!

The **grain line** is indicated with a line that has triangles on both ends. This helps you get your pattern straight on your fabric. When you measure from the tip of both triangles to the edge of your fabric, the two distances should be the same.

Adjustment lines show you where to shorten or lengthen the pattern piece.

Thin, solid lines are used to indicate center fold lines, hemlines, and placements for pockets or trims that go on the outside of the garment.

Notches are the diamond-shaped symbols along the cutting line. They help you join pieces together at the right place. **Dots** are also aids for matching seams and other construction details.

Choosing Your Pattern

Your teacher may decide that everyone in the class should make the same item for his or her first project. If your class is large, this can speed up your progress. You will be able to work with your friends on the same steps or problems. You can individualize your project by choosing unique fabric and trim.

If you can choose your own pattern, you will want to find one that is right for you. There are several factors to consider when doing this. These include the following:

- The pattern should match your sewing skill level.
- The garment should fit into your wardrobe and go with other garments you already have.
- The design should flatter your body shape.
- The garment should be one you will enjoy making.

If you have very little sewing experience, you will want to choose a pattern that is fairly simple. A garment made using a simple pattern can also be made in less time than a more complex pattern. The following terms are used to identify simple patterns: *Yes! It's Easy, See & Sew, Easy Stitch 'n Save,* and *It's So Easy.* Some will indicate a short time period, such as 60 minutes, 90 minutes, or two hours.

Generally, simple patterns have few pieces, and they fit loosely. They do not have pleats, curved yokes, collars, or pockets. You could begin with a simple project like making a pillow, cafe curtains, or a school banner for your room. Sewing straight lines can be easy. If you already have some sewing experience, you may wish to choose a more complex pattern with details you have not made before. This can increase your knowledge of sewing skills and techniques.

You may decide to use a kit to make your first project. Kits come with all the materials needed to complete a project along with step-by-step

grain line
Line with arrows on each end used to help you place the pattern piece on the straight grain of the fabric.

adjustment lines
Two parallel lines that show where to shorten or lengthen a pattern piece.

notches
Diamond-shaped symbols along the cutting line used to show where pattern pieces should be joined.

dots
Solid circles on pattern pieces used for matching seams and other construction details.

instructions. Sweatshirts, shorts, pillows, and stuffed animals are all available in kit form, 19-10. You can choose a kit that is at your sewing skill level and teaches you new techniques as you progress.

If you choose your own pattern, consider what you need. Do you need new sweats? Could you use a new pair of pull-on pants? Do you need a new sweatshirt to go with your jeans? Making a garment makes more sense if you know that you need it in your wardrobe.

If making a decision is a problem, visit a clothing store and look at ready-to-wear garments. Try on several garments in the style you think you like. Is the style flattering to your figure type? Do the colors look good on you? Would you like to make your garment oversized or more fitted? Making these decisions will help you enjoy your sewing project more.

If you can finish your first project quickly and without problems, you will probably learn to enjoy sewing. You will have fun and be proud of your finished product. Then you can go on to make more difficult garments. A simple pattern design is shown in 19-11. Sweats could be just what you need for track practice. You could choose fabrics in your school colors. The project would be fairly simple, and you could save money. See 19-12.

Pineapple Appeal

19-10
These shirts, pants, and shorts are all available in kit form.

Pineapple Appeal

19-11
These shorts and pants are simple projects that can be completed in very little time.

To-Sew

19-12

Sweats are quick and easy to make.

Even if your first garment is a success, you may decide that you would not like to make all of your clothes. Your sewing skills and knowledge will still be helpful to you. You will be able to select ready-to-wear garments more intelligently. Later, when you cannot find the exact garment you want, or when you want to save money, you may decide to try sewing again.

CHAPTER REVIEW

Key Points

- Pattern catalogs show you the patterns that are available in your size. They also have numerical indexes and measurement charts.

- All patterns have three parts: the pattern envelope, the cutting and sewing guide sheet, and the pattern pieces. Each provides the sewer with important information.

- Pattern envelopes may show several views giving you ideas of different fabrics, designs, and details that can be used.

- The cutting and sewing guide sheet gives detailed instructions on how to make your garment.

- Each pattern piece will have a pattern number, size, view number, name of piece, and identification letter printed on it.

- If you have very little sewing experience, you should choose a pattern that is fairly simple.

To Review

1. Why are actual photographs shown in pattern catalogs?

2. In looking for a pattern, you may have forgotten your figure type classification although you remember your measurements. How could you use the pattern catalog to solve your problem?

3. List four things you can learn by looking at the front of the pattern envelope.

4. Where can you find suggestions for the type of fabric to use with your pattern?

5. What directions are given in the cutting layouts section of the cutting and sewing guide sheet?

6. Why should you read through all the steps of the sewing instructions section before you begin sewing?

7. Which pattern symbol shows you where to shorten or lengthen the pattern piece?

8. Explain the advantages of using the same pattern as other students in your class.

9. Name three factors to consider when choosing your own pattern.

10. Name three features generally found on simple patterns.

To Do

1. Ask salespersons or store managers to save old pattern catalogs for use in the classroom. Look through the pattern catalogs. Become familiar with format and all sections.

2. Collect pictures of garments or items that would be easy first projects to sew. Arrange on bulletin board.

3. Select patterns for guys and girls from pattern catalogs and magazines. Make a display using a *Now* caption for beginning projects and a *Later* caption for more difficult patterns.

4. List ideas to individualize a basic pattern. Compare lists.

5. Using sample pattern envelopes from the family and consumer sciences department, make an arrangement on the bulletin board. Select fabric samples to go with each pattern.

6. Select a pattern from the catalog you feel fits your personality. Write a paragraph explaining the type of fabric you would use and suggest accessories. Give reasons for your selections.

7. Draw oversized pattern pieces. Add markings, symbols, and identification words. Make an attractive bulletin board.

8. Write a skit of a poorly prepared student buying fabric and notions from a poorly informed salesperson. Perform it for the class. Discuss what students need to know before going to the store.

To Think About

1. Pattern companies have switched to multisized patterns in recent years. Why do you think they made this change?

2. What are the advantages and disadvantages of using a multisized pattern?

3. Why do you think it is important to choose a pattern suited to your skill level? What might happen if you do not?

4. Compare the use of a sewing kit with the use of a standard pattern and fabric. What are the advantages and disadvantages of each?

5. What would you include in a sewing kit if you were designing one?

CHAPTER 20

Sewing Equipment

Objectives

After studying this chapter, you will be able to

- describe the basic supplies needed for sewing.
- describe additional sewing supplies that will make your sewing job easier.
- identify and give the function of the parts of a sewing machine.
- operate a sewing machine correctly.
- recognize and solve minor sewing machine problems that might occur.
- explain how to care for a sewing machine.

Key Terms

shears
scissors
rotary cutter
pinking or
    scalloping shears
thread clipper
seam ripper
tape measure
skirt marker
sewing gauge
thimble
fasteners
interfacing
press cloth
sleeve board
seam roll
pressing ham

Every kind of job requires special equipment. Some tools are necessary to do the job. Others just make the job easier. To be a successful sewer, you need some special equipment. The list of basic supplies is not long. Other tools can be added as you need them and can afford them. See 20-1 for a list of the basic supplies plus additional supplies you might want to add later on. Do some comparison shopping to get the most for your money.

Cutting Tools

Many types of shears and scissors are available, 20-2. The list of basic supplies includes a pair of shears. Other cutting tools are helpful additions.

Shears and scissors are not the same. **Shears** are usually longer than scissors. The blades are usually 7 to 8 inches long. The handles are not the same size. They are shaped to fit your hand. Left-handed persons should use left-handed shears.

Shears are used to cut pattern pieces from the fabric. *Bent-handled shears* are the most popular cutting tool for fabric. The bent handle allows the fabric to lie flat as it is cut. This results in more accurate cutting.

Scissors are usually short and the handles have small, matching holes. Blades are different widths, but about 4 to 6 inches long. They are used to clip around curves, trim seams, and clip threads. They are lightweight and easy to handle.

A good pair of shears will cost more than most of your other basic supplies. If you care for shears properly, they will last for years. Use them only for cutting fabric—not for cutting string, paper, or anything else. If they become dull, have them sharpened by someone who knows the correct way.

shears
Cutting instrument that is usually longer than scissors and the handles are not the same size.

scissors
Cutting instrument that is usually short with handles that have small, matching holes.

SEWING **SUPPLIES**

Basic Supplies	Additional Supplies
Shears	Scissors
Tape measure	Pinking or scalloping shears
Tracing wheel and paper	Thread clipper or seam ripper
Needles	Sewing gauge
Pins	Yardstick or meter stick
Pincushion	Skirt marker
Thread	Tailor's chalk
Sewing box	Thimble
Iron	Sleeve board
Ironing board	Press cloth
Sewing machine	Pressing ham

20-1
A successful sewer needs these supplies.

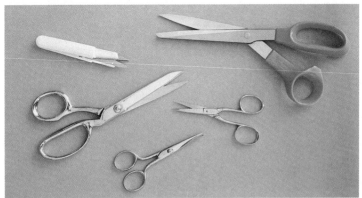

J. Wiss & Sons Co.

20-2
Shears, scissors, and thread clippers come in various shapes and sizes.

pinking shears
A cutting instrument used to give seam edges a finished look with a zigzag edge.

rotary cutter
A cutting device with a round blade.

thread clipper
A cutting device with a spring action that reopens the blade after each cut.

seam ripper
A small gadget with a hook-like blade that is used to remove stitches.

tape measure
A flexible measuring tool used to take body measurements.

skirt marker
A measuring tool used to mark an even hem.

A **rotary cutter** has a round blade that can be used for cutting fabric. It looks like a pizza cutter. A locking mechanism retracts the blade for safety. The rotary cutter is especially good for cutting the straight lines of quilt pieces. It must be used with a special self-healing mat that protects both the work surface and the blade.

Pinking or **scalloping shears** have a zigzag cutting edge or a scalloping cutting edge. They are used to give seam edges a finished look. They can also be used to achieve a decorative look on nonwoven fabrics. They should not be used to cut garment pieces from fabric. The uneven edge is difficult to follow when sewing. Seam edges can be pinked after the garment is made.

A **thread clipper** is used to clip threads at the start and end of every stitching line. Spring action reopens the blade after each cut. This tool can also be used as a seam ripper to undo mistakes in sewing or to remove basting stitches.

Another handy cutting tool is a **seam ripper.** This is a small gadget with a hook-like blade that is used to remove stitches. It can quickly remove an entire row of stitching. You have to be careful, however, that you do not cut the fabric.

Measuring Tools

Measuring tools are needed for accurate sewing. See 20-3. You need a **tape measure** to take body measurements. It is 60 inches long. One made of plastic or strong fabric does not stretch. Metal ends protect it for longer use.

To mark an even hem, you may want to use a **skirt marker.** This is a device that is used to measure and mark hemlines on garments using either pins or chalk. Wearing the garment to be hemmed, stand beside the skirt marker. Your friend or teacher will mark the placement of the hem with pins or powdered chalk, measuring an equal distance from the floor.

A yardstick could also be used to mark hems. It may also be used to make sure patterns are laid on the grain of fabrics. A 12-inch ruler would also be helpful to have. A transparent plastic one is handy for marking buttonholes, pleats, and tucks.

A **sewing gauge** (or seam gauge) is a 6-inch ruler with a sliding marker. It is used to measure hems, seam widths, cuffs,

Prym-Dritz Corp.

20-3
A tape measure, skirt marker, and sewing gauge are helpful measuring tools.

space between buttons, and other short distances. Although this tool is not necessary, it is inexpensive and handy. A *hem gauge* can also be used for measuring hems. It is a thin curved metal or plastic plate with graduated markings.

sewing gauge
A 6-inch ruler with a sliding marker.

Marking Tools

Marking tools are used to transfer pattern markings to the fabric. These markings help you put the pattern pieces together in the right way. Tracing wheels, dressmaker's carbon paper, marking pens, and tailor's chalk are types of marking tools, 20-4. They are inexpensive. You can find them in fabric and craft stores. Do not use ballpoint pens. The ink will soak through the fabric.

Dressmaker's carbon paper and a *tracing wheel* are frequently used to transfer markings. A package of several colors of a special waxed paper can be purchased. The tracing wheel can have a smooth edge or a serrated edge. The colored side of the paper is placed next to the wrong side of the fabric. The wheel marks any pattern markings that need to be transferred. Choose a color close to the color of your fabric. If the color shows through on the right side, you will not notice it. The marks usually can be removed when the garment is washed or dry cleaned.

Fabric marking pens are one of the easiest and fastest ways to mark fabric. These pens contain disappearing ink that makes it possible to mark on either the right or wrong side of the fabric. There are two types, water-soluble pens and evaporating marking pens. Water-soluble pens contain a blue ink that disappears when the marks are treated with water. Evaporating marking pens contain a purple ink that evaporates in less than 48 hours. To be sure your markings will still be there when you need them, do not use this type of pen until just before you are ready to sew.

Tailor's chalk is a clay chalk that comes in red, white, and blue. It is available in a small square form or as a pencil. Chalk marks can generally be brushed away when the mark is no longer needed.

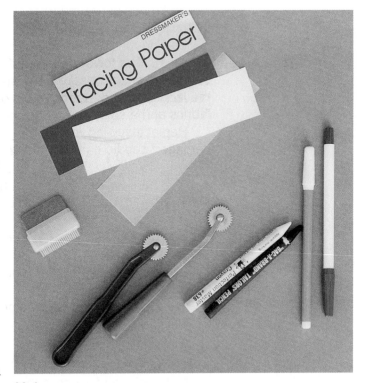

20-4

Choose from these various marking tools to transfer pattern markings to fabric.

Needles

There are many sizes and types of hand needles. Hand sewing is easier when you use the right needle. Coarse needles are for heavy fabrics, and fine needles are for delicate fabrics. A package of assorted sizes would be a good choice.

The sizes for coarse needles are low numbers. The sizes for fine needles are high numbers. Therefore, a size 1 needle is larger than a size 12 needle. Size 7 or 8 is used for most common hand sewing tasks.

Three types of needles are sharps, betweens, and crewel. *Sharps* are most often used for hand sewing. They are average in length and have a small eye. *Betweens* are short needles with a small eye. *Crewel* or *embroidery* needles have larger eyes. They are used for crewel and embroidery projects as well as hand sewing.

Three basic types of machine needles are ballpoint, sharp, and universal. Use a *ballpoint* needle for knits and stretch fabrics. A rounded tip allows the needle to slip between the yarns. It pushes the fabric aside instead of piercing it. Use a *sharp* needle for woven fabrics. It is designed to pierce heavyweight, densely woven fabrics. The *universal* needle has a specially rounded point. It is sharp enough to pierce tightly woven fabrics yet rounded enough to push aside the yarns of a knitted fabric. It is a good all-purpose sewing machine needle.

Sewing machine needles also come in a range of sizes from size 9 to size 18. The lower numbers are the finer needles and the higher numbers are coarser needles. The size used is determined by the weight of the fabric and the size or type of thread used. Use a size 9 or 11 for fine fabrics and a size 16 or 18 for heavier fabrics.

Replace sewing machine needles when they become dull or bent. A damaged needle can harm fabric and cause stitching problems.

Pins

Straight pins are used to attach pattern pieces to fabric and to pin garment pieces together before sewing. Marking should not be done with pins alone because the pins fall out of place before the marking can be used. The following are several types of pins:

- *Dressmaker's* pins are not for "dressmakers" only. They are medium in diameter with sharp points. Since they are brass, they will not rust.

- *Silk pins* are very slender. They have the sharpest points. They were first designed for use with silk or very fine fabrics, so they were called "silk" pins. These pins come in boxes or in paper folders and are made of stainless steel or brass.

- *Ballpoint pins* are recommended for use with knit fabrics. The rounded point slides between the yarns instead of cutting through them, preventing snags.
- *Ball-headed pins* have large, round heads. They are easy to see and to handle.

thimble
Metal or plastic device placed over the middle sewing finger to help push the needle through the fabric.

Pincushions

Never put pins in your mouth. Pins belong in pincushions. You can choose from many shapes and sizes of pincushions. Some can be worn on your wrist to keep the pins handy. Some are magnetic.

Some pincushions have a small strawberry-shaped emery bag attached to them. You can remove a rough spot or a dull point on a needle or pin by pushing it into the bag several times, 20-5. You may prefer to leave the bag in your sewing box rather than have it dangle from your pincushion.

Prym-Dritz Corp.

20-5_____
This pincushion has an emery bag attached for use in sharpening needles and pins.

Thimbles

When sewing by hand, a needle can damage your finger if you are working with thick or tightly woven fabric. A **thimble** is a metal or plastic device that is placed over the middle finger of your sewing hand. You use it to push the needle through the fabric.

Choose a thimble with deep enough grooves to hold the needle securely. Try on a thimble when you buy it. It should be snug but not tight. If it's too loose, you will not be able to use it successfully. It may feel awkward the first time you use it, but it will soon become a helpful tool, 20-6.

Notions

In addition to sewing tools, you need notions. Notions are items other than fabric that become part of a garment or project. Thread, zippers, buttons, snaps, hooks and eyes, hook and loop tape, tapes, trims, elastics, and interfacings are notions. The notions you need for your garment or project will be listed on your pattern envelope under notions or supplies needed.

20-6_____
Choose a thimble that has deep grooves and fits your middle finger of your sewing hand.

Buy your notions at the same time you buy your fabric. This way you can match colors. When selecting notions, keep in mind the care of your finished garment. If you are planning to wash your garment, check to see that your notions are also washable.

Thread

Thread comes in a wide variety of colors. If you are using solid-colored fabric, select thread that is slightly darker. (Thread looks lighter when it is stitched into fabric.) If your fabric is a print or a plaid, try to select thread that matches the background color in the fabric. See 20-7.

Choosing the right fiber content of thread is just as important as choosing the color. There are three main types of thread available. They are polyester/cotton, polyester, and mercerized cotton. There are several types of specialty threads also available.

Polyester/cotton thread is an all-purpose thread that can be used for sewing almost all fabrics. It is strong, stretchable, and has minimum shrinkage. This thread is often used to sew on knit and stretch fabrics because of its strength and ability to "give." It is made with a polyester core that gives the thread strength. This core is then wrapped with cotton to give it smoothness and luster. It comes in an extra fine weight for sewing lightweight fabrics. An all-purpose weight is used for medium to heavyweight fabrics.

Polyester thread is also considered an all-purpose thread. It is strong, abrasion resistant, and has the ability to stretch and recover.

Mercerized cotton thread is used to sew on woven fabrics made of natural fibers. It is smooth and lustrous. Although it sews well, it has limited stretching ability. Seams sewn with it could rip if there is excess strain.

Mercerization is a process that increases the strength, luster, and colorfastness of threads.

Specialty threads are used for specific projects. *Silk thread* is recommended for sewing on sheer and delicate fabrics. It is also used on wool and silk fabrics. *Nylon thread* is used for sewing heavy fabrics such as upholstery. *Heavy-duty* thread is also used for heavier fabrics that require heavy thread. *Buttonhole twist* is used for topstitching and handworked buttonholes. It is thicker than other threads. *Basting* and *quilting threads* are used to make quilts and other craft items. *Metallic thread* adds sparkle to decorative stitches.

Rayon thread is lustrous and silk-like, making it appropriate for decorative stitching. Size 40 rayon thread is suitable for free-hand machine embroidery. Size 30 is a

20-7

Choose a thread color that is slightly darker than the fabric color or matches the background color in a plaid.

heavier thread that gives bolder topstitching and greater fill-in when using programmed decorative stitches.

Fasteners

Fasteners are used to close openings on garments. They include zippers, buttons, hooks and eyes, snaps, and hook and loop tape. The type of fastener you need will be listed on your pattern envelope.

fasteners
Items used to close openings on garments.

Zippers

Zippers are available in various colors, types, and lengths. Like thread, you need to match the color of the zipper to the fabric. Check your pattern envelope for the type and length zipper you need. Zippers are available with both nylon and metal teeth in various weights and thicknesses. The zipper tapes may be made of cotton or manufactured fibers. They may be firmly woven or stretchable.

Different types of zippers have different uses. These include the following:

- *All-purpose zippers* are used most often. They open only from the top.
- *Separating zippers* can come apart at the bottom. They are used on jackets and parkas.
- *Invisible zippers* look like regular seams from the right side of the garment. No stitching is visible. The special way they are sewn gives them this appearance.
- *Two-way zippers* have sliders at the top and the bottom. They can be opened at either end.
- *Trouser zippers* have wider tapes and teeth than other zippers. The teeth are often made of brass.

Buttons

Buttons can be decorative or functional. The size and number of buttons you need are listed on your pattern envelope. A button's size is its diameter. There are two common types of buttons:

- *Sew-through buttons* have two to four holes in them. Thread is stitched through the holes.
- *Shank buttons* have a loop underneath the button. You stitch the thread through the loop.

Hooks, Eyes, and Snaps

Hooks and eyes come in a variety of sizes. Regular hooks and eyes have curved or straight eyes. *Curved eyes* are used on edges that just meet, such as the edge of a collar. *Straight eyes* are used when edges overlap, such as on a waistband. Trouser hooks and eyes are wider and flatter.

Inventions We Can't Live Without

For thousands of years, buttons and belts were the only fasteners used to hold clothes together. Then an engineer named Whitcomb Judson invented his "clasp locker" in 1893. It was really a series of hooks and eyes that closed mechanically. It wasn't a real hit, however, because it was rather crude and tended to come open—not a real plus.

In 1913, Gideon Sundbach developed a similar fastener using metal teeth—the prototype of today's zipper. He sold these fasteners to the U.S. Army for use on soldiers' clothing and gear during World War I. Sundbach is considered the father of the zipper industry.

The word "zipper" was actually coined by B.F. Goodrich in 1923, whose company sold rubber galoshes equipped with zippers. Goodrich named them zippers because of the zipping sound they made when opened and closed.

Velcro® is another fastener that has found many uses. A Swiss engineer named George de Mestral invented it in 1948. He got the idea while hiking. George noticed how burrs (burdock seeds) stuck to his clothing due to their hooklike protrusions. He used this concept to develop Velcro, which consists of one strip of nylon with loops and another with hooks. Though used mainly in apparel, Velcro is also used to fasten many other items. Can you name some of them?

Snaps also come in many sizes. Smaller snaps are used in areas with little strain. Larger snaps can withstand heavy-duty use. They can be used covered or uncovered depending on the garment, 20-8.

Hooks and eyes and snaps usually come in black and silver. Black is usually used on dark-colored fabrics. Silver is often used on light-colored fabrics.

Hook and Loop Tape

Hook and loop tape is made up of two pieces of nylon. One piece has tiny nylon loops. The other has a fuzzy surface. When the two pieces are pressed together, they stick to one another. Hook and loop tape may come in precut shapes such as circles and squares. It is also available in strips by the yard. A common brand of hook and loop tape is Velcro®.

Tapes and Trims

Tapes and trims are available in a variety of types, widths, and colors. They may be firmly woven or stretchable. The type you choose depends on how you will use it.

Tapes and trims can be functional as well as decorative. For instance, colorful seam tape can be used to finish hems and facing edges. Other colorful trims, such as ribbon, lace, and braid, are made into designs to decorate garments. Tapes can be used to cover fabric edges or reinforce seams to keep them from stretching.

A number of tapes and trims are available. They include

- *seam tape*—a woven tape used to finish hem and facing edges
- *twill tape*—a firm tape used to reinforce seams
- *bias tape*—a single-fold or double-fold tape that stretches; used for binding curved or straight edges or for casings and ties
- *hem facing*—a wide type of bias tape used for hems and binding edges
- *piping*—a corded bias strip that can be inserted into a seam for a decorative effect
- *ribbing*—a knitted band used for necklines, sleeves, or lower edges

Check the package directions for how these tapes and trims are to be used and how to apply them. Your pattern may tell you what type and how much to buy for the garment you are making.

Prym-Dritz Corp.

20-8
No-sew decorative snap fasteners are applied with a special type of pliers.

Elastics

Elastic is used to give better fit to garments. It is available in different widths and types. When buying elastic, check to make sure you get the kind you need. *Woven elastic* can be used in a casing (an enclosure to hold elastic) because it stays the same width when stretched. It can also be stitched directly to a garment. *Braided elastic* becomes narrow when it is stretched. It is only used in casings. *Elastic thread* may be thin or heavy. Thin elastic thread may be used on the lower edges of sweaters to help them hold their shape. Heavier elastic thread may be used on jacket waistlines. There is also specially designed elastic for swimwear and lingerie.

Interfacings

interfacing
A fabric that is used under the outer fabric to prevent stretching and provide shape to a garment.

Interfacing is a fabric used under the outer fabric to prevent stretching and provide shape to a garment. It also adds strength to necklines, buttonholes, and front closings. It gives shape to collars, cuffs, waistbands, and pockets.

When choosing interfacing, consider the weight of your fabric. As a rule, choose interfacing the same weight or a little lighter weight than your fabric. Make sure your interfacing has the same care instructions as the other fabric you are using. Interfacings come in both woven and nonwoven types. They are also either sewn into the garment or have a *fusible backing.* Fusible interfacings bond to another fabric when pressed with an iron.

Sewing Box

You will need some kind of container or sewing box to keep your small equipment organized. You can either buy one or make one. If you buy a sewing box, look for one with many sections so you can keep your tools separated. If you make one, use a large box, which will hold several small boxes.

Pressing Equipment

It is important as you construct a garment to press it as you go along. You will need an iron for this. Irons vary in features and cost. A dry iron can be used successfully if you use a damp pressing cloth to supply steam when needed. A steam iron is more convenient and produces a lot of steam. It's not the heat that shapes the garment, but moisture.

press cloth
Cloth used to cover a garment before it is pressed to prevent iron shine.

To prevent iron shine and possible water drops on the fabric, cover your garment with a **press cloth** before you press. You can use an absorbent, light- to medium-weight cotton or linen fabric for a press cloth. A press cloth allows you to remove wrinkles without making the fabric surface shiny. The press cloth can be dampened if you want to provide more steam.

A **sleeve board** is handy for pressing small details. It looks like a small ironing board. A **seam roll** is a long tubular cushion that allows you to press seams open without leaving marks from the seam allowances. Curved seams and darts can be easily pressed with a **pressing ham** (a firm, round cushion). See 20-9. The garment lies flat against its rounded shape and curved edges.

An ironing board should be sturdy, level, and adjustable for different heights. A smooth absorbent padding with a tight-fitting cover is best. A cotton cover absorbs moisture. Keep the cover smooth and clean, 20-10.

The Sewing Machine

Since Elias Howe patented his sewing machine in 1846, many changes in shape and features have been made. The latest change has been the addition of computer technology. Thread tension, stitch length, and button-hole size can be automatically set. Many more stitches are often available.

If you have ever sewn a seam by hand, you can appreciate the efficiency of a sewing machine. It is a complex piece of machinery. Before you sew, you should learn how the machine you will use works. Different models and brands vary in some ways. They may thread differently. Some may have special features. Regardless of the model you use, you must know some basics: threading, starting, controlling the speed, backstitching, and stopping at the desired spot.

sleeve board
A padded sleeve-shaped board used to help press small details in garments.

seam roll
A long tubular cushion that allows you to press seams open without leaving marks from the seam allowances.

pressing ham
A firm, round cushion used to help press curved seams and darts.

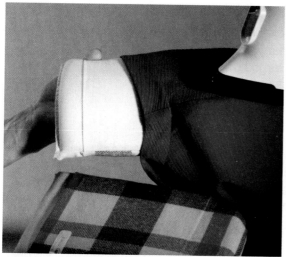

June Tailor, Inc.

20-9
A small pressing mitt helps you get good results when pressing curved areas and seams.

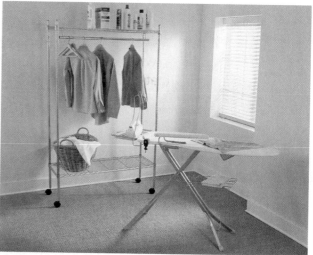

©Spiegel 2000

20-10
A well-equipped pressing area includes an iron, sleeve board, and ironing board for pressing during garment construction.

The Parts of the Sewing Machine

In order to learn how to operate a sewing machine, it helps to have a basic knowledge of its parts. The head of a sewing machine is shown in 20-11. It holds many moving parts that help the machine operate. If you lift it from its storage cabinet, be careful not to drop it. It is heavy and requires both hands for lifting.

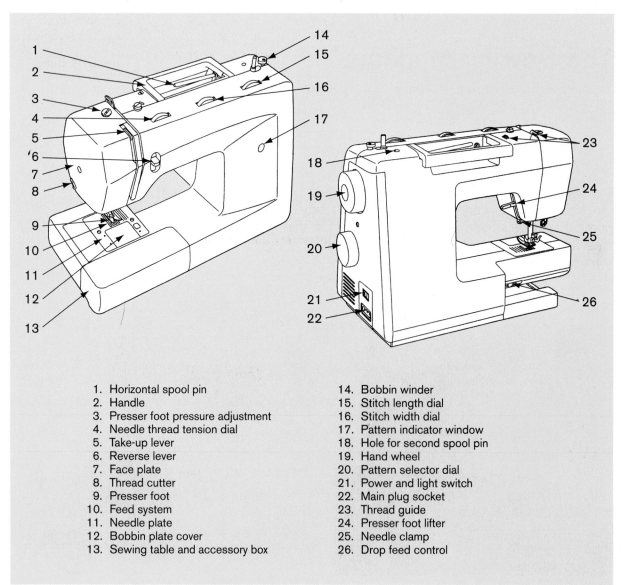

1. Horizontal spool pin
2. Handle
3. Presser foot pressure adjustment
4. Needle thread tension dial
5. Take-up lever
6. Reverse lever
7. Face plate
8. Thread cutter
9. Presser foot
10. Feed system
11. Needle plate
12. Bobbin plate cover
13. Sewing table and accessory box
14. Bobbin winder
15. Stitch length dial
16. Stitch width dial
17. Pattern indicator window
18. Hole for second spool pin
19. Hand wheel
20. Pattern selector dial
21. Power and light switch
22. Main plug socket
23. Thread guide
24. Presser foot lifter
25. Needle clamp
26. Drop feed control

The Singer Sewing Company

20-11
This illustration identifies the various parts of a sewing machine.

There are many makes and models of sewing machines. The following are the main parts of most sewing machines. Locate these parts on the sewing machine you will be using.

- *Hand wheel* controls movement of the take-up lever and needle. It turns as the machine runs. You can move the needle up and down by turning the wheel toward you with your hand.
- *Bobbin winder* guides the thread when filling the bobbin with thread.
- *Spool pin and cap* holds the spool of thread.
- *Presser foot pressure adjustment* controls the amount of pressure the pressor foot places against the feed system.
- *Stitch width dial* controls the width of zigzag stitching. It also positions the needle for straight stitching.
- *Thread guides* lead the thread to the needle.
- *Bobbin winder tension disc* regulates thread tension for bobbin winding.
- *Take-up lever* controls flow of needle thread. It must be at its highest position each time you start to sew. If it is not, the thread will be pulled up and away from the needle as the lever rises, and you will have to thread the needle again.
- *Face plate* swings open for access to movable parts and light.
- *Needle thread tension dial* lets you set the tension for your particular project. Your fabric, stitch, and thread will determine the tension setting you need.
- *Presser foot holds* fabric against feed system teeth.
- *Feed system* (feed dog) moves fabric under the presser foot.
- *Needle plate* has guidelines to help you sew straight, even seams. It also supports the fabric during sewing.
- *Needle clamp* holds the needle in place.
- *Stitch length dial* regulates the length of the stitches. Some models have a special setting for stretch stitching.
- *Reverse lever* lets you stitch backward.
- Presser foot lifter allows you to raise and lower the presser foot.
- *Thread cutter* is on the back of the presser bar for convenience.
- *Slide plate* or bobbin cover plate covers the bobbin and bobbin case.
- *Speed controller* is used to operate the machine. Press down on it to stitch.
- *Power and light switch* turns on machine and sewing light at one time.
- *Drop feed control* allows you to lower the feed dog if you do not want the fabric to move

An important item that comes with your sewing machine is the instruction manual. It shows you the parts of your machine and tells you what they do. It describes any accessories that come with your machine and any special features. Be sure to read the instruction manual thoroughly before you begin using a sewing machine.

Using the Sewing Machine

Machines operate with two threads: the needle thread and the bobbin thread. The needle thread runs from the spool pin, around the tension discs and through the take-up lever, thread guides, and needle. The bobbin thread runs from the bobbin plate up through the throat plate. Your teacher will show you how to thread your particular machine. If you have diagrams, study them carefully.

A problem of most beginners is learning to operate the machine at a moderate speed. They either go too fast or much too slow. You can practice controlling the speed of a sewing machine by stitching on paper patterns without thread.

When you feel you are ready, thread your machine. Begin to sew using some fabric scraps. See if you can do as well on fabric as you did on paper. Use two layers since most sewing is done with two pieces of fabric. Keep your fingers away from the machine needle. Do not lean too close to the machine needle in case it breaks.

Study the chart of sewing machine problems and cures in 20-12. Then you will know what to do if one of these problems should occur. Learn to be your own detective and solve your own problems.

Caring for the Sewing Machine

A sewing machine is a precise instrument that will stitch well if it is given the proper care. Many students will be using the sewing machines in your classroom. The average sewing machine gets far less use. Therefore, you will need to do your part in keeping the machines clean and running smoothly. Your instructor will give you guidelines to follow in your classroom. These may include the following:

- Unplug the sewing machine before cleaning it.

- Remove lint and fluff from the exposed parts using a soft cloth. Clean the machine head, tension discs, take-up lever, thread guides, presser foot bar, and needle bar.

- With a small lint brush, clean behind the face plate and around the feed dog and bobbin case. You may need to remove the entire bobbin case, 20-13.

- Check to see if you are to oil your machine. Many of the newer machines never need to be oiled. If your machine is to be oiled, follow the instruction manual or your teacher's directions. Be sure to only use machine oil. Use only the amount recommended, which is usually just a drop. Then sew a few lines of stitching on a scrap of fabric to remove excess oil. You don't want any oil to get on the garment you are sewing.

- Cover the sewing machine when it is not in use to keep dust away from the machine.

MINOR PROBLEMS AND CURES FOR **SEWING MACHINES**

Problem	Cause	Cure
1. Loud noise as you start to sew and matted threads in seamline.	Machine threaded wrong.	Thread machine again.
2. Lower thread breaks.	Lower tension too tight. Knot in bobbin thread.	Adjust tension screw. Check thread.
3. Puckered seamline.	Tension too tight. Thread too heavy or too light for fabric. Pulling on fabric.	Check by sewing on different weight fabric.
4. Machine locks. Needle will not go up and down.	Thread caught in bobbin.	Turn hand wheel backward to release thread.
5. Skipped stitches.	Needle bent, blunt, too long or short. Needle threaded wrong.	Check needle. Thread needle again.
6. Looped stitches. Top line. Bottom line.	Top tension adjusted wrong. Bottom tension adjusted wrong.	Check tension.
7. Needle picks or pulls thread in line of stitching.	Point of needle bent when it hit a pin.	Insert new needle.
8. Needle breaks.	Presser foot loose and needle hit it. Pulling fabric while stitching.	Tighten presser foot. Do not pull fabric.
9. Machine runs "hard."	Needs cleaning and oiling.	Clean and oil according to instruction booklet.
10. Machine will not run at all.	Machine may be unplugged. Cord or outlet may be defective.	Check to see if plugged in tightly. Check another outlet to see if cord is okay.

20-12
You can save time and frustration by learning to recognize common sewing machine problems and knowing how to solve them.

If you have a sewing machine at home, check the use and care manual that came with your machine. It will tell you how to care for your machine each time it is used. It will also tell you what needs to be done every few months or so to keep your machine running well for many years.

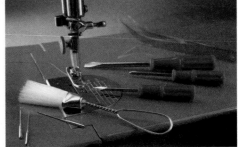

Prym-Dritz Corp.

20-13
Use a lint brush to clean the face plate, feed dog, and bobbin case. Change machine needles whenever they become dull.

CHAPTER REVIEW

Key Points

- To be a successful sewer, you need some special equipment. Some tools are necessary to do the job. Others just make the job easier.

- Cutting tools include shears, scissors, pinking or scalloping shears, thread clippers, and seam rippers. You will need at least a pair of shears to construct a garment.

- Measuring tools include tape measures, skirt markers, yardsticks, rulers, and sewing gauges. You will need to have a tape measure.

- Marking tools are used to transfer pattern markings to the fabric. Most people use dressmaker's carbon paper and a tracing wheel for this task.

- You will need to use both needles (hand and machine) and pins for your sewing project. They come in a variety of types and sizes.

- In addition to sewing tools, you need notions. Notions are items other than fabric that become part of a garment or project. Thread, zippers, buttons, snaps, hooks and eyes, hook and loop tape, tapes, trims, elastics, and interfacings may be needed.

- As you construct a garment, it is important to press it as you go along. You will need an iron and ironing board for this. In addition, you may want to use a press cloth, sleeve board, seam roll, and pressing ham.

- The sewing machine is a complex piece of machinery. Before you sew, you should learn how it works. Different models and brands vary in some ways. Regardless of the model you use, you must know some basics: threading, starting, controlling the speed, backstitching, and stopping. You also need to know how to care for the sewing machine.

To Review

1. Explain the difference between scissors and shears.
2. What is the advantage of bent-handled shears?
3. Describe pinking shears and their use.
4. List two factors to consider in buying a good tape measure.
5. Describe one of the marking tools and how it is used.
6. Which type of needle is most often used for hand sewing?
   A. Sharps.
   B. Betweens.
   C. Crewel.
   D. Ballpoint.
7. Name the best all-purpose sewing machine needle and why it is a good choice for most fabrics.
8. Which pins should be used with knitted fabrics?
9. When is a thimble used and why?
10. Why is polyester/cotton thread a good choice for sewing almost all fabrics?
11. Which type of zipper would you choose if you were sewing a jacket and why?
12. When using hooks and eyes, which type of eye would you use if you want the edges of your garment to just meet?
13. When choosing interfacing fabric, explain how you decide what weight to buy.
14. Which pressing tool would you use to press a curved seam and a dart?
15. What should you use to clean a sewing machine each time it is used?

To Do

1. Have an equipment-marking day at the beginning of the sewing unit. Everyone labels each piece of equipment clearly with name and class period.

2. Select a partner. Choose a piece of sewing equipment. One tells the class factors to consider in purchasing it. The other explains how to use and care for it.

3. Arrange some pieces of small equipment on a bulletin board with this caption: *Use the Right Tools to Build Your Garment.*

4. Try removing a rough spot on a pin by using an emery bag attached to a pincushion.

5. Visit notions departments. Find unusual equipment and items. Prepare a report for the class.

6. Ask older people about sewing equipment they and their grandparents used. Was it different? What changes have been made? Share with the class.

7. Practice using a thimble.

8. Iron a scrap of polyester fabric without using a press cloth. Can you see "iron shine"?

9. Watch your teacher demonstrate how to care for the sewing machines in your classroom.

10. On a classroom sewing machine, demonstrate filling a bobbin, threading the bobbin, controlling speed, following lines, turning corners, and storing the machine.

To Think About

1. Compare the various tools for transferring pattern markings to fabrics. What are the advantages and disadvantages of each?

2. Some people find it awkward to use a thimble. What would you say to them about its use and usefulness?

3. Prepare a list of safety guidelines for using sewing equipment, the sewing machine, and pressing equipment. Post it on the bulletin board.

4. Review the basic sewing supplies listed in Figure 20-1. Which of these would you need to use to make simple clothing repairs and alterations? What does this tell you about the supplies needed to construct a new garment?

5. When sewing for the first time, there are supplies you may need to buy. Brainstorm ways to obtain these supplies if funds are not available.

CHAPTER 21

Getting Ready to Sew

Objectives

After studying this chapter, you will be able to

- check the grain of fabric and prepare fabric for cutting and sewing.
- lay out a pattern and properly pin it to fabric.
- cut out a garment.
- transfer pattern markings to fabric.

Key Terms

preshrunk
true bias
off-grain
layout

The more you know about something, the more at ease you feel working with it. This is true if you are caring for children, playing baseball, talking before a group, or sewing a garment.

Sewing is a complex task, but the more you know about it, the easier it seems. By learning about fabrics, patterns, equipment, and basic sewing techniques, you will avoid frustration and mistakes. Instead, you will enjoy sewing and will have success with your projects.

This chapter explains many preliminary sewing steps. The guide sheet of your pattern gives step-by-step directions for your specific garment. Together, they tell you all you need to know to make your sewing project a success.

Preparing the Fabric

Before pinning the pattern to the fabric, there are some preliminary steps you must follow in preparing the fabric. The fabric may need to be preshrunk. You may also need to straighten the grain of the fabric. Both of these preparation steps will help assure a properly fitted garment when it is finished and ready to wear.

Preshrinking the Fabric

Many of today's fabrics are **preshrunk.** This means they were shrunk during manufacturing to help keep them from shrinking during washing or cleaning. Check the label on the end of the bolt when you buy your fabric. If it has not been preshrunk, you should do it yourself. Then you will be sure that the finished garment will not shrink.

To preshrink your fabric, treat it as if it were the finished garment. If you will machine wash and dry the garment, machine wash and dry the fabric. (You do not need to add detergent.) If you will hand wash the garment and lay it flat to dry, do this to the fabric. If the garment will be dry-cleaned, you may want to dry-clean the fabric.

Also check the notions. Zippers and trims may need to be preshrunk as well. If not, they may shrink after they are attached to the garment. This could cause the garment to pucker.

Understanding Fabric Grain

Woven fabrics have two sets of yarns—warp and filling. (See Chapter 15 for a review of warp and filling yarns.) The direction the yarns run is called *grain*. The warp yarns form the *lengthwise grain*. An easy way to find the lengthwise grain is to look for the selvages of the fabric. The lengthwise grain runs in the same direction as the selvages. See 21-1. When your pattern refers to "straight grain" or "grain line," it means the lengthwise grain.

preshrunk
Fabric that has been treated during manufacturing to help keep it from shrinking during washing or cleaning.

The filling yarns run straight across the fabric from one selvage to the other. This is the *crosswise grain* of the fabric.

The other fabric grain is *bias grain.* This runs diagonally across the fabric. **True bias** runs at a 45 degree angle, as shown in 21-2. It allows the greatest amount of stretch in a woven fabric. To find the true bias, pick up a corner of the fabric. Fold it so the cut edge is parallel to the selvage.

The grain in knitted fabrics is slightly different. Instead of two sets of yarns, these fabrics have rows of loops in two directions. The rows of loops running the length of the fabric form the lengthwise grain. The rows of loops running across the fabric form the crosswise grain. In knitted fabrics, the crosswise grain allows the most stretch.

true bias
Fabric grain that runs at a 45 degree angle to the lengthwise and crosswise grains. It allows the greatest amount of stretch in a woven fabric.

Checking the Grain

If the fabric is **off-grain,** the lengthwise yarns and the crosswise yarns are not at a perfect 90 degree angle to each other. The fabric grain is crooked, and it will be difficult to handle. It may not lie flat as you cut out the pattern pieces. The finished garment will twist, pull to one side, and the hem may be uneven. The fabric grain must be "straight" to make a garment look right.

The first step in checking the straightness of the grain is to see if the fabric was cut along the crosswise grain. (The fabric may not have been

off-grain
The lengthwise and crosswise yarns of a fabric are not at a perfect 90 degree angle to each other.

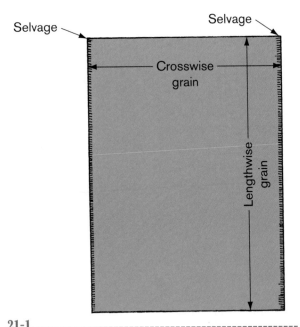

21-1
The lengthwise grain runs parallel to the selvages. The crosswise grain runs between selvages.

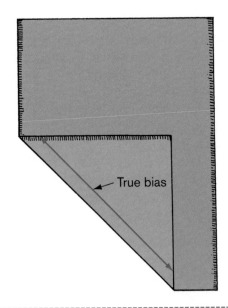

21-2
The true bias runs at a 45 degree angle across the fabric.

cut on the grain when it was cut from the bolt of fabric in the store.) You may be able to see one of the filling yarns. Cut along one of these filling yarns close to the end of the fabric. If you cannot see the yarns clearly, clip through the selvage near the cut edge. Inside the clip, pick up one filling yarn and pull it gently. With your other hand, push the fabric along the pulled yarn as shown in 21-3. This leaves a mark that you can use as a cutting line. If the yarn breaks in the middle of the fabric, cut as far as you can see the line. Pick up the yarn and pull it again. Continue until you have cut all the way across the fabric.

Some firmly woven fabrics can be torn to make the cut edges even. This is risky because the fabric sometimes splits along the lengthwise grain while being torn. If you decide to tear your fabric, clip through the selvages. (They are difficult to tear.) Then tear along the crosswise grain.

Lay the fabric on a large, flat surface. Bring the two selvages together, making a lengthwise fold. If the grain is straight, the fold will be smooth and straight. The selvages will match, and the cut edges on each end will match. The cut edges and the selvages will meet in a right angle. See 21-4.

Straightening the Grain

Suppose the fold is not smooth and straight or that the edges do not match. This could happen if the fabric was twisted as it was rolled onto

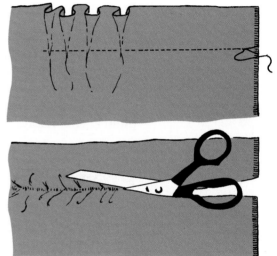

21-3
One way to find the straight crosswise grain is to pull a filling yarn, leaving a mark you can follow when cutting.

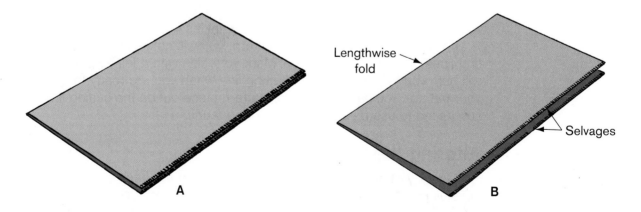

Lengthwise fold

Selvages

A   B

21-4
If the fabric grain is straight, all edges match and the fabric lies flat (A). If the grain is not straight, the selvages and cut edges do not match (B). The grain will need to be straightened.

bolts. It can be straightened by pulling. Two persons can do this better than one. Hold the two opposite corners that are too short. Pull along the bias. Check often to see if you have pulled enough.

Yarns are sometimes forced off-grain during the finishing process. In durable-press fabrics, chemicals and heat are added to help resist wrinkling. If unevenness occurs during the finishing stage, it is "baked" into the fabric. It will have to be used as is. Pulling the fabric to straighten the grain will not work. It will return to the off-grain shape.

Pressing the Fabric

If your fabric needs pressing, do it before you place your pattern pieces on it. Accurate cutting is impossible on wrinkled fabric. Press carefully and thoroughly. Give special attention to the center fold. The crease may be difficult to remove. A damp pressing cloth or a steam iron is often helpful.

Press in the direction of the lengthwise grain. This will keep the fabric grain in line. Fabric stretches very little in the lengthwise direction.

Preparing the Pattern

Remove your pattern pieces from the envelope. Look at the sketches of the pattern pieces on the guide sheet. The guide sheet will state which pattern pieces you need for the garment or view you are making. Many pieces will be printed on one large piece of tissue paper. You will need to cut these apart, but you do not need to cut directly on the cutting line. You will do this later when you cut out your fabric. Return the pattern pieces you will not be using to the envelope.

Write your name and class period number on the center of each pattern piece. Also put your name on your guide sheet and pattern envelope.

If your pattern pieces are badly wrinkled, press them with a dry, warm iron. Be careful not to press tiny wrinkles into each piece.

If you are using a multisized pattern, you will notice three or four cutting lines on each pattern piece. Mark your size with a felt tip pen. This will help you follow the correct cutting line when you are ready to cut out your pattern. You can also cut the pattern piece out on the cutting line you intend to use before pinning it to the fabric.

Altering the Pattern

Check your measurements with the chart on the back of the pattern envelope. If they are not the same (allowing for ease), you will have to *adjust* or *alter* your pattern. Altering patterns is better than altering finished garments. It is more accurate and assures better fit. A finished garment might not have enough extra fabric to make the needed changes.

Altering the Length

The most common adjustments are for length. Many pattern pieces are labeled "lengthen or shorten here" in one or two places. This phrase is often found at the bottom cutting edge of a pattern piece. In this case, lengthen the piece by taping a piece of paper to the bottom. Measure the desired amount from the original cutting line. Draw a new line that is parallel to the original. This method is pictured in 21-5.

To shorten the pattern piece at the bottom edge, measure the desired amount up from the original line. Draw a new cutting line that is parallel to the first. Be sure to lengthen or shorten all pieces the same amount.

Altering the bottom edge of pattern pieces does not solve all fitting problems. An adjustment in the middle of pattern pieces may be needed instead. Look for two parallel lines that are close together. These are the *adjustment lines.* You may find the phrase "lengthen or shorten here" next to them, but not always.

To lengthen the pattern piece, cut between the two lines. Place a piece of paper under the pattern. Spread the pattern the needed distance and tape to the paper. Redraw the cutting lines at the sides to form straight lines. See 21-6.

To shorten the pattern, measure up from the adjustment line the amount to be shortened. Draw a new line. Fold the pattern at the adjustment line and bring the fold to the newly drawn line. Tape in place and redraw the cutting lines. See 21-6.

Altering the Width

It may be necessary to make adjustments in the width of pattern pieces in the waist, hip, or thigh areas. These adjustments should be made in both front and back pieces. If the total amount of the alteration is less than two inches, you can increase or decrease one-fourth the amount needed on each of the side seams. If larger adjustments are needed, you may find a different pattern size to be more appropriate. You might also consult with your teacher or an alterations book for additional adjustment techniques.

To increase the size of a waistline in pants and skirts, tape a strip of paper along the front and back side edges of your pattern pieces from the waist to the hip. Measure out from the cutting line at the waist one-fourth of the total

21-5_____
To lengthen the bottom edge of a pattern, tape extra paper below the cutting line. Draw a new cutting line that is parallel to the original. Fill in the adjacent seam lines and cutting lines.

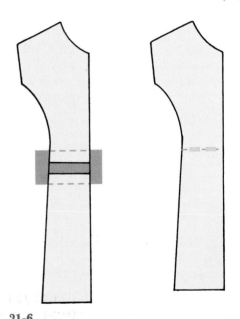

21-6_____
To lengthen, cut between the adjustment lines and spread the pattern apart. To shorten, fold at the adjustment line and tape.

Hemlines— The Highs and the Lows of the Last 100 Years

For hundreds of years, the hemlines of women's skirts always touched the floor. It wasn't until the 1900s that hemline length began to creep upward, and then it wasn't a continual rise. There were highs and lows often related to economics, politics, art, world events, wars, revolutions, and technology. Let's take a closer look at some dates and changes in hemlines.

1908—Hemlines rise just slightly off the floor.

1918—Skirts rise above the ankle for the first time since anyone can remember, just before the Nineteenth Amendment gave women the vote in 1920.

1925—Hemlines rise above the kneecap.

1930—Following the stock market crash, hems plunge to eleven inches off the floor.

1939—Nylon stockings appear, creating the desire for more exposed leg and higher hems.

1941—Hems head north as wartime regulations restrict fabric yardages in dresses.

1943—The jitterbug craze creates the need for more legroom.

1947—Dior unveils his New Look of longer skirts at midcalf, which remained popular through the 1950s.

1961—Oleg Cassini designs Jacqueline Kennedy's inaugural skirt at midknee.

1964—London designer Mary Quant responds to the demands of the youth culture and their modern dances with the invention of the miniskirt, which remains popular throughout the 60s.

1970s—Maxiskirts, reaching midankle, appear on the scene during the Vietnam and Watergate years as the feminist movement takes place.

1980s—Hems are on the rise again as women decide it's OK to be sexy and liberated.

1990s—Some years are up and some are down as women embrace the freedom to choose.

2000s—Hemlines of all lengths are available to suit women's many moods and needs.

Will skirt hemlines ever again hit the floor? Who can predict what lies ahead?

amount to be added. For instance, if the total alteration is one inch, add 1/4 inch to the front and back side seams. Redraw the cutting lines, tapering to the hip line. See 21-7. If there is a waistband or waistline facing, make the same amount of adjustment in these pattern pieces. Cut the waistband pattern apart at the side seam markings. Increase each side one-half the amount necessary.

To decrease the size of the waistline, measure in one-fourth the needed amount at each side seam. Redraw the cutting lines on the pattern pieces, tapering down to the hipline. If there is a waistband, fold out one-half of the amount of the alteration at the side seam markings and tape in place.

To increase the hip and thigh area of straight skirts and pants, tape a strip of paper to the pattern from the waist to the hemline. At the side hipline, measure out from the cutting line one-fourth of the needed amount on the front and back pieces and make a mark with a pencil. Redraw the cutting lines. To do this, taper the lines upward to the original waistline. Measure out from the hemline the same amount as at the hipline and make a mark. Draw a straight line from the hipline mark to the hemline mark. See 21-8.

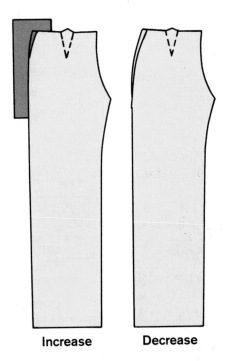

Increase   Decrease

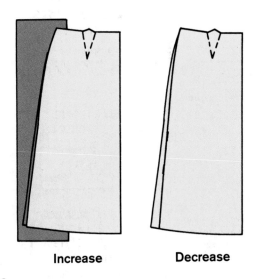

Increase   Decrease

21-7 --
To increase or decrease the width of the waist, measure in or out one-fourth of the needed amount at the wide waistline edge. Redraw the cutting lines, tapering to the hipline.

21-8 --
To increase or decrease the width of the hips, measure in or out one-fourth of the needed amount at the side hipline. Redraw the cutting lines, tapering to the waist and extending down to the hemline.

To decrease the hip and thigh area, measure in from the cutting line at the hipline one-fourth of the total amount needed. Redraw the lines, tapering to the waistline and drawing straight down to the hemline. For pants, some of the width adjustments should be made on the inner leg seams as well as the outer leg seams.

The Pattern Layout

layout
The section of the pattern guide sheet that shows how to lay the pattern pieces on the fabric.

The guide sheet of your pattern suggests many layouts, as shown in 21-9. The **layout** shows you how to lay your pattern pieces on your fabric for cutting. Find the one that matches your pattern size, project or view, and fabric width. You will want to use a "with nap" layout if your fabric has a nap, pile, or one-way design. Draw a circle around it so you can refer to it easily.

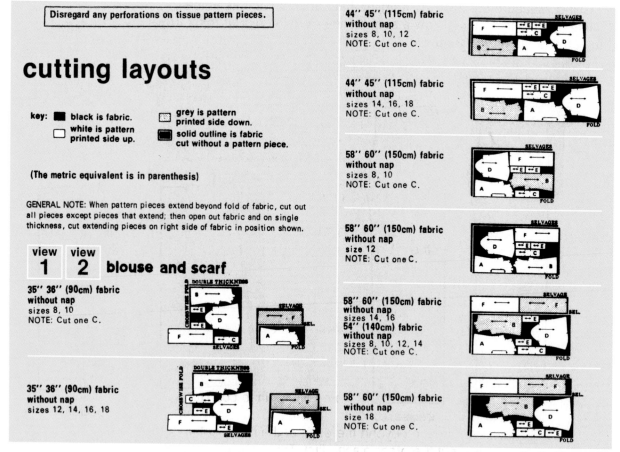

21-9.
Many layouts are shown on the guide sheet of a pattern.

The Simplicity Pattern Co.

Folding the Fabric

The layout diagram will indicate how your fabric should be folded before pinning on the pattern. First, determine which is the right side of your fabric. Some plain weaves are identical on both sides. In that case, you can use either side, but use the same one for all pattern pieces.

Most fabrics are folded with the right sides together. Your pattern may call for one or more of the following types of folds:

- *Lengthwise fold:* Fold the fabric lengthwise so the two fabric selvages are together.

- *Off-center lengthwise fold:* Fold one selvage toward the other. They should not match, but they should be parallel. One part of the fabric is doubled. The other part is single thickness. See 21-10.

- *Double fold:* Fold the fabric lengthwise so the selvages meet in the center.

- *Crosswise fold:* Place the cut edges together and match them.

- *Bias fold:* This fold runs diagonally across the fabric. The selvage is folded so it is parallel to the crosswise grain.

Your fabric may be longer than the table you are using. If so, let one end rest in a chair, as shown in 21-11. This prevents strain on the fabric and keeps it from sliding off the table.

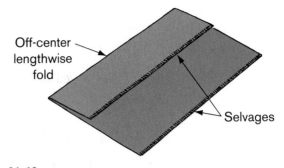

21-10
Some layouts suggest an off-center lengthwise fold.

21-11
Let extra fabric rest on a chair while you work. This reduces the pull on the fabric.

Placing the Pattern Pieces

Most pattern pieces are placed on the fabric with the printed side up. These are white on the cutting layouts. A shaded piece is to be placed printed side down.

Most pieces need to be cut twice. This is why the fabric is doubled before cutting. Check each piece. Some are labeled "cut one" or "cut four."

Lay all pattern pieces on the fabric before you begin to cut. This will assure you that you have enough fabric.

A pattern piece may extend beyond the edge of the fabric in the cutting layout. In this case, cut the other pieces first. Then unfold the fabric to a single thickness and cut that piece.

Pinning the Pattern Pieces

21-12_____
Check these points before you start to pin pattern to fabric.

Before you start to pin the pattern to the fabric, check the points in 21-12. Then begin working with the large pieces at one end of the fabric.

If the pattern piece is to be placed on a fold, you will see a line with a bending arrow at both ends, as in 21-13. The arrows point toward one edge of the pattern piece. Place that edge along the fold of the fabric. Pin along that edge first.

If the piece does not need to be along a fold, the grain line is a straight line with an arrow at each end. See 21-14. This line must be parallel to the grain of the fabric. With the pattern and fabric lying flat on the table, push a pin through all layers at the point of each arrow. Then measure from the point of each arrow to the edge of the fabric. The two distances should

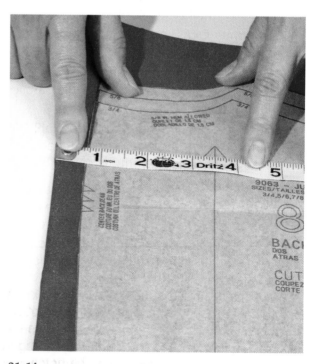

21-14_____
A straight line with arrows represents the lengthwise grain line. Measure from the tip of both ends of the arrow to the fabric edge.

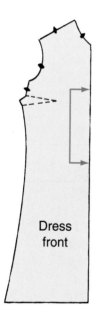

Dress front

21-13_____
Bending arrows point to an edge that should lie on a fold of the fabric.

be the same. If they are different, remove one pin and shift the pattern slightly. Insert the pin again and remeasure. Repeat until the grain line arrow is parallel to the fabric grain.

Smooth the pattern pieces from the grain line or fold line toward the edges as you work. Pat, rather than pull, the pattern and fabric.

Place pins about 6 inches apart, as shown in 21-15. On curved edges or slippery fabric, place them closer together. Point pins at right angles to cutting lines and fold lines. Point them diagonally into corners. Pins should not lie across cutting lines.

When you have finished pinning, check once more with your layout diagram to be certain you have followed it exactly. Measure again from the grain lines to the edge of your fabric. Ask your teacher for final approval before you begin cutting.

You may not have enough time to pin and cut pieces in one class period. If you must wait another day, carefully fold your pattern and fabric in about 12-inch folds. The next day you can carefully unfold it to cut.

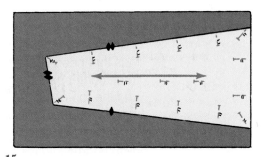

21-15
Notice how the pins are placed in this pattern piece.

21-16
Cut notches to the outside of the seam allowance.

Cutting

Bent-handled shears are the best for cutting out a garment. The design allows the blade to lie flat on the table while cutting. Since the fabric is raised only slightly, you can cut exactly along the cutting lines.

Cut with long, smooth strokes. Keep your free hand lightly on the pattern and fabric near where you are cutting. Cut slowly enough to be aware of notches and any alterations. Do not cut beyond your cutting line. You could ruin a section of fabric that you need for another piece.

As you approach a notch on your cutting line, cut to the base with the points of your scissors. Cut outward to the tip of the notch. Cut back inward to complete the notch, still using the tip of your scissors. Cutting notches outward will give you room to make a smaller seam allowance if you later find this is needed for better fit. Double or triple notches can be cut across the top making one wide notch rather than two or three small ones so close together.

Some patterns show the notches pointing inward only, as shown in 21-16. It is still a good idea to cut the notches outward in case you have to adjust the seams later on.

Save some of the large fabric scraps. You can use them later for practice stitching.

Transferring Pattern Markings

When you have finished cutting your garment, find the pieces with markings that need to be transferred to the fabric. These markings include center front, center back, darts, tucks, pleats, dots, buttons, buttonholes, pockets, and the top of sleeves. They are the markings that will help you put the garment together correctly. If your pattern piece shows seam lines, do not mark them. Most sewing machines have a gauge you can follow to sew straight, even seams. Multisized patterns will not have seam line markings.

Remove only the pins that are in the way of markings you need to make. The other pins are needed to hold the pattern in place.

Several methods can be used to transfer markings to fabrics. A tracing wheel with dressmaker's tracing paper is one of the most common. Other methods include tailor's chalk, fabric marking pens, and basting.

Dressmaker's Tracing Paper and Tracing Wheel

Dressmaker's tracing paper has a special coating that is transferred to the fabric with a tracing wheel. Use only light-colored tracing paper on light-colored fabrics. Dark colors would show on the right side. Use medium- and dark-colored tracing paper for medium- to dark-colored fabrics.

Some tracing paper makes permanent marks, so be careful when using this method of marking. Before you begin, test the paper on a scrap of fabric. Check to see that the markings do not show on the right side.

There are two types of tracing wheels. A *serrated edge tracing wheel* leaves a dotted line on the fabric. This type is suitable for firmly woven or knit fabrics of solid colors or subdued prints. A *smooth edge tracing wheel* leaves a solid line on the fabric and can also be used on these same fabrics. In addition, it can be used for plaids, prints, doubleknits, wool flannel, and delicate fabrics.

To use the tracing paper, place the colored side of the paper next to the wrong side of the fabric. Use a sheet of cardboard to protect the table. Then roll the tracing wheel along the markings you want to transfer. Use a ruler to mark straight lines. See 21-17. Use only enough pressure to make the markings show on the wrong side. Too much pressure will cause the marks to show on the right side.

21-17_____

A tracing wheel and dressmaker's carbon paper are often used for marking. Always mark a fabric scrap as a test before marking the garment.

Tailor's Chalk

Tailor's chalk or a chalk pencil can be used for marking details on most fabrics. Only one layer of fabric is marked at a time. Pins are often used with tailor's chalk for marking.

With the pattern facing upward, push a straight pin through all layers at each point to be marked. Turn the piece upside down. With a ruler as a guide, draw a chalk line between the pins, 21-18. (Draw on the wrong side of the fabric.) Then with this same side facing upward, push pins down through all layers. Turn the piece upside down again. Carefully remove the pattern, easing the tissue over the pinheads. Be careful not to pull out the pins. Again draw chalk lines between the pins.

Chalk lines tend to rub off, so handle the pieces carefully. The chalk will disappear when the garment is laundered or dry-cleaned.

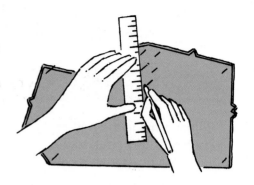

21-18
One way to mark is to insert pins at important construction details. Turn the garment piece over and mark the details with tailor's chalk.

Fabric Marking Pens

Fabric marking pens are another option for transferring pattern markings. These pens contain disappearing ink. Therefore, you can use the pens to transfer markings to either the right or wrong side of your fabric.

The ink may be water soluble, which means that the ink rinses out of the fabric with water. After constructing your garment, wash it to remove the water-soluble pen marks.

Another type of ink evaporates from the fabric. Place air-evaporating pen marks when you are ready to sew. They contain an ink that evaporates in less than 48 hours.

To use a fabric marking pen, stick pins straight through the pattern tissue and both fabric layers at all the marking points. Starting from the outside edges of the pattern, carefully separate the layers of fabric just enough to place an ink dot where the pin is inserted. Mark both layers of fabric. Then remove the pin. Work your way from the outer cut edges to the center or the centerfold until all pins have been marked.

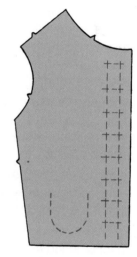

21-19
Marking garments with basting stitches takes time, but it is neat and accurate.

Basting to Transfer Pattern Markings

A good way to mark both the right and wrong sides of a fabric is by basting. To baste, make long, loose stitches by hand or machine. Use a contrasting color for the thread. Basting is sometimes done to transfer other kinds of markings to the right side. These might be used to indicate pockets or buttonholes. See 21-19. Basting takes more time than other marking methods, but it is very accurate. It does not damage the fabric. After the markings have been used, the basting stitches are removed.

When you have finished marking, you may remove all the pins and put the pattern pieces back into the envelope. You may leave the pattern pieces pinned to the fabric until you are ready to sew them together. This makes the pieces easy to identify.

CHAPTER REVIEW

Key Points

- Before pinning the pattern to the fabric, the fabric may need to be preshrunk. You may also need to straighten the grain of the fabric.

- If the fabric is off-grain, the lengthwise yarns and the crosswise yarns are not at a perfect 90 degree angle to each other. The fabric will need to be straightened by pulling opposite corners.

- Check your measurements with the chart on the pattern envelope. If they are not the same, you will have to alter your pattern. Altering patterns is better than altering finished garments.

- The layout shows you how to lay your pattern pieces on your fabric for cutting. Find the one that matches your pattern size, project or view, and fabric width.

- Place pins about 6 inches apart. On curved edges or slippery fabric, place them closer together. Pins should not cross cutting lines.

- Cut with long, smooth strokes. Cut notches outward in case seams need to be adjusted.

- When you have finished cutting your garment, find the pieces with markings that need to be transferred to the fabric. There are several methods you can use to transfer these markings to the fabric.

To Review

1. How do you decide what method to use to preshrink your fabric?
2. How can you find the lengthwise, crosswise, and bias grains of a fabric?
3. Why should the fabric grain be straight before you pin and cut out a garment?
4. Describe one way to find out if the fabric was cut along the crosswise grain.
5. Why should alterations be made in pattern pieces rather than in your garment?
6. Explain how to lengthen a pattern piece in the middle of the pattern.
7. List three fabric folds that pattern layouts sometimes suggest.
8. When pinning a pattern to fabric, pin _____.
   A. at right angles to cutting lines
   B. parallel to cutting lines
9. Explain how to use dressmaker's tracing paper to transfer pattern markings.
10. _____ is a good way to mark both the right and wrong sides of a garment piece.

To Do

1. Bring to class samples of several types of fabrics. Decide how each should be preshrunk, if at all.

2. Pull along the lengthwise, crosswise, and true bias grains of a woven fabric. Notice the lengthwise grain stretches the least. Which stretches the most?

3. Practice adjusting the length of patterns. Lengthen one pattern piece at the bottom edge. Shorten a different piece at the adjustment lines. (Undo all practice alterations before using the pattern pieces.)

4. Study your pattern guide sheet. Make a list of all the types of information provided on the guide sheet.

5. On a length of fabric, demonstrate each of the five types of folds described in this chapter.

6. Bring in a sample of a fabric that would require a cutting layout for a napped fabric and explain why. Compare fabrics that would require using a cutting layout with a nap and without a nap.

7. Try cutting out a pattern piece on a scrap of fabric using a pair of scissors. Then cut out a pattern piece using shears. Which tool is easiest to use and gives the smoothest edge?

8. On a fabric scrap, test three different ways of marking. Compare the results.

To Think About

1. What are the advantages of studying the pattern and guide sheet before you begin using them?

2. How do you decide if you need to preshrink a fabric or not?

3. How do you decide where to make pattern alterations—in the center of the pattern piece or at the edge?

4. If you were sewing a fabric with nap, what might happen if you used a cutting layout for a fabric without nap?

5. What are the advantages and disadvantages of each of the methods of transferring pattern markings?

CHAPTER 22

Basic Sewing Skills

Objectives

After studying this chapter, you will be able to
- operate the sewing machine properly.
- construct darts and seams.
- apply various seam finishes to seams.
- demonstrate how to trim, grade, and clip seams.
- describe how to apply facings and interfacings.
- identify various types of fasteners and zippers and describe how to apply them.
- mark, finish, and secure a hem.
- describe pressing techniques.

Key Terms

seam
seam allowance
backstitching
staystitching
directional
  stitching
basting
easing
gathers
darts
seam finish
trimming
grading
clipping
notching
facings
clean-finish
understitching
stitch in the ditch
hem
double-fold hem

At this point, you know that a sewing machine is a fine, delicate piece of machinery. You are ready to use it carefully and skillfully.

A quick review of terms will remind you that stitches are used to hold two pieces of fabric together. A row of stitches forms a **seam.** The usual **seam allowance** or width between the fabric edge and the seam is 5/8 inch. See 22-1.

Machine Stitching Techniques

As you start to sew, check that the spool and bobbin threads are pulled about 5 inches behind the presser foot. This will prevent tangling and knotting of thread at the beginning of the seam. Is the take-up lever at its highest point? If not, the thread will be pulled out of the needle as you start.

Place the fabric under the presser foot. Keep most of the fabric to the left of the needle so you can see the seam guides on the throat plate. The fabric edges should line up with one of the seam guides. For instance, if you are sewing a 5/8 inch seam, the fabric edges should lie exactly on the 5/8 inch line.

Using your right hand, turn the hand wheel and lower the needle into the starting point. Lower the presser foot with your right hand while holding the fabric with your left hand.

Start to stitch at a slow, constant speed. Keep both hands lightly on the fabric near the presser foot. Do not push or pull the fabric; just guide it. Watch the seam guide, not your line of stitching or the needle, as you sew.

When you stop, move the take-up lever to its highest point by turning the hand wheel. Then raise the presser foot and pull the fabric to the back. Cut threads, leaving about 3 inches if they are to be tied to prevent the stitches from coming loose.

As you sew, it is best to remove each pin as the presser foot comes to it. If your machine has a flexible or "rocking" presser foot, you can sew over the pins. If you do sew over pins, sew very slowly. At a slow speed, if the needle hits a pin, it will slide over it. At a faster speed, the needle could bend or break. It is best to remove pins rather than sewing over them if at all possible.

Sometimes you need to turn a corner while stitching. See 22-2. To do this, stitch to within 5/8 inch of the corner. Stop. Be sure the needle is down into the fabric. Lift the presser foot. Turn the fabric. Lower the presser foot, and continue to sew.

seam
The joining of pieces of fabric together with stitching.

seam allowance
Width between the fabric edge and the seam line.

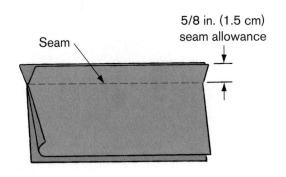

5/8 in. (1.5 cm) seam allowance

Seam

22-1
Notice the relationship between a seam and a seam allowance.

backstitching
Sewing backward and forward in the same place to secure stitching.

staystitching
A line of regular machine stitching on a single thickness to stabilize curves and prevent stretching.

directional stitching
Stitching with the grain to preserve the position of the grain.

basting
Temporarily joining layers of fabric together.

Backstitching

Instead of tying threads at the start and end of each seam, you may wish to secure your thread by **backstitching.** Take three or four stitches forward. Then put your machine in reverse and carefully sew backward, directly over the other stitches. Then sew forward again. This locks your stitches so the seam will not pull apart.

Staystitching

Staystitching is done to stabilize curved or bias fabric edges and prevent them from stretching. Staystitching is a line of regular machine stitching on a single thickness of fabric. It is sewn 1/8 inch or less from the seamline (toward the cut edge). Use the same thread you will use to make the garment. Sew around curves and along bias edges.

For many years, staystitching was used on all fabrics. Today, it is used less often. Many modern fabrics do not stretch or fray. The yarns are "locked" into position with finishes. Loosely woven or flimsy fabrics still require staystitching.

Directional Stitching

To preserve the position of the fabric grain, you should try to stitch with the grain whenever possible. This is called **directional stitching.** It helps keep fabrics from stretching out of shape or curling.

To find which direction to sew, you can test each piece yourself. Rub your finger down along a cut edge of a woven fabric. Then rub it up along the same edge. Which way feels smoother? Sew in that direction. As a rule, sew from a wide area to a narrow area, such as a skirt hem edge to the waist, and from the top of a curve to the bottom. Straight edges can be stitched in either direction. General guidelines are shown in 22-3.

Basting

Basting is a way to temporarily join layers of fabric together until they are permanently stitched on the machine. There are several methods of basting. Using pins is the most common method. Basting can also be done using hand stitching or machine stitching.

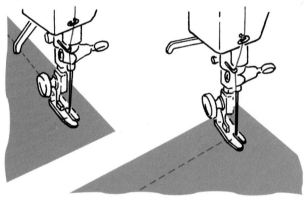

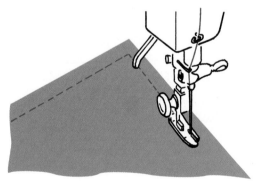

22-2

To turn a corner, insert the needle into the garment. Raise the presser foot, and turn the garment. Lower the foot and sew.

- To *pin baste,* place pins perpendicular to the seamline. Insert the pins right at the seamline. The pin heads should be to the right of the presser foot so they can be removed as you stitch.

- To *hand baste,* use a single thread no longer than your arm. Thread the needle with the end that came off the spool of thread first. Your thread will tangle less as you sew. Make a knot in the other end.

- To *machine baste,* set the stitch control to 6 or 8 stitches per inch and loosen the thread tension. Sew along the regular seamline. Do not backstitch or knot the thread ends.

To remove the basting stitches without damaging the fabric, clip the top thread every few inches. Then pull the bottom thread.

You have already learned that basting stitches are used to transfer pattern markings to garment pieces. Basting is also helpful when you want to check the fit of a garment. After machine-basting the seams, try on the garment. If it fits, sew over the basting stitches for a permanent seam. If you need to sew a narrower or wider seam, rebaste, possibly with another color thread. Remove the first basting stitches, and recheck the fit.

Hand basting is often used in detail areas where pin basting would not be secure enough and machine basting would be too difficult to do. It is also best for sheer or slippery fabrics.

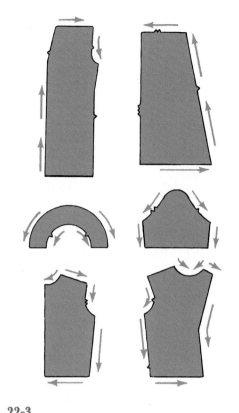

22-3
Directional stitching keeps fabrics from stretching out of shape or curling.

Easing

Easing is used when two edges of fabric are to be joined and one edge is slightly larger than the other. Easing should not cause visible gathers or pleats to form in the seamline. The seam should be smooth when stitched. Easing is used when making set-in sleeves, joining shoulder seams, and attaching waistbands, 22-4.

To ease two edges together, follow these steps:

1. Stitch one row of machine basting close to the seamline in the larger piece of fabric.

2. Stitch a second row of stitches 1/4 inch away from the first row of stitching in the seam allowance.

3. Pin the ends of the two pieces together with the eased side up. Pull the threads and distribute the fullness evenly. Pin in place.

4. Stitch along the seamline being careful to avoid any tucks or folds.

22-4
Set-in sleeves are eased to fit into the armhole of garments.

easing
Joining two edges of fabric together when one edge is slightly larger than the other. No visible gathers should form.

When there is only a small amount of fullness to ease, you may be able to use pins only. To do this, pin the ends of the pieces of fabric together. Then pinning as you work, distribute the fullness of the larger piece evenly across the shorter piece.

Gathering

Gathers are tiny, soft folds of fabric formed when a larger piece of fabric is sewn to a smaller piece. Puffed sleeves and gathered skirts use gathers, 22-5. Gathers are fuller than easing.

To gather, follow these steps:

1. Sew one row of machine basting next to the regular seamline in the seam allowance.
2. Sew another row of machine basting 1/4 inch away from the seamline toward the cut edge. Leave long threads at both ends.
3. With the right sides of the fabric together, pin the edges together matching notches, seams, and other markings.
4. Gently pull both bobbin threads, gathering up the full edge until it lies flat against the shorter edge between the pins. Fasten these threads by wrapping them in a figure eight around the pin at the end, 22-6.
5. Repeat from the other end of the machine stitching.
6. Arrange the gathers evenly and place additional pins crosswise to the stitching.
7. Stitch the gathered piece to the matching piece with the gathered side up. Stitch slowly as you hold the gathers to prevent any folds from forming in the seam.

gathers
Tiny, soft folds of fabric formed when a larger piece of fabric is sewn to a smaller piece.

22-5
The extra fabric in puffed sleeves is gathered to fit into the armhole seam.

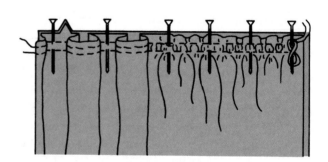

22-6
Secure threads by wrapping them around a pin. Then pull the other ends to gather.

Darts

Darts provide shape and fullness to a garment so it fits the curves of the body. Darts should point to the fullest part of body curves. For instance, on slacks and skirts, darts begin at the waistline and taper to the hipline. This allows fullness around the hips. In jackets, blouses, and shirts, darts taper to the fullest part of the bust or chest.

A dart is made by stitching to a point along a fabric fold. Darts are made before other seams in a garment are sewn. This is because they cross other seamlines.

To make a dart, begin at the widest end of the dart and sew to the point. To prevent the point from puckering, the last three stitches should be made on the fold. See 22-7. At the end of the dart, tie the threads securely.

If you are sewing a dart with two points, start stitching at the center of the dart and stitch to one end. Then turn your work over, and place your needle in the spot where you began for the other end of the dart. Stitch to the other end. Tie the threads at both ends.

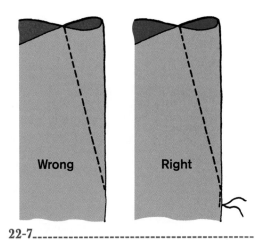

22-7--
To prevent the fabric from puckering at the point of the dart, make the last three stitches of the dart on the fold.

dart
A stitched fold that provides shape and fullness to a garment so that it fits the curves of the body.

Pressing Darts

The next step is to press the darts. Press darts along the stitching line, from the widest end to the point. Use a tailor's ham to add shape as you press. Vertical darts are pressed toward the center front or center back. Horizontal darts are pressed downward. If a dart is wide or made of bulky fabric, it may be slashed to within 1 inch of the point and pressed open.

Seams and Seam Finishes

Most seams used in clothing construction are plain seams. These seams may need a seam finish to prevent the edges from raveling. There are other types of seams that you may want to use. These include the topstitched, flat-fell, welt, and French seams.

Plain Seams

The most common seam is the *plain seam.* It is suitable for all areas of a garment and for most fabrics except sheers and laces.

To make a plain seam:
1. With right sides together, match the cut edges and notches. Place pins about 5 inches apart along the rest of the seamline. Pins should be at right angles to the seamline. The heads of the pins should lie within the seam allowance.

2. Sew along the seamline. Secure threads at both ends by backstitching.

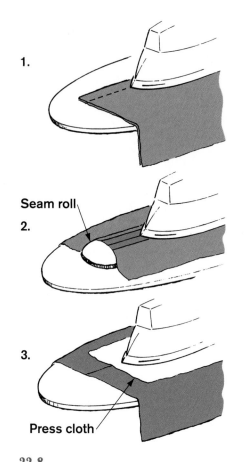

1.

Seam roll
2.

3.

Press cloth

22-8_____
Follow these steps when pressing a plain
seam. 1. Press with right sides together.
2. Press seam open, wrong sides up.
3. Press seam open, right sides up.

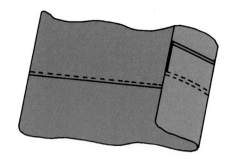

22-9_____
Topstitched seams create a decorative
effect on garments.

The three steps in pressing open a plain seam are
shown in 22-8.

1. Press the seam flat with right sides together.
2. Open the two garment pieces. With wrong sides up,
   press the seam open. For best results, use a seam
   roll for this step. The seam roll lets the garment fall
   away from the seam so the edges of the seam will
   not show through to the right side. Use only the tip
   of the iron when pressing seams open.
3. Press the seam open with right sides up, using a dry
   press cloth.

Topstitched Seams

The *topstitched seam* is a plain seam with a row of
machine stitching on one or both sides of the seamline.
Topstitched seams are often used for a decorative effect
on sport clothes. Topstitching may be found on pockets
and pleats or to emphasize seamlines.

To make a topstitched seam, first stitch a plain seam.
For one row of stitching, press the seam allowance to one
side. Topstitch the desired distance from the seam on the
right side of the fabric through all three thicknesses, 22-9.

For two rows of stitching, press the seam allowance
open. Topstitch on both sides of the seamline through
both layers of fabric.

When topstitching collars, cuffs, or pockets, stitch
carefully and slowly. Use your presser foot as a guide to
sew the same distance from the seamline on each piece.
A slightly longer stitch is often used to create more attractive lines of stitching on the outside of the garment.

Flat-fell Seams

Flat-fell seams are decorative, yet strong and functional. Whenever raw edges are not desirable, this seam
is ideal. They are often used on shirts, underwear,
sportswear, jeans, pajamas, and other clothing receiving
hard wear, 22-10. They are suitable for all fabrics except
those that are very heavy. Straight or slightly curved
areas are appropriate for this type of seam.

To make a flat-fell seam:

1. Stitch a plain seam with the wrong sides together.
2. Trim the under seam allowance to 1/8 inch.

3. Press the seam to one side with the wider part on top.

4. Turn under the edge of the top seam allowance and fold it over the trimmed edge.

5. Stitch close to the folded edge through all thicknesses. Keep the right side of the garment up as you sew.

Welt Seams

Welt seams are a variation of the flat-fell seam, but are less bulky, 22-11. For this reason, they are often used on heavy fabrics. They are easier to sew and can be used on straight or slightly curved seams.

To make a welt seam:

1. Sew a plain seam with right sides together.

2. Trim one seam allowance to 1/4 inch.

3. Press the other seam allowance over the trimmed edge.

4. With right sides up, stitch through the outer fabric and the wider seam allowance. The distance between the seamline and the second row of stitching can vary, depending on the look you want.

5. For a padded look, press the seam, right sides down, over a bath towel.

French Seams

A *French seam* is a narrow seam within a seam. See 22-12. It is used on fabrics that ravel easily. It is also used on sheer fabrics because no raw edges show. French seams are used only for straight seams.

To make a French seam:

1. Place wrong sides together and pin.

2. Stitch about 1/4 inch from the edge.

3. Trim seam to 1/8 inch.

4. Press seam flat.

5. Fold right sides together and stitch 1/4 inch from edge. The first seam will be enclosed in the second seam.

6. Press seam to one side.

Seam Finishes

A **seam finish** is a way of treating a seam edge to prevent raveling and to make the seam stronger and longer wearing. Many firmly woven fabrics do not need seam finishes. The yarns are locked together and do

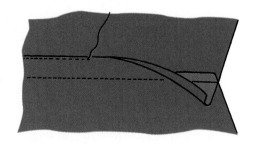

22-10
Flat-fell seams provide sturdy construction on jeans and sportswear.

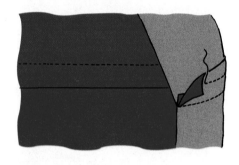

22-11
A welt seam is a good choice for heavy fabrics.

22-12
A French seam provides an attractive finish for sheer fabrics.

seam finish
Treatment of seam edges to prevent raveling and to make the seam stronger and longer

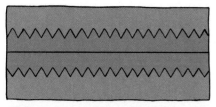

Pinked seams finishes should be used only on fabrics that do not ravel.

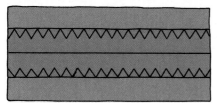

A zigzag finish is easy to do with a zigzag setting on the sewing machine.

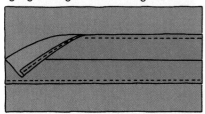

A turned and stitched finish is a good choice for lightweight fabrics.

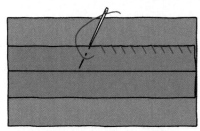

A hand overcast finish prevents raveling on bulky fabrics.

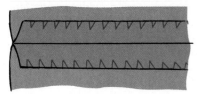

A serger can be used to make a machine overcast finish.

22-13_____

Choose one of these seam finishes based on the weight of the fabric and if it ravels easily.

not ravel. Most knits and nonwoven fabrics do not need seam finishes. Loosely-woven and sheer fabrics do require seam finishes. There are several ways to finish seams. See 22-13.

Pinked Finish

Pinked seam finishes look nice, but they do not prevent raveling. They should be used only on fabrics that do not ravel. To improve the durability of this seam finish, machine stitch 1/4 inch from the edge of the seam allowance before pinking the edges.

After sewing the seam, press it flat. Pink the edges. Then place the seam on a seam roll and press it open.

Machine Zigzag Finish

Your machine may have a zigzag setting or attachment. A *machine zigzag* finish is quick and easy, and it prevents raveling. It puckers less than a line of straight stitches because it has more "give." It works best on medium and heavyweight fabrics.

Press the seam open. Adjust the stitch width, using a narrower stitch width for lightweight fabrics and a wider one for heavyweight fabrics. Stitch close to the edge of the seam allowance through a single layer of fabric.

Turned and Stitched Finish

A *turned and stitched seam finish* looks neat and prevents raveling. This finish is often used for unlined jackets of lightweight fabrics. It is also used on the edges of facings for sheer and lightweight fabrics. It is too bulky for medium and heavyweight fabrics.

Press the seam open. Turn the edges under 1/4 inch. Stitch close to fold.

Hand Overcasting

Hand overcasting is used for fabrics that are bulky or that ravel easily. It prevents raveling, and it leaves a flat seam. The disadvantage is that it takes a lot of time.

Press the seam open. Trim all notches and frayed edges. Using a single thread, use a loose overcast stitch. Each seam allowance is done separately.

Did You Know?

Sewing for a Cause

You are learning a skill you can put to use in helping others. Perhaps you're a member of an FCCLA chapter looking for a service project. Have you thought about using your sewing skills? Clothes, blankets, layettes, and stuffed toys are needed even in your own community. Several nationwide groups support local efforts to sew such items as the following:

- blankets for seriously ill or traumatized children through the organization *Project Linus.* Project Linus has delivered 250,000 "security" blankets to children around the world. For more information, go to projectlinus.org.

- quilts for infants and children who are infected with HIV, affected by drugs or alcohol, or abandoned through the organization *ABC Quilts.* An area coordinator for this organization delivers the quilts to hospitals to assure confidentiality of recipients. For more information, go to abcquilts.org.

- clothes for premature and low birthweight infants in neonatal units of hospitals. *Care Wear* is a nationwide volunteer group providing handmade baby items to hospitals in their local communities. Patterns for making the items can be found on their Web site: carewear.org

- clothes, blankets, and toys for sick and needy newborns in hospitals, especially premature babies who are too tiny to wear regular infant clothing. *Newborns in Need* is a volunteer organization with chapters across the country seeking layette items for needy infants. Go to their Web site at newbornsinneed.org to find information on how to make and donate these layette items.

- chemotherapy turbans and soft hats for cancer patients, wheelchair totes, walker caddies, lap robes, and hospital bed saddlebags are just some of the patterns available at the Home Sewing Association's Web site: sewing.org. This organization also provides advise on organizing group sewing projects and shares stories from groups doing so across the country.

These are just a few of the many ways you can help others using your sewing skills. Can you think of others?

Note: These Web site addresses were accurate at the time this book was printed.

Machine Overcasting

Machine overcasting can be done by sergers and some sewing machines. This finish is used for firm, medium-weight fabrics. The stitches are more bulky than hand overcast stitches.

Press the seam open. Stitch through a single layer of fabric. The needle should move back and forth across the cut edge of the seam allowance. It should reach only slightly outside the cut edge.

Seam Treatments

In some garment areas, a regular seam allowance is too bulky. This is especially so in enclosed areas such as necklines, collars, and cuffs. Curved seams and corners also will be bulky. You can eliminate this bulk by trimming, grading, and clipping seams.

Trimming

Trimming is cutting off part of the seam allowance. To trim a seam, cut away part of the seam allowance, leaving a 1/8 to 1/4 inch seam allowance. Curved areas, such as the underarm section of an armhole seam or the center back seam of pants, are usually trimmed to 1/4 inch.

Corners and points should also be trimmed before they are turned and pressed. Collars and cuffs, for example, will lie smooth and flat if the seams are trimmed before turning. To trim a right-angle corner, cut diagonally across the seam allowance. Cut close to the stitching. See 22-14.

Grading

For heavier fabrics or for places with three layers of fabric, grading is better. **Grading** is trimming each seam allowance to a different width. This prevents a ridge from showing on the outside of the garment. It is most often used on enclosed seams, such as collars, cuffs, pockets, and facings.

When grading a seam, make sure the seam allowance closest to the outside of the garment is the widest. This will prevent press marks from showing on the finished side of the garment. Trim this seam allowance to 1/4 inch. Trim the other seam allowance to 1/8 inch.

If a corner has a sharper point, as the one in 22-15, cut diagonally across the seam allowance as before. Then make another cut on each side of the corner to remove the extra fabric.

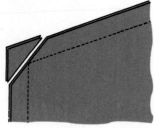

22-14

To remove bulk, trim seams to 1/8 inch or 1/4 inch. Trim corners at right angles.

Clipping and Notching

Curved seams will not lie flat unless they are clipped. **Clipping** is making straight cuts into the seam allowance. It is done after the seam is trimmed or graded.

To clip, use the tips of sharp shears. Cut to within 1/8 inch of the seamline, but not through it. If you have staystitched the seam, clip to the staystitching. Clip every 1/4 inch to 1/2 inch depending on the sharpness of the curve.

When a seam curves inward, as shown in 22-16, clip straight into the seam allowance. Necklines, armholes, and waistlines are inward curves.

When a seam curves outward, also shown in 22-16, clip V-shaped sections from the seam allowance. This is called **notching.** When the seam is opened, the remaining notches will come together to make a flat, even seam. Rounded collars and pockets are outward curves.

Facings

Facings are used to cover raw edges in a garment such as at the armholes, neckline, or other garment openings. In addition to covering the raw edge, facings add some firmness to the open areas and keep them from stretching out of shape. They are usually not meant to be seen on the right side of the garment.

clipping
Making straight cuts into the seam allowance so that curved seams will lie flat.

notching
Clipping V-shaped sections from the seam allowance on seams that curve outward.

facing
A piece of fabric used to finish raw edges in a garment such as at the armholes, neckline, or other garment edges.

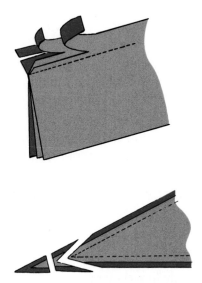

22-15
Grading seams means cutting each seam allowance to a different width. Grade and clip sharp corners as shown.

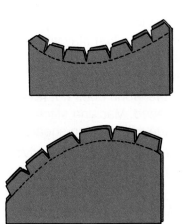

22-16
Clip straight into inward curves. Clip V-shaped sections out of outward curves.

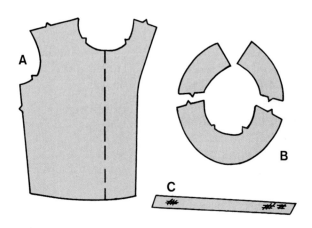

22-17
The three types of facings are (A) extended, (B) fitted, and (C) bias.

There are three main types of facings: extended, fitted, and bias. See 22-17.

- An *extended facing* is cut as part of a garment piece. The facing part is then folded to the inside. Front or back openings often use an extended facing. This will be indicated on your pattern.

- A *fitted facing,* sometimes called a shaped facing, is cut the same shape as the raw edge and is a separate pattern piece. It is stitched to the edge and turned to the inside of the garment.

- Another type of facing is a *bias facing.* This is a narrow bias strip of fabric stitched to the edge to be faced. Necklines, armholes, and other gently curved edges often have bias facings. Bias strips of fabric can be cut or bias tape can be purchased. After the narrow facing is attached to the edge, the free edge is hand stitched or topstitched to the garment.

Stitching the Facing

The first step in constructing a facing is to sew the facing pieces together. The free edges should then be finished to prevent raveling. There are several ways to finish the edges, depending on the weave and weight of the fabric:

clean-finish

A method of finishing the raw edge of a facing, folding and stitching the raw edge under.

- Light to medium-weight fabrics can be clean-finished. To **clean-finish** the edge, first staystitch 1/4 inch from the raw edge. Then fold the edge of the facing under along the line of stitching. Stitch again close to the folded edge.

- If the fabric does not ravel easily, a pinked edge will be all that is needed. Machine stitch 1/4 inch from the unnotched edge. Trim the edge with pinking shears.

- On heavy fabrics that ravel easily, overcast the raw edge either by hand or by machine.

Attaching the Facing

To attach the facing to the garment, follow these steps:

1. Pin the right sides together matching notches and seams.
2. Stitch the facing to the garment.
3. Trim, grade, and clip the seam as needed.

4. Press the seam toward the facing.

5. Understitch the seam to give the edge a crisp finish and to prevent the facing from rolling to the outside. **Understitching** is a row of stitching placed close to the seamline through the facing and the seam allowances. When understitching, sew on the right side of the facing, keeping the seam allowances toward the facing. Pull the fabric slightly on either side of the seamline as you sew, 22-18.

6. Turn the facing to the inside and press.

7. Fasten or tack the free edge of the facing to the seam allowances with hand stitches. A quicker option is to **stitch in the ditch** on the outside of the garment. Using short machine stitches, stitch directly into the "well" of the seam through all layers of fabric.

understitching
A row of stitches on the facing placed close to the seamline through the facing and the seam allowances.

stitch in the ditch
Stitching into the "well" of a seam through all fabric layers.

Interfacing

An interfacing is a layer of fabric placed between the garment and the facing. It is used to add body and firmness to the outer fabric. It also prevents stretching and provides extra reinforcement. Interfacing is used in collars, cuffs, lapels, facings, and waistbands. It is also used in areas of stress such as under buttons and around buttonholes. See 22-19. Garments are better looking and more durable when interfacing is used.

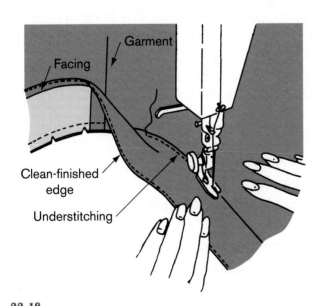

Pellon, Div. of Freudenberg Nonwovens

22-18
Understitching the facing to the seam allowances helps to hold the facing in place.

22-19
Interfacing (white areas) provides a framework within a garment to shape, support, and stabilize.

A wide variety of interfacing fabrics are available. Consider the look you want to achieve. A heavier weight interfacing gives a crisp look whereas a lighter weight gives a softer look. As a general rule, choose an interfacing that is a little lighter in weight than your garment fabric.

Read the care requirements carefully before you buy. The cleaning requirements for the interfacing should be the same as the finished garment. For instance, if you plan to wash the garment, you would want to use an interfacing fabric that is also washable. Also check to see that the interfacing is preshrunk if it is to be used in a washable garment.

Types of Interfacing Fabrics

There are three main types of interfacing fabrics: woven, nonwoven, and fusible.

- *Woven interfacings* have grain so the pattern pieces must be cut on the same grain as the facing and outer fabric. Woven interfacings come in a wide range of weights. They work best with woven fabrics.

- *Nonwoven interfacings* have no grain so they can be cut in any direction. They don't ravel, are preshrunk, and are washable and dry-cleanable. Nonwoven interfacings are available in various weights. All-bias types stretch in all directions. Nonstretchable interfacings are used mainly for craft and decorating projects.

- *Fusible interfacings* have a resin on one side of the fabric that melts with heat and moisture and bonds to the fabric pieces. Fusible interfacings may be woven, nonwoven, or knit. They are best used with garment fabrics that are firm enough that the outline of the interfacing will not show on the outside. They are also useful in waistbands and for stabilizing buttonholes if the fabric ravels easily.

Attaching Interfacing Fabrics

Woven interfacings must be sewn to the garment:

1. Pin the interfacing to the wrong side of your fabric.
2. Machine baste 1/2 inch from the fabric edge.
3. Trim the interfacing close to the stitching line.
4. Cut diagonally 1/4 inch across any corners to reduce bulk.

   To attach fusible interfacings:

1. Trim away all seam allowances, hem allowances, and corners.
2. Place the adhesive side of the interfacing on the wrong side of your fabric.
3. Fuse following the manufacturer's directions, 22-20.

Fusible interfacings can be applied to the garment facings rather than to the outer garment fabric. This prevents the edge of the interfacing from showing on the outside of the garment.

Zippers

Zippers come in all lengths, weights, styles, and colors. The back of your pattern envelope lists the length and type of zipper you need.

Preshrink zippers that have cotton tape. Polyester tapes do not need to be preshrunk. Then press the tape to remove any packaging folds. Do not press the coils (teeth) of nylon or polyester zippers. A hot iron could melt them.

Most zippers are sewn into place by machine. To do this, you must change the regular presser foot to a *zipper foot*. See 22-21. You can stitch closer to the zipper coils when using a zipper foot.

There are several ways to attach a zipper to the garment. These are called zipper applications. Your pattern guide sheet will recommend which method to use. The two most common methods are centered and lapped. Another method is called the invisible application.

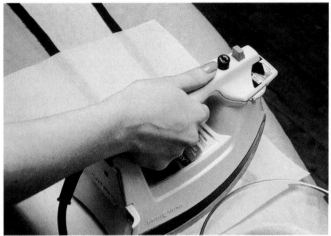

Pellon, Div. of Freudenberg Nonwovens

22-20_____
For fusible interfacing to fuse properly, you need steam, heat, and pressure. Place a press cloth over the garment part.

Centered Zippers

Centered zippers are used at center front and center back openings. The zipper coils are centered in the seamline. Two rows of stitching are used—one on each side of the seamline. The two rows are an equal distance from the seamline.

Follow these steps for a centered zipper application:

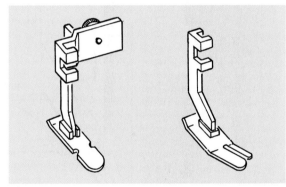

22-21_____
A zipper foot (left) lets you sew closer to the zipper coils than a regular presser foot (right).

1. Find the two garment pieces that will be joined by the zipper. Put the right sides together, and pin along the seamline.

2. Measure the length of the zipper, and add 1 inch. From the top of the seamline, measure down this distance. Mark the point with two pins.

3. Sew a regular seam, beginning at the bottom edge of the garment piece and ending at the two pins. Backstitch to secure thread ends. Then move the stitch control to the longest possible stitch. Baste the rest of the seam.

4. Press the seam open.

5. Remove the presser foot, and attach the zipper foot. Adjust the zipper foot so the foot is to the right of the needle.

6. Open the zipper. Keep the pull tab pointing toward the top of the zipper. Place the zipper face down on the seam allowance. Match the bottom stop of the zipper to the start of the basting stitches. One side of the zipper's coil should lie exactly on the seamline. Pin in place. See 22-22.

7. Machine baste from bottom to top. Stitch through the zipper tape and the seam allowance only. When you sew next to the pull tab, tilt the tab to make the zipper tape lie flat against the fabric.

8. Adjust the zipper foot so it is to the left of the needle. Place the other side of the zipper's coil on the seamline. Pin in place. See 22-23.

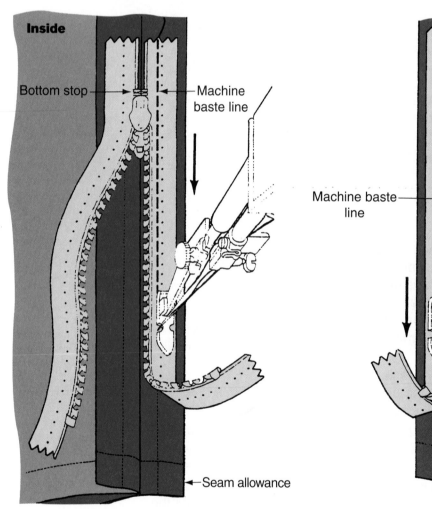

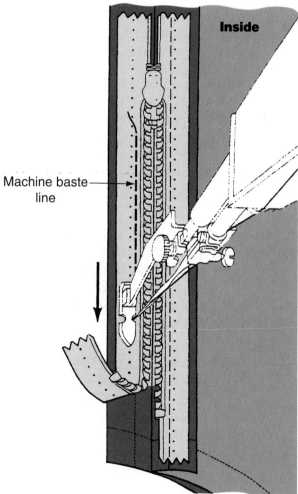

Talon, Inc.

22-22 --
Machine baste the zipper tape to the seam allowance only.

22-23 --
The second row of stitches attaches the other side of the zipper tape to the seam allowance only.

9. Baste from bottom to top, stitching through the zipper tape and the other seam allowance.

10. Close the zipper. Set the stitch control at 10 to 12 stitches per inch. Move the zipper foot to the right side of the needle.

11. Place the garment flat, with wrong sides up. Sew the zipper to the garment, stitching through the garment, seam allowance, and zipper tape. Stitch down one side, across the bottom and up the other side. Keep the rows of stitches an equal distance from the seamline, as shown in 22-24.

12. Remove the basting stitches in the seamline. If the seam puckers, remove the basting stitches in the seam allowances. Press.

Lapped Zippers

In a *lapped zipper* application, one side of the zipper opening forms a lap over the zipper. The zipper coil is less visible in lapped zippers than in centered zippers. Most openings in side seams are closed with lapped zippers because the lap can hide the zipper from view. Lapped zippers can also be used for other garment openings.

Follow these steps for a lapped zipper application:

1. Sew, baste, and press the zipper seam as you would for a centered zipper.

2. Attach the zipper foot so it is to the right of the needle. Open the zipper. Place the bottom stop of the zipper on top of the first basting stitch. The coil should lie exactly on the seamline, 22-25.

3. Machine baste through the zipper tape and one seam allowance, sewing from bottom to top. Stitch very close to the zipper coil. As you sew next to the pull tab, tilt it so you can keep your stitches straight.

4. Close the zipper. Turn it right side up. This creates a fold along the stitches just sewn.

5. Move the zipper foot to the left of the needle. Readjust stitch to regular length. Stitch very close to the edge of the fold, 22-26. Sew from bottom to top.

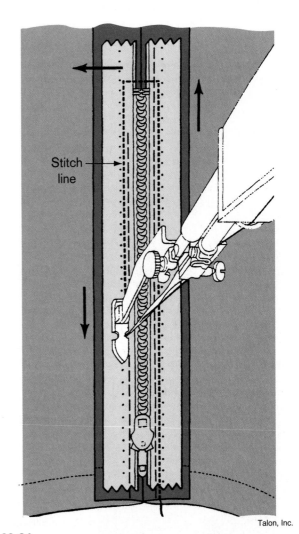

Stitch line

Talon, Inc.

22-24
For the final step, close the zipper and readjust stitch to regular length. Beginning at the top, stitch through the tape, seam allowance, and garment, down one side, across bottom of zipper, and up the other side.

6. With wrong sides up, sew across the bottom and up the side of the zipper. See 22-27. Stitch through the zipper coil, seam allowance, and garment.

7. Pull the threads at the bottom of the zipper to the wrong side. Tie a knot to secure them.

8. Remove the basting stitches.

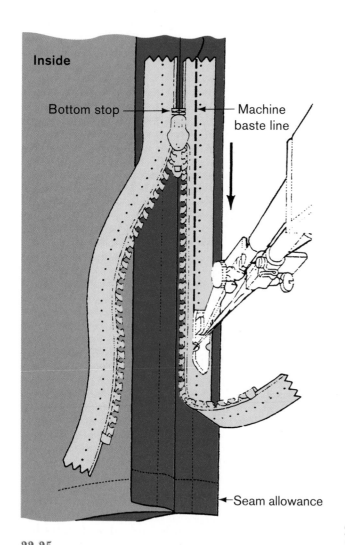

22-25 _____
Machine baste one side of the zipper to the seam allowance only using a zipper foot.

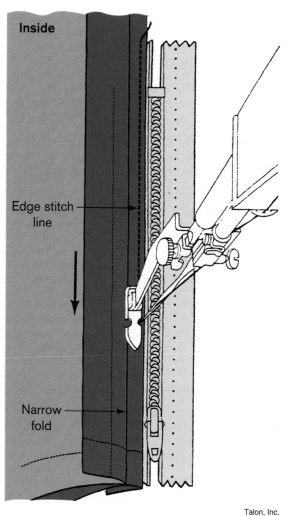

Talon, Inc.

22-26 _____
Readjust stitch to regular length. Close zipper and turn face up. Edge stitch on the fold, beginning at the bottom of the tape.

The *fly front zipper* is a variation of the lapped zipper. The difference is that the seam allowance is extra wide for the fly front zipper to allow for the larger lap. If your pattern calls for a fly front zipper, the guide sheet will give complete directions.

Invisible Zippers

From the right side of a garment, an *invisible zipper* looks like a regular seam. The pull tab is the only clue to the zipper placement. See 22-28.

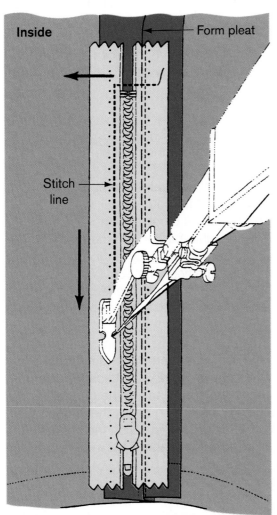

Talon, Inc.

22-27_____
Spread the garment flat with the zipper face down. Stitch across the bottom and up one side of the zipper, stitching through all layers.

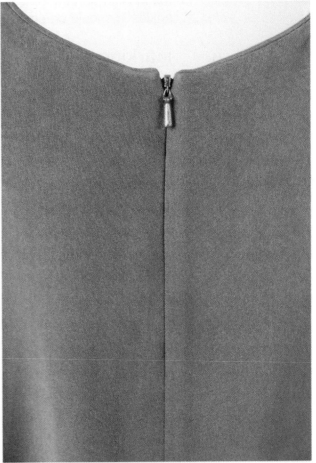

Jack Klasey

22-28_____
Only the pull tab of the invisible zipper can be seen on the outside of the garment. No stitches show.

Invisible zippers are sewn in an open seam. The rest of the seam is sewn after the zipper is in place. To attach this type of zipper, follow the steps provided in the zipper package. A special zipper foot is needed for invisible zippers. You can buy the required zipper foot where you purchase the zipper.

Hems

hem
A finished edge on a garment.

When all other construction steps are done, press the garment and let it hang for a day. This will give it time to stretch to its final shape. Then it will be ready to hem. A **hem** produces a finished edge on a garment.

Hemming is one of the last steps in sewing a garment, but it is one of the most important. Whether the hemline is above the knee or at the ankles, it should be smooth, even, and almost invisible.

Marking a Hem

Try on the garment with the undergarments and shoes you will wear with it. Jackets and belts should also be worn if they will be a part of the finished outfit.

Stand in front of a long mirror, and test several different lengths. When you decide on the length that is best for you, mark it with a pin.

The easiest way to mark an even hem on a dress or skirt is to have someone help you. As you stand still, the other person can move around you. Use a skirt marker, yardstick, or meterstick. Measure from the floor to the desired hemline. Place pins parallel to the floor and about 3 inches apart.

Now is the time to double-check the length. Fold the fabric up at the marked line. Turn it inside the garment, and pin it. Is the hem parallel to the floor? Do you like the length?

Remove the garment. Move the pins so they are at right angles to the cut edge of the hem. Baste close to the hemline, as shown in 22-29. Match the seamlines in the hem to the seamlines in the garment.

For pants, fold under at the top of the shoe in the front. The hem edge should just touch the shoe. In the back, the hemline should be about 1/2 inch longer than the top of the shoe.

Decide how wide the hem should be. The pattern pieces suggest a hem width. Use this as a guide. With a ruler or sewing gauge, measure the desired distance up from the hemline, 22-30. Mark the line with tailor's chalk. Cut along the marked line. Be careful to cut only the extra hem allowance; do not cut into the garment.

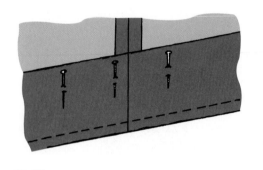

22-29
To hold the hem in place, insert pins at right angles to the cut edge of the hem. Baste close to the hemline.

Removing Extra Fullness in Hems

When a garment is flared, the hem does not lie flat. The extra fabric puckers at the upper edge. This extra fullness must be eased in to fit flat against the garment. To ease:

1. Machine baste 1/4 inch from the cut edge of the hem only using 10 stitches per inch.

2. Turn the hem up. Pin the hem to the garment at each seamline.

3. Pick up the bobbin thread with a pin. Pull up gently to slightly gather the fabric on both sides. See 22-31. Repeat this several times, until all extra fullness is gathered and spread evenly around the garment.

The hem will look smoother if you remove some of the gathered fullness by *shrinking*. This is done with steam. To shrink:

1. Place a piece of brown paper between the hem and the garment to prevent press marks.

2. Hold the steam iron slightly above the hem, letting the steam penetrate the fabric.

3. Flatten the gathers with your fingers being careful to keep your fingers away from the steam.

4. Press the hem.

Some fabrics are difficult to ease and shrink. Remove the extra fullness in these by *tapering* the seam. See 22-32. To taper:

1. Mark the hemline.

2. Insert the sewing machine needle into the seamline slightly above the hemline. Sew along the seamline to the hemline. At the hemline, pivot slightly and angle the seam inward.

3. Remove the original stitches, and trim the seam allowance.

4. Press seams open. Repeat this process on the other seams.

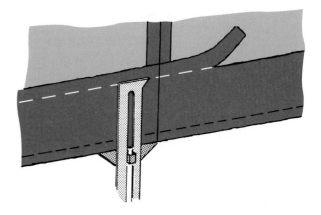

22-30
Mark the width of the hem with tailor's chalk. Cut off the extra fabric.

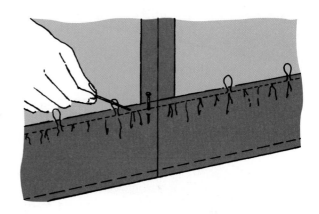

22-31
To ease in extra fullness, pull up gently on the bobbin thread. Repeat several times around hem.

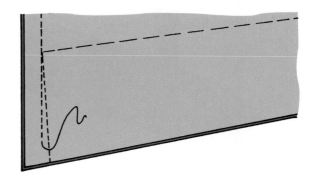

22-32
You can remove extra fullness by tapering seams.

Finishing Hem Edges

Hem finishes are much like seam finishes. The finish you use depends on the garment style and the fabric weight. Choose from these methods, which are illustrated in 22-33:

- **_Pinked finish:_** To finish fabrics that do not ravel, machine stitch 1/4 inch from the cut edge. Then pink the edge.

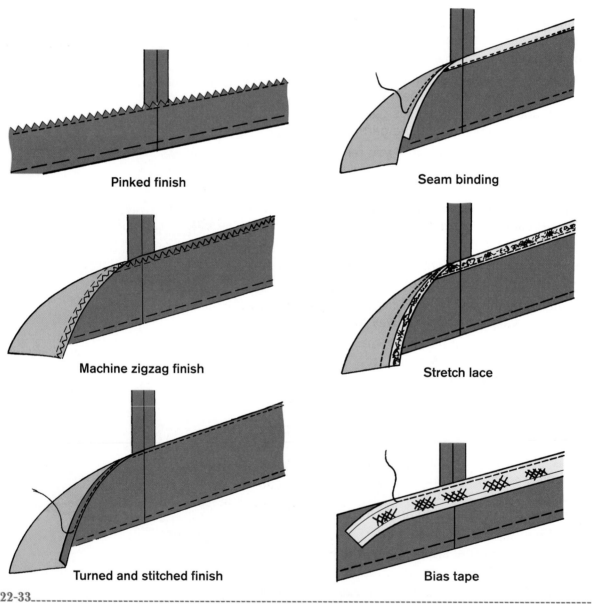

Pinked finish

Seam binding

Machine zigzag finish

Stretch lace

Turned and stitched finish

Bias tape

22-33
The hem finish you choose will depend on the style of the garment, the fabric type, and the fabric weight.

- *Machine zigzag or overcast finish:* For fabrics that do ravel, zigzag or overcast the edge above a row of machine stitching. This method gives a very flat hem. It is great for shirts and blouses that will be tucked into other garments.

- *Turned and stitched finish:* Fabrics that ravel can also be finished in other ways. They can be turned and stitched. Turn edges under 1/4 inch, and stitch close to fold. This method is bulky, so use it on straight hems of medium or lightweight fabrics.

- *Seam binding:* Seam binding is used for medium or heavyweight fabrics. It works best on straight hems. With the right side of the fabric up, lap the tape over the hem edge. Stitch 1/4 inch from the cut edge of the hem.

- *Stretch lace:* Stretch lace is used for medium and lightweight fabrics as well as knits. Because it stretches, it works well on curved hems. Lap it over the right side of the fabric. Stitch 1/4 inch from the cut edge of the hem. Use a straight stitch for woven fabrics and a zigzag stitch for knits.

- *Bias tape:* Bias tape is used for fabrics that ravel a great deal. It is also good to use on circular or very full skirts. It is a bulky finish, so use it only on medium and heavyweight fabrics. Open one fold. With right sides together, sew in the crease to join the tape to the hem allowance. Turn the tape up and over the cut edge of the hem.

Securing Hems

After you have finished the hem edge of the garment, you are ready to secure the hem edge to the garment. This can be done by using hand stitches, machine stitches, or fusing. Most hems are sewn by hand so that no stitches show on the right side of the garment. Machine stitching is fast and easy. It is used for more casual wear, on knits, or when a decorative machine stitch is desired.

Hand-Stitched Hems

Most hems are sewn into place by hand. To secure a hem with hand stitches, use a fine needle with a single thread. Hold the garment so the hem is on top and facing you. Stitch from right to left if you are right-handed. Left-handed persons should stitch from left to right.

Space the stitches evenly for a neat look. They should be loose so the fabric does not pucker.

Several types of hand stitches can be used for securing hems. These include the hemming stitch, slip stitch, blind stitch, and catch stitch. See 22-34 for illustrations of these stitches.

- *Hemming stitch:* The hemming stitch is a strong stitch. It can be used for hems with almost any type of finish.

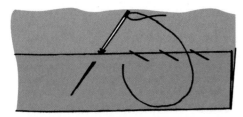

Hemming stitch

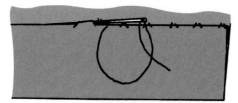

Slip stitch

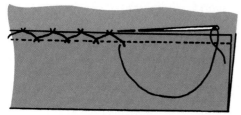

Catch stitch

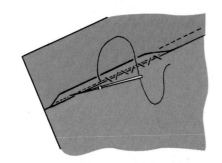

Blind stitch

22-34

Use one of these stitches to secure the hem.

Secure the thread in the hem edge with a knot or small backstitch. Pick up a yarn from the garment. Then bring the needle straight up or at an angle through the hem. Move about 1/4 inch to the left, and pick up another yarn from the garment. Repeat making stitches across the hem edge. When you reach the end of your thread, secure it with a backstitch in the hem edge and begin again.

- **Slip stitch:** The slip stitch hardly shows on either side of the fabric. The thread is hidden under a fold along the hem edge. Since a fold is needed, this stitch is used for hems with a turned and stitched finish or a bias tape finish.

Secure the thread in the hem edge. Pick up a yarn from the garment. Bring the needle straight up and into the fold, then across about 1/4 inch inside the fold. Next, bring the needle straight down, and pick up another yarn from the garment. Repeat around hem.

- **Blind stitch:** The blind stitch shows even less than the slip stitch. The thread is hidden from view because it lies between the hem allowance and the garment. This is an advantage because it prevents the thread from wearing and snagging. The stitches are loose to allow the two layers of fabric to move slightly without pulling.

Secure the thread in the hem edge. Fold the hem edge up, away from the garment. Pick up a yarn from the garment. Move the needle diagonally up and to the left about 1/4 inch. Pick up a yarn from the hem allowance. Move the needle diagonally down and to the left, and pick up a yarn from the garment. Make the stitches loose. Repeat around hem.

- **Catch stitch:** This stitch is good to use with knits and fabrics that stretch because it "gives." It can also be used to attach facings at seams.

Work from left to right with the needle pointing to the left. Take a stitch through the edge of the hem. Take a tiny stitch in the garment 1/4 inch to the right, close to the hem edge. Take the next stitch in the hem so that the stitches form an "X." Continue, alternating stitches between the garment and the hem. Keep stitches fairly loose.

Machine-Stitched Hems

Hems can be secured in other ways. Some sewing machines are equipped to sew a blind stitch. Check your machine's manual, and follow its directions.

A **double-fold hem** is a machine-stitched hem made with two folds of fabric of equal depth. The cut edge is in the crease of the outer fold. One or two rows of stitches show on the right side of the garment. It works best on straight edges where there is no excess fullness. To make a double-fold hem, turn under the hem at the desired length and press. Trim to one inch from the fold. Unfold the edge and turn the raw edge in to meet the pressed fold. Press this fold. Then refold the edge, forming the double-fold hem. Stitch along the inner fold and edgestitch on the outer fold.

double-fold hem
A machine-stitched hem made with two equal folds of fabric.

Fused Hems

A fusible material can also be used to secure hems. The heat of an iron causes it to melt and bond the hem to the garment. This method is quick and easy, but you need to take some special precautions when using it. Always follow the manufacturer's directions. Read the care label to be sure it can be cleaned the same way you will clean the garment. Check to see that the garment is the right length; this type of hem is permanent.

Test a piece of the fusible material on fabric scraps to avoid any problems later. The material should bond the two fabrics together completely. It should not change the color or texture of the fabrics.

Do not let the iron touch the fusible material. Once it melts onto the iron, it is difficult to remove. When you are ready to bond the hem, use a press cloth to protect the garment from the heat of the iron.

Place fusible web between the hem and the garment about 1/4 inch below the top edge of the hem. Pin in place. Press lightly between the pins to hold the layers in place. Remove the pins and cover with a press cloth. Then press a small section at a time.

Butterick Company, Inc.

22-35
The fasteners used on this jacket are both serviceable and decorative.

Fasteners

A variety of fasteners are used to close garments, 22-35. These include buttons, hooks and eyes, snaps, and hook and loop tape. Each can be used alone or in combination with other fasteners. Some are both serviceable and decorative. Your pattern will recommend the type of fastener to use. Many times the choice will depend on whether the opening edges are to meet or to overlap.

Buttons and Buttonholes

Buttons and buttonholes have been used to close garments for many centuries. Buttons are not only functional, but decorative as well. They come in a wide variety of materials and colors. Buttons and buttonholes can be used when the opening to be secured overlaps.

Buttonholes are always made before buttons are sewn into place. Usually they are made on the right front side in girls' and women's garments. On boys' and men's clothing, buttonholes are on the left front side.

There are three types of buttonholes:

- In a **bound buttonhole,** the edges are finished with fabric. Bound buttonholes give tailored garments a custom-made appearance. They are made in the garment before the facing is attached.

- In a **machine-worked buttonhole,** the edges are worked over with thread using a zigzag stitch machine. They are made after the garment is constructed. Machine-worked buttonholes are used for most items of clothing. They are especially durable.

- In a **hand-worked buttonhole,** the edges are worked over with thread using a buttonhole stitch. They are used on very loosely woven and lightweight fabrics.

Marking for Buttons and Buttonholes

Markings for buttonholes need to be transferred from the pattern piece to the outside of the garment. The markings should be accurate and follow the grain of the fabric. Be sure that the marking method that you use does not leave a permanent mark on your garment. Machine basting, hand basting, or tailor's chalk can be used. Mark the location and length of each buttonhole.

The length of the buttonhole you need depends on the size of your buttons. Measure both the diameter and the thickness of the button. The total of these two measurements is the length the buttonholes should be.

Once the buttonholes are completed, the placement of the buttons can be determined. Pin the garment closed. For a horizontal buttonhole, push a pin through the buttonhole 1/8 inch from the outer end. For a vertical buttonhole, push a pin through 1/8 inch below the top of the buttonhole. The buttons should be attached where the pins enter the fabric.

Machine-Worked Buttonholes

Most buttonholes are made by machine. On some machines, buttonholes can be made by adjusting the zigzag stitch. Other sewing machines have a built-in buttonhole setting. Special buttonhole attachments can also be purchased. Follow the directions provided with your machine or buttonhole attachment. Always make a sample buttonhole on a scrap of fabric before making one on your garment.

Use small, sharp scissors to slash the finished buttonholes open. Begin in the center and cut toward each corner. A pin inserted at each end of the buttonhole will keep you from cutting too far.

Hand-Worked Buttonholes

Hand-worked buttonholes can be made using the buttonhole stitch. First machine stitch 1/8 inch on either side and across both ends of the buttonhole marking using a small stitch length. Carefully slash the buttonhole cutting from the center toward each end line. Secure the thread at the end of the opening. Insert the needle through the slash and bring it out just outside the machine stitching line on the right side of the garment. Loop the thread under the end of the needle and the point of the needle. Pull the needle through the fabric so that a knot forms at the cut edge of the slash. See 22-36. Repeat this stitch around the edge and secure threads at the end.

Attaching Buttons

Attach buttons using a double strand of thread. Sew-through buttons have two to four holes through which you sew. A thread shank is usually needed as space for the buttoned garment to lie smoothly. Shank buttons have an attached loop on the back that forms a shank. They need only a small thread shank. Instructions for attaching buttons are given in Chapter 17. Some sewing machines will sew on buttons.

Snaps

Snaps are used to hold overlapping edges together where there will be little strain. They are made of two sections, the ball half and the socket half. Snaps come in various sizes. Large, heavy snaps should be used on sportswear, coats, and jackets.

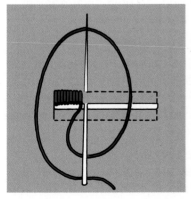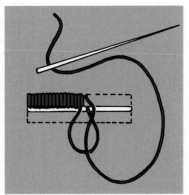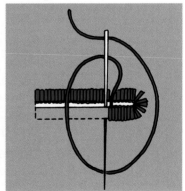

22-36
In hand-worked buttonholes, a knot or "purl" forms at the edge of the opening with each stitch.

To sew on snaps, follow these steps:

1. Place the ball half of the snap on the underside of the overlapping section.
2. Using the buttonhole stitch, take three or four small stitches close together through each hole. Make sure stitches do not show on the right side of the garment.
3. Carry the thread under the snap from hole to hole until all ball sections have been attached.
4. Fasten the thread ends securely with a couple of stitches.
5. To mark the position for the socket part of the snap, overlap the edges. Push a pin through the center hole of the ball part.
6. Attach the socket part at this location using the buttonhole stitch. A pin inserted in the hole in the socket part of the snap will help hold the snap in place as you sew. See Chapter 17 for an illustration.

Hooks and Eyes

Hooks and eyes are more secure than snaps. Use them on parts of garments where there is extra strain. Small sizes are often used at neck edges. Larger hooks and eyes are used on waistbands for pants, shorts, and skirts where there is more strain.

The eyes are either round or straight. Use a round eye when the two edges just meet. If the edges overlap, use a straight eye.

To attach hooks and eyes:

1. Place the hook on the inside of the garment just a slight distance from the edge so it does not show.
2. Stitch around each hole using a buttonhole stitch or an overcast stitch. Make sure stitches do not go through to the outside of the garment.
3. Place a few stitches at the end of the hook to hold it flat against the fabric.
4. Secure the threads.
5. Place the round eye on the inside of the opposite edge so that the loop extends slightly beyond the edge. The garment edges should just meet when the hook and eye is fastened. The straight eye is sewn to the underlap part of the garment exactly opposite the hook. Sew the eye on as you did the hook. See Chapter 17.

Trouser hooks and eyes are often used on the waistbands of jeans, pants, shorts, and sportswear, 22-37. They are very durable. They are sewn, clamped, or hammered into the fabric. It is best to use them on firmly woven fabrics as they could damage lightweight fabrics. To attach, follow the manufacturer's directions on the package.

Hook and Loop Tape

Hook and loop tape is used on edges that overlap. It consists of two strips of nylon fabric. One strip has tiny loops and the other strip is fuzzy. When the two strips are pressed together, they hold fast to one another. To open the garment, pull the two strips apart. The strips of tape can be cut to the desired length, shape, or size. Precut squares and circles can also be purchased. Hook and loop tape is often used on jackets, children's clothes, craft items, camping equipment, and household items.

To attach hook and loop tape:

1. Cut the tape to the desired size.
2. Place the fuzzy side of the strip on the underneath side of the overlapping garment edge, 22-38.
3. Stitch around all four edges by hand or machine.
4. Place the looped side of the strip on the underlap so that the garment closes properly.
5. Stitch in place through all fabric thicknesses.

Pressing Techniques

Good pressing techniques are as important as good sewing techniques. A carefully constructed garment will look better if you press as

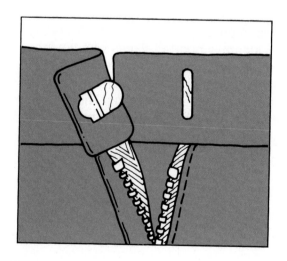

22-37
Trouser hook and eyes are good for use on sportswear and other clothes that take hard wear.

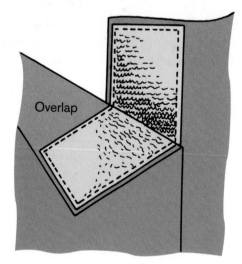

Overlap

22-38
Place the fuzzy side of hook and loop tape on the underside of the overlap. Place the looped side on the underlap.

Simplicity Pattern Co.

22-39

Pressing as you sew will yield professional-looking results. With practice and experience, you can become an expert.

you sew. Press all seams and darts before they are crossed with other lines of stitching. Pressing of the completed garment will take less time and effort. The end result will be a professional-looking garment, 22-39. As you set up your machine to sew, set up your pressing equipment. This includes your iron, ironing board, pressing ham, and press cloth.

Remember that pressing is not ironing. Pressing is lifting the iron and setting it down again on the fabric. The heat, steam, and weight of the iron do the work. The iron is not moved back and forth, as in ironing. Pressing is usually all that is needed during garment construction. Ironing is often done after laundering to remove wrinkles.

The temperature setting on the iron is determined by the fiber content of the fabric. Press a scrap of your fabric to check the temperature setting before you begin. If the iron sticks to the fabric or if the fabric puckers or melts, the temperature is too hot.

Press on the wrong side of the garment whenever possible. This will prevent a shine from appearing on the outside of the garment. Seams and darts can be easily pressed from the wrong side. If you must press on the right side, use a press cloth, especially with dark fabrics. A press cloth can be dampened if more steam is needed. Press with the fabric grain, in the direction of your stitching. Be careful not to stretch edges or curves out of shape. Do not press over pins. The soleplate of the iron could be scratched and the pins may leave an impression in the fabric.

Use care when working with fusible fabrics. If the adhesive comes in contact with the iron, it will melt and stick to it. This can be difficult to remove from the iron. Ironing over a piece of waxed paper will help restore the smooth surface.

Pressing gathers requires extra care. Place the garment over the end of the ironing board, wrong side up. Press the gathers below the seamline by sliding the iron point up into the gathers. This will keep the gathers from being flattened and having a pleated look. Press the seam allowance away from the seamline with the point of the iron. Then press the seam allowances flat to reduce bulk.

Press curved seams and darts over a rounded surface such as a pressing ham. The pressing ham allows curved garment sections to lie smoothly against the firm, rounded surface. Sleeves can be pressed without creases when a sleeve board is used, 22-40. Never press any sharp creases in your garment until the fit has been checked.

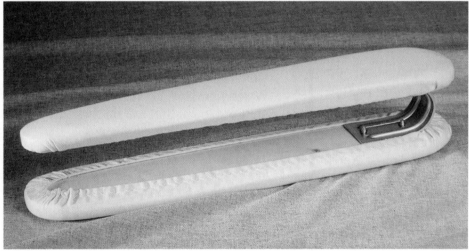

June Tailor, Inc.

22-40

A sleeve board allows you to press sleeve seams open without forming creases.

CHAPTER REVIEW

Key Points

- Both staystitching and directional stitching help to maintain the shape of the garment.
- Darts provide shape and fullness to a garment so it fits the curves of the body.
- Most seams used in clothing construction are plain seams. These seams may need a seam finish to prevent the edges from raveling. Other types of seams are the top-stitched, flat-fell, welt, and French seams.
- In some garment areas, a regular seam allowance is too bulky. You can eliminate this bulk by trimming, grading, and clipping seams.
- Facings are used to cover raw edges in a garment such as at the armholes, neckline, or other garment openings. Facings may be extended from the garment piece, separate fitted or shaped pieces, or a strip of bias fabric.
- A wide variety of interfacing fabrics are available. A heavier weight interfacing gives a crisp look whereas a lighter weight gives a softer look.
- Zippers come in all lengths, weights, styles, and colors. There are several ways to attach a zipper to the garment. The two most common methods are centered and lapped.
- Hemming is one of the last steps in sewing a garment. It should be smooth, even, and almost invisible on the outside of the garment.
- A variety of fasteners are used to close garments. These include buttons, hooks and eyes, snaps, and hook and loop tape. Each can be used alone or in combination with other fasteners. Some are both serviceable and decorative.
- Good pressing techniques are as important as good sewing techniques. A carefully constructed garment will look better if you press as you sew.

To Review

1. What should you do to make sure the thread will not be pulled out of the needle when you start to sew?
2. Why is staystitching done?
3. Explain the difference between the appearance of easing and gathering.
4. How do you prevent a pucker from forming at the end of a dart?
5. Which seam would you use for a sheer fabric that ravels easily?
6. Press seam open. Turn edges under 1/4 inch. Stitch close to fold. These are the directions for the _____ seam finish.
7. Explain the difference between clipping and notching.
8. What is the purpose of understitching?
9. Name two reasons for using interfacing.
10. Which zipper application, centered or lapped, would you use for a side seam?
11. Which hem finish could you use on a shirt or blouse that will be tucked into another garment?
12. The blind stitch is often used to secure a hem. Explain how it is done.
13. Which type of fastener would you use for an edge that just meets?
14. List two guidelines to follow when pressing during the construction of a garment.

To Do

1. Practice using the sewing machine. Learn to start and stop, sew straight, sew around curves, turn corners, and backstitch.

2. Practice directional stitching. Cut diagonally across two fabric scraps. Stitch up one of the edges. Stitch down the other edge. Compare.

3. Ease one edge of a fabric sample. Gather the edge of another fabric sample. Attach both to a third fabric sample. See if you can attach the eased sample without forming any gathers or tucks.

4. Cut two pieces of fabric 6 inches by 8 inches. Mark dart lines on each piece. Sew one dart with three stitches taken along the fold at the point. Sew the other dart without taking these stitches. Press over a tailor's ham. Which dart puckers and which lies smoothly?

5. Make samples of each type of seam and seam finish using 6 by 8 inch fabric swatches.

6. Use three different methods to sew a zipper in fabric samples.

7. Practice securing a hem.

8. Prepare a demonstration showing how to use various pieces of pressing equipment.

To Think About

1. When would you use backstitching to secure a seam? When would it be better to secure a seam by tying the threads?

2. Select ten ready-to-wear items of clothing from your wardrobe. Identify the types of seams and seam finishes used. Analyze why the clothing manufacturer might have used each.

3. What will happen to a curved, fitted facing if it is not trimmed, graded, and clipped before it is turned and pressed?

4. What are the advantages and disadvantages of each of the three types of interfacing fabrics?

5. Some people do not like to take the time to press as they sew. How would you explain to them the importance of this practice?

CHAPTER 23

Advanced Sewing Skills

Objectives

After studying this chapter, you will be able to

- identify various types of collars, sleeves, pockets, waistline treatments, and casings.
- construct various types of collars, sleeves, pockets, waistline treatments, and casings.
- attach a collar with or without a facing.
- describe how elastic is used when constructing garments.
- summarize guidelines for sewing with knits and pile fabrics.

Key Terms

flat collar
rolled collar
standing collar
kimono sleeve
raglan sleeve
set-in sleeve
patch pocket
in-seam pocket
front hip pocket
waistband
waistline facing
casing
self-casing
applied casing
pile
nap

After you have become successful making simple garments, you may be ready to construct something more difficult and detailed. Advanced sewing skills can enable you to make items that feature collars, sleeves, and pockets. Advanced sewing projects may include waistbands, faced waistlines, and casings. Some fabrics are more difficult to sew than others. These require special handling techniques. Learning these advanced sewing skills will enable you to make many styles of shirts, blouses, slacks, and jackets. These garments may take longer to construct, but you will feel a sense of pride and accomplishment when you have completed your project.

Collars

Collars are used on all types of garments. You will find them in a variety of shapes and sizes. Since collars are close to the face, it is important they be well made and fit properly.

In a well-made collar, both sides of the collar should be identical. Curves should be smooth and points precise. The underside of the collar should not show along the edge.

There are three basic types of collars: flat, rolled, and standing, 23-1. The flat collar lies flat against the garment. It is used on dresses, blouses, and children's clothing. The **flat collar** is sometimes called a *Peter Pan collar* or a *shaped collar*. The notched edge of the collar is almost identical to the shape of the neck edge of the garment. This shaping allows the collar to lie flat. The upper and lower collar pieces are cut from the same pattern.

The **rolled collar** stands up from the neck slightly and forms a roll around the neck. Separate pattern pieces are used for the upper and lower layers of the collar. The undercollar is usually cut slightly smaller, in two pieces, and on the bias. This causes the collar to form a roll.

The **standing collar** stands up from the neck edge of the garment. It is also known as a *band collar* or *mandarin collar*. It may fold over for a *turtleneck style*. The standing collar may be cut from either a shaped or a straight piece of fabric. If the collar is to turn over, it is cut on the bias.

Shirt collars are sometimes called standing collars. They consist of two parts: the collar and a neckband. Both are usually interfaced. The collar is first attached to a band, and then the band is attached to the shirt.

flat collar
A collar that lies flat against the garment.

rolled collar
A collar that stands up from the neck slightly and then forms a roll around the neck.

standing collar
A collar that stands up from the neck edge of the garment.

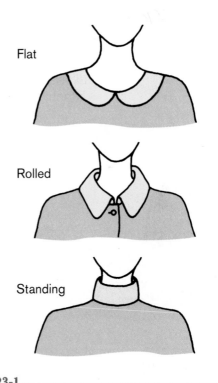

Flat

Rolled

Standing

23-1
The three basic styles of collars are flat, rolled, and standing.

Constructing a Collar

Most collars are sewn together before they are attached to garments. Though collar styles vary, most are constructed in the following manner.

Collars need the support provided by interfacing. Trim off corners of interfacing on pointed collars before attaching. This will reduce bulk in the points. Either stitch or fuse the interfacing to the wrong side of the under collar. Trim the interfacing close to the stitching.

Pin the right sides of the collar pieces together. Stitch along the unnotched edge. Leave the notched edge open so the collar can be turned right side out. Reinforce corners and curves with shorter stitches. Trim and grade the seam allowances. Clip at curves. Understitch the under collar to the seam allowances. This will prevent the under collar from rolling out at the seam line and showing along the edges. Turn to the right side and press.

Attaching a Collar

There are several different methods used to attach the collar to the garment. Most collars are attached using a full fitted facing, a partial facing, or no facing at all. Facings hide the neckline seam allowances. When there is no facing, the collar is attached so the garment neckline seam allowances are between the layers of the collar. Specific directions for attaching collars are given on your pattern guide sheet.

Collars with Full Fitted Facings

When attaching a collar using a full fitted facing, first prepare the facing as described in Chapter 22. Then follow these steps:

1. Staystitch and clip the neckline edge of the garment.

2. Pin the collar to the neck edge matching notches and other markings. Machine baste the collar in place stitching just inside the seam line.

3. Pin the facing over the collar with right sides together. Match notches and other markings. Stitch through all thicknesses.

4. Trim, grade, and clip the seam allowances.

5. Understitch the facing to the seam allowances, 23-2.

6. Press the collar and facing. Tack the facing edge to the shoulder seam allowances.

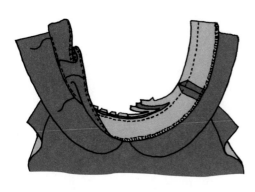

23-2
After stitching the facing to the neckline edge, trim, grade, and clip the seam allowances. Understitch the facing to the seam allowances.

Collars with Partial Facings

Flat and rolled collars are usually attached using a partial facing. Follow these steps:

1. Staystitch the neckline edge of the garment and clip.
2. Pin the collar to the neck edge of the garment matching notches. Machine baste the collar to the neck edge from the front opening to the shoulder markings.
3. Machine baste the under collar only to the back neck edge between the shoulder markings.
4. With right sides together, pin the front facings to the neckline. Clip neck edge at shoulder markings.
5. Stitch entire neck seam, but do not catch the free edge of the collar back in the seam.
6. Trim, grade, and clip the seam allowances.
7. Turn the facing to the inside and press.
8. Understitch the facing to the neckline seam allowance.
9. Turn under the free edge of the collar 5/8 inch and trim to 1/4 inch.
10. Using a slip stitch, attach the free edge to the back neck seam.

Collars with No Facing

A standing collar is usually attached with no facing. When attaching a collar without a facing, follow these steps:

1. Clip the neck edge of the garment to the staystitching.
2. Pin the right side of the collar to the garment neck edge, leaving the other layer of the collar free. Match notches and other markings.
3. Stitch, grade, and clip the seam, 23-3.
4. Press the seam allowances toward the collar. Press under the seam allowance on the free layer of the collar and trim to 1/4 inch.
5. Pin the folded edge over the neckline seam. Stitch the folded edge in place by hand using a slipstitch.

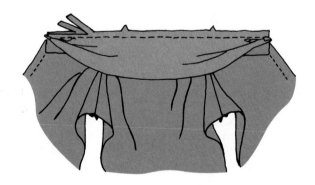

23-3————————————————————————————————————
Be careful not to catch the other layer of the collar in the stitching line.

Sleeves

There are many different styles and lengths of sleeves. The three most common styles are kimono, raglan, and set-in, 23-4.

Kimono sleeves are formed as continuous extensions out from the shoulder area. There is no seam line connecting the garment and sleeve.

Raglan sleeves are attached to the garment by front and back diagonal seams from the underarm to the neckline. A curved seam or a shaped dart creates shoulder shaping. Raglan sleeves are a good choice for hard-to-fit shoulders. The seams can be adjusted for differences in body shape.

Set-in sleeves are attached to the garment with a seam that goes around the armhole at the tip of the shoulders. The area of the sleeve at the end of the shoulders must be shaped and curved to fit smoothly over the arms. The set-in sleeve is larger than the armhole to which it is joined. This allows the arm to move freely. Some set-in sleeves are styled with a great deal of fullness that is gathered and then attached to the armhole edge. Other styles require the sleeve to be eased into the armhole. This creates a smooth appearance with no visible gathers. Set-in sleeves are the most difficult to sew of the three styles.

Kimono Sleeves

To make a kimono sleeve, follow these steps:

1. Pin the garment front and back together at the underarm and side seams. Match markings and notches.

2. Beginning at the lower edge of the garment, stitch the seam line. Try not to stretch the fabric around the curve.

3. Reinforce the underarm seam by stitching again around the curved area just outside the seam line, 23-5.

4. Clip the seam at the curve and press the seam open.

kimono sleeve
A sleeve formed as a continuous extension of the shoulder area.

raglan sleeve
A sleeve attached to the garment by front and back diagonal seams from the underarm to the neckline.

set-in sleeve
A sleeve attached to the garment with a seam that goes around the armhole at the tip of the shoulders.

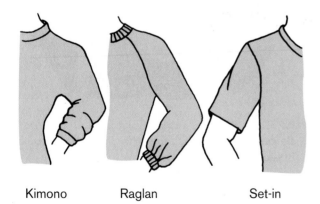

Kimono   Raglan   Set-in

23-4
Most sleeves are variations of these three basic styles.

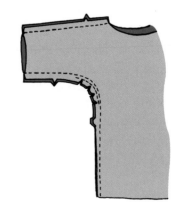

23-5
Kimono sleeves need to be reinforced at the underarm curve.

Your pattern guide sheet may ask you to further reinforce the seam by sewing a strip of seam binding or bias tape into the seam line. Follow the instructions given on your guide sheet.

Raglan Sleeves

The following are the steps in sewing a raglan sleeve:

1. Stitch the shoulder dart.
2. Slash the dart and press it open.
3. With right sides together, pin the diagonal seams of the sleeves to the garment, matching notches.
4. Stitch each seam, and then stitch the seam again just outside the first row of stitches to reinforce the seam.
5. Clip the seam below the notches and press the seam open, 23-6.
6. Stitch the entire underarm and side seam.

Set-In Sleeves

Set-in sleeves can be sewn to the garment in two ways. They can be joined to the garment before the underarm sleeve seams and side seams are sewn. They can also be joined to the garment after these seams are sewn. Your pattern guide sheet will indicate the best method to use. However, you may find that you prefer one method over the other.

To set in the sleeves after the seams are sewn, first construct the sleeve. Follow these steps:

1. To ease in the excess fullness in the sleeve, machine baste two rows of stitches around the sleeve top between the notches, 23-7. Stitch one row just outside the 5/8 inch seam line. Stitch the other row 3/8 inch from the edge. Leave a couple of inches of thread at the end of each row of stitching.
2. Stitch the underarm seam and press open.
3. With the garment wrong side out and the sleeve right side out, slip the sleeve into the armhole. Pin right sides together at the markings, notches, and underarm seam.
4. Pull up the basting threads until the sleeve fits the armhole, 23-8. Adjust the fullness evenly between the notches and markings. Pin about every 1/2 inch.

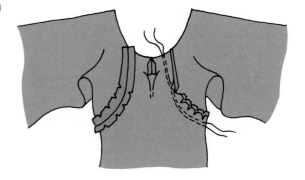

23-6_____
The diagonal seams in the raglan sleeve are clipped and pressed open before the underarm seam is joined.

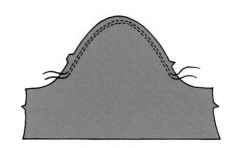

23-7_____
Machine basting the sleeve cap allows you to ease in the extra fullness.

5. With the sleeve side up, stitch the sleeve to the armhole, 23-9. Stitch carefully to avoid puckers or tucks.

6. Make a second row of stitching between the notches in the underarm area to reinforce the seam. Stitch 3/8 inch from the edge.

7. Trim the seam allowances in the underarm area only.

8. Press the seam allowances together and then turn them toward the sleeve. Do not press the sleeve seam along the cap area after the sleeve is set in.

Set-in sleeves can also be joined to the garment before the side seams and underarm seams are sewn. This method is best used for sleeves that fit smoothly and have little fullness to be eased into the armhole. Shirts are often made in this manner.

To attach sleeves before the side seams and underarms seams are sewn, follow these steps:

1. Machine baste the sleeve cap area if your pattern guide sheet suggests that you do so. Some sleeves can be attached without machine basting.

2. With right sides together, pin the sleeve to the armhole matching notches and ends. Adjust fullness if necessary.

3. Stitch the seam with the sleeve side up.

4. Press seam allowances toward the sleeve.

5. If your pattern suggests topstitching the seam, press the seam allowances toward the garment. See 23-10. Topstitch close to the seam line.

6. Stitch the entire underarm and side seam.

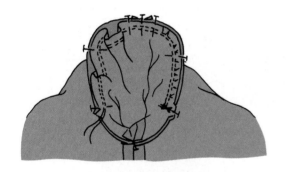

23-8
Pull the basting threads until the sleeve is eased against the armhole edge.

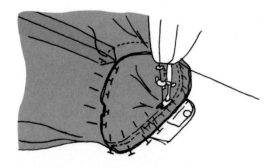

23-9
Carefully stitch the sleeve into the armhole to avoid tucks and puckers.

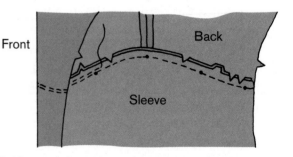

Front Back

Sleeve

23-10
Set-in sleeves can be attached before underarm seams are sewn.

Pockets

Pockets are a very important feature in many garment designs. They are not only decorative, but also functional. Because they may be a prominent design feature, it is important that they be constructed well.

There are many different types of pockets. **Patch pockets** are made from fabric pieces that are stitched on the outside of a garment. These are often used on shirts, blouses, skirts, pants, and shorts. Pockets that are sewn in the side seam of a garment are called **in-seam pockets.** If they are made properly, they do not show when the garment is worn. A variation of the in-seam pocket is the **front hip pocket.** This is an angular pocket often used on the front of pants and skirts.

Patch Pockets

Patch pockets can be made from the same fabric as the garment or of a contrasting fabric. Most pockets are unlined, but if the fabric is thin and soft, you may want to line the pockets.

To make an unlined patch pocket:

1. Finish the top edge of the pocket.
   - For light- to medium-weight fabrics, turn under 1/4 inch along the top and stitch to form a hem.
   - For heavier fabrics, zigzag or serge the hem edge. Turn the hem to the right side along the fold line. Stitch ends on the seam line and trim, 23-11.

2. If the pocket has rounded edges:
   - Machine baste 3/8 inch from the curved edges. See 23-11.
   - Pull up the threads until the seam allowance curves in and lies flat against the pocket.
   - Trim and notch the seam allowance to reduce bulk and avoid puckers.
   - Press the pocket.

3. If the pocket has square corners:
   - Staystitch around the pocket on the seam line. This forms a guide for turning and pressing the edge of the pocket before it is attached to the garment, 23-12.
   - Press the corners diagonally to the wrong side. Trim the corners.
   - Press all seam allowances under along the staystitching line, mitering the corners to form sharp points.

patch pocket
A pocket formed from a separate piece of fabric stitched on the outside of a garment.

in-seam pocket
A pocket sewn in the side seam of a garment that does not show when the garment is worn.

front hip pocket
An angular pocket often used on the front of pants and skirts.

23-11_____
Trim the seam allowance on the hem of the patch pocket. Machine baste the curved edges.

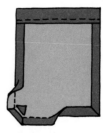

23-12_____
To form a straight edge on the sides of a square patch pocket, staystitch on the seam line. Press under along the stitching line, trimming and mitering the corners.

4. To attach the patch pocket to the garment:
- Pin the pocket to the outside of the garment on the marking line.
- Stitch the pocket to the garment close to the edge of the pocket. Backstitch at the upper corners to prevent the pocket from pulling loose.
- The pocket can also be topstitched to the garment, stitching 1/4 inch from the edge, or sewn on with hand stitches.

In-Seam Pockets

In-seam pockets are the simplest pockets to make. They are either cut from a separate pattern piece or are an extension of the garment front and back. Cut separate pattern pieces from lining fabric to reduce the bulk and give a flatter look.

To make an in-seam pocket:

1. Stitch the pocket to the front and back if the pockets are separate pieces.
2. Press the seam allowances toward the pockets.
3. Pin the back to the front at sides, matching notches and markings. Pin pocket edges together.
4. Stitch the side seam and around the pocket.
5. Clip the back seam allowance above and below the pocket, 23-13.
6. Press the garment seam allowances open. Press the pocket seam allowances flat. Turn the pocket toward the front and press lightly at the pocket opening.

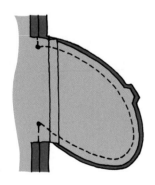

23-13..

Clip only the back seam allowance above and below the pocket so the seam can be pressed open.

Front Hip Pockets

Many jeans, pants, shorts, and skirts have partially hidden hipline pockets sometimes called slant pockets or Western pockets. Front hip pockets include two different pieces. The back portion forms a part of the garment that is attached at the waist and side seams. The other piece is the pocket facing, which finishes the opening edge.

To make the front hip pocket:

1. Stitch a piece of seam binding along the upper side edge of the front. This will prevent the pocket from stretching.
2. Stitch the pocket facing to the upper side edge of the front, right sides together.
3. Trim the seam, being careful not to cut the seam binding.

4. Turn the pocket to the inside and press, 23-14.

5. Topstitch the seam if desired.

6. Stitch the back portion of the pocket to the pocket facing, right sides together. Keep the front free as you stitch.

7. Press the pocket.

8. Baste the upper and side edges of the pocket to the garment along the seam lines.

9. Stitch the front to the back along the side seams.

Waistline Treatments

The waistline edge of pants, shorts, and skirts must be finished in some way. The three most common ways of finishing waistlines are with a waistband, a facing, or a casing.

- A **waistband** is a strip of fabric attached at the waistline edge of the garment. It may be straight or curved and is visible above the waistline.

- A **waistline facing** is a curved piece of fabric attached at the waistline edge that folds to the inside of the garment. It is not visible above the waistline.

- A **casing** is a fabric piece that encloses a drawstring or elastic that draws the garment snugly against the figure. Casings will be discussed later in this chapter.

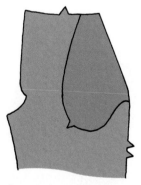
A. Attach the pocket facing at the pocket opening.

B. Sew the back portion of the pocket to the pocket facing.

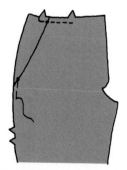
C. Baste the pocket in place along the seam lines and complete the garment.

23-14
To make a front hip pocket, follow these steps.

Waistbands

When the garment you are making includes a waistband, it should be interfaced. Interfacing prevents the waistband from stretching and rolling over when the garment is worn. The interfacing is attached to the waistband before the waistband is sewn to the garment. Follow these construction steps:

1. Machine baste the interfacing to the waistband as your pattern guide sheet explains. A fusible interfacing can also be used.
2. Press under the seam allowance on the long unnotched edge of the band and trim to 1/4 inch.
3. With right sides together, pin the notched edge of the band to the waistline, 23-15. Match notches, seams, and other markings. Ease to fit if necessary.
4. Stitch, trim, and grade the seam. Clip if it is a curved seam.
5. Press the seam allowances toward the waistband.
6. You are now ready to stitch the ends of the band. With right sides together, fold the waistband along the foldline. See 23-16. Match the folded edge of the band exactly with the seam line. Stitch across the ends.
7. Trim the seams and corners to reduce bulk.
8. Turn the band right side out and press.
9. Pin the free folded edge of the band over the waist seam line.
10. Slipstitch the entire band in place by hand, making sure stitches do not show on the outside of the garment.

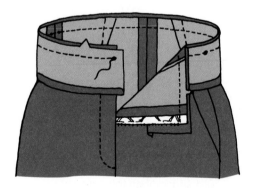

23-15
Baste or fuse interfacing to the waistband. With right sides together, stitch the band to the waist.

23-16
With right sides together, fold the waistband along the foldline. Stitch the ends and trim.

Sometimes a pattern will feature a waistband that is topstitched on the outside of the garment. The steps for attaching a waistband in this manner are similar to the steps given on the previous page. However, when you first sew the waistband to the garment, pin the right side of the band to the wrong side of the garment. The long folded edge of the band will later be brought to the right side of the garment. Then, after pinning the folded edge over the seam line, stitch close to the folded edge of the waistband.

Waistline Facings

A facing may be used to finish the waistline edge of a garment. Interfacing should be used to reinforce the waist area. It can be sewn to the facing pieces, or to the waistline edge of the garment. Your pattern may also suggest that seam binding or tape be used to prevent stretching. It should be placed over the seam line on the inside of the garment. Machine baste in place on the seam line.

To attach a waistline facing, follow these steps:

1. Join the side seams of the facing.
2. Finish the unnotched edge of the facing as described in Chapter 22.
3. Pin the facing to the garment, right sides together. Stitch, easing the garment to fit.
4. Trim, grade, and clip the seam.
5. Press the seam allowances toward the facing.
6. Understitch the seam allowances to the facing.
7. Turn the facing to the inside and press.
8. Tack the facing to the seam allowances with a few hand stitches. Turn under the ends of the facing and hand stitch in place.

Casings

Casings, fabric pieces that are used to enclose drawstrings or elastic, are often found in sportswear. Shorts, skirts, slacks, sweats, and swim trunks often use casings at the waistlines. Casings are also used at sleeve edges on shirts and dresses and hemlines on sweatpants. Necklines sometimes feature casings. Casings are comfortable to wear because they easily adapt to the shape of the body.

Casings are quick and easy to make. They are generally made one of two ways. A casing that is formed by turning back the edge of the garment piece is called a **self-casing.** When a separate piece of fabric or bias tape is attached to the garment to form the casing, it is called an **applied casing.**

self-casing
A casing formed by turning back the edge of the garment.

applied casing
A casing formed by a separate piece of fabric or bias tape attached to a garment.

Self-Casings

To make a self-casing, follow these steps:

1. Turn under 1/4 inch along the casing edge of the garment and press. (The amount to be turned under may vary. It will be specified on your pattern guide sheet.) If the fabric is bulky, finish the raw edge with a zigzag stitch or overedge using a serger.

2. Turn the casing edge to the inside along the foldline and press again, 23-17.

3. Stitch close to the inner edge, leaving an opening to insert the drawstring or elastic. Your pattern may suggest that you also stitch close to the upper edge.

Applied Casings

To make an applied casing, follow these steps:

1. With right sides together, pin the casing to the garment. Turn in the ends.

2. Stitch in a 1/4 inch seam.

3. Press the seam allowance toward the casing and understitch.

4. Fold the casing to the inside. Turn under 1/4 inch along the raw edge of the casing, or zigzag or serge the edge.

5. Stitch the edge of the casing to the garment leaving an opening for the elastic. See 23-18.

Sometimes a pattern may call for a separate band at the waist or sleeve openings. Elastic is inserted into the band. This method is often used with knit fabrics. The serger can be used with this method. First stitch the band into a circle. Then press in half lengthwise, wrong sides

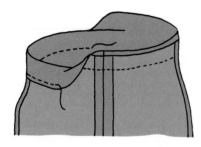

23-17_____

For a self-casing, turn the casing edge to the inside and stitch close to the edge.

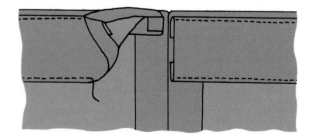

23-18_____

An applied casing is stitched to the garment edge. It is then folded to the inside and stitched again.

together. Divide the band into quarters and mark with pins. Pin the band to the garment, right sides together. Match seams and markings. Serge the band to the garment leaving an opening to insert the elastic.

A one-piece dress or jacket may call for an applied casing using a strip of bias fabric or bias tape. If you are using a strip of fabric, turn under the long edges of the casing 1/4 inch and press. Bias tape is already folded along both sides. Pin the casing in place following the markings on the pattern. Turn in the ends of the casing so the edges just meet. Stitch close to both long edges of the casing, 23-19. Leave the ends open to insert the elastic or drawstring.

Inserting Elastic in Casings

Once the casing is sewn, elastic is usually inserted. Elastic is available in different types and widths. In selecting elastic for a casing, choose one that is about 1/4 inch narrower than the casing width. This will allow room for the elastic to be inserted easily. If the elastic is too narrow, it will twist and roll inside the casing. Your pattern envelope will recommend the type and size of elastic to use.

To determine the length of elastic to use, hold a piece of elastic around the body where the casing is to be located. Pull the elastic snugly, but not too tight. Add 1 inch to this length to overlap the ends of the elastic.

Insert the elastic through the casing. This can be done by fastening a safety pin to one end of the elastic. Insert the pin into the casing opening and work the pin through to the other end. Leave several inches of elastic extending from each end. Overlap the ends 1/2 inch and pin together with the safety pin. Try on the garment to check the fit and adjust if needed. Zigzag or straight stitch several times across the overlapping ends of the elastic. Stitch the opening in the casing.

Attaching Elastic Directly to Garment

Elastic is sometimes attached directly to a waistline, sleeve, or pant leg edge. The elastic is then folded inside to form a casing. This is a good method to use with knit fabrics. A serger makes the technique especially easy and quick.

To attach elastic directly to a garment, follow these steps:

1. Cut a piece of elastic to the desired length.

2. Overlap the ends of the elastic and stitch securely.

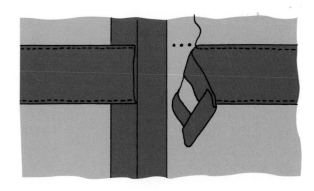

23-19

A bias strip of fabric or bias tape may be sewn on to form a casing on one-piece dresses or jackets.

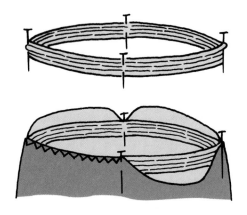

23-20--

To attach elastic directly to a garment edge, first divide the elastic into four sections. Divide the garment edge into four sections also. Match the pins and stitch the edges together.

3. Divide the elastic into four sections and mark with pins, 23-20.
4. Divide the garment edge into four sections and mark with pins.
5. Place the elastic on the wrong side of the garment with the edges even. Match the pins and pin in place.
6. Serge or zigzag the elastic to the garment. Stretch the elastic to fit the garment as you sew.
7. Turn the elastic and casing to the inside.
8. Using a straight stitch, sew through the casing, elastic, and garment. Again, stretch the elastic as you sew.

Sewing with Knits

Clothes made of knit fabrics are popular among teens. Knits are comfortable to wear and easy to maintain. Because knitted fabrics stretch more than woven fabrics, they are ideal for activewear.

There are many different types of knits available. Select the weight and type of knit recommended for your pattern. Choose from the following:

- Lightweight knits include single knits, jerseys, and tricots. These knits stretch more crosswise than lengthwise. They are suitable for softly styled garments with fluid lines, 23-21.
- Medium-weight knits such as cotton knits and wool jerseys are used mainly for sportswear.
- Heavier knits include double knits and sweatshirt knits. These stretch very little and hold their shape well.

Sewing with knits requires some special handling techniques. It is best to wash knits before cutting. Even if the fabric is preshrunk, excess sizing should be removed. Sizing can cause your sewing machine to skip stitches. Steam out any center foldlines.

Pinning and Cutting Knits

When pinning and cutting, lay knits on a large, flat surface. The fabric will stretch if allowed to hang over the edge. Though knits have no grain, locate lengthwise ribs

The McCall Pattern Co.

23-21----------------------

Garments made of lightweight knits are soft and fluid.

Fleece— A Popular Choice for Cold-Weather Wear

You can sew a warm top quickly by choosing a fleece fabric. Fleece fabrics are knitted then brushed to create a fuzzy, downy surface on both sides of the fabric. They retain very little water, so they are good for outerwear. In addition, they won't run, ravel, or shrink.

When sewing with fleece, it may be hard to tell the right side from the wrong side. To check, stretch the fabric on the crosswise grain. Fleece fabrics generally curl to the wrong side. It's still best to mark the right side when each garment piece is cut out.

Follow these pointers when sewing fleece:

- Use polyester thread and a universal or ballpoint machine needle.

- Choose a needle size based on the weight of the fleece, but use the smallest size possible.

- Set the stitch length at 7 to 9 stitches per inch for most loose-fitting garments and low-stress seams. If seams need to "give," shorten the stitch length to 12 to 14 stitches per inch. This provides more strength in high-stress seams.

- If using a serger, use a three/four thread seam.

- Because fleece does not ravel, you can eliminate bulk on collars, cuffs, and pockets by using the cut edge as the finished edge.

Pressing is not recommended, but if it is necessary during construction, hold the iron above the fabric and steam only. Then press with your fingers so the fleece lies in the desired position. Never place the iron directly on the fleece as this contact may leave a permanent imprint or melt the fabric.

Butterick Co., Inc.

in the fabric. Make certain grainline arrows follow these ribs. Use the "with nap" pattern layout to avoid any color differences in the finished garment.

Use very sharp shears for cutting to avoid snags. Make sure pins are sharp also. When marking, use chalk, marking pen, or tailor's tacks. Tracing wheels can snag knits or leave permanent markings.

Sewing Knit Fabrics

Your sewing machine should have a ballpoint needle. Ballpoint needles gently separate the yarns as they enter the fabric. Pointed needles pierce the yarns causing runs.

Select a needle size appropriate for the weight of the fabric. Lightweight knits use lower numbers (size 9 or 11) than heavier knits (size 14 or 16).

Make sure the needle is sharp. Dull needles can cause snags, runs, and skipped stitches.

Thread should have some elasticity to prevent stitches from breaking. Choose all-purpose polyester or cotton-wrapped polyester thread.

Seams in knits should have some stretch to them. This prevents the stitches from breaking. Use one of the following methods:

- If you use a straight stitch, stretch the seam slightly as you sew. Stitch on the seam line. Then stitch again 1/4 inch from the seam line in the seam allowance. Trim close to the second stitching.

- A second method is to use a narrow zigzag stitch. Trim the seam to 1/4 inch and then zigzag or overcast the edge.

- A third method is to use a serger machine. It is ideal to use with knits because it is fast and easy. The machine sews the seam, trims the seam allowance, and overcasts the edge in one motion. The 3-thread or 3/4-thread overlock stitches are good ones to use.

Some seams, such as at the shoulder or waistline, should not stretch. These seams should be stabilized by sewing twill tape or seam binding into the seam. Topstitching will also stabilize seams.

In the button and buttonhole areas, apply fusible interfacing. This prevents stretching and gives needed stability.

Before hemming your garment, allow it to hang for a day or so. Any stretching will occur before you sew the hem.

There are several ways to hem knits. Choose from the following:

- On sportswear, topstitching or a zigzag stitch give a casual look.

- A serger can be used to create an overedged hem.

- If hand sewing is your choice, the catch stitch allows for the greatest give.

Sewing with Pile Fabrics

If you are sewing a pile fabric, you will need to follow a few guidelines. A **pile** fabric has ends or loops of yarn extending above the surface of the fabric. Terry cloth is a pile fabric with a looped surface. If the loops are cut, it is called a *cut pile* fabric. Examples of cut pile fabrics are corduroy, velvet, and velour. Fleece fabrics are also pile fabrics that have become quite popular. Most fleece fabrics have a knit backing, 23-22.

A pile creates a nap on the fabric. A **nap** is a layer of fiber ends above the fabric surface. The nap lies in one direction on a pile fabric. If you run your hand in the direction of the nap, it will feel smooth. If you stroke your hand in the opposite direction, it will feel rough. This texture affects the color of the napped fabric.

When you sew with napped fabrics, it is important that the nap run in the same direction in the entire garment. If a section is cut in the opposite direction, a difference in color or shading will be noticed.

When sewing with pile fabrics, follow these guidelines:

- Choose a simple design with few seams.
- Follow the cutting layout for "with nap" fabrics. For richer color, the pile should go upward.
- Pretrim pattern pieces for easier cutting of high-loft fabrics.
- Use long pins to pin pattern to bulky fabrics.
- Mark with tailor's tacks or pins and chalk.
- Use a size 14 stretch machine needle, which has a longer shaft to prevent skipping of stitches. Set stitch length for 9 stitches per inch.
- Hand basting may be necessary to prevent slippage, or use a double-sided basting tape.

Pressing pile fabrics requires special techniques to prevent the pile from being crushed. Always place a piece of the pile fabric against the pile of the garment. When pressing the garment on the wrong side, place the piece of fabric on the ironing board, pile side up. When pressing the garment on the right side, lay the piece of pile fabric against the right side of the garment before pressing. Press lightly with steam.

For high-loft fabrics such as fleece, pressing is not recommended. The iron may leave a permanent imprint on these fabrics. Hold the iron above the fabric and steam. Set down the iron, and finger press to set the fabric in the desired position.

pile
Yarn ends or loops extending above the surface of a fabric.

nap
A layer of fiber ends above the fabric surface.

23-22
Pile knits, such as this fleece fabric, are best suited for garments with few seams.

CHAPTER REVIEW

Key Points

- There are three types of collars: flat, rolled, and standing. They can be attached with a full fitted facing, a partial facing, or with no facing.

- The three most common styles of sleeves are kimono, raglan, and set-in. The easiest to make is the kimono sleeve. The set-in sleeve is the most difficult to sew. It is attached to the garment with a seam that goes around the armhole.

- Patch pockets, in-seam pockets, and front hip pockets are the most common styles of pockets. Patch pockets can be made from the same fabric or a contrasting fabric.

- The waistline edge of pants, shorts, and skirts must be finished in some way. The three most common ways of finishing waistlines are with a waistband, a facing, or a casing.

- Casings, fabric pieces that are used to enclose drawstrings or elastic, are often found in sportswear. Shorts, skirts, slacks, sweats, and swim trunks often use casings at the waistline.

- Sewing with knits and pile fabrics require some special handling techniques. When you sew with napped fabrics, it is important that the nap run in the same direction in the entire garment. If not, a slight difference in color might be noticed between the parts of the garment.

To Review

1. What causes a collar to roll rather than to lie flat?
2. What can you do to keep the under collar from rolling out and showing at the edge of a collar?
3. Which sleeve style has a diagonal seam extending from the underarm to the neckline?
4. Describe how to ease in the fullness in a set-in sleeve.
5. Which type of pocket is not visible when the garment is worn?
6. Describe how to make straight sides and sharp corners on a square pocket.
7. What can be done to stabilize seams and keep them from stretching, such as on a front hip pocket?
8. How does a waistband differ from a waistline facing?
9. List four places where casings might be used on a garment.
10. If a casing is 1 inch wide, what width of elastic should you use?
11. Describe three techniques for sewing with knits discussed in this chapter.
12. What might cause parts of a velvet garment to appear a different color?
13. List two clothing construction steps described in this chapter where using a serger was suggested.

To Do

1. Make a collage of pictures of various garments. Identify the types of collars, sleeves, pockets, and waistline treatments featured in each design.

2. Practice making curved and square patch pockets using the patterns provided by your teacher.

3. Compare different methods used to finish fabric edges. Experiment with a zigzag stitch, an overcast stitch on the serger, and a hemmed edge. Use the same methods on both woven fabrics and knit fabrics. Write a paper summarizing your results.

4. Prepare a demonstration for the class on one of the construction techniques described in this chapter.

5. Collect and mount samples of various knit fabrics. Identify and classify the knits by type. List garment styles that would be appropriate for each type of knit.

6. Cut 4-inch square samples of three types of knit fabrics. Measure the amount of lengthwise and crosswise stretch in each fabric. Choose a pattern that would be suitable for each fabric.

7. Press a piece of pile fabric on a flat surface and then against a piece of the same fabric. Compare the results.

To Think About

1. Compare the advantages and disadvantages of the three styles of sleeves. Consider appearance, wearability, and ease of construction.

2. Compare the three waistline treatments described in this chapter. Consider appearance, wearability, and ease of construction.

3. To make a shirt, you might use several of the sewing techniques described in this chapter, such as collars, set-in sleeves, and patch pockets. Compare the pros and cons of buying a ready-to-wear shirt with sewing a similar shirt. Consider dollar costs as well as time involved.

4. How can the sewing techniques described in this chapter be used to restyle garments to accommodate individuals with special needs?

5. Why is it more difficult to sew with knit fabrics? with pile fabrics?

CHAPTER 24

Serging Skills

Objectives

After studying this chapter, you will be able to

- explain how the serger functions and identify machine parts.
- identify basic serger stitches.
- thread and operate the serger, adjusting thread tensions and stitches as needed.
- use a serger to construct a garment.
- serge various types of seams.
- perform routine care of the serger.

Key Terms

sergers
cones
loopers
overedge stitch
flatlock stitch
rolled edge stitch
overlock stitch
cover stitch
chainstitch
cone adapter
spool cap
thread net
chaining off
continuous overcasting technique
narrow double-stitched seam
mock flat-felled seam
flat method of construction
stabilizing

Sergers, also called overlock or overedge machines, provide a factory-like finish to home-sewn garments, 24-1. These machines join two layers of fabric to form a seam, trim away extra seam allowance width, and overcast (finish) the fabric edges all in one step. See 24-2.

Sergers first became available for home use in the early 1970s. Before that time, they were used only in the garment industry. They were not immediately accepted, however, due to their limitations. It was nearly ten years later before they really began to gain widespread use. Home sewers liked the job sergers did of stitching and finishing seams in one fast and easy step, but sergers could not be used for all sewing tasks.

Recently, improvements made in serger machines have made them more suitable for more sewing tasks. The newer ones have many new stitches that are similar to regular sewing machine stitches. The only things many of today's sergers cannot do is embroider and make buttonholes.

In spite of the improvements made, most home sewers use the serger to supplement a conventional sewing machine—not replace it. Most sergers stitch on the edge of the fabric only. They are not used for inside areas, such as inserting zippers.

The serger works well on fabrics from lightweight chiffon to heavyweight denim. Most serger stitches are stretchable so they can be used on knit fabrics as well as on wovens.

Whether you make something to wear or something for your home, serging can enhance its appearance both on the inside and outside. A professional seam finish can be given to garments such as unlined jackets. Hems and ruffles can be done quickly and easily with a serger. You can also give a professional look to items such as curtains and placemats with a serger.

How the Serger Functions

A serger uses two, three, four, or five spools of thread or **cones,** depending on the model. They use one or two needles, but some models can use three. Sergers do not have bobbins but have loopers,

sergers
Machines that join two layers of fabric to form a seam, trim away extra seam allowance width, and overcast the fabric edges all in one step.

cones
Large spools of thread.

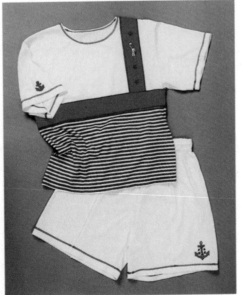

Bernina of America, Inc.

24-1
This serged child's T-shirt and shorts makes use of the decorative 5-thread reversible cover stitch to create a unique outfit.

Bernina of America, Inc.

24-2
A serger can give your finished sewing project a professional look.

loopers
The parts of the serger that form the stitch.

both upper and lower. **Loopers** are the parts of the serger that form the stitch. Unlike sewing machines, which create stitches by interlocking bobbin and needle threads, a serger loops thread around the needle thread, encasing the fabric edge. Looper threads do not penetrate the fabric. The needles and loopers form the stitches over the fabric edge as the fabric passes through the machine. See 24-3. Knife blades trim off the fabric as it is stitched.

The serger performs many functions at the same time to create the stitches. The fabric is fed into the machine, reaching the feed dogs first. As the fabric is moved along, the knives trim the edge. Then the loopers and needles form the stitches on the fabric. The fabric is then fed off the stitch finger behind the needle.

Since the serger performs three functions at once, and since it runs much faster than a conventional sewing machine, it can reduce the sewing time of a project by as much as half. Some sergers can stitch at a speed of 1300 to 1500 stitches per minute. The average top speed of a conventional sewing machine is 900 to 1000 stitches per minute.

Bernina of America, Inc.

24-3.
A serger forms a seam, trims away excess seam allowance, and overcasts the edges to produce a factory like finish.

Serger Machine Parts

Although there are a variety of types and models of sergers, they have many similarities. Following is a list of the names and functions of the basic parts found on most sergers. As you read about each part, locate it on the machine diagram in 24-4.

- *Thread guides* (1). Guide the threads from the spools to the needles and loopers.

- *Spool pins* (2). Hold spools, cones, or tubes of thread.

- *Stitch length regulator* (3). Adjusts the number of stitches per inch. Adjustments may be made by loosening a screw, moving a lever, or turning a dial.

- *Differential feed regulator* (4). Adjusts the front and back feed dogs to operate at different speeds. Not all sergers have this control.

- *Hand wheel* (5). Turns to raise or lower the needles.

- *Power and light switch* (6). Turns on the serger and light.

- *Tension regulators* (7). Apply tension to the threads leading to one or two needles so they feed at a constant rate.

- *Stitch width regulator* (8). Adjusts the position of the knives and stitch finger. Not all sergers have this control.

- *Throat plate* (9). Covers the area below the needle and presser foot.

- *Stitch finger* (10). A metal prong around which stitches are formed. The stitch finger may be located on the throat plate or the presser foot.

- *Pressure regulator* (11). Adjusts the amount of pressure applied to the presser foot and the fabric.

- *Needle clamp screws* (12). Hold needles in place.

- *Presser foot* (13). Holds fabric in place as the serger stitches.

- *Feed dogs* (14). Move fabric under the presser foot.

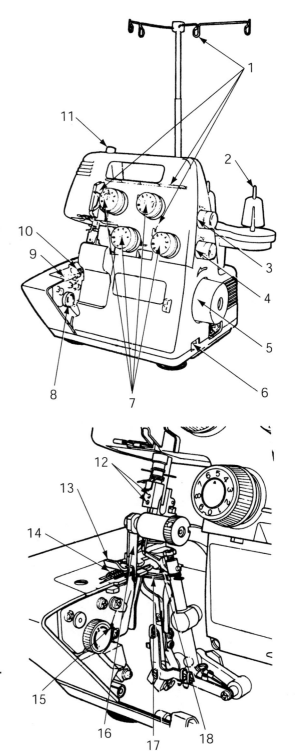

Bernina of America, Inc.

24-4
These diagrams show the major parts of the serger.

- *Knives* (15 and 16). Trim seam allowances as stitches are formed. Sergers have upper and lower knives. On some sergers, the knives can be disengaged when trimming is not desired.
- *Loopers* (17 and 18). Are necessary in forming stitches. Sergers have one to three loopers. They are referred to as the upper and lower. The two threads that come up from underneath the needle plate are called the *lower looper thread* and the *upper looper thread.* Each has its own tension regulator.

Basic Serger Stitches

Serger stitches vary with machine make and model. Knowledge of the various serger stitches will help you select the serger best suited to your needs. Listed below are the most common serger stitches. Decorative stitches can be produced with the serger to achieve a special effect. Decorative specialty threads can produce an interesting look, adding extra emphasis to the stitches. Refer to 24-5 as the stitches are described.

- The **overedge stitch** is a two-thread stitch used solely as an edge finish on garments. It cannot be used for seaming purposes. It uses one needle and one looper. The overedge stitch gives a quick, durable, and professional seam finish to any fabric sewn on your conventional sewing machine. It is the least bulky and is good for sheer and lightweight fabrics. Unlined jackets, facing edges, hem finishes, and fabrics that require an edge finish to prevent raveling are good choices for the overedge stitch.
- The **flatlock stitch** is a two-thread stitch that uses one needle and one looper to join a seam. A three-thread stitch uses two loopers. The flatlock stitch is used primarily for sportswear or lingerie elastic application. The flatlock stitch is produced by unbalancing the machine tension. This allows the fabric edges to be pulled open and flattened once a seam has been stitched. The seam produced is visible from the face side of the garment creating a decorative "ladder" effect.
- The **rolled edge stitch** is a two- or three-thread stitch. Most three-thread machines will stitch a narrow rolled hem, while only some two-thread machines can produce the stitch. A narrow rolled hem is produced by unbalancing the machine tension, allowing fabric to roll into a narrow hem. This is a timesaving way to finish scarves, napkins, lingerie, ruffles, or anywhere a narrow hem might be used. It is also useful as a seaming technique on sheers, laces, or silk fabrics. The three-thread rolled edge, which uses two loopers, gives a bulkier edge more suited to light- to medium-weight fabrics.

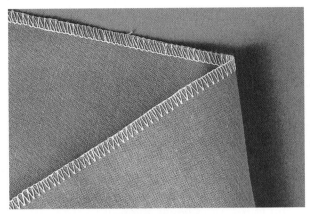

Overedge stitch

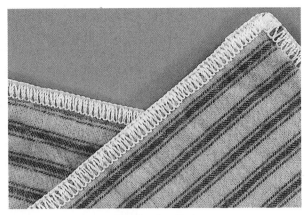

Overlock stitch

Flatlock stitch

Cover stitch

Rolled edge stitch

Chainstitch

Bernina of America, Inc.

24-5 These are the six basic stitches created by the serger. They have various uses.

- The **overlock stitch** is a three-, four-, or five-thread stitch used for seaming purposes. It can stitch, trim, and overedge a seam in one operation similar to the seams found in ready-to-wear. This stitch is the "core" of any serger. Adjusting the stitch width and length can make the stitch suitable for a wide variety of weights and types of fabric.

- The **cover stitch** is mainly used for hemming knits. It is one of the newest stitches that sergers can now do. On the top side, this stretchable stitch resembles two or three parallel rows of topstitching. On the underside, one looper thread interlocks all the needle threads. The cutting blade is not used when making this stitch. The three-thread cover stitch uses two needles and one looper, creating two rows of topstitching. The four-thread cover stitch uses three needles and one looper, creating three rows of topstitching.

- The **chainstitch** does not overlock the edge of the fabric. It can function as a standard straight stitch as the cutter is disengaged. The top side looks like a straight stitch, and the underside resembles a chain. The two-thread chainstitch uses one needle and the lower looper on the 4- and 5- thread machines. The chainstitch is sometimes referred to as a safety stitch.

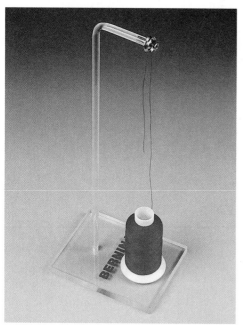

Bernina of America, Inc.

24-6
Buy serger thread on cones or tubes as more thread is used than in conventional sewing.

Selecting Thread and Accessories

Regular sewing thread can be used on your serger, but special serger threads offer the following advantages:

- fineness for more delicate finishing and less bulk
- strength
- cross-winding for smooth top feeding during high-speed sewing
- larger quantities
- economy

Because sergers use more thread than conventional sewing machines, serger thread is usually sold on cones or tubes. Tubes can have as much as 1,000 yards of thread on them while cones can hold up to 6,000 yards, 24-6.

Serger threads are generally lighter than regular sewing threads. Because more thread is used in a serger seam, a lighter-weight thread reduces the bulk. The thread must be strong, however, because the serger sews very fast and there is more tension on the thread. It is very important to use quality thread to minimize breakage.

The following types of thread are suitable for serging:

- *Cotton-covered polyester or 100 percent polyester serger thread.* This is a finer thread than that used for conventional sewing. The polyester makes the thread strong and provides stretch. The cotton wrap provides smoothness and luster.

- *Nylon serger thread.* This is a very strong thread that is recommended for knitted swimwear, lingerie, and active sportswear. It works well for rolled hems.

- *Decorative threads.* Several types of threads are commonly used to create decorative effects when serging. These include metallic thread, silk thread, woolly (texturized) nylon, pearl cotton (a crochet thread), machine embroidery thread, lightweight ribbons, and baby yarns.

Because thread color selection is more limited with serger threads, you may not be able to find an exact color match for your fabric. Try selecting a color that blends rather than matches. Also choose a color slightly darker than the fabric. If you have only one thread that matches the fabric, use it for the needle thread, which is more likely to be seen.

A cone adapter and spool cap may come with your serger. The **cone adapter** is used when the thread is on a cone. If using a thread on a tube, remove the adapter. If using thread from a spool, a **spool cap** (or unreeling disk) is placed over the spool to provide even feeding of thread to the machine. Place the spool of thread on the thread stand with the notch down. A **thread net** is sometimes used with specialty threads that may tangle or slip off the spools. A thread net is especially helpful when using slippery threads. See 24-7.

Threading the Serger

Thread the serger according to the manual provided with your serger. To make it easier to thread the machine, many manufacturers label the path of the threads with different symbols or colors. A color-coded threading guide is often placed directly on the machine. The newer machines are easier to thread. Many have a special looper threading aide and a

cone adapter
A device that allows a cone of thread to be used on a spool pin.

spool cap
A device placed over the spool to provide even feeding of thread to the serger.

thread net
A plastic circular net placed over spools of thread to keep threads from tangling or slipping off the spools.

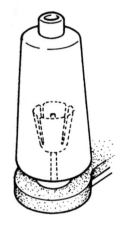

Cone adapter

Spool cap

Thread net

Bernina of America, Inc.

24-7 --

A cone adapter, spool cap, and thread net are helpful serger accessories.

chaining off
Serging off the end of the fabric until a 2- to 3-inch thread chain forms.

needle threader. Heavier threads should be threaded through the loopers, not the needles.

It is very important to thread the loopers and needles in the correct order. Threads may break or stitches may not form if the machine is not threaded correctly. The loopers are always threaded before the needles—the upper looper first. The lower looper is the most difficult to thread. You may find that tweezers will make this job easier.

Rather than rethread completely each time you change thread, you can tie the new thread to the old thread. Follow these steps:

1. Clip the current threads below the thread guides located above the spools.
2. Replace the old spools of thread with the new spools.
3. Tie the threads from the new spools to the old threads using square knots. Tug on the knots to make sure they are secure, and trim the thread ends one inch from knots, 24-8.
4. Lift the presser foot and raise the needle. Remove the threads from the tension dials and carefully pull the knots through the guides pulling from behind the presser foot.
5. Do not pull knots through the needles, but clip the knots in front of the needles.
6. Replace threads in tension dials and thread the needles.

Operating the Serger

After threading the serger, practice using it with fabric scraps. Always use a double layer of fabric in order to check the stitch formation and thread tension. It is also a good idea to use a different color of thread for each looper and needle. This will help you learn which thread forms which part of the stitch. Follow these steps:

Needle thread — Upper looper thread — Lower looper thread

The McCall Pattern Company

24-8
Tying threads from new spools to the old threads will save you time in rethreading your serger.

1. Set all tension dials to 5.
2. Check that the upper knife is lowered and in the cutting position.
3. Lower the presser foot. It can remain in this lowered position.
4. Holding the thread chain or tails lightly behind the presser foot, serge a 2- to 3-inch thread chain. This is called **chaining off.**

5. Place the fabric in front of the presser foot where the longer feed dogs will pull the fabric forward. Do not push or pull the fabric. Watch the stitching guidelines on the machine for the proper seam width.

6. At the end of the seam, continue sewing to form a 3 inch (8 cm) thread chain. Do not raise the presser foot. See A in 24-9.

7. Holding the fabric in one hand pull the thread chain over the thread cutter on the presser foot shank, B in 24-9.

Check your trial run. See 24-10 and check for the following:

- The upper looper thread (1) lies on the upper side of the fabric and the lower looper thread (2) lies on the underside of the fabric. The loops formed by both threads meet exactly on the edge of the fabric.

- The overlock needle thread (3) anchors both looper threads. It forms a straight stitch on the upper side of the fabric and appears as tiny dots on the underside.

- The double chain needle thread (5) forms a separate straight stitch on the upper side of the fabric and appears as tiny dots on the underside.

- The double chain looper thread (4) can only be seen on the underside of the fabric and joins the dots together to form a double chain stitch.

Now do a trial run using only one color thread and compare the two samples. Check the tension on the same basis as the colored-thread sample and note the differences between the upper and underside of the stitch. Remember, it is not necessary to rethread the machine for this. Cut off the threads above the cones or spools, replace them, and knot this thread onto existing colored thread.

If the stitch formation varies considerably from what it should be, check the following points:

- Is the machine threaded correctly?

- Is the thread lying properly between the tension discs?

- Are all the tension dials set at 5? (Varies by serger model.)

- Is the thread caught?

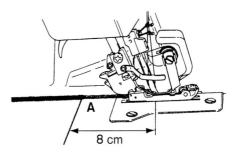

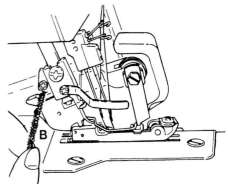

Bernina of America, Inc.

24-9_____
Be sure to leave a 2- to 3-inch thread chain by continuing to sew off the edge of the fabric (A). Cut the thread chain using the thread cutter (B).

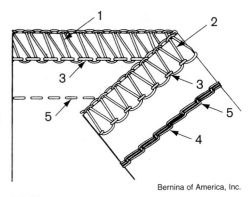

Bernina of America, Inc.

24-10_____
Check these five points when evaluating your 5-thread overlock chainstitch.

Adjusting Thread Tension

When using the serger, you may need to adjust the thread tensions. Adjustments may be needed when you change fabric, thread, or stitch. A serger can have as many as five tension regulators—one for each thread. You will need to recognize which thread tension needs to be adjusted and by how much. With practice, this will become easier.

When tension adjustments are needed, turn the tension dial by only half or one number. Then test sew again and check the results. The following descriptions, and the illustrations in 24-11, will help you recognize thread tension problems:

- If the looper threads meet on the underside of the fabric, tighten the upper looper thread tension or loosen the lower looper thread tension. (A)

- If the looper threads meet on the upper side of the fabric, tighten the lower looper thread tension or loosen the upper looper thread tension. (B)

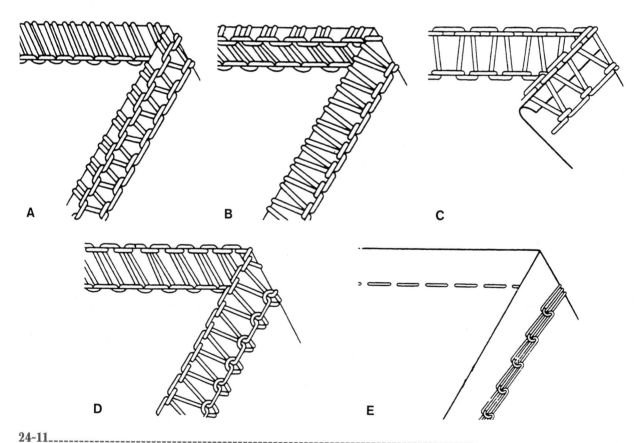

24-11
The illustrations above will help you learn to adjust the thread tension on your serger. Turn the dial by only half or one number and then test again.

- If the edge of the fabric curls, the tension of both looper threads is too tight. Loosen upper and lower looper thread tension. (C)
- When the overlock (right-hand) needle thread forms loops on the underside, tighten the overlock needle thread tension. (D)
- The double chain (left-hand) needle thread may form loops on the underside. If so, tighten the double chain needle thread tension. (E)

Other types of problems can occur when sewing with a serger. The chart in 24-12 will help you determine possible solutions to some common problems.

SERGER PROBLEMS AND SOLUTIONS

Problem	Possible Solutions
Skipped stitches	• Check threading: change type of thread; rethread. • Check needle: tighten needle; replace dull or damaged needle; change type or size. • Check tension: loosen slightly.
Thread breaks	• Check threading: check for tangled or caught thread; check sequence. • Change to higher-quality thread. • Check needle: insert correctly; replace dull or damaged needle. • Check tension: loosen slightly.
Fabric jams	• Check for tangled or caught thread; chain off after completing stitching. • Lengthen stitch length. • Increase presser foot pressure for heavy fabrics. • Decrease presser foot pressure for light fabrics.
Needle breaks	• Check for tangled or caught thread. • Check if needle is inserted correctly. • Change to larger needle. • Tighten needle screw.
Fabric puckers	• Loosen right- or left-hand needle thread tension. • Check threading; look for tangled or caught thread. • Shorten stitch length. • Hold fabric taut in front of and behind presser foot while sewing. • Adjust differential feed, if available.

24-12
If you are having problems with your serging, check this chart for possible solutions.

Trends Making News

Sewing— Not Just for Grandma Anymore

What was once thought as a dying art is making a comeback, but for different reasons. Just a few decades ago, people sewed clothes as a way to save money. Today's sewers are more likely to be hobbyists who find a creative outlet in designing and sewing their own clothes or home decor. Many enjoy creating unique, one-of-a-kind quilts. There has been a huge resurgence in quilting over the past decade alone. About 15.5 million Americans are spending $1.6 billion on quilt fabrics and supplies each year. It is not unusual for a dedicated quilter to spend $400 a year on supplies.

Sewing is included in the top ten list of women's leisure activities according to a Gallup poll. Though home sewers can save 50 to 70 percent off ready-made costs, most sewers do so for pleasure and a sense of accomplishment. A *SewNews* reader survey found 93.5 percent sew because they enjoy it, while 59 percent find sewing relaxing. Another study reported that people sew because it makes them feel energetic, creative, and optimistic. Research also shows sewing reduces stress. A significant drop in heart rate, blood pressure, and perspiration rate when compared to other leisure activities evidences this.

New and better sewing equipment has also attracted new sewers. Whereas handmade items used to take hours and hours to create, unique and clever items can be quickly embroidered or monogrammed using today's electronic sewing machines. With computerized machines, designs can be scanned from any source and embroidered onto a garment or home accessory. Sergers are also popular today because they can cut garment construction time in half.

Adjusting Stitch Length and Width

Adjustments may be needed in the stitch length and width whenever you change fabrics, threads, or stitches. As a general rule, you will use shorter, narrower stitches for lightweight fabrics and longer, wider stitches for heavyweight fabrics.

To vary the length of the stitch, use the stitch length regulator. The length of the stitch is the distance in millimeters (mm) between the needle penetrations. See 24-13. The range is generally from 1 mm to 5 mm. If the fabric jams, the stitch length may be too short for the fabric you are using.

The width of the stitch represents the distance in millimeters between the needle thread and the trimmed edge of the fabric. This range can be from 1.5 mm to 7.5 mm depending upon the machine you are using. To change the width of the stitch, your serger may have a dial that can be adjusted. Other sergers may require a change in the needle plate. The method for your machine will be explained in the instruction manual.

Using a Serger in Clothing Construction

There are three ways you can use the serger in clothing construction:

- The first is to use the one-step operation where seams are stitched, trimmed, and overcast all at one time by the serger. For this method, the needle stitches on the seam line. The knives will automatically trim the correct amount. If the machine has two needles, the left needle stitches on the seam line. When 5/8 inch seam allowances are used, the left needle is 5/8 inch from the fabric edge, 24-14.

- The second way is to use the serger only to finish the raw seam edges of the garment. The garment is then stitched together with a sewing machine. This method is recommended for tailored garments sewn from wools, linens, and silk. It is also best to use when fit is uncertain to allow for letting out seams. If this method is used, the serger knife should just skim the edge of the fabric so nothing is trimmed off the seam allowance.

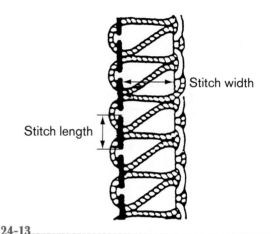

Stitch width

Stitch length

24-13
The length and width of stitches are shown in this diagram. They will need to vary depending on the fabric, thread, and stitch you are using.

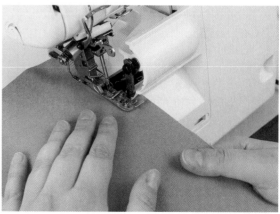

Bernina of America, Inc.

24-14
The left needle is stitching on the 5/8 inch seam line.

**continuous over-
casting technique**
Lining up several
garment sections so
the stitching is not
broken as you move
from the edge of
one garment section
to the next.

To speed this process up, you can use the **continuous overcasting technique.** The garment sections are lined up so the stitching is not broken as you move from the edge of one garment section to the next. Once all of the overcasting is finished, the thread chains are clipped and the garment sections are separated.

- The third method involves first stitching the garment seams together on the sewing machine using the standard 5/8 inch seam. Afterward the two seam allowances are treated as one and serged together, placing the needle 1/8 inch from the first line of stitching. This is called a **narrow double-stitched seam** or a *reinforced seam*. It is often used on light- to medium-weight woven fabrics. It is also used with knit fabrics where a seam needs to have a moderate amount of stretch. It is also used to reinforce areas of stress in a garment, such as crotch seams or the underarm area of a set-in sleeve.

Another seam that is also made using both the conventional sewing machine and the serger is called the **mock flat-felled seam.** This seam is often used with denim and other heavyweight woven fabrics. To make this seam, you once again stitch a standard seam with right sides together using the sewing machine. Then with the serger, overlock the seam allowances together, trimming slightly. Press the seam allowances toward one side. Once again with the sewing machine, topstitch from the right side next to the seamline. Then topstitch again, 1/4 inch away through all layers.

Selecting a Pattern

Many commercial patterns are designed specifically for sewing on the serger. However, do not limit your pattern selection to those with instructions only for the serger. Any pattern can be constructed to some degree using the serger. Before beginning construction, think through the design, outlining how to make it efficiently with the serger. As you use your serger more, this will quickly become second nature to you. The list in 24-15 suggests the many ways you can use a serger in clothing construction.

Because sergers trim the seam allowance as you sew, they are best used with garments that do not require precise fitting. Loose, unfitted garments are good choices, or garments made with knits where fit is achieved through the stretch of the fabric.

USING THE SERGER IN GARMENT **CONSTRUCTION**

- Seams can be stitched, trimmed, and overcast in one operation.
- Seams stitched using a conventional sewing machine can be overcast to prevent raveling.
- Outer edges of garments can be finished, eliminating the need for facings, ribbings, and bands.
- The inside of unlined garments can have a finished look.
- Narrow or rolled hems can be created quickly on ruffles, flared skirts, or tablecloths and napkins.
- A blindstitch hem can be used instead of hemming garments by hand.
- Lace and elastic can be applied easily.
- Stretch fabrics can be stitched without the worry of broken stitches in the seams when the garment is worn.
- Decorative flatlock stitching using lightweight yarns, metallic threads, and even thin ribbons can be combined to create one-of-a-kind garments and household items.

24-15_____
The serger can be used in many ways when constructing a garment.

Transferring Pattern Markings

Mark garment pattern pieces with a water-soluble or air-erasable marking pen instead of notches or snips. Stitching with a serger removes the notches and sews the snips together, making them difficult, if not impossible to locate. Tailor's tacks or chalk can also be used.

Fit Before You Sew

Be sure to fit before you sew! Once a seam is stitched, the seam allowance is trimmed away, making it virtually impossible to alter seams. Instead, on garment areas where fit is critical, baste seams together with a conventional machine to test for fit. After the garment is correctly fitted, treat the seam allowances as one and serge together, leaving a 1/4-inch to 3/8-inch seam allowance.

Construction Order

The best way to assemble a serged garment is to use the **flat method of construction** whenever possible. With this method, you sew flat pieces rather than pieces "in the round." For example, you will finish necklines, armseyes, sleeves, and hems before serging underarm and side seams. This differs from the usual order for assembling garments. When using the flat method of constructing a T-shirt, the order would be as shown in 24-16.

The pattern guide sheet will often follow the flat method of construction. Refer to it when deciding construction order.

narrow double-stitched seam
After stitching garment seams together on the sewing machine, they are serged together, placing the needle 1/8 inch from the stitching line.

mock flat-felled seam
A seam formed using both the sewing machine and the serger. Topstitching completes the seam on the outside of the garment.

flat method of construction
Serging flat pieces together rather than pieces "in the round."

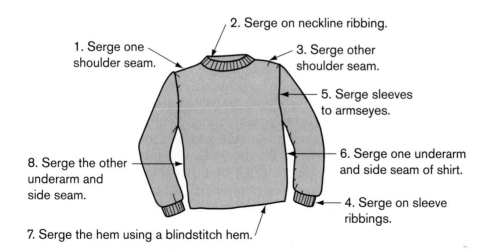

1. Serge one shoulder seam.
2. Serge on neckline ribbing.
3. Serge other shoulder seam.
4. Serge on sleeve ribbings.
5. Serge sleeves to armseyes.
6. Serge one underarm and side seam of shirt.
7. Serge the hem using a blindstitch hem.
8. Serge the other underarm and side seam.

24-16

Construct a basic T-shirt in the order shown here.

Serging Seams

Sewing seams with a serger is fast and easy. If you are using the serger to construct a garment, you will need to know the different types of seams you can use. You will also need to know how to serge curves and corners, and how to begin and end a seam. You may need to know how to remove a seam if you make a mistake.

Types of Seams

There are many ways seams can be sewn using a serger. The type you choose will depend on the garment design, type of fabric used, and durability desired. If you are using a pattern, the guide sheet may suggest the type of seam to use.

The basic types of seams include the following:

- **Overlock seam.** The basic overlock seam can be made using three or four threads. The four-thread seam will be stronger. This seam can be used on a wide variety of garments. It is suitable for woven fabrics, but it can be used with knits too because the seam will stretch. Because the seam allowance will be cut off as the seam is sewn, you must be sure of the fit before you stitch. To make this seam, place right sides of the fabric together and serge on the 5/8 inch seamline.

- **Serged and topstitched seam.** This may also be called an exposed seam because the stitches are "exposed" on the right side of the garment. Decorative thread can be used for this purpose. It is best used with light- to medium-weight fabrics. To make this seam, serge the wrong sides together. For added durability, or to flatten this seam, it can be topstitched to the garment using a sewing machine. First open the fabric and press the seam to one side. Then topstitch the seam to the fabric, 24-17.

- **Lapped seam.** This seam gives a decorative effect on the outside of the garment. It can also be used for reversible garments or for thick, loosely woven fabrics to provide strength. To make this seam, serge to the seamline on one side of the seam. On the other side of the seam, skim the edge of the seam with serging, leaving the seam allowance. Lap the trimmed seam edge over the other, aligning the 5/8 inch seamlines. Fusible web or fabric glue can be used to hold the layers in place. Using a conventional sewing machine, topstitch the seam together.

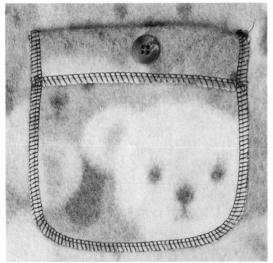

Bernina of America, Inc.

24-17

A 4-thread overlock stitch was used to give a decorative edge to these patch pockets. They were then stitched to the garment using a conventional sewing machine.

- *Flatlocked seam.* This seam is used for its decorative effect and is often seen on knit sportswear, 24-18. It is suitable for many fabric weights, but should not be used with fabrics that ravel. To make this seam, adjust your serger for flatlocking according to the serger manual. The thread tensions will need to be loosened. Then serge the two layers of fabric together. Pull the two layers apart so the seam allowance lies flat inside the stitching and the cut edges meet.

24-18 The 2-thread flatlock seam gives a distinctive look to sportswear. The ladder effect is also used for its decorative look on the outside as well.

When serging seams, try to stitch in a continuous manner as described for overcasting seam edges. For example, sew seam after seam without cutting the stitching between the pieces. Leave four inches of serger chain between pieces and cut in the middle when separating pieces.

Sewing over pins is not possible with a serger because of the cutting blades. Use water soluble basting tape, a water soluble glue stick, or pins placed parallel to the left of the seamline to hold seams in place. If you choose to use pins, make certain to remove all pins before they reach the cutting area. Also place them about one inch from the seamline. If a pin should accidentally hit the knives, your serger can be damaged. Pins are not as essential with a serger due to the longer presser foot and feed dog. Fabrics shift very little when sewn on a serger.

Serging Curves and Corners

With practice, you will easily master curved edges and corners. To accurately serge inside or outside curves, watch the knife rather than the needle, as you would with a conventional machine. Remember, the serger cuts before it sews. Feed the fabric slowly with your hands at the front of the presser foot.

You may want to serge in a circle, beginning and ending at the same place. This is often used on hem edges. When serging in a circle, serge all the way around, overlapping stitching for one inch at the end and serging off the fabric edge. If you want a more attractive finish, overlap only a few stitches at the end. Then lift the presser foot and needles and pull the unchained threads from the serger. Tie knots in the threads and trim.

For outside corners, you can stitch along one side of the fabric and off the edge, leaving a chain. Then stitch the next side, crossing and securing the first line of stitching. This also cuts off the chain end of the previous row of stitches. This is the easiest method to use.

stabilizing
Adding extra
strength to seams
and areas that
receive stress during
wearing.

For inside corners, stitch to the corner, stopping when the blade reaches the edge of the fabric. Pull the fabric toward you so the edge is straight, but a pleat forms to the left. Then continue stitching. The fabric will lie flat after serging.

It is not possible to pull threads on a serger once a stitch is formed. A little slack in the stitch is helpful in turning corners or removing a possible thread jam. To achieve the necessary slack, pull to loosen the needle thread between the needle and last thread guide. Gently slide the threads and fabric to the back, off the stitch finger. Continue pulling needle thread and pulling the fabric to the back until you have the needed slack.

Securing Seam Ends

Since backstitching is not possible with a serger, stitches will need to be secured in some other way. If not secured, they will unravel. If seams or stitching are crossed by other stitching, this will secure the ends. If the seam will not be crossed, you will need to secure the ends in some manner. There are several ways to do this, including the following:

- ● *Knot the thread chain.* Place the knot close to the fabric edge.
- ● *Bury the chain.* After stitching, pull the chain to smooth it out. Thread it through a large-eyed needle or loop turner and run it under 1 to 2 inches of overlocked stitches. See 24-19. Trim the excess thread.

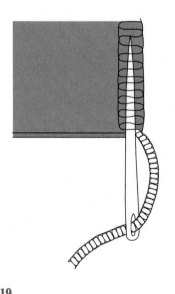

- ● *Secure the threads while stitching.* At the beginning of a seam, take two stitches. Stop, lift the presser foot, and bring the chain to the front. Place the chain on the seamline, lower the presser foot, and serge over the chain. At the end of the seam, stitch off the fabric one stitch. Lift the presser foot and needle. Slip the chain off the stitch finger. Flip the fabric over and to the front. Lower presser foot and serge over the last few stitches and off the fabric.
- ● *Use liquid seam sealant.* Put a dab of sealant on the thread chain and stitches at end of seam. After it has completely dried, cut the thread tails. Sealant will stiffen and may darken the fabric. This method is best used where it will not show.

Stabilizing Seams

Garment seams stitched with a serger may need to be stabilized. **Stabilizing** is a means of adding extra strength to areas that receive stress during wearing. Shoulder and neckline seams, front areas, and crotch seams are often stabilized. Facings and interfacings will help to stabilize necklines and front opening edges.

24-19
You can "bury" the thread chain by threading it through a needle and running it under the stitches.

One method of stabilizing seams is to use a row of straight stitching along the seamline. Use a conventional sewing machine for this. Then serge the seam, stitching close to the first row of stitching.

You can also serge over twill tape, seam tape, or ribbon. Cut the tape the length of the seam and place it over the seamline. Stitch the seam through the tape, being careful not to cut the tape.

Garments made of knits or loosely woven fabrics generally require more stabilizing. Sew loosely woven fabrics using the serger only as a seam finish. Stitches tend to pull out of a serged seam when the seam is stitched, trimmed, and overcast in one step.

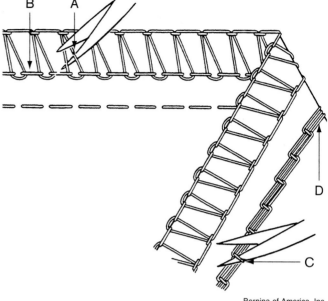

Bernina of America, Inc.

24-20 _____
Follow these steps to unpick overlock stitches.

Unpicking Seams

Serger stitches can be easily ripped out. Use a seam ripper or sharp scissors. To remove seams, use the following methods:

- Two-thread overlock: Slide a seam ripper or scissors under the stitches. Pull out the cut threads.

- Three-thread overlock: Using sharp scissors cut the loops every three or four stitches. See A in 24-20. Pull the needle thread and the stitches will come undone. (B)

- Two-thread double chain stitch: Cut the needle thread at the end of the seam. (C) Pull the looper thread and the stitches will come undone. (D)

Serger Care

The serger will operate effectively if it is properly maintained, 24-21. It needs to be cleaned and oiled regularly as specified by the manufacturer. Sergers operate at high speeds causing internal parts to rotate more often than conventional sewing machines. Because the fabric is cut as the machine stitches, lint accumulates quickly.

Use a soft brush to remove the lint from the knife area. Also replace needles if stitches are not forming properly. Replace blades when fabric is not cut smoothly. Oil the machine as described in the owner's manual using sewing machine oil. This is a special type of oil formulated for sewing machines.

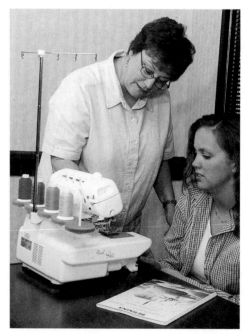

Bernina of America, Inc.

24-21 _____
Your instructor will explain how to care for the serger to keep it operating effectively.

CHAPTER
REVIEW

Key Points

- A serger uses two, three, four, or five spools of thread or cones, depending on the model. They use one, two, or three needles. Sergers do not have bobbins but have loopers, both upper and lower.

- Serger stitches vary with machine make and model. The most common stitches include the following: overedge stitch, flatlock stitch, rolled edge stitch, overlock stitch, cover stitch, and chainstitch.

- Special thread designed for serger use offers a number of advantages. Serger thread is generally sold on cones or tubes, which can hold from 1,000 to 6,000 yards of thread.

- Thread tensions and stitch length and width generally need to be adjusted when you change fabrics, threads, or stitches.

- You can use the serger to construct a garment completely or in combination with a conventional sewing machine.

- The flat method of construction should be used when serging a garment. With this method, you sew flat pieces rather than pieces in the round.

- There are many ways seams can be sewn using a serger. The type you choose will depend on the garment design, type of fabric used, and durability desired.

- The serger will operate effectively if it is properly maintained. It needs to be cleaned and oiled regularly as specified by the manufacturer.

To Review

1. Name the three main functions performed by a serger.
2. What two sewing tasks can a serger *not* perform?
3. The _____ _____ is a metal prong around which stitches are formed on a serger.
4. The _____ stitch is visible from the face side of the garment and creates a decorative "ladder" effect when the fabric edges are pulled open and flattened.
5. Name two advantages in using thread specifically made for sergers.
6. Explain how to chain off when operating the serger.
7. If the stitch formation is not what it should be, what four things should you check?
8. What is the general rule for selecting stitch length and width?
9. Name the three ways you can use a serger in clothing construction.
10. What methods of transferring pattern markings should *not* be used when serging seams together?
11. Why is it important to fit before you sew when using the serger?
12. Explain how to serge an outside corner.
13. Describe one way to secure the end of a seam.
14. Describe one way to stabilize a seam.

To Do

1. Take a survey of your home. List as many items as you can that could be made with a serger.
2. In small groups, make lists of what a serger can and cannot do. Then compare with a conventional sewing machine.
3. Using the instruction manual that came with the serger you will be using, locate and explain the function of each part of the serger. What machine parts does the serger have that the conventional sewing machine does not have?
4. Practice doing the following:
   A. Remove and replace the serger needle.
   B. Thread the serger using a different color thread for each spool. Use a cone adapter or spool cap.
   C. Change threads in the serger by tying new threads to old threads.
   D. Practice making the various types of stitches your serger can make.
   E. Practice making various types of seams with the serger. For each seam, cut two 6- by 2-inch fabric samples.
5. Select a pattern from a pattern catalog supplied by your teacher. Mount on a sheet of notebook paper. Evaluate the pattern in terms of its suitability for serger construction. How could you use the serger? What would you need to do with a conventional sewing machine?
6. If you are making a serged garment, outline the steps using the flat method of construction and continuous stitching. If using a conventional sewing machine, how would the order of the steps differ?
7. Using the Internet, visit Web sites for various manufacturers of sergers. Learn about the models they offer and the newest features.
8. If you are having a problem with serging, use the Internet to visit Web sites that can give you help with your serger. Share what you learn online with the class.

To Think About

1. Why do you think it took a number of years for sergers to become popular with home sewers?
2. If you could buy only one machine, would you purchase a conventional sewing machine or a serger? Why?
3. How does using a serger affect the pattern and fabric you select?
4. If you were using a serger to make a garment and you were not certain about the fit of the pattern, what would you do?
5. How would you explain the flat construction method to someone?

25

Sewing and Needlecrafts for Fun and Profit

Objectives

After studying this chapter, you will be able to

- summarize the benefits of doing sewing and needlecraft projects.
- list points to consider when choosing sewing and needlecraft projects.
- select sewing projects to match your interests and abilities.
- describe the basic equipment and techniques used in patchwork, quilting, embroidery, knitting, and crochet.
- explain how to choose, price, and market sewing and craft projects to sell.

Key Terms

batting
crewel
stabilizer fabric
crochet
entrepreneur

Sewing and needlecrafts can be fun outlets for your self-expression. You can sew clothes that are fun to wear. You can quilt, embroider, knit, and crochet gifts that are fun to give, 25-1. You can also make useful items to sell for profit.

Using your creativity to make something can give you a good feeling. When others admire your work, you can take even more pride in your skills.

Benefits of Sewing and Needlecraft Projects

Doing sewing or needlecraft projects can have a number of benefits. First of all, sewing and needlecrafts make excellent hobbies. Taking a break from your daily tasks to do something that you enjoy is relaxing. Many projects don't require your full concentration. Therefore, you can take part in conversation, listen to music, or watch TV while you do them. Meeting with friends to work on projects together is also fun.

Variety is a benefit of sewing and needlecraft projects. The kinds of items you can make are limited only by your imagination. With so many choices of projects to do, you are not likely to become bored with your hobby.

Uniqueness is another benefit of sewing and needlecraft projects. When you are done with your project, you have something that is one-of-a-kind. You may use the same pattern as someone else, but the colors and trims you select will add a personal touch.

Handmade items make special gifts. You could sew or make projects to give to family members and friends as birthday and holiday gifts. A handmade gift means more to the person receiving it. It says you spent time and thought to make something just for that person. See 25-2.

Another advantage of sewing and needlecraft projects is the speed with which they can be done. You can often "make it today and use it tomorrow." Pillows, hats, and wall hangings are easy-to-make items.

Saving money is another reason for doing sewing and needlecraft projects. Garments, accessories, and gift items can be made for less money than you pay for ready-mades. Labor is a major factor in determining the cost of any product. When you do the labor yourself, you save

The McCall Pattern Co.

25-1
You can sew fun clothes for yourself or others. Adding embroidery and glitter gives them a special look.

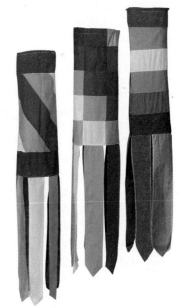

Pineapple Appeal

25-2
A friend might appreciate a handmade gift such as one of these windsocks.

Trends Making News

Crafts Gaining New Converts

Maybe it's sitting at a computer all day long where you can see something on a screen, but you can't touch it or feel it that's leading to a renewed interest in handcrafts. Handcrafters are people who like to touch things. They enjoy the tactile kinds of crafts where they can use their hands to create clever or beautiful items.

The new crafters today are typically working women. They enjoy the creative process, but they don't have hours and hours to spend on projects. They often like projects they can take with them to do while waiting in a doctor's office or carpooling.

According to the Craft Yarn Council of America, 36 percent of all American women knit or crochet. The biggest age group to take on knitting is the youngest group. Since 2002, participation has increased more than 150 percent among 25- to 34-year-olds and 100 percent in the under-18 set.

Many women go to yarn shops or coffeehouses to knit and crochet. They join knitting groups to share information with other stitchers. In yarn shops, they can see the latest yarns and accessories while getting ideas for projects from other customers. Knitting clubs have many chapters in major cities often holding monthly meetings at libraries. Some clubs offer classes and seminars with renowned master knitters.

This new type of crafter has helped push the national sales of craft and hobby products to more than $10 billion per year. What the craft manufacturers have provided are products that are faster, easier, and provide better results. The industry has also moved away from cute and country to include more sophisticated looks. There are more choices of simple craft projects that can be done in just a few hours.

People today take great pride in doing things for themselves and being able to say I made it myself. Many have even become home-based entrepreneurs who sell their one-of-a-kind creations.

Many young entrepreneurs are crocheting and knitting garments and accessories for the young crowd. Dresses, jackets, T-shirt tops, and skirts are popular because of their unique one-of-a-kind appeal.

money. Many projects can be made from scraps, so you can also save money on materials. See 25-3.

Not only can sewing and needlecrafts save you money, they can help you make money, too. Selling items you have made can bring you a nice source of extra income.

Choosing a Project

Many people start sewing or needlecraft projects that they never finish. Giving some thought to your choice of projects will help you avoid this.

Doing your project will be more fun if you think about your interests when you choose it. Choose a project that will allow you to use a skill you enjoy. In other words, don't choose a knitting project unless you like to knit. Your project may tie into some of your other interests, too. For instance, if you like to play tennis, you might want to sew a tennis bag to carry your equipment. See 25-4.

Consider the amount of time you have to spend when choosing a project. If your time is limited, you may want to choose a small project or use a kit. When your work speed or your free time increases, you can move on to bigger projects.

Also think about the amount of money you have to invest in your project. Find out what supplies and equipment you will need. Some craft supplies can be expensive. See if you already have some of the needed materials at home. Many projects can be made from scraps.

Simplicity Pattern Co.

25-3 --
The small purse and iPod carrier can be made from leftover fabric in very little time.

Kit Projects

If you are learning a new skill, a kit project may be a good choice for you. Kits are available for both sewing and needlecraft projects. Kits for sewing projects include items such as jackets, vests, sweatshirts, shorts, pants, bags, comforters, and toys. Needlecraft kits can be purchased to make pillows, wall hangings, baby clothes, afghans, and many other items.

Kits come ready to assemble to make a professional-looking item. They include fabric, yarn, or other

Pineapple Appeal

25-4 --
If you participate in sports, an equipment bag might be a good project to choose.

materials needed to construct the project. They also contain all notions such as buckles, snaps, buttons, zippers, and trims. Polyester fiberfill or down is often included for stuffed articles. Step-by-step directions are included with each kit. Kits are sold in a range of prices and are designed for a variety of skill levels. See 25-5.

When ordering or buying kits, be sure you choose the correct size for garments such as jackets and coats. If you order by mail, you may be responsible for paying the return postage if an item doesn't fit. Returning can also cause delays in completing your project on time.

An advantage of using a kit is the quickness with which you can finish a project. You can choose kits that match your skills, and you can learn new techniques as you progress. You must follow directions carefully in order not to damage a part or section of the item. Using kits is a fun way to gain practice in following directions and using a new skill.

Sewing Projects

Patterns are available for a wide range of sewing projects. For some simple items, you may even want to make your own patterns. The ideas suggested here are all fairly easy projects. They are fun items to make for yourself. They also make good projects to sell because they can be made quickly.

Garments

Sweatshirts, sweatpants, shorts, and tops are quick and easy to make and fun to wear, 25-6. These garments need little fitting, so they make great sewing projects for beginners. You can practice your sewing skills making these simple garments. Then you may want to try making more fitted garments that require more advanced sewing techniques.

Pineapple Appeal

25-5
Everything you need to make these bags is included in a kit.

Bags

It seems that almost everywhere people go, they take some of their belongings with them. People need beach bags, book bags, lunch bags, gym bags, fanny packs, and makeup cases to help them carry their possessions. Making bags can be a quick and easy sewing project. See 25-7.

Kits are available to make various types of bags. You can even use your creativity to make your own patterns in the shapes and sizes you like. Since these items are small, leftover fabric scraps could be used to make them. You can use embroidery, bright trims, or special fabrics to personalize them.

Sports Equipment

Clothes and accessories for a wide variety of sports activities make great sewing projects. You can save up to half the cost of ready-mades if you sew your own. Some items you can make are vests, sweaters, jackets, pillows, backpacks, hoods, and ski mitts. You can also make swimwear, tennis and bicycle bags, exercise mats, and head covers for golf clubs. Seat cushions make an excellent project for spectator sports.

Pineapple Appeal

25-6
The shorts, pants, and tops shown here are all easy for beginners to sew.

The McCall Pattern Company

25-7
Bags are quick and useful sewing projects.

Some of these items are available as kits. There are kits designed for beginners, but those with sewing experience can make more difficult items.

Stuffed Toys

Stuffed toys give you a chance to express your creativity and use your imagination. Use your originality to create one-of-a-kind designs. They may be used as accessories for your room or as gifts for friends and children.

A wide variety of patterns for toys can be found in pattern catalogs. These include balls, clowns, and a wide variety of animals and other items, 25-8. With extra time, you could create your own pattern. If time is short, stuffed toy kits can be used.

When making stuffed toys for small children, select a sturdy fabric. Use polyester fiberfill for the stuffing so the toy can be safely laundered. If details such as eyes and nose are added, use fabric that can be sewn onto the toy. If you use button eyes, be sure they are attached securely so that they cannot be pulled off and swallowed.

Pillows

Making pillows can be one of the fastest ways to add a decorative touch to your room. They can be made in a variety of shapes. Pillow kits are available like those in 25-9. You can also use your imagination to create pillows from various fabrics. Firmly woven or knitted medium- to heavyweight fabrics work best for pillows. Patchwork can also be used.

Simplicity Pattern Co., Inc.

25-8
Any child would love receiving one of these cute, cuddly stuffed toys.

Pineapple Appeal

25-9
You can have a real conversation piece with one of these fun pillows on your bed.

Your pillow can be stuffed with polyester fiberfill, or pillow forms can be used. A zipper can be stitched into one seam of the cover. Then the cover can be easily removed for washing. Add machine-washable trims to personalize your pillow. Fabric paints can also be used to give a personal touch.

You may want to make a large floor pillow to provide a comfortable place to sit while reading or watching television. Make it firmer than other types of pillows. This will help it to keep its shape and last longer. Like other pillows, floor pillows can be stuffed with polyester fiberfill or a pillow form.

Patchwork

Patchwork can be a fun way to use fabric scraps in a creative way. *Patchwork* is sewing small pieces and shapes of fabric together to form larger pieces. Once you have a larger piece of fabric to work with, there are any number of ways you can use it.

In earlier times, patchwork was a way of reusing old pieces of fabric. They were often made into quilts. Today, patchwork can be used to make sections of a garment, such as a collar or pockets, or an entire garment, such as a vest. It can also be used to make accessories, such as purses and ties. Home accessories often feature patchwork in pillows, bedspreads, placemats, and wall hangings.

Patchwork does not have to be a way of using scraps of fabric. Many patchwork fabrics are specifically designed around certain colors and fabric patterns. When selecting fabrics to create a patchwork design, keep the following points in mind:

- All fabrics should have the same care requirements.
- All fabrics should be of a similar weight for even wear.
- The colors and patterns should coordinate or complement each other.
- The fabric patterns should be in proportion to the size of the patches. The larger the patch, the larger the pattern can be.

Choose a simple design for your first project that uses squares and triangles, 25-10. The size of each patch should be no smaller than 2 inches and no larger than 8 inches. Cut a pattern out of cardboard allowing 1/4 inch seam allowances.

Make sure your fabrics are on grain. Use your pattern to mark the pieces on the wrong side of the fabric. Cut the pieces out using shears.

To-Sew

25-10

A simple patchwork pillow uses squares and triangles.

Sew all seams using a 1/4 inch seam and 12-15 stitches per inch. If using triangles in your design, sew these first to form squares. Then sew the square patches together to form rows. Press all seams open before joining the rows. Finally, sew the rows together to form the fabric. Your patchwork is now ready to be made into a garment or home accessory.

Quilting

Quilting is the joining together of two layers of fabric and an in-between layer of padding with stitches. The stitching, which is both decorative and functional, can be done by hand or machine.

Quilting has enjoyed a renewed interest in recent years. Many people are enjoying making their own quilts. Quilts are most often used as warm covers for beds. Other uses include wall hangings, tote bags, place mats, and vests.

The top layer of the quilt is often made with patchwork. The top layer can also be made of one piece of fabric with a printed design on it, or a design may be appliquéd to the upper fabric. If a solid color fabric is used, the rows of stitches create a pattern in the quilt. Parallel rows of stitching form a geometric design.

batting
The inner layer of a quilt, which is often made of polyester fiberfill, down, or cotton.

The inner layer, called **batting,** is often made of polyester fiberfill, down, or cotton. Polyester fleece can also be used. This inner layer gives warmth to the quilt. The bottom layer, called the lining or backing, is usually one piece of firmly woven fabric.

If a quilt is to be sewn by hand, as they were traditionally made, the three layers of the quilt are often stretched on a quilting frame. Quilting begins in the center and proceeds outward. Small stitches are made through all layers. Handmade quilts are treasured more because of the time it takes to make them. They are also more expensive than those made by machine. Antique quilts can be very valuable heirlooms, 25-11.

Machine Quilting

Quilting can also be done by machine. Most people who do quilting today sew the quilts by machine. The newest sewing machines offer many features that make the repetitive actions quick and easy to do. Special presser feet help keep the layers of fabric from sliding when stitched.

If you plan to use a pattern for a garment or accessory, quilt the fabric before cutting out the pattern sections. Quilting reduces the size of the fabric.

25-11
Quilts often become family heirlooms.

Follow these steps when machine quilting:

1. Press the top and back fabrics.

2. Layer the fabrics beginning with the backing fabric. Place on a flat surface right side down. Then place the filler fabric on top. Finally, place the top fabric over the filler with the right side of the fabric face up.

3. Hand-baste all layers together from the center outward to prevent shifting. Use long, loose stitches.

4. Set your machine stitch length at 6 to 8 stitches per inch and reduce the pressure on the presser foot. If you have a *walking presser foot,* the layers will be less likely to shift while sewing.

5. If you are following a design, begin sewing in the center of the project and work outward.

6. If you are making parallel rows of stitching, work from one side to the other. Mark one line along the edge of the fabric and stitch on this line. Then, using a *quilting attachment* as a guide, stitch the remaining rows an equal distance apart.

Needlecraft Projects

Embroidery, knitting, and crochet have been favorite needlecrafts for years. These are only a few of the types of needlecrafts available. Counted cross-stitch, shadow stitching, macramé, and soft sculpture are others you could try. Check a local fabric or craft store to learn about a new handcraft that interests you.

Embroidery

Embroidery is decorative stitching made by using needle and thread. You can embroider almost any design on almost any item made from fabric. Embroidery can be used to decorate everything from garments to bed linens. Personalized items embroidered with people's names make popular products to sell. Embroidery can be done by hand or machine, 25-12.

Hand Embroidery

Hand embroidery requires only a few pieces of equipment. The supplies needed for a project can also be bought in kits.

The McCall Pattern Co.

25-12--
The delicate embroidery on the collar and front of this jacket could be done by hand or machine.

Supplies Needed

Embroidery floss is a six-ply yarn. This means there are six strands of thread lightly twisted together. For a thick, solid look, use all six strands. They can be separated to achieve special effects. For instance, the thin stem of a plant could be made using only one or two strands. Experiment to see what effect you like best.

Special embroidery needles are available, but any needle can be used if its eye is large enough for the thread. Most threads slip through the needle eye easily. If you have one that won't, cutting on a slant may help. Bulky threads can be a problem. Fold these back about an inch at one end. Pinch the fold and squeeze it through the eye of the needle.

Although any type of scissors can be used, a small, sharp-pointed pair is best. They will cut deeper into corners and closer to stitches. Always cut with the points. You may cut too far and damage your fabric if you use the back part of the blades.

An *embroidery hoop* is a set of two metal, plastic, or wooden rings. One ring fits inside the other. Fabric is held taut (tightly and smoothly) between the rings to prevent puckering as you embroider. A hoop with an adjustable screw on the outside ring is best. This type of hoop allows you to work with either thin or thick fabrics.

Techniques

Your embroidery thread should be no longer than your arm. Twisting, knotting, and fraying result when you work with longer lengths.

The first step in embroidery is to anchor the thread. This can be done in two ways. You can knot the thread end and insert it into the fabric from the wrong side. You can also make several small stitches and a back-stitch close to the starting point. Then bring the needle through to the right side of the fabric.

Most embroidery is done using a few basic stitches. Choose designs within your ability. Once you master the basic stitches, you can vary them for creative effects. As your embroidery skills increase, you may wish to tackle more complex designs.

To end your work, make a tiny backstitch on the wrong side. Then weave the thread through several of the completed stitches. Clip the thread close to the fabric.

Practice basic embroidery stitches until you can comfortably handle the needle, thread, fabric, and hoop. Later, you may want to use some of your samples as decorative patches.

Crewel

crewel
A type of hand embroidery that uses wool or wool-like yarn instead of thread.

Crewel is a type of hand embroidery that is done with a different type of thread. Wool or wool-like yarn is used in crewel. Since yarn is thicker than embroidery floss, the work goes faster. The rest of the equipment and the techniques used in embroidery are also used in crewel.

Machine Embroidery

Machine embroidery is a quick and easy way to duplicate hand embroidery. Some simple machine embroidery can be done with a basic zigzag sewing machine. However, the more sophisticated computerized sewing machines available today can be programmed to create very complicated embroidery designs, which would take hours of work if done by hand. See 25-13. Designs can be selected from those programmed into the machine, or custom designs can be created by combining different designs and adding lettering. Additional computer software can be purchased to give you more designs from which to choose. Some machines can be connected to your personal computer so you can design your own patterns, or you can use a scanner to copy a design into the computer.

An embroidery hoop must be used with machine embroidery as in hand embroidery. In addition, a stabilizer fabric should be used. The **stabilizer fabric** is placed under the fabric to be embroidered to support the machine stitches. It prevents puckering and tunneling, resulting in a smooth embroidery design. The stabilizer fabric is removed after the embroidery stitching is completed. There are several types of stabilizer fabrics from which to choose. These include the following:

stabilizer fabric
A special type of fabric used when machine embroidering to support stitches and prevent puckering.

- *Tear-away stabilizers* are made from a fiber that will tear easily. This type works well with stable woven fabrics. The excess stabilizer is torn away after stitching. Some tear-away stabilizers are available as iron-on fabrics. They are fused to the wrong side of the fabric before it is embroidered.

- *Cut-away stabilizers* must be cut from the outer edges of the embroidery. Some stabilizer fabric remains behind the embroidery. This type is recommended when embroidering ready-to-wear T-shirts.

- *Water soluble stabilizer* looks like a clear plastic sheet but it dissolves in water. After stitching, the excess is torn away. Then the work is placed in water to remove any residues. This type is good to use if all stabilizer fabric needs to be removed after stitching. It is also good to use when transferring designs for free motion embroidery.

Butterick Company, Inc.

25-13
The row of machine embroidery down the side of this dress creates a lovely and special look.

Placing the fabric correctly in the hoop is an important element for quality embroidery. See 25-14. Choose a hoop size large enough to contain the entire design. Loosen the hoop screw enough to get the fabric into the hoop without distorting it. Place the larger outside hoop on a sturdy flat surface. Then place the stabilizer and fabric over it, right side up. Set the smaller inner hoop on top and press down firmly to hoop the fabric. Tighten the hoop screw so the fabric is very taut in the hoop. Once the fabric is in the hoop, do not pull on it. This causes distortion and stretches out the fabric resulting in puckered embroidery.

Use a fine or extra fine rayon or cotton embroidery-weight thread for the upper thread. A regular thread can be used for the bobbin. A universal point machine needle is also recommended. Press the finished embroidery on a well padded surface from the wrong side.

Free-motion embroidery can be done with a regular zigzag sewing machine. A design is traced onto the fabric and the fabric is placed in a hoop. Set the stitch width at a wide zigzag setting (4 mm). Lower or cover the feed dogs on the machine. Remove the presser foot and attach a darning foot. Place the hoop under the needle and lower the presser foot lever. Place your hands on the rim of the embroidery hoop—not inside the hoop. Use a fast machine speed as you slowly move the hoop forward, backward, and to the side. Stitches should be close enough so no fabric shows through but the threads do not pile up. Outlining movements and fill-in movements are used to create the design.

Brother International

25-14

A hoop that contains the entire design is important for quality results. This computerized machine allows the user to select and view the design on an LCD display before it is created.

Knitting

Knitting is making a garment or article by looping and twisting yarn when using two knitting needles. A single yarn is looped off of one needle and onto the other needle.

Knitting projects make good products to sell because they are unique. Knitting items for yourself or to give as gifts can be fun. Sweaters, scarves, ponchos, and hats are popular knitting projects, 25-15.

Supplies Needed

Yarn and knitting needles are the main pieces of equipment needed to make most knitted projects. Most knitting yarns are made of either wool or acrylic fibers. Yarn is packaged in skeins that vary in weight from 1/3 to 4 ounces. Two-, three-, or four-ply yarns can be used. (Four-ply yarn is thicker than two-ply yarn.) The directions for your project will tell you what type of yarn and how many skeins to buy.

Be sure to buy all the yarn you need for a project at one time. All yarn that is dyed at the same time is given a certain dye lot number. You can be sure skeins with the same dye lot number are exactly the same color. Exact colors are almost impossible to reproduce. If you go back later to buy more yarn, you may have to buy a skein with a different dye lot number. It may be a slightly different color.

Knitting needles may be made of either plastic or metal. Sizes range from 00 (small) to 50 (large). They are from 7 to 14 inches long. For easy handling, choose a pair of needles that are size 5 or larger and no longer than 10 inches. When you follow printed directions, the needle size is specified.

Beginners should use single-pointed needles. Experienced knitters can create special effects and patterns by using double-pointed needles. Circular needles are used for making tube-shaped items, such as cuffs, turtleneck collars, and larger circular areas. These articles are seamless.

Reading Instructions

Instructions for any knitting project should be read carefully. Every word is important. If you skip over something, your project could be ruined. Underlining each step as it is completed will help prevent mistakes.

To make directions shorter and simpler, abbreviations are used. All knitters use the same abbreviations. Once you learn them, you will be able to read any knitting directions.

To make sure that a knitted item will be the correct size, a gauge is given. A *gauge* is the number of stitches per inch and the number of rows per inch. If you use the correct size yarn, needles, and knitting tension, a sample of your knitting should match the gauge given in the instructions. If it does not, the item will be either too small or too large.

Techniques

Casting on is the first step in knitting. This means putting the first row of stitches on the knitting needle. Your instructions will tell you how many stitches you need.

Knit and *purl stitches* are the basic stitches in knitting. Combinations of these two stitches form

Reproduced courtesy of Coats & Clark

25-15

These knitted ponchos are popular with all ages.

many patterns and designs. Other knitting stitches include the *stockinette, garter,* and *ribbing stitches.* To shape items, you need to know how to *increase* and *decrease* stitches.

Try not to put your work down while you are in the middle of a row. If possible, knit to the end of a row. Then push the stitches to the back of the needle so they cannot accidentally slip off the needle. If the needle is full with stitches, wind a small rubber band around the point of the needle. This will keep the stitches from slipping off the needle. A point protector can be purchased to serve the same function.

When you are not working on your project, roll your work loosely around the needles. Put it into a bag to keep it from getting soiled.

When you have finished knitting a project, you have to *cast* off. Stitches are looped together leaving a finished edge. The yarn at the end is knotted to prevent raveling.

As soon as you know how to determine gauge, cast on, knit, purl, and cast off, you can start a project. One of the fun things about knitting is being able to unravel your work and start over if you wish. You will need practice. Most people feel awkward at first. Try to establish good habits. Later, you will be able to relax and work more comfortably with better results.

crochet
Similar to knitting, but only one needle is used to pull the thread through a loop or series of loops.

Crochet

Crochet is similar to knitting, but only one needle is used. The needle is used to pull the thread through a loop or series of loops.

Many articles and garments can be crocheted. Projects made with bulky yarns and bright colors are popular. Scarves, hats, belts, afghans, vests, sweaters, skirts, and shawls are often crocheted, 25-16. Many instruction booklets are available for making these items.

Supplies Needed

The tool used to crochet is called a *crochet hook.* Hooks can be made of steel, aluminum, plastic, or wood. In steel, the sizes range from 14 (small) to 00 (large). In aluminum, plastic, and wood, sizes are designated by either numbers or letters of the alphabet. The smallest is A or zero. The size of hook you need is determined by what you are making and the weight of your yarn.

Any yarn can be used for crochet, from fine to bulky. Yarn is sold according to weight and ply. A thicker ply results in a heavier yarn. Buy all the yarn you need at one time to be assured it is from the same dye lot. If the dye lot number on all the labels match, the colors will be exactly alike. See 25-17.

Reproduced coutesy of Coats & Clark

25-16

Scarves are quick and easy projects to crochet.

Techniques

As in knitting, you must control your gauge so your finished project will be the right size. The instructions for any project list a gauge. Learning how to hold the yarn and the hook to get the correct tension will help you get the proper gauge. Measure a 3-inch square practice piece to determine if your gauge is correct. If you have too many stitches, use a larger hook. If you have too few stitches, use a smaller hook.

A *slip knot* is used to start any crochet project. The next step is to form a *starting chain*. A few basic stitches are used to make most crochet projects. These stitches are looped through the chain to form the first row of your project. Rows are looped through rows according to the instructions until the project is completed. By varying, enlarging, or combining basic stitches, you can make all other stitches.

25-17_____

Checking the dye lot number on each skein of yarn will assure you that all your yarn is exactly the same color.

Reproduced courtesy of Coats & Clark

25-18_____

String ponchos you crochet yourself would be popular with other teens.

Entrepreneurship: Profiting from Your Skills

You can turn your sewing and needlecraft skills into a source of income by selling the items you make, 25-18. An **entrepreneur** is someone who organizes and manages his or her own business. If this idea interests you, you have some decisions to make. First, you must decide what you will sell. You must also decide how much you will charge for your products and where you will sell them. These are just a few of the many decisions you will need to make as an entrepreneur.

What to Sell

In choosing an item to sell, you will need to consider what your customers will want to buy. Items that you make to sell should be unique and original. Items made from kits are not likely to sell as well as items you've designed yourself. People realize they can do kit projects themselves. Try to find a few items that you enjoy making and that you can make quickly and inexpensively.

entrepreneur
A person who organizes, manages, and assumes the risk of his or her own business.

Haan Crafts

25-19_____
Duffel bags sell well at craft fairs, especially if they are made in your school colors.

You can get ideas for marketable sewing or needlecraft projects from a number of sources. Start at a fabric store. Pattern catalogs are loaded with fun sewing ideas. Many fabric stores also carry kits, craft supplies, and how-to project books. These can give you ideas for needlecraft projects you might enjoy.

A craft shop is another place to get project ideas. Many craft shops offer classes. You can learn a new handcraft skill and make a project to take home with you. With practice, you can use your new skill to create products to sell.

Craft fairs can also give you ideas for items you might enjoy selling. Seeing products other people have found profitable may give you some thoughts of your own, 25-19.

Pricing Your Product

You must consider all of your costs when pricing your products. One of these costs is the cost of your materials. Be sure to include the cost of all your notions, too. Trims, buttons, thread, and even your price tags cost money. Even if you make your products from scraps, the scraps have value that should be figured into your sales price. Suppose you are making stuffed animals to sell. Each animal takes a yard of fabric, two buttons, and a yard of ribbon to make. Your costs for materials might look like this:

Fabric	$4.00
Buttons	3.90
Ribbon	1.00
Stuffing	1.90
Miscellaneous (thread, price tags, bags, etc.)	.95
Total	$11.75

Your time must also be considered when pricing your product. Decide how much you want to earn per hour. Carefully figure how much time it takes you to make each item. Then multiply your wages by your time to calculate your labor costs. This cost must be added to the price of each item. Suppose you can cut out and sew a stuffed animal in two hours. If you want to earn $6.00 per hour, you have to include $12.00 in the price of each animal to cover the cost of your labor ($6.00 x 2 = $12.00).

Your sales time must also be included in the price of your products. Suppose you sell your stuffed animals at a craft fair. If you sell six animals per hour, it costs you $1.00 in sales time to sell each animal ($6.00 ÷ 6 = $1.00). You would want to sell your animals for at least $24.75 to be sure to cover all your expenses ($11.75 + 12.00 + 1.00 = $24.75).

You may find that the price you must charge is more than most customers are willing to pay. See 25-20. If this happens, try looking for ways to reduce your costs. You may be able to find a less expensive source of materials. Sometimes you can save money by buying large quantities of materials. However, be sure you will use all that you buy before you invest in large amounts. You may decide to lower your labor costs. However, avoid working for less than minimum wage. If you find you are making only $2.00 per hour, you may become frustrated. This frustration may cause you to abandon your business. If you can't find a way to reduce your product costs, you may have to sell a different product.

Market Your Product

Once you have decided what to sell and how much to charge, you must decide where you will sell your products. You may have several options. Choose the one that you feel will be most enjoyable as well as profitable for you.

Schools, churches, and shopping malls often hold art fairs and craft shows featuring displays of handmade items. Many community flea markets also include tables of craft items. These events give you the opportunity to sell to a lot of people in a short time. However, there is usually a charge for booth or table space at these events. Remember to figure this cost into the cost of your products. See 25-21.

Another option for selling your products may be to market them through gift shops and boutiques. You may be able to arrange for shop owners to display items and take orders for you. You will have to share your profits with the shop owners. However, you will avoid the expenses of booth space and selling time.

You can advertise your wares through newspaper ads and posters on community bulletin boards. You can also create your own Web site. Word of mouth from satisfied customers may soon become your best advertising.

Some people do not like selling. They feel uncomfortable trying to convince other people to make purchases. However, if you like your products and believe in their quality, you will find them easy to sell. In fact, many handmade items are so appealing they practically sell themselves.

The McCall Pattern Co.

25-20

The labor costs required to make a tailored jacket like this one might make it too expensive to sell.

25-21

People who have turned their sewing and needlecraft skills into businesses often sell their products at craft shows.

CHAPTER REVIEW

Key Points

- Sewing and needlecrafts can be fun outlets for your self-expression. Using your creativity to make something can give you a good feeling. There are other benefits as well.

- There are several factors to consider when choosing a project. If you are learning a new skill, a kit project may be a good choice for you. Kits are available for both sewing and needlecraft projects.

- Patterns are available for a wide range of sewing projects such as sweatshirts, shorts, bags, sports equipment, and stuffed toys. Patchwork and quilting have gained new popularity in recent years.

- Embroidery, knitting, and crochet have been favorite needlecrafts for years. Machine embroidery is easy with the new electronic sewing machines.

- You can turn your sewing and needlecraft skills into a source of income by selling the items you make. If this idea interests you, you will need to decide what to sell, how much to charge, and how to market your product.

To Review

1. List four benefits of doing sewing and needlecraft projects.
2. What are three key points to consider when choosing sewing and needlecraft projects?
3. True or false. Sewing and needlecraft kits contain the basic materials needed to construct a project, but they do not include notions.
4. Give two guidelines that should be followed when making stuffed toys for small children.
5. Name two factors to keep in mind when choosing fabrics for a patchwork design.
6. Why should a fabric be quilted before the pattern pieces for a quilted vest are cut out?
7. What is the difference between embroidery and crewel?
8. Why should all the yarn needed for a project be bought at one time?
9. The number of stitches per inch and the number of rows per inch in knitting and crochet is called _____.
10. List three sources of ideas for marketable sewing and needlecraft ideas.
11. Explain how to figure the labor cost that must be added to the price of sewing and needlecraft items sold for profit.
12. What is a disadvantage of selling sewing and needlecraft items at craft shows and flea markets?

To Do

1. Ask students and adults who like to sew and do needlecrafts for a list of their favorite projects. Compile a master list from all students in class.

2. Write a one-page real or fictional account of a gift-giving occasion in which someone received a handmade gift. Describe the gift and explain why being handmade made it seem extra special.

3. Record the price of a sewn or needle-crafted item you see in a gift shop. Then go to a fabric or craft store and price the materials needed to make a similar item. Compute the cost of making the item yourself. Compare the costs and share your findings in class.

4. After completing a kit project, write a brief evaluation of the kit. Your evaluation should include answers to the following questions:

   - Did the kit include all the materials you needed?
   - Were the instructions easy to follow?
   - Did the project turn out as you expected?
   - Would you recommend this kit to a friend? Explain why or why not.

5. Visit a craft show. Give an oral report to the class on what you observed. Describe the types of products sold, the price range of the products, and the location of the show. Also describe the number and types of people who attended the event.

6. If you have embroidery sewing machines, scanners, and a computer program that creates custom embroidery designs in your classroom, offer to embroider logos and designs for clubs and organizations in your school as a fund-raising project. Review the section of the chapter that explains how to charge for your services. Profits can be used to purchase more software and equipment for the classroom.

To Think About

1. Compare the benefits and drawbacks of doing sewing and needlecraft projects.

2. What factors would you consider if you were selecting a sewing or needlecraft project for yourself? What project would you select? Why?

3. Why do you think there is a renewed interest in quilting and embroidery in recent years?

4. Is there a needlecraft that one of your grandparents did that few people know how to do today? What do you think is the future for hand needlework? Are they becoming dying art forms? Does this concern you?

5. Identify a sewing or needlecraft item that you could make and sell. Write up a business plan that includes an analysis of your costs and what you would charge for your product. Explain where you would sell your product.

6

Career Preparation

Chapters

Preparing for the World of Work

Objectives

After studying this chapter, you will be able to

○ define leadership and describe leadership traits.

○ summarize the skills involved in being an effective team member.

○ identify student organizations that help prepare students for the world of work.

○ explain the order of business during meetings that are conducted according to parliamentary procedure.

○ describe the process of getting a job, including finding job openings, preparing a resume, writing letters of application, filling out job application forms, and interviewing.

○ explain what it takes to succeed on the job and the best way to leave a job.

○ evaluate entrepreneurial opportunities.

When you were a small child, people may have asked you, "What do you want to be when you grow up?" You probably had a ready answer—a nurse, truck driver, doctor, or football player. That decision may have been made because you knew or admired someone in that career. Perhaps a television show or movie influenced you.

Now other factors will influence your career decisions. You are thinking about how your interests, aptitudes, and skills relate to various careers. You may be investigating how much education you would need for a certain career. You might also want to know what the payoffs would be through the years in terms of job satisfaction, promotions, salary, and fringe benefits. You may even want to think about how a career choice would influence your lifestyle. For instance, a job may dictate where you would live and what hours you would work. You may also want to consider how family life would blend with your work and what people you would meet through your work.

Right now, you may not know what career to choose. Depending on your age, you may have some time to think about this decision. You can use this time to learn about the possibilities that are open to you, 26-1. Meanwhile, you can develop leadership and teamwork skills that will help you succeed in any career. There are many organizations you can join now that will help you practice these skills.

26-1.
A part-time job is a great way to explore career possibilities and the world of work.

Leadership

A **leader** is a person who guides a group toward its goals. **Leadership** is the capacity to lead or to direct others on a course or in a direction. Leadership is needed for the successful operation of schools, businesses, cities, and nations.

Why is it important to develop leadership skills? They help you build your self-confidence and self-esteem. They help you succeed in school and on the job. If you have leadership skills, you can take charge of a project and get it done, 26-2. Others learn they can rely on you.

Leadership skills are necessary for a class president, football captain, or committee chairperson. They are also important if you work with classmates on a science project. Also consider a job setting. You may be asked to work with two other salespersons to design a window display for a clothing store. Leadership skills will help you accomplish that goal.

Leadership Traits

Leaders are often described in terms of their traits. The following are leadership traits you may want to develop. Leaders

- are self-confident and show a strong sense of responsibility.
- have good communication skills and can express their thoughts clearly and effectively.

Nancy Henke-Konopasek

26-2
Working on a project and completing it helps you to develop leadership skills.

- are enthusiastic and can motivate others to do their best.
- stress cooperation and set good examples. They do their share of work just as everyone else does.
- help their teams reach their goals.
- are flexible. They can accept change and can help others accept change, too.
- keep an open mind about decisions and situations and are willing to listen to new ideas.
- are able to delegate responsibilities. They do not do all the work themselves, but assign tasks to those best qualified.
- are good problem-solvers. They can identify a problem and consider all the alternatives and consequences.
- have the confidence to make a decision and carry it out.

teamwork
Individuals work together to reach a common goal.

Because the traits and skills of a leader are helpful in so many ways, they are worth developing. In school, you have the opportunity to lead in various clubs and organizations. Join one or more groups that interest you and get involved. Volunteer for committee work. Run for an office. The experience and skills you gain will prepare you for leadership roles as an adult.

Being an Effective Team Member

Emphasis in the workplace today is on sharing responsibility to get a job done. Teamwork is stressed. **Teamwork** means individuals working together to reach a common goal. Using the talents and skills of team members, work is done more efficiently, 26-3. Productivity is increased.

Team members have a wide variety of personalities and abilities. By recognizing and using the strengths of each member, the goals of the group can be accomplished. For the team to be successful, every member must complete his or her assignments. They must be willing to share ideas, listen to each other, and cooperate to reach group goals.

26-3
Humansville, Missouri, FCCLA members make a quilt as their annual fundraiser. This quilt raised funds for the relief effort following the September 11 attacks.

interpersonal skills
Skills needed to get along well with other people and to be an effective team member.

empathy
The ability to understand and be sensitive to the feelings, thoughts, and experiences of others.

The Interpersonal Skills Needed

To be an effective team member, a variety of **interpersonal skills** are required. These are the skills you need to get along well with other people and to be an effective team member. When you join a club or organization, you have the opportunity to be with other people who have similar interests as you. You will be able to practice your interpersonal skills. As a future employee, these skills will be of benefit to you.

The following interpersonal skills will help you in organizations that you belong to now. They will also help you be a better employee.

- Develop **empathy.** This is the ability to understand and be sensitive to the feelings, thoughts, and experience of others. With empathy, you are better able to interpret why people think or behave as they do.

- Show respect for other people's feelings and needs. Make requests rather than demands using a pleasant tone of voice and a calm manner. Be courteous to others.

- Be willing to give and take when differences arise. Respect the opinions of others even though they may differ from yours.

- Be able to accept criticism without taking offense. If you must criticize someone else, do so in a tactful manner that does not cause hurt feelings.

- Have a sense of humor. This is especially helpful when tension mounts. It improves relationships and allows communication to flow more easily.

- Keep a positive attitude. If you have a positive attitude, you tend to see the good side of situations and other people. You are optimistic, pleasant, and cheerful. You see life as worthwhile and enjoyable. This makes you pleasant to be around.

- Be honest and trustworthy. Keeping promises and dealing fairly with people are important attributes. Others need to know they can trust you.

- Dependability means people can rely on you. You do what you say you will do. If you say you will be at a meeting, you are there. If you say you will take on a certain responsibility, you can be counted on to complete the task.

Communication Skills

For both leaders and team members, communication skills are important. They will help you in your personal relationships and in the groups you join. When you enter the world of work, they will be an important factor in your career success.

communication
The process of exchanging thoughts, ideas, or information with others.

Communication is the process of exchanging thoughts, ideas, or information with others. As a worker, you may communicate with supervisors, coworkers, and customers. You may write letters, answer phone calls, or speak to clients. As a member of a student organization, you will communicate with fellow club members, committee members, or officers. You might need to share information on club activities or give a committee report at a club meeting. In either setting, it is important that all messages are understood and interpreted correctly.

There are two ways of communicating. **Verbal communication** involves using words—speaking or writing. **Nonverbal communication** involves sending messages without words. The way a person looks, acts, and reacts all communicate nonverbal messages. Both forms may be used together to communicate a single message.

Verbal Communication

Verbal communication is used to send a message between two or more people. With any form of verbal communication, there is a sender and a receiver. The *sender* begins the process by initiating a conversation, phone call, letter, or e-mail message. The *receiver* is the one who receives the message and interprets it. The communication process is completed when the receiver responds to the message with an accurate interpretation or response. See 26-4.

Most communications involve a speaker and a listener. Both play an important role in making sure the communication process is completed. Speakers must provide clear and accurate messages. Listeners must stay attentive and focused. Remember that listening and hearing are not the same. You hear with your ears, but you have to use your brain in order to listen.

To make sure your verbal messages are received accurately, follow the tips in 26-5. Likewise, to be a good listener, follow the tips for listeners. Poor listening habits at work can be costly to employers. Mistakes and misunderstandings can lead to lost productivity and dissatisfied customers.

verbal communication
Communication that uses words—speaking or writing.

nonverbal communication
Sending messages through facial expressions and actions without using words.

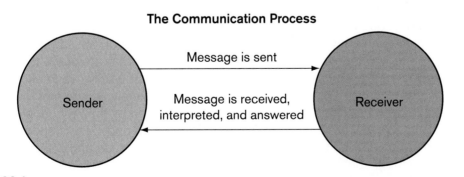

26-4
In the communication process, both sender and receiver must communicate clearly.

IMPROVING YOUR COMMUNICATION **SKILLS**

Tips for Improving Your Speaking Skills	Tips for Improving Your Listening Skills
✓ Speak slowly, clearly, and distinctly. Avoid running words together.	✓ Pay attention to the speaker. Stop talking, remove any distractions, and stay focused.
✓ Establish eye contact and speak to the listener.	✓ Use eye contact and body language to show you are interested.
✓ Use a friendly, courteous tone in an upbeat and positive manner.	✓ Empathize with the speaker by trying to understand his or her point of view.
✓ Be respectful and considerate of listeners' feelings. Avoid hurtful comments or talking down to a person.	✓ Be patient. Allow the speaker time to make his or her point.
✓ Use words with precise, familiar meanings. Avoid the use of slang.	✓ Do not interrupt the speaker.
✓ Keep your messages short and to the point.	✓ Do not let your mind race ahead of the speaker. You will lose the speaker's train of thought.
✓ Make your points in order.	✓ Ask questions that show you are receiving and understanding the message in the two-way communication process.
✓ Pause before you begin new thoughts.	✓ Reflect back to the speaker what you think was said. This allows the speaker to see if the message was misinterpreted.
✓ Build on your listeners' past knowledge and lead them from there.	✓ Listen to the speaker's tone of voice. Sometimes the way something is said is as important as what is said.
✓ Ask questions to be sure your message is being interpreted correctly.	✓ Give nonverbal feedback by nodding and smiling.

26-5

Follow these tips to improve both your speaking and listening skills.

Nonverbal Communication

The nonverbal messages people send are also important to understand. Body language is the use of body movements, such as facial expressions and body gestures, to convey messages. Your message is interpreted by what others see. Sometimes you may be aware of the messages you are sending through your body language. You may even send intentional signals. At other times, you may be completely unaware of the messages you are sending. You may even be shocked by the way people react sometimes. Then there are moments when your body reacts spontaneously, such as when you receive good news and jump up and scream.

Everything about you sends signals—the way you sit, the way you stand, the way you hold your arms, and what you do with your hands. Your facial expressions are especially revealing. You can look happy, sad, interested, bored, excited, silly, angry, worried, or confused. Even though your words may be saying one thing, your body language could be sending an entirely different message.

Your overall appearance is another important part of nonverbal communication. Your clothes and your appearance send the first message to people you meet for the first time. Before you say anything, your appearance speaks for you. What is the message you are sending? If you want to make the best possible first impression, such as for a job interview, take a close look at yourself in the mirror. What is the message your appearance is sending? Is it what you want to say? If not, begin making changes in those areas where improvements can be made.

Student Organizations

Many opportunities for leadership and teamwork experience are available in student organizations. Each club needs members who are willing to work for the good of the club. Only a few can be officers, but everyone can take an active role. Everyone can attend meetings, learn parliamentary procedure, and participate in club activities. Everyone should have an opportunity to serve on a committee at least once a year. All members can work toward the development of leadership traits and interpersonal skills.

Although any organization can be beneficial, career and technical student organizations have extra advantages. They help students learn about career opportunities in various fields. Your school may already have a student organization that is related to your career interests. If not, one can be started with your school's approval. The following organizations offer opportunities for participation at local, state, and national levels.

Family, Career and Community Leaders of America

26-6--
Participation in FCCLA gives members the opportunity to develop skills for life such as communication skills, planning, goal setting, and decision making.

- *Family, Career and Community Leaders of America (FCCLA)* is available to students in family and consumer sciences classes. The focus is on the multiple roles of family member, wage earner, and community leader. The organization helps young men and women become leaders and address important personal, family, work, and societal issues through family and consumer sciences education, 26-6. Careers related to family and consumer sciences are also explored. Examples of these careers are fashion merchandising, clothing services, food services, and child care services.

- *National FFA Organization (FFA)* is for students interested in the science, business, and technology of agriculture. It strives to promote leadership, character development, cooperation, service, improved agriculture, and citizenship.
- *DECA—An Association of Marketing Students* is open to all students in marketing education. Chapter activities help students develop leadership skills and learn more about marketing, management, entrepreneurship, and related careers.
- *Future Business Leaders of America (FBLA)* is for students interested in business careers. Its purpose is to help students choose business occupations and to develop competent, aggressive business leaders.
- *Health Occupations Students of America (HOSA)* is open to students interested in health and health-science related occupations. It helps members develop the traits necessary to become competent leaders and health care workers.
- *SkillsUSA* is for all students in occupational courses preparing for trade, industrial, technical, and health careers. Its motto is "Preparing for leadership in the world of work." SkillsUSA strives to develop students' social and leadership skills as well as their occupational skills, 26-7.

Clay Allen for SkillsUSA

26-7
These students are participating in a SkillsUSA national meeting. As members of this organization, they are preparing for trade, industrial, technical, and health careers.

Conducting Meetings

As you attend meetings of organizations, you will find that they usually follow the same pattern. Most groups conduct their meetings according to **parliamentary procedure.** This is an orderly way of conducting a meeting and discussing group business. Its purpose is to help groups run their meetings fairly and efficiently.

parliamentary procedure
An orderly way of conducting a meeting and discussing group business.

The terms listed in 26-8 are often used during meetings. Once you know these terms, you will understand what happens during meetings. You will be able to participate effectively.

The sequence of events during meetings is called the order of business. Most meetings follow the order of business outlined in Robert's Rules of Order, a well-known book on parliamentary procedure.

The order of business includes these steps:

1. ***Call to order:*** A meeting is called to order by the president or presiding officer of the group. He or she may rap a gavel and say, "This meeting will now come to order."

2. ***Reading and approving of minutes:*** The secretary reads the minutes. The president then says, "Are there any corrections to the minutes?" Any member may point out corrections or additions that should be made to the minutes.

3. ***Reports of officers:*** The president calls on the officers of the group to give any reports they may have. In most groups, the only officer to give a report at every meeting is the treasurer.

4. ***Standing committee reports:*** Standing committees are permanent committees of the group as specified in the group's bylaws. Examples include membership, program, and refreshment committees.

5. ***Special committee reports:*** Special committees are those that are set up for a certain purpose only. Once their work is completed, they no longer meet.

6. ***Unfinished business:*** Unfinished business might include motions that have been tabled from previous meetings.

TERMS USED IN PARLIAMENTARY **PROCEDURE**

Adjourn—To end a meeting.

Agenda—A list of things to be done and discussed at a meeting.

Amend the motion—To change the wording of a motion that has been made.

Chair—The presiding officer at a meeting, such as the president or chairperson.

Debate—To speak for or against a motion. Every member has a right to debate an issue.

Majority—At least one more than half of the members present at the meeting.

Minutes—A written record of the business covered at a meeting.

Motion—A suggestion by a member that certain action be taken by the group.

Quorum—The number of members who must be present to legally conduct business at a meeting.

Second the motion—The approval of a motion by another member.

Table the question—To delay making a decision on a motion.

The floor—The right to speak in a meeting without interruption from others.

The question—The motion upon which members are called to vote.

26-8
Knowing the terms of parliamentary procedure will help you participate effectively in group meetings.

7. ***New business:*** During this part of the meeting, ideas for future activities are discussed. Goals may be set, and special committees may be formed.

8. ***The program:*** This is the heart of the meeting. Programs are usually informative. They may be entertaining as well as educational. Worthwhile programs encourage current members to attend meetings, and they attract new members to the group.

9. ***Announcements:*** At this time, committees may be thanked for their work, or individuals may be congratulated for special achievements. Members are reminded of upcoming events of interest. The date, time, and place of the next meeting is announced.

10. ***Adjournment:*** To end the meeting, the president asks for a motion to adjourn, and the motion is voted on.

A Job for You

Many young people are choosing to have part-time jobs while they are still attending school. If you are one of them, you know how difficult it can be to find time for schoolwork, home chores, and friends, 26-9. Some young people feel they need to work in order to have spending money or to save for college. Others choose jobs to get some experience in a career field that interests them.

There are benefits to having a job. You can meet new people and learn new skills. You may be able to get a job in the field you are considering for your future career. That is the best way of testing your interest and ability.

If you think you might want to get a job, there are some factors to consider. You will want to talk with your parents about how your work will fit in with your school and home responsibilities. You will need to consider transportation. Will you be able to walk to work? Is public transportation available? Will you need to drive a car or have someone else drive you to and from work? You will also need to think about what kinds of work you would like to do and what jobs are available in your area.

26-9

When you have a job while you are still in school, you need to learn to manage your time well.

You will need to find out what types of jobs federal and state labor laws allow you to do. These laws place some restrictions on the kinds of work that teens can do. Once you have reached the age of 16, you have few restrictions. Employment of 14- and 15-year-old minors is much more limited. The work they do must not interfere with their schooling, health, or well being. To find out what your state and local laws are, contact your state's Department of Labor, Wage and Hour Division.

The *Teen Worker's Bill of Rights* shown in 26-10 was developed by the U.S. Department of Labor to help young workers understand their rights in the workplace. You can also visit the Department of Labor's Web site at www.dol.gov for more information on teen safety at work.

Finding Job Openings

When looking for a job, don't be bashful. Talk to people. Let them know you want to work. Friends, neighbors, relatives, religious leaders, teachers, coaches, and counselors may be able to help. They may know of job openings in your community.

Keep your eyes and ears open. Look for "Help wanted" signs in the windows of local businesses. Read notices on community bulletin boards in supermarkets, drug stores, and community centers. Listen to classmates as they talk about their jobs. If one has just quit a job, that job may be available. Listening to peers may also give you ideas about

TEEN WORKER'S BILL OF **RIGHTS**

- **Right one: It pays to work...and work must pay**

I have the right to a fair and full day's pay for a fair and full day's work.

- **Right two: Overtime work = Overtime pay**

I have the right to overtime pay (at least time and one half my regular rate of pay) for every hour I work beyond 40 hours a week, with some exemptions.

- **Right three: Safety is part of the job**

I have the right to a safe workplace and the right to file a complaint if the job is unsafe. I have the right to required safety clothing, equipment, and training. If I am under 18, I am prohibited from certain tasks.

- **Right four: No harassment hassles**

I have the right to equal employment opportunity without regard to race, color, religion, sex, national origin, or disability in an environment free of sexual and physical harassment.

26-10

If you are a young worker, know your rights according to the U.S. Department of Labor.

Help Wanted

BRIDAL SHOP: Part time help needed. Experience with bridal and better making a must. Flexible hours, days or evenings, for ★Presser ★Alterations ★Sales Apply in person Monday thru Friday, 11am to 5pm, no calls.
Mademoiselle Of Munster

CUTTER
Exp'd work clothing, Wheeler. 4330 W. Belmont

Designer
PRODUCT DESIGN

Craft product distributor - immediate opening - sewing and pattern making a must. Craft knowledge, 3 dimensional art, good writing skills and tole painting a plus. Ideal for recent college graduate. Samples required. Non smokers only. Send resume or call Joanne, Monday-Friday 9-1 at:

FIBRE CRAFT
MATERIALS CORP.
equal opportunity employer m/f

DRY CLEANING
Experienced in prespotting, dry cleaning and pressing. Call Ray collect:
Day: Eves:

PART TIME
• 20-25 hours per week
• Merchandise costume jewelry displays
• 1 Person Northbrook, Deerfield, Wheeling area.
• 1 Person Oaklawn area.
• Flexible hours
• No weekends, evenings or sales required
• Competitive hourly wage
• Organized, self-motivated, fashion minded person with dependable transportation
• Retail experience helpful
• Local Interviews
SUPERIOR JEWELRY CO.
Established 1939
Monday, October 26
8 a.m. - 4 p.m.
EEO M/F

Retail
★★★★★★★★★★★
●ASST. MANAGER●
SPECIALTY STORE
FASHION SPORTSWEAR
FOR MEN AND WOMEN

If you're interested in contemporary fashion and have supervisory ready-to wear exp., we'd like to talk to you!

COMPETITIVE SALARY
FULL BENEFITS PACKAGE
OPPT'Y. FOR GROWTH

★★★★★★★★★★★

Retail
LOOMCRAFT
Home Decorating Fabrics
is looking for full and part time employees to fill positions in our new stores. Fabric and design experience helpful.

Retail
MANAGEMENT

LADIES APPAREL

In line with our continuous expansion and current new store openings, we welcome experienced specialty shop retailers. Quick thinking individuals who are dedicated to customer service, able to set priorities and inspire others.

City and suburban locations.

Retail
DEPARTMENT STORE MANAGER

LOOKING FOR A NEW CHALLENGE?

Local specialty department store looking for an experienced Store Manager. Candidate must have:
• Strong quality retail background dealing with men's, women's and children's merchandise
• A minimum of 2 years retail experience as a Store Manager
• Volume responsibility for at least $10 million
Competitive salary and benefits package. Qualified candidate please send resume with salary history to:
P.O. Box
Chicago, Il. 60680
equal opportunity employer m/f

Retail **SHOE SALES**

We seek an experienced shoe sales person to sell top quality men's footwear in our FLAGSHIP Loop location.

Join a prestigious men's wear retailer with top benefits and earning opportunity.

CAPPER & CAPPER

ROBERT BUTLER
A HARTMARX COMPANY
equal opportunity employer

RETAIL SALES
FULL & PART TIME
COACH LEATHERWARE, the distinctive manufacturer of quality leather goods, is looking for bright, responsible people with a strong sense of classic style to join our staff at our new store opening in the OAKBROOK TERRACE SHOPPING CENTER. Most important is an appreciation & understanding of our customers, and a desire to serve them.
CALL
The COACH STORE
equal opportunity employer m/f

TAILOR/FITTER
FULL AND PART TIME.
HOURS FLEX. GOOD PAY.
Chicago. Prospect Hts. Darien.
CALL FOR APPOINTMENT.

26-11 ——————————————————————
The classified ads in your local newspaper can be a source of job leads.

where you would like to work. Some jobs are better than others. You may want to apply for these jobs even if there are no immediate openings. You could fill out a job application and ask to be called when a job is available.

The classified ads (want ads) in local newspapers are another source of information about job openings. See 26-11. They give brief descriptions of all kinds of available jobs. If you see an ad that interests you, respond quickly. Job openings listed in classified ads are often filled a day or two after the ads appear. Newspapers often post their classified ads on their Web sites.

Many people find jobs using the Internet. If you have access to the Internet, you can search Internet sites providing employment information and job listings. There are various government Web sites that provide information about the job market. Special job-search sites may list jobs by type, title, and location. These sites may list educational requirements, allow you to post your resume, and provide direct links to companies with job openings.

Public employment offices have been set up in every state by the federal government. They help people find jobs in and out of government. They do not charge fees for their services. Check the telephone book to see if the state employment service has an office near you. If so, you may want to go there to fill out an application and talk with a job counselor. If a job opening matches your interests and skills, an interview will be arranged for you.

Private employment agencies charge fees for their services. Either the employer or the job seeker pays the bill. Many private agencies specialize, dealing only with office workers, salespeople, accountants, or engineers. If a contract is offered to you, be sure to read it carefully. Know exactly what you are agreeing to pay if you accept a job the agency finds for you. Do not sign any contract until you understand all the terms of the agreement.

Preparing a Resume

Before you actually apply for a job, you will need to prepare a **resume.** A resume is a brief account of your education, work experience, and other qualifications for employment.

Your resume should help you make a good impression on potential employers. It should be short—just one or two pages. It should be neat, well organized, free of errors, and easy to read, 26-12. Print your resume on good quality paper. If your resume is sloppy or confusing, it won't be read, and you won't be hired.

An example of a well-written resume is shown in 26-13. It includes the information a company needs to know about the applicant. The information is organized under appropriate headings.

List the most important information first: your name, address, and telephone number. You want to be sure the employer can reach you to set up an interview and offer you a job.

resume
A brief account of a person's education, work experience, and other qualifications for employment.

Job Objective

After your name, address, and telephone number comes your job objective. This tells what kind of job you want. You can be very specific such as "Machine operator in the alterations department of a fashion boutique." You can also be general and write "A challenging position in sales." A specific job objective is great if it matches the job opening. On the other hand, a general job objective shows that you are flexible. Thus, you may be considered for more than just one job opening.

If you are interested in several types of work, you may need to prepare several resumes. Each could have a different job objective. Another option is to not include a job objective. However, most career counselors recommend including a job or career objective on every resume.

Education

Under this heading, list all the high schools, vocational schools, colleges, and other schools you have attended. (You do not need to list schools you attended before high school.) List them in reverse order, with the most recent school first.

Give the name and location of each school. Tell when you attended each school, and list graduation dates. Describe diplomas, certificates,

26-12
Take time to prepare a neat, well-organized resume.

Susan L. Wang
624 Pine Street
Irvine, California 92714
(714) 555-3674

Job Objective

Salesperson in a clothing store

Education

Woodbridge High School, Irvine, CA
Expected date of graduation: June, 2008
Related courses: fashion merchandising, clothing, general business
Overall grade point average: 3.5 (A=4.0)

Work Experience

Waitress, Garden Cafe, Irvine, CA, from March, 2006 to present; part-time during the school year and full-time during the summer. My duties include taking orders, serving food, operating the cash register, and keeping my station clean.

Wardrobe Assistant, Women's League of Orange County, February, 2006. As a volunteer, I worked backstage to assist the models in a fashion show.

Honors And Activities

First-place award in the "Young Designers Contest" sponsored by the Women's League of Orange County.

Member of FCCLA for three years; have served as vice president and as chairperson of the program committee.

Member of Drama Club for two years; have served as chairperson of the costume committee.

Member of Woodbridge Marching Band for four years.

Member of softball and volleyball teams for two years.

Interests

Designing clothes, sewing, swimming, cooking, photography.

References upon request.

26-13
Your resume is your advertisement of yourself. A well-written resume can help you make a good impression on an employer.

or degrees you have earned and major programs you have studied. If you received good grades, you may want to mention your grade point average.

Work Experience

Employers are especially interested in the listings under this heading. They know if you have had work experience, you have had to assume responsibility.

List your work experiences in reverse order, with the most recent one first. If you have never had a regular job, you could list volunteer work, yard work, or baby-sitting in this section. If you have had several regular jobs, list just those. Your goal is to show that you are capable of being a responsible, dependable, valuable employee.

For each work experience you list, include your job title, the employer's name, and the location. Also give a brief description of the work you did on the job.

The order of the sections on work experience and education varies. Sometimes education is first. Sometimes work experience is first. You should design your resume to highlight your strengths. If you feel qualified for a job because of the education you have had, list education first. If you have had valuable work experience related to the job you are seeking, list work experience first.

Honors and Activities

This section allows you to highlight your achievements. List honors, awards, and scholarships you have received. List school and community organizations to which you belong. Be sure to mention any leadership positions you have held. If you did not mention volunteer work you have done under "Work experience," you can list it here.

The name of this section should relate to the items you list in it. You may prefer to call it "Activities," "Organizations," or "Honors and Organizations." It should point out your accomplishments, but it should not be overdone or exaggerated.

Skills and Interests

Include this section only if you have skills or hobbies that you believe would enhance your job performance. Examples might be computer skills or the ability to speak a second language.

Personal

You are not required to give any personal information. By law, employers cannot ask you about some of your personal qualifications. However, if you think some of your personal qualifications might help you get the job, include them. On the other hand, do not include any personal information that would hurt your chances. Think of your resume as an advertisement. Be truthful and point out your best features.

References

Most people do not list references on their resume. Instead, they write the phrase "References available upon request." A potential employer can ask the job seeker for his or her references. Most will not do so unless they are seriously interested in you as a job candidate. Then you must be prepared to give them your list of references.

If you include references, give the names, titles (if applicable), and addresses of three or four people. These should be people who know you well and who could discuss your qualifications with employers. Do not use relatives as references. Former employers, club advisors, teachers, and religious leaders are better choices. Before listing someone as a reference, be sure to ask for his or her permission. Failing to do so would be rude. It can hurt your chances of getting a prompt and favorable response to an employer's inquiry.

A Portfolio

portfolio
A well-organized collection of materials that shows a person's abilities and accomplishments.

Starting a portfolio while you are in school is a good habit. A **portfolio** is a well-organized collection of materials that shows your abilities and accomplishments. Place honors or awards you receive in your portfolio. Also include news releases mentioning your name. Samples of articles you write are good to include. Also put in examples of work you have done that shows your abilities. Include your resume. Organize your portfolio attractively and place it in an attractive binder. You might want to make a table of contents. Some potential employers will want to see your portfolio.

Letters of Application

letter of application
A letter sent to a potential employer along with a resume to get the employer interested in interviewing you.

When you send a resume to a potential employer, a **letter of application** should accompany it. The purpose of the letter is to get the employer interested enough to arrange an interview with you.

A letter of application should be sent to the person within a company who has the authority to hire you. In large companies, this is usually the personnel manager. In other cases, it may be the head of a department or the president of the company. If you do not know the person to contact, call the company and talk with the receptionist. Ask for the name and title of the person to whom a letter of application should be sent. Ask the receptionist to spell the name so you are sure to get it right.

A letter of application should follow the format of a standard business letter. It looks best when prepared on a computer. A letter of application should be printed on good quality paper. It should be an original, not a copy.

A good letter of application is brief and to the point. Only three paragraphs are needed. The first should explain why you are writing. The second should tell why you think you are right for the job. If you are sending a resume, mention it here. The last paragraph should ask for an interview. A sample letter of application is shown in 26-14.

624 Pine Street
Irvine, CA 92714
May 20, 2007

Catherine Griffin, Personnel Director
High Fashions, Inc.
300 N. Main Street
Irvine, CA 92714

Dear Ms. Griffin:

The fashion merchandising course I am taking in high school has fascinated me. I would like to enter the field of fashion merchandising by working part-time as a salesperson at the High Fashions store in Irvine. The high quality and broad selection of clothes in your stores have always appealed to me.

With the knowledge I have gained in my class, I believe I could be a successful salesperson. My background and qualifications are described in my resume, which is enclosed.

May I have an interview to discuss the possibility of working for High Fashions? I can be reached between 4 p.m. and 6 p.m. at 555-3647. I will appreciate the opportunity to talk with you.

Sincerely,

Susan L. Wang

Susan L. Wang

26-14
A good letter of application should attract attention to your qualifications.

Job Application Forms

When you apply for a job, you will probably be asked to fill out a job application form. If so, take this task seriously. Employers often compare the application forms of several job candidates. You will want yours to look neat with accurate information in the correct spaces. A sample job application form is shown in 26-15.

When you fill out a job application form, use your resume as a guide. It contains most of the information you will need. However, don't expect to be able to substitute your resume for an application form. Most companies require all job seekers to complete their standard application forms.

Keep the following tips in mind when you fill out application forms.

- Read through the entire application form before you begin writing. Be sure you understand how to respond to all the questions.
- Look for specific directions such as type, print, or use black ink. Usually these directions are given at the top of an application, but sometimes they are at the end. Follow all directions carefully. Be sure not to write in sections marked "For office use only."
- Write as neatly as possible.
- Respond to every question. If a question does not apply to you, draw a line through the space or write "Does not apply." If you simply leave it blank, the employer may think you carelessly skipped over the question.
- Give complete and accurate information. Never lie.
- Be prepared to give the names, titles (if applicable), and addresses of at least three references. Be sure you have asked these people in advance for permission to use them as references.

Job Interviews

The goal of your resume, letter of application, and job application form is to get a job interview. The goal of the job interview is to get a job.

The job interview is the single most important part of the job hunt. It gives the employer a chance to ask questions about your qualifications, work habits, and career goals. It gives you a chance to learn more about the job and the company.

Preparing for the Interview

Since the job interview is so important, you will want to prepare yourself for it. Being prepared will help you make a good impression on the employer. It will also help you feel more relaxed and confident.

APPLICATION FOR EMPLOYMENT

PERSONAL INFORMATION

Date _____

Social Security Number _____

Name _____
        Last   First   Middle

Present Address _____
        Street   City   State

Permanent Address _____
        Street   City   State

Phone No. _____

If related to anyone in our employ, state name and department _____

Referred by _____

EMPLOYMENT DESIRED

Position _____

Date you can start _____

Salary desired _____

Are you employed now? _____

If so, may we inquire of your present employer? _____

Ever applied to this company before? _____ Where _____ When _____

EDUCATION

	Name and Location of School	Years Completed	Subjects Studied
Grammar School			
High School			
College			
Trade, Business or Correspondence School			

Subject of special study or research work _____

What foreign languages do you speak fluently? _____ Read _____ Write _____

(Continued)

26-15
Complete application forms accurately and neatly. This sample shows the types of information you may need to provide.

U.S. Military or Naval service	Rank	Present membership in National Guard or Reserves

Activities other than religious (civic, athletic, fraternal, etc.). Exclude organizations the name or character of which indicates the race, creed, color or national origin of its members. _____

FORMER EMPLOYERS List below last three employers starting with last one first.

Date Month and Year	Name and Address of Employer	Salary	Position	Reason for Leaving
From				
To				
From				
To				
From				
To				

REFERENCES Give below the names of two persons not related to you, whom you have known at least one year.

	Name	Address	Job title	Years Acquainted
1				
2				

PHYSICAL RECORD

Have you any defects in hearing, vision, or speech which might affect your job performance?

_____

In case of emergency notify

Name	Address	Phone No.

I authorize investigation of all statements contained in this application. I understand that misrepresentation or omission of facts called for is cause for dismissal.

Date _____   Signature _____

26-15

Continued

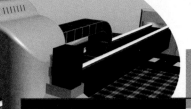

Focus on Technology

Technology and the Interview Process Join Forces

It's Monday morning and you're anxious to call about a job opening you saw in Sunday's newspaper. You call the 800 number given and find yourself talking to a computer! Welcome to one of the latest ways large companies are using technology to reduce the costs of recruiting and interviewing.

As you begin a job search today, you may encounter any of the following interview methods before you even meet someone from the company:

- *Telephone/computerized interviewing.* Applicants call an 800 number and respond to an automated set of questions for the position. Employers then download the responses and sort out those applicants they wish to call for a personal interview.

- *Computerized interviewing.* Companies use a computer to administer a structured interview of all applicants. As a question appears on the screen, the applicant enters his or her response. Printed reports are then generated, and the company selects the applicants to call for personal interviews.

- *Video interviewing.* A video camera tapes the applicant's interview at a prearranged location. The applicant is given a list of questions to answer designed for the specific position. Employers can then view the tape to evaluate the individual.

- *Videoconferencing.* Video equipment is used as an interactive tool between the recruiter and the applicant. A "live" interview takes place, but in separate locations. Interviewees speak to the applicants and maintain visual contact using monitors. The screens may use picture-in-a-picture technology so both parties can see each other. This method allows two-way communication, unlike video interviewing.

High-tech interviewing is here to stay. As you begin preparing for the world of work, also be prepared for these new interviewing methods.

The first step in preparing for an interview is to research the company. Try to find out the following:

- What products or services does the company offer?
- Who are its customers?
- How large is the company?
- What is its potential for growth?
- Are most of the employees engineers, accountants, carpenters, or factory workers?

Some information may be available in libraries. Check references such as *Standard and Poor's Register of Corporations, Moody's Industrial Manual,* and state business directories. People are good sources of information, too. Talk to people who work for the company or to people who know others who work there.

Also check to see if the company has a home page on the Internet. There you will often find information on the company's history, products, and employment needs, 26-16. Look for Internet addresses in TV commercials and magazine ads.

Once you have done your research, start thinking about how you might fit into the company. Prepare yourself for questions the interviewer could ask you, such as the following:

- What do you know about our company?
- What kind of work do you want to do?
- Why do you want to work here?
- Why should we hire you?
- What are your career goals?

You should also make a list of questions to ask during the interview. Like good answers, good questions show that you are serious enough about the job to have done some research. Ask questions about the job and the company. They may help you decide if you really want to work there. You might ask the following:

- How would I be trained for this job?
- What duties would I have, and what tasks would I perform?
- What hours would I work?
- What opportunities are there for advancement?

Avoid asking questions about wages and fringe benefits. Those are topics to be discussed after the job is offered.

26-16
Using the Internet to learn about a company is a good way to prepare for an interview.

Going to the Interview

First impressions are important in interviews. You will want to look your best. Strive for a clean, neat appearance from head to toe. Your hair should be clean and neatly styled. Men should be cleanly shaven, and women should be conservative in their use of makeup. Clothes should be clean and pressed. A general rule is to wear clothes that are equal to or a step above what you would wear on the job, 26-17.

As you go to the interview, take all the items you might need. These include a pen, a pencil, and a copy of your resume. You may want to take the list of questions you plan to ask. If you are applying for a job as a writer, illustrator, or photographer, you should take samples of your work.

There is one thing you should not take with you—another person. You want to show that you are mature, responsible, and independent.

Finally, be sure you have all the facts. Double-check the date, time, and place of the interview. Know how to get there and how long it will take you to get there. Be sure you know the name of the company, the name of the interviewer, and the job title for which you are applying. Allow yourself plenty of time so you arrive a few minutes early. That will help you begin the interview feeling calm and collected.

During the Interview

Begin the interview by greeting the interviewer with a firm handshake. When a seat is offered, sit in a comfortable position, but do not slouch. Try to look and act interested and alert, but relaxed. Do not smoke or chew gum.

Listen carefully to what the interviewer says and the questions he or she asks. Some questions require just a yes or no answer. Others require longer responses. Think before you speak, so your answers are appropriate. Speak slowly and clearly, using good grammar. Do not brag, but don't be bashful about your accomplishments. Be enthusiastic, but not pushy or insincere. Above all, be honest. It is never to your advantage to lie.

Be prepared to answer questions about education, work experiences, interests, skills, and goals. You may be asked about your best and worst subjects in school. You may be asked about your personal strengths and weaknesses. There will be questions about other jobs you have had and which you enjoyed most (or least). Be prepared to explain why you left previous jobs, and if you have ever been fired. Your expectations for the job and your plans for the future may also be questioned. You will be asked what you expect to be paid

26-17

An interview is your chance to sell yourself to a potential employer. You should look your best.

and how many hours a week you can work. Many interviewers ask what you plan to be doing 5, 10, or 20 years from now.

When the interviewer has all the necessary information about you, he or she will probably ask if you have any questions. This is the time for you to ask the questions you have prepared. After finding out more about the job during the interview, you may have some additional questions you would like to ask.

You might be offered the job right then. If so, you would need to know when you would start, what hours you would work, and how much you would be paid. You would also want to know about any fringe benefits. If everything sounded good, you could accept right away. If you wanted to think about it, the interviewer would probably give you a deadline for your decision.

In most interviews, the job applicant is not offered a job. Instead, the interviewer usually takes time to consider your qualifications as well as those of other applicants. The interviewer may tell you that he or she will call you on a certain date, or you may be asked to call the interviewer at a later date. If nothing is said, ask when a decision will be made. You have the right to know what to expect next.

Regardless of what conclusions are reached, end the interview by shaking the interviewer's hand. Thank him or her for taking the time to talk with you and to consider your qualifications. If you are seriously interested in the job, be sure to say so.

After the Interview

As soon as you have a chance to be alone, go over the interview in your mind. Make notes about the questions you were asked. Were there any that took you by surprise? Think about your answers to all of the questions. Which were your best ones? Which do you need to improve?

follow-up letter
A letter thanking an interviewer for a job interview.

Evaluating your performance during an interview will help you do even better in your next interview. It will also help you decide what to write in your follow-up letter, 26-18. The main purpose of the **follow-up letter** is to thank the interviewer for taking the time to talk with you. It also gives you an opportunity to fill in any gaps left open after the interview. If you forgot to mention an important fact during the interview, you can include it in the follow-up letter. Suppose you think the interviewer still doubts your ability to handle the job. You could explain in your follow-up letter why you believe you are qualified. The follow-up letter gives you another chance to state your case and show your enthusiasm. It keeps your name in front of the interviewer, and it may help you get the job.

If the interviewer promised to call you on a certain date, be sure you are available to receive the call. If you were asked to call the interviewer, be sure to do so. Suppose you were told you would "hear something in about two weeks," but two weeks go by without word. Then you have the right to call the interviewer and politely ask if a decision has been made.

624 Pine Street
Irvine, CA 92714
May 30, 2007

Catherine Griffin, Personnel Director
High Fashions, Inc.
300 N. Main Street
Irvine, CA 92714

Dear Ms. Griffin:

Thank you for taking the time to talk with me yesterday. I enjoyed learning more about your stores and the duties of your sales staff.

After meeting with you, I am even more enthusiastic about working for High Fashions. I am confident that I could be a successful salesperson.

I look forward to hearing your decision and hope it will be a favorable one.

Sincerely,

Susan L. Wang

Susan L. Wang

26-18
After a job interview, it is a good idea to send a follow-up letter.

Don't be too discouraged if you don't get the job. Few job seekers get a job after just one or two interviews. Try to maintain a positive attitude. Think of each interview as a learning experience. Eventually, you should be able to get a job that is just right for you.

Succeeding on the Job

Getting a job is the end of the job hunt, but it is just the start of a new work experience. It is a chance to earn money, but also to learn new skills, gain experience in the world of work, and develop a work ethic.

A positive attitude is important when you start a new job. Listen carefully when your duties are explained to you. Follow directions. Concentrate on your work so you will be able to do it well. Perform your duties to the best of your ability, without complaining. Once you can handle your job well, watch for opportunities to assume new responsibilities, 26-19. That's how you learn even more skills and advance in the world of work.

Getting along with coworkers is a major factor in succeeding on the job. You will need to use your interpersonal skills, including the following:

- Be pleasant and courteous.
- Do your share of the work, and respect others for the work that they do.
- Show you are responsible by completing your assigned tasks. Look for ways to help your coworkers if you have the time.
- Use good communication skills. Avoid gossip, and learn to control your emotions. If you get angry, find a way to cool down.

26-19
This employee knows he can advance to department manager if he does a good job in his present position.

- Learn from your mistakes and accept any criticism that might come your way. If you do something wrong, don't try to hide it from your supervisor. Admit your error, and ask how to correct the situation.
- Be enthusiastic and show an interest in your work.
- Cooperate with your coworkers and set a good example.
- Keep an open mind, and listen to new ideas.

Getting along with your coworkers will help you enjoy your work and achieve success.

Develop a Work Ethic

As you work, you will develop a work ethic. A **work ethic** is a standard of conduct for job performance. Your concepts of fairness, right and wrong, and good and bad affect your work ethic.

A traditional work ethic is to give an honest day's work for an honest day's pay. Adopting this work ethic benefits both you and the company. The company gets the results of your hard work, done to the best of your ability. You get not only a paycheck, but also personal satisfaction. When you are a conscientious worker, you feel good about the work you do every day. Such pride and personal satisfaction make your work seem important and enjoyable.

work ethic
A standard of conduct for job performance.

Use Communication Devices Effectively

There are many ways to communicate in today's workplace. You have learned some important tips on speaking and listening. Almost 75 percent of workplace communication takes place through speaking and listening. You've also read in previous sections about how to write letters. Two other methods of communicating are important in the workplace—using the telephone and e-mail.

Telephone Skills

If you have a job that involves using the telephone, it is important to use good telephone manners. Your telephone manners can help or hurt your employer. You and your company may be judged by your promptness in answering the phone, as well as your attitude, 26-20.

26-20
How you relate to customers over the telephone can impact the success of the company that employs you.

The following pointers will help you effectively handle phone calls at work:

- Answer the telephone promptly.
- Greet the caller pleasantly, and identify yourself and the company.
- Speak clearly and naturally using a pleasant tone of voice.
- Do not chew gum, eat, or drink when answering a call.
- Listen carefully.
- Write down the name and telephone number of the caller and a brief message. Indicate the time and date of the call.
- If the call is a complaint, remain calm and poised. Take any needed action, but avoid blaming others.
- End the call pleasantly. If you received the call, thank the person for calling. If you placed the call, thank the person for his or her assistance or cooperation.

E-Mail Skills

e-mail
A message delivered electronically from one computer to another.

In today's workplace, e-mail is an important method of communication. **E-mail** is the shortened term for *electronic mail,* which is a message delivered from one computer to another. E-mail may replace many office memos. Even communications between companies often take place via the Internet. An e-mail message may contain a few lines of text or several hundred. It can travel around the world in seconds in contrast to the days it takes a letter to travel by mail.

Though e-mail is often a less formal type of communication, when used in business certain guidelines apply. Your employer will expect you to use e-mail professionally, including the use of correct grammar, spelling, and punctuation. Follow the guidelines given in 26-21.

Leaving a Job

You will have many jobs during the course of your lifetime. Job changes are common today. Employee turnover is high for all age groups.

There are many reasons why people leave their jobs. Sometimes they leave for higher pay, more hours, or better working conditions. A change in their personal life can lead to a job change. Marriage, divorce, death, or the birth of children can create new job requirements. Some people change jobs to advance their careers, hoping a new job will lead to new challenges or better use of their skills. Others leave their jobs to further their education.

Before a job change is made, it is important to think through your options. Is this the best course of action at this time? Carefully weigh the pros and cons of leaving your current job for another job. If you decide a change is needed, start looking for a new job before leaving your old job, if possible.

USING E-MAIL AT **WORK**

- **Check grammar, spelling, and punctuation.** Your e-mail may be viewed as regular business correspondence, so appearance counts.
- **Be positive.** A positive tone to your messages will make them more understandable and also get better responses from the receivers.
- **Don't yell.** Using all upper-case letters is considered YELLING. Use upper- and lower-case letters, just as you would in business reports or letters.
- **Fill the e-mail window accurately.** Be sure to completely fill in the information for To, Date, From, and Subject.
- **Make the subject line informative.** A few carefully chosen words tell receivers what the message is about. The information contained in the subject line may determine whether the e-mail message gets read or is deleted without being opened.
- **Remember e-mail is not private.** Write messages that are appropriate for others in the company to read. Also remember that e-mail is not yet considered a legal document.

26-21

These guidelines should be followed when using e-mail at work.

There is a right way to leave your job. You want to leave under the best possible circumstances. Inform your employer before you tell your coworkers. Do so at least two weeks prior to your leaving. This allows your employer time to find your replacement.

A **letter of resignation** is appropriate in most businesses. This letter should state when and why you are leaving. It can be brief, but it should be positive. Thank the company for the opportunity to work there.

During the two weeks before you leave, continue to do your job as you always have. Return any office supplies and organize your workstation. Be pleasant to your coworkers as you may work with them again in a different job. Thank them for their help and friendship.

letter of resignation
A letter written by an employee informing the employer of his or her resignation.

Entrepreneurship

A growing number of people are choosing to be their own bosses by becoming entrepreneurs. The career paths of entrepreneurs are varied, as the following examples show. Sherry began cutting her neighbor's grass when she was a teenager. After graduating from high school, she worked at a local nursery. She worked hard and learned a lot about lawns, trees, shrubs, and flowers. When she felt ready, she began her own landscaping and yard care business.

Joel grew up in a family with four younger siblings. He enjoyed helping his parents care for them. As a teenager, he was a popular neighborhood baby-sitter. In college, he majored in child development. After working in a few different child care centers, he opened his own.

Rhoda took clothing classes at school and worked in the alternations department of a large clothing store for three years. Later, when she and her husband had their first child, Rhoda decided she wanted to stay at home with the baby. She opened up an alterations business in her home.

For some people, entrepreneurship is a lifelong career goal. By chance or by plan, they develop a hobby, a special talent, or turn a part-time job into a full-time career.

For others, entrepreneurship fulfills short-term career goals during a certain stage of the life cycle. Parents who want to spend more time with their children while maintaining a place in the world of work often begin their own businesses. When their children are grown, they may or may not continue those businesses. In other cases, people work as employees until retirement age. Then they begin businesses of their own.

The Pros and Cons of Entrepreneurship

Entrepreneurship has both pros and cons. On the positive side, people generally enjoy the chance to be their own bosses. They relish the freedom and responsibility this brings. They like the flexibility of controlling their own time. They also welcome the challenge of seeing how much money they can make. Entrepreneurs can control their working conditions. Many view the ability to work at home as a big plus.

On the other hand, the lack of interaction with other adults can be a negative. It can be lonely in the beginning if you are the only employee. You also have sole responsibility for the success or failure of your business. You risk losing not only your own money but also that of investors. You may not have enough money to pay yourself. Earnings can rise or fall depending upon the success of the business.

Beginning entrepreneurs may be frustrated with the length of time it takes to establish their businesses. They may have to work extra long hours to get their business going. Unexpected problems can also come up that must be solved.

Characteristics of Successful Entrepreneurs

Not everyone has what it takes to become a successful business owner. What does it take to succeed? The following are characteristics that most successful entrepreneurs have in common:

- Energetic with great physical stamina and the ability to handle stress
- Highly motivated to work hard and achieve goals
- Well organized and self-disciplined

- Adaptable to new situations
- Gets along well with other people
- A risk taker
- Self-confident
- Competitive
- Persuasive

Preparing to Be an Entrepreneur

Those thinking about entrepreneurship should work to prepare themselves. They should acquire some knowledge of accounting, business management, and business law. They need communication skills, decision-making skills, time management skills, and self-discipline. They also need a thorough understanding of the specialty areas of their businesses. They should discuss their ideas with attorneys, financial advisors, and business counselors. They may want to contact an office of the Small Business Administration (SBA). The SBA was established by the federal government to help people get into business and stay in business. It offers a number of different programs.

Entrepreneurial Opportunities Related to Clothing

Entrepreneurial opportunities related to clothing are varied. They can be either of two types: a product or a service. A *product* is something that exists, such as an item of clothing, which can be sold to customers. For example, you could open a boutique, specializing in teenage fashions, bridal wear, children's clothes, or athletic wear. You could make and sell hand-knitted ponchos, purses, and sweaters or embroidered clothing items.

A *service* is work that provides time, skills, or expertise in exchange for money. Examples include an alterations business or a dressmaking and tailoring shop, 26-22. You could run a laundry and dry-cleaning business. Another option is a wardrobe consulting business. You could help people plan and build wardrobes to meet their business, social, and leisure needs. The possibilities are many and varied. That's what makes the idea of entrepreneurship so intriguing.

26-22
This woman has used her weaving skills to develop her own specialized business.

CHAPTER REVIEW

Key Points

- Leadership is the capacity to lead or to direct others on a course or in a direction. Leaders are often described in terms of their traits.

- Emphasis in the workplace today is on teamwork. Using the talents and skills of team members, work is done more efficiently. Interpersonal skills and communication skills are necessary for teams to accomplish their goals.

- Many opportunities for leadership and teamwork experience are available by joining career and technical student organizations.

- Most groups conduct their meetings according to parliamentary procedure. This is an orderly way of conducting a meeting and discussing group business.

- Many young people seek part-time jobs while they are still in school. They need to know how to find job openings, prepare a resume, write a letter of application, fill out a job application form, and interview for a job.

- A positive attitude is important when you start a new job. Listen carefully when your duties are explained to you. Learn to use the telephone and e-mail as your employer recommends.

- There is a right way to leave a job. You want to leave under the best possible circumstances.

- A growing number of people are choosing to be their own bosses. They are known as entrepreneurs. They organize, manage, and assume the risks of their own businesses.

To Review

1. Name five leadership traits.
2. Describe three interpersonal skills that will help you be an effective team member.
3. What are the full names of the following organizations?
   A. FCCLA
   B. FFA
   C. FBLA
   D. HOSA
4. Name one advantage and one disadvantage of having a job while going to school.
5. What is the purpose of the job objective on a resume?
6. To whom should a letter of application be sent?
7. List three steps in preparing for an interview.
8. What are two purposes of the follow-up letter?
9. A traditional work ethic is to give an _____ for an _____.
10. True or false. Because e-mail is a less formal type of business communication, the rules of grammar and punctuation are not as important.
11. State two recommended practices for leaving a job.
12. What are two advantages and two disadvantages of entrepreneurship?

To Do

1. Work in small groups to prepare skits showing leadership and interpersonal skills being used in school or job settings.

2. Choose a historical figure who was considered to be a great leader. Research and write a paper describing the traits that made this person a famous leader.

3. Estimate the amount of time you spend using each of the following forms of communication in an average day: reading, writing, speaking, and listening. Research to find out what studies show to be the average communication usage in the workplace. Compare and contrast your estimates with the research studies.

4. Find out what career and technical student organizations are available in your school. Ask a representative from each organization to tell your class about the group's activities and goals.

5. Conduct a meeting according to parliamentary procedure. Plan ahead so you have the necessary officers and committee chairpersons, business to discuss, and a program.

6. As a class, discuss the pros and cons of having a job while going to school.

7. Look in the want ads to find a job opening that appeals to you. Prepare a resume with that job in mind. Write a letter of application. (Whether or not you send it and actually apply for the job is up to you.) Prepare for an interview for the job, and write a follow-up letter.

8. Write a description of the "ideal" employee from an employer's point of view.

9. Ask three entrepreneurs in your community to talk to your class about their experiences in establishing their own businesses.

10. Design a bulletin board on the theme *Entrepreneurial Opportunities Related to Clothing.*

To Think About

1. Make a list of ten characteristics of a good leader. Then rank them in order from the most important characteristic to the least important. Be prepared to defend your ranking.

2. Why is trust important for effective teamwork? How would you describe a trustworthy person?

3. What can you learn from being a member of a student organization that you cannot learn in the classroom?

4. Why do teens you know have part-time jobs today? Do you think these are good reasons for working while still in school? What sacrifices do they make in order to hold jobs? Do the benefits outweigh the sacrifices?

5. Do you think it is important to use proper grammar, spelling, and punctuation when sending e-mail messages? Is it more or less important than when writing letters?

Careers
in Textiles
and Apparel

Objectives

After studying this chapter, you will be able to

- describe careers in the textile industry, apparel production, and fashion merchandising.
- state the preparation requirements and personal traits needed for these careers.
- list questions to ask yourself when choosing a career.
- give examples of how to manage multiple roles.

Key Terms

job
career
research
development
marketing
wholesale
retail
custom-made
commission
dual-career
 families

Do you love clothes? Are you always eager to see what the new fashions will be for the next season? Are you fascinated by fibers that can be made into thousands of items from bridal gowns to bulletproof vests? If so, a career in the exciting, creative field of textiles and clothing could be for you, 27-1.

As you read this chapter, you will find the terms *job* and *career* used frequently. What is the difference between these two terms? A **job** refers to a group of tasks performed by a worker, usually to earn money. You might have a job as a sales associate at a fashion boutique or a job on the production line at a clothing manufacturing plant. A person rarely stays at the same job for a lifetime. Instead, a series of increasingly challenging but related jobs leads to a career. A **career** is a succession of related jobs a person has over a span of time that results in professional growth and personal satisfaction.

If you choose a career in textiles and clothing, it might be in one of three areas: the textile industry, apparel production, or fashion merchandising. Each is a separate field, but all are related to textiles and clothing.

The textile industry deals with fibers, yarns, dyes, finishes, and methods of fabric production. Apparel production includes the designing and making of garments. Fashion merchandising is concerned with promoting and selling new fashions. This means people are shown what is new in designs, colors, and fabrics and are convinced to buy them.

job
A group of tasks performed by a worker.

career
A succession of related jobs a person has over a span of time that results in professional growth and personal satisfaction.

27-1 ___
Many exciting and rewarding careers are available in the field of textiles and apparel.

The Textile Industry

A wide variety of job opportunities exist within the textile industry. As in any industry, production workers outnumber management personnel.

Many jobs require college degrees; others are available with a high school education. A number of colleges offer undergraduate and graduate degrees related to textiles. Such programs include computer science, management, chemistry, engineering, and other specialized studies. Technical schools, trade schools, and community colleges also offer training for employment in the textile industry.

Textile Designing

Textile designers develop designs for fabric, colors, patterns, prints, and weaves. In some textile companies, designers work at drawing boards to sketch their designs. Some designs are then tried on hand looms. Most designers today use computer design programs to create their designs, 27-2. Finally, the designs go into the production of fabric.

The difference between textile designing and fashion designing is important. Textile designers produce fabric designs. Fashion designers work with finished fabrics. They design garments and accessories for men, women, and children.

Textile designers must have a technical background as well as creative skills. They need to understand what machines can and cannot do in the production of fabric. They must also be familiar with the latest changes in finishes, dyes, and equipment. They need to understand production costs. In this way, they can be creative and still meet the needs of the company.

Manufacturing

More people are employed in the manufacturing phase than in any other phase of the textile industry. All skill levels are involved.

Textile plant operations include many processes such as spinning, dyeing, weaving, knitting, and finishing. Each of these steps requires special machinery, 27-3. The textile industry depends on the people who operate these machines. The nature of each job varies with the kind of machine used in the job. Most are operated by electronic or computerized controls.

Pendleton Woolen Mills

27-2

This textile designer for Pendleton uses CAD software to aid her in the creation of new textile patterns.

Textile machines must be handled with a great degree of skill and responsibility. People who control them must be able to operate them alone and without constant supervision. On-the-job training is generally given to these operators. A high school education is often adequate background for some beginning machine operators.

Some employees who use machines in their work are *spinners, colorists, loom operators,* and *machine operators.* They are usually paid on an hourly scale. Their wages vary according to how long they have worked and what machines they operate.

Machine technicians are responsible for keeping the textile machinery in good working order. They may be called upon to solve problems in every type of production machine in the plant. One day they may work on a large gear chain or the delicate controls of a knitting machine. Another day they may solve problems in a computer system.

Textile Engineers

Textile engineers play an important part in textile manufacturing. They need college degrees and may have to go through a training program to become familiar with the operations of the plant.

Textile engineers may have a degree in chemical, computer, electrical, industrial, or mechanical engineering. Each degree prepares engineers for different engineering jobs. A *chemical engineer* might work in a department where fabric dyeing or printing is handled, 27-4. A *computer engineer* might be sure the machines that produce the fabrics are correctly programmed. *Industrial engineers* are responsible for seeing that all the production operations are performed. They look for better and less expensive ways of handling production without reducing quality. Industrial engineers must be experts in work method, efficiency, and production standards. As materials are passed from one department to the next, they determine the pattern of workflow and what each machine will do.

Opportunities to climb the career ladder as a textile engineer are good. There are many areas where they may work, such as new product development,

American Textile Manufacturers Institute

27-3_____
This man is operating a machine that slits circular knit fabric in tubular form to make flat fabric.

Agricultural Research Service, USDA

27-4_____
These textile chemists are researching how to dye wool and cotton blended fabrics.

quality control, or project management. They might move from one area to another. In this way, other manufacturing processes will become familiar to them. Then, they might advance to higher levels of management responsibility. As they advance, so does their value to the company and, thereby, their income. Some industrial engineers become plant engineers.

Plant engineers make sure that all systems are operating properly. These include machinery operation, heating, air conditioning, electrical, materials handling, and environmental control. They must be expert problem-solvers in all areas of production.

Textile Converters

Many decisions about the production of fibers, yarns, and fabrics are the responsibilities of *textile converters.* They decide what fibers to use, what widths and weights of fabrics to weave or knit, and how many yards to produce. They select dye colors and choose finishes that will help the fabrics perform as expected.

Setting prices is another task of textile converters. This is known as "costing the fabric." All the costs involved in producing the fabric are computed. Then a margin of profit is added to determine the fabric's selling price.

Large textile firms may employ many converters and assistant converters. Each might be a specialist in certain types of fabrics for a particular market. For example, fabrics produced for a manufacturer of children's clothing must be strong and durable. Fabrics produced for ladies' scarves must be lightweight and delicate.

Textile converters must always be aware of the needs of their customers. They should be good at details and record keeping. Other valuable assets include good organizational skills, the ability to work under pressure, and good communication skills.

Laboratory Technicians

Laboratory technicians are trained to perform tests on fibers, yarns, and fabrics in a laboratory, 27-5. They make sure the products meet certain standards of quality. Machines are designed to test how well and how long a fabric will wear under certain conditions. Various tests are performed during many steps of production. They are done to assure quality control throughout the process, resulting in a superior finished product.

Agricultural Research Service, USDA

27-5

A laboratory technician is testing the effects of various dyes on textile samples.

Lab technicians complete textile technology programs in colleges or technical schools. They must be able to organize their own work and to follow precise instructions. They should enjoy doing detailed work, and they should be able to write accurate and thorough reports of test results.

Research and Development

Developing new products to meet consumer demand and finding ways to produce these products are important parts of the textile industry. **Research** is working to find new products such as fibers, weaves, dyes, and finishing techniques. **Development** means finding practical ways to use the products the researchers create.

A couple of examples will show how the process of research and development works. Researchers created finishes to make fabrics wrinkle resistant. People who worked in development found ways to apply these finishes on fabrics, and ironing chores were lessened. At about the same time, textile researchers worked on ways to prevent fabrics from getting dirty. People in development worked to apply the researchers' findings. As a result, we have soil-resistant carpets, upholstery fabrics, and garments.

Other products of textile research and development include space suits, inflatable buildings, and flame-retardant sleepwear. People in this part of the textile industry may also be asked to find ways to lower production costs. They may work to improve current machines and manufacturing processes or to design new ones.

A career in textile research and development requires education in chemical, mechanical, electrical, or textile engineering; physics; or textile chemistry. An advanced degree increases the researcher's value to the company and may be required for some jobs, 27-6.

In addition to education, people in research and development need certain traits such as creativity, flexibility, and dedication. They must be able to find solutions to real problems. They must be open-minded enough to find ways to improve quality, reduce costs, and increase efficiency. They must be dedicated enough to stick with a project from the original idea to the end result.

research
Developing new products such as fibers, weaves, dyes, and finishing techniques.

development
Finding practical ways to use the products researchers create.

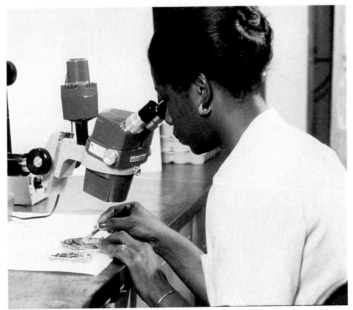

Manufactured Fiber Manufacturers Assoc.

27-6.
Advanced textile technology courses could lead to a career in research and development.

Marketing

Marketing is the process of buying and selling goods. Before fabrics can be sold, other processes take place. Raw materials such as fibers and yarns must be purchased. Manufacturers must decide what raw materials to buy and what fabrics to manufacture. They base their decisions on careful studies of what consumers want.

Market analysts are the people who study fashion changes and consumer demands. They tell manufacturers what fabrics will be needed for the new fashions. Their research is done far in advance so the fabrics will be ready when the clothing manufacturers want to buy them.

Textile salespeople are another part of the marketing division. Selling is the last step in the marketing process. Salespeople show fabric samples to manufacturers of men's, women's, and children's clothing. The manufacturers buy the fabrics they will use to produce garments for the next fashion season. Salespeople also sell their fabrics to fabric departments in stores and to fabric shops.

Marketing and sales are highly competitive fields. Careers in these areas often require a great deal of travel. They are exciting, but full of pressure, competition, and hard work.

Administration

Developing, producing, and marketing fabrics are the principle functions of a textile plant. However, for these functions to run smoothly, they must be organized and coordinated. The people who do this are called *administrators.* Some of their titles may include *financial managers, office managers, personnel managers, purchasing agents,* and *accountants. Public relations specialists, transportation managers,* and *tax specialists* could also be included.

The education required depends on the particular job. Advancement depends on a person's ability to do the job well and to get along with people.

Computers in the Textile Industry

Computers have changed the way many textile companies do business. Jobs that were once handled by several people are now done faster and more easily by one person and a computer.

Textile designers use computers to develop their designs, 27-7. Machines that weave or knit are operated by computers.

Fashion Institute of Technology

27-7.

Textile designers can view designs in different colors on computer screens.

Administrators of textile companies use computers to figure the costs of fabrics and to analyze and record sales. Computers keep track of inventory, shipping, billing, and payroll.

Jobs in *computer programming* require special training. Career and technical schools have specialized courses in computer training. A college degree in computer science or business administration would help you advance faster in the computer field. You would be able to design software as needed for the production of fibers, fabrics, and apparel.

Computer technicians are needed to repair computers. Vocational and technical schools offer courses in this area. Computer manufacturers offer training for the repair of their particular models.

Apparel Production

Apparel production includes all the people and processes involved in designing and making garments. Many career opportunities are available in this vast manufacturing industry.

New technology has changed, and most likely will continue to change, apparel design and production methods. CAD (computer-aided design) and CAM (computer-aided manufacturing) are computer-based systems. CAM is used in planning and monitoring garment production. Chart 27-8 lists some of the advantages of CAD and CAM in apparel design and production.

COMPUTER-BASED SYSTEMS IN APPAREL **DESIGN** AND **PRODUCTION**

CAD:
- Reduces production costs by reducing the time and numbers of people needed to make a pattern and prepare it for cutting.
- Increases quality and consistency.
- Enhances production flexibility.
- Reduces the reaction time to changes in market demands. More time is available for creativity.
- Standard details may be reproduced quickly.
- Drawings are more accurate.

CAM:
- Allows production of more work with fewer people.
- Operator efficiency is increased.
- Payroll information can be accurately recorded.
- Operation costs are reduced.
- Inventory can be monitored.
- Style data can be controlled.

27-8
Computer-based systems are changing design and production methods. This new technology has several advantages over more traditional production methods.

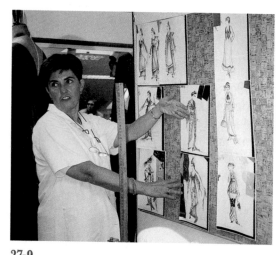

27-9

This fashion designer has sketched her creations, which are now ready to be created in fabric.

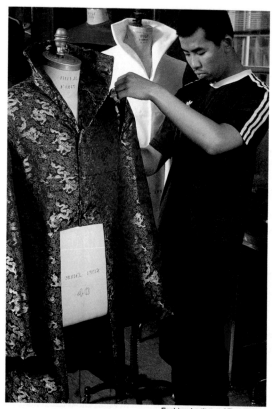

Fashion Institute of Technology

27-10

A sketched design is being "draped" onto a figure form.

CAD and CAM are growing fields. Many trade schools and colleges offer courses in these areas. However, in addition to CAD and CAM courses, an understanding of basic apparel design, pattern making, and production procedures is still necessary.

Fashion Designing

Fashion designers create new designs and ideas for new clothes and accessories. They may specialize in women's, men's, or children's clothing. They may specialize further in certain types of garments such as men's coats, women's dresses, or children's sleepwear. Some may choose to specialize in an accessory such as shoes, hats, or handbags.

Designers must be creative and imaginative. They must have artistic ability and a flair for clothing. They must be knowledgeable about fabrics. All the processes used in making fabrics and garments should be familiar to them. They need this knowledge to be sure the items they design can be produced within a given price range.

Where do designers get their ideas for new styles? Many designers get their inspiration from examining new swatches of fabrics from the textile plants. Many use museum exhibits of historical clothing, art galleries, and libraries as resources. World events often influence fashion trends.

A fashion designer is the first person involved in making a garment. The first step is an idea. Sketches are made until the designer is satisfied with one, 27-9. Then fabric is cut and fitted to a dress form following the details of the sketched lines. This is called *draping*, 27-10. Later, the fabric pieces are removed from the dress form and are sewn together by a *sample maker*. A live model then shows the sample garment to production managers. They consider the design itself, the latest fashion trends, and the costs of making garments from that design. If the design is accepted, the garment is put into production.

Many fashion designers today use CAD, computer-aided design, to develop their ideas. CAD can be used to create, modify, and communicate pattern designs. Using a computer, a designer can change seam lines, move darts, or change darts into pleats or gathers. The designer can try different color combinations and different trims until the right look is achieved. A pattern can be plotted on a screen and then printed out, 27-11. The sample maker then creates the design.

Designers are generally expected to create two or more collections or *lines* each year. There is usually a new line for each season. In large companies, there may be as many as 40 to 75 new items in each line.

Designing is done for low, moderate, and high-priced clothing. Less costly garments are often copies of more expensive ones. For example, an expensive suit may be made of silk. The less expensive one in the same design may be made of polyester. Leather buttons and belts may be replaced with vinyl ones. Less expensive garments would require less fabric and fewer, less detailed steps in construction.

Very few designers get a first job as a top designer. They usually begin in another position. Eventually they move up into a design position. Some entry-level jobs that may lead to design are *sample maker, sketching assistant, sketcher,* and *design assistant.*

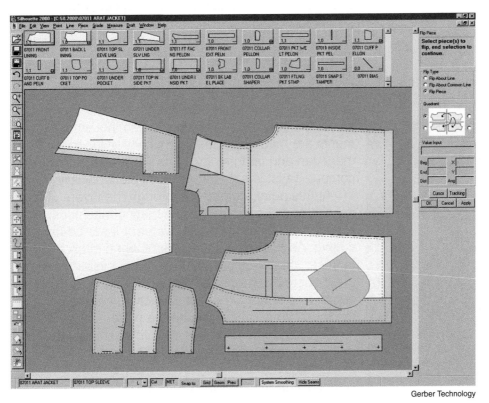

Gerber Technology

27-11
Pattern design is carried out electronically using CAD software. Revisions are done quickly and easily. All patterns are stored electronically preventing loss in the event of fire or water damage.

To become a designer, special training is needed. High school courses in art, clothing and textiles, computer science, history, and psychology would be helpful. Specialized fashion design programs of two or four years are offered in fashion institutes, trade schools, and universities.

The Production Line

The process of making a garment involves many steps that are performed by many workers. After the sample maker completes the designer's new garment, changes or additions may be made. Then a production *pattern maker* makes a perfect master pattern. See 27-12. *Pattern graders* take the master pattern and make it into a wide range of sizes. Each piece of the master pattern is reduced or enlarged to get the different sizes. Most manufacturers now use computer programs to create the master patterns and the various sizes.

After the graded or sized patterns are made, *spreaders* lay out the fabric on a long table. The fabric must be smooth and straight. A machine helps spreaders create many layers of fabric.

Markers are employees who decide how the pattern pieces should be placed so that as much of the fabric can be used as possible. When thousands of garments are made, saving a few inches of fabric per garment can add up to many yards. Most plants now have computer systems that can do this electronically, 27-13.

At this point, *cutters* cut through the layers of fabric with power saws or electric cutting machines. Newer machines use jets of water or laser beams for cutting. As many as 100 layers of fabric often a foot high can be cut at a time. If computer systems were used to create the pattern, pattern outlines are in the computer memory. A special machine can then cut the fabric automatically without a pattern.

The hundreds of pieces of cloth are numbered, gathered, and put into bundles by *sorters* or assemblers. The bundles are then taken to the sewing room. Here *sewing machine operators* sew the pieces together. The operators work as specialists in one specific task needed for each garment. This may be sewing on sleeves, making buttonholes, or attaching labels, 27-14. Sewing machines are often computerized. They

Fashion Institute of Technology

27-12.
Pattern making is both an art and a skill. These students are learning about this important step in apparel production.

Gerber Technology

27-13.
This high-speed plotter prints full-size markers on paper to guide cutters or to identify cut parts in automated cutting.

are designed to do a specific task such as making pleats or sewing on cuffs of shirts. In very expensive clothes, each sewing machine operator may sew an entire garment.

The sewn garments are given to *finishers.* They add outside stitching or any hand sewing that may be required to finish the garments. *Trimmers* remove loose threads, lint, and spots from the finished products. *Pressers* iron out the wrinkles and press creases and pleats in place, 27-15. *Inspectors* check the garments and send them to the shipping room. Here the garments are packed and sent to wholesalers by *shipping clerks.*

Many entry-level jobs in apparel production do not require education beyond high school. Because of the technical nature of most jobs on the production line, apprenticeship programs or on-the-job training is offered. However, training at trade or vocational schools could be helpful in getting a job or advancing to a better job. Knowing how to handle production equipment would be an advantage. For instance, special training is needed to operate the sewing machines used in production. They are much faster and more powerful than those used for home sewing. Someone with such training would be hired before someone without it.

27-14

The work of sewing machine operators is highly specialized.

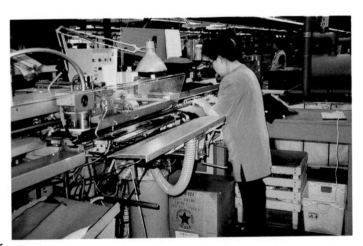

27-15

Pressers make sure wrinkles are smoothed and creases and pleats are pressed.

Engineering and Management

In addition to production line workers, other people have careers in the production process. These people may have college degrees in apparel production, apparel management, or engineering. Some courses required for these positions include production management, methods engineering, plant engineering, and managerial accounting. Good communication and problem-solving skills are necessary. These workers must deal with people with varied personalities. They must be able to give instructions clearly and accurately.

Positions in engineering and management include the following:

- *Production engineers* handle a variety of engineering projects. One such project may be a time-and-motion study. This study can determine how quickly and efficiently each step in the production process should be completed. These engineers also work with other production systems. They help select machinery and choose operation methods for top performance.

- *Costing engineers* determine the price of producing an item of clothing or an accessory.

- *Quality control engineers* develop standards of quality for garments and are responsible for seeing that those standards are met. They conduct tests of products at each step in the manufacturing process to check for quality.

- *Production managers* estimate production costs and schedule for flow of work in the plant. They supervise all aspects of production activities in the plant.

- *Plant managers* have total responsibility for what happens in the company. They are sometimes called chief engineers.

Marketing

Marketing in the apparel industry is primarily wholesale. To understand wholesale, you must understand retail. The selling of quantities of goods for resale is known as **wholesale.** Selling small quantities of goods to consumers is known as **retail.** In the apparel industry, manufacturers sell to retail buyers who represent shops and department stores (wholesale). Shops and department stores sell to individual customers (retail).

New fashions are created at least a "season" or six months before they are ready for sale in stores. After samples are made, they are placed in showrooms for retail buyers to see. The buyers order the styles and amounts they believe customers of their stores will buy.

Special fashion shows are often held for buyers. Models wear the new clothing designs to help convince buyers to order them. Fashion writers and fashion promotion specialists are also invited to these shows. They gather information about the new fashions. When they return to their home cities, they inform the public about the newest fashions and colors for the coming season.

As manufacturers receive orders from retail buyers, the clothes are scheduled for production. The stores will have deliveries in about three months. The clothes that buyers order in spring are in stores by summer so customers can buy them in time to wear for fall.

wholesale
The selling of quantities of goods for resale.

retail
Selling small quantities of goods to individual consumers.

Custom Work in Apparel Production

If you like to sew, tailoring or alterations work may be a career for you. Many people have their clothing **custom-made.** This means they ask someone to make garments especially for them. A desire to have one-of-a-kind garments could be one reason for wearing custom-made clothes. Figure faults that prevent ready-made clothing from fitting well may be another reason.

Tailoring is a form of custom work. Suits and coats are the garments most often tailored. It is time-consuming, but many people are willing to pay high prices for well-tailored garments, 27-16.

Tailors take a great deal of pride in their work. The finished garments look nicer and fit better than most ready-to-wear clothing. Fabric is often sold at the tailor's shop, which provides additional income for the tailor.

Many clothing stores hire an *alterations person.* Altering clothes can be more difficult than doing the original construction. To have a full- or part-time career in alterations, you must be able to sew well, work fast, and fit clothing properly. You may be able to work for more than one store, if the stores are small. Sometimes you can do the work in your own home.

Some duties of alterations specialists are

- deciding what fitting problems exist
- marking and pinning garments before altering them
- shortening or lengthening sleeves, hems, waistlines, and darts
- repairing merchandise that is damaged before the customer buys it
- changing trims or buttons to satisfy the customer

If you are considering a job in this field, take all the courses related to clothing and textiles that you can. Knowledge of construction techniques and fabric characteristics will be helpful. Specialized training is available in many trade and vocational schools. Steady employment is seldom a problem. Trained people in this area are in demand.

custom-made
Something made to the individual order of a customer or to fit particular specifications.

Fashion Merchandising

Fashion merchandising includes all the phases of buying and selling clothes and accessories. It is closely related to the field of fashion promotion. *Fashion promotion* includes all the efforts made to inform people of what is new in fashion and convincing them to buy it.

27-16_____
Tailors create custom-made garments for their clients.

Many people are involved in fashion merchandising and promotion. Some of their job titles are merchandise managers, buyers, salespeople, stock clerks, market researchers, fashion coordinators, display directors, illustrators, writers, models, and photographers.

The world of fashion offers many exciting careers. Backgrounds in writing, art, clothing and textiles, public speaking, psychology, and business are all helpful. Many careers require a college degree or additional training after high school.

27-17_____

Merchandise managers are responsible for overseeing the operations of one or more departments within a store.

Merchandise Managers

Merchandise managers are responsible for the operation of one or more departments within a store, 27-17. This could be women's coats, children's wear, or men's shoes. New shops within the store such as boutiques may be the result of creative merchandise managers.

Merchandising managers plan seasonal sales, promotional sales, and special events. Deciding what merchandise is to be sold and at what price is their responsibility. Long-range planning is necessary for successful events.

Merchandise managers work closely with salespeople to help them keep their departments looking attractive and up-to-date. In-service meetings and training programs keep salespeople aware of the latest trends in fashion and new methods of selling merchandise. The merchandising managers schedule these.

Merchandising managers are in charge of the store's buyers. They set the budgets for the buyers, which tell them how much money they may spend at market for new merchandise.

Long hours of work under pressure are normal for most merchandising managers. They must complete schedules and meet deadlines for their special events.

Merchandising managers often begin their careers as salespersons. They are often promoted to buyers before moving up to managers.

A high school education could eventually lead to a merchandise manager's job after many years in retailing. However, a college degree with a major in fashion merchandising, business, or marketing is preferred, and advancement would be easier.

Buyers

Buyers are responsible for selecting the clothes and accessories to be sold in the stores they represent. They may go to major fashion centers, called the "market," several times a year. The showrooms at the market display manufacturers' merchandise. Buyers order the items and amounts they want to be delivered to their stores. Buyers who work for large stores or chains of stores may travel worldwide looking for unusual merchandise for their customers.

In a specialty shop, a buyer may be responsible for all the merchandise sold in the store. Large stores may have buyers for each department. In a small store, the merchandising manager and buyer may be the same person, 27-18.

Keeping tabs on what customers are buying in their stores is a major job of buyers. Such records are usually computerized. Buyers are interested in what styles, colors, and sizes are selling best. The profits of a store depend largely on the decisions of its buyers. If merchandise is bought that does not sell, the price will have to be lowered, possibly several times. The store may not make any profit, or it may even lose money.

Buyers work closely with merchandise managers, display directors, fashion coordinators, and salespeople. Everyone must work together to maintain the image the store wants to present to the public. This could be as an exclusive boutique, a high-end department store, or the best budget-priced store in town.

A high school education is a must for buyers. Further education in a college, vocational school, or fashion institute is best. Business courses are valuable because of the budgeting and pricing that buyers must do. Training in display and advertising may also make a buyer's job easier and advancement faster.

27-18
Buyers are responsible for selecting the merchandise to be sold in stores.

Salespeople

Salespeople are important employees in a store. They often develop long-term relationships with devoted customers. They learn the tastes of these customers and inform them when garments they might like arrive at the store.

Salespeople are the only store employees that most customers ever meet. When salespeople are pleasant and helpful, customers are impressed. They are also pleased when salespeople can answer questions about fabrics, fashions, garment construction, and care instructions. Customers who are treated well leave with a favorable impression of the store, 27-19.

Good salespeople keep the displays of merchandise attractive. They receive payments and package items that are sold. They may also be responsible for handling exchanges and returns.

Many beginning retail selling positions pay a flat salary or an hourly wage. Some salespeople are paid a salary plus a percentage of their total sales. This percentage is called a **commission.** Salespeople may also get an employee discount on merchandise they purchase from the store.

A high school diploma is usually required for a full-time job as a salesperson. Many stores have on-the-job training as well as a short training period before a person starts to work.

commission
A percentage of total sales paid to a salesperson.

27-19
A salesperson often determines whether or not a customer returns to shop again in the store.

A degree in merchandising, marketing, retailing, or a related area will allow a person to move up the career ladder quickly. Colleges and fashion institutes offer courses in fashion merchandising, sales promotion, consumer motivation, retail store management, accounting, and business law.

Stock Clerk

A starting position or entry-level job in retail is often as a *stock clerk*. This is not to be considered an unimportant job. It is necessary for the smooth running of any business. Salespeople depend on stock clerks for many duties. Some could include

- receiving merchandise from the delivery trucks
- comparing the delivery tickets with the actual merchandise received
- checking for damaged items
- putting new stock items on records
- preparing price tags and attaching them
- placing merchandise in departments
- handling returned merchandise
- helping with inventory

A stock clerk could advance to the position of head of stock or into sales. Responsibilities and wages would increase.

Market Research

Market researchers study what customers want and need, 27-20. They survey boutiques, department stores, discount stores, and other retail outlets. They find out what is selling and what customers would buy if it were on the market. For instance, they may find a need for more athletic shoes or for brightly colored shirts.

This information is sent to manufacturers, designers, and buyers. It influences the textile industry and apparel production as well as fashion merchandising and promotion. A college degree in marketing is generally needed for this career.

27-20 A fashion forecaster interprets various types of information to determine what the public might buy in the year ahead.

Fashion Coordinators

Fashion coordinators work to promote stores and the stores' merchandise. They visit wholesale and retail markets to see what is happening in the fashion world. They relay the information gathered on these trips to merchandise managers and buyers. They also work with their stores' advertising and publicity departments. This allows the stores to coordinate their efforts in advertising, promotional events, and merchandising.

Planning fashion shows is usually a responsibility of fashion coordinators. They select garments and accessories from different departments within their stores. They hire the models and write the scripts for the shows. The day of a show, the fashion coordinator is generally the person who presents the show.

Classes for new salespeople on color, line, clothing construction, and clothing care could be taught by fashion coordinators. They might also offer classes on planning and coordinating a wardrobe to customers. Talking to students and members of community organizations about fashion trends may also be included in their responsibilities.

Fashion coordinators are sometimes called fashion directors, promotion directors, or fashion consultants. They work for magazines, advertising agencies, and mail-order companies as well as retail stores. Most have degrees from colleges or professional schools of fashion. A few have climbed the career ladder from sales positions. Successful fashion coordinators share certain important traits. They are able to work tactfully with people, speak to large audiences, and schedule time wisely.

Knowledge of fashion merchandising and broad retail experience is required for fashion coordinators. They must have a highly developed fashion sense plus imagination. They must have flair for fashion. They are expected to dress in the latest styles.

27-21

A display director designed this arrangement of men's clothing to attract the attention of potential buyers.

Display Directors

Display directors create the attractive displays you see in store windows, 27-21. When a suit or dress is shown, all the accessories to go with it are also shown. With a suit may be a shirt, necktie, handkerchief, belt, socks, and shoes. A dress may be displayed with jewelry, belts, scarves, and shoes. All of this is shown in a planned theme such as vacation time or the beginning of spring. You are encouraged to buy not only the main garment, but everything that goes with it, too.

The fashion coordinator works closely with the display director. They want to be sure the displays present the right fashion image of the store. Together they plan the total displays.

There may be several artists working with the display director. They must be creative and imaginative. Being able to sketch their ideas is necessary as they plan their displays.

A high school education is required. Courses in technical art, design, and fashion illustration would be valuable. Trade schools, community colleges, and universities offer these courses. Being an assistant could be a way to work up the career ladder to display director.

Fashion Illustrators

Fashion illustrators work for retail stores, pattern companies, and advertising agencies. The work of fashion illustrators is complex. In each illustration, they show construction details (seams, topstitching, trims), fabric textures (stiff, bulky, flimsy), fabric designs (prints, plaids, solids), and fashionable accessories (hats, shoes, jewelry). In addition, each one must be an attractive picture that will catch the eye of the viewer.

To be successful, fashion illustrators must have artistic ability, creativity, and an interest in clothing. They also need further education at a university or a special school of art or fashion. Courses they should take include art, clothing and textiles, history, and psychology, 27-22.

Fashion Writers

Fashion writers must keep in contact with manufacturers and key people in the fashion industry. Then they can tell the public about new trends in fashion as soon as they occur. Press kits are sent to fashion writers from manufacturers and advertisers. They include detailed descriptions and photographs of new fashions.

These writers work under pressure with deadlines to meet. They must be able to write quickly, thoroughly, and accurately. They spend much time keeping up-to-date on new trends and products. Almost all jobs for fashion writers require a college degree in journalism and/or textiles and clothing.

Large newspapers have fashion writers and editors. They show and explain new fashions to readers. Often they have a daily column.

Fashion Institute of Technology

27-22

These students are studying fashion illustration in preparation for their fashion careers.

Mail-order catalog companies employ many writers. They must be able to accurately describe an item using few words. Consumers are interested in knowing as much as possible about the fabric, design, and care of a garment before they order it.

Television script writing is an interesting career. The scripts may be for either general viewing or educational programs. In some cities, a daily fashion program is produced. Men's, women's, and children's clothing may be shown. Descriptive material must be prepared. Preparing educational programs such as sewing classes for television requires informational material.

Many fashion writers and editors work for magazines and trade journals. Often their assignments are in a specific area such as clothing, textiles, accessories, hairstyles, or makeup. A flair for writing and a keen sense of fashion trends are needed to be successful.

Pattern companies need writers who have a thorough knowledge of sewing techniques. These writers prepare booklets, charts, and videos to be used by marketing departments. They write instructional materials for patterns, including cutting and sewing techniques and directions. They also prepare educational materials for use in fabric shops and classrooms.

Fashion Models

Fashion models are needed in photos for press releases, mail-order catalogs, pattern catalogs, and advertisements. Models are also needed in fashion shows. Seminars, trade shows, and conventions are popular places for fashion shows. Some large department stores and leading restaurants also feature them. They are often held at mid-day for shoppers to see the latest fashions.

For models, beauty is not as important as posture. Their goal is to make the garments look their best, as in 27-23. A flair for effective movements and an outgoing personality are needed traits.

Most models are tall and thin. This is because clothes are more attractive on tall, thin persons and because photographs seem to make people look heavier.

To be a model, a person must be well groomed and have a pleasing personality. He or she must also be able to wear garments of a certain size without altering them. Modeling school is recommended. The opportunities in the field are limited, and the competition is keen. For those who succeed, the wages are high.

Not all models are in their twenties. A small number of younger boys and girls and older men and women model clothing. A few models begin their careers while they are still in junior and senior high school.

27-23
Successful models work to make clothes look as good as possible.

Fashion Photographers

A career in *fashion photography* often stems from an early interest in taking pictures. Those who specialize in fashion photography work to make clothes and accessories look their best. They are also responsible for suggesting creative backgrounds for photos as in 27-24. In addition to still photography, they often work with film and videotape for advertisements and promotions.

Making a Career Choice

A career in the field of textiles and clothing offers many options. Selecting one career path is not an easy decision. The following are questions you might want to ask yourself as you consider each job possibility:

- What does this job entail?
- What preparation is required for this job?
- Do I have the personal traits needed for this job?
- Is this an area that interests me?
- Do I have the skills and abilities needed for this job?
- Will this job help me reach my career goals?
- Do I like to work with people or alone?
- Do I like work that is repetitious or work that is continually changing?
- Do I work best in a calm, relaxed atmosphere, or do I work better under pressure?
- Would I like to travel or do I prefer working in the same place every day?
- Am I willing to start at an entry-level position, or would I rather obtain further education and start at a higher level?
- If I marry, what are my ideas about sharing household responsibilities?

By doing a self-study of your personal needs and wants and exploring your career options, you will be able to choose a career that is right for you. You will be ready for the challenges and rewards that await you.

Pendleton Woolen Mills

27-24 _____

The fashion photographer must plan and find interesting backgrounds.

dual-career families
Families in which both parents are employed outside the home.

Managing Multiple Roles

Throughout your life, you will have many roles. Right now you are a student, a son, or a daughter. You may also be a brother or a sister, a friend, a class officer, or an employee. Each role requires that you fulfill certain responsibilities. Sometimes you may find it difficult to fulfill all of your responsibilities. For instance, as a student you may be required to write a term paper. Suppose it is due tomorrow and you are not quite finished. A friend of yours invites you to go to a movie tonight. How will you manage your roles as a student and as a friend?

As you get older, you may take on parenting and career roles. In **dual-career families,** both parents work outside the home. Meeting both family and career responsibilities is challenging. However, balancing multiple roles can also be exciting and rewarding.

Striking a balance between these roles is the key. However, there is no magic way to do this. This is where management skills, such as planning, organizing, decision making, and being flexible must be used.

Decision-making skills are important. For instance, suppose you have a family. You value spending time with your family. You want to be a good parent and spouse. However, you are offered a position as a buyer that involves a great deal of travel. You may enjoy traveling. It may also help you move ahead in your career, which could help your family financially. How do you decide what to do? One way is to follow the decision-making method described in Chapter 5 of this text. (The decision-making skills discussed in Chapter 5 were in relation to making clothing decisions. These same skills can be applied to personal decisions.)

Balancing roles requires managing your time. Time must be distributed among several roles, 27-25. For instance, you will want to be able to spend time with your children as well as with your spouse. How much time will you need to devote to your career? How much time will you want to retain for yourself?

It helps if you can be flexible. Being flexible means that you are able to adapt to new situations. For example, suppose you and your spouse are working parents. One of your children becomes ill and is unable to go to school. Can you and your spouse make alternative arrangements at the last minute?

Whatever career you choose, there will be many challenges and rewards. Hard work and dedication are required. Enthusiasm and perseverance will help you along the way. The end result will be a lifetime of success and happiness.

27-25
Managing several roles for working parents requires managing your time wisely.

Job Hunting Made Easier Via the Internet

If you have access to the Internet, you have a tool that you can use in a number of ways to help you find that perfect job.

First, use the Internet to find out more about a career that interests you. Maybe one of the careers described in this chapter appeals to you. You can use a search engine and simply enter the job title. A list of sources for information about that career will come up. Other options are to visit Web sites that are designed to provide career information such as America's Career Info Net at www.acinet.org, sponsored by the U.S. Department of Labor.

If you are looking for a job, you can search job postings on the Internet. America's Job Bank at www.ajb.dni.us contains positions representing every line of work. For fashion careers, try www.fashion.net. You can learn about various fashion sites and designers, as well as current job openings. In addition, most large newspapers post their "Help Wanted" sections on their Web sites.

If you're considering a specific job, you can use the Internet to learn about the company. Larger companies have their own Web sites where you can gather background information. This can help you decide if you want to work for this company. The information gathered can also help you prepare for a job interview. Companies may also list their job vacancies on-line. The jobs are described and the company's e-mail address and phone number are often provided.

Another way you can use the Internet is to post your resume on-line on a commercial Web site designed for this purpose. Employers review the resumes posted and contact those people who might fit their needs. Usually, either the job seeker or the employer is charged a fee.

Though the Internet is another tool you can use to help you find the right job, the job search still remains basically the same. It will take effort on your part to finally secure that perfect job.

CHAPTER REVIEW

Key Points

- Careers in textiles and clothing can be grouped into three areas: the textile industry, apparel production, and fashion merchandising. Each is a separate field, but all are related.

- A wide variety of job opportunities exist within the textile industry. As in any industry, production workers outnumber management personnel. Many jobs require college degrees; others are available with a high school education.

- Apparel production includes all the people and processes involved in designing and making garments. Many career opportunities are available in this vast manufacturing industry, which begins with fashion design.

- Fashion merchandising includes all the phases of buying and selling clothes and accessories. It is closely related to the field of fashion promotion, which includes all the efforts made to inform people of what is new in fashion and convincing them to buy.

- Selecting one career path is not an easy decision. You need to ask yourself a number of questions.

- In dual-career families, both parents work outside the home. Meeting both family and career responsibilities is challenging. Management skills, such as planning, organizing, decision making, and being flexible, must be used.

To Review

1. What is the difference between textile designers and fashion designers?

2. More people are employed in _____ than in any other phase of the textile industry.

3. What information do market analysts provide to textile manufacturers?

4. List two places where fashion designers may get ideas for new garment designs.

5. Which of these factors helps determine the cost of producing a garment?
   - A. The type and amount of fabric.
   - B. The type and amount of trims.
   - C. The number and difficulty of steps in construction.
   - D. All of the above.

6. What is the job title of the person who plans sales, schedules in-service meetings for salespeople, and sets the budgets for buyers?

7. Buyers need access to records that show which _____, _____, and _____ of garments are selling best in their stores.

8. The goal of a fashion model is to _____.
   - A. be beautiful
   - B. develop good grooming habits
   - C. be tall and thin
   - D. make clothes and accessories look as good as possible

9. List three questions to ask yourself when choosing a career field.

To Do

1. Do an Internet search to find the names and addresses of textile manufacturers in your state. Then write to the manufacturers for information about jobs available, education requirements, job descriptions, and salaries, or obtain this information from their Web sites.

2. Create textile designs for a man's shirt, a woman's evening dress, and a chair's upholstery. Sketch the designs, or, if available, use a CAD program.

3. Select one career in the textile industry and do further research on it. Find out more about job qualifications, duties and responsibilities, working conditions, and wages.

4. Work in small groups to outline the creation and production of a garment. List all the people and all the steps involved in getting the garment to a manufacturer's showroom. Present your work in the form of a written report or PowerPoint presentation.

5. Create a garment design. Sketch the design, or use a CAD program.

6. Role-play situations in which salespeople interact with customers. Focus on how the attitudes and actions of salespeople influence the attitudes of customers.

7. Select a career in fashion merchandising or promotion and come up with a creative idea a person in that career could use. For example, as a merchandise manager, plan a seasonal sale. As a fashion coordinator, plan a fashion show. As a display director, design a store window display.

8. Research trade schools, community colleges, fashion schools, and universities in your state that offer courses for textile and apparel careers. Compare course offerings, costs, and other factors important in selecting a school.

To Think About

1. Which job or career described in this chapter has the most appeal to you? Why?

2. Computers are taking over more and more jobs in the textiles and apparel industry. Is this good or bad? Are there some jobs they cannot do? Explain your answers.

3. What is the difference between a job and a career? Is one career better than another? Explain your answer.

4. Review the list of questions to ask yourself when choosing a career. Why is each question important when making a career decision?

5. How would you advise someone to balance the multiple roles involving a family and a career?

Glossary

A

accented neutral color scheme. A color scheme using a neutral color combined with a bright accent color. (10)

accessories. Items such as shoes, scarves, legwear, handbags, billfolds, hats, neckties, jewelry, and belts; the items needed to complete an outfit. (4)

acne. A disorder of the skin's oil glands that results in plugged pores and outbreaks of lesions. (12)

adjustment lines. Two parallel lines that show where to shorten or lengthen a pattern piece. (19)

agitation. The action that helps to loosen and remove soil from clothes during the wash cycle. (16)

alterations. Changes made in the size, length, or style of a garment so it will fit properly. (8)

alternatives. Various ways to solve a problem or reach a goal. (5)

analogous color scheme. A color scheme using adjacent colors on the color wheel. (10)

anorexia nervosa. A disorder in which a person avoids eating. (12)

antiperspirants. Personal care products that control perspiration by reducing the flow of moisture. (12)

apparel marts. Large buildings in Atlanta, Dallas, and Chicago where many garment manufacturers have showrooms and sales offices. (3)

applied casing. A casing formed by a separate piece of fabric or bias tape attached to a garment. (23)

appliqué. Sewing one or more small pieces of fabric to a larger piece of fabric or a garment to add a decorative touch. (17)

B

backstitching. Sewing backward and forward in the same place for a few stitches to secure ends of stitching. (22)

balance. The arrangement of objects in an even, pleasing way; a principle of design. (11)

balance of trade. The relationship between the value of a country's imports compared to its exports. (3)

ballpoint pins. Pins with rounded points that are recommended for use with knits. (20)

bargain. A sale in which money is saved on items needed. (7)

basting. Temporarily joining layers of fabric together until they are permanently stitched on the machine. (22)

batting. The inner layer of a quilt, which is often made of polyester fiberfill, down, or cotton. (25)

bleach. A laundry product that removes stains and whitens or brightens fabrics. (16)

blend. Yarn made by spinning different types of staple fibers together into a single yarn. (15)

blueing. A product used to counteract the natural yellowing in some fabrics. (16)

body language. Nonverbal communication, such as facial expressions and posture; the way a person uses his or her body, such as the eyes, arms, and hands. (1)

body measurements. The actual dimensions of the body. (18)

bonding. The process of permanently fastening one fabric to another. (15)

bound buttonhole. A buttonhole in which the edges are finished with fabric. (22)

budget. A spending plan that can help people manage money. (5)

bulimia. An eating disorder where victims eat large amounts of food and then expel the food by vomiting or purging. (12)

C

CAD (computer-aided design). A computer system used to create textile and garment designs on a display screen. (3)

calories. The units of energy or "body fuel" provided by the foods a person eats. (12)

CAM (computer-aided manufacturing). A computer system used to control specific steps in the production of textiles and garments. (3)

carding. A process that pulls the cotton fibers from the lap, cleans them, and straightens them. (14)

Care Labeling Rule. A rule issued by the Federal Trade Commission that requires all clothing (except hosiery) give clear, uniform, and detailed instructions for care and maintenance. (6)

career. A succession of related jobs a person has over a span of time that results in professional growth and personal satisfaction. (27)

casing. A fabric piece that encloses a drawstring or elastic, which draws the garment snugly against the figure. (23)

cellulosic fibers. Fibers made from vegetable (plant) sources. Cotton and flax are the major natural cellulosic fibers used for clothing. (14)

chaining off. Serging off the end of the fabric until a 2- to 3-inch thread chain forms. (24)

chainstitch. A serger stitch that does not overlock the edge of the fabric, but functions as a standard straight stitch when the cutter is disengaged. (24)

chain stores. Groups of 12 or more stores owned and managed by a central office and carrying the same line or products. (7)

classic. A style that stays in fashion for a long time. (2)

clean-finish. A method of finishing the raw edge of a facing. Stitch 1/4 inch from the edge, turn under on the stitching line, and stitch again close to the edge. (22)

clearance sale. A sale planned when a store wants to sell items to make room for new merchandise. (7)

clipping. Making straight cuts into the seam allowance so that curved seams will lie flat. (22)

colorfast. Able to resist a change in color in spite of a certain influence such as washing, dry cleaning, perspiration, sunlight, or rubbing. (15)

color scheme. An appealing combination of colors. (10)

color wheel. A chart that shows the relationship among colors or hues. (10)

combination yarn. Yarn made by twisting two different types of single yarns into a ply yarn. (15)

combing. A process that makes fibers even more parallel and removes any short fibers. This leaves longer fibers that make smoother, stronger yarns called combed sliver. (14)

commission. A percentage of total sales paid to a salesperson. (27)

communication. The process of exchanging thoughts, ideas, or information with others. (26)

comparison shopping. Looking at different brands of the same or similar products in several stores to compare prices, quality, features, and store services before buying. (7)

complementary colors. Colors located opposite one another on the color wheel. (10)

complementary color scheme. A color scheme using colors opposite each other on the color wheel. (10)

compromise. An agreement that requires each person to give up a little. (5)

computer imaging. A computer program that allows an image on a display screen to be turned to any angle in a three-dimensional effect. (3)

cone adapter. A device that allows a cone of thread to be used on a spool pin. (24)

cones. Large spools of thread. (24)

conformity. Following or obeying some set standard or authority. (1)

consumer. A person who uses goods and services; a buyer of goods and services. (6)

contact lenses. Vision correction devices worn directly on the eyes. (13)

continuous overcasting technique. Lining up several garment sections so the stitching is not broken as you move from the edge of one garment section to the next. (24)

cool colors. Blue, green, and purple. They are relaxing colors. Because they make objects seem farther away, they are also called receding colors. (10)

cord yarn. Yarn made by twisting ply yarns together. Ropes are often made from cord yarns. (15)

costume jewelry. Jewelry designed for wear with current fashions and usually made from inexpensive materials. (8)

cotton. A natural cellulosic fiber obtained from the cotton plant. (14)

cover stitch. A serger stitch used mainly for hemming, producing two or three parallel rows of top-stitching on one side. (24)

credit. A promise to pay in the future for what is purchased today. (7)

crewel. A type of hand embroidery that uses wool or wool-like yarn instead of thread. (25)

crochet. Similar to knitting, but only one needle is used to pull the thread through a loop or series of loops. (25)

culture. The beliefs and customs of a particular racial, religious, or social group. (1)

custom. A tradition or practice that has been handed down from one generation to the next. (2)

custom-made. Something made to the individual order of a customer or to fit particular specifications. (27)

cuticle. The skin at the base of the nail. (13)

cutting and sewing guide sheet. A printed sheet that gives detailed instructions on how to make a garment. (19)

cutting line. The bold outline around the edge of each pattern piece. (19)

D

dart. A stitched fold that provides shape and fullness to a garment so that it fits the curves of the body. (22)

debit card. A card issued by banks that allows the user to deduct money electronically from the user's bank account in payment for goods or services. (7)

decision-making process. A series of steps that you go through to help you make choices and solve problems. (5)

decorative lines. Lines added to a garment to add interest. (11)

deodorant. Personal care product that controls body odor while allowing the person to perspire normally. (12)

department stores. Stores that sell a variety of items and clothing in a wide range of styles, qualities, and prices. (7)

dermatologist. Doctor who specializes in diseases and disorders of the skin. (12)

design. The arrangement of elements or details in a product or work of art. (11)

design ease. An extra amount of fullness provided in patterns to give the garment its special look or silhouette. (18)

detergent. A chemical mixture made from petroleum and natural fats and oils used to remove dirt from clothes. (16)

development. Finding practical ways to use the products researchers create. (27)

directional stitching. Stitching with the fabric grain to preserve the position of the grain and to keep fabrics from stretching out of shape or curling. (22)

disability. A condition that interferes with a person's ability to perform tasks like walking or lifting. It may be the result of an injury, an illness, or a birth defect. (9)

discount stores. Stores where items are sold at lower prices than department stores. (7)

dots. Solid circles on pattern pieces used for matching seams and other construction details. (19)

double-fold hem. A machine-stitched hem made with two equal folds of fabric. (22)

drawing. A process that combines many carded slivers of cotton into a single drawn sliver, which is then stretched. (14)

dry cleaning. A process of cleaning clothes using organic chemical solvents instead of water. (16)

dual-career families. Families in which both parents are employed outside the home. (27)

dyes. Coloring agents used to add color to fibers, yarns, fabrics, or garments. (15)

E

easing. Joining two edges of fabric together when one edge is slightly larger than the other. No visible gathers should form. (22)

economics. How a society chooses to produce, distribute, and consume its goods and services. (2)

elements of design. Color, line, form, and texture. (11)

e-mail. A message delivered electronically from one computer to another. (26)

embroidery. Decorative hand or machine stitching that creates a pattern or a design on the fabric. (17)

emery board. Pieces of thin cardboard covered with a grainy paper used to smooth edges and shape nails. (13)

empathy. The ability to understand and be sensitive to the feelings, thoughts, and experiences of others. (26)

emphasis. The center of interest; a principle of design. (11)

entrepreneur. People who organize, manage, and assume the risks of their own businesses. (25)

environment. Everything around you including your family, friends, school, and community. (1)

enzyme presoak. A laundry product specially formulated to help remove stains before washing. (16)

evaluate. To determine the worth of something. (4)

exports. Products sent out of a country to other countries. (3)

F

fabric. Textile product usually made by knitting or weaving yarns together. (14)

fabric finish. Any treatment given to fibers, yarns, or fabrics that makes the final product look, feel, or perform differently. (15)

fabric softener. Laundry product used to make garments soft and fluffy and to reduce wrinkles and static electricity. Some fabric softeners are used in the washer; others are used in the dryer. (16)

facing. A piece of fabric used to finish raw edges in a garment such as at the armholes, neckline, or other garment edges; the facing also adds some firmness to open areas and keeps them from stretching out of shape. (22)

factory outlet stores. Stores operated by manufacturers that sell only their own merchandise. (7)

fad. Something new that is popular for only a short period of time. (2)

Fair Labor Standards Act. A 1938 federal law that established a minimum wage and a maximum work week of 40 hours. It also included child labor regulations. (3)

family life cycle. Stages in the life of a family beginning with marriage. (5)

farsighted. Able to see things that are far away more clearly than things that are near. (13)

fashion. The particular style of clothing that is popular at a given time. (2)

fashion centers. Cities such as New York, Los Angeles, Dallas, Chicago, Atlanta, and Miami where retail store buyers come during fashion weeks to view the new collections and make their selections. (3)

fashion cycle. The periodic return of specific styles and general shapes. (2)

fashion merchandising. A field that includes all the phases of planning, buying, and selling clothes and accessories. (3)

fashion promotion. A field that includes all the efforts made to inform people through advertising of what is new in fashion and convincing them to buy it. (3)

fashion trend. The direction in which a particular change or fashion is moving. (2)

fasteners. Items used to close openings on garments. (20)

felt. Fabric made from short wool fibers that interlock to form a solid mass when heat, moisture, and pressure are applied. (15)

fiber. Basic unit of all textiles. (3)

fiber dyeing. Process of dyeing fibers before they are spun into yarns; includes both solution dyeing and stock dyeing. (15)

figure types. Sizing standards used by pattern companies to group figures according to height and proportion. (18)

filament. A continuous strand of fiber. Any manufactured fiber can be made in filament form. Silk is the only natural fiber that is a filament. (14)

filling yarns. The shorter yarns that lie crosswise in woven fabric. (15)

films. Fabrics made of thin sheets of vinyl and urethane; often used as a coating on other fabrics. (15)

finance charge. An extra charge you pay for the use of credit. (7)

fine jewelry. Jewelry usually made from gold, silver, or platinum. (8)

flame-resistant. A term used in relation to fabrics that are self-extinguishing or easy to extinguish. (9)

Flammable Fabrics Act. A law that specifies flammability standards for household textiles and apparel. (6)

flat collar. A collar that lies flat against the garment, also called a Peter Pan collar or shaped collar. (23)

flatlock stitch. A 2-thread stitch that uses one needle and one looper to join a seam. Fabric edges can be pulled open and flattened to produce a decorative "ladder" effect. (24)

flat method of construction. Serging flat pieces together rather than pieces "in the round." (24)

flax. The natural fiber used to make linen fabric. (14)

follow-up letter. A letter thanking the interviewer for taking the time to talk with the applicant. It is also an opportunity to fill in any gaps left open after the interview. (26)

form. The three-dimensional shape of an object; an element of design. (11)

front hip pocket. An angular pocket often used on the front of pants and skirts. (23)

fusible fabric. A sheer adhesive-coated fabric that joins two other fabrics together when ironed. (17)

G

gathers. Tiny, soft folds of fabric formed when a larger piece of fabric is sewn to a smaller piece. Gathers are fuller than easing. (22)

generic groups. Groups of manufactured fibers that are chemically alike. The Federal Trade Commission has identified 21 generic groups of fibers. (6)

goals. Something a person wants to accomplish. (5)

grading. Trimming each seam allowance to a different width. (22)

grain. The direction the lengthwise and crosswise yarns run. (15)

grain line. Line with arrows on each end used to help you place the pattern piece on the straight grain of the fabric. (19)

greige goods. Unfinished fabric ready to be dyed or printed. (15)

grooming. Taking care of your body through good health habits and personal cleanliness. (12)

H

hangnails. The tiny, loose pieces of skin along the side of nails. (13)

hangtags. Tags made of heavy paper or cardboard that are attached to purchased clothes. They are not required by law and are removed from garments before they are worn. (6)

harmony. A sense of unity achieved when the elements of design are used according to the principles of design, creating a pleasing visual image. All parts look as if they belong together. (11)

hem. A finished edge on a garment. (22)

heritage. The customs and traditions passed down from predecessors. (2)

hook and loop tape. A type of fastener that has tiny hooks on one strip and loops on the other that hold together when pressed with the fingers. (9)

hue. The name of a color. (10)

human resources. All the resources you have within yourself such as skills, knowledge, and experience. (5)

I

imports. Products that come into a country from foreign sources. (3)

impulse buying. Unplanned consumer purchases or "spur of the moment" buying of merchandise on display. (7)

individuality. What sets one person apart from others. (1)

Industrial Revolution. A movement in the late 1700s marked by major changes in the economy due to the invention of many machines, the introduction of steam power, and the development of the factory system. (3)

in-seam pocket. A pocket sewn in the side seam of a garment that does not show when the garment is worn. (23)

intensity. The brightness or dullness of a color. (10)

interfacing. A fabric that is used under the outer fabric to prevent stretching and provide shape to a garment. (20)

intermediate colors. Colors made by combining equal amounts of a primary color and a secondary color; red-violet, blue-violet, blue-green, yellow-green, yellow-orange, red-orange. (10)

interpersonal skills. Skills needed to get along well with other people and to be an effective team member. (26)

inventory. An itemized list of goods, possessions, or resources. A wardrobe inventory is an itemized list of clothes and accessories. (4)

ironing. The process of removing wrinkles from damp, washable clothing using a gliding motion. (16)

irregulars. Items with slight defects. (7)

J

job. A group of tasks performed by a worker. (27)

jute. A rough, coarse natural fiber that has a natural odor. It is used for burlap. (14)

K

kimono sleeve. A sleeve formed as a continuous extension of the shoulder area. (23)

knitting. Looping yarns together with a knitting machine to produce fabric. (15)

L

labels. Small pieces of ribbon or fabric, firmly attached to the inside of garments, that provide important information. Garment labels are required by law to state fiber content and care instructions. (6)

laundering. The washing of clothes with water and laundry products. (16)

layaway buying. Placing a small deposit on an item so that the store will reserve it for a buyer. (7)

layout. The section of the pattern guide sheet that shows how to lay the pattern pieces on the fabric. (21)

leader. A person who guides a group toward its goals. (26)

leadership. The capacity to lead or to direct others on a course or in a direction. (26)

letter of application. A letter sent to a potential employer along with a resume to get the employer interested in interviewing you. (26)

letter of resignation. A letter written by an employee informing the employer of his or her resignation and explaining when and why the person is leaving. (26)

line. An element of design that gives a sense of movement and direction. (11)

linen. A cloth made from the cellulosic fiber called flax. (14)

loopers. The parts of the serger that form the stitch. (24)

M

mail-order shopping. A type of shopping that allows a person to shop at home by mail. (7)

manicure. A treatment for the care of hands and fingernails. (13)

manufactured fibers. Fibers not found in nature. Rayon, acetate, and triacetate are made from cellulose. Other manufactured fibers are made primarily from carbon, oxygen, hydrogen, and nitrogen. (3)

marketing. The process of buying and selling goods. (27)

mass production. A manufacturing process that allows large numbers of items to be made at the same time. (3)

merchandising plan. The producer's plans for creating a line of designs for a given season. (3)

mix-and-match wardrobe. A wardrobe in which garments can be combined with many other garments to create several different outfits. (4)

mock flat-felled seam. A seam formed using both the sewing machine and the serger. Topstitching completes the seam on the outside of the garment. (24)

modesty. Covering the body according to what is considered proper by the society in which you live. (1)

monochromatic color scheme. A color scheme using several values and intensities of one color. (10)

monofilament yarns. Yarns made from a single filament. (15)

multifilament yarns. Yarns made from a group of filaments. (15)

multisized patterns. Patterns having several sizes printed on the same pattern tissue. (18)

MyPyramid. An individualized food guidance system that will help you eat a well-balanced diet. (12)

N

nap. A layer of fiber ends above the fabric surface. (23)

narrow double-stitched seam. After stitching garment seams together on the sewing machine, they are serged together, placing the needle 1/8 inch from the stitching line. (24)

natural fibers. Fibers made from natural sources (plant or animal) and changed slightly during processing. Cotton, wool, silk, and linen are the most common natural fibers. (3)

nearsighted. Able to see things that are near more clearly than things far away. (13)

need. Something required for a person's continued survival. (1)

neutrals. Black, white, and gray are neutrals. White, the absence of color, reflects light. Black absorbs all colors. Gray is a blend of black and white. (10)

nonhuman resources. Material things you have or can use to help you achieve goals, such as money, tools, and time. (5)

nonverbal communication. Sending messages through facial expressions and actions without using words. (26)

notches. Diamond-shaped symbols along the cutting line used to show where pattern pieces should be joined. (19)

notching. Clipping V-shaped sections from the seam allowance on seams that curve outward. (22)

notions. Items other than fabric that become part of a garment. Thread, fasteners, and interfacing are examples. (19)

nutrients. The substances that a person gets from foods that help the body to grow and stay healthy. (12)

nutrition. Eating a variety of nourishing foods that will keep the body working properly. (12)

O

Occupational Safety and Health Act. This 1970 act calls for safe and healthful working conditions in the workplace. The Occupational Safety and Health Administration (OSHA) was formed to set and enforce job safety and health standards. (3)

off-grain. The lengthwise and crosswise yarns of a fabric are not at a perfect 90 degree angle to each other. (21)

off-price discount stores. A type of discount store that features brand name or designer merchandise at below normal prices. (7)

online shopping. A type of shopping that allows a person to order items from retailers' Web sites using a computer that is connected to the Internet. (7)

optical illusion. A misleading image or visual impression presented to the eyes. (11)

order of business. The sequence of events during meetings. (26)

order of priority. Items are listed from the most important to the least important. (4)

overedge stitch. A 2-thread serger stitch used as an edge finish on garments, but not as a seam. (24)

overlock stitch. A 3-, 4-, or 5-thread serger stitch that stitches, trims, and overcasts a seam in one operation. The basic serger stitch. (24)

overrun. Item that was produced by a manufacturer but not ordered by retailers. (7)

P

parliamentary procedure. An orderly way of conducting a meeting and discussing group business. (26)

patching. A garment repair technique in which a small piece of fabric is sewed over a hole. (17)

patch pocket. A pocket formed from a separate piece of fabric stitched on the outside of a garment. (23)

patchwork. Small pieces of fabric cut into shapes then sewn together by hand or machine to form a pattern. Quilts are made by patchwork. (17)

pattern. Tissue paper pieces to follow when cutting out fabric for making a garment. (19)

pattern ease. Extra room built into a pattern so that clothes will be comfortable. (18)

pattern grading. The process of adjusting pattern pieces to make garments in a range of sizes. This process is now computerized. (3)

pedicure. A treatment for the care of feet and toenails. (13)

peer pressure. The force that makes you want to be like friends your age (peers). (1)

personality. Everything about a person that makes that person unique. (1)

piece dyeing. The process of dyeing in which color is added after the fabric has been made; the most common method of dyeing and generally the least expensive. (15)

piecework. Work done one piece or one step at a time for which payment is made at a set rate per unit. (3)

pile. Yarn ends or loops extending above the surface of a fabric. (23)

pills. Small balls of fiber that form on the surface of a fabric. Pilling usually occurs on places of wear, as the elbows of sweaters. (15)

pinking shears. A cutting instrument used to give seam edges a finished look with a zigzag edge. (20)

plain weave. A weave made by passing a filling yarn over one warp yarn and then under one warp yarn. (15)

plaque. A layer of film on teeth that contains harmful bacteria, which can cause tooth decay and gum disease. (12)

ply yarn. Yarn made by twisting two or more single yarns together. Each part of the yarn is called a ply. Ply yarns are larger and stronger than single yarns. (15)

podiatrist. Physician who specializes in foot problems. (13)

portfolio. A well-organized collection of materials that shows a person's abilities and accomplishments. (26)

preshrunk. Fabric that has been treated during manufacturing to help keep it from shrinking during washing or cleaning. (21)

press cloth. Cloth used to cover a garment before it is pressed to prevent iron shine. (20)

pressing. The process of removing wrinkles from clothing using steam and a lifting motion. (16)

pressing ham. A firm, round cushion used to help press curved seams and darts. (20)

prewash soil and stain removers. Products that help remove oily stains and heavy soil from fabrics. (16)

primary colors. The three colors from which all other colors can be made; red, yellow, and blue. (10)

principles of design. Guides that tell how the elements of design should be combined. Balance, proportion, rhythm, and emphasis are the principles of design. (11)

printing. Process of adding color, pattern, or design to the surface of fabrics. (15)

priorities. Ranking of the importance of items or options. (5)

proportion. The relationship between one part to another and of all the parts to the whole; a principle of design. (11)

protein fibers. Natural fibers from animal sources. Wool and silk are the two major protein fibers used for clothing. (14)

Q

quality. The performance characteristics of an item. (8)

quilting. The process of adding a layer of padding between two layers of fabrics held together with stitches. (15)

R

raglan sleeve. A sleeve attached to the garment by front and back diagonal seams from the underarm to the neckline. (23)

ramie. A fiber often called "China grass." It comes from a shrubby plant often grown in China and India. (14)

ready-to-wear. Clothing made in factories in standard sizes. (2)

recycled wool. Wool fibers from previously made wool fabrics are used in the fabric. (14)

recycling. To reuse. Clothing can be recycled. Wool fabrics might be recycled and made into new fabrics. (17)

redesigning. To change a garment in its appearance or function. (17)

regular charge account. A charge account that allows a person to charge purchases in exchange for a promise to pay in full within 10 to 30 days after the billing date. (7)

resale shops. Stores that sell clothing that has been owned or worn before. (7)

research. Developing new products such as fibers, weaves, dyes, and finishing techniques. (27)

resources. The objects or abilities that can be used to reach goals. (5)

restyling. Giving a garment a new and different look. (17)

resume. A brief account of a person's education, work experience, and other qualifications for employment. (26)

retail. Selling small quantities of goods to individual consumers. (27)

retailers. Businesses that buy from manufacturers and sell goods to customers. (3)

revolving charge account. A charge account that allows a person to make purchases up to a limit set by the creditor and the customer when the account was opened. (7)

rhythm. The feeling of movement created by line, shape, or color; a principle of design. (11)

robotic machine. A machine that operates automatically and is controlled by a computer. (3)

rolled collar. A collar that stands up from the neck slightly and then forms a roll around the neck. (23)

rolled edge stitch. A 2- or 3-thread serger stitch that produces a narrow rolled hem. (24)

rotary cutter. A cutting device with a round blade. (20)

S

satin weave. Weave made by floating a yarn from one direction over four or more yarns from the other direction and then under one yarn. The satin weave is used to make fabrics with a smooth, shiny surface. (15)

scalloping shears. Cutting instrument much like pinking shears, but with a more curved shape. (20)

scissors. Cutting instrument that is usually short with handles that have small, matching holes. Blades are different widths. (20)

seam. A row of stitches joining pieces of fabric together. (22)

seam allowance. Fabric between the seam and the garment edge, usually 5/8 in. (1.5 cm). (22)

seam finish. Treatment of seam edges to prevent raveling and to make the seam stronger and longer wearing. (22)

seam ripper. A small gadget with a hook-like blade that is used to remove stitches. (20)

seam roll. A long tubular cushion that allows you to press seams open without leaving marks from the seam allowances. (20)

secondary colors. Colors made by combining equal amounts of two primary colors; orange, green, and violet. (10)

seconds. Items that are soiled or have flaws. (7)

self-actualization. The highest level of need according to Maslow. These needs are related to success in personal achievements, expressions of personal creativity, and self-fulfillment. To reach this level, the other levels of needs must be at least partially fulfilled. (1)

self-adornment. Decorating the body in some manner. (1)

self-casing. A casing formed by turning back the edge of the garment. (23)

self-concept. The mental image a person has of himself or herself. (1)

self-esteem. A feeling of personal self-worth. (1)

self-help features. Easy-to-work openings and closures in clothes that make it easier for children to dress themselves. (9)

selvage. Side edges of a woven fabric, running in the direction of the lengthwise grain. Selvages are formed by the filling yarns as they are turned to go back across the warp yarns. Selvages are very strong and will not ravel. (15)

sergers. Machines that provide a factory-like finish to home-sewn garments. These machines join two layers of fabric to form a seam, trim away extra seam allowance width, and overcast the fabric edges all in one step. Also called overlock machines. (24)

set-in sleeve. A sleeve attached to the garment with a seam that goes around the armhole at the tip of the shoulders. (23)

sewing gauge. A 6-inch ruler with a sliding marker; used to measure hems, cuffs, space between buttons, and other short distances. (20)

shade. Dark value of a color made by adding black to the color. (10)

shape. The outline of an object made up of lines. (11)

shears. Cutting instrument that is usually longer than scissors and the handles are not the same size. (20)

silk. A natural protein fiber obtained by unwinding the cocoons of silkworms. (14)

skirt marker. A measuring tool used to mark an even hem. (20)

sleeve board. A padded sleeve-shaped board used to help press small details in garments. (20)

societies. Groups of people living and working together. (2)

solution dyeing. The process of dyeing manufactured fibers by adding dye to the liquid before the fiber is forced through the spinneret. (15)

solvent. A liquid substance used to dissolve greasy stains. (16)

sorting. Grouping clothes in piles according to the way they will be laundered. (16)

specialty shops. Shops that sell specific kinds of merchandise. (7)

spinneret. A small nozzle with many tiny holes through which a thick liquid is extruded, making manufactured fibers. (14)

split-complementary color scheme. A color scheme using one color with the two colors on the sides of its opposite complement. (10)

spool cap. A device placed over the spool to provide even feeding of thread to the serger. (24)

spun yarn. Yarn made from short, staple fibers. (15)

stabilizer fabric. A special type of fabric used when machine embroidering to support stitches and prevent puckering. (25)

stabilizing. Adding extra strength to seams and areas that receive stress during wearing. (24)

stain. A spot or discoloration caused by various liquids or solid materials. (16)

standard. A set of criteria established by authorities who judge products to verify certain levels of quality. (6)

standard sizes. The set of body measurements used by most pattern companies. (18)

standing collar. A collar that stands up from the neck edge of the garment. Also known as a band collar or mandarin collar. (23)

staple fiber. Short strand of fiber. All natural fibers except silk are staple fibers. All manufactured fibers can be produced in staple form. (14)

starch. A laundry product that produces a crisp, smooth surface on fabrics. (16)

status. Refers to a person's position in relation to others. (1)

staystitching. Sewing a line of regular machine stitching on a single thickness of fabric to stabilize curved or bias edges and prevent stretching. (22)

stitching line. The broken line just inside the cutting line on single-sized pattern pieces. (19)

stitch in the ditch. Stitching into the "well" of a seam through all fabric layers. (22)

stock dyeing. Process of adding dye to loose fibers. (15)

structural lines. Lines formed as the pieces of a garment are sewn together. (11)

style. Type of garment that has specific characteristics that make it unique. (2)

sweatshop. A manufacturing plant that may use child labor, pay less than minimum wages, not pay overtime, or have unclean or unsafe facilities. (3)

synthetics. Manufactured fibers. (3)

T

tape measure. A flexible measuring tool used to take body measurements. (20)

tartar. A hard, crusty substance that results when plaque is left on the teeth. (12)

teamwork. Individuals work together to reach a common goal. (26)

technology. The manner of accomplishing a task using current technical methods or knowledge. (2)

textiles. Products made of cloth. (3)

Textile Fiber Products Identification Act. Requires labels to tell what fibers are in the textiles. (6)

texture. How a fabric feels and how it looks on the surface; an element of design. (11)

texturing. Twisting, crimping, coiling, or looping fibers to vary the appearance and stretch of yarns. (14)

thimble. Metal or plastic device placed over the middle sewing finger to help push the needle through the fabric. (20)

thread clipper. A cutting device with a spring action that reopens the blade after each cut. (20)

thread net. A plastic circular net placed over spools of thread to keep threads from tangling or slipping off the spools. (24)

thrift shops. Shops that carry leftovers from other stores and some out-of-style garments. (7)

tie-dyeing. A method of dyeing where sections of fabric are folded or gathered and tied tightly with string or wrapped with rubber bands. When the fabric is dyed, the tied or wrapped portions resist the dye, resulting in a design. (17)

tint. Light value of a color made by adding white to the color. (10)

trade deficit. Imports of a country exceed its exports, causing a negative trade balance. Money flows out of the country in payment for imports. (3)

trademark. Identifying name, symbol, or design that sets a manufacturer's product apart from similar products or competitors. (6)

trade surplus. Exports of a country exceed its imports, allowing money to flow into the country in payment. (3)

traits. The personal qualities that make a person different from everyone else. (1)

trendsetter. A person who takes the lead or sets an example. They aren't afraid to try new styles. (2)

triad color scheme. A color scheme using three colors that form an equal-sided triangle on the color wheel. (10)

trimming. Evenly cutting away part of the seam allowance; usually done on lightweight fabrics. (22)

true bias. Fabric grain that runs at a 45 degree angle to the lengthwise and crosswise grains. It allows the greatest amount of stretch in a woven fabric. (21)

twill weave. A weave made when the filling yarns float over one and under two or more warp yarns. Each float begins one yarn over from the last one. The floats can be either filling or warp yarns. (15)

U

understitching. A row of stitches on the facing placed close to the seamline through the facing and the seam allowances. This keeps the facing from rolling to the outside of the garment. (22)

unisex. Patterns that are designed for either males or females. (18)

V

value. The qualities, standards, principles, and ideals you consider important or desirable, which guide your actions and influence your decisions. (1) The lightness or darkness of a color. (10)

verbal communication. Communication that uses words—speaking or writing. (26)

virgin wool. The fibers have never been used before for a fabric or garment. (14)

W

waistband. A strip of fabric attached at the waistline edge of the garment. It is visible above the waistline. (23)

waistline facing. A curved piece of fabric attached at the waistline that folds to the inside of the garment. (23)

wardrobe. All the clothes and accessories a person has to wear. (4)

wardrobe plan. A plan that includes the clothes you have now and what you will need to add in the future. (4)

warm colors. Red, yellow, and orange. They are stimulating colors, and they draw attention. Because they make objects seem nearer, they are sometimes called advancing colors. (10)

warp knitting. Process of knitting in which the loops are made by one or more sets of warp yarns. All warp knits are made on flat machines. (15)

warp yarns. The longer yarns that run the length of fabric. (15)

water hardness. The amount of minerals, such as calcium and magnesium, contained in water. (16)

water softener. A product or device used to soften water. (16)

wearing ease. Extra room allowed in patterns for wearing comfort. (18)

weaving. Process of interlacing yarns at right angles to each other to make fabric. (15)

weft knitting. Process of knitting in which loops are made as yarn is added in the crosswise direction of the fabric. This can be done by either hand or machine, on either circular or flat machines. (15)

wholesale. The selling of quantities of goods for resale. (27)

wool. A natural protein fiber made from the fleece of sheep or lambs. (14)

Wool Products Labeling Act. A law that requires any textile product that contains some wool be labeled with the percentage and type of wool present and its country of origin. (14)

woolen yarns. Wool yarns made from short fibers (less than two inches). (14)

worked buttonhole. The edges of the buttonhole that are worked over with thread by hand or by machine. (22)

work ethic. A standard of conduct for job performance. (26)

worsted yarns. Wool yarns made from combed sliver using longer fibers. (14)

woven fabric. Fabric made by interlacing yarns at right angles to each other. (15)

Y

yarn. A continuous strand made of fibers. (14)

yarn dyeing. A dyeing process in which yarns are first wound onto spools and then placed in a dye bath. Yarn dyeing is usually used for making plaid and striped fabrics. (15)

Index